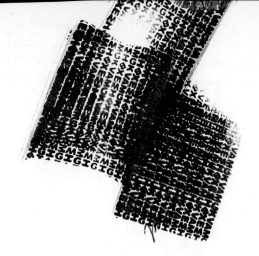

Developing
Reading
Skills

Developing
Reading
Skills

Deanne Milan
City College of San Francisco

McGraw-Hill, Inc.

New York St. Louis San Francisco Auckland Bogotá Caracas
Lisbon London Madrid Mexico City Milan Montreal New Delhi
San Juan Singapore Sydney Tokyo Toronto

Developing Reading Skills

Permissions Acknowledgments appear on pages 557–561 and on this page
by reference.

 This book is printed on recycled, acid-free paper containing
10% postconsumer waste.

2 3 4 5 6 7 8 9 0   AGM AGM   9 0 9 8 7 6 5

ISBN 0-07-041914-0

This book was set in Stone Serif by The Clarinda Company.
The editors were Laurie PiSierra and James R. Belser;
the design was done by A Good Thing, Inc.;
the production supervisor was Leroy A. Young.
Arcata Graphics/Martinsburg was printer and binder.

Library of Congress Cataloging-in-Publication Data

Milan, Deanne K.
    Developing reading skills / Deanne Milan. — 4th ed.
      p.   cm.
    Includes index.
    ISBN 0-07-041914-0
     1. Reading (Higher education)   2. Reading comprehension.
I. Title.
LB2395.3.M55   1995
428.4′07′11—dc20   94-7827

About the Author

After receiving a B.A. and an M.A. in Comparative Literature from the University of Southern California, Deanne Milan worked for a management consultant firm as a junior editor. A few months of delivering mail, typing, and correcting the consultants' grammar convinced her that a business career was not for her. She found a part-time job teaching at Los Angeles Valley College, taught for a while at Rio Hondo Community College, and in 1968 joined the English Department at City College of San Francisco. She has done postgraduate work at San Francisco State University, studying logic, anthropology, and literature. At City College of San Francisco she teaches reading and composition courses. In addition to this text, she is the author of an intermediate reading book, *Improving Reading Skills* (2d ed.), published by McGraw-Hill.

For Charlotte, as she goes out into the wider world

The man who has not the habit of reading is imprisoned in his immediate world, in respect to time and place. His life falls into a set routine; he is limited in contact and conversation with a few friends and acquaintances, and he sees only what happens in his immediate neighborhood. From this prison there is no escape.

—Lin Yu-T'ang, "The Art of Reading"

Message printed on a T-shirt:

A person who does not read is no better off than one who can't read.

Contents

Preface   xvii

To the Student   xxi

Introduction: The Reading Process   **1**

Characteristics of a Good Reader   1

Improving Your Vocabulary   4

Learning New Words   8
Using Context Clues   10

Exercises   12

Part I

Reading and Analyzing Paragraphs

17

1. The Fundamentals of Reading Paragraphs   **19**

The Structure of the Paragraph   19

The Direction of Paragraphs—How Writers Write   22

The Placement of the Main Idea   26

Levels of Support   30

Modes of Discourse: The Author's Purpose   32

Narration   33
Description   34
Exposition   37
Persuasion   38

Exercises   40

Selection 1: Liam O'Flaherty, "The Sniper"   41

Selection 2: Peter Farb and George Armalagos, *Consuming Passions: The Anthropology of Eating*   42

Selection 3: James Stevenson, "People Start Running"   43

Practice Essay: Richard Kluger, "Topeka, 1951"   45

2. Four Methods of Paragraph Development 51

Examples and Illustration   51

Process   53

Comparison and Contrast   56

Definition   57

Exercises   60

Selection 1: Edward T. Hall, from *The Hidden Dimension*   60
Selection 2: Lewis Thomas, "Clever Animals"   61
Selection 3: Mark Crispin Miller, "Black and White"   63

Practice Essay: Rose Del Castillo Guilbault, "Book of Dreams: The Sears Roebuck Catalog"   65

3. More Methods of Paragraph Development 71

Analysis and Classification   71

Cause and Effect   74

Analogy   77

Combination of Methods   80

Exercises   82

Selection 1: Desmond Morris, from *Manwatching: A Field Guide to Human Behaviour*   82
Selection 2: Sallie Tisdale, "The Only Harmless Great Thing"   83
Selection 3: Mark Twain, from *Life on the Mississippi*   85

Practice Essay: Peter Farb, "How to Talk about the World"   87

4. Patterns of Paragraph Organization 94

Unity and Coherence in Paragraphs   94

Transitions   96

Patterns of Organization   100

Chronological Order   100
Spatial Order   101
Deductive Order   103
A Variation of Deductive Order   104
Inductive Order   105
Emphatic Order   106

Punctuation and Meaning   106

Commas   107
Semicolons   108
Colons   108
Parentheses   109
Dashes   109
Exercises   110

Selection 1: Jonathan Norton Leonard, from *Ancient America*   110
Selection 2: Jan Yoors, from *The Gypsies*   112
Selection 3: Edwin O. Wilson, from *The Diversity of Life*   113

Practice Essay: David Attenborough, "Penguins"   115

PART II
Discovering Meaning through Language

123

5. Making Accurate Inferences   125

Inferences Defined   125

Practicing Making Inferences   126

Open-Ended Inferences   133

Exercises   134

Selection 1: Ian Frazier, "Bear News"   134
Selection 2: Bill McKibben, "Reflections: Television"   136
Selection 3: Diane Ackerman, from *A Natural History of the Senses*   139

Practice Essay: Larry Woiwode, "Guns"   141

6. Language   146

Denotation and Connotation   146

Language Misused and Abused   150

Weasel Words   151
Euphemisms   154
Sneer Words   155
Doublespeak   156
Politically Correct Language   157
Jargon   158
Clichés   160

Figurative Language   161

Exercises: Part 1—Analyzing Figurative Language   164

Exercises: Part 2   166

Selection 1: Gerald Durrell, from *The Overloaded Ark*   166
Selection 2: Ella Leffland, from *Rumors of Peace*   168
Selection 3: Margaret Atwood, "The View from the Backyard"   169

Practice Essay: Perri Klass, "Learning the Language"   172

7. Tone   179

An Explanation of Tone   179

The Ironic Stance   186

Wit   188
Irony   189
Satire   190
Cynicism   192
Sarcasm   193

Special Effects   195

Exercises: Part 1—Determining Tone   196

Selection 1: Letter to "Dear Abby"   196
Selection 2: Irving Howe, from *World of Our Fathers*   197
Selection 3: Edward Abbey, from *Desert Solitaire*   198
Selection 4: Winston Churchill, "Adolf Hitler"   198
Selection 5: David Grimes, "Florida—The Mildew State"   199
Selection 6: John Updike, "A & P"   200

Allusions   201

Symbols   202

Exercises: Part 2   203

Selection 1: Chinua Achebe, "Hopes and Impediments"   203
Selection 2: John McPhee, from *Encounters with the Archdruid*   205
Selection 3: Elspeth Huxley, from *Out in the Midday Sun*   207

Practice Essay: John Updike, "Venezuela for Visitors"   209

PART III
Reading Critically: Evaluating What You Read

217

Critical Reading Defined   218

The Reader's Responsibility   218

Developing a World View   220

Uncovering Arguments   224

Unstated Assumptions   228

Kinds of Evidence   230

Exercises: Part 1—Evaluating Evidence   230

Selection 1: Marie Winn, from *Children without Childhood*   230
Selection 2: Andrew Hacker, from *Two Nations: Black and White, Separate, Hostile, Unequal*   231
Selection 3: Ellyn Bache, "Vietnamese Refugees: Overcoming Culture Clash"   232

Balance   233

Kinds of Reasoning   236

Inductive Reasoning   237
Problems with Inductive Reasoning   238
Sweeping Generalization   238
Hasty Generalization   238
Incorrect Sampling   238

Deductive Reasoning   241

Exercises: Part 2—Evaluating Arguments   245

Appeals in Arguments   247

Appeals to the Emotions   247
Transfer   248
Plain Folks   248
Testimonial   248
Bandwagon Appeal   249
Flattery   249

Appeal to Authority   249
Appeal to Fear   250
Appeal to Patriotism   250
Appeal to Prejudice   250
Appeal to Sympathy   251
Appeal to Tradition   251

Logical Fallacies   252

Ad Hominem Argument   252
Begging the Question   252
Either/Or Fallacy   253
False Analogy   253
False Cause   254
Oversimplification   255
Non Sequitur   255
Post Hoc, Ergo Propter Hoc   256
Slippery Slope   256
Two Wrongs Make a Right   257

Exercises: Part 3—Identifying Logical Fallacies and False Appeals   257

Other Manipulative Techniques   261

Authority   261
Bias   262
Lying with the Facts   266
Misleading Statistics   267

Exercises: Part 4—Analyzing Editorials   268

Selection 1: Anna Quindlen, "A New Kind of Battle in the Abortion Wars"   269

Selection 2: Dan Wetzel, "A Question of Oppression at U. Mass.: Freedom of the Press or Racism?"   270

Selection 3: Raymond Bonner, "A Conservationist Argument for Hunting"   272

Selection 4: Mike Barnicle, "The Legacy of Lies and Fears"   274

Selection 5: Patrick J. Buchanan, "It's Evil, Pure and Simple"   276

Selection 6: Arthur Schlesinger, Jr., "How to Think about Bosnia"   278

PART IV
Reading Essays and Articles

283

Why Read Essays in the First Place?   283

The Characteristics of an Essay   284

The Parts of an Essay   285

Finding the Thesis   285
Separating the Essay's Parts   285

How to Read an Essay   286

Questions to Consider While Reading   287

Sample Essay: Alexander Petrunkevitch, "The Spider and the Wasp"   288

Why Write Summaries?   295

How to Write a Summary   295

Sample Essay: Lewis Thomas, "On the Need for Asylums"   296

Essays: Group 1   303

Selection 1: Solomon Northrup, "A Slave Witness of a Slave Auction"   303

Selection 2: Amy Tan, "Mother Tongue"   308

Selection 3: Richard Wright, "The Ethics of Living Jim Crow"   316

Selection 4: Malcolm Cowley, "The View from 80"   329

Selection 5: Diane Ackerman, "Anosmia"   342

Essays: Group 2   347

Selection 6: Sissela Bok, "Harmless Lying"   347

Selection 7: Nancy Mitford, "A Bad Time"   353

Selection 8: Nien Cheng, "Solitary Confinement"   367

Selection 9: Diana Hume George, "Wounded Chevy at Wounded Knee"   388

Selection 10: Shelby Steele, "The Recoloring of Campus Life"   404

Essays: Group 3   422

Selection 11: Loren Eiseley, "The Brown Wasps"   422

Selection 12: "America's Decadent Puritans," from *The Economist*   431

Selection 13: Michael Arlen, "Ode to Thanksgiving"   437

Selection 14: Stephen Jay Gould, "Carrie Buck's Daughter"   443

Selection 15: Aristides (Joseph Epstein), "Student Evaluations"   456

PART V
**Reading
Short
Stories**

473

Analyzing the Short Story   473

The Short Story Defined   474

The Parts of a Short Story   474

Diagramming the Plot   476

Questions about Short Stories   477

Questions about Plot   477
Questions about Character   478
Questions about Theme   478

Short Story 1: Anton Chekhov, "The Lady with the Pet Dog"   478

Short Story 2: Bobbie Ann Mason, "Shiloh"   492

Short Story 3: Katherine Mansfield, "Miss Brill"   504

Short Story 4: Raymond Carver, "Cathedral"   509

PART VI
**Reading and
Studying
Textbook
Material**

523

The Structure of Modern Textbooks   523

Making Efficient Use of Study Time   524

The SQ3R Study Skills Method   525

Applying the SQ3R Method   527

Textbook Selection 1: David G. Myers, "Gender Roles," from *Social
Psychology*   527

Textbook Selection 2: Stephen E. Lucas, "Listening," from *The Art of
Public Speaking*   541

Permissions Acknowledgments   557

Index   562

Preface

A fourth edition offers an author the chance to refine, to clarify, to make the book as good as it can possibly be. The fourth edition of *Developing Reading Skills* represents a more extensive revision than the second and third editions. Instructors who have not used the text before will benefit from the many suggestions and responses gathered from our experiences with the first three editions. Instructors who have used earlier editions will find much that is familiar; and while the changes are not radical, I hope they find the text significantly improved in physical layout, in the arrangement of topics, and, most significantly, in the choice of readings. These changes should make the book more useful and appealing to students and instructors alike.

The basic tenet underlying all four editions has remained constant, and this may account for the book's success: Good reading and clear thinking go hand in hand. The text is organized around the principle that students can best improve their reading, first, by intensive, analytical practice with high-quality short reading passages, followed by practice applying these skills to longer and increasingly more challenging essays and articles.

As in the three earlier editions, the reprinted selections represent a variety of topics intended to appeal to students and to general readers alike. I always tell my students at the beginning of the semester that I want them to learn something about the world as they read this book. Accordingly, the topics cover a wide range: anthropology, sports, human behavior, social and political issues, cross-cultural awareness, scientific observation, personal reminiscence, history, the minority experience, education, and so forth. The readings reflect what students can expect to encounter in their college courses and in their daily lives. It makes sense that they learn to read—with ease and confidence—all kinds of material, no matter how abstract or how potentially uninteresting to them, and to read these assignments carefully, critically, and analytically.

Developing analytical skills requires concentration and an intense engagement with the text. Accordingly, *Developing Reading Skills,* like its three predecessors, deliberately does not cover speed techniques. The wisdom of this decision has been borne out as the nation's teachers have become increasingly concerned about the difficulty students

have—at all levels—reading perceptively and thinking critically. This concern is further reflected in the inclusion of critical thinking and reading skills in the nation's elementary and high school curricula and in the increased offering of critical-thinking courses in colleges.

With these concerns in mind and taking into account reviewers' and McGraw-Hill editors' comments, I rethought the book's scheme. Here is what is new in the fourth edition:

- Slightly less than 75 percent of the readings are new, and just under 70 percent were published after 1980. Of the seven practice essays at the end of Chapters 1–7, five are new. Of the fifteen essays in Part IV, eleven are new, as are three of the four short stories in Part V. Both excerpts from textbooks in Part VI are new.

- Approximately 30 percent of the readings are by women or by minority writers.

- The introduction now begins with a discussion of the characteristics of good readers and concludes with a stronger explanation of context clues as a means of developing a good reading vocabulary.

- Part I, "Reading and Analyzing Paragraphs"—includes Chapters 1–4 more or less in their original form; Part II, "Discovering Meaning through Language"—includes Chapters 5–7. Inference skills (in previous editions discussed in the introduction) are now covered in Chapter 5. Chapters 6 and 7 explore language and tone, as before. The progression is more clearly from basic reading skills to more advanced techniques.

- New topics in Chapters 1–7 include a discussion of the way writers write, punctuation and its effect on meaning, special effects, allusion, symbol, and politically correct language. Chapter 5, "Making Accurate Inferences," begins with simpler, more "obvious" inference questions. Then the student is introduced to other types of inference questions (multiple-choice and fill-in-the blanks).

- The number of exercises following Chapters 1–7 has been reduced to keep the book from becoming too unwieldy, to allow for a more open design, and to give teachers a chance to move more quickly from these fundamental skills to the critical reading, essay, and short story sections.

- Part III, "Reading Critically: Evaluating What You Read"—has been considerably strengthened with new sections on cross-cultural awareness, the concept of a "world view" (including the hazards of ethnocentrism), lying with the facts, and misleading statistics. Part III also offers more extensive coverage than it did in the third edition of evidence, bias, arguments, unstated assumptions, balance, deductive and inductive reasoning, various kinds of emotional appeals, and logical fallacies.

- Part IV, "Reading Essays and Articles"—now includes, besides an explanation of how to read an essay, information on how to write a summary.

Summarizing is an excellent test of both students' comprehension and writing skills. The summary process is demonstrated with Lewis Thomas's persuasive essay, "On the Need for Asylums"; students are shown how an experienced reader and writer annotates with marginal notes. A summary of Thomas's essay follows.

- The instructor's manual retains all the features of the third edition's manual with these additions: suggestions for teaching each long selection in Parts I, II, and IV and topics for short essays for those instructors who like to give writing assignments; a discussion of ways to incorporate collaborative-learning exercises in the classroom; and a list of readings in the text that are especially appropriate for developing cross-cultural awareness.

Within the text's framework, the six sections and the accompanying exercises are directed at improving these specific skills:

- Improving vocabulary, with particular emphasis on using context clues
- Identifying the main idea in a paragraph and the thesis of an essay
- Determining the author's purpose and predominant mode of discourse
- Discerning methods of development, patterns of organization, and logical relationships between ideas
- Making accurate inferences
- Determining the author's tone, including the ability to recognize the many shades and subtleties of irony
- Understanding and analyzing connotative and figurative language
- Distinguishing between fact and opinion, weighing evidence
- Finding unstated assumptions, determining appeals, and evaluating arguments in expository prose and editorials
- Identifying several common logical fallacies

From the comments of students, instructors, and reviewers, the most appealing feature of *Developing Reading Skills* is the quality of the readings. I hope the fourth edition lives up to this reputation. The premise underlying the choice of readings remains the same. Students should practice with first-rate material, not only because good writing is easier to read (by virtue of its clarity), but also because students should not be intimidated by good writing.

Instructors should find their old favorites, but this edition continues to emphasize human-interest reading, with such selections as Rose Del Castillo Guilbault's "Book of Dreams: The Sears Roebuck Catalog"; Perri Klass's amusing look at how she learned medical school lingo in "Learning the Language"; Solomon Northrup's plaintive and bleak eyewitness account of a slave auction; Amy Tan's fond but funny description of her mother's "broken" English in "Mother Tongue"; Richard

Wright's childhood experiences with racial intolerance in "The Ethics of Living Jim Crow"; Malcolm Cowley's wry look at the vices, virtues, and compensations of being an octogenarian in "The View from 80"; Nancy Mitford's "A Bad Time," an account of Scott's disastrous expedition to the South Pole; Oliver Sack's profile of a Canadian neurosurgeon who suffers from Tourette's syndrome in "A Neurologist's Notebook: A Surgeon's Life"; Diana Hume George's episodic look at Native Americans in "Wounded Chevy at Wounded Knee"; and Stephen Jay Gould's thoughtful essay "Carrie Buck's Daughter," in which he examines the case of a Virginia woman who was involuntarily sterilized.

Short stories are included because they are a good way to get students involved in reading imaginative literature, to sharpen their interpretive skills, and to provide enjoyment for students and instructors alike.

A packet of tests is available for instructors who adopt the fourth edition.

Acknowledgments

The following people deserve special thanks for their continuing help: David Spears, Michael Hulbert, Robert Stamps, Don Cunningham, all members of the English Department at City College of San Francisco, and the many people at McGraw-Hill who worked on the book: Laurie PiSierra, Tim Julet, and James R. Belser. Also deserving thanks is Alison Zetterquist, whose support was greatly appreciated.

I would also like to thank the following reviewers for their insightful comments about the third edition, nearly all of which I agreed with and took to heart: Paulette Babner, Cape Cod Community College; Elizabeth Balakian, Fresno City College; Sam Chatham, Long Beach City College; Cherry Conrad, Jackson Community College; Mary Ann DeArmand, San Antonio College; Kathleen Engstrom, Fullerton College; Amy Girone, Glendale Community College; Karen Haas, Manatee Community College; Corin Kagan, Normandale Community College; Betty Murray, St. Petersburg Junior College; Dorothy Scully, Modesto Junior College; Merritt Stark, Henderson State University; and Laurie Stevens, University of St. Thomas.

Deanne Milan

To the Student

A couple of years ago I was shopping with a friend and his twelve-year-old daughter in downtown San Francisco. An older African-American man, a street musician whom my friend happened to know from his own musician days, was playing the tenor saxophone on a streetcorner. His name is Clifford, and he had attracted a crowd with his wonderful performance. After he finished, my friend introduced him to me and his daughter. Clifford asked her if she played an instrument, and when she replied that she was taking trumpet lessons and played in her junior high school band, he said, "That's fine, little lady. Learn your instrument well and you can play anything."

Somehow these simple yet wise words struck me as appropriate not only for a budding trumpet player but also for a reader. If you learn to read well, you can read anything you want—not just the daily newspapers and mass circulation magazines, but more difficult material like philosophy, anthropology, film criticism, military history—whatever interests you as your confidence grows. You would not be limited in any way. Assuming you had the vocabulary—or at least a good dictionary at your side—you could pick up a book, concentrate on it, and make sense of the author's words.

Because in the United States reading instruction often ends at elementary school, students sometimes have difficulty as they progress through school. The reading material gets harder and harder, yet they still must tackle their assignments armed only with their elementary school reading skills. The result, too often, is frustration and loss of confidence. And the assigned reading in your college courses will be even greater than they were in high school—both in content and in the amount of reading assigned. *Developing Reading Skills* is designed to accomplish several tasks: to show you the skills that will enable you to read with greater comprehension and retention, to help you tackle reading assignments with confidence, and to teach you to become an active reader.

Reading is an almost magical process that involves more than merely decoding print. It requires internal translation. In other words, you must internalize the author's words, so that you understand not only their surface meaning but also what the words suggest beyond that. Rather than reading passively, sitting back and letting the author

do all the work, you must learn to interact with the text. When you read, you enter into a peculiar relationship with the writer, a two-way process of communication. Although the writer is physically absent, the words on the page are nonetheless there to be analyzed, interpreted, questioned, perhaps even challenged. In this way, the active reader engages in a kind of silent dialogue with the author.

Along the way, to understand what you read more accurately, you must learn to see relationships between ideas, to determine the author's tone and purpose, to make accurate inferences, to distinguish between fact and opinion, and to detect bias, unstated assumptions, false appeals, logical fallacies, distortions, lack of balance, and the like.

Because the bulk of the reading you must do in college is expository—that is, prose writing that explains, shows, and informs—the readings in this book mostly reflect this kind of writing, although textbook material, editorials, and fiction are included as well. The text will provide you with a variety of engaging readings and many exercises to give you intensive practice in comprehension and analysis. You should take some time to look through the table of contents to become familiar with the book's layout.

As you glance through Parts I and II, you will see that the seven chapters deal extensively with the paragraph, using explanations, illustrative passages, and exercises. At first it may seem odd, or possibly artificial, to devote so much time to single paragraphs, which, after all, are seldom read in isolation. Yet concentrating on short passages promotes careful reading. The paragraph is the basic unit of writing (it is often referred to as the main building block of the essay). Studying its structure closely and examining paragraphs for placement of main idea, methods of development, patterns of organization, inferences, language (especially connotation and figurative language), and tone will help you learn to analyze on a small scale. Certainly it is less intimidating to practice with a hundred-word paragraph than with a five-page essay. Once you become proficient with paragraphs, you can then apply the same skills to longer works.

Entirely too much emphasis has been placed on increasing reading speed, on skimming and scanning, on zooming through material simply to get the "drift" of what the author is saying. These techniques are useful under certain circumstances—for example, for the sports fan who wants to find out which team won, for the student looking through the print or electronic card catalog for likely research sources, or for the reader of "Dear Abby" in the daily newspaper. But they are inappropriate for the major part of the reading you will have to do in college. For this reason, *Developing Reading Skills* does not include a discussion of speed techniques.

One final comment. During the course, as you sharpen your skills, your work should have two results. The first will be an improvement in your own writing. There is much evidence to support the connection

between good reading skills and good writing skills. When you understand how professional writers organize, develop, and support their ideas, you will become more aware of how to deal with your own writing assignments. Second, and more important, you will learn to be a better thinker as well. All of these skills will serve you well for the rest of your life.

Deanne Milan

Introduction: The Reading Process

Characteristics of a Good Reader

Developing confidence in reading is crucial both for improving your academic reading skills and for becoming not merely a competent reader, but a good one. What are the characteristics of a good reader?

The crucial characteristic, it seems to me, is the ability to read carefully, thoughtfully, and confidently. The good reader knows what to look for and is actively involved in the text—by thinking, questioning, and evaluating. Once the individual words are decoded—that is, recognized and pronounced—to himself or herself—the good reader looks up any unfamiliar words rather than taking a chance and guessing incorrectly at their meaning.

Although knowing the meanings of individual words is obviously important, the real meaning of a text lies in the relationship these words have to each other. First ask yourself, what is the author saying? What is the main idea of the passage? What is he or she trying to get across about the main idea? Can you paraphrase the writer's ideas by putting each sentence into your own words? Then look at the relation-

ship between the words and sentences. Do you see a pattern? How is the main idea supported?

Next, evaluate the author's ideas. Do they seem reasonable to you? Has the writer offered sufficient support? What other information do you need before you can intelligently accept or reject them? How does the writer's thinking accord with your own experience, values, observations, or thoughts? Is any pertinent information missing? Is the author biased? Is there an underlying but unstated motive?

To repeat: The good reader is active; he or she thinks and questions all the way through the text. (Using a pencil to make brief marginal notations is an excellent way to sharpen your comprehension and critical reading skills, as will be explained further in Part IV.)

To show you what a good reader does subconsciously, let us practice with a short paragraph. The title of the article from which it's taken, "Marriage as a Wretched Institution," suggests the author's probable point of view, and so we can anticipate before we read that he is going to criticize the institution of marriage. Now read the paragraph through once:

> Marriage was not designed as a mechanism for providing friendship, erotic experience, romantic love, personal fulfillment, continuous lay psychotherapy, or recreation. The Western European family was not designed to carry a lifelong load of highly emotional romantic freight. Given its present structure, it simply has to fail when asked to do so. The very idea of an irrevocable contract obligating the parties concerned to a lifetime of romantic effort is utterly absurd.
>
> Mervyn Cadwallader, "Marriage as a Wretched Institution," *Atlantic Monthly*

After you have read through the paragraph once, go back to see whether there are any unfamiliar words in it that might make your understanding less than perfect. Three words, in particular, might cause some difficulty. The first, "lay" in the phrase "lay psychotherapy," is used as an adjective, so you can ignore the verb definitions in the dictionary. Of the three following adjective definitions, which seems most appropriate?

1. Pertaining to, coming from, or serving the laity; secular: *a lay preacher.* 2. Practicing psychoanalysis but not having a medical degree: *a lay analyst.* 3. Of, or typical of, the average or common man: *lay opinion.*

Because of the context clue "psychotherapy," definition 2 is the suitable one for this usage.

The second word, "freight," in the phrase "a lifelong load of highly emotional romantic freight," is used in an unusual way—metaphorical-

ly rather than literally. We can infer here that "freight" refers not to a railroad car, but to a burden (literally, "something carried along").

The third difficult word is "irrevocable," which can easily be broken into its component parts to obtain a working definition. Embedded in the middle is the root "revoke," meaning "to cancel." The prefix *-ir* means "not," and the suffix *-able* is self-evident, "able to." Putting all this together, then, yields this definition: "not able to be canceled."

However, the pronunciation of this word is tricky. Although it looks as if it should be pronounced (ĭ-rĭ vōk'ə bəl), the accent is on the second syllable (ĭ RĔV' ə kə bəl).

A good reader also puts an author's ideas—especially if they are difficult or abstract—into his or her own words. (If you can restate the author's ideas accurately, then you can say that you have truly understood them.) To give yourself some practice, try this step. Write each of Cadwallader's sentences in your own words, then compare your version with the one provided here.

> *Sentence 1:* Marriage is not designed as an institution to provide friendship, sexual experience, romantic love, personal fulfillment for one's ambitions, constant amateur psychological therapy, or recreation.
>
> *Sentence 2:* The Western European family (meaning marriage) was not intended to be burdened with a lifelong commitment to romantic love.
>
> *Sentence 3:* Because of the way marriage is now regarded, it can only fail when the partners are asked to make that lifelong commitment.
>
> *Sentence 4:* It is ridiculous to expect marriage to be an irrevocable contract that commits the partners to a lifelong romantic effort.

Notice that the phrase "when asked to do so" in the third original sentence refers to the *last* part of sentence 2—"carrying a lifelong load of highly emotional romantic freight." This kind of omission, called an *elliptical remark,* can confuse the unwary reader because the writer assumes that the reader sees the connection between the initial phrase and the unstated second one.

Now we can summarize the paragraph in a single sentence: The Western European institution of marriage is destined to fail when spouses expect that romantic love will last a lifetime.

Next, consider the pattern that Cadwallader imposes on his ideas. Sentences 1 and 2 state what marriage was *not* designed to do. Sentence 3 draws a conclusion, and sentence 4 restates the main idea, ending with an emphatic statement: that our high expectations for marriage are utterly absurd. Essentially, then, Cadwallader's paragraph shows a cause-effect relationship.

Having come to an accurate literal understanding of the passage, the careful reader considers whether the ideas represent factual infor-

mation or a subjective opinion. Since there is no way to "prove" what Cadwallader says, we can conclude that it represents an opinion. And although there is no support, we must remember that this excerpt is the opening paragraph of a magazine article and is therefore taken out of context. We can reasonably expect that the remainder of the article will support his view. Even without support, however, what he says may correspond with what we already know about human relationships: Intense romantic feelings don't last forever.

Finally, the careful reader asks questions that go beyond the scope of the passage. In this book you will learn to evaluate ideas from other perspectives, to see that there are other ways of looking at ideas, customs, institutions, and practices that we take for granted. For example, do North Americans have unrealistic expectations about marriage? We know from cultural experience that Americans believe in marrying for love. Further, since our marriage customs are derived from the European tradition, we can assume that Cadwallader's observations pertain to American attitudes as well. How do other cultures view marriage? Why do people in other cultures marry? Are we wrong to expect that romantic love will endure for a lifetime? If we know lifelong romantic love is illusory, why do so many people marry for this very reason? If other cultures are more realistic about marriage, are their divorce rates lower than ours? Is the diminishing of romantic love the reason people get divorced, or are there other, more substantive factors at work? These questions show the close alliance between reading and thinking. Even a little four-sentence paragraph provides a lot for us to think about.

In the everyday world of reading and studying, it is obviously impractical to paraphrase everything you read as we have done here. But in those cases where you do read analytically, remember that although the method might initially seem tedious, you get will get better and faster with practice. As you work through this book, you will find yourself analytically reading many passages—some much longer than Cadwallader's—and accomplishing more and more in a shorter time, because the process will gradually become automatic. Careful and intensive practice with short pieces is the best way to improve your critical and analytical skills, and that is the aim of everything in this text.

Improving Your Vocabulary

A good vocabulary is probably the single most important prerequisite for good reading. Every other skill—comprehension, retention, making inferences, drawing conclusions, evaluating—depends on whether you know what the words on the page mean in relation to each other and according to the context. After all, if you don't know what the words you are reading mean, you cannot fully understand what the writer is

saying. Sometimes it is possible to "wing it," meaning that you can get the drift of the writer's main idea even if some words remain unfamiliar. Most often, however, and especially with the careful reading you will be asked to do in this volume, your understanding of a passage may depend solely on the meaning of a single word, a situation in which guessing is hazardous.

To illustrate how imperative your understanding of unfamiliar words is, consider the following passage, which comes from an opening section of a newspaper article. In December 1992, the United Nations, aided by U.S. Marines, sent forces into Somalia to ensure the delivery of food shipments to the starving populace. This article is about the amphetamine drug *khat,* which is widely used in Somalia and other parts of the world.

[1]*Bardera, Somalia.* Young men huddle at the edge of the airstrip in the late afternoon sun, machine guns slung loosely over their shoulders, oblivious to the roaring airplane full of foreign food aid they are supposed to help unload.

[2]Their eyes are glazed, but the conversation is animated, led by a man in an orange T-shirt that reads: "I'm the Boss." A wad of green paste bulges in the side of his mouth, sticking to the edges of his teeth when he talks and sending a trickle of dark liquid down his chin.

[3]A few more twigs of khat are added to freshen the wad, fueling the amphetamine high, quickening the discussion and dulling any desire to return to work. It is the fourth hour the men have spent doing little else but chewing the substance; the session could last another six or eight.

[4]It is a ritual repeated each day by millions of people in the Horn of Africa, the Arab peninsula and other parts of the world.

[5]The exploding use of khat in Somalia, however, has proved shattering. It has helped cripple the country's economy, starved its children and enervated a generation. It now fuels the internecine civil war here and exacerbates a culture of guns and violence.

[6]"Healthwise, economically, politically and socially khat is destructive—it has destroyed Somalia," said Mohamud Abshir, a spokesman for the Somali Salvation Democratic Front. "It is the worst enemy we have."

Mary Gooderham, "Khat—the Drug That Saps Somalia,"
San Francisco Chronicle

The main idea is expressed in paragraph 6. According to the author, khat is helping to destroy Somalia. Although most of the vocabulary in the passage is fairly simple, there are some exceptions. Do you know what these words mean: "oblivious," paragraph 1; "animated," paragraph 2; "enervated," paragraph 5; "internecine," paragraph 5; and "ex-

acerbates," paragraph 5? If not, insert these definitions of the italicized words into the original context:

- "Young men . . . *oblivious* to the roaring airplane"—unaware, unmindful of
- "the conversation is *animated*"—lively, spirited
- "It has . . . *enervated* a generation"—deprived of vitality, weakened
- "It now fuels the *internecine* [ĭn'tər-nĕs'ēn'] civil war"—mutually destructive, ruinous to both sides, relating to struggle within a nation
- "It now . . . *exacerbates* a culture of guns and violence"—increases the severity of, makes worse

From this little exercise, it should immediately be clear that it is measurably more satisfying to read the passage if you know exactly what all the words mean. A hazy notion or an ill-considered guess about a word's meaning can lead to a misinterpretation. For example, consider the word "enervate" from the article above. The form of the word makes it look as if it has something to do with providing energy, when it fact it means exactly the opposite. Although the context might suggest that "enervate" has a negative connotation (its emotional association), you are much safer to consult a dictionary if you are not sure. A good rule of thumb is: When in doubt, look it up.

Even seemingly common words can cause problems in reading. When a writer uses an ordinary word in an unusual way, the unwary reader may get confused, and the meaning that pops into his or her head may not work in a different context. To demonstrate this, read the following short passage by James Baldwin.

> [1]The projects in Harlem are hated. They are hated almost as much as policemen, and this is saying a great deal. And they are hated for the same reason: both reveal, unbearably, the real attitude of the white world, no matter how many liberal speeches are made, no matter how many lofty editorials are written, no matter how many civil-rights commissions are set up.

> [2]The projects are hideous, of course, there being a law, apparently respected throughout the world, that popular housing shall be as cheerless as a prison. They are lumped all over Harlem, colorless, bleak, high, and revolting. The wide windows look out on Harlem's invincible and indescribable squalor: the Park Avenue railroad tracks, around which, about forty years ago, the present dark community began; the unrehabilitated houses, bowed down, it would seem, under the great weight of frustration and bitterness they contain; the dark, the ominous schoolhouses from which the child may emerge maimed, blinded, hooked, or enraged for life; and the churches, churches, block upon block of churches, niched in the walls like cannon in the walls of a fortress. Even if the administration of the projects were not so insanely humiliating (for example: one must report raises in

salary to the management, which will then eat up the profit by raising one's rent; the management has the right to know who is staying in your apartment; the management can ask you to leave, at their discretion), the projects would still be hated because they are an insult to the meanest intelligence.

James Baldwin, "Fifth Avenue, Uptown: A Letter from Harlem,"
Nobody Knows My Name: More Notes of a Native Son

Look again at the first sentence of paragraph 2. What does "popular" mean in the phrase "popular housing?" Here are six dictionary definitions for this word from *The American Heritage Dictionary*. Which is the appropriate one for the context?

1. Widely liked or appreciated. 2. Liked by friends, associates, or acquaintances; sought after for company. 3. Of, representing, or carried on by the common people or the people at large. 4. Fit for or reflecting the taste and intelligence of the people at large. 5. Accepted by or prevalent among the people in general: *a popular misunderstanding.* 6. Suited to or within the means of people: *popular prices.*

Although we probably think of "widely liked" when we think of the word *popular,* the best choice for this context is the third definition, because Baldwin is criticizing, not praising, Harlem housing projects. Definitions 4–6 are closer to the mark than numbers 1 and 2, but all convey a more positive connotation than Baldwin intends. *Popular* here means simply "for the people."

"Meanest" in the last sentence is another tricky word. Here are eight dictionary definitions from *The American Heritage Dictionary.* Which is best?

1. Low in quality or grade; inferior. 2. Low in social status; of humble origin or rank. 3. Characteristic of humble folk; common or poor in appearance; shabby. 4. Ignoble. 5. Low in value or amount; paltry. 6. Miserly; stingy. 7. Lacking elevating human qualities, as kindness and good will: a. Reluctant to oblige or accommodate. b. Cruel; malicious; spiteful. 8. *Informal:* Ill-tempered.

Judging from the context, the first definition is most appropriate. "Cruel" or "ill-tempered," more typical definitions of *mean,* appear at the end of the list and are labeled "informal." Because Baldwin's discourse is more formal than informal, this is a case in which you can use this usage label to help you choose the best definition.

The task of improving your vocabulary is inescapable, and it is a lifelong one as well. At first, learning dozens of new words may seem like a staggering task, but it *is* possible and eminently satisfying. Everyone has to start somewhere, and everyone's vocabulary can be im-

proved, because the number of words in the English language is sufficiently vast to make even the best reader reach for the dictionary occasionally. (Modern unabridged dictionaries generally have around 150,000 entries, but it has been estimated that the English language has well over 1,000,000 words.)

Learning New Words

An exhaustive treatment of vocabulary acquisition is not within the scope of this book, and any number of excellent vocabulary guides are available. The best way to acquire new words is to read a lot; most of the words you recognize in reading you know because of your prior exposure to them. Memorizing lists of words in isolation is tempting but inefficient. You won't remember many of them, nor will you understand their nuances, their subtleties in meaning, or their meanings in various contexts. New words are best learned (and retained) when you encounter them in your reading. Aside from that warning, however, here are some suggestions to get you started on an active program to learn the new words you encounter in your reading.

First, you should have two dictionaries: an abridged (shortened) paperback edition for class, and an unabridged (complete) edition to use at home while you study. There are several excellent dictionaries of both varieties on the market. Ask your instructor to recommend one, or choose one from this list:

> *The Random House Dictionary of the English Language*
> *The American Heritage Dictionary of the English Language*
> *Webster's New World Dictionary*
> *Merriam Webster's Collegiate Dictionary*
> *The Oxford American Dictionary*

Because the language is constantly changing, be sure that your dictionary is a current edition. Trying to save money by using a parent's hand-me-down, twenty-five-year-old dictionary is misguided thrift. For example, my faithful 1970 edition of *The American Heritage Dictionary* does not include the informal meaning of the word *clout,* "having influence or power" (as in "having political clout"), although it is listed in the 1989 edition.

Second, develop an interest in language. When you look words up in an unabridged dictionary, look at their etymology, or history, because many words have unusual origins. The etymology of a word is always printed in brackets [ ] following the definitions; it explains and traces the derivation of the word and gives the original meaning in the language (or languages) that the word is derived from.

For instance, one dictionary traces the history of the word *nice* as follows:

[Middle English, foolish, wanton, shy, from Old French, silly, from Latin *nescius,* ignorant, from *nescire,* to be ignorant]

You can easily see how radically this ordinary (and now nearly meaningless) adjective has changed over the centuries as it moved from language to language.

Here's a second example. The word *curfew* comes from medieval French. Because most houses were made of wood and had thatched roofs, the danger of fire was always great, particularly at night. Every evening residents had to put out their candles when a bell was rung, signaling the order "Cover fire." The French word *couvre-feu,* brought to England by the Norman conquerors, eventually became today's word *curfew.*

Finally, try to think of words that share similar meanings and origins as belonging to groups or families. The word *matriarchy,* for example, referring to a society where the dominant authority is held by women, derives from these word parts: *mater* (Latin for "mother") and the Greek suffix *-archy* (rule or government). From the root *mater,* we have the related words *maternal; maternity; matricide* (killing one's mother); *matrilineal* (tracing one's descent through one's mother); and *alma mater* (the school one graduated from, from Latin, "cherishing or fostering mother"). The suffix *-archy* can also be found in *monarchy* (rule by one); *oligarchy* (rule by a small group); and *anarchy* (absence of rule, from the Greek prefix *a-* or *an-* meaning "without").

The Latin root *fides* gives us the word *fidelity* (faithfulness), its negative form, *infidelity* (lack of religious faith, also adultery), and the stereotypical name for a dog, *Fido.* Studying the common Latin and Greek prefixes, roots, and suffixes is a good way to build your stock of vocabulary.

Last, devise a system for learning important new words you look up. Write new words and their meanings—and the context, if possible—in a small notebook or on index cards. Reviewing this list periodically will ensure your mastery of them. On index cards you might use a form something like this:

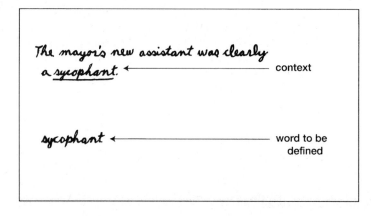

```
┌─────────────────────────────────────────────────────────┐
│                     Reverse Side                        │
│                                                         │
│   sycophant—one who tries to win favor by              │
│     flattering people with influence; a                │
│     servile self-seeker ◄──────────────── definition    │
│     (noun) ◄────────────────────────── part of speech   │
│                                                         │
│     (siḱə fənt) ◄──────────────────── pronunciation     │
│                                                         │
└─────────────────────────────────────────────────────────┘
```

Using Context Clues

A good dictionary is clearly an indispensable item as you study, yet it is probably unrealistic and certainly overwhelming to look up every unfamiliar word in the dictionary. Relying on context clues should not be a substitute for looking up exact meanings in the dictionary, nor will every sentence containing an unfamiliar word necessarily provide you with a clue. But when they do occur, they are a good shortcut toward more efficient reading, especially when you can understand the main point without knowing the exact meaning. There are four kinds of context clues: (1) synonyms; (2) antonyms; (3) examples and illustrations; and (4) opinion and tone.

1. Synonyms

A synonym is the most frequently used context clue. The writer may provide a word similar in meaning to the unfamiliar one. Although it may not have the exact same meaning, it may be close enough to give you an approximate definition. For example:

> The student was so *reticent* about getting up in front of his speech class that his long silences made everyone feel uncomfortable yet sympathetic.

The phrase, "long silences," is the context clue, and from that you could probably determine that *reticent* means "unwilling to speak." Consider this example:

> We can all point to many instances of *inequity,* injustice, and unfairness in American society.

Does the word *inequity* most likely mean (a) evil practices; (b) racial hostility; (c) inequality; or (d) instability? Which words provide context clues?

2. Antonyms

In sentences suggesting a contrast or a contradiction, the context clue may be in the form of an *antonym,* a word that means the opposite of the word in question. If you know the antonym, then you may be able to figure out the new word. For example:

> Although her instructor wants his composition students to develop a concise writing style, Sally's papers are always returned with the comment that her style is too *verbose.*

In this instance, the opposite of *verbose* (meaning overly wordy) is clearly *concise.* These words are antonyms or opposites.

Here is another example where a contrasting situation can be used as the context clue:

> A well-known writer was most upset when he learned that his publisher planned to release his newest novel, which contained profanity, in an *expurgated* edition. Instead, he canceled his contract and found a publisher who would accept his book and release it without removing any of the objectionable parts.

Does expurgated mean (a) thoroughly revised; (b) simplified, made easier to understand; (c) grammatically correct; (d) having the offensive matter taken out? Which words provide the context clue?

3. Examples and Illustrations

A writer may suggest the meaning of an unfamiliar word by examples and illustrations. In this case, no one word or phrase implies the definition, but, taken together, the examples allow us to infer the meaning. For example:

> The *squalid* conditions of many of America's inner cities—with their burned-out buildings, high crime rates, distressing poverty levels, malnutrition, and high unemployment—have too long been neglected by our political officials.

By considering carefully the examples of these conditions printed between the dashes, you can probably determine that *squalid* means "wretched and neglected," reinforced further by the last part of the sentence.

Try this example:

> Those involved in conspiracies usually arrange *clandestine* meetings to plan their illicit activities. They meet in unfamiliar locations, perhaps wear disguises, demand a password before newcomers are

allowed entrance, and cover up their subversive activities with legitimate-sounding names.

Does *clandestine* mean (a) secret; (b) open, publicly announced; (c) hastily arranged; (d) numerous?

4. Opinion and Tone

This last kind of context clue is less direct and consequently more difficult to rely on with accuracy. The writer's tone—that is, his or her attitude toward the subject or the opinions expressed—may give you a clue for an unfamiliar word. Consider this example:

> Every day Winston came home from school in tears. He could no longer endure his classmates' taunts on the bus ride home, their constant teasing and ridicule of his clothes, his name, his glasses, the braces on his teeth. Finally, driven by *solicitude* for her son's well-being, Winston's mother filed a complaint with the school principal.

The author's tone here is obviously one of sympathy for this child; therefore, we can infer that *solicitude* means "showing active care or concern."

Here is another example:

> A famous painter whose works often were sold to collectors for thousands of dollars once refused to have his new paintings exhibited in the same gallery as a relatively unknown new artist. He sneered that the artist was not really a painter at all, but only a *dilettante* who had learned his craft by doing paint-by-number kits.

According to the context, is a *dilettante* (a) a master artist; (b) an amateur artist; (c) a technical genius; (d) a pushy intruder?

Exercises

Exercise 1

Read each item carefully and underline the word or phrase that serves as a context clue for the italicized word. Then decide what kind of context clue you are given and write *your* definition in the first blank. Finally, look the word up in the dictionary and write the dictionary definition in the third blank.

1. The *belligerent* relations between the warring factions in the former Eastern European country of Yugoslavia have threatened to disrupt the peaceful relations between the other European nations.
    Kind of context clue _____
    Your definition _____
    Dictionary definition _____

2. When the student looked up, he realized with dismay that the teacher had observed him copying test answers from his notes. He knew from her *grave* expression that he was in serious trouble.
    Kind of context clue _____
    Your definition _____
    Dictionary definition _____

3. Mel's term paper was anything but *lucid.* His thoughts wandered and his paragraphs were hard to understand.
    Kind of context clue _____
    Your definition _____
    Dictionary definition _____

4. The guest speaker spoke for thirty minutes while the bored guests fidgeted and yawned. The chairman, on the other hand, spoke with *brevity* for only ten minutes.
    Kind of context clue _____
    Your definition _____
    Dictionary definition _____

5. The priestess at Delphi gave the Greek hero a *cryptic* answer in the form of a riddle. No matter how hard he tried to solve it, he found her message puzzling.
    Kind of context clue _____
    Your definition _____
    Dictionary definition _____

6. My neighbor's twins are different in every way. Charlotte is friendly and outgoing, while Lisa is withdrawn and *dour.*
    Kind of context clue _____
    Your definition _____
    Dictionary definition _____

7. Mr. Spears' English composition class is a *heterogeneous* mix of students representing all ages, races, and ethnic groups.
    Kind of context clue _____
    Your definition _____
    Dictionary definition _____

8. Both political candidates engaged in a dirty-tricks campaign, yet each accused the other of *nefarious* and underhanded practices to win the election.
    Kind of context clue _____
    Your definition _____
    Dictionary definition _____

9. O'Henry's story, "The Ransom of Red Chief," ends *ironically.* The kidnapped child is so obnoxious that the kidnappers are desperate to send him home.

Kind of context clue _____

Your definition _____

Dictionary definition _____

10. Whether rightly or wrongly, salesclerks often judge their customers by their dress. Although they may behave arrogantly with customers they deem poorly dressed, they often act very differently with the stylishly dressed, treating them *obsequiously,* as if they were royalty, much to the annoyance of the rest of us.

Kind of context clue _____

Your definition _____

Dictionary definition _____

Exercise 2

Now try your hand at determining the meaning of words using context clues with these more difficult passages from reprint material. Read the passage carefully and, for the first five, choose the definition that best fits the way the italicized word is used in context.

_____ 1. Tide pools contain mysterious worlds within their depths, where all the beauty of the sea is subtly suggested and portrayed in miniature. Some of these pools occupy deep *crevices* or fissures. . . . (Rachel Carson)
(a) deep, wide holes; (b) narrow cracks; (c) earthquake faults; (d) unexplored areas.

_____ 2. The hot dry season in India. . . . A corrosive wind drives rivulets of sand across the land; *torpid* animals stand at the edge of dried-up water holes. The earth is cracked and in the rivers the sluggish, falling waters have exposed the sludge of the mud flats. (Peggy and Pierre Streit)
(a) physically inactive; (b) domestic; (c) skittish and excitable; (d) malnourished, excessively thin.

_____ 3. The history of the word "creole" itself dates back to the slave trade. After slaves had been gathered from many parts of Africa, they were imprisoned in West African camps, *euphemistically* called "factories," for "processing" before being shipped out to "markets." (Peter Farb)
Describing words that (a) are examples of jargon, the specialized language of a particular profession; (b) accurately depict reality; (c) are less offensive substitutions for offensive words or phrases; (d) are substitutions for overly difficult words.

_____ 4. No aspect of the civil rights movement has generated so much controversy and so little agreement as affirmative action. The idea is a simple one: To help *redress* the long history of racial and gender discrimination in this country, racial minorities and

women should be given preference over white males in education, jobs training, hiring and promotion. (Daniel McLoughlin)
(a) understand; (b) embellish, decorate; (c) set right, remedy; (d) aggravate, make worse.

_____ 5. Cooking that does not apply heat directly to food, but transmits it through another medium, is most probably a more recent invention. When the medium is water, the process is boiling; when it is oil, the process is frying. Whereas roasting could have been discovered by accident, hot water is a rare natural *phenomenon,* not easily produced by humans in the absence of containers that are to some degree water proof and fireproof. It was therefore long believed that boiling and frying did not develop until after ceramics and metallurgy had been invented. . . . (Peter Farb and George Armalagos)
(a) any observable fact or occurrence; (b) something that impresses the observer as extraordinary, a marvel; (c) a person outstanding for some achievement; (d) an apparition, a figment of the imagination.

For these last five exercises, write the definition in your own words according to the context.

6. Our sense of smell can be extraordinarily precise, yet it's almost impossible to describe how something smells to someone who hasn't smelled it. The smell of the glossy pages of a new book, for example, or the first solvent-damp sheets from a mimeograph machine, or a dead body, or the subtle differences in odors given off by flowers like bee balm, dogwood, or lilac. Smell is the mute sense, the one without words. Lacking a vocabulary, we are left tongue-tied, groping for words in a sea of *inarticulate* pleasure and exaltation. (Diane Ackerman)
Inarticulate _____

7. In an increasingly complex society it was no longer possible for children simply to melt into the adult world and function as somewhat inferior but nevertheless useful versions of adults. This had worked in past centuries, when children served as agricultural helpers or as workers in cottage industries or as apprentices to craftsmen. In such an economy the *attributes* required to carry out their assigned tasks successfully were persistence, perseverance, courage, and independence, virtues more readily acquired if a child is set loose early from intimate ties with those who nurtured him in infancy. (Marie Winn)
Attributes _____

8. One of my earliest discoveries in the field of intercultural communication was that the position of the bodies of people in conversation varies with the culture. Even so, it used to puzzle me that a special

Arab friend seemed unable to walk and talk at the same time. After years of living in the United States, he could not bring himself to stroll along, facing forward while talking. Our progress would be *arrested* while he edged ahead, cutting slightly in front of me and turning sideways so we could see each other. Once in this position, he would stop. His behavior was explained when I learned that for the Arabs to view the other person *peripherally* is regarded as impolite, and to sit or stand back-to-back, is considered very rude. You must be involved when interacting with Arabs who are friends. (Edward T. Hall)

Arrested _____

Peripherally _____

9. Termites make *percussive* sounds to each other by beating their heads against the floor in the dark, resonating corridors of their nests. The sound has been described as resembling, to the human ear, sand falling on paper, but spectrographic analysis of sound records has recently revealed a high degree of organization in the drumming; the beats occur in regular, rhythmic phrases. (Lewis Thomas)

*Percussive*_____

10. Consider this familiar *paradox* of biological diversity: almost all the species that ever lived are extinct, and yet more are alive today than at any time in the past. The solution of the paradox is simple. The life and death of species have been spread across more than three billion years. If most species last an average of, say, a million years, then it follows that most have expired across that vast stretch of geological time, in the same sense that all the people who ever lived during the past 10,000 years are dead though the human population is larger than it has ever been. (Edwin O. Wilson)

Paradox _____

You should now be well prepared for the material in Part 1.

PART

Reading and Analyzing Paragraphs

The Fundamentals of Reading Paragraphs

The Structure of the Paragraph

The paragraph is the fundamental unit of written thought. Simply defined, a paragraph is a group of related sentences that develops and supports one idea, whether stated or not. A paragraph may be any length as long as it keeps to that one idea. The main idea—a general statement telling the reader what the paragraph is about—may be explicitly present in a sentence that *often* appears at or near the beginning of the paragraph. (As you will see later in the chapter, however, many essay writers do not adhere to this pattern. The main idea may be buried in the middle of the paragraph, it may be at the end, or to complicate matters, it may not be there at all.)

Most books use the term *topic sentence* to describe the main idea of a paragraph, but since there may not be a single explicit topic sentence, I prefer to use the term *main idea*. If there is a main idea sentence in the paragraph, it consists of two parts: the *topic* and the *controlling idea*. The

topic is what the paragraph is about: the general subject (not necessarily the grammatical subject). The controlling idea—usually a word or phrase—limits, qualifies, or narrows down the topic to make it manageable. Another way of looking at the main idea is to ask yourself two questions: What is the topic? What does the author want me to understand about the topic? The answers to these two questions will usually give you the topic and controlling idea. Diagrammed, the typical main idea sentence might look like this:

Main Idea = Topic + Controlling Idea

Consider this sentence:

> The American presidency is an increasingly grueling and unrewarding job.

In this example, the topic is the phrase "The American presidency," and the controlling idea or limiting phrase is "a grueling and increasingly unrewarding job." If the writer shifted direction and changed the controlling idea, the paragraph would be committed to develop an entirely different idea, for example:

> The American presidency increasingly resembles that of a teacher who must control a group of unruly, quarreling students in his dealings with the public, the press, and Congress.

Here is another example:

Topic: The high cost of living in the United States has resulted in

Controlling idea: the majority of married couples with children needing two incomes to survive.

When you analyze a main idea, it is helpful to label these parts separately by underlining the topic once and the controlling idea twice. Irrelevant information need not be labeled, as this illustration shows:

> Although there are some diehard writers who still bang away on their typewriters, the widespread availability of inexpensive personal computers has undoubtedly simplified the task of writing for students and professionals alike.

You do not need to include the first clause ("although . . . typewriters") because the author is most likely uninterested in the disadvantages of writing on a typewriter. The author mentions this fact only to concede a truth and to avoid generalizing. The topic is "the widespread availability of inexpensive personal computers," and the controlling idea narrows that topic to include only the *results* of the computer revolution, "has made the task of writing much easier for students and professional writers alike."

This pattern—topic + controlling idea—is the typical one, but main idea sentences need not follow it. In this revised sentence, these elements are reversed. The meaning is the same, whether the topic precedes the controlling idea or follows it:

> Students and professional writers alike have found the task of writing greatly simplified by the wide availability of inexpensive personal computers.

Being able to identify the writer's controlling idea helps you keep on track and makes it easier to follow the idea's development, as you will see in the next section.

Here is a short exercise in labeling main ideas. For each, underline the topic once and the controlling idea twice.

1. The bathroom is the most dangerous room in the house.
2. The most dangerous room in the house is the bathroom.
3. The complexity of the mating "dance" performed by some fish is often astonishing.
4. It is astonishing to observe the complexity of the mating "dance" performed by some fish.
5. The threat of starvation in the world's poor countries is the most tragic effect of failed population control measures.
6. The most tragic effect of failed population control measures is the threat of starvation in the world's poor countries.
7. The cow is considered a sacred animal in India for many reasons.
8. Many Eastern European nations, most notably the former Yugoslavia, have been torn apart by long-simmering ethnic conflicts that resurfaced after the breakup of the Communist empire.
9. The search for water is a paramount concern in the lives of desert dwellers, whether animal or human.
10. Psychologists agree that children who watch too much television may have difficulty distinguishing between fantasy and reality.
11. If one hopes to get ahead in the business world, a knowledge of computers is an absolute necessity.
12. The most useful book a college student can own is an unabridged dictionary.
13. Los Angeles is a city of great contrasts: a burgeoning downtown skyline and blighted ghetto neighborhoods, opulent wealth and abject poverty.
14. Part of the appeal of popular music, since the emergence of rock 'n' roll in the early 1950s, is its ability to antagonize people.
15. Success is best measured by the number of imitations a new idea gives rise to, as evidenced by the many television spin-offs of programs like *Melrose Place*.

Now that you have had some practice separating the components of main-idea sentences, let us move to the paragraph as a whole. As you read through the following paragraph, label each sentence either with a *G* (for general statement) or an *S* (for supporting statements.) Then try to discern a pattern. Which sentences represent main idea, supporting details, and conclusion?

_S_ Language originates in magic. _S_ The first "words" of a baby are not words at all, but magic incantations, sounds uttered for pleasure and enjoyed indiscriminately to bring about a desired event. _G_ Sometime in the last quarter of the first year the baby makes the sounds "mama" or "dada." _S_ The baby is surprised and pleased at the excitement he creates in his parents and can easily be induced to repeat this performance dozens of times a day. _G_ Unfortunately, he doesn't know who or what "mama" is. _S_ He will look right into your eyes and say "mama" and you melt at the lovely sound, and he will look right into his father's eyes and say "mama" and his father, embarrassed, corrects him. _S_ He will pursue the dog's tail chanting "mama," and he will reach for a cookie yelling "mama" and he will lie in his crib murmuring "mamamamamamamama"—and he hasn't a thought in his head for M-O-T-H-E-R and the millions of things she gave him. _S_ He doesn't connect the word and the person at this point.

Selma H. Fraiberg, The Magic Years

Let's see how you did. You should have marked sentences 1, 2, and 8 as general statements and the remaining sentences as supporting ones. This paragraph represents a traditional pattern: Sentence 1 makes a broad generalization; sentence 2 explains the first sentence and narrows the generalization down to a manageable topic. The sentences in the body of the paragraph (3 through 7) provide specific examples of a baby's unconscious mimicking of sounds and the parents' reaction to it; and sentence 8 concludes from the foregoing evidence that the baby does not yet connect the word "mama" with his mother.

The Direction of Paragraphs— How Writers Write

As a college reader, you must learn to cope with an infinite variety of writing styles and techniques; this necessitates revising some of the "rules" you may have been taught in the past. For example, most students learn—usually during junior high school—that the first sentence in a paragraph is the topic sentence. But as noted earlier, a main idea can appear anywhere in the paragraph, and some paragraphs lack a main idea sentence altogether. Adult prose is not so neatly formulaic as stu-

dents would like it to be, and the careful reader has to be alert and ready for any variation. A glance at the paragraphs in the essays in Part IV or at the essays in any freshman English anthology will confirm that the old rules you were taught in the past may no longer be wholly reliable.

Reading and writing go hand in hand, and you may find it instructive to examine what Richard Marius, director of the Expository Writing Program at Harvard College since 1978, says about the way a writer thinks. This information in turn will help you follow a writer's ideas so that you don't get "lost," even in long passages. In his text, *A Writer's Companion,* which is widely used in college writing courses, Marius first says:

[1]A lot of nonsense has been written about paragraphs; much of it is not only wrong but harmful. Much of the nonsense arises from the false notion that every paragraph is a short essay and that the thesis for the essay should be expressed in a *topic sentence.* Some books teach that a topic sentence may be at the beginning, the middle, or the end of a paragraph. Many teachers command students to underline the topic sentence, and students dutifully obey whether the paragraph has a topic sentence or not.

[2]The topic sentence is said to be a general statement that is supported by the evidence in the rest of the paragraph. A good topic sentence is supposed to develop paragraph unity.

[3]No doubt, paragraph unity is important. In our reading we do not like to be jerked around from thought to thought without seeing any connections between those thoughts. Smooth-flowing paragraphs take us from thought to thought, from detail to detail. Sometimes a paragraph does develop an idea stated in a general statement that fits the standard textbook definition of the topic sentence. The other sentences in the paragraph provide some reason to accept the generalization. Such paragraphs usually explain things. In most other paragraphs, no textbook topic sentence can be found.

Then he continues:

[4]But many paragraphs—most paragraphs, in fact—are not introduced by general statements. Here, for example, is a paragraph from James Baldwin's "Notes of a Native Son":

> On the 29th of July, in 1943, my father died. On the same day, a few hours later, his last child was born. Over a month before this, while all our energies were concentrated in waiting for these events, there had been, in Detroit, one of the bloodiest race riots of the century. A few hours after my father's funeral, while he lay in state in the undertaker's chapel, a race riot broke out in Harlem. On the morning of the 3rd of August, we drove my father to the graveyard through a wilderness of smashed plate glass.

We could summarize the paragraph above in a general topic sentence such as this: "Several interesting things happened on the day my father died." Such a sentence would be tedious and unnecessary. As Baldwin tells us what happened, event by event, we easily follow along. We see the unity of the paragraph as we read it.

[5]But how do paragraphs work? What do paragraphs with general topic sentences have in common with paragraphs that lack such sentences? Paragraphs have unity. But how do writers attain this unity?

[6]I believe that we write with a sense in our heads of when we are going to make a slight shift in the subject we are treating. When we wish to move on to another point, another idea, another incident, we indent and write a sentence. The first sentence of the paragraph contains some ideas we wish to expand in the next sentence. We pick up one of those ideas and use it in that next sentence. We connect the two sentences by some repetition—a word, a pronoun, or a synonym for an idea in the first sentence.

[7]Let's examine that process in the paragraph from James Baldwin.

> On the 29th of July, in 1943, my father died.

Think for a moment of all the possibilities in this sentence. We have several key thoughts—"29th of July," "1943," "my father," and "died."

[8]Baldwin picks up the thought of the date and the thought of the father. The important topic here is "when." He develops them in this sentence:

> On the same day, a few hours later, his last child was born.

"On the same day," is a synonym for "On the 29th of July, in 1943," and "his" refers to "my father." Baldwin develops a thought of what happens on July 29, 1943. Now he develops a further thought, also related to the question "when."

> Over a month before this, while all our energies were concentrated in waiting for these events, there had been, in Detroit, one of the bloodiest race riots of the century.

Two thoughts are picked up here. "Over a month before this" develops the thought of "On the 29th of July, in 1943," and "On the same day." "While all our energies were concentrated in waiting for these events" relates to the ideas of the death of Baldwin's father and the birth of the father's last child.

[9]Baldwin continues in the next sentence to develop the idea of "when," also referring to his father's death by mentioning the funeral:

> A few hours after my father's funeral, while he lay in state in the undertaker's chapel, a race riot broke out in Harlem.

Again referring to his father's funeral, and also referring to the race riot mentioned in this sentence, he develops the next sentence:

On the morning of the 3rd of August, we drove my father to the graveyard through a wilderness of smashed plate glass.

This sentence concludes the paragraph. We see in these sentences a network of interlocking thoughts that begin with the first sentence. That first sentence is not a general topic sentence; it is a simple declaration of fact. The other sentences are similar declarations of fact, but they are all tied to the first sentence by the words they use. Every sentence picks up some words or ideas from the previous sentence and adds something new.

[10]These are qualities of all paragraphs, whether they have a general topic sentence or not. They reflect the writer's mind.

Richard Marius, *A Writer's Companion*

Let us apply what Marius says about unity in the Baldwin paragraph to another passage, this one from an essay by Alexander Petrunkevitch. (This essay is reprinted in its entirety at the beginning of Part IV.) As you read it, follow the lines and circles to see how one sentence leads logically and naturally to the next, as Marius says, to create "a network of interlocking thoughts."

The entire body of a tarantula especially its legs, is thickly clothed with hair. Some of it is short and wooly, some long and stiff. Touching this body hair produces one of two distinct reactions. When the spider is hungry, it responds with an immediate and swift attack. At the touch of a cricket's antennae the tarantula seizes the insect so swiftly that a motion picture taken at the rate of 64 frames per second shows only the result and not the process of capture. But when the spider is not hungry, the stimulation of its hairs merely causes it to shake the touched limb. An insect can walk under its hairy belly unharmed.

Alexander Petrunkevitch, "The Spider and the Wasp"
Scientific American

Here is another short passage for you to practice with. This one is from a popular book about anthropology. Using a pencil, make the connections between ideas by drawing circles and lines as in the previous example.

[1]Early in the present century, anthropologists were surprised to discover that certain primitive tribes engaged in conspicuous consumption and conspicuous waste to a degree unmatched by even the most wasteful of modern consumer economies. Ambitious, status-hungry men were found competing with each other for approval by giving huge feasts. The rival feast givers judged each other by the amount of food they provided, and a feast was a success only if the guests could eat until they were stupefied, stagger off into the bush, stick their fingers down their throats, vomit, and come back for more.

[2]The most bizarre instance of status seeking was discovered among the American Indians who formerly inhabited the coastal regions of Southern Alaska, British Columbia, and Washington. Here the status seekers practiced what seems like a maniacal form of conspicuous consumption and conspicuous waste known as *potlatch*. The object of potlatch was to give away or destroy more wealth than one's rival. If the potlatch giver was a powerful chief, he might attempt to shame his rivals and gain everlasting admiration from his followers by destroying food, clothing, and money. Sometimes he might even seek prestige by burning down his own house.

Marvin Harris, *Cows, Pigs, Wars, and Witches*

You can improve your comprehension enormously by looking for these logical connections between ideas and by seeing how each sentence looks back to a word or phrase in a previous sentence and points ahead to the ideas in the next sentence.

The Placement of the Main Idea

Now we can begin to put everything together. Let us examine a few paragraphs to see both the placement of the main idea and the direction of the ideas. As you read this first paragraph, which reflects the typical pattern of main idea + support, first look for the main idea sentence; then separate it into its component parts of topic and controlling idea. (Hanoi, mentioned in sentence 1, is the capital of North Vietnam.)

Just as the Red River Delta, where the poverty of the North is so conspicuous, has become one of the most densely populated rural environments in Asia, so Hanoi has become one of Asia's most crowded urban environ-

ments. In the central part of the city, the population density runs to about thirteen hundred persons per hectare, or thirty-two hundred and fifty people per acre—one of the highest densities on earth. Some of the worst crowding occurs in the ancient part of Hanoi, where thirty-six picturesque streets, so narrow that they are actually lanes, are knit together into a section just above the city's most famous lake, the Lake of the Restored Sword. Many of the buildings there are of one or two stories and are hundreds of years old. Since plumbing is virtually nonexistent in them, a nightly ritual is to take the children down to the sidewalk to urinate before bedtime. The number of Vietnamese packed into once-spacious villas in the former European sections can be astonishing. In the late nineteen-eighties, the Australian Embassy, which was in need of more room for its staff, leased two adjacent two-story buildings from the Hanoi city government. When the Vietnamese residents were evicted so that the buildings could be refurbished, the Australians discovered to their dismay that a hundred and twenty-seven Vietnamese had been living in just one of the houses.

Neil and Susan Sheehan, "Vietnam," The New Yorker

The main idea is stated in the *second* part of the first sentence. The topic is simply "Hanoi," and the controlling idea is "one of Asia's most crowded urban environments." This phrase unifies the details in the remainder of the paragraph. Each sentence following the main idea develops and extends that controlling idea. Notice that the Sheehans keep us on track by repeating the controlling idea ("most crowded") in different words: "population density," "highest densities," "worst crowding," and "packed."

However, not all paragraphs are so conventionally organized. In this next paragraph, the first sentences *introduces* the general subject, and the main idea—that all species of lichens are slow-growing—is reserved for the second sentence. The rest of the paragraph supports that assertion with a single dramatic example.

There are some 16,000 species of lichens in the world. All are slow-growing, but those that encrust the rocks of mountain peaks are particularly so. At high altitudes, there may be only a single day in a whole year when growth is possible and a lichen may take as long as sixty years to cover just one square centimetre. Lichens as big as plates, which are very common, are therefore likely to be hundreds if not thousands of years old.

David Attenborough, The Living Planet

Writers may also *delay* the main idea for several sentences. Sometimes the introductory sentences provide background or orient us to

the subject. David Rieff uses this delayed topic sentence pattern in the following paragraph on the Cuban presence in Miami.

> In Miami, Cuba is with you everywhere. Its presence can be felt immediately by the traveler arriving at Miami International Airport. The predominant language of passersby there is Spanish. Over the public-address system, many flight announcements are routinely given in both Spanish and English—far more often, in fact, than in the airports of a city as international as New York or as Hispanic as Los Angeles. And in Miami the Spanish that one hears is neither schooled Castilian nor the leisurely accents of Mexico but, rather, that fast, jolting Cuban variant of the language which was once described to me by a Cuban-American friend as "Spanish jazzed up on amphetamine—Spanish in overdrive." In the crowded terminal are a number of small stands whose signs say simply "Café Cubano." There Cuban-American airport workers banter comfortably in Spanish with the women serving the coffee while befuddled tourists worry about what the coffee will cost (it is in fact absurdly cheap: thirty-five cents for a tiny cup called a *chiquito,* and ninety-five cents for what in a restaurant would be called a triple *espresso*), and even about whether an order given in English will be understood or heeded. Indeed, many tourists seem to act as if they had landed not in a provincial American resort city but in the capital of a foreign country.
>
> David Rieff, "The Second Havana," *The New Yorker*

Rieff begins with a broad generalization: the Cuban presence is everywhere in Miami. The second and third sentences narrow this generalization to the main idea—the impact of the Cuban influence at Miami International Airport—a more manageable topic than the one represented in the first sentence would have been. Following the main idea are several examples of the pervasiveness of the Spanish language at the airport. The final sentence represents a conclusion, unifying the paragraph by restating the main idea in different words.

Another technique writers often use is to establish at the beginning of a paragraph an assertion or popular assumption that they wish to disprove, as you can see in this next example. The first short paragraph presents the common way of thinking; the second explains why Regan believes this approach is deficient.

> [1]Someone might think that though what one person thinks or feels about moral issues does not settle matters, what all or most people think or feel does. A single individual is only one voice; what most or all people think or feel is a great deal more. There is strength in numbers. Thus, the correct method for answering questions about right and wrong is to find out what most or all people think or feel; opinion polls should be conducted, statistics compiled. That will reveal the truth.

²This approach to moral questions is deficient. All that opinion polls can reveal is what all or most people think or feel about some moral question—for example, "Is capital punishment morally right or wrong?" What such polls cannot determine is whether what all or most people think about such an issue is true or that what all or most people feel is appropriate. There may be strength in numbers, but not truth, at least not necessarily. This does not mean that "what we all think (or feel)" is irrelevant to answering moral questions. Later on, in fact . . . . , we will see how, given that certain conditions have been met, "what we all think" might provide us with a place from which to begin our search for what is right and wrong, and why. Nevertheless, *merely* to establish that all (or most) people think that, say, capital punishment is morally justified is not to establish that it *is* morally justified. In times past, most (possibly even all) people thought the world is flat. And possibly most (or all) people felt pleased or relieved to think of the world as having this shape. But what they thought and felt did not make it true that the world is flat. The question of its shape had to be answered without relying on what most people think or feel. There is no reason to believe moral questions differ in this respect. Questions of right and wrong cannot be answered just by counting heads.

Tom Regan, Matters of Life and Death

Some writers suggest the main idea over a series of several sentences, requiring you to take bits and pieces from them to formulate a main idea of your own. Consider this example:

Sagebrush covers 58,000 square miles of Wyoming. The biggest city has a population of fifty thousand, and there are only five settlements that could be called cities in the whole state. The rest are towns, scattered across the expanse with as much as sixty miles between them, their populations two thousand, fifty, or ten. They are fugitive-looking, perched on a barren, windblown bench, or tagged onto a river or a railroad, or laid out straight in a farming valley with implement stores and a block-long Mormon church. In the eastern part of the state, which slides down into the Great Plains, the new mining settlements are boomtowns, trailer cities, metal knots on flat land.

Greta Ehrlich, The Solace of Open Spaces

A main idea sentence would be superfluous because the details readily suggest the main point: Wyoming is sparsely populated.

Here is one final example of a paragraph whose point is readily discernible even though it does not have a main idea. By piling up detail after detail about the kinds of people who shop at the Sunshine Market in the Queens (a borough of New York City), we see immediately that

all different kinds of people come to shop at this store to buy an incredible array of products.

> The people who shop at Sunshine Market, a grocery store in Jackson Heights, Queens, are thin and beautiful. They are also fat and plain, relaxed and frantic, Colombian, Italian, Jewish, Indian, African-American, Bolivian, Uruguayan, Vietnamese, young, middle-aged, elderly, rowdy, meek, cheerful, world-weary, rich, and broke. They buy health food. They buy Ding Dongs and Diet Coke. They have just come to America. They have lived in America, in Jackson Heights, in the same apartment, with the same furniture in the same arrangement, for sixty years. They are in a big hurry. They are in no rush and hoping to bump into their neighbors for a chat. They are in minks. They are in their pajamas, wearing stacks of hair curlers and no makeup. They are buying the works for a dinner party. They are buying a Lean Cuisine Chicken Fettucini to eat alone. They come in every single day and buy the same three things: a gallon of bottled water, a banana, a skinless boneless chicken breast. They come in once a week and weave up and down every aisle and arrive at the cash register, exhausted, with a tipsy heap of groceries. They are immigrants hunting for Goya Guanabana Nectar or Manischewitz Low Calorie Borscht or Trappey's India-Pep Pepper Sauce. They are immigrants who desire Planters Cheez Balls, Salerno Scooter-Pies, Maxwell House Coffee, Chef Boyardee Pac-Man Pasta in Spaghetti Sauce with Mini-Meat Balls, Count Chocula, Pringles potato crisps, Frank Sinatra's Marinara Sauce, Newman's Own Olive Oil and Vinegar Dressing, and a copy of the *Sun* ("WORLD'S SMALLEST MOM! She's Just 34 Inches Tall—But Has a 6-Foot Son!"). They do their shopping with their own red pushcarts, or with eco-conscious green string bags, or with their napping babies in Graco strollers, in which, if the baby is average-sized, they can also fit a small package of lean ground beef, half a dozen peaches, and two bars of Dove.
>
> Susan Orleans, "All Mixed Up," *The New Yorker*

Levels of Support

Now we can turn our attention to the paragraph's support—the body sentences. A useful skill in analytical reading is the ability to distinguish between *major* supporting statements and *minor* ones. Briefly, major statements directly relate to, and develop, the main idea, while minor ones further explain or illustrate or otherwise develop the major ones. Analysis of levels of support trains you to think logically because you must weigh the relative importance of ideas in relation to the main idea. Diagrammed, using an ideal model paragraph, the supporting sentences might look like this:

> **Main Idea (topic sentence)**
> **Major Support**
>   **Minor Support**
>   **Minor Support**
> **Major Support**
>   **Minor Support**
>   **Minor Support**
> **Conclusion**

The following paragraph nicely exemplifies the model above. Notice that each minor supporting sentence is printed in parentheses, each parenthetical sentence serving to state the author's opinion of each type of book owner.

[1]There are three kinds of book owners. [2]The first has all the standard sets and best-sellers—unread, untouched. [3](This deluded individual owns wood-pulp and ink, not books.) [4]The second has a great many books—a few of them read through, most of them dipped into, but all of them as clean and shiny as the day they were bought. [5](This person would probably like to make books his own, but is restrained by a false respect for their physical appearance.) [6]The third has a few books or many—every one of them dog-eared and dilapidated, shaken and loosened by continual use, marked and scribbled in front to back. [7](This man owns books.)

Mortimer Adler, "How to Mark a Book," Saturday Review

Here is another example with a different pattern of major and minor supporting details. (You will recall that you practiced following the direction of ideas with this paragraph about tarantulas earlier in the chapter.) The first two sentences describe the insect's body, and sentence 3 represents the main idea. Read the remainder of the paragraph carefully and label sentences 4 through 7 according to whether they represent major support (MA) or minor support (MI):

[1]The entire body of a tarantula, especially its legs, is thickly clothed with hair. [2]Some of it is short and woolly, some long and stiff. [3]Touching this body hair produces one of two distinct reactions. [4]When the spider is hungry, it responds with an immediate and swift attack. [5]At the touch of a cricket's antennae the tarantula seizes the insect so swiftly that a motion picture taken at the rate of 64 frames per second shows only the result and not the process of capture. [6]But when the spider is not hungry, the stimulation of its hairs merely causes it to shake the touched limb. [7]An insect can walk under its hairy belly unharmed.

Alexander Petrunkevitch, "The Spider and the Wasp," Scientific American

You should have marked sentences 4 and 6 as *major* support (MA) and sentences 5 and 7 as *minor* support (MI). The paragraph is beautifully constructed so that the supporting statements are balanced. Diagrammed, Petrunkevitch's paragraph would look like this:

Sentences 1 and 2:	**Descriptive details**
Sentence 3:	**Topic sentence**
Sentence 4:	**Major support**
Sentence 5:	**Minor support**
Sentence 6:	**Major support**
Sentence 7:	**Minor support**

Unhappily, not every paragraph works out as well as this one does. At the end of this chapter, a few of the exercises will ask you to distinguish between major supporting ideas (those that directly reinforce the topic), and minor ones (those that merely add to or explain the major details).

Now try your hand at distinguishing between the two kinds of support in the following exercise. In the space before each sentence, indicate whether the sentence represents the main idea (MAIN), major support (MA), or minor support (MI):

_____ People feel safer behind some kind of physical barrier. _____ If a social situation is in any way threatening, then there is an immediate urge to set up such a barricade. _____ For a tiny child faced with a stranger, the problem is usually solved by hiding behind its mother's body and peeping out at the intruder to see what he or she will do next. _____ If the mother's body is not available, then a chair or some other piece of solid furniture will do. _____ If the stranger insists on coming closer, then the peeping face must be hidden too. _____ If the insensitive intruder continues to approach despite these obvious signals of fear, then there is nothing for it but to scream or flee.

Desmond Morris, *Manwatching: A Field Guide to Human Behaviour*

You should have marked the sentences as follows: MAIN, MA, MI, MI, MI, and MI.

Modes of Discourse: The Author's Purpose

Finally, a good reader also must learn to establish the writer's purpose. If you can ascertain the purpose you will later be able to accomplish other, more difficult skills (such as detecting bias, understanding the

reason one method of development was chosen over another, understanding word choice and connotation, and so on).

The traditional term, *modes of discourse,* actually refers to the kind of writing a piece of nonfiction prose represents. There are four modes or types: (1) narration; (2) description; (3) exposition; (4) and persuasion. But in simpler terms, you can think of mode of discourse as synonymous with the author's purpose. In other words, the choice of one mode over another reflects the author's purpose in writing.

Narration

The first and most easily recognized mode of discourse is *narration,* which means simply telling a story. A writer uses the narrative mode because his or her purpose is to relate events, either real or imagined, in chronological order, usually to provide evidence for some larger truth. One of the simplest forms of narration is the fable, a short tale written or told to illustrate a moral truth, as in this fable by Aesop:

The Fox and the Grapes

One hot summer's day a Fox was strolling through an orchard till he came to a bunch of Grapes just ripening on a vine which had been trained over a lofty branch. "Just the thing to quench my thirst," quoth he. Drawing back a few paces, he took a run and a jump, and just missed the bunch. Turning around again with a One, Two, Three, he jumped up, but with no greater success. Again and again he tried after the tempting morsel, but at last had to give it up, and walked away with his nose in the air, saying, "I am sure they are sour."

"It Is Easy to Despise What You Cannot Get,"
Folk-Lore and Fable: Aesop, Grimm, Andersen

This fable is the source of the expression, "sour grapes," meaning, as the fable tells us, the human tendency to criticize what we cannot have.

Typically, however, narration is used along with the other modes of discourse to support an idea or to illustrate a theory, as Lewis Thomas does in this passage.

[1]We may be about to rediscover that dying is not such a bad thing to do after all. Sir William Osler took this view: he disapproved of people who spoke of the agony of death, maintaining there was no such thing.

[2]In a nineteenth-century memoir on an expedition in Africa, there is a story by David Livingston about his own experience of near-death. He was caught by a lion, crushed across the chest in the animal's great jaws, and saved in the instant by a lucky shot from a friend. Later, he remembered the episode in clear detail. He was so amazed by the extraordinary sense of peace, calm, and total painlessness associated with being killed that he

constructed a theory that all creatures are provided with a protective physiologic mechanism, switched on at the verge of death, carrying them through in a haze of tranquillity.

Lewis Thomas, "The Long Habit," *Lives of a Cell*

Description

The *descriptive mode* shows what someone or something looks like or what something feels like. The author's purpose is to paint a picture in words. Description almost always relies on sensory details—that is, words that appeal to the reader's senses. Furthermore, although descriptive writing by itself does not have a main idea, there usually is a *dominant impression*. In this paragraph, the mystery writer Raymond Chandler shows us what Bunker Hill, a derelict area near downtown Los Angeles, looked like in the 1940s. (Today the old buildings of Bunker Hill have been completely razed, and the area is filled with condominiums and office buildings. There is little trace now of either its former grandeur or dereliction, as Chandler describes it.)

[1]Bunker Hill is old town, lost town, shabby town, crook town. Once, very long ago, it was the choice residential district of the city, and there are still standing a few of the jigsaw Gothic mansions with wide porches and walls covered with round-end shingles and full corner bay windows with spindle turrets. They are all rooming houses now, their parquetry floors are scratched and worn through the once glossy finish and the wide sweeping staircases are dark with time and with cheap varnish laid on over generations of dirt. In the tall rooms haggard landladies bicker with shifty tenants. On the wide cool front porches, reaching their cracked shoes into the sun, and staring at nothing, sit the old men with faces like lost battles.

[2]In and around the old houses there are flyblown restaurants and Italian fruitstands and cheap apartment houses and little candy stores where you can buy even nastier things than their candy. And there are ratty hotels where nobody except people named Smith and Jones sign the register and where the night clerk is half watchdog and half pander.

[3]Out of the apartment houses come women who should be young but have faces like stale beer; men with pulled-down hats and quick eyes that look the street over behind the cupped hand that shields the match flame; worn intellectuals with cigarette coughs and no money in the bank; fly cops with granite faces and unwavering eyes; cokies and coke peddlers; people who look like nothing in particular and know it, and once in a while even men that actually go to work. But they come out early, when the wide cracked sidewalks are empty and still have dew on them.

Raymond Chandler, *The High Window*

What dominant impression of Bunker Hill does Chandler convey?

In this next descriptive passage, the travel writer Paul Theroux describes his impressions of the Great Wall of China, using both sensory details and figurative language, to fancifully compare the Wall to an undulating dragon.

[1]The Wall is an intimidating thing, less a fortification than a visual statement announcing imperiously: I am the Son of Heaven and this is the proof that I can encircle the earth. It somewhat resembles, in intention, the sort of achievement of that barmy man Christo, who giftwrapped the Golden Gate Bridge. The Wall goes steeply up and down mountainsides. To what purpose? Certainly not to repel invaders, who could never cling to those cliffs. Wasn't it another example of the Chinese love of taking possession of the land and whipping it into shape?

[2]Anyway, it was not empty. It swarmed with tourists. They scampered on it and darkened it like fleas on a dead snake.

[3]That gave me an idea. "Snake" was very close, but what it actually looked like was a dragon. The dragon is the favorite Chinese creature ("just after man in the hierarchy of living beings") and until fairly recently—eighty or a hundred years ago—the Chinese believed they existed. Many people reported seeing them alive—and of course fossilized dragon skeletons had been unearthed. It was a good omen and, especially, a guardian. The marauding dragon and the dragon slayer are unknown in China. It is one of China's friendliest and most enduring symbols. And I found a bewitching similarity between the Chinese dragon and the Great Wall of China—the way it flexed and slithered up and down the Mongolian mountains; the way its crenellations looked like the fins on a dragon's back, and its bricks like scales; the way it looked serpentine and protective, undulating endlessly from one end of the world to the other.

Paul Theroux, *Riding the Iron Rooster*

In both fiction (imaginative writing, such as short stories and novels) and nonfiction, narration and description frequently appear together. The narrative elements advance the action of the story, and the descriptive elements give us a picture of what the environment, characters, scenery, and so forth look like. This combination is well illustrated in the following excerpt from an essay by Annie Dillard, in which she recounts the experience of seeing a weasel near her suburban home. As you read it, try to identify the narrative and descriptive elements.

[1]I have been reading about weasels because I saw one last week. I startled a weasel who startled me, and we exchanged a long glance.

²Twenty minutes from my house, through the woods by the quarry and across the highway, is Hollins Pond, a remarkable piece of shallowness, where I like to go at sunset and sit on a tree trunk. Hollins Pond is also called Murray's Pond; it covers two acres of bottomland near Tinker Creek with six inches of water and six thousand lily pads. In winter, brown-and-white steers stand in the middle of it, merely dampening their hooves; from the distant shore they look like miracle itself, complete with miracle's nonchalance. Now, in summer, the steers are gone. The water lilies have blossomed and spread to a green horizontal plane that is terra firma to plodding blackbirds, and tremulous ceiling to black leeches, crayfish, and carp.

³This is, mind you, suburbia. It is a five-minute walk in three directions to rows of houses, though none is visible here. There's a 55 mph highway at one end of the pond, and a nesting pair of wood ducks at the other. Under every bush is a muskrat hole or a beer can. The far end is an alternating series of fields and woods, fields and woods, threaded everywhere with motorcycle tracks—in whose bare clay wild turtles lay eggs.

⁴So. I had crossed the highway, stepped over two low barbed-wire fences, and traced the motorcycle path in all gratitude through the wild rose and poison ivy of the pond's shoreline up into high grassy fields. Then I cut down through the woods to the mossy fallen tree where I sit. This tree is excellent. It makes a dry, upholstered bench at the upper, marshy end of the pond, a plush jetty raised from the thorny shore between a shallow blue body of water and a deep blue body of sky.

⁵The sun had just set. I was relaxed on the tree trunk, ensconced in the lap of lichen, watching the lily pads at my feet tremble and part dreamily over the thrusting path of a carp. A yellow bird appeared to my right and flew behind me. It caught my eye; I swiveled around—and the next instant, inexplicably, I was looking down at a weasel, who was looking up at me.

⁶Weasel! I'd never seen one wild before. He was ten inches long, thin as a curve, a muscled ribbon, brown as fruitwood, soft-furred, alert. His face was fierce, small and pointed as a lizard's; he would have made a good arrowhead. There was just a dot of chin, maybe two brown hairs' worth, and then the pure white fur began that spread down his underside. He had two black eyes I didn't see, any more than you see a window.

⁷The weasel was stunned into stillness as he was emerging from beneath an enormous shaggy wild rose bush four feet away. I was stunned into stillness twisted backward on the tree trunk. Our eyes locked, and someone threw away the key.

⁸Our look was as if two lovers, or deadly enemies, met unexpectedly on an overgrown path when each had been thinking of something else: a clearing blow to the gut. It was also a bright blow to the brain, or a sudden beating of brains, with all the charge and intimate grate of rubbed bal-

loons. It emptied our lungs. It felled the forest, moved the fields, and drained the pond; the world dismantled and tumbled into that black hole of eyes. If you and I looked at each other that way, our skulls would split and drop to our shoulders. But we don't. We keep our skulls. So.

⁹He disappeared. This was only last week, and already I don't remember what shattered the enchantment. I think I blinked, I think I retrieved my brain from the weasel's brain, and tried to memorize what I was seeing, and the weasel felt the yank of separation, the careening splashdown into real life and the urgent current of instinct. He vanished under the wild rose. I waited motionless, my mind suddenly full of data and my spirit with pleadings, but he didn't return.

Annie Dillard, "Living Like Weasels,"
Teaching a Stone to Talk: Expeditions and Encounters

Exposition

Exposition, or expository writing, is the most common kind of writing you will encounter in your college reading. It is essentially factual writing with a straightforward purpose: to inform, to explain, to make clear, to discuss, or to set forth. In this first example, Genelle Morain explains the significance of eyes to babies in two cultures, Japan and America. (Argyle in the last sentence is a reference to a book by Michael Argyle entitled *Bodily Communication*.)

Whether the eyes are "the windows of the soul" is debatable; that they are intensely important in interpersonal communication is a fact. During the first two months of a baby's life, the stimulus that produces a smile is a pair of eyes. The eyes need not be real: a mask with two dots will produce a smile. Significantly, a real human face with eyes covered will not motivate a smile, nor will the sight of only one eye when the face is presented in profile. This attraction to eyes as opposed to the nose or mouth continues as the baby matures. In one study, when American four-year-olds were asked to draw people, 75 percent of them drew people with mouths, but 99 percent of them drew people with eyes. In Japan, however, where babies are carried on their mother's back, infants do not acquire as much attachment to eyes as they do in other cultures. As a result, Japanese adults make little use of the face either to encode or decode meaning. In fact, Argyle reveals that the "proper place to focus one's gaze during a conversation in Japan is on the neck of one's conversation partner."

Genelle G. Moraine, "Kinesics and Cross-Cultural Understanding,"
Language in Education: Theory and Practice

Even potentially inflammatory or controversial topics can be treated in the expository mode. In this excerpt Dinesh D'Souza uses a series of rhetorical questions—questions intended to make us think—about the issue of affirmative action. Even though he is a conservative with

serious reservations about affirmative action policies, he does not give his own opinion. He merely informs us of the changes brought about as we move toward being a multiracial, multicultural society.

> [1]The result [of America's becoming a multiracial, multicultural society] is a new diversity of pigments and lifestyles. When America loses her predominantly white stamp, what impact will that have on her Western cultural traditions? On what terms will the evanescent majority and the emerging minorities, both foreign and domestic, relate to each other? How should society cope with the agenda of increasingly powerful minority groups, which claim to speak for blacks, Hispanics, women, and homosexuals? These challenges are currently being faced by the leadership of institutions of higher education.
>
> [2]Universities are a microcosm of society. But they are more than a reflection or mirror; they are a leading indicator. In universities, an environment where students live, eat, and study together, racial and cultural differences come together in the closest possible way. Of all American institutions, perhaps only the military brings people of such different backgrounds into more intimate contact. With coeducation now a reality in colleges, and with the confident emergence of homosexual groups, the American campus is now sexually democratized as well. University leaders see it as a useful laboratory experiment in training young people for a multicultural habitat. Michael Sovern, president of Columbia, observes, "I like to think that we are leading society by grappling earnestly and creatively with the challenges posed by diversity."
>
> Dinesh D'Souza, *Illiberal Education*

Persuasion

This last kind of writing is sometimes called *argumentation,* though technically there is a difference. Argumentation traditionally refers to the setting up of logically valid arguments that can be used in defense of a specific issue. In contrast, *persuasion* is an attempt to change another person's feelings or opinions by any effective means. A writer persuades when he or she wants to *convince* the reader that a particular idea or opinion is worth holding, to win the reader over to a certain viewpoint, or to get the reader to change his or her mind.

By its very nature, persuasive writing relies more on opinion than on fact, since by definition, it represents the writer's subjective point of view. In this first example, the author persuades us to put the influence of television on the state of our literacy into perspective:

> It will not do to blame television for the state of our literacy. Television watching does reduce reading and often encroaches on homework. Much of it is admittedly the intellectual equivalent of junk food. But in some respects, such as its use of standard written English, television watching is

acculturative. Moreover, as Herbert Walberg points out, the schools them-selves must be held partly responsible for excessive television watching, be-cause they have not firmly insisted that students complete significant amounts of homework, an obvious way to increase time spent on reading and writing. Nor should our schools be excused by an appeal to the effects of the decline of the family or the vicious circle of poverty, important as these factors are. Schools have, or should have, children for six or seven hours a day, five days a week, nine months a year, for thirteen years or more. To assert that they are powerless to make a significant impact on what their students learn would be to make a claim about American educa-tion that few parents, teachers, or students would find it easy to accept.

E. D. Hirsch, Jr., *Cultural Literacy: What Every American Needs to Know*

Here is a second, more difficult example in which African-American writer Gerald Early offers his subjective opinion of the Miss America Pageant.

Adults, older girls, shops, magazines, newspapers, window signs—all the world had agreed that a blue-eyed, yellow-haired, pink-skinned doll was what every girl child treasured.

—Toni Morrison, *The Bluest Eye*

It is now fast become a tradition—if one can use that word to describe a habit about which I still feel a certain amount of shamefacedness—for our household to watch the Miss America contest on television every year. The source of my embarrassment is that this program remains, despite its at-tempts in recent years to modernize its frightfully antique quality of "women on parade," a kind of maddeningly barbarous example of the per-sistent, hard, crass urge to sell: from the plugs for the sponsor that are made a part of the script (that being an antique of fifties and sixties televi-sion; the show does not remember its history so much as it seems bent on repeating it) to the constant references to the success of some of the previ-ous contestants and the reminders that this is some sort of scholarship competition, the program has all the cheap earnestness of a social uplift project being played as a musical revue in Las Vegas. Paradoxically, it wish-es to convince the public that it is a common entertainment while simulta-neously wishing to convey that it is more than mere entertainment. The Miss America pageant is the worst sort of "Americanism," the soft smile of sex and the hard sell of toothpaste and hair dye ads wrapped in the dreamy ideological gauze of "making it through one's own effort." In a perverse way, I like the show; it is the only live television left other than sports, news broadcasts, performing arts awards programs, and speeches by the president. I miss live TV. It was the closest thing to theater for the masses. And the Miss America contest is, as it has been for some time, the most perfectly rendered theater in our culture, for it so perfectly captures what we yearn for: a low-class ritual, a polished restatement of vulgarity,

that wants to open the door to high-class respectability by way of plain middle-class anxiety and ambition. Am I doing all right? the contestants seem to ask in a kind of reassuring, if numbed, way. The contest brings together all the American classes in a show-biz spectacle of classlessness and tastelessness.

Gerald Early, "Life with Daughters: Watching the Miss America Pageant," *The Kenyon Review*

Each of the passages you have examined thus far in this section represents one dominant mode. But prose writers often combine modes, as you saw earlier in the Annie Dillard example. In this passage James Fallows combines exposition, description, and persuasion as he informs us about the primitive system of farming in Vietnam. As you read it, see if you can isolate the different modes.

The problem of Vietnam's economy is that the average level of existence is so low. The farming system is more brutally primitive than anything else I've seen in Asia, including China, Burma, and rural Java. Growing rice involves a lot of hand labor wherever it's done. Even in supermodern Japan it's not unusual to see people stooped over in the fields during the most labor-intensive stages of the rice cycle: transplanting the little seedlings into the paddies, and cutting the mature stalks and tying them into neat bundles. In Vietnam every stage seems to rely on human labor. In the arid central part of the country, between Da Nang and Nha Trang, the paddies are irrigated in more or less the way the ancient Egyptians did it. Boys stand over well holes, dip buckets into the wells, and haul the water out bucket by bucket to slosh into the paddies. Once or twice I saw a crude mechanical threshing device, resembling a large grinding wheel. As the wheel spins, women hold sheaves of rice against it and the mature rice grains are stripped off. Exactly once in nine days I saw a tractor in a field. People, sometimes with buffaloes, did the rest of the work themselves. Highway 1 is the main, and usually the only, north-south route in the country. For most of its length rice grains are laid out in foot-wide swaths along the side of the road, to dry in the sun.

James Fallows, "No Hard Feelings," *The Atlantic Monthly*

Exercises

The three short excerpts and practice essay that comprise the exercises will test you on your understanding and mastery of main idea, levels of support, and modes of discourse, in addition to inference and vocabulary in context. For words that are not part of your active reading vocabulary, try first to determine the meaning from context. Often you will be able to choose the appropriate definition in this way. However, if you are unsure, turn to the dictionary rather than taking a blind stab. It is not cheating to look up

words you don't know even while you are working through exercises. You should follow this procedure for all the multiple-choice vocabulary exercises in this book.

Selection 1

[1]The long June twilight faded into night. [2]Dublin lay enveloped in darkness but for the dim light of the moon that shone through fleecy clouds, casting a pale light as of approaching dawn over the streets and the dark waters of the Liffey. [3]Around the beleaguered Four Courts the heavy guns roared. [4]Here and there through the city, machine guns and rifles broke the silence of the night, spasmodically, like dogs barking on lone farms. [5]Republicans and Free Staters were waging civil war.

Liam O'Flaherty, "The Sniper," Spring Sowing

A. Vocabulary

For each italicized word from the paragraph, choose the best definition according to the context.

1. *beleaguered* [sentence 3]: (a) conquered, defeated; (b) besieged; surrounded; (c) betrayed, compromised; (d) heavily populated.
2. *spasmodically* [4]: (a) continually; (b) loudly; (c) intermittently; (d) annoyingly.
3. *waging* [5]: (a) pledging; (b) fighting; (c) threatening; (d) engaging in.

B. Content and Structure

Choose the best answer.

1. The main idea of this paragraph is expressed in sentence ___5___.
2. Which mode of discourse is represented in the first two sentences? (a) narration; (b) description; (c) exposition; (d) persuasion.
3. Sentence 2 suggests a contrast between (a) Republicans and Free Staters; (b) night and day; (c) light and dark; (d) war and peace.
4. The Liffey, mentioned in sentence 2, probably refers to (a) an ocean; (b) a river; (c) a swimming pool; (d) a park.
5. By mentioning the weapon activity, O'Flaherty suggests that (a) the Republicans were the stronger faction; (b) ammunition and weapons were in short supply; (c) outbursts of fighting occurred even at night; (d) most of the fighting took place in the countryside.

Selection 2

[1]*De gustibus non est disputandum*—"There is no arguing about taste"—runs the Latin proverb. [2]But taste did not just happen. [3]Cultural, historical, and ecological events have interacted to cause frogs, for example, to be esteemed as a del-

icacy in southern China but to be regarded with revulsion in northern China. [4]Even though much remains unknown, tastes cannot be dismissed as inarguable or illogical; an attempt will be made here to discover why, as Lucretius* put it, "What is food to one man may be fierce poison to others."

[5]Among the approximately thirty million tribal people of India, a total of 250 animal species are avoided by one group or another. [6]Most of these people will not eat meat from a tiger or any of various snakes, particularly the cobra. [7]Although they say they feel a kinship with these animals, it is obvious that both are highly dangerous and that hunting them systematically would be foolish. [8]Monkeys are avoided, probably because of their close resemblance to human beings; in these tribes, cannibalism is viewed with extreme horror. [9]A reluctance to eat the females of edible species of animals has been attributed to veneration for the maternal role, but it could also be due to a policy of allowing the females to reproduce and provide more edible young. [10] Many tribes avoid eating any animal that has died of unknown causes, an intelligent attitude in view of the possibility that the animal might have died from an infectious disease that could spread to humans. [11]Animals that consume excrement or garbage are similarly avoided, an adaptive step that prevents contact with parasites, and that might explain why members of one tribe eat any of twenty-one different species of rats, but not the house rat.

Peter Farb and George Armalagos,
Consuming Passions: The Anthropology of Eating

*A Roman poet and philosopher.

A. Vocabulary

1. *ecological* [sentence 3]: Describing the relationship between (a) people and their governments; (b) organisms and their environment; (c) people and the food they eat; (d) animals and their habitat.
2. *revulsion* [3]: (a) criticism; (b) hostility; (c) respect; (d) disgust.
3. *esteemed* [3]: (a) regarded with distaste; (b) regarded highly; (c) preferred; (d) came to mean.
4. *attributed* [9]: (a) attached; (b) characterized by; (c) blamed on; (d) considered as caused by.
5. *veneration* [9]: (a) profound respect; (b) concern; (c) protectiveness; (d) indifference.

B. Content and Structure

Choose the best answer.

1. The mode of discourse in the passage is (a) narration; (b) description; (c) exposition; (d) persuasion.

2. In your own words, write a sentence that states the main idea.

_____

_____

_____

3. Specifically, the authors' purpose is (a) to provide a list of animals we should avoid eating; (b) to explain some of the reasons that tastes differ from culture to culture; (c) to persuade us that cultural practices involving food taboos are foolish and illogical; (d) to describe human eating habits.

4. The authors strongly suggest that (a) many cultural inhibitions regarding the eating of certain animals have a practical basis; (b) cannibalism is universally abhorred; (c) most arguments about taste are inconclusive; (d) the scientific community is largely responsible for food taboos and prejudices.

5. Sentence 8 suggests that the Indian tribal people (a) are prohibited by law from eating monkeys; (b) dislike the taste of monkeys; (c) consider eating monkeys to be the same as eating a human being; (d) believe that monkeys are poisonous.

6. In relation to the main idea, mark these supporting sentences as MA (major) or MI (minor):

    _MA_ sentence 5   _MI_ sentence 9

    _MI_ sentence 6   _MI_ sentence 10

    _MI_ sentence 7   _MI_ sentence 11

    _MI_ sentence 8

Selection 3

[1]Partway down the long, very steep slope of Loma Vista Drive, descending through Beverly Hills, with the city of Los Angeles spread out far below the houses of sparkling opulence on either side, there is a sign warning "Use Lowest Gear" and, shortly after that, a sign that says "Runaway Vehicle Escape Lane 600 Feet Ahead." [2]Just before Loma Vista crosses Doheny Road, it expands on the right into a third lane, composed of a succession of low, uneven piles of loose gravel nestled against cement block set in an embankment. [3]The operator of a runaway vehicle is apparently expected to steer his car into this soft and receptive lane and come to a halt like a baseball player sliding into third. [4]It seems a perfectly reasonable solution; the unsettling aspect is the underlying assumption that automobiles will so frequently go berserk hereabouts that some accommodation must be made for them. [5]Similarly, along the heavily populated canyon roads of Beverly Hills there are signs forbidding cigarettes and matches: these dry hills may burst into flame at any time. [6]The houses above Sunset Boulevard are stuck in the nearly vertical slopes like cloves in a ham; how they stay there is mysterious. [7]It seems likely that, if they do not catch fire first, a good rain will send them tumbling down the mountain; already, earth has slid out from under retaining walls, terraces, swimming pools,

driveways, even roads. [8]In some places, tons of concrete have been poured like icing over a section of hillside to hold it back—and the concrete has even been painted green—but the earth has begun to slip away beneath that, too, leaving edges of concrete sticking out against the sky. [9]In addition, of course, the entire area sits close to the quiescent but menacing San Andreas Fault.* [10]Gazing up the perilous roads at the plucky, high-risk homes perched in the tinderlike hills near the great rift, a visitor feels that this may be a community where desire and imagination automatically take precedence over danger, and even over reality.

James Stevenson, "People Start Running," The New Yorker

*The major earthquake fault line that runs north and south through a large portion of California.

A. Vocabulary

For each italicized word from the paragraph, choose the best definition according to the context.

1. *opulence* [sentence 1]: (a) construction, design; (b) decoration, adornment; (c) brilliance, luster; (d) wealth, affluence.
2. *unsettling* [4]: (a) disturbing; (b) ridiculous; (c) unproved; (d) common.
3. *quiescent* [9]: (a) invisible; (b) threatening; (c) famous; (d) inactive.
4. *perilous* [10]: (a) steep; (b) dangerous; (c) well-maintained; (d) curving.
5. *plucky* [10]: (a) expensive to build and maintain; (b) innovative in design and construction; (c) spirited in the face of unfavorable odds; (d) jutting out, unsuitable for the landscape.
6. *rift* [10]: (a) valley; (b) mountain; (c) flatland; (d) opening.
7. *take precedence over* [10]: (a) are less important than; (b) are more important than; (c) have no logical relationship to; (d) have priority over.

B. Content and Structure

Choose the best answer.

1. Which *two* modes of discourse are evident in this paragraph? (a) narration; (b) description; (c) exposition; (d) persuasion.
2. The main idea is expressed in sentence _10_.
3. Stevenson supports the main idea with (a) definitions of key terms; (b) contrasting details; (c) specific examples; (d) reasons.
4. From his discussion of Los Angeles and the way the houses are built he intends to emphasize the city's (a) sense of beauty; (b) great wealth; (c) social inequities; (d) unrealistic attitudes.
5. Stevenson suggests that Los Angeles is unique because (a) its inhabitants are divided into rich or poor, with no middle class; (b) its design-

ers and residents pay little attention to physical or geographic limitations; (c) its houses are innovatively designed; (d) it is more polluted than other major cities.

6. Read sentence 3 again. Explain what Stevenson means in comparing a car driver's using the runaway lane to a baseball player sliding into third base. _____

_____

_____

7. Why do you think that some concrete retaining walls on Los Angeles hillsides have been painted green? _____

Practice Essay

The following selection gives you the opportunity to practice your new skills with a short essay. Read the passage carefully once. Then read it again, this time looking up any unfamiliar words in the dictionary. Next, answer the comprehension questions without looking back at the selection. Check your answers against the text. Then answer the remaining questions. As you work through the subsequent exercises, feel free to refer to the selection if necessary.

Topeka, 1951
Richard Kluger

Born in 1934, Richard Kluger, a writer on legal matters, has worked for a number of national newspapers and publishing houses. His book, Simple Justice: A History of Brown v. Board of Education, *from which this selection comes, documents the 1954 landmark Supreme Court decision which outlawed the practice of segregation in the nation's public schools. The book was nominated for the National Book Award in 1976.*

1   Whatever else it was in 1951, Topeka was also a Jim Crow* town. It had been one as long as anyone could remember.

2   There were no separate waiting rooms at the train and bus stations, and Negroes did not have to ride in the back of the local buses, but in most other ways it was segregated by law and, more effectively, by custom. There were eighteen elementary schools for whites and four for blacks. There was one colored hotel, the Dunbar, and all the rest were for whites. Almost no restaurants downtown served colored customers. Before the Second World War, a number of the better beaneries in town

*Jim Crow laws refer to the systematic practice of segregating and suppressing blacks, common in the first half of this century.

had a sign in the window reading: "Negroes and Mexicans served in sacks only," meaning they could take out food in bags but not eat on the premises. One movie theater in town admitted colored people to its balcony. Another, called the Apex, was for colored only. The other five movie houses were for whites only. The swimming pool at Gage Park was off-limits to colored, except one day a year when they were allowed in for a gala picnic.

3   Worse yet was the employment picture. Blacks had won some jobs at the Santa Fe shops during a strike in the early Twenties, but there were few black union members in Topeka and fewer held white-collar positions of any kind. A black clerk at a retail shop or a black stenographer at an insurance company was almost unknown. Mrs. Inza Brown, who had been a legal secretary to the only black lawyer in town for thirteen years in the Twenties and Thirties, won a civil-service job at the State Department of Health, where, as she remembers, "They didn't know what to do with a black woman, so they lent me out to the city health department. In two years there, I was never offered a cup of coffee from the office coffee wagon. I had to go around the corner to get some. Topeka was one prejudiced town then, let me tell you."

4   Unwelcomed by most white employers, Topeka blacks retreated into their own world and tried to make do. The principal black businesses in town were beauty and barber shops, barbecue restaurants, after-hours bars, and whorehouses. A black-owned drugstore started up and, serving black clientele only, folded after a year. Few colored retailers could command credit from the banks; few could get management experience at any white-owned store. A hundred or so professionals made a living in town—black teachers teaching black children, black preachers serving black churches, a few physicians tending the black sick. The only other work blacks had a corner on in Topeka was the most menial sort: the janitorial jobs in the statehouse, the mop-up work at the hotels, the maids and laundresses and cooks and gardeners and chimneysweeps of the white people. A black laborer was much more likely to find an honest day's work in Detroit or Pittsburgh or back South.

5   Until the Second World War, black Topeka took it all quietly. Things were worse elsewhere, they said. The head of the local NAACP branch, who had been a lieutenant in the First World War and was the first Negro to work in the Topeka post office, was no firebrand. "We've got to learn to crawl before we can walk," he was wont to say with the solemnity of Booker Washington. The war, though, began to change things on both sides of the color line. Says Tom Lee Kiene, a native Topekan who served seventeen years on the staff of the Topeka *Capital-Journal* before becoming its executive editor in 1959: "Blacks who participated in civic drives selling war bonds or raising money for the Red

Cross began to come to banquets—it seemed the patriotic thing to ask them—and we whites started remarking to each other that it didn't seem to spoil our dinners."

6   In the black community, a few enlightened discontents began to emerge, like Lucinda Todd, an ex-schoolteacher who had been forcibly retired by the then common rule that married women could not teach. Mrs. Todd was especially sensitive to the education her daughter, Nancy, received and was increasingly disturbed when she found that it was not as rich as that offered white youngsters. She had wanted her daughter to play the violin, for example, but there was no musical instruction at any of the black schools. Then one day she saw a notice in the newspaper about a concert by the grade-school orchestra representing all eighteen schools in town, and she exploded. "I got on the phone to the music supervisor," she remembers, "and told him there were twenty-two grade schools in town, not eighteen, and why weren't the black children offered music instruction?" She was directed to the coordinator of black schools in Topeka, who assured her that colored folks did not want music instruction and could not afford to buy the instruments. She brought her case to the Board of Education and won it. There was another time—in 1944, she places it—when Mrs. Todd bought a ticket to the Grand movie theater, the one that admitted Negroes to a section of the balcony, and when she climbed up there the two dozen or so seats reserved for colored were filled, so she took a seat right across the aisle in the white section. A policeman came and told her that she could not do that and would have to sit in the colored section or nowhere. They gave her her money back. "They did things like that all the time," Lucinda Todd recalls. Soon she became active in the NAACP, was elected secretary of the branch, and once had Walter White as an overnight guest in her residence.

7   But there were few such proud and angry Negroes in Topeka who were ready to do something about their degraded standing in the community. Things would pick up after the war, everybody said. It was no time to rock the boat. In fact, though, very little opened up after the war. Remembers Negro attorney Charles Scott, who went to Washburn Law School after military service prior to joining his father's firm: "You'd look up and down Kansas Avenue early in the morning, and all you could see were blacks washing windows. That wasn't anything, but at least it was work. There was still no chance for a black man to become a bank teller or a store clerk or a brick mason. The few blacks with union jobs at Goodyear almost never advanced, and people were retiring from the Santa Fe shops after holding the same job for twenty or twenty-five years. A lot of hopes got dashed."

8   The 1950 U.S. Census documents the job plight of Topeka Negroes:

	WHITE	NON-WHITE
Bookkeepers (female)	541	2
Stenographers, secretaries and typists	2,225	16
Bus drivers	86	1
Electricians	215	1
Salesmen and sales clerks in retail trade	2,158	11
Accountants and auditors	425	1
Plumbers and pipefitters	197	4
Compositors and typesetters	214	2
Pharmacists	71	2
Dentists	57	2
Managers, officials, proprietors (self-employed)	1,600	30
Managers, officials, proprietors (salaried)	1,684	32
Janitors, porters, charwomen	293	318
Private household workers		
(living out)	320	347
(living in)	120	14

A. Comprehension

Choose the answer that best completes each statement. Do not refer to the selection while doing this exercise.

1. Which of the following represents the main idea of the passage? (a) in 1951, Jim Crow laws made it difficult for black residents of Topeka to get decent jobs; (b) in 1951, blacks in Topeka experienced segregation in all aspects of their lives, both by law and by custom; (c) in 1951, waiting rooms at Topeka's train and bus stations were integrated, and blacks did not have to ride in the back of the bus; (d) Topeka was more segregated in 1951 than other cities in the Midwest.

2. Even worse for blacks in Topeka than their exclusion from public facilities, according to Kluger, was a lack of (a) adequate health care; (b) extracurricular school programs; (c) employment opportunities; (d) strong leadership.

3. Mrs. Inza Brown, who had a civil-service job with the city health department, remembers that in the two years she worked there, (a) no one spoke to her; (b) no one offered her a cup of coffee; (c) no one invited her home for a visit; (d) no one asked her to go to lunch.

4. Kluger writes that when Topeka blacks were rejected for jobs by white employers, they (a) staged demonstrations and protests; (b) became

bitter and disillusioned; (c) moved away to northern industrial cities where the opportunities were better; (d) retreated into their own world and opened businesses catering to a black clientele.

5. Lucinda Todd, a former schoolteacher, complained to school officials because her daughter, who attended one of the city's black schools, (a) was not offered music instruction; (b) was not allowed to participate in sports; (c) had out-of-date textbooks; (d) was not offered the same academic curriculum as white students.

6. The U.S. Census figures for 1950 show (a) blacks holding only union jobs in manufacturing; (b) blacks increasingly working as managers or in other white-collar occupations; (c) blacks systematically being relegated to menial, unskilled jobs; (d) blacks largely unemployed or on welfare.

B. Structure

1. The mode of discourse in the passage is primarily (a) narration; (b) description; (c) exposition; (d) persuasion.

2. Look again at the details the author presents to support the main idea in paragraph 2. Which of the following general categories would include all of them? (a) privately owned facilities; (b) facilities intended for public use; (c) government institutions; (d) entertainment facilities.

3. The following statements are rewritten from paragraph 2. Label them according to whether they represent the main idea of the selection (MAIN), major support (MA), or minor support (MI).

_____ a. There were no separate waiting rooms at the train and bus stations, and Negroes did not have to ride in the back of the local buses.

MAIN b. But in most other ways it [Topeka] was segregated by law and, more effectively, by custom.

_____ c. There were eighteen elementary schools for whites and four for blacks.

_____ d. There was one colored hotel, the Dunbar, and all the rest were for whites.

_____ e. Almost no restaurants served colored customers.

_____ f. Before World War II, a number of the better beaneries in town had a sign in the window reading: "Negroes and Mexicans served in sacks only."

_____ g. One movie theater in town admitted colored people to its balcony.

_____ h. The swimming pool at Gage Park was off-limits to colored, except one day a year when they were allowed in for a gala picnic.

4. In paragraph 2, why does Kluger translate the sign stating that blacks and Mexicans would be allowed to buy only take-out food?

_____

_____

5. When Kluger writes in paragraph 2 that blacks were allowed into the swimming pool at Gage Park once a year for "a gala picnic," he is being (a) witty; (b) skeptical; (c) objective; (d) sarcastic.

6. The method of development in paragraph 4 is primarily (a) steps in a process; (b) definition of unfamiliar terms; (c) comparison; (d) contrast; (e) examples.

7. In paragraph 5, what does the statement by the head of the local NAACP branch, "We've got to learn to crawl before we can walk," suggest about blacks' attitudes toward their plight? _____

_____

8. Why does Kluger reprint the data from the 1950 U.S. Census?

_____

C. Vocabulary

For each italicized word from the selection, choose the best definition according to the context in which it appears.

1. the most *menial* sort [paragraph 4]: (a) pertaining to a servant; (b) low-paying; (c) undesirable; (d) requiring little education.

2. he was no *firebrand* [5]: (a) an intellectual; (b) a representative; (c) a person who fits the stereotype; (d) a person who stirs up trouble.

3. he was *wont* to say [5]: (a) accustomed; (b) correct; (c) willing; (d) quick.

4. their *degraded* standing [7]: (a) impoverished; (b) improved in quality; (c) reduced in quality; (d) unclear, ambiguous.

5. a lot of hopes got *dashed* [7]: (a) exploited; (b) raised; (c) destroyed; (d) changed.

6. the job *plight* of Topeka Negroes [8]: (a) dilemma; (b) difficult situation; (c) tragedy; (d) opportunity.

D. Questions for Analysis and Discussion

1. From what Kluger both states directly and implies, why was the job situation so difficult for blacks in Topeka during the early 1950s?

2. How much has the situation improved for blacks and other minorities in this country in the past forty years? What gains have they made in employment and educational opportunities? What examples of exclusion because of prejudice still exist?

Four Methods of Paragraph Development

Now that you have practiced with the main idea, levels of support, and modes of discourse, you can analyze the structure of paragraphs. The next skill we will learn is how to determine the method a writer uses to develop or support the main idea. In this chapter you will be introduced to the first four methods of paragraph development: (1) examples and illustration; (2) process; (3) comparison and contrast; and (4) definition.

These four methods refer to the particular kinds of *evidence* the writer uses in the body of the paragraph. (The other three methods are more difficult and will be taken up in Chapter 3.) As you study these sample paragraphs, you will see that the majority are expository; in fact, some composition textbooks refer to these as *expository* methods of development.

Examples and Illustration

This method of development is the most common and the easiest to recognize. A writer supports a general statement, either by citing a series

of specific *examples,* or instances, of the main idea, or by using a single, longer *illustration.* The methods are clearly related and have the same function: both support and clarify some larger idea by pointing to typical and concrete instances.

In real life we use examples all the time. If a New Yorker says to someone visiting from a small Midwestern town that rents are high in Manhattan, the Midwesterner may have no inkling of what is actually meant by "high." The $800 rent that the New Yorker might consider a good deal might well be twice what the Midwesterner would expect to pay. But citing specific examples of what constitutes a high rent in New York would establish a common ground and support the initial observation that New York rents are high.

If you tell your friend that you have a rule not to do any "hard work" on weekends, she may not know what you are referring to unless you provide some examples of what you mean by "hard work"–planting a vegetable garden or writing a twenty-page term paper perhaps, or babysitting for your three nieces or cooking a lavish dinner for a dozen people or taking apart, repairing, and reassembling a carburetor. Without the examples, "hard work" is a relative term with a different meaning for everyone. It is the same with writing. Examples reinforce general concepts and get us on an equal footing with the author so that we are not obliged to supply our own instances, which, of course, would come from a different set of experiences.

The only difference between examples and illustrations is that examples are short and are usually found in clusters, whereas an illustration demonstrates a general idea in more detail. In this paragraph, the authors use a cluster of short examples to show that, by modern standards, medieval courtiers' table manners were pretty repulsive.

Among the important societal rules that represent one component of cuisine are table manners. As a socially instilled form of conduct, they reveal the attitudes typical of a society. Changes in table manners through time, as they have been documented for western Europe, likewise reflect fundamental changes in human relationships. Medieval courtiers saw their table manners as distinguishing them from crude peasants; but by modern standards, the manners were not exactly refined. Feudal lords used their unwashed hands to scoop food from a common bowl and they passed around a single goblet from which all drank. A finger or two would be extended while eating, so as to be kept free of grease and thus available for the next course, or for dipping into spices and condiments— possibly accounting for today's "polite" custom of extending the little finger while holding a spoon or small fork. Soups and sauces were commonly drunk by lifting the bowl to the mouth; several diners frequently ate from the same bread trencher. Even lords and nobles would toss gnawed bones back into the common dish, wolf down their food, spit onto the

table (preferred conduct called for spitting under it), and blow their noses into the tablecloth.

Peter Farb and George Armelagos, *Consuming Passions:*
The Anthropology of Eating

Here is another paragraph developed with examples. ("Verbal bobbles" are blunders from hearing language improperly.)

[1]The treasury of verbal bobbles is enriched each hour each day in every land on earth. . . . When my daughter was eight, she described something she had seen "as I was towardsing home"; when she was ten, she told a story that ended flatly, "This is my virgin of what happened"; when she was eleven, she sighed morosely, "I am a middle-aged child."

[2]In a Winnetka kindergarten some years ago, one lad drew a man with tiny creatures creeping all over him. When the foolish teacher asked what the drawing meant, young Raphael explained: "That's John, with all the mice on him." What John? What mice? "From the poem: 'Diddle, diddle dumpling, mice on John' ['my son John']." I can find no way of faulting such peerless imagery. Or that of the tot who sang, "London britches falling down. . . ." These delightful inventions are not, of course, in the same immortal league as the line, uttered by a child, which has surely been savored ten thousand times: "The equator is a menagerie lion that runs around the middle of the earth."

Leo Rosten, *Rome Wasn't Built in a Day*

Here are some other errors like those Rosten describes: "donzerly," as in the "dawn's early light" from "The Star Spangled Banner"; "hippy hollers," as in "if he hollers, let him go"; "Round John Virgin" from "Silent Night"; and "Happy the Cross-Eyed Bear" from the hymn actually titled "Gladly the Cross I'd Bear."

Process

A second method of paragraph development is *process*. There are two kinds of process writing. In the first, called *directive* process writing, the author explains the steps—in chronological order—that one must follow to perform a task, such as how to study for final exams, how to develop a photograph, or how to lose ten pounds. Directive process writing is found most often in laboratory or technical manuals or in how-to and self-help books. The following paragraph from a newspaper article on eating explains step by step how one goes about learning to use chopsticks.

Learning to use chopsticks takes only a practice session or two, and using them does enhance the enjoyment of Chinese food: Form a loose fist with your thumb facing up. Slip the lower chopstick into the crux of your hand and over the tip of your middle finger, with the narrow end of the chopstick jutting about 5 inches beyond the tip of your finger. Grip the upper chopstick something like a pencil between the thumb and forefinger. The tips of the chopsticks should be even. To pick up food, move the top chopstick up and down with your index finger. The lower chopstick, held in place with your thumb, should remain stationary.

Bruce Cost, "Mom Might Faint, But It's OK to
Slurp in Chinese Eateries," *San Francisco Chronicle*

The second kind of process writing, called *informative* process writing, describes a phenomenon—how something works or how something developed or came into existence. The author uses chronological order, just as in the directive kind, but the underlying purpose is different. In this kind of process writing the writer does not expect us to duplicate the process described. This excerpt is from an article about traveling in the Sahara Desert. The author uses process here to show how something happens, in this case, death by thirst, a potential threat to any desert traveler. Notice that the steps in the process are held together with time markers—*transitions*—that help keep us on track: "first," "a two percent loss," "a five percent loss," "beyond that," "at 10 percent," "now," and finally, "the end comes."

[1]Water is the largest component of our bodies, but we have little to spare. In the hottest desert we can lose it (mostly by sweating) at the rate of two gallons a day while resting in the shade, or four gallons a day walking. Because sweating keeps us cool, we function well in extreme heat as long as we have plenty of water. We need a *lot* of water—say, half again as much as a camel over the course of a year. The rule is to drink until your thirst is gone and then drink a little more. If water is available, you naturally maintain your fluid content within a range of a quarter of a percent. If water is not available, juice, Coke, or beer is just as good. Apparently, radiator coolant also works. But what happens when it all runs out? Inevitably this becomes the question for anyone stranded in the Sahara. I can only list the symptoms.

[2]Thirst is first felt when the body has lost about 0.5 percent of its weight to dehydration. For a 180-pound man that amounts to about a pint. With a two percent loss (say, two quarts) the stomach is no longer big enough to hold as much as the body needs, and people stop drinking before they have replenished their loss, even if they are given ample water. This is called voluntary dehydration, though it is not a conscious choice. Up to a five percent loss (about one gallon) the symptoms include fatigue, loss of appetite, flushed skin, irritability, increased pulse rate, and mild fever. Be-

yond that lie dizziness, headache, labored breathing, absence of salivation, circulatory problems, blue skin, and slurred speech. At 10 percent a person can no longer walk. The point of no return is around 12 percent (about three gallons), when the tongue swells, the mouth loses all sensation, and swallowing becomes impossible. A person this dehydrated cannot recover without medical assistance. In the Sahara it may take only half a day to get to this stage. Now the skin shrinks against the bones and cracks, the eyes sink, and vision and hearing become dim. Urine is dark and urination is painful. Delirium sets in. In a hot desert climate, as the body dehydrates, a disproportionate amount of water is drawn from the circulating blood. The blood thickens and finally can no longer fulfill its functions, one of which is to transport heat generated within the body to the surface. It is this heat that ultimately kills. The end comes with an explosive rise in body temperature, convulsions, and blissful death.

William Langewiesche, "The World in Its Extreme," *The Atlantic Monthly*

In the next example, William Finnegan uses the informative process expository method to explain the experience of surfing. As you read through the passage, locate the transitional time marker phrases. ("Rails" are the edges of the surfboard, and "face" is the front of the wave where the surfer rides.)

A wave comes. It swings silently through the kelp bed, a long, tapering wall, darkening upcoast. I paddle across the grain of the water streaming toward the wave across the reef, angling to meet the hollow of a small peak ghosting across the face. For a moment, in the gully just in front of the wave, my board loses forward momentum as the water rushing off the reef sucks it back up the face. Then the wave lifts me up—I've met the steepest part of the peak, and swerved into its shoreward track—and with two hard strokes I'm aboard. It's a clean takeoff: a sudden sense of height fusing with a deep surge of speed. I hop to my feet and drive to the bottom, drawing out the turn and sensing, more than seeing, what the wave plans to do ahead—the low sun is blinding off the water looking south. Halfway through the first turn, I can feel the wave starting to stand up ahead. I change rails, bank off the lower part of the face, and start driving down the line. The first section flies past, and the wave—it's slightly overhead, and changing angle as it breaks, so that it now blocks out the sun—stands revealed: a long, steep, satiny arc curving all the way to the channel. I work my board from rail to rail for speed, trimming carefully through two more short sections. Gaining confidence that I will in fact make this wave, I start turning harder, slicing higher up the face and, when a last bowl section looms beside the channel, stalling briefly before driving through in a half crouch, my face pressed close to the glassy, rumbling, pea-green wall. The silver edge of the lip's axe flashes harmlessly past on

my left. A second later, I'm coasting onto flat water, leaning into a pull-out, and mindlessly shouting "My God!"

William Finnegan, "Surfing," The New Yorker

Comparison and Contrast

The comparison and contrast method is used to explain similarities and differences between two things. The less common of the two, *comparison,* involves a discussion of *similarities* between two seemingly unlike or unrelated things. For example, a writer might explain what the seemingly unrelated situations of interviewing for a new job and meeting a new girlfriend's or boyfriend's parents have in common.

Contrast properly refers to a discussion of the *differences* between two related or like things—for example, the Bush and Clinton administrations, the Korean and Vietnam wars, or two models of cars. You may find comparison and contrast used together or singly, depending on the subject.

The following paragraph uses only comparison. The author's purpose is to show the similarities between excessive television viewing and excessive use of alcohol. Notice that these seemingly unrelated activities are linked in a meaningful way.

Not unlike drugs or alcohol, the television experience allows the participant to blot out the real world and enter into a pleasurable and passive mental state. The worries and anxieties of reality are as effectively deferred by becoming absorbed in a television program as by going on a "trip" induced by drugs or alcohol. And just as alcoholics are only inchoately aware of their addiction, feeling that they control their drinking more than they really do ("I can cut it out any time I want—I just like to have three or four drinks before dinner"), people similarly overestimate their control over television watching. Even as they put off other activities to spend hour after hour watching television, they feel they could easily resume living in a different, less passive style. But somehow or other while the television set is present in their homes, the click doesn't sound. With television pleasures available, those other experiences seem less attractive, more difficult somehow.

Marie Winn, The Plug-In Drug

The next paragraph, by Bill McKibben, uses only contrast to show the differences between the ways television and newspapers present the news:

Perhaps the greatest distortion of TV news comes from the very fact of its seeming comprehensiveness. Each day, it fills its allotted hours no matter

what, and each day it fills them with a crackling urgency. A newspaper comes out every day, too, but a newspaper has various ways of letting you know whether or not an event is important. The single most useful thing about the *Times* is that the width and type size of the lead headline each morning let you know how it compares, in the view of the paper's editors, with all the other lead stories since the *Times* began. It has a way of saying to its readers, "Nothing earthshaking happened today; it's O.K. to read the reviews or the sports." TV has almost no flexibility of this sort.

Bill McKibben, "Reflections: Television," The New Yorker

The final example comes from Joan Didion's book *Miami,* in which she explains the differences between the use of Spanish in Miami and in other major American cities like Los Angeles, Houston, and New York. Contrast is used more subtly here, with only the phrases "in Miami" and "in New York or Los Angeles" to point to the main distinction.

This question of language was curious. The sound of spoken Spanish was common in Miami, but it was also common in Los Angeles, and Houston, and even in the cities of the Northeast. What was unusual about Spanish in Miami was not that it was so often spoken, but that it was so often heard: In, say, Los Angeles, Spanish remained a language only barely registered by the Anglo population, part of the ambient noise, the language spoken by the people who worked in the car wash and came to trim the trees and cleared the tables in restaurants. In Miami Spanish was spoken by the people who ate in the restaurants, the people who owned the cars and the trees, which made, on the socio-auditory scale, a considerable difference. Exiles who felt isolated or declassed by language in New York or Los Angeles thrived in Miami. An entrepreneur who spoke no English could still, in Miami, buy, sell, negotiate, leverage assets, float bonds, and, if he were so inclined, attend galas twice a week, in black tie. "I have been after the *Herald* ten times to do a story about millionaires in Miami who do not speak more than two words in English," one prominent exile told me. "'Yes' and 'no.' Those are the two words. They come here with five dollars in their pockets and without speaking another word of English they are millionaires."

Joan Didion, Miami

Definition

Unlike the other methods described thus far, *definition* is most often used in conjunction with other methods of development. As a method, it is nearly self-explanatory, but writers' purposes in using the definition method may differ, as we shall see in the following examples. In the

first, Charles Earle Funk explains the origin of the word *blackguard* (pronounced blăg´ərd). He defines the word by explaining its etymology (its origin) and the eventual change in its meaning:

 ## blackguard

Four or five centuries ago it was not so easy as it is today to move from one's winter residence to his place in the country for the summer and to make the reverse move in the fall. Today, the very wealthy may have a retinue of servants at each place, and the actual change of residence may be accomplished by automobile or airplane with little inconvenience in a matter of a few hours. But in the sixteenth century even the king was compelled to shift his entire retinue—and the retinue of the royal house or of any of the noble houses ran into large numbers. The more important members went before on horseback. Huge springless wagons carried the linens and the multitudinous boxes of raiment. Bringing up the rear were the unsightly but necessary men and women of the kitchen, the lowest menials of the household, the scullions and knaves who performed the needful dirty work of the smoky kitchen; they, with their black and sooty pots and pans, had one large wagon to themselves, or rode on mules or traveled on foot, loaded with their clattering greasy implements. In playful allusion to the appearance and most unmilitary equipment of these tailenders, they were called "the black guard." In later years, whether or not these kitchen menials were drawn from or became loafers and criminals, the name became attached to that class, and still later, as at present, *blackguard* came to denote a low, vicious person, addicted to or ready for crime.

Charles Earle Funk, *Thereby Hangs a Tale: Stories of Curious Word Origins*

The most common use of definition occurs when a writer clarifies a term because it is open to varying interpretations or subject to misinterpretation. This type of definition is especially useful for abstract terms like *machismo* or *honor* or *tolerance*. It is for this reason that Susan Faludi defines the word *feminism* in the next paragraph by citing the beliefs and tenets of the feminist movement, thus lessening the possibility of misinterpretation.

The meaning of the word "feminist" has not really changed since it first appeared in a book review in the *Athenaeum* of April 27, 1895, describing a woman who "has in her the capacity of fighting her way back to independence." It is the basic proposition that, as Nora put it in Ibsen's *A Doll's House* a century ago, "Before everything else I'm a human being." It is the simply worded sign hoisted by a little girl in the 1970 Women's Strike for Equality: I AM NOT A BARBIE DOLL. Feminism asks the world to recognize at long last that women aren't decorative ornaments, worthy vessels, members of a "special-interest group." They are half (in fact, now more than

half) of the national population, and just as deserving of rights and opportunities, just as capable of participating in the world's events, as the other half. Feminism's agenda is basic: It asks that women not be forced to "choose" between public justice and private happiness. It asks that women be free to define themselves—instead of having their identity defined for them, time and again, by their culture and their men.

Susan Faludi, *Backlash: The Undeclared War Against American Women*

In traditional rhetoric, the definition method follows this classic model:

Term to be defined = class + distinguishing characteristics

For example, we could define the word *sofa* like this, using the classic model.

Sofa **(term)** = *a piece of furniture* **(class)** + *having an upholstered seat and back intended to seat two or three people* **(distinguishing characteristics)**

Here is another:

Schizophrenia **(term)** = *a psychotic mental disorder* **(class)** + *marked by withdrawal from reality, bizarre behavior, and sometimes delusional behavior* **(distinguishing characteristics)**

In the next paragraph, scientist Edwin O. Wilson uses the classic scheme to define the term *evolutionary event* in the opening sentence. Following this, he clarifies the definition further by examples and explanations.

The fundamental evolutionary event is a change in the frequency of genes and chromosome configurations in a population. If a population of butterflies shifts through time from 40 percent blue individuals to 60 percent blue individuals, and if the color blue is hereditary, evolution of a simple kind has occurred. Larger transformations are accomplished by a great many such statistical changes in combination. Shifts can occur purely in the genes, with no effect on wing color or any other outward trait. But whatever their nature or magnitude, the changes in progress are always expressed in percentages of individuals within or among populations. Evolution is absolutely a phenomenon of populations. Individuals and their immediate descendants do not evolve. Populations evolve, in the sense that the proportions of carriers of different genes change through time. This conception of evolution at the population level fol-

lows ineluctably from the idea of natural selection, which is the core of Darwinism. There are other causes of evolution, but natural selection is overwhelmingly dominant.

Edwin O. Wilson, *The Diversity of Life*

Exercises

Selection 1

[1]The concept that no two people see exactly the same thing when actively using their eyes in a natural situation is shocking to some people because it implies that not all men relate to the world around them in the same way. [2]Without recognition of these differences, however, the process of translating from one perceptual world to another cannot take place. [3]The distance between the perceptual worlds of two people of the same culture is certainly less than that between two people of different cultures, but it can still present problems. [4]As a young man, I spent several summers with students making archaeological surveys in the high deserts of northern Arizona and southern Utah. [5]Everyone on these expeditions was highly motivated to find stone artifacts, arrowheads in particular. [6]We marched along in single file with the typical head-down, ground-scanning gaze of an archaeological field party. [7]In spite of their high motivation, my students would repeatedly walk right over arrowheads lying on top of the ground. [8]Much to their chagrin, I would lean down to pick up what they had not seen simply because I had learned to "attend" some things and to ignore others. [9]I had been doing it longer and knew what to look for, yet I could not identify the cues that made the image of the arrowhead stand out so clearly.

[10]I may be able to spot arrowheads on the desert but a refrigerator is a jungle in which I am easily lost. [11]My wife, however, will unerringly point out that the cheese or the leftover roast is hiding right in front of my eyes. [12]Hundreds of such experiences convince me that men and women often inhabit quite different visual worlds. [13]These are differences which cannot be attributed to variations in visual acuity. [14]Men and women simply have learned to use their eyes in very different ways.

Edward T. Hall, *The Hidden Dimension*

A. Vocabulary

For each italicized word from the selection, choose the best definition according to the context in which it appears.

1. *perceptual* [sentences 2 and 3]: pertaining to (a) observing with the senses; (b) making careful distinctions; (c) developing the imagination; (d) experiencing physical sensations.

2. *chagrin* [8]: A feeling of (a) hostility, resentment; (b) confusion, perplexity; (c) embarrassment caused by failure; (d) displeasure, unhappiness.
3. *unerringly* [11]: (a) patiently; (b) arrogantly; (c) without understanding; (d) consistently and accurately.
4. *attributed* [13]: (a) characterized by; (b) said to be the result of; (c) substituted; (d) defined as.
5. *acuity* [13]: (a) keenness; (b) ability; (c) training; (d) sensitivity.

B. Content and Structure

Choose the best answer.

1. The mode of discourse in the passage is (a) narration; (b) description; (c) exposition; (d) persuasion.
2. The main idea is that (a) men and women perceive the world differently; (b) people of different cultures perceive the world differently; (c) it is more difficult to perceive things in nature than things in one's home; (d) for reasons not fully understood, no two people see exactly the same thing when they use their eyes.
3. Hall develops the main idea by means of (a) steps in a process; (b) definition; (c) comparison; (d) examples and illustrations.
4. The word *distance* as Hall uses it in sentence 3 means (a) literally the distance from one place to another; (b) the degree of difference; (c) an interval separating two events; (d) a feeling of reservation or aloofness.
5. Hall strongly suggests that much of our ability to perceive comes from our (a) genetic inheritance; (b) experience in looking at things around us; (c) level of intelligence; (d) our desire to learn.
6. Isolating the factors that cause people to perceive the same thing differently is (a) possible; (b) a waste of time; (c) difficult, if not impossible; (d) necessary.

Selection 2

[1]Scientists who work on animal behavior are occupationally obliged to live chancier lives than most of their colleagues, always at risk of being fooled by the animals they are studying or, worse, fooling themselves. [2]Whether their experiments involve domesticated laboratory animals or wild creatures in the field, there is no end to the surprises that an animal can think up in the presence of an investigator. [3]Sometimes it seems as if animals are genetically programmed to puzzle human beings, especially psychologists.

[4]The risks are especially high when the scientist is engaged in training the animal to do something or other and must bank his professional reputation on the integrity of his experimental subject. [5]The most famous case in point is that of Clever Hans, the turn-of-the-century German horse now immortalized in the

lexicon of behavioral science by the technical term, the "Clever Hans Error." [6]The horse, owned and trained by Herr von Osten, could not only solve complex arithmetical problems, but even read the instructions on a blackboard and tap out infallibly, with one hoof, the right answer. [7]What is more, he could perform the same computations when total strangers posed questions to him, with his trainer nowhere nearby. [8]For several years Clever Hans was studied intensively by groups of puzzled scientists and taken seriously as a horse with something very like a human brain, quite possibly even better than human. [9]But finally in 1911, it was discovered by Professor O. Pfungst that Hans was not really doing arithmetic at all; he was simply observing the behavior of the human experimenter. [10]Subtle, unconscious gestures—nods of the head, the holding of breath, the cessation of nodding when the correct count was reached—were accurately read by the horse as cues to stop tapping.

Lewis Thomas, "Clever Animals,"
Late Night Thoughts on Listening to Mahler's Ninth Symphony

A. Vocabulary

For each italicized word from the selection, choose the best definition according to the context in which it appears.

1. *integrity* [sentence 4]: (a) responsibility; (b) loyalty; (c) soundness; (d) reputation.
2. *lexicon* [5]: (a) a body of terms used in a particular profession; (b) legendary stories handed down from generation to generation; (c) written history; (d) published reports.
3. *infallibly* [6]: (a) faithfully; (b) habitually; (c) singly, one at a time; (d) without error.
4. *subtle* [10]: (a) strong; (b) barely noticeable; (c) deliberate; (d) invisible.
5. *cessation* [10]: (a) ceasing; (b) beginning again; (c) counting; (d) activity.

B. Content and Structure

Choose the best answer.

1. Which *two* modes of discourse are most evident in this passage? (a) narration; (b) description; (c) exposition; (d) persuasion.
2. The main point Thomas emphasizes about Clever Hans is that he (a) really could do arithmetic; (b) had been taught by his trainer deliberately to deceive his audiences; (c) had learned to read subtle clues in his questioners' behavior and body language, enabling him to "do arithmetic"; (d) was the most intelligent horse that ever lived.

3. The "Clever Hans Error" means essentially that (a) horse trainers often do not know their animals as well as they should; (b) animals are more intelligent than most people give them credit for being; (c) researchers can easily be fooled by the animal subjects they study; (d) it is wrong to assume that animals cannot be taught human computational skills.

4. Paraphrase this phrase from sentence 4: "[the scientist] must bank his professional reputation on the integrity of his experimental subject."

   _____

   _____

5. What is the relationship between paragraphs 1 and 2? (a) steps in a process; (b) general statement and a supporting illustration; (c) contrast; (d) introduction to an unfamiliar term and a definition of it.

6. At the end of sentence 3, when Thomas writes that "it sometimes appears as if animals are genetically programmed to puzzle human beings, especially psychologists," his attitude—toward psychologists, at least—expresses (a) admiration; (b) sarcasm; (c) indifference; (d) hostility.

Selection 3

[1]The word "racism" ought to be as complex as the tangled thing which it denotes; and so it should be handled carefully, as a delicate gauge to help assess an old and varied problem. [2]All too often, however, the word is used as a blunt instrument, cutting conversations short and making people circumspect. [3]Thus wielded, it is not an analytic or descriptive term, but a mere accusation, based on a limited conception of racism. [4]It is, first of all, a reduction of the whole range and history of our interracial struggles to the crude oppression of one side by the other. [5]And this "racism" is as abstract as it is one-sided. [6]It is not a social or historical phenomenon but merely a dark impulse, atavistic and irrational, lurking in every white heart and nowhere else.

[7]Although the charge of "racism" is ostensibly intended to expose the secret thoughts and deeds of bigotry, it is actually a means of concealment. [8]It inhibits frank discussion of what really happens between blacks and whites today; it demands the suppression of any experience that might contradict the sentimental myth of simple, unilateral persecution. [9]The charge of "racism," in other words, forces us to ignore the very conflicts that have kept racism going: it demands not that we resolve our differences, but that we repress them, and this insistence on repression has perverted all our thinking about race. [10]What we often consider "racist" nowadays is not the mistreatment of one race by another, but the mere acknowledgment of differences between blacks and whites—different histories, different cultures, unequal origins within these borders.

Mark Crispin Miller, "Black and White," *Boxed In: The Culture of TV*

A. Vocabulary

For each italicized word from the selection, choose the best definition according to the context in which it appears.

1. *denotes* [sentence 1]: (a) symbolizes; (b) uses, employs; (c) indicates, points to; (d) causes confusion over.
2. *circumspect* [2]: (a) watchful, cautious; (b) nervous, tense; (c) angry, hostile; (d) tolerant, open-minded.
3. *wielded* [3]: Here, used metaphorically to mean (a) stated; (b) threatened; (c) used as a weapon; (d) introduced.
4. *atavistic* [6]: Referring to the characteristics of (a) a fierce warrior; (b) a remote or primitive ancestor; (c) an evil, malicious person; (c) a crazy person.
5. *ostensibly* [7]: (a) outwardly, apparently; (b) usually, most of the time; (c) ideally, perfectly; (d) blatantly, extremely.
6. *bigotry* [7]: (a) hatred; (b) distrust; (c) the criminal mind; (d) intolerance.
7. *inhibits* [8]: (a) allows, permits; (b) denies, cancels; (c) restrains, prevents; (d) pretends to be, assumes.
8. *repress* [9]: (a) ignore; (b) hold back; (c) recognize; (d) aggravate.

B. Content and Structure

Choose the best answer.

1. Which mode of discourse does this passage represent? (a) narration; (b) description; (c) exposition; (d) persuasion.
2. Explain the reason you chose the answer to question 1 above by citing evidence from the passage. _____
   _____
   _____
3. The method of development most evident in the paragraph is (a) example; (b) steps in a process; (c) comparison; (d) definition.
4. What, apparently, does the author want us to understand about the word "racism"? (a) The word is used by ignorant people who do not understand its true meaning; (b) The word has unfortunately come to be used as a weapon, preventing people from confronting true instances of racism; (c) The word no longer applies to the kinds of racial problems the U.S. experiences today; (d) The word should no longer be used because it merely inflames racial misunderstandings and tension.
5. Explain in your own words what Miller means in sentence 3 when he says that the word "racism," as it is often used, is "based on a limited

conception of racism." _____

_____

_____

6. In relation to the phrase at the end of sentence 7, "a means of
    concealment," what is the function of sentence 8? (a) to cite a
    contradictory example; (b) to explain further what that phrase
    means; (c) to provide an illustration of the phrase; (d) to draw a
    conclusion.

7. Find the phrase in the passage where Miller gives us an accurate
    definition of the word "racism." _____

    _____

8. From what he writes in sentence 9, we can assume that the author
    thinks that (a) being aware of our differences and not repressing them
    is the way to solve racial tensions; (b) the country's racial problems are
    unsolvable; (c) both whites and blacks are equally guilty of unfairly
    charging others with racism; (d) we should change our behavior before
    we start tampering with the language.

Practice Essay

Book of Dreams: The Sears Roebuck Catalog
Rose Del Castillo Guilbault

*In early 1993 Sears Roebuck & Company announced that it would stop pub-
lishing its mail-order catalog, a venerable institution begun in 1886. For generations Americans had shopped at home with the catalog; it was especially
important to farm families who made infrequent trips to town. (In the Depression, hard-pressed farm families "recycled" their old Sears and Mont-
gomery Ward catalogs and used them as toilet paper in their outhouses.) But
as Rose Del Castillo points out in this article from the* San Francisco Chronicle *the Sears catalog represented something abstract and metaphorical to her
immigrant family—the possibility of becoming a full-fledged part of the
American dream.*

*Guilbault was born in Mexico and later immigrated with her family to
the U.S., where they settled in the Salinas Valley, an agricultural area in central California. She formerly wrote a column for the Sunday* San Francisco
Chronicle *called "Hispanic, USA" and is now director of public affairs and
editorials for the ABC affiliate in San Francisco, KGO-TV.*

1   The news that Sears is closing 113 stores and folding its 97-year-old
catalog sent me scurrying through the basement in search of one of my
favorite possessions, a 1941 Sears Roebuck & Company catalog. I was

relieved to find it, still inside a metal filing cabinet, underneath a jumble of old Chronicles and a 1939 *Liberty* magazine.

2   I've always had an affinity for the 1940s. I love the Big Band music, the movies and the fashions. As a child I sat mesmerized, listening to my mother's stories about dances under the stars where local groups played and my young mother and her sisters flirted the night away.

3   But that's not the only reason I've held onto this ragged catalog through college, marriage, children and numerous moves. It symbolizes the America my parents and I believed in when we arrived in this country from Mexico. An America where everything you could possibly want was in an emporium inside a book. A book that came to your home from which you could leisurely, conveniently choose items that would be delivered to your doorstep. The concept was amazing to us. This wasn't about accumulating goods but about obtaining a piece of the American pie.

4   Many of today's immigrants are easily caught in this country's web of materialism, easy credit and easy debt. But in the early '60s, the values in rural areas were different. These "wish books" were a metaphor for America's bounty and what could be had with hard work.

5   Every new catalog was savored. We all had our own dream sections. Papa, eyes sparkling, would ease himself into his chair after dinner and briskly examine the tools, hunting rifles and cameras. Then he'd pass the catalog to Mama, who—for what seemed to me to be hours—studied the pretty dresses, household appliances, dishes and plants.

6   By the time the catalog made its way into my hands, my palms itched with anxiety. At Easter time, I would lose myself in pages of frilly, pastel dresses with matching hats and purses. In the Christmas season, which brought my favorite edition of the year, I would sit for hours, staring glassy-eyed at the pages of toys, dolls and games.

7   But nothing frivolous was ever ordered. We lived on a farm in the Salinas Valley, miles and miles from a big city and miles from the nearest small town. To get there, you'd turn off the main paved road onto a bumpy dirt trail that led to two farmhouses—one big one where the boss and his family lived, and a small, four-room cottage where we lived. The inside was sparsely furnished, mostly with hand-me-down furniture from the boss, except for the spindly TV and a cheap, forest-green nylon sofa set my father bought my mother as a wedding gift.

8   Extravagances were unaffordable. Only the most practical and necessary items would be given consideration—my mother's first washing machine, a school coat for me, and thick, dark denim overalls to keep Papa warm in the frostiest of dawns.

9   The Sears catalog had other uses. I'd cut out the models and use them as paper dolls. My mother would match English words with pic-

tures, *"Y estas ollas? Seran "pots" en ingles?"* And in my most desperate hours of boredom, when only sports programs dominated afternoon television, rain fell outdoors, and absolutely nothing interested me indoors, I'd pick up the thick catalog, sit in the bedroom with the faded cabbage-rose print linoleum and spin fantasies about living the good life I imagined the Americans in the catalogs lived.

10   In the front of my 1941 Sears catalog are two stories about typical Sears customers. One profiles the Browns of Washington state, who arrived there as homesteaders, lived in a tent with their children until their farm produced enough for them to build a two-room shack, and eventually built a comfortable white clapboard farmhouse on their land. Photos show Mr. and Mrs. Brown with their new cream separator, daughter Evelyn with her new Elgin bicycle, and the whole family listening to their silver-tone radio-phonograph—all from Sears, of course.

11   The second article describes the Yeamens of Glendale, in Los Angeles County. Mr. Yeamen works at Lockheed Aviation, a mile and a half commute from their "modern, five-room bungalow . . . with a barbecue grill in the back yard and a view of the mountains from every window." Photographs show the various family members with their Sears products: Dad relaxing on a glider swing in the back yard, Mom putting avocado sandwiches in lunch boxes and the kids romping in their stylish clothes.

12   The Browns and Yeamens, the catalog summarizes, are what all of us want to be—good, solid, dependable Americans.

13   As corny and blatantly commercial as these stories are, I like reading them. It reminds me of the America of my youth, or perhaps of my imagination. Even though my family of Mexican immigrants probably didn't have a whole lot in common with the Browns and the Yeamens, we all shopped from that Sears catalog—a book that made us believe everything was reachable, and ours to have.

14   My family prospered too. Not in great leaps and bounds like the Browns of Washington state, but little by little. Our progress was marked by the occasional splurge from the Sears catalog.

15   When I got to the point where I had to own my own clarinet or drop out of the school band—there was a limit to how long we could borrow from the music department—my family had to make a choice. I was not a great musician; we all knew that. But the band was a wholesome activity that integrated me into school life, into America. One evening after dinner, my parents called me into the living room. I searched their faces for a clue, but they remained mysteriously impassive until my father brought out a wrinkled brown package from behind his back.

16   My heart began pounding when I saw the Sears return address. Out came a compact gray and white case, and inside it, lying on an elegant bed of royal blue rayon velvet, were the pieces of a brand-new ebony

clarinet. Never in my stolen afternoons with the Sears catalog had I imagined possessing something so fine!

17   Somehow I can't envision today's kids reminiscing about a Land's End or Victoria's Secret catalog. Times have changed, and so have demographics. People in rural America no longer need a catalog. They now have K Marts or Wal-Marts in their own mini-malls.

18   Newspapers articles reporting on the Sears closures have described the catalog as "the best record of American material culture." But to many of us, this catalog wasn't about materialism at all. It was about making dreams come true.

A. Comprehension

Choose the answer that best completes each statement. Do not refer to the selection while doing this exercise.

1. The main idea of the article is that, for Guilbault, the Sears Roebuck catalog represented (a) a vision of America that she and her family could never obtain; (b) the possibility of obtaining a piece of the American pie; (c) a way of life that typified the simpler, less stressful era of the 1940s; (d) a convenient way to shop at home to buy both the necessities and expensive luxuries.

2. For the author and her family, the most important American virtue was (a) a competitive spirit; (b) generosity; (c) hard work; (d) the desire for an education.

3. The kinds of things the author's family ordered from the Sears catalog were (a) toys and games; (b) fancy dress clothing; (c) frivolous things; (d) useful items like warm clothing.

4. Guilbault's mother looked at the catalog not only to enjoy the pictures of clothing and household items, but also to (a) think of gifts for the family; (b) practice her English; (c) get ideas for making homemade clothing; (d) dream of the good life in America.

5. The catalog's description of the model families—the Browns and the Yeamans—suggested to her that (a) her family was just like them; (b) America was not really the land of opportunity; (c) it was important to buy one's belongings from Sears; (d) everything in America was reachable for her family.

6. Guilbault remembers one especially memorable acquisition, a clarinet. Aside from marking her family's economic prosperity, this purchase was also significant because (a) she could become a great musician; (b) she would improve her status in the class; (c) she would be integrated into American life; (d) she could play music for her family.

B. Structure

Choose the best answer.

1. Which *two* modes of discourse are evident in the article? (a) narration; (b) description; (c) exposition; (d) persuasion.
2. This article has a clear beginning, middle, and end. Write the number of the paragraph where the body begins. ____
    Write the number of the paragraph where the conclusion begins. ____
3. Which of the following adjectives best represents the author's point of view? (a) nostalgic; (b) objective; (c) envious; (d) philosophical; (e) self-pitying.
4. What method of development is used in paragraph 4? (a) example; (b) steps in a process; (c) contrast; (d) definition.
5. What primary method of development is used in paragraphs 5–9? (a) example; (b) comparison; (c) contrast; (d) definition.
6. Look again at paragraph 14 and paragraphs 15 and 16. What is the relationship between them? (a) All represent steps in a process; (b) paragraph 14 includes a term to be defined, and the other two define it; (c) paragraphs 15 and 16 offer a contrast to paragraph 14; (d) paragraph 14 makes a general statement, and paragraphs 15 and 16 serve as a supporting illustration.

C. Vocabulary

For each italicized word from the selection, choose the best definition according to the context in which it appears.

1. an *affinity* for the 1940s [paragraph 2]: (a) natural attraction; (b) obsession; (c) slight interest in; (d) reaction.
2. I sat *mesmerized* [2]: (a) silent; (b) amazed; (c) enthralled; (d) withdrawn.
3. an *emporium* inside a book [3]: (a) playground; (b) educational center; (c) imaginary toyland; (d) large retail store.
4. a metaphor for America's *bounty* [4]: (a) high reputation; (b) amalgamation of goods and services; (c) generosity, liberality in giving; (d) treasure chest.
5. every new catalog was *savored* [5]: (a) fought over; (b) relished, enjoyed; (c) perused from cover to cover; (d) worn ragged from use.
6. nothing *frivolous* was ever ordered [7]: (a) insignificant, trivial; (b) attractive, beautiful; (c) expensive; (d) of good quality.
7. the inside was *sparsely* furnished [7]: (a) lavishly, expensively; (b) skimpily, meagerly; (c) poorly, cheaply; (d) cozily, comfortably.

8. as corny and *blatantly* commercial [13]: (a) offensively; (b) typically; (c) ridiculously; (d) obviously.

9. they remained mysteriously *impassive* [15]: (a) silent, withdrawn; (b) showing no emotion; (c) excited, jubilant; (d) embarrassed.

10. times have changed, and so have *demographics* [17]: the study of (a) social values; (b) populations and their characteristics; (c) ethnic groups; (d) social classes.

D. Questions for Analysis and Discussion

1. In paragraph 4, Guilbault implicitly criticizes today's culture for its emphasis on materialism, yet it is clear that the Sears catalog, too, promoted materialism. Guilbault suggests a difference, however. What is it?

2. In paragraph 17, Guilbault writes, "Somehow I can't envision today's kids reminiscing about a Land's End or Victoria's Secret catalog." What does she mean? Do you agree with her?

3

More Methods of Paragraph Development

In this chapter we will be concerned with three additional methods of paragraph development: (1) analysis and classification; (2) cause and effect; and (3) analogy. These methods are a bit more difficult to recognize than the ones you studied in Chapter 2.

Analysis and Classification

Analysis and classification are traditionally considered together. Although they are actually separate methods, their underlying purpose is the same. Both involve the author's taking apart a larger subject and examining its separate parts to see how each relates to the whole. A writer might *analyze* a single entity—a speech given by a political candidate, for example—by discussing its separate features—its quality of thought, its language and style, and the candidate's delivery. The same writer might *classify* another single entity—the audience of students, business leaders, and journalists listening to the speech, for example—by dividing its members into types, or *classes,* and describing the distinguishing characteristics of each group. If you read a paragraph that begins, "At

the tourist trap where I work during the summers, have observed three different kinds of customers," or "There are five subspecies of fish called darters," you can expect the writer to use the classification method to develop the topic.

In the following excerpt, Page Smith, a historian now in his seventies, classifies dreams, especially old people's dreams, into three categories. You can easily predict that he will use the classification method from the first sentence:

[1]It seems to me that there are two or three quite different categories of dreams. There are dreams that are just what they seem to be—dreams of trying to find a bathroom (increasingly common in old age), dreams of erotic conquest (ageless), dreams of finding money or valuable and highly desired "things." Then there are dreams of doing effortlessly what in real life is plainly difficult or impossible. I have frequent dreams of running effortlessly over forbidding terrain. The more my old joints creak, the more, it seems, I dream of gliding through space. Sometimes I have dreams that revolve around intractable problems, around feelings of guilt. I have been exonerated in dreams for faults and failings. I used to dream, from time to time, that the secret of life was about to be revealed to me; I always woke up before the revelation.

[2]Then there are dreams that are utterly mysterious, that seem without rhyme or reason. There are nightmares, terrifying dreams, dreams of danger and imminent death. These we could all clearly do without. Sweet dreams, we say. We can hope for sweet dreams, but dreams are clearly the one aspect of our lives over which we have little or no control. Most dreams are ephemeral, yet some remain in memory for a lifetime.

Page Smith, "To Sleep (II): Perchance to Dream," *San Francisco Chronicle*

The topic of the next example is decidedly more grisly. In a chapter describing the horrors inflicted on residents of the Central African Republic by its former leader Bokassa, Alex Shoumatoff classifies cannibalism into four types. (In passing, the writer alludes to the Uruguayan soccer team whose plane crashed in the Andes. Their experiences have been recorded in a fine book by Piers Paul Read, *Alive!*, which was also made into a 1993 film of the same name.)

There are many kinds of cannibalism. Revenge cannibalism—the gloating, triumphant ingestion of a slain enemy's heart, liver, or other vital parts—is common at the warring-chiefdom stage of social evolution. Emergency cannibalism was resorted to by the Uruguayan soccer team whose plane crashed in the Andes. Ritual endocannibalism is practiced by certain tribes like the Yanonamo of northern Amazonia, whose women drink the pulverized ashes of slain kin mixed with banana gruel before their men go off on

a raiding party. In the Kindu region of Zaire there are to this day leopard men who wear leopard skins, smear their bodies with leopard grease (which protects them even from lions), chip their teeth to points, and attack and eat people. Among their victims were some Italian soldiers who were part of the U.N. peace-keeping force during the turbulence after independence in 1960. The rarest kind of cannibals are gustatory cannibals— people who are actually partial to the taste of human flesh.

Alex Shoumatoff, "The Emperor Who Ate His People," *African Madness*

As stated before, analysis examines a *single* idea by looking at its separate parts. Consider this paragraph by Robert N. Bellah and others from their study of American values, in which they analyze the cowboy's characteristics and his significance in American culture. (Notice that the authors also use a secondary method of development, examples—the Lone Ranger, the film character Shane from the movie of the same name, and the cowboy hero of *High Noon,* Will Kane.)

America is also the inventor of that most mythic individual hero, the cowboy, who again and again saves a society he can never completely fit into. The cowboy has a special talent—he can shoot straighter and faster than other men—and a special sense of justice. But these characteristics make him so unique that he can never fully belong to society. His destiny is to defend society without ever really joining it. He rides off alone into the sunset like Shane, or like the Lone Ranger moves on accompanied only by his Indian companion. But the cowboy's importance is not that he is isolated or antisocial. Rather, his significance lies in his unique, individual virtue and special skill and it is because of those qualities that society needs and welcomes him. Shane, after all, starts as a real outsider, but ends up with the gratitude of the community and the love of a woman and a boy. And while the Lone Ranger never settles down and marries the local schoolteacher, he always leaves with the affection and gratitude of the people he has helped. It is as if the myth says you can be a truly good person, worthy of admiration and love, only if you resist fully joining the group. But sometimes the tension leads to an irreparable break. Will Kane, the hero of *High Noon,* abandoned by the cowardly townspeople, saves them from an unrestrained killer, but then throws his sheriff's badge in the dust and goes off into the desert with his bride. One is left wondering where they will go, for there is no longer any link with any town.

Robert N. Bellah et. al., *Habits of the Heart*

In the next example, Richard Preston uses analysis to explain the elusive nature of pi (3.14). This excerpt is from an article about the Chudnovsky brothers, who have assembled gigantic computers capable

of expanding the decimal numbers of pi to thousands of places to see if they can discern a pattern. So far, the decimal places make no sense.

[1]Pi which is denoted by the Greek letter π, is the most famous ratio in mathematics, and is one of the most ancient numbers known to humanity. Pi is approximately 3.14—the number of times that a circle's diameter will fit around the circle. Here is a circle, with its diameter:

[2]Pi goes on forever, and can't be calculated to perfect precision:

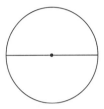

3.14159265358979323846264338327950288841971693993751. . . . This is known as the decimal expansion of pi. It is a bloody mess. No apparent pattern emerges in the succession of digits. The digits of pi march to infinity in a predestined yet unfathomable code: they do not repeat periodically, seeming to pop up by blind chance, lacking any perceivable order, rule, reason, or design—"random" integers, ad infinitum. If a deep and beautiful design hides in the digits of pi, no one knows what it is, and no one has ever been able to see it by staring at the digits. Among mathematicians, there is a nearly universal feeling that it will never be possible, in principle, for an inhabitant of our finite universe to discover the system in the digits of pi. But for the present, if you want to attempt it, you need a supercomputer to probe the endless scrap of leftover pi.

Richard Preston, "Profiles: David and Gregory Chudnovsky," *The New Yorker*

Cause and Effect

You might think of the cause-and-effect method of paragraph development as a way of finding *reasons* to explain events, problems, or issues and the *consequences* that result. The phrase *cause and effect* refers both to a logical relationship between ideas and to a method of development. A writer may discuss only causes, or only effects, or both, and they can be presented in any order.

For example, a writer interested in exploring the question of why the Communist empire disintegrated in the former USSR and its satellite nations might focus on the *causes* alone: the entrenched corruption in the Communist party; an increasingly divisive inequality between party members and ordinary citizens; a desire for an improved standard

of living closer to that enjoyed by Western nations; a critical lack of ordinary consumer goods; and the citizens' demands for democratization after the *perestroika* ("openness") era of Gorbachev, among others.

The *effects* of the end of the Communist era have been extremely far-reaching. (It is important to remember that complicated issues have complicated causes and often complicated effects as well, much like the ripple effect that occurs when you throw a pebble into a pond.) The immediate effect was a sense of elation and openness as one country after another declared its independence from the former USSR and toppled the Communist regimes. But the transition from government-managed economies to market economies in nearly every country has been very painful. Two ultimate results have been the emergence of warring factions prepared to commit appalling atrocities in the former Yugoslavia (Serbia, Croatia, Bosnia), and the skyrocketing costs resulting from the reunification of West and East Germany. But the effects of the end of the Cold War have not just been limited to Eastern Europe. Improved relations between East and West and the East's collapsing economies have meant that there has been less need for defense spending—leading, in turn, to less government spending for armaments, military development, and weapons research. Decreased defense spending in the United States has further led to high unemployment in areas like Southern California where defense industries are concentrated, contributing—at least in part—to the 1990–1993 recession. A related effect is the closing of several U.S. military bases around the nation, leading further to unemployment both for military and nonmilitary personnel. It is conceivable that a storeowner who depended on business from, say, Homestead Air Force Base in Florida, which in 1993 was scheduled for closure, could trace his financial insecurity—at least indirectly—to the collapse of communism in Eastern Europe.

The cause-and-effect pattern always involves the question *why?* whether stated or implied. If you read a paragraph that begins, "America's continued dependence on foreign oil poses serious economic problems for the future," you can predict that the writer will examine the probable economic consequences (the *effects*) of our oil consumption (the *cause*), even though words like "reason," "effect," "consequence," or "result" are not present.

Let us examine a paragraph with a fairly obvious cause-and-effect relationship. The author begins with a question: What does large school size and large class size mean? This situation is the *cause*. He then examines the consequences, or *effects*, of large class sizes.

What does large school size and large class size mean from the standpoint of the teenager's efforts at self-definition? One clear consequence is the loss of what has been called *mentoring*. In the autobiographies of many men and women who became successful despite adversity, one repeatedly finds that a

significant person in their lives recognized their special gifts and devoted time, energy, and skill to helping them realize their abilities. More often than not, this significant person was a teacher or coach whom the successful person first encountered in school. Although teacher and pupil did not meet at school, the importance of the role of the mentor is best illustrated by the case of Helen Keller. As a young child she was not only deaf and blind but nearly demented in her behavior. It took the insight, dedication, and hard work of her teacher, Anne Sullivan, to enable Helen Keller to realize her intellectual and artistic gifts. The establishment of a mentor relationship is much more likely in the small high school, with its small classes, than in the large high school. It is next to impossible, for example, for an English teacher who sees two hundred students a day to single out a few to work with intensively. Many gifted and talented students fail to realize their potential because the bigness of today's schools militates against the mentoring of such students by individual faculty members.

David Elkind, *All Grown Up and No Place to Go*

Elkind cites two consequences (in the second sentence and in the last sentence). Notice, too, that he uses two other methods of development, namely example and definition.

In this next example, Sissela Bok explains the effects of lying on those who have been lied to. Notice that the cause-and-effect relationship here is only implied:

Those who learn that they have been lied to in an important matter—say, the identity of their parents, the affection of their spouse, or the integrity of their government—are resentful, disappointed, and suspicious. They feel wronged; they are wary of new overtures. And they look back on their past beliefs and actions in the new light of the discovered lies. They see that they were manipulated, that the deceit made them unable to make choices for themselves according to the most adequate information available, unable to act as they would have wanted to act had they known all along.

Sissela Bok, *Lying: Moral Choice in Public and Private Life*

In this last example, William Finnegan examines the historical role of surfing in Hawaii, among other things. According to Finnegan, what caused—at least temporarily—the decline in surfing in Hawaii?

[1]Before the arrival of Europeans in the Pacific, surfing was practiced throughout Oceania—in Hawaii, Polynesia, New Guinea, even New Zealand. Captain James Cook, the British explorer, saw canoe surfing and bodysurfing in the Society Islands in 1777 and standup board surfing in

the Hawaiian Islands in 1778. Cook was fascinated, and so were many of the traders, missionaries, and journalists who followed him, including Mark Twain and Jack London. In Hawaii, surfing had religious significance—after prayers and offerings, skilled craftsmen made boards from sacred koa or wiliwili trees—and it was practiced by men and women, young and old, royalty and peasantry. As Leonard Lueras notes in "Surfing: The Ultimate Pleasure," the sport allowed for fashion statements; a visiting British sea captain, a cousin of Lord Byron, wrote that "to have a neat floatboard, wellkept, and dried, is to a Sandwich Islander what a tilbury or cabriolet, or whatever light carriage may be in fashion is to a young English man." When the surf was good, "all thought of work is at an end, only that of sport is left," wrote Kepelino Keauokalani, a nineteenth-century Hawaiian scholar. "All day there is nothing but surfing. Many go out surfing as early as four in the morning."

[2]This was not what the Calvinist missionaries who began arriving in Hawaii in 1820 had in mind for the islanders as a way of life. Hiram Bingham, who led the first missionary party, which found itself in a crowd of surfers before it had even landed, wrote, "The appearance of destitution, degradation, and barbarism, among the chattering, and almost naked savages, whose heads and feet, and much of their sunburnt skins were bare, was appalling. Some of our number, with gushing tears, turned away from the spectacle." Twenty-seven years later, Bingham wrote, "The decline and discontinuance of the use of the surfboard, as civilization advances, may be accounted for by the increase in modesty, industry or religion." He was not wrong about the decline of surfing. Hawaiian culture had been destroyed and the people decimated by European diseases; between 1778 and 1893, the Hawaiian population shrank from three hundred thousand to forty thousand, and by the end of the last century surfing had all but disappeared.

William Finnegan, "Surfing," *The New Yorker*

(In addition to an implied cause-and-effect relationship between ideas, Finnegan also uses contrast, specifically to show the native conception of surfing and the changes that occurred after the missionaries came to spread their work. This might be called a "then-and-now" form of contrast.)

Analogy

Analogy, the last method of development, is perhaps the most difficult method for readers to perceive and understand well. An analogy is an *extended metaphor;* that is, the writer develops the topic by setting up an imaginative comparison between two unlike things. In yoking these two things together, the writer emphasizes shared characteristics and

also provides a fresh insight. A writer might, for instance, explain the functioning of a human heart in terms of the way a more familiar object—a pump—works. The human eye is often compared by means of an analogy to a camera.

The analogy always begins with a metaphor, but rather than being expressed in (typically) a single phrase or sentence, an analogy is a *sustained* metaphor. This means that the comparison is usually extended through a paragraph or occasionally even throughout a longer piece. The following two examples illustrate the common link and the difference between metaphor and analogy. In 1990 when former Soviet president Mikhail Gorbachev was trying to change the economic and political course of the USSR, Jeff Trimble and Dianne Rinehart in *U.S. News & World Report* described the situation like this:

> In the view of Gorbachev's own people, documented in public opinion surveys, the Soviet Union today resembles nothing so much as a patient opened for surgery by a chief doctor who has no idea what to do next.

This is a simple metaphor: The USSR is compared to a patient undergoing surgery, and Gorbachev is unflatteringly compared to an incompetent surgeon. How, then, does a metaphor become an analogy? In this next example a different writer uses a strikingly similar comparison. To explain the political and economic turmoil in Poland, he *extends* the comparison throughout the paragraph, thereby developing the paragraph with a true analogy.

> "An unskilled team of surgeons is performing a complicated procedure" is how *Gazeta's* senior political columnist, Ernest Skalski, recently described political developments in Poland after last October's parliamentary elections. "They're not doing great, but somehow they're managing. Suddenly, in the middle of the operation, a new team shows up, insisting that it, too, has the right to try its hand. The patient is lying there cut open, his guts all splayed out, the anesthesia is wearing off, and now the two teams take to pushing and struggling among themselves all around the table. Finally, the new guys wrest control and start in, but they presently acknowledge that actually they'll only be submitting their plan of operation in some two months' time."
>
> Lawrence Weschler, "A Reporter at Large: Poland," *The New Yorker*

What is being compared to what? Poland's political situation is being compared to a patient undergoing surgery, and its leaders are described first as an "unskilled team of surgeons." We can all imagine this horrifying scene: Surgery has begun; the team is doing its best to operate on the patient to save his life. In literal terms, of course, Weschler

means that the leaders have a plan of action to reform the country, even if they are not exactly sure of what they are doing. But then another team of political leaders shows up and demands that they be allowed to try to fix the country. In the meantime, Poland—again compared metaphorically to a patient who has been opened up—is suffering terribly. The two teams argue and fight about who will have control. The new leaders win the battle, but then admit that they really have no immediate plan to fix the country's ills, which can only become worse.

As you read a paragraph that is developed by analogy, you have to keep its actual subject in mind. The literal subject in this case is Poland and its warring political leaders, *not* a sick patient undergoing surgery and teams of inept surgeons. Good analogies like this one are remarkably effective and powerful: they are attention-getting devices, but they also provide a point of view far more convincing and engaging than a literal description would be.

Here is another example of a short paragraph using analogy. It represents the opening sentences of a news article on the terrible fires during the summer of 1988 that destroyed 25 percent of Yellowstone National Park.

> Visiting this fire-scarred but still magnificent park is like watching one of those Hollywood melodramas in which the gorgeous heroine suffers some horrible accident and wakes up in the next scene with her face covered in white bandages. The audience can only wait in suspense to know whether she will still be beautiful when the gauze is removed.
>
> T. R. Reid, "New Yellowstone to Rise from Ashes," *The Washington Post*

In the preceding example the author mentions the true subject— the burned parkland—only once. Then he introduces the analogy with the crucial word "like." A literal description ("A visitor to Yellowstone wonders what the long-term effects of the fire will be") would be dull and does not convey the suspense that the analogy permits.

This next example by African-American writer Eddy L. Harris is from a book he wrote about a trip to Africa during which he visited Abidjan, the capital of Ivory Coast (now Côte d'Ivoire). What picture does Harris convey about the city of Abidjan?

> A hot wind blows slowly across the land and moisture hangs heavy in the air. The desert has come at last to an end, the sand giving way first to hard red laterite, then to rocky soil and scrub bushes, and finally now to the dark loamy soil of the rain forest.
>
> Here where forest and sea come together teeters Abidjan, a modern city on the edge of a shelf of antiques, a city where cardboard shacks lie in the

shadow of skyscrapers, glass and steel, 50 stories tall. In Abidjan the two worlds are poised side by side, like crippled legs of uneven lengths belonging to a lame man. When he walks there is pain and discomfort. He manages to hobble, but not without a great deal of effort.

Eddy L. Harris, Native Stranger

Analogies can also be misused (See the discussion of *False Analogy* in the section called Logical Fallacies in Part III, Reading Critically.)

Combination of Methods

Finally, you should recognize that, like many of life's challenges, the task of reading is a complex undertaking. Not all paragraphs can be as neatly categorized as the ones you have examined here. Although some writers use an easily recognizable method of development, many do not. Within an essay or article, a writer may use several different methods as well as paragraphs that use a combination of methods. The following paragraph is a good example of a piece of writing that employs a mix of the methods you have studied thus far.

The manatee is, of course, a member of that curious group the water mammals. It is a large beast, shaped like a tapered balloon, weighing around a thousand pounds, and measuring ten feet or so in length. Like the whale and the seal, the manatee is a creature whose ancestors moved from land back to a life in the sea. It has been altered by its years in the sea less than the whale but more than the seal, which still spends some time on land. The manatee never leaves the water, but it is not equipped, as whales are, for life in the open ocean. It spends its time in rivers and estuaries and along the fringes of the land. Whales, seals, and manatees, despite their similarities, are not close cousins but the descendants of different beasts, which took to the water at different times. Improbable as it sounds, the nearest relative of the manatee is thought to be the elephant. Like the elephant, the manatee is completely herbivorous, it grazes on river and sea grasses. And like the elephant's, the manatee's mammary glands are pectoral. The manatee's teeth resemble the elephant's; it has no incisors or canines—only molars. Lacking front teeth to crop its food, the manatee uses its long, muscular upper lip, which is cleft in the middle and equipped with stout bristles, to grasp food and push it into its mouth. The manatee has lost its hind legs (though vestigial bones remain), and its forelegs have become flippers. Though the bones are hidden within the flipper, the Florida manatee still has three nails at the end of each flipper—reminders of its terrestrial existence. The flippers are highly flexible. Manatees use them

not for fast swimming but for close maneuvering, for support when they rest on the bottom, and for embracing each other.

Faith McNulty, "Manatees," The New Yorker

In this example McNulty combines several methods:

1. Definition (defining manatees by placing them in the water mammal group)
2. Comparison (comparing manatees to whales, seals, and elephants)
3. Contrast (contrasting the manatee with whales and seals)
4. Analysis (analyzing the structure of the manatee's body)

And appropriate to her purpose, she combines two modes of discourse, exposition and description, although neither predominates.

The last passage, by Bill Barich, a writer on contemporary music, is concerned with the phenomenon known as the Deadheads, the faithful band that follow Jerry Garcia and the Grateful Dead from concert to concert. See if you can determine the three methods of paragraph development it embodies.

[1]Deadheads are everywhere at present. For the band, they are a blessing and a curse. Their fealty translates into huge profits, but they also imply an unwanted responsibility. Sometimes they make a prisoner of Garcia. He can't wander about in Marin County or anywhere else the way he once did. When the Deadhead phenomenon began to snowball, five or six years ago, he was concerned about its cultlike implications and tried to sabotage it by being nonresponsive and pretending that it didn't exist, but since then he has seen that it's too directionless to amount to a serious threat. He accepts it as a logical consequence of the Dead's tribal impulse. Besides, Deadheads are quick to be critical, he says, whenever the band is lazy, sloppy, dull, or just plain bad. Still, he isn't entirely comfortable with them, and never speaks a word from the stage, because he's afraid of how it might be interpreted.

[2]Garcia puzzles over the Deadheads. He is trapped inside their obsession and can only probe at it from the inside. He thinks that the band affords its followers "a tear in reality"—a brief vacation from the mundane. The Dead design their shows and their music to be ambiguous and open-ended, he says; they intend an evening to be both reactive and interactive. A Deadhead gets to join in on an experiment that may or may not be going anywhere in particular, and such an opportunity is rare in American life. The Deadhead world is multireferential and feeds on itself. A fan's capital is measured by his or her involvement with the band over time, by the number of shows attended and the amount of trivia digested.

Bill Barich, "Still Truckin'," The New Yorker

Exercises

Selection 1

¹Those of us who have to spend a great deal of time in crowded conditions become gradually better able to adjust, but no one can ever become completely immune to invasions of Personal Space. ²This is because they remain forever associated with either powerful hostile or equally powerful loving feelings. ³All through our childhood we will have been held to be loved and held to be hurt, and anyone who invades our Personal Space when we are adults is, in effect, threatening to extend his behaviour into one of these two highly charged areas of human interaction. ⁴Even if his motives are clearly neither hostile nor sexual, we still find it hard to suppress our reactions to his close approach. ⁵Unfortunately, different countries have different ideas about exactly how close is close. ⁶It is easy enough to test your own "space reaction": when you are talking to someone in the street or in any open space, reach out with your arm and see where the nearest point on his body comes. ⁷If you hail from western Europe, you will find that he is at roughly fingertip distance from you. ⁸In other words, as you reach out, your fingertips will just about make contact with his shoulder. ⁹If you come from eastern Europe you will find you are standing at "wrist distance." ¹⁰If you come from the Mediterranean region you will find that you are much closer to your companion, at little more than "elbow distance."

¹¹Trouble begins when a member of one of these cultures meets and talks to one from another. ¹²Say a British diplomat meets an Italian or an Arab diplomat at an embassy function. ¹³They start talking in a friendly way, but soon the fingertips man begins to feel uneasy. ¹⁴Without knowing quite why, he starts to back away gently from his companion. ¹⁵The companion edges forward again. ¹⁶Each tries in this way to set up a Personal Space relationship that suits his own background. ¹⁷But it is impossible to do. ¹⁸Every time the Mediterranean diplomat advances to a distance that feels comfortable for him, the British diplomat feels threatened. ¹⁹Every time the Briton moves back, the other feels rejected. ²⁰Attempts to adjust this situation often lead to a talking pair shifting slowly across a room, and many an embassy reception is dotted with western-European fingertip-distance men pinned against the walls by eager elbow-distance men. ²¹Until such differences are fully understood, and allowances made, these minor differences in "body territories" will continue to act as an alienation factor which may interfere in a subtle way with diplomatic harmony and other forms of international transaction.

Desmond Morris, *Manwatching: A Field Guide to Human Behaviour*

A. Vocabulary

For each italicized word from the selection, choose the best definition according to the context in which it appears.

1.   *immune to* [sentence 1]: (a) indifferent to; (b) endangered by; (c) unconcerned about; (d) unaffected by.

2. *charged* [3]: (a) intensified; (b) challenged; (c) excitable; (d) loaded.
3. *suppress* [4]: (a) alter; (b) give into; (c) reduce; (d) hold back.
4. *alienation* [21]: Describing a state of (a) unawareness; (b) being disturbed; (c) isolation; (d) irritation.

B. **Content and Structure**

Choose the best answer.

1. The mode of discourse in this passage is (a) narration; (b) description; (c) exposition; (d) persuasion.
2. This passage reflects a combination of various methods of development. Write the method represented in these sentences:

      sentences 1–4:   _____
      sentences 2–4:   _____
      sentences 6–10:   _____
      sentences 11–20: _____

3. What is the relationship between sentences 2 and 3? (a) both show steps in a process; (b) sentence 2 shows contrast from sentence 1; (c) sentence 2 introduces an important term, and sentence 3 defines it; (d) sentence 2 represents a cause, and sentence 3 shows its effect; (e) sentence 2 presents a general idea, and sentence 3 clarifies and explains it further.
4. The main idea of the passage is that (a) diplomats need special training in other cultures' definition of Personal Space; (b) the concept of Personal Space is not very well understood; (c) every culture has its own perception of Personal Space; (d) all of us have difficulty responding to invasions of our Personal Space.
5. Look again at sentences 13–19. From Morris's description of this hypothetical conversation between diplomats, it is likely that (a) both the Briton and the Mediterranean feel equally offended; (b) the Briton is more offended than the Mediterranean; (c) the Mediterranean is more offended than the Briton; (d) both diplomats are violating the other's Personal Space on purpose to establish dominance.
6. The tone—that is, the emotional feeling conveyed—in sentence 20 is (a) sneering, ridiculing; (b) objective, impartial; (c) mildly humorous; (d) highly negative, critical.

Selection 2

[1]There are between twenty-five thousand Asian elephants left in the world. [2]Their gradual elimination in the wild is the result of a number of changes, most of them recent and a few subtle. [3]The invention of the chain saw, for in-

stance, made forest-clearing much easier and quicker work. [4]But basically there is just not enough room in Southeast Asia for both elephants and people. [5]The elephant's jungle habitat is being replaced by cropland, and many of the crops are delectable to the now homeless elephant. [6]The elephant raids the millet and sugarcane, and is killed for his efforts, and kills in turn; in India, nearly a hundred and fifty people are killed by elephants every year. [7]Wild elephants are found from India to Indonesia; most inhabit shrinking parks and preserves, in shrinking populations, separated from each other by human settlements as uncrossable as an ocean. [8]Bulls, being more aggressive, are killed far more often than cows. [9]Not only does this deplete the gene pool but the cows' opportunities to breed grow fewer, and as the birth rate falls their mean age increases. [10]Because elephants will feed on the youngest, tenderest trees available, finding them the most appetizing, herds quickly denude small parks beyond the point of natural recovery. [11]Several countries, notably Thailand and India, are attempting to conserve these insular environments and to confront the problems of the diminished gene pool and male-to-female ratio, but quite a few people in elephant biology wonder whether the wild elephant is past saving. [12]There are estimated to be a million elephants left in Africa; however, their numbers are also dropping. [13]Certainly its future, one way or another, resides in zoos.

Sallie Tisdale, "The Only Harmless Great Thing," *The New Yorker*

A. Vocabulary

For each italicized word from the selection, choose the best definition according to the context in which it appears.

1. *subtle* [sentence 2]: (a) not immediately obvious; (b) of great concern; (c) quickly apparent; (d) old, traditional.
2. *delectable* [5]: (a) poisonous; (b) off-limits; (c) nourishing; (d) greatly pleasing.
3. *deplete* [9]: (a) ruin, destroy; (b) use up, diminish; (c) change, alter; (d) enhance, add to.
4. *mean* [9]: (a) average; (b) inferior; (c) productive; (d) useful.
5. *denude* [10]: (a) trample; (b) take refuge in; (c) make bare of vegetation; (d) dominate.
6. *insular* [11]: (a) protected, like a refuge; (b) isolated, standing alone; (c) manmade, artificial; (d) natural, genuine.

B. Content and Structure

Choose the best answer.

1. In your own words, state the main idea of the paragraph.

   _____

2. The method of development in this paragraph is clearly cause and effect. In the following spaces, state first the effect and then briefly list the chain of causes Tisdale provides as evidence.

Effect: _____

Cause 1: _____

Cause 2: _____

Cause 3: _____

Cause 4: _____

Cause 5: _____

3. Label the following sentences according to whether they represent major support (MA) or minor support (MI) with respect to the main idea: sentence 4 _____ ; sentence 5_____ ; sentence 6 _____ ; sentence 7 _____ ; sentence 8 _____.

4. What is the relationship between sentences 8 and 9? (a) general idea and a supporting example; (b) cause and effect; (c) contrast; (d) classification; (e) analogy.

5. In sentence 11, when the author writes that elephant biologists wonder whether the wild elephant is "past saving," she means that it (a) is not worth saving; (b) can be saved; (c) may not be able to be saved; (d) is many years away from being saved.

6. From her discussion, the author is (a) more sympathetic to the human population than to the elephant; (b) more sympathetic to the elephant population than to the human; (c) equally sympathetic to both populations; (d) completely neutral.

Selection 3

[1]One cannot easily realize what a tremendous thing it is to know every trivial detail of twelve hundred miles of river and know it with absolute exactness. [2]If you will take the longest street in New York, and travel up and down it, conning* its features patiently until you know every house and window and door and lamp-post and big and little sign by heart, and know them so accurately that you can instantly name the one you are abreast of when you are set down at random in that street in the middle of an inky black night, you will then have a tolerable notion of the amount and the exactness of a pilot's knowledge who carries the Mississippi River in his head. [3]And then if you will go on until you know every street crossing, the character, size, and position of the crossing-stones, and the varying depth of mud in each of those numberless places, you will have some idea of what the pilot must know in order to keep a Mississippi steamer out of trouble. [4]Next, if you will take half of the signs in that long street, and *change their places* once a month, and still manage to know their new positions accurately on dark nights, and keep up with these repeated

changes without making any mistakes, you will understand what is required of a pilot's peerless memory by the fickle Mississippi.

Mark Twain, *Life on the Mississippi*

*Studying, examining carefully so as to memorize.

A. Vocabulary

For each italicized word from the selection, choose the best definition according to the context in which it appears.

1. *trivial* [sentence 1]: (a) silly; (b) ordinary; (c) of little significance; (d) unobserved.
2. *abreast of* [2]: (a) in the vicinity of; (b) near; (c) alongside; (d) behind.
3. *tolerable* [2]: (a) fair, adequate; (b) able to be endured; (c) permissible; (d) exact, accurate.
4. *peerless* [4]: (a) reliable; (b) well-trained; (c) hazy; (d) unmatched.
5. *fickle* [4]: (a) hard to get along with; (b) changeable; (c) undependable; (d) complicated.

B. Content and Structure

1. The method of development in this paragraph is clearly analogy. Explain first what Twain is comparing to what.

    _____ is compared
    to _____.

2. Now explain in your own words what, in literal terms, the analogy means—that is, what is required of a Mississippi river pilot.

    _____
    _____
    _____

3. Twain probably uses this particular analogy because (a) we can understand the difficulty of learning all of a street's characteristics; (b) the familiar can be explained better in terms of the unfamiliar; (c) a river and a street have nearly identical characteristics; (d) everybody should know the characteristics of a single street as well as Twain suggests.

4. It is apparent from sentence 2 that learning to be a Mississippi riverboat pilot (a) takes an enormous amount of patience; (b) can be quickly accomplished; (c) requires a person who can follow orders; (d) requires a person who can make quick life-and-death decisions.

5. Of the tasks described in sentences 2, 3, or 4, which—in literal terms for the riverboat captain—would probably be the most difficult to accomplish? _____

What clue does Twain provide to help you arrive at this answer?

_____

6. We usually reserve the word *fickle* to describe human behavior. From what Twain suggests in sentence 4, what are some factors that would cause a river to be described as fickle? _____

_____

Practice Essay

How to Talk about the World

Peter Farb

Until his untimely death in 1980 at the age of forty-nine, Peter Farb was a naturalist, an anthropologist, and a writer who popularized the natural sciences. His specialty was Indian languages—in the United States as well as in Mexico, Central America, and Brazil. He is the author of Man's Rise to Civilization as Shown by the Indians of North America and Face of North America, *of* Consuming Passions: The Anthropology of Eating *(with George Armelagos), and of* Word Play, *a highly readable introduction to the field of linguistics, from which this excerpt comes.*

1   If human beings paid attention to all the sights, sounds, and smells that besiege them, their ability to codify and recall information would be swamped. Instead, they simplify the information by grouping it into broad verbal categories. For example, human eyes have the extraordinary power to discriminate some ten million colors, but the English language reduces these to no more than four thousand color words, of which only eleven basic terms are commonly used. That is why a driver stops at all traffic lights whose color he categorizes as *red,* even though the lights vary slightly from one to another in their hues of redness. Categorization allows people to respond to their environment in a way that has great survival value. If they hear a high-pitched sound, they do not enumerate the long list of possible causes of such sounds: a human cry of fear, a scream for help, a policeman's whistle, and so on. Instead they become alert because they have categorized high-pitched sounds as indicators of possible danger.

2   Words, therefore, are more than simply labels for specific objects; they are also parts of sets of related principles. To a very young child, the word *chair* may at first refer only to his highchair. Soon afterward, he learns that the four-legged object on which his parents sit at mealtimes is also called a *chair.* So is the thing with only three legs, referred to by his parents as a *broken chair,* and so is the upholstered piece of furniture in the living room. These objects form a category, *chair,* which is

set apart from all other categories by a unique combination of features. A *chair* must possess a seat, legs, and back; it may also, but not necessarily, have arms; it must accommodate only one person. An object that possesses these features with but a single exception—it accomodates three people—does not belong to the category *chair* but rather to the category *couch,* and that category in turn is described by a set of unique features.

3   Furthermore, Americans think of *chairs* and *couches* as being related to each other because they both belong to a category known in English as *household furniture.* But such a relationship between the category *chair* and the category *couch* is entirely arbitrary on the part of English and some other speech communities. Nothing in the external world decrees that a language must place these two categories together. In some African speech communities, for example, the category *chair* would most likely be thought of in relation to the category *spear,* since both are emblems of a ruler's authority.

4   The analysis of words by their categories for the purpose of determining what they mean to speakers of a particular language—that is, what the native speaker, and not some visiting linguist, feels are the distinguishing features or components of that word—is known as "componential analysis" or "formal semantic analysis." The aim, in brief, is to determine the components or features that native speakers use to distinguish similar terms from one another so that more exact meanings can be achieved.

5   Anyone who visits an exotic culture quickly learns that the people are linguistically deaf to categories he considers obvious, yet they are extraordinarily perceptive in talking about things he has no easy way to describe. An English-speaking anthropologist studying the Koyas of India, for example, soon discovers that their language does not distinguish between dew, fog, and snow. When questioned about these natural phenomena, the Koyas can find a way to describe them, but normally their language attaches no significance to making such distinctions and provides no highly codable words for the purpose. On the other hand, a Koya has the linguistic resources to speak easily about seven different kinds of bamboo—resources that the visiting anthropologist utterly lacks in his own language. More important than the significance, or the lack of it, that a language places on objects and ideas is the way that language categorizes the information it does find significant. A *pig,* for example, can be categorized in several ways: a mammal with cloven hoofs and bristly hairs and adapted for digging with its snout; a mold in which metal is cast; a British sixpence coin. The Koyas categorize the pig in none of these ways; they simply place it in the category of animals that are edible. Their neighbors, Muslims, think of it in a different way by placing it in the category of defiled animals.

6   Everyone, whether he realizes it or not, classifies the items he finds in his environment. Most speakers of English recognize a category that

they call *livestock,* which is made up of other categories known as *cattle, horses, sheep,* and *swine* of different ages and sexes. An English speaker who is knowledgeable about farm life categorizes a barnyardful of these animals in a way that establishes relationships based on distinguishing features. For example, he feels that a *cow* and a *mare,* even though they belong to different species, are somehow in a relationship to each other. And of course they are, because they both belong to the category of Female Animal under the general category of Livestock. The speaker of English unconsciously groups certain animals into various sub-categories that exclude other animals:

Livestock

	CATTLE	HORSES	SHEEP	SWINE
Female	cow	mare	ewe	sow
Intact Male	bull	stallion	ram	boar
Castrated Male	steer	gelding	wether	barrow
Immature	heifer	colt/filly	lamb	shoat/gilt
Newborn	calf	foal	yeanling	piglet

A table such as this shows that speakers of English are intuitively aware of certain contrasts. They regard a bull and a steer as different—which they are, because one belongs to a category of Intact Males and the other to a category of Castrated Males. In addition to discriminations made on the basis of livestock's sex, speakers of English also contrast mature and immature animals. A *foal* is a newborn horse and a *stallion* is a mature male horse.

7   The conceptual labels by which English-speaking peoples talk about barnyard animals can now be understood. The animal is defined by the point at which two distinctive features intersect: sex (male, female, or castrated) and maturity (mature, immature, or newborn). A *stallion* belongs to a category of horse that is both intact male and mature; a *filly* belongs to a category of horse that is both female and immature. Nothing in external reality dictates that barnyard animals should be talked about in this way; it is strictly a convention of English and some other languages.

8   In contrast, imagine that an Amazonian Indian is brought to the United States so that linguists can intensively study his language. When the Indian returns to his native forests, his friends and relatives listen in disbelief as he tells about all the fantastic things he saw. He summarizes his impressions of America in terms of the familiar categories his language has accustomed him to. He relates that at first he was bewildered by the strange animals he saw on an American farm because each animal not only looked different but also seemed to represent a unique concept to the natives of the North American tribe. But after consider-

able observation of the curious folkways of these peculiar people, at last he understood American barnyard animals. He figured out that some animals are good for work and that some are good for food. Using these two components—rather than the Americans' features of sex and maturity—his classification of livestock is considerably different. He categorized *stallion, mare,* and *gelding* as belonging to both the Inedible and Work (Riding) categories. The *bull* also belonged to the Inedible category but it was used for a different kind of Work as a draught animal. He further placed a large number of animals—*cow, ewe, lamb, sow,* and so on—in the category of Edible but Useless for Work. Since his method of categorizing the barnyard failed to take into account the breeding process, which depends upon the categories of sex and maturity, he no doubt found it inexplicable that some animals—*ram, colt, boar,* and so on—were raised even though they could not be eaten or used for work.

9   To an American, the Amazonian Indian's classification of barnyard animals appears quite foolish, yet it is no more foolish than the American's system of classification by the features of sex and maturity. Speakers of each language have the right to recognize whatever features they care to. And they have a similar right to then organize these features according to the rules of their own speech communities. No one system is better than another in making sense out of the world in terms that can be talked about; the systems are simply different. A speaker of English who defines a *stallion* as a mature, male horse is no wiser than the Amazonian who claims it is inedible and used for riding. Both the speaker of English and the speaker of the Amazonian language have brought order out of the multitudes of things in the environment—and, in the process, both have shown something about how their languages and their minds work.

A.   Comprehension

Choose the answer that best completes each statement. Do not refer to the selection while doing this exercise.

1.   The main idea of the entire passage is that (a) the English system of classifying items in the environment is more logical than and therefore superior to systems used by other linguistic groups; (b) language is an arbitrary collection of words; (c) each culture has its own logical system for classifying items found in that particular environment; (d) the process of naming things shows the intricate working of the human mind.

2.   The author stresses that human beings in any culture find it necessary to (a) learn a foreign language; (b) study linguistics; (c) categorize information into broad categories; (d) understand the origin of their vocabulary.

3. According to Farb, the English speaker places *chair* and *couch* together in the category of *household furniture,* whereas, because both words represent a ruler's authority, some speakers of African languages would classify *chair* with the word (a) *king;* (b) *spear;* (c) *throne;* (d) *cattle.*

4. English speakers label barnyard animals according to the way these two distinguishing features intersect, namely (a) usefulness and size; (b) sex and maturity; (c) edible and inedible; (d) companion or pet and sex.

5. Farb emphasizes throughout the excerpt that every culture's labeling of things in the environment (a) is simply different from every other culture's, and one is not necessarily better or worse than another; (b) is irrational and usually makes little sense; (c) is difficult to learn and explain to outsiders; (d) is based solely on tradition and custom.

6. The hypothetical Amazonian Indian would be puzzled by the American system of naming barnyard animals because, according to *his* system, animals are classified according to whether they are good for (a) breeding or eating; (b) work or food; (c) domestication or nondomestication; (d) recreation or work.

B. **Structure**

Choose the best answer.

1. The mode of discourse in this passage is (a) narration; (b) description; (c) exposition; (d) persuasion.

2. Consider again the first two sentences in paragraph 1. What is the relationship between them? (a) steps in a process; (b) term and its definition; (c) general statement and a specific example; (d) contrasting ideas.

3. Indicate *three* methods of development evident in paragraphs 2 and 3. (a) example; (b) definition; (c) analogy; (d) comparison; (e) classification; (f) contrast; (g) cause-and-effect.

4. From the information provided in paragraph 5, it is likely that (a) the English language has even more words for bamboo than do the Koyas of India; (b) bamboo is not an especially important plant in India; (c) dew, fog, and snow are probably not very common natural phenomena in India where the Koyas live; (d) Eskimos probably have hundreds of words to describe snow and ice.

5. Look again at the chart reprinted in paragraph 6. Consult an unabridged dictionary if necessary and decide in which category in the far left column you would put these specific kinds of chickens. (Note: one of the following labels has no counterpart in this chart.)

chick	_____	poulard	_____
hen	_____	capon	_____
rooster	_____		

6. Look again at paragraphs 6–9, which suggest a contrast. What two things is Farb contrasting? _____ _____ and _____

7. Explain the point Farb is trying to make at the end of paragraph 8. Specifically, an Amazonian Indian would not understand why Americans raise animals like rams, colts, and boars, which can neither be eaten or used for work. Why, then, do Americans raise them?

_____

8. The author, as you remember, is an anthropologist and linguist. In your own words, explain how his tone—the way he expresses his ideas— reflects his occupation?_____

_____

C. Vocabulary

For each italicized word from the selection, choose the best definition according to the context in which it appears.

1. to *discriminate* some ten million colors [paragraph 1]: (a) perceive; (b) take in through the senses; (c) tell the difference between; (d) name, codify.

2. a relationship is entirely *arbitrary* [3]: (a) relatively unimportant; (b) logical, precise; (c) not well understood; (d) not based on rational principles or rules.

3. nothing in the external world *decrees* [3]: (a) orders authoritatively; (b) determines precisely; (c) makes effective use of; (d) implies, suggests.

4. both are *emblems* of authority [3]: (a) examples; (b) symbols; (c) tangible objects; (d) mottoes.

5. anyone who visits an *exotic* culture [5]: (a) foreign, unfamiliar; (b) lush, tropical; (c) economically undeveloped; (d) popular with tourists.

6. the category of *defiled* animals [5]: (a) inedible; (b) unclean; (c) lined up in rows; (d) vicious.

7. speakers of English are *intuitively aware* [6]: (a) able to describe a thing's characteristics; (b) skilled at contrasting one thing with another; (c) having knowledge of something without having to use reason; (d) adept at making intelligent decisions.

8. two distinctive features *intersect* [7]: (a) split up, divide; (b) overlap, come together at a point; (c) become identical; (d) contradict, contrast.

9. as a *draught animal* [8] (Note: "draught" is the British spelling of "draft"): (a) an animal that is difficult to domesticate; (b) an animal that serves primarily as a pet; (c) an animal suited for pulling heavy loads; (d) a cloven-hoofed animal.

10. he no doubt found it *inexplicable* [8]: (a) impossible to understand; (b) unclassifiable; (c) unrecognizable; (d) difficult to explain.

D. Questions for Analysis and Discussion

1. Look around your room and choose a common household object, for example, a lamp, a chest of drawers, a nightstand, or a book. Subject it to the same method to define it, according to its essential characteristics, as Farb does in paragraphs 2 and 3. Then find its distinguishing characteristics. For instance, how does a nightstand differ from a coffee table? How does a book differ from a magazine or a newspaper, two items belonging in the same category?

2. If possible, discuss Farb's ideas with one of your classmates who is from a different culture and speaks another language in addition to English. For example, compare the names of colors and shades; or categorize groups of objects, such as foods eaten at various times of the day or ways of naming relatives. (The English system of naming relatives is quite limited in comparison to those used in other cultures, particularly for relatives like sisters- or brothers-in-law and cousins.)

4

Patterns of Paragraph Organization

Unity and Coherence in Paragraphs

As you learned at the beginning of Chapter 1, a paragraph is defined as a series of sentences that develops a single idea. Whether a writer uses a single method of development or a combination, he or she is careful to help you follow the main idea by ensuring that the paragraph has *unity,* or singleness of purpose. Every sentence in the paragraph—whether short or long—should relate to the topic sentence. There are no irrelevant or extraneous sentences to lead you astray. (In the same way, as you will see later in Part IV, every paragraph in an essay relates to and develops the main idea or thesis statement.)

This attention on the part of a good writer means that if you make a serious effort to concentrate and to follow his or her path, you should not have too much difficulty following the direction of the ideas. Let us look at a rather long paragraph to see how one writer maintains unity.

This excerpt by Page Smith concerns the Bhagwan Shree Rajneesh, who, during the 1970s, moved his commune (called a *puram*) to rural eastern Oregon, where he attracted a large number of followers and lived a lavish life. Stories began to circulate about the Bhagwan's physical cruelty to his devotees as well as allegations of free and open sex, as Smith describes here. (The Bhagwan was subsequently indicted for tax evasion and deported to India, his native country.) As you read this passage, first find the main idea, paying particular attention to the adjective that serves as the controlling idea. This adjective is later repeated. Notice, too, that every example in support of the main idea *directly* bears out this controlling idea.

Of all modern cults, that of the Bhagwan Shree Rajneesh in Oregon may well be the most bizarre. After presiding over a puram or Buddhist religious commune in Poona, India, the Bhagwan transferred his operation to a ranch in Oregon. There, as a brochure informed the curious, the Bhagwan (God) and his disciples would "live together in a non-possessive way, neither possessing things nor possessing persons; people living together, creating together, celebrating together and still allowing each one his own space; people creating a certain climate of meditativeness, of love, of living in that climate." Hard to argue with any of that. It was, indeed, the classic utopian dream; it was the aim of the earliest Christian communities and the hope of succeeding generations. Uncounted numbers of men and women have gathered together to live by similar principles throughout history. What was truly bizarre about the Bhagwan's commune was the strain that it might be thought to have imposed on the credulity of the highly—one is tempted to say, extravagantly—educated men and women who flocked to it. What the skeptic saw was a dissipated, self-indulgent Indian guru who encouraged every wild excess from physical violence of the most brutal and degrading kind to ingeniously aberrant sex; who was arbitrary and tyrannical almost beyond belief; who collected jeweled watches and Rolls-Royces on a hitherto unimagined scale. All this was acquiesced in, supported, and praised by his infatuated followers, the great majority of them people with college degrees and many with advanced degrees. Ph.D.'s were a dime a dozen in the puram, and the largest professional group represented were psychologists. Many of the Rajneeshees had given all their worldly goods to the Bhagwan. When the journalist Frances Fitzgerald visited the puram, she was astonished at the professional backgrounds of the Rajneeshees. The commune's city planner, Swami Deva Wadud, had been a professional city planner in San Mateo, California, and boasted an M.A. from the Harvard Graduate School of Design. His assistant was an Australian with a Ph.D. in linguistic philosophy. Another disciple had a degree from Harvard in "visual and environmental studies." The "president" of the commune had been a systems analyst for IBM and Uni-

vac and studied computer sciences at the University of London. The list seemed endless. The chief publicist had a Ph.D. from Yale.

Page Smith, *Killing the Spirit: Higher Education in America*

Besides unity, well-constructed paragraphs also have *coherence,* (literally, the quality of "sticking together"). You may remember from Chapter 1 that good writing is characterized by a network of interlocking thoughts, so that, ideally, each sentence leads smoothly and logically to the next. This is essentially what coherence means. At first glance, studying the ways writers achieve coherence may seem more appropriate for a composition course than for a reading course. However, seeing these methods may help you more accurately understand what you read; sometimes your correct understanding of a passage may depend on a seemingly unimportant little word like *but* or *yet.*

In this analysis of the effects of aging on taste and smell, Olga Knopf both repeats key words and uses pronouns referring to important nouns to keep the reader on track. These repetitions and pronouns have been italicized so that you can see how they function more clearly.

Taste and smell are also affected by *aging,* but *their* changes are less understood and appreciated. People who are in contact with *the elderly* will tell you *they* have two major *complaints—food* and their children. The *complaint about food* is easily explained when one considers how *the taste buds work.* Distributed over the tongue, *they* last no longer than a few days each and then are replaced. In keeping with the general slowing-down process, *they* are renewed more slowly than *they* are used up. This means that the total number of effective *taste buds* declines, and, therefore, *food tastes less savory.* Extensive dentures that cover a large portion of the oral cavity *diminish the perception of taste* even further. In addition, there is the close interrelationship between *smell and taste.* Anyone who has ever had a cold can testify to the fact that while the cold lasts, not only is *the sense of smell reduced,* but *food loses its taste* as well. There is *a similar deterioration in the sense of smell* as a result of *the process of aging.*

Olga Knopf, *Successful Aging*

Transitions

Another way that writers establish coherence between ideas is to use signposts or markers, called *transitions,* to indicate either a logical relationship or a shift in direction. Transitions can be either single words or phrases, and they may appear at the beginning of sentences, but this is not a hard and fast rule. In the Knopf paragraph above, *therefore* signals a cause-and-effect relationship: The number of taste buds declines *(cause);* therefore, food doesn't taste as good *(effect).* Similarly, *in addi-*

tion introduces another reason to explain the decline in old people's experience of and ability to taste.

To show you how crucial transitions may be to understanding some writers' prose, here is a paragraph by George Orwell printed without the transitions:

> After getting into the water the toad concentrates on building up his strength by eating small insects. He has swollen to his normal size again. He goes through a phase of intense sexiness. All he knows, at least if he is a male toad, is that he wants to get his arms round something. If you offer him a stick, or even your finger, he will cling to it with surprising strength and take a long time to discover that it is not a female toad. One comes upon shapeless masses of ten or twenty toads rolling over and over in the water, one clinging to another without distinction of sex. They sort themselves out into couples, with the male duly sitting on the female's back. You can distinguish males from females. The male is smaller, darker, and sits on top, with his arms tightly clasped round the female's neck. The spawn is laid in long strings which wind themselves in and out of the reeds and soon become invisible. The water is alive with masses of tiny tadpoles which rapidly grow larger, sprout hind legs, then forelegs, then shed their tails. The new generation of toads, smaller than one's thumbnail but perfect in every particular, crawl out of the water to begin the game anew.

Obviously something is wrong here. Reading this paragraph is like reading a novel with every tenth page missing, or like trying to put a bicycle together when the manufacturer has left out all the screws you need. It just does not hold together, and the sentences sound monotonous and choppy. Here is the actual version, this time printed with the transitions restored and italicized, making it much less tedious to read.

> *For a few days* after getting into the water the toad concentrates on building up his strength by eating small insects. *Presently* he has swollen to his normal size again, *and then* he goes through a phase of intense sexiness. All he knows, at least if he is a male toad, is that he wants to get his arms round something, *and* if you offer him a stick, or even your finger, he will cling to it with surprising strength and take a long time to discover that it is not a female toad. *Frequently* one comes upon shapeless masses of ten or twenty toads rolling over and over in the water, one clinging to another without distinction of sex. *By degrees, however,* they sort themselves out into couples, with the male duly sitting on the female's back. You can *now* distinguish males from females, *because* the male is smaller, darker and sits on top, with his arms tightly clasped round the female's neck. *After a day or two* the spawn is laid in long strings which wind themselves in and out of

the reeds and soon become invisible. A *few more weeks, and* the water is alive with masses of tiny tadpoles which rapidly grow larger, sprout hind legs, then forelegs, then shed their tails; *and finally, about the middle of the summer,* the new generation of toads, smaller than one's thumbnail but perfect in every particular, crawl out of the water to begin the game anew.

George Orwell, "Some Thoughts on the Common Toad," *The Orwell Reader*

Here is a list of transitions classified by function, meaning the relationship they suggest between the words they precede and the words they follow:

1. **Transitions signaling an additional statement** (usually of equal importance): *and, in addition (to), additionally, as well as, besides, furthermore, moreover*

   Example: The house was badly neglected. The windows were broken *and* the paint was blistered. *Moreover,* what had once been a well-tended lawn was only an overgrown weed patch.

2. **Transitions signaling a contrast:** *but, yet, however, nevertheless, nonetheless, while, whereas, on the other hand, in contrast (to), contrary to*

   Example: Labrador retrievers are known for their exuberant friendliness. *In contrast,* many breeds of terriers are high-strung and highly excitable.

3. **Transitions signaling an example or illustration:** *for example, as an example, to illustrate, as an illustration, for instance, namely, specifically, a case in point*

   Example: The level of violence directed at abortion clinics and the physicians who perform abortions has seriously escalated in recent months. *For example,* in March 1993, Dr. David Gunn was shot in the back by a prolife activist, the first instance of a murder connected with abortion protests.

4. **Transitions signaling steps in a process or chronological order:** *first, second, third, next, the next step, further, then, before, after that, finally, last, in July, last week, in a few days, in 1994,* and the like

   Example: To make an omelette, *first* beat three eggs until fluffy. *Then* cook them slowly in a lightly buttered pan. *Finally,* add cheese, mushrooms, or onions, fold over, and serve.

5. **Transitions signaling a conclusion:** *therefore, thus, then, to conclude, in conclusion, in summary, to summarize, consequently, hence*

    Example: Charlotte spent two hours a day working in the reading laboratory, and she looked up every unfamiliar word she encountered. *As a result,* there was a dramatic improvement in her reading comprehension by the end of the semester.

6. **Transitions signaling emphasis:** *indeed, in fact, certainly, without a doubt, undoubtedly, admittedly, unquestionably, truly*

    Example: The little boy sat on the curb, his chin in his hands, as he looked at his bent and twisted bicycle. *Indeed,* he looked inconsolable.

7. **Transitions signaling a concession or an admission of truth:** *although, even though, in spite of, despite*

    Example: Although the yearly cost of a college education, especially at private institutions, rises more than the annual inflation rate, the number of applicants has increased dramatically in the last ten years, the result of many social and demographic factors.

8. **Transitions signaling spatial order:** *above, below, to the right, to the left, nearby, from afar, beyond, further on, up the road, on top, below, underneath,* and so on

    Example: "Where the mountains meet the sea" is the official motto of Camden, Maine, a New England village known for its splendid harbor. No wonder. *Behind the harbor, not far from* where the schooners, sailboats, and cabin cruisers are anchored, Ragged Mountain rises precipitously. *Near the peak of the mountain* one can find Maiden Cliffs, where, according to legend, an Indian maiden leaped to her death because of an unhappy love affair.

Not all writers use transitions. But when transitional words and phrases are present, their presence will help both your comprehension and your reasoning ability. To give you practice in locating these devices, read the following discussion of racial divisions in the United States. You will immediately see that Andrew Hacker's purpose is to contrast blacks' and whites' situations, and that he uses transitions that reinforce this contrast. As you read it, underline these transitions and determine how each functions.

[1]Race has been an American obsession since the first Europeans sighted "savages" on these shores. In time, those original inhabitants would be subdued or slaughtered, and finally sequestered out of view. But race in America took on a deeper and more disturbing meaning with the importation of Africans as slaves. Bondage would later be condemned as an awful injustice and the nation's shame, even as we have come to acknowledge the stamina and skill it took to survive in a system where humans could be bought and sold and punished like animals. Nor are these antecedents buried away in the past. That Americans of African origin once wore the chains of chattels remains alive in the memory of both races and continues to separate them.

[2]Black Americans are Americans, yet they still subsist as aliens in the only land they know. Other groups may remain outside the mainstream—some religious sects, for example—but they do so voluntarily. In contrast, blacks must endure a segregation that is far from freely chosen. So America may be seen as two separate nations. Of course, there are places where the races mingle. Yet in most significant respects, the separation is pervasive and penetrating. As a social and human division, it surpasses all others—even gender—in intensity and subordination.

> Andrew Hacker, *Two Nations: Black and White, Separate, Hostile, Unequal*

Patterns of Organization

Now that you understand how unity and coherence work in a paragraph, we can turn our attention to patterns of organization within paragraphs. This term refers to the various ways ideas in a paragraph may be arranged. Although, as you have seen, the paragraph is remarkably flexible, we can nevertheless isolate a few typical patterns. In the remainder of this chapter we shall consider six basic patterns or orders: (1) chronological, (2) spatial, (3) deductive, (4) a variation of deductive, (5) inductive, and (6) emphatic. The first and second patterns are found most often in narrative and descriptive writing; the others tend to occur more in expository or persuasive writing.

Chronological Order

Chronological, or time, order, the easiest pattern to recognize, refers to the order in which events happen. It is used to tell a story, to relate an incident, to recount a historical event, or to describe the steps in a process. In this example, Eugene Kinkead uses time order to explain how snail darters reproduce.

During the spawning season, a female darter lays around six hundred eggs in the swift water of the gravel shoals in the shallowest parts of a river. The eggs, rolling along the bottom, have a sticky exterior, and will fasten onto

a stone. There, for about two weeks, the embryos inside develop. Upon hatching, they drift downstream to a pool of deep water—if they are lucky, that is; infant mortality, as with most fish, is very high. Probably less than one or two per cent of the eggs laid produce adults. All kinds of darters, including snail darters, probably eat snail-darter eggs and larvae. The deep-water pools act as snail-darter nurseries. For some weeks, the larvae live on the unconsumed egg yolk they carry with them. They are strange, still embryonic-looking things, less than a quarter of an inch long. After the egg yolk is gone, they stay in the pool, feeding on microcrustaceans through the summer. By fall, the diet shifts to snails, and the fish make their way back upstream to the shallows.

Eugene Kinkead, "Tennessee Small Fry," *The New Yorker*

Kinkead signals chronological order with these transitional phrases: "during the spawning season," "for about two weeks," "upon hatching," "for some weeks," and "by fall."

Spatial Order

The term *spatial* comes from the word *space*. Spatial order refers to the arrangement of things in an environment. Most often in descriptive writing, spatial order helps a writer organize the details he or she is describing so that we see them in a coherent fashion. It makes it easy for the reader to picture what might otherwise be a jumble of unrelated impressions.

Some typical ways writers arrange details spatially are from left to right or right to left, near to far or far to near, top to bottom or the reverse. Again, transitions help the reader visualize the scene. The next passage by Sallie Tisdale describes a cabin her family owned in southern Oregon in the Klamath National Forest. To help the reader visualize the cabin's appearance, she makes extensive use of prepositional phrases to move our eye from one part of the cabin to another. As you read, underline these phrases so that you become aware of their function.

The cabin was a small, boxy two-story building with a deck, which we called the porch, perched on stilts outside the front door—a room-size platform with a rail on three sides and a dusty porch swing in constant shade. On the first floor was a long, narrow kitchen, which was lined—floor, walls, and ceiling—with a wood so old that it was black from years of lamp-oil and wood smoke. Across from it was a square open stairway, which led to a single room twice as large as the kitchen and extending up the stretch of a hill. To the right at the top of the stairs was the bathroom; the floor of the shower was always gritty with sand, and the shower head yielded no more than a drizzle of cold water. Over the kitchen, facing the river, was a sleeping porch—a narrow screened room with several iron beds, each one piled with musty, lumpy mattresses two or three deep. I

slept on them in perfect peace. Oilcloth curtains hung in the kitchen windows but were never closed, even in the blackest night. By the front door was a wooden counter with a chipped white sink, and on the counter there always stood a silvery pail with a ladle. When we arrived, I would grab the pail and run out the back door and down three steps to a spring that trickled from beneath the house. The ground there was boggy, and the plants were wet with dew condensing in the shadows, and I held in my fist the knowledge that we were here for a long time, an infinite time. I would hold the pail under the trickle and wait happily while it filled, inhaling the exuberant scent of the woods, my bare feet cold in the spreading edge of the clear water.

Sallie Tisdale, "The Pacific Northwest," *The New Yorker*

In the last example, Kenneth Boulding uses spatial order in a highly unusual way: to locate himself in first his narrow environment and then, more philosophically, in the whole galaxy. By repeating the key preposition *beyond,* we follow his imaginative journey easily.

As I sit at my desk, I know where I am. I see before me a window; beyond that some trees; beyond that the red roofs of the campus of Stanford University; beyond them the trees and the roof tops which mark the town of Palo Alto; beyond them the bare golden hills of the Hamilton Range. I know, however, more than I see. Behind me, although I am not looking in that direction, I know there is a window, and beyond that the little campus of the Center for the Advanced Study in the Behavioral Sciences; beyond that the Coast Range; beyond that the Pacific Ocean. Looking ahead of me again, I know that beyond the mountains that close my present horizon, there is a broad valley; beyond that a still higher range of mountains; beyond that other mountains, range upon range, until we come to the Rockies; beyond that the Great Plains and the Mississippi; beyond that the Alleghenies; beyond that the eastern seaboard; beyond that the Atlantic Ocean; beyond that is Europe; beyond that is Asia. I know, furthermore, that if I go far enough I will come back to where I am now. In other words, I have a picture of the earth as round. I visualize it as a globe. I am a little hazy on some of the details. I am not quite sure, for instance, whether Tanganyika is north or south of Nyasaland. I probably could not draw a very good map of Indonesia, but I have a fair idea where everything is located on the face of this globe. Looking further, I visualize the globe as a small speck circling around a bright star which is the sun, in the company of many other similar specks, the planets. Looking still further, I see our star the sun as a member of millions upon millions of others in the Galaxy. Looking still further, I visualize the Galaxy as one of millions upon millions of others in the universe.

Kenneth Boulding, *The Image*

Deductive Order   *Deductive* order is the most common pattern in the English paragraph. You saw deductive order in the section on placement of main ideas in Chapter 1. Deductive order is sometimes called *general-to-specific* order, because deductively organized paragraphs begin with a general statement (the main idea), which is then supported by a series of specific statements. The pattern of organization, in this case, is determined by the topic sentence's location. It is easy to visualize deductive order if you imagine an inverted triangle with the base at the top:

Typically, expository paragraphs use deductive order, as Lewis Thomas does in the following example. Notice that the main idea in sentence 1 is supported with a single effective illustration.

> Animals seem to have an instinct for performing death alone, hidden. Even the largest, most conspicuous ones find ways to conceal themselves in time. If an elephant missteps and dies in an open place, the herd will not leave him there; the others will pick him up and carry the body from place to place, finally putting it down in some inexplicably suitable location. When elephants encounter the skeleton of an elephant out in the open, they methodically take up each of the bones and distribute them, in a ponderous ceremony, over neighboring acres.
>
> Lewis Thomas, *Lives of a Cell*

In the next example, the authors, both anthropologists, combine two modes of discourse: narration and exposition. The paragraph, like the preceding one, begins with a main idea followed by support in the form of a narrative. This one, however, ends with a conclusion drawn from the support.

> The value of past experience is neatly demonstrated in an anecdote reported by Colin Turnbull, an American anthropologist who has studied the pygmies of the Congo region. The BaMbuti (the general name given to all pygmies in the Forest of Ituri) spend their entire lives so deeply surrounded

by vegetation that the greatest distance they are likely to have experienced is no more than the few tens of yards between them and the other side of a river or a clearing. For the rest of the time their visual world is pressed in closely around them. It is against this background they interpret the size and distance of objects they see. One day Turnbull took Kenge, one of the BaMbuti, with him on a long drive out of the forest and up a mountain overlooking Lake Albert. There Kenge, who found it almost impossible to believe in a world without trees, made a classic perceptual blunder. Pointing to a herd of buffalo grazing several miles away, he asked, "What insects are those?" It took Turnbull a while to realize what Kenge was talking about. Because at that distance buffalo looked so small Kenge supposed they *were* small, in fact no bigger than insects. To a far greater extent than we realize, like Kenge, we "see" what through experience we have come to expect to see.

Richard E. Leakey and Roger Lewin, *Origins*

A Variation of Deductive Order

In this pattern, the writer uses deductive order—beginning with a main idea followed by supporting sentences—but he or she then *restates* the main idea at the end of the pattern, thereby underscoring its importance. You can visualize this pattern if you imagine not a triangle, but a tri-level square.

Main Idea	General ▼
Supporting Statements	Specific
Restated Main Idea	▲ General

Using this variant deductive pattern, James Herriot, author of several books recounting his experience as a veterinarian in the north of England, humorously explains why one local resident viewed vets as useless. (The word *knacker,* incidentally, is British for a person who buys worn-out or dead livestock and sells the animals' meat or hide.)

[1]Vets are useless creatures, parasites on the agricultural community, expensive layabouts who really know nothing about animals or their diseases. You might as well get Jeff Mallock the knacker man as send for a vet.

[2]At least that was the opinion, frequently expressed, of the Sidlow family. In fact, when you came right down to it, just about the only person for miles around who knew how to treat sick beasts was Mr Sidlow himself. If any of their cows or horses fell ill it was Mr Sidlow who stepped forward

with his armoury of sovereign remedies. He enjoyed a God-like prestige with his wife and large family and it was an article of their faith that father was infallible in these matters; the only other being who had ever approached his skill was long-dead Grandpa Sidlow from whom father had learned so many of his cures.

[3]Mind you, Mr Sidlow was a just and humane man. After maybe five or six days of dedicated nursing during which he would perhaps push half-a-pound of lard and raisins down the cow's throat three times a day, rub its udder vigorously with turpentine or maybe cut a bit off the end of the tail to let the bad out, he always in the end called the vet. Not that it would do any good, but he liked to give the animal every chance. When the vet arrived he invariably found a sunken-eyed, dying creature and the despairing treatment he gave was like a figurative administration of the last rites. The animal always died so the Sidlows were repeatedly confirmed in their opinion—vets were useless.

James Herriot, *All Creatures Great and Small*

Inductive Order

The opposite of deductive order is the *inductive* pattern, sometimes called *specific-to-general* order. This pattern actually derives from a kind of thinking called induction, which you'll learn more about in Part III, Critical Reading. For now, it's enough to know that inductive order involves a series of specific statements leading to a generalization (the main idea) that the reader can validly infer from those statements.

A diagram of an inductively arranged paragraph looks like this:

In the next paragraph, the author, a linguist, provides background information in sentences 1 and 2. (These sentences are not the main idea.) Following that, she uses two expository modes, example and contrast, which in turn lead up to the main idea expressed in the last sentence.

Members of the same culture share a common body idiom—that is, they tend to read a given nonverbal signal in the same way. If two people read a signal in a different way, it is partial evidence that they belong to different

cultures. In Colombia, an American Peace Corps worker relaxes with his feet up on the furniture; his shocked Colombian hostess perceives the gesture as disgusting. Back in the United States, a university president poses for a photograph with his feet up on the desk; newspaper readers react with affection for "good old President Jones." While Americans use the feet-on-furniture gesture to signal "I'm relaxed and at home here," or "See how casual and folksy I am," neither message is received by a Colombian, who reads the signal as "boor!" An understanding of the role gestures play within a culture is critical to sensitive communication.

Genelle G. Morain, "Kinesis and Cross-Cultural Understanding,"
Language in Education: Theory and Practice

Emphatic Order

The same principle that leads a good trial lawyer to save the best argument for last governs the way writers arrange their supporting statements, particularly within deductive paragraphs, so that they build in intensity from the least important to the most important. Hence the term *emphatic* order. Whether this actually deserves to be a separate category is open to question, because a paragraph arranged deductively may also use emphatic order for the arrangement of details.

Here, Diane Ackerman analyzes the function of skin in organisms. After presenting a series of skin's various characteristics, she ends with a final emphatic sentence, indicated by the transitional phrase "but, most of all."

Our skin is what stands between us and the world. If you think about it, no other part of us makes contact with something not us but the skin. It imprisons us, but it also gives us individual shape, protects us from invaders, cools us down or heats us up as need be, produces vitamin D, holds in our body fluids. Most amazing, perhaps, is that it can mend itself when necessary, and it is constantly renewing itself. Weighing from six to ten pounds, it's the largest organ of the body, and the key organ of sexual attraction. Skin can take a startling variety of shapes: claws, spines, hooves, feathers, scales, hair. It's waterproof, washable, and elastic. Although it may cascade or roam as we grow older, it lasts surprisingly well. For most cultures, it's the ideal canvas to decorate with paints, tattoos, and jewelry. But, most of all, it harbors the sense of touch.

Diane Ackerman, *A Natural History of the Senses*

Punctuation and Meaning

An extensive discussion of grammar and punctuation is outside the scope of this text. However, as a closing note to this chapter and as a

prefatory section to Part II, it may be worthwhile to review some marks of punctuation, especially the more sophisticated ones like parentheses, dashes, semicolons, and colons. Punctuation marks go beyond the usual definitions of enclosing and separating. Careful writers choose punctuation marks precisely—to enclose and to separate, but also to emphasize, or to slow us down, or to speed us up, or to clarify. Like carefully chosen transitions, punctuation marks can help you follow the writer's ideas. The writer's words are meant to be heard in your head. Punctuation marks—little marks that enclose and separate words—allow us to recreate them as the author intended us to.

Punctuation often conveys meaning. Even *apostrophes,* which we don't hear when we speak, can affect meaning. Consider, for instance, these two nearly identical sentences:

- The butler stood at the door and called the guests names as they entered the mansion.
- The butler stood at the door and called the guests' names as they entered the mansion.

In which sentence is the butler insulting the guests?

Commas

Let us begin with the *comma.* There are many and various rules for the use of commas—you can consult any good grammar handbook for a list. But one thing about this punctuation mark remains constant wherever it appears and however it's used: it always indicates that we should pause, however briefly. Commas determine and affect the rhythm of the prose. To demonstrate this, read aloud this short passage by Greta Ehrlich. Notice as you read how these little markers enhance the rhythm and flow of her description. Ehrlich here explains and describes winter in Wyoming.

[1]The name Wyoming comes from an Indian word meaning "at the great plains," but the plains are really valleys, great arid valleys, 1600 square miles, with the horizon bending up on all sides into mountain ranges. This gives the vastness a sheltering look.

[2]Winter lasts six months here. Prevailing winds spill snowdrifts to the east, and new storms from the northwest replenish them. This white bulk is sometimes dizzying, even nauseating, to look at. At twenty, thirty, and forty degrees below zero, not only does your car not work but neither do your mind and body. The landscape hardens into a dungeon of space. During the winter, while I was riding to find a new calf, my legs froze to the saddle, and in the silence that such cold creates I felt like the first person on earth, or the last.

Greta Ehrlich, *The Solace of Open Spaces*

Notice that although the comma following "earth" in the last sentence is grammatically unnecessary, its presence definitely contributes to the effect. What is its purpose?

Semicolons

The semicolon is useful for joining together two independent clauses that have a clear and logical connection with each other. Stronger than a comma but not quite as strong as a period, the semicolon shows that the writer wants you to consider the clauses as a unit, usually because there is some logical connection between them, for example, cause-and-effect or contrast or general-to-specific. Often a transition indicating the logical relationship is placed between the two clauses, as in the first of the following examples.

- But however immature they are, these lovers are not dull characters; on the contrary, they are hauntingly and embarrassingly real. (Arthur Mizener, *The Far Side of Paradise*)
- Steeped in new moods and ideas, I bought a ream of paper and tried to write; but nothing would come, or what did come was flat beyond telling. (Richard Wright, *Black Boy*)
- No other fairy tale renders so well as the "Cinderella" stories the inner experiences of the young child in the throes of sibling rivalry, when he feels hopelessly outclassed by his brothers and sisters. Cinderella is pushed down and degraded by her stepsisters; her interests are sacrificed to theirs by her (step)mother; she is expected to do the dirtiest work and although she performs it well, she receives no credit for it; only more is demanded of her. (Bruno Bettelheim, *The Uses of Enchantment*)
- The man who has not the habit of reading is imprisoned in his immediate world, in respect to time and space. His life falls into a set routine; he is limited to contact and conversation with a few friends and acquaintances, and he sees only what happens in his immediate neighborhood. From this prison there is no escape. (Lin Yu-T'ang, "The Art of Reading," *The Importance of Understanding*)

Colons

Besides introducing lists, the *colon* has a special function within independent clauses. A writer may use a colon to separate a clause when it introduces something to be explained, as in the following examples.

- Indeed, the life of a sharecropper's wife, which often demanded twelve-hour days in the fields, normally allowed little time for food preparation at all. Typically, she would rise at 4 a.m. in a one- or two-room cabin to prepare breakfast: thinly sliced fat salt pork fried over an open fire and corn bread spread with fat and molasses. (Harvey Levenstein, *Revolution at the Table: The Transformation of the American Diet*)

- Because of Columbus's exaggerated report and promises, his second expedition was given seventeen ships and more than twelve hundred men. The aim was clear: slaves and gold. (Howard Zinn, *A People's History of the United States*)
- The vanity of older people is an easier weakness to explain, and to condone. With less to look forward to, they yearn for recognition of what they have been: the reigning beauty, the athlete, the soldier, the scholar. (Malcolm Cowley, *The View From 80*) Note: In this example, consider the effect of the comma after the word "explain," which is not required grammatically. What is its effect?

Parentheses

Parentheses enclose additional or "extra" information within a sentence. The term *parenthetical* refers to explanatory or qualifying information usually contained in parentheses. (Note: A parenthetical expression is sometimes enclosed within commas to suggest that the material is not very important or within dashes to suggest that the material is important and is meant to be emphasized.) The use of parentheses suggests that the material enclosed could be dropped without any significant loss of meaning.

- Franz Kafka (1883–1924), the famous Austrian writer, is best known for his novels *The Trial* and *The Castle*.
- Packs of wild dogs and wolves, in which both males and females join in the hunt, have only a weak hierarchy, functioning only within each of the sexes (though the pack is usually led by an *alpha* male). (Richard E. Leakey and Roger Lewin, *Origins*)
- For generations, this has been the pattern. Immigrant parents have sent their children to school (simply, they thought) to acquire the "skills" to survive in the city. The child returned home with a voice his parents barely recognized or understood, couldn't trust, and didn't like. (Richard Rodriguez, *Hunger of Memory*)
- A further reason for football's intensity is that the game is played like a war. The idea is to win by going through, around, or over the opposing team and the battle lines, quite literally, are drawn on every play. Violence is somewhere at the heart of the game, and the combat quality is reflected in football's army language ("blitz," "trap," "zone," "bomb," "trenches," etc.). (Murray Ross, "Football Red and Baseball Green")

Dashes

The *dash* is a dramatic mark of punctuation. One of its functions is to introduce an afterthought or a punchline at the end of a joke, as you can see in this example:

- People who live in Maine say that they have two seasons—winter and July.

  As noted earlier, the dash can also be used to enclose parenthetical elements, especially for emphasis. It can also signal an abrupt interruption. Study these remaining examples. Then mentally substitute parentheses for the dashes to see the difference.

- After a few moments he [the wolf] flops on his side, rises, stretches, and moves a few feet to inspect—minutely, delicately—a crevice in the rock outcropping and finds or doesn't find what draws him there. (Barry Holstun Lopez, *Of Wolves and Men)* Note: The brackets [ ] used in this example indicate that the *editor* has inserted words to clarify or to comment on something in *quoted* material. Parentheses are reserved for the *writer's* parenthetical remarks.
- Without question, it would have pleased me to have heard my teachers address me in Spanish when I entered the classroom. . . . But I would have delayed—postponed for how long?—having to learn the language of public society. I would have evaded—and for how long?—learning the great lesson of school: that I had a public identity. (Richard Rodriguez, *Hunger of Memory)*
- The season of hibernating begins quite early for some of the creatures of outdoors. It is not alone the cold which causes it; there are a multiplicity of other factors—diminishing food supply; increased darkness as the fall days shorten; silence—frequently decisive. (Alan Devoe, *Lives Around Us)*

Exercises

Selection 1

¹A Maya city still untouched—and there are plenty of them—is a strange and somewhat frightening sight. ²From a high-flying airplane the jungle looks like an endless expanse of massed broccoli, the rounded treetops standing close together and giving no glimpse of the ground. ³If the airplane circles lower, a few crumbling walls of light-gray limestone appear above the green, like rocky islets poking out of a sea. ⁴Sometimes the eye catches a glimpse of a steep-sided pyramid rising from below. ⁵Approached on foot the scene is strikingly different. ⁶The jungle floor is deeply shaded, with only occasional flecks of sunlight filtering through from the sky. ⁷There is little undergrowth: the ground is soft with rotting humus, and great trees stand solemnly with thick vines dripping down from their tops. ⁸Their buttressed trunks march up the sides of the pyramids, and exposed roots writhe like boa constrictors, pry-

ing the stones apart. ⁹Trees often sprout from the very apex of a pyramid and they cover lesser structures completely.

Jonathan Norton Leonard, *Ancient America*

A. Vocabulary

For each italicized word from the selection, choose the best definition according to the context in which it appears.

1. *glimpse* [sentences 2 and 4]: (a) representation; (b) incomplete look; (c) sign, omen; (d) understanding.
2. *islets* [3]: (a) little pyramids; (b) little walls; (c) little passageways; (d) little islands.
3. *buttressed* [8]: (a) growing tightly together; (b) spread out over a wide area; (c) supported, propped; (d) gouged, cracked.
4. *writhe* [8]: (a) twist; (b) become tightly curled or coiled; (c) threaten to overtake; (d) spread poisonous substances.
5. *apex* [9]: (a) steep sides; (b) face; (c) bottom; (d) top.

B. Content and Structure

1. This paragraph is a combination of two modes of discourse: (a) narration; (b) description; (c) exposition; (d) persuasion.
2. The main idea of the first paragraph is expressed in sentence _____ ; the main idea of the second paragraph is in sentence _____.
3. In addition to deductive order within each paragraph in the passage, another pattern of organization evident in the passage is (a) inductive; (b) variation of deductive; (c) spatial; (d) chronological.
4. Write any transitions that helped you arrive at your answer for question 3 above. _____

_____

5. In sentence 2 the author uses an imaginative comparison, in this case a simile. Tell what is being compared to what: _____
_____ is compared to _____
In using this comparison, what does the writer want us to see?

_____

6. In sentence 3 he uses another figure of speech or simile. Again, tell what is being compared to what: _____
_____ is compared to _____
7. Sentences 8 and 9 suggest that jungle vegetation (a) cannot thrive without sunlight; (b) is so lush it can easily take over manmade structures; (c) is being cleared to make way for farms; (d) is home to a diverse animal and plant population.

8. A good title for this paragraph would be (a) "Lost Cities"; (b) "Untouched Maya Cities"; (c) "The Pyramids in the Jungle"; (d) "A Frightening Sight."

Selection 2

¹As I approached the Gypsy camp for the first time, yellow, wild-looking, stiff-haired dogs howled and barked. ²Fifteen covered wagons were spread out in a wide half circle, partly hiding the Gypsies from the road. ³Around the camp-fires sat women draped in deep-colored dresses, their big, expressive eyes and strong, white teeth standing out against their beautiful dark matte skin. ⁴The many gold pieces they wore as earrings, necklaces and bracelets sharpened their color even more. ⁵Their shiny blue-black hair was long and braided, the skirts of their dresses were ankle-length, very full and worn in many layers, and their bodices loose and low-cut. ⁶My first impression of them was one of health and vitality. ⁷Hordes of small barefoot children ran all over the campsite, a few dressed in rags but most nearly naked, rollicking like young animals. ⁸At the far end of the encampment a number of horses, tethered to long chains, were grazing; and of course there were the ever-present half-wild growling dogs. ⁹Several men lay in the shade of an oak tree. ¹⁰Thin corkscrews of bluish smoke rose skyward and the pungent, penetrating smell of burning wood permeated the air. ¹¹Even from a distance the loud, clear voices of these Gypsies resound-ed with an intensity I was not accustomed to. ¹²Mingling with them, farther away, were the dull thuds of an ax, the snorting and neighing of horses, the occasional snapping of a whip and the high-pitched wail of an infant, contrast-ing with the whisper of the immediate surroundings of the camp itself.

Jan Yoors, *The Gypsies*

A. Vocabulary

For each italicized word from the selection, choose the best definition ac-cording to the context in which it appears.

1. *bodices* [sentence 5]: (a) full skirts; (b) long sleeves; (c) top portions of dresses; (d) shawls.
2. *vitality* [6]: (a) laziness; (b) enthusiasm; (c) curiosity; (d) energy.
3. *rollicking* [7]: (a) rolling; (b) prancing; (c) behaving; (d) romping.
4. *tethered* [8]: (a) restricted; (b) bound; (c) braided; (d) harnessed.
5. *pungent* [10]: (a) sweetish; (b) biting; (c) sickening; (d) familiar.
6. *permeated* [10]: (a) perfumed; (b) polluted; (c) wafted through; (d) spread throughout.

B. Content and Structure

1. The mode of discourse in this paragraph is (a) narration; (b) description; (c) exposition; (d) persuasion.

2. The pattern of organization is (a) deductive; (b) spatial; (c) chronological; (d) inductive; (e) emphatic.

3. Write any transitional phrases that helped you arrive at your answer for question 2 above. _____
   _____

4. Find the two nouns that Yoors uses to characterize these Gypsies.
   _____ and _____

5. A good title for this paragraph would be (a) "A Study of Gypsy Life"; (b) "The Survival of the Gypsies"; (c) "I Decide to Become a Gypsy"; (d) "First Impressions of a Gypsy Camp."

6. Yoors uses many words that appeal to our senses. Which sense is *not* emphasized? Words pertaining to (a) sight; (b) smell; (c) sound; (d) touch; (e) color.

Selection 3

Note: In sentence 4 of this selection the word *outliers* (pronounced out lī' ərz) means, in this context, far-ranging locales or widely separated environments. And, as suggested in sentence 6, the offspring of a lion and tiger who have mated is called a liger if the father is a lion and a tiglon if the father is a tiger.

[1]At the height of the Roman Empire, when North Africa was covered by fertile savannas—and it was possible to travel from Carthage to Alexandria in the shade of trees—expeditions of soldiers armed with net and spear captured lions for display in zoos and in coliseum spectacles. [2]A few centuries earlier, lions were still abundant in southeastern Europe and the Middle East. [3]They preyed on humans in the forests of Attica while being hunted themselves for sport by Assyrian kings. [4]From these outliers they ranged eastward to India, where they still thrived during British rule in the nineteenth century. [5]Tigers ranged in turn from northern Iran eastward across India, thence north to Korea and Siberia and south to Bali. [6]To the best of our knowledge, no tiglons or ligers were recorded from the zone of overlap. [7]This absence is especially notable in the case of India, where under the British Raj trophies were hunted and records of game animals kept for more than a century.

[8]We have a good idea why the two species of big cats, despite their historical proximity, failed to hybridize in nature. [9]First, they liked different habitats. [10]Lions stayed mostly in open savanna and grassland and tigers in forests, although the segregation was far from perfect. [11]Second, their behavior was and is radically different in ways that count for the choice of mates. [12]Lions are the only social cats. [13]They live in prides, whose enduring centers are closely bonded females and their young. [14]Upon maturing, males leave their birth pride and join other groups, often as pairs of brothers. [15]The adult males and females hunt together, with the females taking the lead role. [16]Tigers, like all other cat species except lions, are solitary. [17]The males produce a different urinary scent

from that of lions to mark their territories and approach one another and the females only briefly during the breeding season. [18]In short, there appears to have been little opportunity for adults of the two species to meet and bond long enough to produce offspring.

Edwin O. Wilson, The Diversity of Life

A. Vocabulary

For each italicized word from the selection, choose the best definition according to the context in which it appears.

1. *savannas* [sentences 1 and 10]: (a) dense jungles or rain forests; (b) open grasslands; (c) mountain terrain; (d) densely wooded forests.
2. *proximity* [8]: (a) connection; (b) similarity; (c) closeness; (d) interdependency.
3. *hybridize* [8]: (a) live together peaceably; (b) develop shared characteristics; (c) develop a symbiotic, or mutually dependent, relationship; (d) crossbreed.
4. *enduring* [13]: (a) tolerating; (b) centralized; (c) lasting; (d) constantly changing.
5. *bonded* [13]: (a) linked, joined; (b) related by blood; (c) living in captivity; (d) superior, dominant.

B. Content and Structure

1. The main idea of this passage is that (a) because they inhabited the same geographical regions, tigers and lions often crossbreed and produce tiglons or ligers; (b) despite their presence in the same geographical regions, tigers and lions fail to interbreed in the wild; (c) tigers and lions are incapable of interbreeding; (d) the offspring of tigers and lions who have mated are noted for representing the best characteristics of each parent.
2. The information in sentences 1–5 shows that (a) throughout history people have been fascinated by lions and tigers; (b) lions have resided in zoos since ancient times; (c) lions and tigers were once found over a wide area of Europe, Africa, and Asia and, in fact, often occupied overlapping regions; (d) the lion and tiger population has severely declined in recent years.
3. Sentences 6 and 7 provide important evidence to support the main idea, suggesting (a) that if tiglons and ligers had been common in India, there would be written records of their existence; (b) the Indian government killed too many game animals, threatening their numbers; (c) the geography of India is too varied for lions and tigers to interbreed; (d) the tiglons and ligers produced in India were killed as game animals.

4. Two methods of development that are evident in sentences 8–18 are
    (a) example; (b) classification; (c) cause-and-effect; (d) definition; (e)
    steps in a process; (f) comparison; (g) contrast.
5. The pattern of organization in the second paragraph is (a) deductive;
    (b) inductive; (c) chronological; (d) spatial.
6. List and briefly explain the two major supporting details in the second
    paragraph. _____
    _____ and _____
    _____
7. The transitional phrase "in short" at the beginning of sentence 18
    suggests that what follows is (a) an example; (b) the main idea; (c) a
    contrast; (d) a concession; (e) a conclusion.
8. What conclusion can you draw about the hybridizing of tigers and lions
    from these two facts? The words *tiglon* and *liger* exist in the English
    language; yet the two species of big cats have failed to hybridize in
    nature. _____
    _____
    _____

Practice Essay

Penguins
David Attenborough

Educated as a zoologist at Cambridge University in England, David Attenborough has for many years been associated with the British Broadcasting Corporation (BBC). He first produced a program titled Zoo Quest, *which ran for several years. His next venture for the BBC was* Life on Earth, *a series adapted from the book of the same name, from which this excerpt is taken.*

1   The characteristic birds of the Antarctic, which are often taken, indeed, as the very symbol of the far frozen south, are, of course, the penguins. In fact, the evidence of fossils suggests that though the family originated in the southern hemisphere, it did so in the warmer parts of it. Even today, some species of penguin live in the relatively warm waters of southern Africa and south Australia. One lives actually on the equator, in the Galapagos. Penguins are superbly adapted to the swimming life. Their wings have become modified into flippers with which they beat the water and drive themselves along. Their feet are used for steering and are placed in the best position for the purpose, at the very end of their body. This gives them their characteristic upright stance when they come out of water. Swimming everywhere demands good in-

sulation and the penguins have developed their feathers to provide it. They are very long and thin, with tips that turn downwards towards the body. The shaft not only has filaments along the blade but, at the base, fluffy tufts that mat together and form a layer that is virtually impenetrable to wind or water. This feather coat covers more of their body than does that of any other bird. It extends low down on the legs of most of them, and the little Adelie penguin, which is one of only two species that lives on Antarctica, even has feathers growing on its stubby beak. Underneath this feather coat is a layer of blubber. So effectively protected are penguins that, like the vicuna, they run a real risk of overheating. They deal with that when necessary by ruffling their feathers and by holding their flippers out from their body to increase their radiating surface.

2   With such efficient insulation penguins have been able to colonise most of the waters of the southern oceans and in places they flourish in astronomic numbers. On Zavodovski, a small volcanic island in the South Sandwich group only 6 kilometres across, 14 million pairs of chinstrap penguins nest. They are small creatures, standing no higher than a man's knees. At the beginning of the Antarctic summer they come in to land, the huge swell hurling them on to the rocks with such violence that they seem certain to be smashed. But they have the resilience of rubber balls and as the surf drains back from the rocks it leaves them unharmed and undismayed and they waddle perkily inland. There on the bare volcanic ash they excavate simple scoops, squabbling ferociously and with ear-splitting shrieks over the pebbles with which they want to line them. In these meagre scrapes, they lay two eggs. The male incubates them while the female goes down to feed. If, as sometimes happens, the pair have chosen to nest in a gully where the ash is underlain by ice, then the heat of his body will melt the ice which drains away leaving him with his eggs sitting, in a rather bewildered way, in a deep hole. When the young hatch, the parents take it in turn to feed them. They grow rapidly so that by the time the short Antarctic summer is over, they are fully fledged and capable of swimming and feeding for themselves.

3   The largest of all the penguins is the emperor. It stands waist-high to a man and weighs 16 kilos, which makes it one of the biggest and heaviest of all sea birds. This great size may well be an adaptation to the cold, for the emperor lives and breeds on the Antarctic continent itself and is the only animal of any kind that is able to live through the extreme cold of the Antarctic interior during the winter. However, while their size undoubtedly helps them to retain heat, it also causes them great difficulties. Penguin chicks cannot feed themselves until they are fully developed and have their seagoing feathers. But large chicks take a long time to hatch and grow to their full size. Emperor penguin chicks cannot achieve this within the few weeks of the Antarctic summer as chinstrap or other smaller penguins manage to do. The emperors have

dealt with this difficulty by adopting a breeding timetable that is exactly the reverse of that followed by most other birds. Instead of laying in the spring and rearing their offspring through the warmer months of summer when food is easy to get, the emperors start the whole process at the beginning of winter.

4   They spend the summer feeding at sea and at the end of it are as fat and as fit as they will ever be. In March, a few weeks before the long darkness of the winter begins, the adults come ashore on the sea-ice. It already extends a considerable way out from the shore and the penguins have to walk south for many miles to reach their traditional breeding grounds close to the coast. Throughout the dark months of April and May, the birds display to one another and finally mate. The pair claim no particular territory for themselves, nor make any nest, for they are standing on sea-ice and there is no vegetation or stones with which to line a scrape. The female produces just one egg, large and very rich in yolk. As soon as it emerges, she must lift it from the surface of the ice before it freezes. She does this by pushing it towards her toes with the underside of her beak and taking it up on to the top of her feet. There it is covered by a fold of feathered skin that hangs down from her abdomen. Almost immediately her mate comes to her and in a ceremony that is the climax of the breeding ritual, takes the egg from her on to his own feet and tucks it beneath his own apron. Her immediate task is done. She leaves him and sets off through the deepening darkness to the edge of the sea-ice where she can at last feed. But winter is now more advanced and the ice extends even farther away from the coast. She may, therefore, have to travel as much as 150 kilometres before she reaches open water.

5   Meanwhile, her mate has remained standing upright, his precious egg on his feet, warm beneath his stomach fold. He does little, shuffling around to huddle together with the rest of the incubating males so that they give one another a little protection, turning his back against the driving snow and the screaming winds. He has no energy to waste on unnecessary movement or needless displays. When he first arrived here from the sea, he had a thick layer of fat beneath his feathers that made up almost half his body weight. He has already drawn upon that to sustain him through the exertions of his courtship. Now it must last him for another two months while he incubates his egg.

6   At last, sixty days after it was laid, the egg hatches. The young chick is not yet able to generate its own body heat and remains squatting on its father's feet, beneath his apron and warmed by his body. Almost unbelievably, the male manages to find from his stomach enough food to regurgitate and provide a meal to his newly-hatched offspring. And then, with extraordinary accuracy of timing, the female reappears. She has put on a great deal of weight. There is no nest site for her to remember. The male, in any case, may have shuffled quite a long way across the ice from where she last left him. She finds him by calling and recognis-

ing the individual tones of his reply. As soon as the pair are reunited, the female gives their chick a feed of regurgitated half-digested fish. The reunion is a critical one. If she had been caught by a leopard seal and failed to return, the chick would die of starvation within the next few days. Even if she is a day or so late, she may not be in time to provide it with the food it urgently needs. It will have perished before she reaches it.

7   The male, having stood and starved for weeks, is now free to find food for himself. Leaving the chick in the charge of his mate, he sets off for the sea. He is pitifully thin, having lost at least a third of his weight, but if he succeeds in reaching the edge of the ice, he dives into the sea and begins to gorge. For two weeks, he has a holiday. Then with a stomach and a crop full of fish, he sets off on the long trek back to his chick.

8   The youngster has had nothing more to eat than the fish carried in by the female, and some juice from her stomach. It is more than ready for further food from its father. It is still dressed in its chick's coat of fluffy grey feathers. All the chicks stand together in a huddle, but each is nonetheless recognisable individually to its parents by its voice. For the remaining weeks of the winter, the parents take it in turn to go fishing and bring back food for their youngster. At long last, the horizon begins to lighten, the temperature rises infinitesimally and cracks begin to appear in the sea-ice. Leads of open water develop closer and closer to the nurseries. Eventually one comes close enough for the chicks to reach. They shuffle down to it and dive in, excellent swimmers from the moment they hit the water. The adult birds join them in the feasting. They have a mere two months to restore their fat reserves before they must start the whole cycle over again.

9   The breeding process has been fraught with dangers and difficulties. Safety margins have been tiny. Weather just fractionally worse than usual, fishing just a little less productive, a parent just a day or so late—any such variation could result in the death of the chick. The majority, in fact, do die. If four out of ten of them reach maturity, the emperors have had a good year.

A. Comprehension

Choose the answer that best completes each statement. Do not refer to the selection while doing this exercise.

1. Attenborough states that penguins are (a) the most adaptable bird in nature; (b) the symbol of the far frozen south; (c) not particularly well suited to the harshness of their environment; (d) the only birds to have an upright stance.

2. Penguins are well suited for the swimming life because of their flippers and their (a) efficient insulation; (b) fast speed; (c) love of the water; (d) effective ratio of muscle to body fat.

3.   After the chinstrap penguins lay two eggs in their "meagre scrapes," they are incubated by (a) the females; (b) the males; (c) the males and females, taking equal turns; (d) females who have no mates.

4.   The Emperor penguins have a special problem—how to allow enough time for the chicks to get big enough to survive—which they have solved by (a) migrating to the warm northern waters in the summer and breeding there; (b) reversing the usual process and beginning the breeding process in the winter; (c) producing only one chick every other year; (d) stockpiling food to nourish the chick during the long dark winter months.

5.   Critical to the survival of an emperor penguin chick is (a) the male's ability to leave the egg and forage for food; (b) the female's huddling together with other females for warmth and safety from predators; (c) the presence of fish and other food in the immediate vicinity where the egg is being incubated; (d) the female's timely return to begin feeding the chick which has hatched in her absence.

6.   Penguins communicate and recognize each other (a) by their distinctive markings; (b) by their individual appearance; (c) by their position on the ice; (d) by their voices.

B.   Structure

Choose the best answer.

1.   Locate and write the sentence that represents Attenborough's main point about emperor penguins' breeding habits. _____
_____

2.   The mode of discourse in the passage as a whole is (a) narration; (b) description; (c) exposition; (d) persuasion.

3.   The method of development in paragraph 1 is (a) example; (b) steps in a process; (c) analysis; (d) analogy; (e) contrast.

4.   The method of development in paragraphs 4–8 is (a) definition; (b) steps in a process; (c) cause-and-effect; (d) comparison; (e) classification.

5.   The pattern of organization in paragraphs 4–6 is (a) chronological; (b) deductive; (c) inductive; (d) spatial.

6.   Locate and write the transitions in paragraphs 4–6 that helped you arrive at your answer to question 5 above. _____
_____
_____

7.   Complete this outline of the passage; that is, write down a brief phrase indicating the topic taken up in the following sections. The first answer has been done for you.

Paragraph 1: *The physical characteristics that enable penguins to adapt to their environment* _____

Paragraph 2: _____

Paragraph 3: _____

Paragraphs 4–8: _____

Paragraph 9: _____

8. Read paragraph 5 again. Which of the following is most appropriate to characterize the way the author describes the males' situation during the incubation period? (a) serious and straightforward; (b) witty and ironic; (c) sad, almost tragic; (d) pathetic and slightly humorous.

C. Vocabulary

For each italicized word from the selection, choose the best definition according to the context in which it appears.

1. characteristic upright *stance* [paragraph 1]: (a) appearance; (b) trait; (c) emotional attitude; (d) position.
2. the shaft has *filaments* [1]: (a) barbs, hooks; (b) slender appendages; (c) insulating material; (d) tiny wires.
3. The *resilience* of rubber balls [2]: (a) ability to stretch and twist; (b) changeability; (c) ability to recover quickly, bounce back; (d) adaptability.
4. leaves them unharmed and *undismayed* [2]: (a) not discouraged or frightened; (b) not embarrassed; (c) in one piece, whole; (d) not endangered.
5. they waddle *perkily* inland [2]: (a) ponderously; (b) clumsily; (c) cheerfully; (d) lazily.
6. in these *meagre* scrapes [2] (Note: "meagre" is the British spelling of "meager"): (a) scanty, shallow; (b) deep; (c) well-formed; (d) rocky.
7. the *exertions* of courtship [5]: (a) rituals, customs; (b) prescribed forms, rules; (c) strenuous efforts; (d) mysteries, puzzles.
8. enough food to *regurgitate* [6]: (a) nourish; (b) provide sufficient sustenance; (c) chew slowly; (d) vomit.
9. the temperature rises *infinitesimally* [8]: (a) by a large amount; (b) immeasurably, minutely; (c) quickly; (d) noticeably.
10. *fraught with* dangers [9]: (a) determined by; (b) made possible because of; (c) accompanied by; (d) minimized by.

D. Questions for Discussion and Analysis

1. What are some of the techniques that Attenborough uses to make this selection readable rather than dry and dull as a discussion of penguin breeding processes could very well be?

2. What particular hardships does the author emphasize in his discussion? Find some examples of his choice of words that suggest the severity of these hardships.

PART **II**

Discovering Meaning through Language

5

Making Accurate Inferences

The three chapters in Part II will introduce you to more sophisticated reading skills. Now that you are probably comfortable with the fundamentals of paragraph structure—placement of main idea, modes of discourse, methods of development, and organizational patterns—you can refine your skills by paying more careful attention to words and the way writers use them. First, in this chapter, you will learn how to make inferences. In Chapter 6 you will learn some complex uses of language, including denotation, connotation, and figures of speech. In Chapter 7 there will be a discussion of tone as it is suggested by the author's language.

Inferences Defined

The inference process goes beyond mere literal comprehension. First, we need to distinguish between two often confused verbs: "imply" and "infer." To *imply* means to hint at or suggest an idea indirectly. To *infer* means to draw a conclusion from what has been implied. In other words, when you make inferences, you "read between the lines." The legal definition of inference is instructive and precise.

A presumption of fact or an inference is nothing more than a probable or natural explanation of facts . . . and arises from the commonly accepted

experiences of mankind and the inferences which reasonable men would draw from these experiences.

American Jurisprudence

In real life, we make inferences by drawing conclusions from our observations or from a set of facts. For example, we infer that a man wearing a ring on the fourth finger of his left hand is married. We may infer that a library book with a shabby cover and torn pages is frequently borrowed. If a yard contains a sandbox and swing set, we probably infer that children live in the house. Based on our "commonly accepted experiences," these inferences are *probably* accurate, but they are not necessarily true. The man wearing the wedding ring may be a widower. The book may be shabby because the library does not have the time, staff, or funds to repair tattered books. As for the play equipment in the yard, perhaps the owners of the house operate a day-care center and do not have any children of their own.

Inferences, then, are merely reasonable or *probably accurate* conclusions you may draw from a situation or from the printed page. Your life experiences and cultural heritage play a key role in making inferences. To illustrate with the wedding ring example, in North America a ring on the fourth finger of a person's left hand generally suggests that the wearer is married. However, in many European countries, married men and women wear their wedding bands on the *right* hand. An American might wrongly infer that a European man with no ring on his left hand is unmarried, merely because of differing cultural practices.

Practicing Making Inferences

Let us see how the inference process works in reading simple sentences. Consider this example from a history textbook.

> During the 1950s, Germany and Japan prospered once again, because American aid helped them recover from the losses they suffered in World War II.

Based on the sentence, these inferences are *probably accurate:*

- Germany and Japan had been prosperous before their defeat.
- America thought helping to rebuild Japan and Germany was important.
- Without American aid, Germany and Japan might not have regained prosperity so quickly.

You can label an inference statement probably accurate if—based on the author's words—it is very likely true or accurate. The inference is a logical statement that follows from the sentence; it does not misinterpret the author's words.

Based on the same sentence, this inference is *probably inaccurate:*

- Germany and Japan could have recovered just as quickly without American aid.

The word *because* establishes a definite cause-and-effect relationship between the two factual statements, making this statement, then, a misinterpretation.

These inferences should be labeled as *insufficient evidence:*

- The American public favored foreign aid to Germany and Japan.
- In contrast to Germany and Japan, America remained economically strong during World War II.

The sentence says nothing about the American public sentiment or about America's own economy; therefore, these inferences cannot be made one way or another.

You will see from these examples that an inference in reading can be made safely only from the author's words, and thus it must be fairly narrow. You should not go beyond the limits of the author's words because, as you will see later, inferring based on your own experiences, attitudes, or values may result in misreading. In many of the exercises in Parts II and IV in the text, you will need to label inferences in this way. Be sure you understand the distinctions between the labels *probably accurate, probably inaccurate,* and *insufficient evidence.* The best way to become adept and comfortable with making inferences is to study several examples and the explanation that follows them.

Here are two short practice examples. The first comes from Nien Cheng's autobiographical work, *Life and Death in Shanghai,* which describes her experiences during the Cultural Revolution in mainland China, instigated by the former premier, Mao Zedong, in the 1960s.

> In Mao Zedong's China, going to prison did not mean the same thing as it did in the democracies. A man was always presumed guilty until he could prove himself innocent. The accused were judged not by their own deeds but by the acreage of land once possessed by their ancestors. A cloud of suspicion always hung over the heads of those with the wrong class origins.
>
> Nien Cheng, *Life and Death in Shanghai*

Label these statements as *probably accurate* (PA), *probably inaccurate* (PI), or *insufficient evidence* (IE).

_____ 1. In a democracy like the United States, one is presumed innocent until proven guilty.

_____ 2. During the Cultural Revolution, one's socioeconomic class had no political significance.

_____ 3. Nien Cheng, the author of the passage, was sent to prison for participating in illegal revolutionary activities.

Here are the answers. (1) PA; (2) PI; (3) IE.

Let us go through these answers one by one. The first inference should be labeled PA because sentence 1 contrasts Mao Zedong's China with democratic nations. In our country, there is the presumption of innocence until one's guilt has been proved. Cheng turns around this familiar democratic tenet, suggesting that the opposite was the case in China during the Cultural Revolution.

The second inference is probably inaccurate because of what sentence 3 implies: that one's deeds did not matter as much as economic class, represented by the amount of land one's family owned. The last sentence further confirms the inaccuracy with the phrase "a cloud of suspicion." And in the final inference, which should be marked IE, Cheng does not indicate her own "crime" or even her reason for writing on this subject. There is nothing about her in the passage.

Here is a second passage.

> In the last few months I have visited several cities around the country, and in each of them I have found the same thing: more and more people in the streets, more and more suffering. (There are at least 350,000 homeless people in the country, perhaps as many as 3 million.) And in talking to the good citizens of these cities, I found, almost always, the same thing: confusion and ignorance, or simple indifference, but anger, too, and fear.
>
> Peter Marin, "Helping and Hating the Homeless," *The New York Times*

Mark these inferences as you did before.

_____ 1. Peter Marin traveled around the country specifically to study the homeless problem firsthand.

_____ 2. Peter Marin is an expert on the homeless problem.

_____ 3. The homeless problem has become worse in the last few months.

_____ 4. It is difficult to make an accurate count of the homeless population in the U.S.

_____ 5. Most of the homeless people in American cities are Vietnam veterans and the mentally ill.

_____ 6. Americans' attitudes toward the homeless are simple and straightforward.

Here are the answers: (1) IE; (2) IE; (3) PA; (4) PA; (5) IE; (6) PI.

Let us analyze these statements one by one. The passage does not hint at the reason for Marin's *travels*. Similarly, we cannot infer—again, one way or the other—whether Marin is an expert on the homeless. Questions like this involve slippery words—what exactly is an "expert"? Marin does not provide us with his qualifications—beyond his personal observations. Notice, too, that his attitude, based on the way he expresses himself, is one of concern and sympathy. He sounds more personal, not remote as an academic writing a sociological study would sound.

The third inference, in contrast, should be labeled *probably accurate* because of the words at the end of sentence 1. People who are forced—for whatever reason—to live in the streets are clearly suffering, and they do constitute a serious social and economic problem, not just for themselves but for other citizens as well. Finally, Marin's repetition of the phrase "more and more" confirms that this is a worsening situation.

The next inference is also *probably accurate* based on the statistics in sentence 2, and there is an enormous difference between 350,000 and 3 million, suggesting that the homeless population, by virtue of its transience, is very difficult to count.

The fifth statement is an example of an inference that cannot be made since the passage gives no evidence for it. Marin does not suggest anything of the backgrounds of the homeless he met; and we should not be seduced by the word "most," which is another slippery qualifier.

In the last sentence Marin characterizes the citizens' attitudes toward the homeless as exemplifying "confusion," "ignorance," "simple indifference," "anger," and "fear," from which we can infer that Americans aren't sure what to think about the homeless or how to solve their problems. Our attitudes are therefore complicated, *not* simple and straightforward. This last inference contradicts the author's words, and thus should be labeled *probably inaccurate*.

To give you more practice, read this well-known fable.

A dispute once arose between the Wind and the Sun as to which was the stronger of the two. They agreed, therefore, to try their strength upon a traveler to see which should be able to take his cloak off first. The Wind began and blew with all his might and main, a cold and fierce blast; but the stronger he blew the closer the traveler wrapped his cloak about him and the tighter he grasped it with his hands. Then broke out the Sun and with his welcome beams he dispersed the vapor and the cold. The traveler

felt the genial warmth and as the Sun shone brighter and brighter, he sat down, overcome with the heat, and cast his cloak on the ground. Thus the Sun was declared the conqueror.

"The Wind and the Sun," from *Aesop's Fables*

Which of these moral truths can you accurately infer from this fable?

1. The mighty rule the world.
2. The meek shall inherit the earth.
3. Force is more effective than persuasion.
4. Persuasion is more effective than force.
5. Competition breeds jealousy.

This fable embodies the moral truth stated in 4, since the gentle warmth of the Sun's rays—in other words, persuasion—was more effective than the harsh force of the Wind's blowing.

The next fable is slightly more difficult.

Death speaks:

[1]There was a merchant in Bagdad who sent his servant to market to buy provisions and in a little while the servant came back, white and trembling, and said, Master, just now when I was in the market-place I was jostled by a woman in the crowd and when I turned I saw it was Death that jostled me. [2]She looked at me and made a threatening gesture; now, lend me your horse, and I will ride away from this city and avoid my fate. [3]I will go to Samarra and there Death will not find me. [4]The merchant lent him his horse, and the servant mounted it, and he dug his spurs in its flanks and as fast as the horse could gallop he went. [5]Then the merchant went down to the market-place and he saw me standing in the crowd and he came to me and said, Why did you make a threatening gesture to my servant when you saw him this morning? [6]That was not a threatening gesture, I said, it was only a start of surprise. [7]I was astonished to see him in Bagdad, for I had an appointment with him tonight in Samarra.

W. Somerset Maugham, "Death Speaks," *Sheppey*

Based on the evidence in the fable, label these inferences PA, PI, or IE.

_____ 1. The servant misinterpreted Death's gesture in the market-place.

_____ 2. The merchant thought his servant was foolish to go to Samarra.

_____ 3.   The time and place of our death is predetermined before we
             are born.

_____ 4.   Ironically, the servant was the cause of his own death.

_____ 5.   The servant thought he was smarter than Death and could
             outwit her.

Here are the answers: (1) PA; (2) PI; (3) IE; (4) PA; (5) PA.

The first inference is clearly accurate, based on the information in
sentences 6 and 7, though arriving at this deduction means that we
must accept Death's version of her gesture and reject the servant's. The
second inference is labeled _probably inaccurate_ because sentence 4 implies that the merchant willingly lent his horse, thereby suggesting that
he agreed with his servant's decision to flee Death's threatening gesture.
And later he scolded Death for frightening his servant. Also, a good
master would not want his servant to die. This inference statement thus
misinterprets the events of the story.

The third inference is an example of an inference that cannot be
drawn one way or another because there is no evidence for it. The servant suggests his belief that fate has determined the place of his death
(since he mentions that he is going to Samarra to "avoid my fate"); but
these words do not imply _when_ our death is predetermined. This inference is an example of _insufficient evidence_ (and not PI), because you cannot point to a word, phrase, or sentence that suggests it one way or another.

The last two inferences are clearly suggested by the irony of the situation, meaning that in attempting to outwit and escape his fate, the
servant, instead, must succumb to it. We and Death know what the servant does not.

As should be plain by now, these inference questions make you
think! While some of these inferences may seem trivial or even picky,
they do force you to look carefully at a passage. The questions should
help you both to become an active, questioning reader and a better
thinker. And as you become better at making accurate inferences, you
will find that you do this automatically as you read, assessing the author's words and seeing implications beyond the literal.

Here is a more difficult passage for you to practice labeling inference statements.

[1]The man who invented Coca-Cola was not a native Atlantan, but on the
day of his funeral every drugstore in town testimonially shut up shop. [2]He
was John Styth Pemberton, born in 1833 in Knoxville, Georgia, eighty
miles away. [3]Sometimes known as Doctor, Pemberton was a pharmacist
who, during the Civil War, led a cavalry troop under General Joe Wheeler.
[4]He settled in Atlanta in 1869, and soon began brewing such patent medicines as Triplex Liver Pills and Globe of Flower Cough Syrup. [5]In 1885, he

registered a trademark for something called French Wine Coca—Ideal Nerve and Tonic Stimulant; a few months later he formed the Pemberton Chemical Company, and recruited the services of a bookkeeper named Frank M. Robinson, who not only had a good head for figures but, attached to it, so exceptional a nose that he could audit the composition of a batch of syrup merely by sniffing it. [6]In 1886—a year in which, as contemporary Coca-Cola officials like to point out, Conan Doyle unveiled Sherlock Holmes and France unveiled the Statue of Liberty—Pemberton unveiled a syrup that he called Coca-Cola. [7]It was a modification of his French Wine Coca. [8]He had taken out the wine and added a pinch of caffeine, and, when the end product tasted awful, had thrown in some extract of cola (or kola) nut and a few other oils, blending the mixture in a three-legged iron pot in his back yard and swishing it around with an oar. [9]He distributed it to soda fountains in used beer bottles, and Robinson, with his flowing bookkeeper's script, presently devised a label, on which "Coca-Cola" was written in the fashion that is still employed. [10]Pemberton looked upon his concoction less as a refreshment than as a headache cure, especially for people whose throbbing temples could be traced to overindulgence. [11]On a morning late in 1886, one such victim of the night before dragged himself into an Atlanta drugstore and asked for a dollop of Coca-Cola. [12]Druggists customarily stirred a teaspoonful of syrup into a glass of water, but in this instance the factotum on duty was too lazy to walk to the fresh-water tap, a couple of feet off. [13]Instead, he mixed the syrup with some charged water, which was closer at hand. [14]The suffering customer perked up almost at once, and word quickly spread that the best Coca-Cola was a fizzy one.

E. J. Kahn, *The Big Drink*

Label these statements as you did before.

_____ 1. John Styth Pemberton, the man who invented Coca-Cola, was well-respected in the Atlanta community.

_____ 2. Pemberton was known as Doctor because he liked to dispense free medical advice to his customers.

_____ 3. Pemberton's first patent medicines, Triplex Liver Pills and Globe of Flower cough syrup, were medically quite effective.

_____ 4. Pemberton took out the wine and added a pinch of caffeine to make his new syrup taste better.

_____ 5. The original Coca-Cola syrup contained cocaine and was thought to be highly addictive.

_____ 6. Pemberton measured all his ingredients carefully and prepared the syrup following a precise formula.

_____ 7. Pemberton recognized immediately that Coca-Cola, his new invention, would be used mostly as a refreshment.

_____ 8. The invention of the carbonated Coca-Cola we drink today can be traced to a soda jerk's laziness.

Many students find the inference questions in the text quite challenging. As you work through them, be sure you look back at the text to find the phrase or sentence that pertains to each question. Remember that in making inferences, there is some degree of "gray"—that is, you may not be wholly certain that the inference is verifiably true, only that, based on our "commonly accepted experiences" and the author's words, it is *probably* accurate or *probably* inaccurate. If you disagree with an answer, first look back at the passage to see if you can determine where you went wrong by yourself, and, if you are still unsure, ask your instructor for help.

Open-Ended Inferences

Another kind of inference exercise involves *open-ended* questions, after which you are asked to write the inferences yourself after you examine a particular sentence or paragraph. To practice this, read this passage by Diane Ackerman on separation experiments performed on monkeys.

[1]At the University of Colorado School of Medicine, researchers conducted a separation experiment with monkeys, in which they removed the mother. [2]The infant showed signs of helplessness, confusion, and depression, and only the return of its mother and continuous holding for a few days would help it return to normal. [3]During separation, changes occurred in the heart rate, body temperature, brain-wave patterns, sleep patterns, and immune system function. [4]Electronic monitoring of deprived infants showed that touch deprivation caused physical and psychological disturbances. [5]But when the mother was put back, only the psychological disturbances seemed to disappear; true, the infant's behavior reverted to normal, but the physical distresses—susceptibility to disease, and so on—persisted. [6]Among this experiment's implications is that damage is not reversible, and that the lack of maternal contact may lead to possible long-term damage.

[7]Another separation study with monkeys took place at the University of Wisconsin, where researchers separated an infant from its mother by a glass screen. [8]They could still see, hear, and smell each other, only touch was missing, but that created a void so serious that the baby cried steadily and paced frantically. [9]In another group, the dividing screen had holes, so the mother and baby could touch through it, which was apparently sufficient because the infants didn't develop serious behavior problems. [10]Those infants who suffered short-term deprivation became adolescents

who clung to one another obsessively instead of developing into independent, confident individuals. [11]When they suffered long-term deprivation,
they avoided one another and became aggressive when they did come in
contact, violent loners who didn't form good relationships.

Diane Ackerman, A Natural History of the Senses

Write a sentence or two stating the inference you can accurately
make from the passage. Try also to explain the origin of your thinking—that is, the words, phrases, or sentences that helped you arrive at
your answer.

1. According to the passage as a whole, what can you infer about the
   effects of touch deprivation in baby monkeys? _____
   _____

2. From the passage, what can you infer about the implications of
   touch deprivation in human infants? _____
   _____

3. From sentences 8–9, which of the five senses can you infer is the
   most important for normal development of infant monkeys?
   _____

4. What can you infer about Ackerman's attitude toward experiments
   like these conducted on monkeys by medical researchers at the University of Colorado and Wisconsin? _____
   _____

Exercises

Selection 1

[1]The first time I ever saw a bear in the wild, I was on my way back from fishing
in a beaver meadow on state land next to the Flathead National Forest, about
ten miles from the town of Bigfork, Montana. [2]I was coming around a bend on
an overgrown logging road when I saw up ahead a large black animal see me
and duck into some thimbleberry bushes. [3]I knew it was a bear. [4]I didn't move
and he didn't move for maybe three minutes. [5]There was no likely tree nearby
for me to climb. [6]Then the bear hopped out of the bushes, took a look at me
over his shoulder, and galloped like crazy down the trail. [7]As he ran, his hind
feet seemed to reach higher than his head. [8]He splashed water up and made
the rocks clack as he crossed a little creek, and then he went into the brush on
the other side with a racket that sounded like a car crashing through there.
[9]For some reason, I picked up a rock. [10]I felt the weight of the rock in my hand,
I smelled the breath from a wild rosebush, I saw the sun on the tops of the
mountains, I felt the clothes on my back. [11]I felt like a man—skinny, bipedal,
weak, slow, and basically kind of a silly idea. [12]I felt as if I had eyes all over my

head. [13]I proceeded, a procession of feelings, down the trail where the bear had run. [14]I saw the dark blots on the trail where he had splashed water from the creek. [15]I kept saying, "A bear! I saw a bear!" [16]I found myself looking over my shoulder for the instant-replay screen. [17]I could not believe that this had happened and then gone by in a second, like trillions of completely unremarkable events. [18]I quickly passed the spot where the bear had disappeared, and then I became happier and happier. [19]I had just moved to Montana at the time, and did not know anyone there. [20]I walked home through the charged twilight and went through the screen door and picked up the telephone and began to call my friends before I even took off my waders.

Ian Frazier, "Bear News," *The New Yorker*

A. Vocabulary

For each italicized word from the selection, choose the best definition according to the context in which it appears.

1. *likely* [sentence 5]: (a) sufficiently tall; (b) nearby; (c) suitable; (d) possible.
2. *bipedal* [11]: two (a) hands; (b) feet; (c) arms; (d) eyes.
3. *procession* [13]: (a) a continuous course; (b) a mixture; (c) a list; (d) a parade.
4. *charged* [20]: (a) tense, filled with dread; (b) filled with a sense of wonder and awe; (c) illuminated by electric lights; (d) intensified, saturated.

B. Content and Structure

Choose the best answer.

1. The mode of discourse in this paragraph is primarily (a) narration; (b) description; (c) exposition; (d) persuasion. Explain your answer.

    _____

    _____

2. The pattern of organization is (a) deductive; (b) inductive; (c) spatial; (d) chronological; (e) emphatic.
3. When it first spotted the author, the bear reacted with (a) excitement; (b) curiosity; (c) fear; (d) indifference.
4. Read sentence 8 again. When the author writes that the bear "went into the brush on the other side with a racket that sounded like a car crashing through there," what does he intend this simile to suggest?

    _____

    _____

5. Sentences 10 and 11 suggest that this encounter with the bear made the author feel—at least in relation to this animal—(a) strong and powerful; (b) vulnerable and open to attack; (c) courageous and daring; (d) small and insignificant.

C. Inferences

On the basis of the evidence in the passage, mark these statements as follows: PA for inferences that are probably accurate; PI for inferences that are probably inaccurate; and IE for insufficient evidence.

_____ 1. Since this incident, the author has probably observed other bears in the wild.

_____ 2. Bears are nocturnal animals.

_____ 3. This bear was more frightened of the author than the author was of the bear.

_____ 4. This particular bear was probably a grizzly.

_____ 5. Bears are common in this part of Montana.

Selection 2

[1]Even magnificent programs, or the smaller good things that happen each day, are doomed, I think, not to make much difference. [2]This is because of the characteristic that really sets TV apart—not its ability to transmit sight and sound but its ubiquity. [3]There it stands, twenty-four hours a day, ready to pour out information and amusement. [4]Which means that if something exceptional happens it hardly matters—it is quickly averaged out, eroded by this ceaseless flood. [5]On "Good Morning America," Teddy Kollek, the mayor of Jerusalem, is being interviewed, and is saying a few interesting things about a recent visit from Václav Havel.* [6]But as soon as he's finished, or maybe slightly before, the host is saying, "Mr. Mayor—always outspoken, always feisty, good to see you. [7]Fifteen minutes past the hour. [8]How to prepare for a record invasion of gypsy moths that may be coming when 'Good Morning America' continues." [9]If the only TV you heard all day was this six-minute talk with Teddy Kollek, it might linger in your mind—you could mull it over. [10]But it's quickly replaced by a man who's talking about egg masses and how a female gypsy moth resembles a 747, and then it's Western Omelette McMuffin and Tom Berenger† and a chat with Brent Musburger‡ and a movie review and a chat among the various hosts about their upcoming trip to the British Isles. [11]This takes less than an hour.

[12]A few years ago, the people of an isolated Colombian Indian tribe, the Kogi, decided they needed to send a message to the rest of the world. [13]The snow-

*A Czech playwright who became president of what is now the Czech Republic after the breakup of the Communist empire.
†An American actor.
‡An American TV news correspondent.

pack that watered their mountain range was disappearing; their seers insisted that human activity was destroying the environment around the entire planet. [14]So they made the unprecedented decision to allow a BBC producer into their villages to film a documentary. [15]"It was not at all clear to them what 'the BBC' was," the producer said later. [16]"Some clearly formed the view that it was a kin group of some sort." [17]But though they had no idea that the world was round, they grasped the magical power of television. [18]Their message—that they "have seen the changes start that mark the end of life; the world is beginning to die"—could instantly and simultaneously be transmitted to most of the people of the world. [19]So the film crew came, with helicopters and lights and cameras; the documentary was made, and it was shown in Britain and America and around the world; and quite a few people watched, and many of them must have found it sobering, for here was a long-lived culture speaking out of nowhere at the same time and with the same message as our leading scientists. [20]It was uncanny. [21]But then it was over, and something else came on, and the warning passed unheeded.

Bill McKibben, "Reflections: Television," *The New Yorker*

A. Vocabulary

For each italicized word from the selection, choose the best definition according to the context in which it appears.

1. *ubiquity* [sentence 2]: (a) existing everywhere at once; (b) tremendous power; (c) influence on public opinion; (d) mediocre quality.
2. *eroded* [4]: (a) increased in intensity; (b) minimized, made less important; (c) worn away; (d) made irrelevant, unimportant.
3. *mull it over* [9]: (a) talk about it; (b) get angry about it; (c) think it over; (d) do research about it.
4. *seers* [13]: (a) political leaders; (b) prophets; (c) scientists; (d) television viewers.
5. *unprecedented* [14]: (a) never before done or experienced; (b) carefully considered; (c) radical, revolutionary; (d) foolish, ill-considered.
6. *sobering* [19]: (a) fascinating, absorbing; (b) gloomy, dreary; (c) boring, tiresome; (d) serious, grave.
7. *uncanny* [20]: (a) uncomfortably strange; (b) miraculous; (c) unpredictable; (d) confusing.
8. *unheeded* [21]: (a) unappreciated; (b) ignored, not paid attention to; (c) unobserved, invisible; (d) carefully considered.

B. Content and Structure

Choose the best answer.

1. The mode of discourse in this paragraph is primarily (a) narration; (b) description; (c) exposition; (d) persuasion.

2. State the main idea of this paragraph in your own words.

_____

_____

_____

3. The author supports the main idea primarily by (a) examples and illustration; (b) steps in a process; (c) comparison; (d) contrast; (e) definition.

4. According to McKibben, the problem with the way television presents news is that (a) it airs too many trivial stories; (b) it pays too much attention to the demands of advertising sponsors; (c) it is limited because of time constraints so that commercials interrupt important stories; (d) it presents important and trivial news stories and advertisements as if they were equally important.

5. In sentences 12–20, the author cites the experience of Columbian Indian tribe, the Kogi. From what the author says, which of the following are accurate conclusions? Mark any that apply. (a) The story was both boring and confusing; (b) The viewers who watched the story had no interest in a story about the depletion of the ozone layer; (c) The Kogi were overly optimistic about the impact their story would have on the viewing public; (d) The nature of television news shows resulted in this story's being buried amid all the other stories in the broadcast.

C. Inferences

On the basis of the evidence in the paragraph, answer these inference questions in your own words.

1. Look at sentence 2 again. When McKibben writes that it is the ubiquitous nature of television that sets it apart, what does he mean? Apart from what? _____

_____

2. Read sentences 5–11. From the details he includes, what are we meant to infer about all these stories and announcements?

_____

_____

3. In sentence 6, what does the author imply about the way the host ended his interview with Teddy Kollek, and why did he end it in this way? _____

_____

4. Look up the word *understatement* in an unabridged dictionary. How does this term apply to the information we are given in sentence 19?

_____

_____

5. What inference can you make about the reason the Kogi message of "the end of life" went unheeded by the viewing public?

_____

_____

Selection 3

[1]In Japan, specially licensed chefs prepare the rarest sashimi delicacy: the white flesh of the puffer fish, served raw and arranged in elaborate floral patterns on a platter. [2]Diners pay large sums of money for the carefully prepared dish, which has a light, faintly sweet taste, like raw pompano. [3]It had better be carefully prepared, because, unlike pompano, puffer fish is ferociously poisonous. [4]You wouldn't think a puffer fish would need such chemical armor, since its main form of defense is to swallow great gulps of water and become so bloated it is too large for most predators to swallow. [5]And yet its skin, ovaries, liver, and intestines contain tetrodotoxin, one of the most poisonous chemicals in the world, hundreds of times more lethal than strychnine or cyanide. [6]A shred small enough to fit under one's fingernail could kill an entire family. [7]Unless the poison is completely removed by a deft, experienced chef, the diner will die midmeal. [8]That's the appeal of the dish; eating the possibility of death, a fright your lips spell out as you dine. [9]Yet preparing it is a traditional art form in Japan, with widespread aficionados. [10]The most highly respected *fugu* chefs are the ones who manage to leave in the barest touch of the poison, just enough for the diner's lips to tingle from his brush with mortality but not enough to actually kill him. [11]Of course, a certain number of diners do die every year from eating *fugu,* but that doesn't stop intrepid *fugu*-fanciers. [12]The ultimate *fugu* connoisseur orders *chiri,* puffer flesh lightly cooked in a broth made of the poisonous livers and intestines. [13]It's not that diners don't understand the bizarre danger of puffer-fish toxin. [14]Ancient Egyptian, Chinese, Japanese, and other cultures all describe *fugu* poisoning in excruciating detail: It first produces dizziness, numbness of the mouth and lips, breathing trouble, cramps, blue lips, a desperate itchiness as of insects crawling all over one's body, vomiting, dilated pupils, and then a zombielike sleep, really a kind of neurological paralysis during which the victims are often aware of what's going on around them, and from which they die. [15]But sometimes they wake. [16]If a Japanese man or woman dies of *fugu* poison, the family waits a few days before burying them, just in case they wake up. [17]Every now and then someone poisoned by *fugu* is nearly buried alive, coming to at the last moment to describe in horrifying detail their own funeral and burial, during which, although they desperately tried to cry out or signal that they were still alive, they simply couldn't move.

Diane Ackerman, *A Natural History of the Senses*

A. Vocabulary

For each italicized word from the paragraph, choose the best definition according to the context.

1. *bloated* [sentence 4]: (a) poisonous; (b) swollen; (c) unappealing; (d) intimidating.
2. *lethal* [5]: (a) powerful; (b) bitter-tasting; (c) causing death; (d) dangerous.
3. *deft* [7]: (a) skillful; (b) efficient; (c) clever; (d) well-trained.
4. *aficionados* [9]: (a) customers; (b) trendsetters; (c) gourmets; (d) enthusiastic followers.
5. *intrepid* [11]: (a) serious; (b) courageous; (c) foolish; (d) stubborn.
6. *ultimate* [12]: representing (a) the farthest extreme; (b) the first in a sequence; (c) the largest; (d) the most flavorful.
7. *connoisseur* [12]: (a) a newcomer, novice; (b) a daredevil; (c) a person who does not consider the consequences of his or her actions; (d) a person who has knowledge about food or other esthetic matters.
8. *excruciating* [14]: (a) intensely painful and exact; (b) overly simplified; (c) boring, monotonous; (d) nauseating, sickening.

B. Content and Structure

Choose the best answer.

1. In your own words explain what the appeal of eating puffer fish is, according to Ackerman. _____
    _____
    _____

2. The mode of discourse in this passage is (a) narration; (b) description; (c) exposition; (d) persuasion.
3. Ackerman's purpose in writing is (a) to persuade and encourage the reader to sample puffer fish; (b) to warn the reader about the dangers of eating puffer fish; (c) to explain the preparation and appeal of puffer fish; (d) to ridicule those who eat this dish.
4. The relationship between sentences 3 and 4 and between sentences 8 and 9 is (a) general idea and a supporting statement; (b) term and its definition; (c) steps in a process; (d) contrast.
5. Which of the following best describes Ackerman's attitude toward puffer fish connoisseurs? (a) She thinks they are weird; (b) She thinks they are foolish; (c) She thinks they are admirable; (d) Her attitude is not evident.
6. Mark any of the following that we can *reasonably* conclude are characteristics of puffer fish connoisseurs, according to Ackerman's discussion. They are (a) thrill-seeking; (b) cowardly; (c) trusting; (d) courageous; (e) stupid.

C. **Inferences**

On the basis of the evidence in the passage, mark these statements as follows: PA for inferences that are probably accurate; PI for inferences that are probably inaccurate; and IE for insufficient evidence.

_____ 1. *Fugu* is another word for puffer fish.

_____ 2. The puffer fish is poisonous only when it is served raw as sashimi.

_____ 3. The danger in eating puffer fish results from the possibility that the chef may leave in a lethal dose of poison.

_____ 4. Connoisseurs who order *chiri* are referred to in the passage as "ultimate connoisseurs" because they are getting a double dose of poison.

_____ 5. Eating puffer fish should be made illegal.

_____ 6. Ackerman has sampled puffer fish.

Practice Essay

Guns

Larry Woiwode

Larry Woiwode, a writer of fiction and essays, was born in Carrington, North Dakota, in 1941. He is a graduate of the University of Illinois, and has been a writer-in-residence at the University of Wisconsin, as well as a Guggenheim fellow. His first novel, What I'm Going to Do, I Think, *won the William Faulkner Award for Best First Novel. He is also the author of a second novel,* Beyond the Bedroom Wall, *and a frequent contributor to* The New Yorker, *the* Atlantic Monthly, Esquire, McCall's, Mademoiselle, Partisan Review, *and other national magazines. This essay first appeared in* Esquire.

1   Once in the middle of a Wisconsin winter I shot a deer, my only one, while my wife and daughter watched. It had been hit by a delivery truck along a country road a few miles from where we lived and one of its rear legs was torn off at the hock; a shattered shin and hoof lay steaming in the red-beaded snow. The driver of the truck and I stood and watched as it tried to leap a fence, kicked a while at the top wire it was entangled in, flailing the area with fresh ropes of blood, and then went hobbling across a pasture toward a wooded hill. Placid cows followed it with a curious awe. "Do you have a rifle with you?" the driver asked. "No, not with me. At home." He looked once more at the deer, then got in his truck and drove off.

2   I went back to our Jeep where my wife and daughter were waiting, pale and withdrawn, and told them what I was about to do, and suggested that they'd better stay at home. No, they wanted to be with me, they said; they wanted to watch. My daughter was three and a half at the time. I got my rifle, a .22, a foolishly puny weapon to use on a deer but the only one I had, and we came back and saw that the deer was lying in some low brush near the base of the hill; no need to trail its blatant spoor. When I got about a hundred yards off, marveling at how it could have made it so far in its condition through snow that came over my boot tops, the deer tried to push itself up with its front legs, then collapsed. I aimed at the center of its skull, thinking, *This will be the quickest,* and heard the bullet ricochet off and go singing through the woods.

3   The deer was on its feet, shaking its head as though stung, and I fired again at the same spot, quickly, and apparently missed. It was now moving at its fastest hobble up the hill, broadside to me, and I took my time to sight a heart shot. Before the report even registered in my mind, the deer went down in an explosion of snow and lay struggling there, spouting blood from its stump and a chest wound. I was shaking by now. Deer are color-blind as far as science can say, and as I went toward its quieting body to deliver the coup de grace, I realized I was being seen in black and white, and then the deer's eye seemed to home in on me, and I was struck with the understanding that I was its vision of approaching death. And then I seemed to enter its realm through its eye and saw the countryside and myself in shades of white and gray. *But I see the deer in color,* I thought.

4   A few yards away, I aimed at its head once more, and there was the crack of a shot, the next-to-last round left in the magazine. The deer's head came up, and I could see its eye clearly now, dark, placid, filled with an appeal, it seemed, and then felt the surge of black and white surround and subsume me again. The second shot, or one of them, had pierced its neck; a gray-blue tongue hung out over its jaw; urine was trickling from below its tail; a doe. I held the rifle barrel inches from its forehead, conscious of my wife's and daughter's eyes on me from behind, and as I fired off the final and fatal shot, felt myself drawn by them back into my multicolored, many-faceted world again.

A. Comprehension

Choose the answer that best completes each statement. Do not refer to the selection while doing this exercise.

1. The deer that is the subject of this selection had been (a) attacked by a mountain lion; (b) run over accidentally by the author's car; (c) shot and left for dead by a hunter; (d) hit by a truck.

2. After being hurt, the deer (a) tried to attack those who had hurt her; (b) tried to escape; (c) fell over and appeared to be dead; (d) lay quivering as if in terrible pain.

3. The author's wife and daughter (a) went off to get help; (b) went home to get a rifle; (c) attempted to help Woiwode with the deer; (d) decided to stay and watch.

4. When Woiwode first fired at the deer, (a) the first shot hit her, and she died peacefully; (b) he aimed at her head, but somehow missed; (c) he fired wildly and completely missed her; (d) the gun misfired.

5. Apparently deer (a) are blind during the daytime; (b) are blind at night; (c) see only in black and white; (d) see only in color.

B. Inferences

On the basis of the evidence in the passage, mark these statements as follows: PA for inferences that are probably accurate; PI for inferences that are probably inaccurate; and IE for insufficient evidence.

_____ 1. Woiwode had extensive experience with firearms and felt comfortable being around them.

_____ 2. The truck driver who had struck the deer left probably because he did not want to get involved.

_____ 3. Woiwode's wife and daughter wanted to stay and watch Woiwode out of morbid curiosity.

_____ 4. The first shot Woiwode aimed at the deer missed because the gun he used was too small.

_____ 5. Woiwode remained impassive and emotionally distant during this incident.

_____ 6. After this experience, the author decided never to use a firearm again.

C. Structure

Choose the best answer.

1. The primary mode of discourse, or type of writing, this selection represents is (a) narration; (b) description; (c) exposition; (d) persuasion. Justify your answer.

_____

2. Apart from the mode of discourse, the passage suggests a secondary purpose, specifically (a) to criticize Americans' fascination with guns and violence; (b) to show the author's discomfort in the face of an animal's suffering; (c) to justify the author's killing the deer; (d) to describe the deer's suffering and death.

3. Throughout the passage, particularly when he shows us the deer he emphasizes (a) colors; (b) shapes; (c) sounds; (d) smells.

4. In paragraphs 3 and 4, Woiwode presents a contrast. What is being contrasted?

    _____

5. Look at the end of paragraph 3 again, in particular this sentence: "And then I seemed to enter its realm through its eye and saw the countryside and myself in shades of white and gray. *But I see the deer in color,* I thought." Explain in your own words what Woiwode means.

    _____

    _____

6. Consider again this sentence from paragraph 4: "The deer's head came up, and I could see its eye clearly now, dark, placid, filled with an appeal, it seemed, and then felt the surge of black and white surround and subsume me again." In the first part of this sentence, Woiwode's tone suggests that his attitude toward the deer is (a) indifferent; (b) greatly sympathetic; (c) bewildered; (d) impossible to discern.

7. In the second part of the same sentence, Woiwode strongly implies that (a) he felt the need to withdraw from the deer's suffering; (b) he was confused and ambivalent about what to do; (c) he was temporarily drawn into the deer's world and could look at her suffering from her point of view; (d) he was glad that the ordeal was finally over.

8. Woiwode's reaction to this incident is best described as one of (a) revulsion; (b) anxiety; (c) curiosity; (d) dismay.

D. Vocabulary

For each italicized word from the selection, choose the best definition according to the context in which it appears.

1. *flailing* the area [paragraph 1]: (a) covering; (b) striking; (c) soaking; (d) saturating.

2. *placid* cows followed [1 and 4]: (a) curious; (b) sleepy; (c) agitated; (d) undisturbed.

3. with a curious *awe* [1]: An overwhelming feeling of (a) fear and dread; (b) excitement; (c) curiosity; (d) happiness.

4. a foolishly *puny* weapon [2]: (a) outdated, obsolete; (b) of an inferior size; (c) rusty, corroded; (d) overly complicated, elaborate.

5. to trail its *blatant* spoor [2]: (a) glaring, notorious; (b) loud; (c) offensive to one's sense of smell; (d) overly obvious.

6. to trail its blatant *spoor* [2]: (a) trail, track; (b) origins; (c) hiding place; (d) final resting place.

7. to deliver the *coup de grace* [pronounced from French, küd ə gräs'] [3]: (a) decision; (b) finishing strike; (c) surprise attack; (d) overthrow.
8. then felt the surge surround and *subsume* me again [4]: (a) draw in; (b) overwhelm; (c) separate; (d) make aware.

E. Questions for Discussion and Analysis

1. Discuss your own experience with guns and your attitude toward them. Has this essay changed your thinking in any way?
2. Are you for or against the banning of privately owned weapons as a means of controlling the violence in our society?

6

Language

In this chapter, we will be concerned with language in prose writing—with words and the effect the writer intends them to have on you. Specifically, we will examine the denotation and connotation of words; the misuse and abuse of words; levels of language; allusions; and figurative language, in particular, metaphors and similes.

Denotation and Connotation

Good writers choose their words carefully to suggest certain ideas, feelings, or attitudes. Much of the pleasure in reading is the ability to savor the emotional associations of the words we read. Doing so can greatly improve your literal understanding and enhance your enjoyment of reading.

Word choice, or *diction,* involves both denotation and connotation. Some words are used to arouse positive feelings, some are meant to be neutral or literal, while others are meant to convey a negative impression. *Denotation* refers to a word's explicit, or literal, meaning. Sometimes denotation is called the dictionary definition of a word. Denotatively, the word *lemon,* for example, refers to a yellow-skinned sour citrus fruit. In the sentence, "The lemon tree produced a good crop this year," the speaker or writer is using *lemon* denotatively; no judgment is implied. However, in the sentence, "Gary's new car turned out to be a lemon; every conceivable mechanical thing has gone wrong with it since he bought it," *lemon* has a decidedly unfavorable meaning. The

dictionary bears this out, giving as an informal meaning of *lemon,* something that proves "unsatisfactory or defective."

This latter negative association is the function of the word's connotation in the context. *Connotation* refers to the cluster of suggestions, emotional responses, or implications—whether positive or negative—that a word carries with it. The connotation extends the meaning beyond its literal or explicit meaning (its denotation).

Richard Altick, author of *Preface to Critical Reading,* has written: "Nothing is more essential to intelligent, profitable reading than sensitivity to connotation." However, no one can teach you this sensitivity. It comes from a wide exposure to reading and a willingness to consult dictionary definitions and the accompanying usage notes for help. This sensitivity may take years to develop.

To begin, consider the verb *walk.* It is purely neutral, denoting a forward movement by taking steps. But what of these related verbs: *stride, saunter, stroll, meander, glide, mince, lumber, plod, trudge, stagger, lurch, stomp,* and *march?*

Here are the connotations of these verbs.

Stride: Suggests walking purposefully or resolutely.

Saunter and *stroll:* Both terms suggest walking in a leisurely, unhurried way.

Meander: Suggests walking in no particular direction, wandering here and there with no fixed destination.

Glide: Suggests walking in an elegant, graceful manner.

Mince: Carries a negative connotation, suggesting walking in little steps with exaggerated affectation or primness.

Lumber: Suggests walking with heavy clumsiness. It is a word often reserved for describing the movement of large, bulky animals like bears.

Plod and *trudge:* Both terms suggest walking in a heavy or laborious way. *Trudge* can also suggest discouragement or defeat.

Stagger and *lurch:* Both words suggest walking in an unsteady manner, whether because of illness, drunkenness, or some other affliction. *Stagger* is stronger than *lurch.*

Stomp: Suggests walking with purposely heavy steps, typically in anger.

March: Used in a military sense, this word refers to a formal way of walking in a regiment. Used in an ordinary or civilian sense, the word may suggest walking purposefully or steadily.

Now consider these pairs of words. If the word carries a positive connotation, mark it with a plus sign; if its connotation is negative, label it with a minus sign. Consult a dictionary if necessary.

secret	underhanded
plump	obese
macho	masculine/manly
binge	spree
pro-life	anti-abortion
nude	naked
childlike	childish
purebred	cur
devious	evasive
motionless	passive
energetic	frenetic
frantic	concerned
swamp	wetland

To see how connotation works in prose passages, consider these two excerpts on the same topic, one by the American novelist John Steinbeck, the other by Ray Allen Billington, an American historian. Both passages are concerned with the westward migration following the 1849 Gold Rush, but you will immediately see that the authors' word choice is radically different, reflecting their radically different points of view.

The railroads brought new hordes of land-crazy people, and the new Americans moved like locusts across the continent until the western sea put a boundary to their movements. Coal and copper and gold drew them on; they savaged the land, gold-dredged the rivers to skeletons of pebbles and debris. An aroused and fearful government made laws for the distribution of public lands—a quarter section, one hundred and sixty acres, per person—and a claim had to be proved and improved; but there were ways of getting around this, and legally. My own grandfather proved out a quarter section for himself, one for his wife, one for each of his children, and, I suspect, acreage for children he hoped and expected to have. Marginal lands, of course, suitable only for grazing, went in larger pieces. One of the largest landholding families in California took its richest holdings by a trick: By law a man could take up all the swamp or water-covered land he wanted. The founder of this great holding mounted a scow on wheels and drove his horses over thousands of acres of the best bottom land, then reported that he had explored it in a boat, which was true, and confirmed his title. I need not mention his name: his descendants will remember.

John Steinbeck, *America and Americans*

[1]Opportunity was the magnet that drew men westward during those three centuries, for nature's untapped riches promised pioneers the fortunes that

fate had denied them in older societies. There, where a king's ransom in furs could be had for the taking, where lush grasslands beckoned the herdsman, where fortunes in gold and silver lay scarcely hidden, where virgin soils awaited only the magic touch of man to yield their wealth, men and women could begin life anew with only their brains and brawn and courage to sustain them. There they could realize the social equality that was the goal of every democratically inclined American. These were the lures that drew the frontiersmen ever westward toward the Pacific.

[2]They moved in an orderly procession. The fur trappers came first, roaming far in advance of the settled areas as they gathered the bales of shiny beaver peltry that would gladden the hearts of Europe's elite. Then came the miners, who also left civilization far behind as they prospected mountain streams and desert wastes in their endless quest for gold or silver. Behind them were the cattlemen, seeking the grassy pastures where their herds could graze without the confinement of fences. Cowboys were a familiar sight on the frontiers of Virginia or Kentucky or Illinois long before they won their places in the sun and cinema on the High Plains of the Far West. These shock troops of civilization made little impression on the wilderness; instead they adapted themselves so completely to the forest environment that they altered the face of the country but slightly.

Ray Allen Billington, "The Frontier Disappears," *The American Story*

Even though each author has a different perspective on the westward migration—Billington takes the broader view, while Steinbeck establishes the background to lead into his grandfather's clever way of evading the homestead law—the difference in connotative words is striking. Billington clearly admires the westward march. To see this for yourself, underline the words in his passage that convey a positive impression. Even his characterization of cowboys as the "shock troops of civilization," which initially sounds negative, turns out to be positive, since he says that their effect on the environment was minimal. Compare this laudatory view with Steinbeck's, whose first two sentences sound extremely negative, almost stridently so.

Lewis Thomas, a noted scientific and medical writer, in this next passage criticizes our destruction of the environment. Study the passage, paying particular attention to his word choice. After you read the passage, try to determine (1) what he is criticizing, and (2) whether his word choice is effective in expressing that criticism.

Human beings have never before had such a bad press. By all reports, we are unable to get anything right these days, and there seems to be almost nothing good to say for ourselves. In just the past century we have increased our population threefold and will double it before the next has run out. We have swarmed over the open face of the earth, occupied every

available acre of livable space, displaced numberless other creatures from their accustomed niches, caused one extinction after another—with more to come—and polluted all our waterways and even parts of the oceans. Now, in our efforts to make energy and keep warm, we appear to be witlessly altering the earth's climate by inserting too much carbon dioxide into the atmosphere; if we do not pull up short, we will produce a new greenhouse around the planet, melting the Antarctic ice shelf and swamping all coastlines.

Lewis Thomas, "Man's Role on Earth," The New York Times

Thomas is concerned about humans' destruction of the environment, but his criticism is muted. His words seem to be chosen for their simple denotative effect, reflecting an almost restrained, gentle manner. There are exceptions, however—specifically "swarmed" and "displaced," which both have negative connotations.

Besides nonfiction prose, you will also encounter connotative words in literature. Writers may use descriptive details that suggest a particular emotional response to their characters. These details help you both to visualize the character and to assess his or her behavior, motivation, and actions. In this paragraph from *David Copperfield,* Charles Dickens introduces the reader to a highly objectionable character named Miss Murdstone. Notice that his description uses several words associated with metal, so that their connotative effect, when taken together, is of a highly unpleasant and inflexible character.

It was Miss Murdstone who was arrived, and a gloomy-looking lady she was: dark, like her brother, whom she greatly resembled in face and voice, and with very heavy eyebrows, nearly meeting over her large nose, as if, being disabled by the wrongs of her sex from wearing whiskers, she had carried them to that account. She brought with her two uncompromising hard black boxes, with her initials on the lids in hard brass nails. When she paid the coachman she took her money out of a hard steel purse, and she kept the purse in a very jail of a bag which hung upon her arm by a heavy chain, and shut up like a bite. I had never, at that time, seen such a metallic lady altogether as Miss Murdstone was.

Charles Dickens, David Copperfield

Language Misused and Abused

A writer can use language unscrupulously to manipulate the reader, to incite or inflame passions, or to soften the impact of ideas that might otherwise be more realistically or harshly interpreted. As a critical read-

er, you should be particularly alert to language that attempts to manip-ulate you not through careful, reasoned thought, but through appeals to your emotions or through the clever misuse of words. We call this kind of verbal manipulation *slanted language*. In this section, we will look briefly at some ways language can be misused and abused: weasel words, euphemisms, sneer words, doublespeak, jargon, and clichés.

Weasel Words

In a clever chapter titled "Weasel Words" on the advertising industry in his book *I Can Sell You Anything,* Carl Wrighter defines *weasel words* like this:

> A weasel word is "a word used in order to evade or retreat from a direct or forthright statement or position" (Webster). In other words, if we can't say it, we'll weasel it. And, in fact, a weasel word has become more than just an evasion or retreat. We've trained our weasels. They can do anything. They can make you hear things that aren't being said, accept as truths things that have only been implied, and believe things that have only been suggested. Come to think of it, not only do we have our weasels trained, but they, in turn, have got you trained. When *you* hear a weasel word, you automatically hear the implication. Not the real meaning, but the meaning *it* wants *you* to hear.

Here are a few excerpts from Wrighter's classification of weasel words:

Words That Mean Things They Really Don't Mean

"HELP"
That's it. "Help." It means "aid" or "assist." Nothing more. Yet, "help" is the one single word which, in all the annals of advertising, has done the most to say something that couldn't be said. Because "help" is the great qualifier; once you say it, you can say almost anything after it. In short, "help" has helped us the most.

Helps keep you young
Helps prevent cavities
Helps keep your house germ-free

"LIKE"
Coming in second, but only losing out by a nose, is the word "like," used in comparison. Watch:

It's like getting one bar free
Cleans like a white tornado
It's like taking a trip to Portugal

Okay. "Like" is a qualifier, and is used in much the same way as "help." But "like" is also a comparative element, with a very specific purpose; we use "like" to get you to stop thinking about the product per se, and to get you thinking about something that is bigger or better or different from the product we're selling. In other words, we can make you believe that the product is more than it is by likening it to something else.

"VIRTUAL" OR "VIRTUALLY"

How many times have you responded to an ad that said:

> Virtually trouble-free . . .
> Virtually foolproof . . .
> Virtually never needs service . . .

Ever remember what "virtual" means? It means "in essence or effect, but not in fact." Important—"but not in fact." Yet today the word "virtually" is interpreted by you as meaning "almost or just about the same as . . ." Well, gang, it just isn't true. "Not," in fact, means not, in fact. I was scanning, rather longingly I must confess, through the brochure Chevrolet publishes for its Corvette, and I came to this phrase: "The seats in the . . . Corvette are virtually handmade." They had me, for a minute. I almost took the bait of that lovely little weasel. I almost decided that those seats were just about completely handmade. And then I remembered. Those seats were not, *in fact,* handmade. Remember, "virtually" means "not, in fact," or you will, in fact, get sold down the river.

"ACTS" OR "WORKS"

These two action words are rarely used alone, and are generally accompanied by "like." They need help to work, mostly because they are verbs, but their implied meaning is deadly, nonetheless. Here are the key phrases:

> Acts like . . .
> Acts against . . .
> Works like . . .
> Works against . . .
> Works to prevent (or help prevent) . . .

You see what happens? "Acts" or "works" brings an action to the product that might not otherwise be there. When we say that a certain cough syrup "acts on the cough control center," the implication is that the syrup goes to this mysterious organ and immediately makes it bet-

ter. But the implication here far exceeds what the truthful promise should be. An act is simply a deed. So the claim "acts on" simply means it performs a deed on. What that deed is, we may never know.

Words That Have No Specific Meaning

"THE LOOK OF" OR "LOOKS LIKE"

"Look" is the same as "feel," our subjective opinion. Did you ever walk into a Woolworth's and see those $29.95 masterpieces hanging in their "Art Gallery"? "The look of a real oil painting," it will say. "But it isn't," you will now reply. And probably be $29.95 richer for it.

If you have kids, then you have all kinds of breakfast cereals in the house. When I was a kid, it was Rice Krispies, the breakfast cereal that went snap, crackle, and pop. (One hell of a claim for a product that is supposed to offer nutritional benefits.) Or Wheaties, the breakfast of champions, whatever that means. Nowadays, we're forced to a confrontation with Quisp, Quake, Lucky Stars, Cocoa-Puffs, Clunkers, Blooies, Snarkles and Razzmatazz. And they all have one thing in common: they're all "fortified." Some are simply "fortified with vitamins," while others are specifically "fortified with vitamin D," or some other letter. But what does it all mean?

"Fortified" means "added on to." But "fortified," like so many other weasel words of indefinite meaning, simply doesn't tell us enough. If, for instance, a cereal were to contain one unit of vitamin D, and the manufacturers added some chemical which would produce two units of vitamin D, they could then claim that the cereal was "fortified with twice as much vitamin D." So what? It would still be about as nutritional as sawdust.

Summary

A weasel word is a word that's used to imply a meaning that cannot be truthfully stated. Some weasels imply meanings that are not the same as their actual definition, such as "help," "like," or "fortified." They can act as qualifiers and/or comparatives. Other weasels, such as "taste" and "flavor," have no definite meanings, and are simply subjective opinions offered by the manufacturer. A weasel of omission is one that implies a claim so strongly that it forces you to supply the bogus fact. Adjectives are weasels used to convey feelings and emotions to a greater extent than the product itself can.

In dealing with weasels, you must strip away the innuendos and try to ascertain the facts, if any. To do this, you need to ask questions such as: How? Why? How many? How much? Stick to basic definitions of words. Look them up if you have to. Then, apply the strict definition to the text of the advertisement or commercial. "Like" means similar to, but not the same as. "Virtually" means the same in essence, but not in fact.

Above all, never underestimate the devious qualities of a weasel. Weasels twist and turn and hide in dark shadows. You must come to grips with them, or advertising will rule you forever.

My advice to you is: Beware of weasels. They are nasty and untrainable, and they attack pocketbooks.

Carl Wrighter, *I Can Sell You Anything*

Euphemisms

A *euphemism* is a supposedly inoffensive word or phrase substituted for an offensive one. Writers use euphemisms to make less harsh our perception of unpleasant events, to change our beliefs, even to cover up wrongdoing. Because euphemisms are so pervasive in our culture, this section contains several examples so that you can learn to spot them readily and to recognize the intent behind them.

During World War II, Japanese-Americans living on the West Coast were forced to move to what the government called "relocation centers." However, the Nazis in Germany and the Soviets imprisoned Jews and other undesirables in "concentration camps," a term of disparagement used by the Allies. "Relocation centers" sounded less sinister than "concentration camps."

During the Vietnam era, euphemisms were widely used in government and military reports about the American presence in Southeast Asia. The 1970 American invasion of Cambodia was described in more positive terms as an "incursion." Bombs were known as "antipersonnel weapons." Herbicides (used to kill the foliage so that North Vietnamese troop movements would be more visible from the air) were called "defoliants." The war itself (which in fact was never declared by Congress and which, ironically, accounted for more dead than any other war America has been involved in) was referred to as a "conflict."

Some euphemisms are more amusing than troubling. For example, a used car lot in New York has gone one step beyond calling its cars "pre-owned." They are now called "pre-enjoyed" cars. A *Jeopardy!* contestant whose occupation is being a bookie called himself a "turf information specialist." A California community college renamed its physical education department the "Department of Human Performance." A school district, charged with distributing condoms to its high school students, referred in the accompanying instructions to sexual intercourse as "penile insertive behavior."

These euphemisms seem harmless, even rather silly, but there is no doubt that euphemisms can color our perception of reality. As an illustration, consider these alternative examples to the so-called buzzwords that tour guides at Sea World in Orlando, Florida, must learn. They are reprinted from the park's training manual, excerpts of which appeared in the November 24, 1991, issue of *Florida,* the Sunday magazine of the *Orlando Sentinel* and were subsequently reprinted in *Harper's.*

Certain words and phrases have negative connotations. At Sea World, we call these "buzzwords." Avoid buzzwords and use more positive words— you'll give guests a better overall impression.

Buzzword	*Alternative*
sick	ill
hurt	injured
captured	acquired
cage	enclosure
tank	aquarium
captivity	controlled environment
wild	natural environment
tricks	behavior
sex	courtship behavior

Other Words to Avoid

dead, die	If people ask you about a particular animal that you know has passed away, please say "I don't know."
kill	This word sounds very negative. Say "eat" or "prey upon."
play, talk, enjoy	Anthropomorphic; they give human traits to animals.
evolve	Because evolution is a controversial theory, use the word "adapt."

"Chickens of the Sea," *Harper's*

Nevertheless, not all euphemisms are bad. They may be used deliberately to change our thinking in a relatively harmless way. For example, a federal agency is currently trying to promote increased consumption of fish to improve Americans' diet. But because fish is so expensive, the government has tried to induce Americans to eat less expensive varieties. The problem is that these fish often have unappetizing names, like croaker, ratfish, gruntfish, hagfish, dogfish, or stump knockers. After all, who wants to look at a piece of hagfish on a dinner plate? So the agency is preparing a list of substitute names—in other words, euphemisms—to make these fish sound more appealing to consumers.

Sneer Words

As we saw in the section on euphemisms, a writer can shape our perception of events, making things seem less bad than they actually are. Similarly, a writer can intensify an already bad situation by using *sneer words,* words with strong negative connotations suggesting derision and scorn. When a foreign political leader is out of favor with the American government, he is routinely described by administration sources as a "strongman." This is the way Manual Noriega of Panama and Slobodan Milosevic of Serbia have routinely been characterized in the American media. Oddly, Saddam Hussein of Iraq is generally accorded more respect, being called "president" or "leader," even though his stronghold

on Iraq is every bit as ruthless as Noriega's and Milosevic's control over their countries has been. The sneer word "strongman" suggests something far more negative than would the more neutral terms "leader" or "president." Here are some other common sneer words:

Lackey: Not only means "servant" but also suggests a fawning, servile follower who does anything the master dictates.

Hack: Refers to a writer who writes only for money.

Do-gooder: Denotes someone who naively or unrealistically tries to make the world a better place.

Zealot (as in religious zealot, pro-life zealot): Suggests a fanatic, someone who will stop at nothing to promote his or her ideas.

Self-styled, self-proclaimed, purported (e.g., self-styled leader, self-proclaimed expert, purported authority): Like "so-called," these three terms suggest that the status or reputation of the people being described is not deserved and has only been conferred by the people themselves.

Doublespeak

Some of the examples of euphemisms we saw earlier are merely humorous, others are ridiculous, but some are truly pernicious and devious, constituting what is sometimes called *doublespeak*. This term was coined from the two words "doublethink" and "newspeak," words that George Orwell used in his novel *1984* to describe a future in which the government twists words to manipulate its citizens' thoughts.

William D. Lutz, a member of Rutgers University's English department, edits the *Quarterly Review of Doublespeak*, a periodical dedicated to publishing especially egregious examples of doublespeak. In the introduction to his book *Doublespeak*, Lutz compares it to "an infection that sickens the language through the pollution of words carefully chosen." Lutz further defines this "pollution of words" as follows.

Doublespeak is language that makes the bad seem good, the negative appear positive, the unpleasant appear attractive or at least tolerable. Doublespeak is language that avoids or shifts responsibility, language that is at variance with its real or purported meaning. It is language that conceals or prevents thought; rather than extending thought, doublespeak limits it.

Each year the review gives awards for conspicuous examples of language that is "grossly deceptive, evasive, euphemistic, confusing or self-contradictory," with the potential for "pernicious social or political consequences." (Lynn Ludlow, "Doublespeak Grows More Common, Says Man Who Collects It," *San Francisco Examiner*, November 20, 1988.) In this sense, then, doublespeak is potentially far more harmful than are euphemisms.

Here is a sampler of items that Lutz has published in various issues of the *Quarterly Review of Doublespeak:*

Predawn vertical insertion: A White House term, used during the Bush Administration, to refer to the invasion of Grenada by parachutists

Wood interdental stimulator: A Pentagon euphemism for a toothpick

High-velocity, multipurpose air circulator: An electric fan

Monitored retrievable storage site: A nuclear fuel dump

Contained depression: An economic recession

Unique retail biosphere: A farmer's market

Wastewater conveyance facility: A sewage plant

Wet disposition: Acid rain

Mental activity at the margins: Insanity

Uncontrolled contact with the ground: A safety expert's term for an airplane crash

Avoidance of collateral damage: A military term for trying not to kill enemy civilians

Ordinance: A military term for a bomb or bombs

Grain-consuming animal units: An agricultural spokesman's term for pigs and cows

Vertical-transportation corps member: An elevator operator

Nutritional avoidance therapy: A diet

Therapeutic misadventure or *diagnostic malpractice of a high magnitude:* The medical profession's terms for medical incompetence that result in a patient's death

Ground-mounted confirmatory route markers: Road signs

A different version of the facts or *reality augmentation:* Lying

Payroll adjustments, permanent downsizing, releasing resources, repositioning: The business world's terms for laying off staff

Unfortunately, doublespeak is not confined to the United States. Here are some examples from other nations:

Ethnic cleansing: The Serbian government's term for forcibly removing and massacring Serbia's Muslim population—in other words, genocide

Foreign guests: What Iraqi president Saddam Hussein called hostages held prisoner by his government

Administrative control: A new term for censorship, according to the Cameroon government

Acquiescent nonvolunteers: The phrase used by British and Hong Kong officials for Vietnamese refugees forcibly returned to Vietnam

Decommissioned aggressor quantum: A bizarre British military term for dead enemy soldiers

Irregular activities: The South African government's term for political assassinations

Politically Correct Language

During the 1980s, the concept of "political correctness" (PC) emerged. Briefly, this doctrine holds that our everyday language is filled with expressions and words that offend or alienate certain groups or call into question their differences. Thus a whole new vocabulary of *politically correct language* has been born. Many of these terms are considered

jokes, but many of them have been adopted by oversensitive people who dare not risk offending anyone or do not want to be offended themselves.

Thus it is no longer acceptable to call someone "blind." He or she should be called "visually challenged." Short people are "vertically challenged," and the disabled, formerly described by the euphemism "handicapped" are sometimes referred to as "physically challenged." Animal rights activists, concerned over man's exploitation of animals, now advocate the term "companion animals" rather than the more negative "pets." As you can see, these PC terms straddle the line between euphemism and doublespeak.

A complete guide to PC terms can be found in the often hilarious book *The Official Politically Correct Dictionary and Handbook* compiled by Henry Beard and Christopher Cerf. Here are some short excerpts:

> *Nontraditional shopper:* Looter, shoplifter
>
> *Stolen products:* Products, such as eggs, milk, cheese, honey, and wool, taken from nonhuman animals by human ones. The use of such items, even when they are obtained in a "humane" manner, is increasingly regarded as an unconscionable violation of nonhuman animal rights. Example: *The politically correct nutritionist outlined the four basic food groups.* 1. **Stolen products.** 2. *Brutally betrayed botanical companions.* 3. *Hapless victims of speciesist slaughter.* 4. *Fortuitarian comestibles.*
>
> *Part white:* The only correct label for describing individuals once commonly referred to as "part black," "part Native American," "part Asian," etc. These obsolete phrases are inappropriate because they assume that white is the standard.
>
> *Melanin impoverished:* White. The term was inspired by Professor Leonard Jeffries of the City College of New York, who has written that "white folks are deficient in melanin," and thus are "less biologically proficient" than blacks. Example: *Todd's favorite politically correct fairy tale was "Snow* **Melanin-Impoverished** *and the Seven Vertically Challenged Individuals.**

*Henry Beard and Christopher Cerf, *The Official Politically Correct Dictionary and Handbook* (New York: Villard Books, 1992).

Jargon

Jargon refers to the specialized language used by members of a particular trade, group, or profession. Although not technically in the same category as slanted language, jargon—like doublespeak, weasel words, and the like—can be used to deceive. The use of jargon can make the writer or speaker sound more intelligent or learned than if he or she used ordinary discourse. In and of itself, jargon is not necessarily harmful, at least not in the same way as the other kinds of slanted language we have examined are. It is certainly natural and probably necessary for specialists in a field to have their own special terminology that outsiders might not understand.

For example, while most of us associate the word *holiday* with a day at the beach or simply a day when we can sleep late, to a house painter, a holiday means a spot on the wall that his brush has missed. Similarly, the terms *widows* and *orphans* mean something quite different to stockbrokers and book designers than they do to ordinary citizens. To a stockbroker, a "widows and orphans" stock is one that involves absolutely no risk—i.e., it is even safe enough for widows and orphans, people who cannot afford to risk a penny of their money. However, to a book designer or desktop publisher, a "widow" refers to a short line of type—the last line of a paragraph that is printed all by itself at the top of a page, for example—while an "orphan" refers to the first line of a new paragraph when it appears on the last line of a page. (Because widows and orphans, in this context, are unattractive, book designers and layout artists try to avoid them.)

These are inoffensive uses of jargon that the reader could probably figure out from the context. At its best, jargon is useful, providing a verbal shorthand among people who are fluent in the terminology and the subject. At its worst, however, jargon is pretentious, obscure, and often nearly impossible to comprehend.

A professor at Rutgers University, Ross Baker, has written a parody of the first line of the Declaration of Independence, using computerese (jargon from the computer field) and jargon from the communications field.

> When at a given point in time in the human-events cycle, the phase-out of political relationships is mandated, a clear signal needs to be communicated to the world as to why we are putting independence on-line.
>
> Quoted in Donald Hall, "A Fear of Metaphors,"
> *New York Times Magazine*, July 14, 1985

Ross Baker's parody is meant to make us chuckle, but the jargon rampant in the real world is used in complete seriousness, especially (and unfortunately) among college instructors, who, probably because of the "publish-or-perish" atmosphere, are compelled to make their mark in the academic world by delivering high-flown papers at meetings and writing articles and books in their fields. What follows are some titles chosen at random from the schedule of workshops and presentations at the Sixteenth Annual Boston University Conference on Language Development, held in October 1991.*

"Degree-O" Learnability, Morphology, and Binding Domains
Principle B and Contrastive Stress

---

*I am indebted to Gerry Coletti, late of the English Department at City College of San Francisco, for the list of talks delivered at this conference.

Quantification over Events in Early Universal Quantification

Universal Properties in the L2 Acquisition of Wh-Questions: A Comparison of Learners from Movement and Non-Movement L1 Backgrounds

Lexical Biases in Dynamic and Static Locative Expressions

Automatic Syntactic Analysis of Longitudinal L2 Production Data

An Empirical Investigation of the Information Sources for Language Acquisition: Cross-Situational vs. Cross-Syntactic Observation

The Role of Sublexical Phonological Structure in Developmental Dysgraphia: Evidence from Case Reports and a Group Study

Acquisition of Language-Specific Prosodic Features: Evidence from Syllable Amplitude Patterns in the Reduplicative Babbling of French- and English-Learning Infants

The problem with these topics is that their meaning is impenetrable and hard to unravel. When you encounter jargon in your reading, especially in your textbooks, here are two suggestions: (1) consult the text's glossary if one is provided and (2) discuss the author's style with your instructor. Ask him or her to explain the meaning of obscure terms.

Clichés

Clichés—fossilized, stale, overused expressions—tell the careful reader that a lazy writer is at work. Good writers avoid clichés because such expressions are tired, having lost their effectiveness long ago. Some clichés do not even make any sense. For example, "Her complexion is like peaches and cream." (Why would anyone want orange and white skin?) Some clichés probably made sense at one time but now, at the end of the twentieth century, sound like nonsense. Yet we still hear people using such phrases as "having an ax to grind," "grist for the mill," or "fight tooth and nail."

For fun, you might begin your own list of clichés to add to this one.

pretty as a picture	an agonizing defeat
dead as a doornail	snatch victory from the jaws of
chip off the old block	defeat
like water off a duck's back	at death's door
no skin off my teeth	labor of love
by the skin of the teeth	leave no stone unturned
work like a dog	proud as a peacock
as right as rain	rich as Croesus
bolt from the blue	a nose for news
hale and hearty	out of harm's way
healthy as a horse	

Figurative Language

Finally, we come to the most difficult, yet the most inventive and interesting use of language: *figures of speech* or *figurative language,* which refers to the use of language not in its literal sense, but in a metaphorical or imaginative way. Although you may associate figures of speech primarily with poetry, prose writers also use them to give immediacy or drama to their writing or to create a striking visual image that the reader can "see." A pleasing figure of speech can give the reader an entirely new perspective on an otherwise commonplace idea.

The two most common figures of speech are metaphors and similes. Both are characterized by imaginative comparisons between two essentially unlike things. A *metaphor* refers to a *direct* comparison in which a particular quality or characteristic of one thing (the figurative) is transferred to another (the literal). Such transfer of meaning does not make literal sense, but the reader knows to interpret it as an imaginative comparison.

For example, consider this sentence: "The farmer's leathery, lined face revealed years of toil in the sun." The writer is directly comparing the farmer's skin to leather, suggesting that the man's skin is browned, thick, and tough—the characteristics of leather.

A *simile* is an imaginative comparison stated indirectly with the words "like," "as," "as though," "as if," "seem." For example, if we change the metaphor above to a simile, it would be stated like this: "The farmer's lined face looked like leather, revealing years of toil in the sun." It is probably fair to say that metaphors are stronger than similes, only because the comparison is more direct.

Let us look at two more examples. In Bobbie Ann Mason's short story, "Shiloh," (reprinted in Part V), the main character, Leroy, has returned to live with his wife in the small rural town in western Kentucky where he grew up. Commenting on the residential development that has taken place during his absence, Mason writes, "[Leroy] notices how much the town has changed. Subdivisions are spreading across western Kentucky like an oil slick."

To analyze any figure of speech, you first must know what is being compared to what. Mason is comparing residential sprawl, specifically, new housing subdivisions, to an oil slick; he is *not* comparing an oil slick to a housing development. What does this simile mean? An oil slick is a kind of pollution, the result of oil's leaking from a tanker and covering a large area of ocean. Not only is it unattractive to look at, it also harms the natural environment and is difficult to control. These are the associations Mason intends you to have: housing subdivisions cover the landscape and form a kind of visual pollution in the same way that oil slicks pollute oceans and

kill sea life. The simile is effective because it makes us think and consider the effects of paving over farmland to build housing developments in a new way.

In another example, Paul Theroux, in his book, *To the Ends of the Earth,* describes a river in India, using a simile: "The river itself made no sound, though it moved powerfully, eddying like a swarm of greasy snakes in the ravine." The word *eddying* means moving against the main current. Theroux intends us to see how the water swirls around and moves in a circular fashion as a swarm of greasy snakes would. The visual picture is disturbing but powerful.

In both these cases the writers have directly stated the terms of the figurative language, but not all writers do this, and often the metaphorical part of the figure of speech or its characteristics must be inferred. Consider, for example, this newspaper headline from the 1992 presidential campaign: "CLINTON TO 'JUMP-START' THE ECONOMY." Here Clinton was metaphorically comparing the economy to a car with a dead battery—meaning that the economy was stalled and needed an emergency infusion of energy to get it going again.

Figures of speech can be effective with philosophical and abstract ideas, as well. In June 1992 the Supreme Court in *Planned Parenthood v. Casey* upheld certain provisions of a Pennsylvania state law restricting abortions, at the same time reaffirming American women's right to have abortions under *Roe v. Wade,* the original 1973 ruling. The vote in *Planned Parenthood v. Casey* was a narrow 5–4.

Justice Harry Blackman, author of *Roe v. Wade* and an abortion proponent, issued a separate opinion, recalling that in the past, four members of the court had called for overturning the abortion right. He wrote, "But now, just when so many expected the darkness to fall, the flame has grown bright." But he cautioned that the slim majority might not last: "I fear for the darkness as four justices anxiously await the single vote necessary to extinguish the light. I am 83 years old. I cannot stay on this court forever." What does the darkness represent? What is the light?

The similarity between metaphors and analogies has probably occurred to you. As you may recall from Chapter 4, an analogy begins with a metaphor, an imaginative comparison, but the analogy is *extended,* usually taking up a few sentences. The following passage clearly shows the process by which a metaphor becomes a full-fledged analogy. In this excerpt, Lowell Cohn, a sports columnist for the *San Francisco Chronicle,* contrasts the performance of two football teams—Stanford and the University of Washington—following their game in October 1992. Cohn begins with a metaphor and then extends it into an analogy. (Bill Walsh, the coach of the San Francisco 49ers who led them to three Super Bowl victories, returned to Stanford as head coach in 1992. In this game Stanford lost to the Huskies, 41–7.)

[1]The day before Stanford played Washington, I suggested that Cardinal coach Bill Walsh was about to find out what kind of car he's driving, with "car" being a metaphor for his team.

[2]We can say without hesitation that the wheels came off in the Washington game. By the end, Stanford resembled one of those abandoned vehicles by the side of the road with the wheels stripped and the windows smashed and the upholstery slashed.

[3]OK, we know Walsh had a serious crash in Husky Stadium, but we still haven't said what kind of car he's driving. It's definitely not a Porsche or a Ferrari. When Stanford played Texas A&M, Arizona and Washington, we discovered that the Cardinal is not fast and cannot handle speed in an opponent—in Stanford's case, speed kills.

[4]In a few years, after Walsh has been able to bring in his own recruits, he may be able to build a little Testarossa down on the Farm. But what's he got right now?

[5]Well, he's got two different cars, if you want to be precise—one on offense and another on defense. They're pretty good cars, but both have limitations.

[6]The Stanford offense is a big old Buick, vintage late '50s or early '60s. Those were nice cars, stable and comfortable on the highway. They were big and stylish and solid. But you couldn't zip around the hairpin turns of the Coast Highway; you couldn't cut in and out of traffic on the Bayshore.

[7]And that's the story of the Stanford offense. It's solid and stately and slow. It gets beaten off the ball by the really quick teams. It's a Buick.

Not Up to Speed

[8]What's the defense?

[9]A Honda Accord.

[10]The Honda Accord is a fabulous car for the money. It handles well and has some power, but it's no match for the top-of-the-line Mercedes or BMW or Lexus.

[11]Last Saturday, the Husky offense was a big fast Mercedes and the Stanford Accord was no match for it.

[12]Washington was saying, "We know what you're trying to do and we don't care." Then the Mercedes would drive right over the Accord.

[13]Looked at another way, the Washington-Stanford game defined echelons in college football for local fans. In the top echelon are Washington, Miami and Michigan. Most of the other teams fall into a middle ground. Stanford and Cal are in that territory—they're good teams which sometimes can rise to an occasion, and occasionally will fall below an occasion.

[14]Stanford has to make sure it doesn't fall too often. What happens in the final three games will determine whether this season is a success—leading to a bowl game, although not the Rose Bowl—or if this season turns into one of promise unfulfilled, of lasting regrets.

Lowell Cohn, "It's Time for Stanford to Shift Gears," *San Francisco Chronicle*

Exercises: Part 1— Analyzing Figurative Language

Here are some short passages containing figurative language for you to analyze. Using a separate sheet of paper, decide first whether the figure of speech is a metaphor or a simile. Then decide what is being compared to what. Finally, explain briefly the meaning of the figure of speech. (Note: Some of the examples may contain more than one figure of speech.)

1. Disappointment and fear stuck like fishbones in her throat. (Ruthanne Lum McCunn, *Thousand Pieces of Gold*)

2. . . . We watched some of the little brown forest skinks hunting among the roots of the trees around us. These little lizards always looked neat and shining, as though they had been cast in chocolate and had just that second stepped out of the mould, gleaming and immaculate. (Gerald Durrell, *A Zoo in My Luggage*)

3. It was noon, without a breath of wind, and the sky seemed like a blazing aluminum lid clamped over the world. (Philip Caputo, *A Rumor of War*)

4. The persistent cloud cover, the almost constant patter of rain, are narcotic. They seem to seal Seattle inside a damp, cozy cocoon, muffling reality and beckoning residents to snuggle up with a good book and a cup of coffee or a glass of wine. (Mary Bruno, "Seattle Under Siege," *Lear's*)

5. We have waited for more than 340 years for our constitutional and God-given rights. The nations of Asia and Africa are moving with jetlike speed toward gaining political independence, but we still creep at horse-and-buggy pace toward gaining a cup of coffee at a lunch counter. (Martin Luther King, Jr., "Letter from Birmingham Jail")

6. And then, abruptly, she woke up beside him in her own bed one early spring morning and knew she loathed him and couldn't wait to get him out of the house. She felt guilty, but guilty in the way one feels guilty when about to discommode some clinging slug that has managed to attach itself to one's arm or leg. (Gail Godwin, "Amanuensis," *Mr. Bedford and the Muses*)

7. The student's biggest problem was a slave mentality which had been built into him by years of carrot-and-whip grading, a mule mentality which said, "If you don't whip me, I won't work." He didn't get whipped. He

didn't work. And the cart of civilization, which he supposedly was being trained to pull, was just going to creak along a little slower without him. (Robert M. Pirsig, *Zen and the Art of Motorcycle Maintenance*)

8. . . . So few lies are solitary ones. It is easy, a wit observed, to tell a lie, but hard to tell only one. The first lie "must be thatched with another or it will rain through." More and more lies may come to be needed; the liar always has more mending to do. And the strains on him become greater each time—many have noted that it takes an excellent memory to keep one's untruths in good repair and disentangled. The sheer energy the liar has to devote to shoring them up is energy the honest man can dispose of freely. (Sissela Bok, *Lying: Moral Choice in Public and Private Life*)

9. The volume of blood had steadily increased, and now it spurted from the wound as if propelled by the beat of the pulse. The mat before the lieutenant was drenched red with spattered blood, and more blood overflowed onto it from pools which gathered in the folds of the lieutenant's khaki trousers. A spot, like a bird, came flying across to Reiko and settled on the lap of her white silk kimono. (Yukio Mishima, "Patriotism," *Death in Midsummer and Other Stories*)

10. He seemed to be made of reinforced concrete: he was enormous, with hair all over his body except on his head, a mustache like a housepainter's brush, a voice like a capstan, which would have been his alone, and an exquisite courtesy. (Gabriel Garcia Marquez, *Love in the Time of Cholera*)

11. Parker's wife was sitting on the front porch floor, snapping beans. Parker was sitting on the step, some distance away, watching her sullenly. She was plain, plain. The skin on her face was thin and drawn as tight as the skin on an onion and her eyes were grey and sharp like the points of two toothpicks. (Flannery O'Connor, "Parker's Back," *The Complete Stories of Flannery O'Connor*)

12. As I looked about me I felt that the grass was the country, as the water is the sea. The red of the grass made all the great prairie the color of winestains or of certain seaweeds when they are first washed up. And there was so much motion in it; the whole country seemed, somehow, to be running. (Willa Cather, *My Antonia*)

13. At a time when everyone's mind is on the explosions of the moment, it might seem obtuse of me to discuss the fourteenth century. But I think a backward look at that disordered, violent, bewildered, disintegrating, and calamity-prone age can be consoling and possibly instructive in a time of similar disarray. Reflected in a six-hundred-year-old mirror, a more revealing image of ourselves and our species might be seen than is visible in the clutter of circumstances under our noses. (Barbara Tuchman, *A Distant Mirror: The Calamitous 14th Century*)

14. There is no way to measure the absolute amount of biological diversity vanishing year by year in rain forests around the world, as opposed to percentage losses, even in groups as well known as the birds. Nevertheless, to give an idea of the dimension of the hemorrhaging, let me provide the most conservative estimate that can be reasonably based on our current knowledge of the extinction process. I will consider only species

being lost by reduction in forest area, taking the lowest z^* value permissible (0.15). I will not include overharvesting or invasion by alien organisms. I will assume a number of species living in the rain forests, 10 million (on the low side), and I will further suppose that many of the species enjoy wide geographical ranges. Even with these cautious parameters, selected in a biased manner to draw a maximally optimistic conclusion, the number of species doomed each year is 27,000. Each day it is 74, and each hour 3. (Edwin O. Wilson, *The Diversity of Life*)

15. Time is but the stream I go a-fishing in. I drink at it; but while I drink I see the sandy bottom and detect how shallow it is. Its thin current slides away, but eternity remains. (Henry Thoreau, "Where I Lived, and What I Lived For")

16. A long-limbed languorous type of showgirl blond lay at her ease in one of the chairs, with her feet raised on a padded rest and a tall misted glass at her elbow, near a silver ice bucket and a Scotch bottle. She looked at us lazily as we came over the grass. From thirty feet away she looked like a lot of class. From ten feet away; she looked like something made up to be seen from thirty feet away. Her mouth was too wide, her eyes were too blue, her makeup was too vivid, the thin arch of her eyebrows was almost fantastic in its curve and spread, and the mascara was so thick on her eyelashes that they looked like miniature iron railings.

    She wore white duck slacks, blue and white open-toed sandals over bare feet and crimson lake toenails, a white silk blouse and a necklace of green stones that were not square cut emeralds. Her hair was as artificial as a night club lobby. (Raymond Chandler, *The High Window*)

*The degree to which organisms are able to disperse to a new environment if their habitat is destroyed.

Exercises: Part 2

Selection 1

[1]N'da Ali[†] was the largest mountain in the vicinity. [2]It crouched at our backs, glowering over the landscape, the village, and our little hill. [3]From almost every vantage point you were aware of the mountain's mist-entangled, cloud-veiled shape brooding over everything, its heights guarded by sheer cliffs of gnarled granite so steep that no plant life could get a foothold. [4]Every day I had looked longingly at the summit, and every day I had watched N'da Ali in its many moods. [5]In the early morning it was a great mist-whitened monster; at noon it was all green and golden glitter of forest, its cliffs flushing pink in the sun; at night it was purple and shapeless, fading to black as the sun sank. [6]Sometimes it would go into hiding, drawing the white clouds around itself and brooding in their depths for two or three days at a time. [7]Every day I gazed at those great cliffs that guarded the way to the thick forest on its ridged

†A mountain in Cameroon, a country in West Africa

back, and each day I grew more determined that I would go up there and see
what it had to offer me.

Gerald Durrell, The Overloaded Ark

A.   Vocabulary

For each italicized word from the selection, choose the best definition according to the context in which it appears.

1. *glowering* [sentence 2]: (a) staring angrily; (b) guarding, protecting; (c) shimmering brightly; (d) towering, dominating.
2. *vantage point* [3]: (a) corner, nook; (b) position that provides a commanding view; (c) position that gives one superiority; (d) general vicinity.
3. *brooding* [3 and 6]: (a) protecting, keeping watch; (b) enveloping, enclosing; (c) hiding, obscuring; (d) sulking moodily.
4. *sheer* [3]: (a) transparent, clear; (b) undiluted, pure; (c) nearly perpendicular, steep; (d) rocky.
5. *gnarled* [3]: (a) difficult to walk on; (b) contorted, twisted; (c) smooth and shiny; (d) rugged, misshapen.
6. *gazed at* [7]: (a) looked intently at; (b) questioned; (c) marveled over; (d) measured, mapped out.

B.   Content and Structure

Answer the following questions.

1. The mode of discourse in the paragraph is (a) narration; (b) description; (c) exposition; (d) persuasion.
2. The dominant impression Durrell wants to create is of N'da Ali's (a) reputation as a sacred mountain; (b) reputation as a dangerous mountain for climbers; (c) changing moods; (d) remarkably beautiful appearance.
3. We can infer that for Durrell the mountain was (a) intimidating; (b) intriguing; (c) magical; (d) mesmerizing.
4. The words "crouched," "glowering," and "brooding" are (a) denotative; (b) connotative with positive overtones; (c) connotative with negative overtones; (d) euphemisms; (e) sneer words.
5. What phrase does Durrell use in sentence 5 to characterize the mountain that relates directly to the descriptive words in question 4 above? (a) early morning; (b) great mist-whitened monster; (c) green and golden glitter of forest; (d) purple and shapeless.

6. Also in sentence 5 which does Durrell emphasize? (a) shapes; (b) sounds; (c) textures; (d) colors.

7. In sentence 6, when Durrell writes that sometimes "it would go into hiding, drawing the white clouds around itself," we can infer that he is imaginatively comparing the mountain to _____, and the clouds are being compared metaphorically to _____ .

8. From the phrases "sheer cliffs," "gnarled granite so steep," "great cliffs," and "ridged back," we can infer that N'da Ali (a) was the only mountain in the vicinity; (b) was an inhospitable environment; (c) had never been explored by people before; (d) offered a commanding view of the entire region.

Selection 2

¹. . . It was so hot that I went down to the creek instead, to cool my feet in one of its stagnant sumps, a poor substitute for my Red Cross swims, which had just ended, but at least water.

²The heat was always more intense in the creek, more dusty and dry and piercing than anywhere else. ³Crackling and powdery, it stung the nostrils and eyes, prickled in little hives all over the body. ⁴Beds of gravel glared; dragonflies glittered in tall, chalky weeds; cicadas droned, broke off, droned again. ⁵Sweat rolled down my ribs as I walked, patching my shirt and gathering damply in the band of my shorts. ⁶When I saw a swarm of gnats, I plodded over to it and with the toe of my tennis shoe splashed aside the scum of a sunken pool. ⁷Then, after pulling off my shoes, I stepped in and stood immersed to the ankles. ⁸The water was sun-filled, warm, the clear golden brown of cider. ⁹I scratched my prickling body, rubbed my stinging eyes until little stars revolved, then slowly took off my shorts and shirt, and then my undershirt, and stretched out full length in the shallow water, rolling with lazy greed until I was wet all over. ¹⁰After getting up again, I stood looking down my glistening body for a while, then, picking up my clothes and shoes, walked on in my underpants. ¹¹I felt sun-dazed, reckless, like an African animal, sleepy, yet somehow intent and ready for anything, a hot, loose-limbed beast prowling.

Ella Leffland, *Rumors of Peace*

A. Vocabulary

For each italicized word from the selection, choose the best definition according to the context in which it appears.

1. *stagnant* [sentence 1]: (a) polluted; poisoned; (b) lacking liveliness; (c) not moving or flowing; (d) muddy; sticky.

2. *piercing* [2]: (a) scorching; (b) penetrating; (c) stinging; (d) burning.

B. Content and Structure

Choose the best answer.

1. The mode of discourse in this passage is primarily (a) narration; (b) description; (c) exposition; (d) persuasion.
2. The dominant impression of the creek is that it is (a) open and spacious; (b) clear and cool; (c) hot and dusty; (d) lonely and isolated.
3. Which *two* patterns of organization are evident in the paragraph? (a) spatial; (b) chronological; (c) deductive; (d) inductive; (e) emphatic.
4. We can infer that the narrator of the passage is probably (a) a little girl of about five or six; (b) a girl of about twelve or thirteen; (c) a young woman of nineteen or twenty; (d) an adult woman.
5. Write the evidence from the paragraph that you used to arrive at your answer in question 4 above. _____

_____

C. Language Analysis

1. How would you characterize the word *sumps* as it is used in sentence 1 in reference to the creek? (a) denotative; (b) connotative with positive overtones; (c) connotative with negative overtones; (d) figurative.
2. In sentence 3, which of the five senses is Leffland appealing to?

_____

3. As it is used in sentence 4, how would you characterize the word *glared?* (a) denotative; (b) connotative with positive overtones; (c) connotative with negative overtones; (d) figurative.
4. Would you characterize the sensation described in the figure of speech in sentence 8 as pleasant or unpleasant?_____
5. As used in sentence 11, is the adjective *reckless* (a) denotative; (b) connotative with positive overtones; (c) connotative with negative overtones; (d) figurative?
6. Also in sentence 11, the adjective *hot* seems to be used ambiguously, suggesting two different meanings. What are they?

_____

7. Finally, in sentence 11, is the figure of speech a metaphor or simile? _____ What is being compared to what? _____ is being compared to _____ Explain the figure of speech. What quality does Leffland emphasize in choosing this comparison? _____

Selection 3

[1]The noses of a great many Canadians resemble Porky Pig's. This comes from spending so much time pressing them against the longest undefended one-

way mirror in the world. The Canadians looking through this mirror behave the way people on the hidden side of such mirrors usually do: They observe, analyze, ponder, snoop and wonder what all the activity on the other side means in decipherable human terms.

[2]The Americans, bless their innocent little hearts, are rarely aware that they are even being watched, much less by the Canadians. They just go on doing body language, playing in the sandbox of the world, bashing one another on the head and planning how to blow things up, same as always. If they think about Canada at all, it's only when things get a bit snowy, or the water goes off, or the Canadians start fussing over some piddly detail, such as fish. Then they regard them as unpatriotic; for Americans don't really see Canadians as foreigners, not like the Mexicans, unless they do something weird like speak French or beat the New York Yankees at baseball. Really, think the Americans, the Canadians are just like us, or would be if they could.

[3]Or we could switch metaphors and call the border the longest undefended backyard fence in the world. The Canadians are the folks in the neat little bungalow with the tidy little garden and the duck pond. The Americans are the other folks, the ones in the sprawly mansion with the bad-taste statues on the lawn. There's a perpetual party, or something, going on there—loud music, raucous laughter, smoke billowing from the barbecue. Beer bottles and Coke cans land among the peonies. The Canadians have their own beer bottles and barbecue smoke, but they tend to overlook it. Your own mess is always more forgivable than the mess someone else makes on your patio.

[4]The Canadians can't exactly call the police—they suspect that the Americans are the police—and part of their distress, which seems permanent, comes from their uncertainty as to whether or not they've been invited. Sometimes they do drop by next door, and find it exciting but scary. Sometimes the Americans drop by their house and find it clean. This worries the Canadians. They worry a lot. Maybe that Americans want to buy up their duck pond, with all the money they seem to have, and turn it into a cesspool or a waterskiing emporium.

Margaret Atwood, "The View from the Backyard," The Nation

A. Vocabulary

For each italicized word from the selection, choose the best definition according to the context in which it appears.

1. *ponder* [paragraph 1]: (a) argue about; (b) criticize; (c) make estimates about; (d) consider carefully.
2. *snoop* [1]: (a) interrogate, question; (b) pry into others' affairs; (c) establish official surveillance posts; (d) admire unquestioningly.
3. *decipherable* [1]: (a) clearly visible; (b) able to be interpreted accurately; (c) controllable; (d) able to be judged fairly.

4. *piddly* [2—slang for *piddling*]: (a) necessary; (b) insignificant;
   (c) irrelevant; (d) incomprehensible.
5. *sprawly* [3—slang for *sprawling*]: (a) tasteful; (b) elegant; (c) spread out;
   (d) garish.
6. *raucous* [3]: (a) tinkling, musical; (b) bitter, scornful; (c) good-natured;
   (d) loud, harsh.
7. *distress* [4]: (a) anxiety; (b) unhappiness; (c) lack of concern; (d) lack of
   certainty.
8. *emporium* [4]: (a) educational exhibit; (b) business enterprise;
   (c) school; (d) vacation spot.

B. **Content and Structure**

Choose the best answer.

1. The mode of discourse in the passage is (a) narration; (b) description;
   (c) exposition; (d) persuasion.
2. In your own words, write a sentence or two stating Atwood's main
   idea. _____
   _____
   _____
3. When Atwood writes at the beginning of paragraph 2 in referring to
   Americans, "bless their innocent little hearts," she is being (a) honest;
   (b) scornful; (c) sarcastic; (d) hostile; (e) laudatory.
4. From what Atwood implies in paragraph 2, explain what Americans
   think about Canadians. _____
   _____
5. From the information in paragraph 4, why specifically do Canadians
   "worry a lot" about their southern neighbors? _____
   _____
6. What are the broader implications of Atwood's passage? What is the
   central inference you can make about the relationship between Canada
   and the United States? _____
   _____
   _____

C. **Language Analysis**

Answer the following questions.

1. Paragraph 1 contains two metaphors. Why do Canadians' noses resemble Porky Pig's? _____ What does Atwood
   mean when she refers to the border between Canada and the United

States as a "one-way mirror." What does this say about Canadians? about Americans? _____

_____

2. Atwood says in paragraph 2 that Americans go on "playing in the sandbox of the world, bashing one another on the head and planning how to blow things up, same as always." What, literally, does the sandbox metaphor refer to? _____

    Explain what the metaphor means. _____
    _____ From this metaphor, how would you describe Atwood's attitude toward Americans?

    _____

3. Irony is the difference between what we expect and what actually occurs. How is the word "unpatriotic" in paragraph 3 used ironically?

    _____

4. In paragraph 3 Atwood switches metaphors, comparing the border between Canada and the U.S. to "the longest undefended backyard fence in the world." In your own words, explain Atwood's thinking about how these neighboring nations get along. Specifically, try to determine what she means when she refers to the Canadians' "neat little bungalow," the Americans' "sprawly mansion," and the "perpetual party" with the "raucous laughter" and beer bottles and Coke cans thrown in the peonies. _____

    _____

5. In paragraph 4, what is the literal meaning of this excerpt? "Sometimes they do drop by next door, and find it exciting but scary. Sometimes the Americans drop by their house and find it clean." _____

    _____

Practice Essay

Learning the Language
Perri Klass

Perri Klass's first book, A Not Entirely Benign Procedure: Four Years as a Medical Student, *from which this essay is taken, concerns her experiences while attending Harvard Medical School. She is also the author of* Recombinations, I Am Having an Adventure, *and* Baby Doctor, *along with numerous stories and magazine articles. As the title of her last book suggests, she is now a practicing pediatrician in Boston, Massachusetts.*

1   "Mrs. Tolstoy is your basic LOL in NAD, admitted for a soft rule-out MI," the intern announces. I scribble that on my patient list. In other words, Mrs. Tolstoy is a Little Old Lady in No Apparent Distress who is in the hospital to make sure she hasn't had a heart attack (rule out a Myocardial Infarction). And we think it's unlikely that she has had a heart attack (a *soft* rule-out).

2   If I learned nothing else during my first three months of working in the hospital as a medical student, I learned endless jargon and abbreviations. I started out in a state of primeval innocence, in which I didn't even know that "s̄ CP, SOB, N/V" meant "without chest pain, shortness of breath, or nausea and vomiting." By the end I took the abbreviations so much for granted that I would complain to my mother the English professor, "And can you believe I had to put down *three* NG tubes last night?"

3   "You'll have to tell me what an NG tube is if you want me to sympathize properly," my mother said. NG, nasogastric—isn't it obvious?

4   I picked up not only the specific expressions but also the patterns of speech and the grammatical conventions; for example, you never say that a patient's blood pressure fell or that his cardiac enzymes rose. Instead, the patient is always the subject of the verb: "He dropped his pressure." "He bumped his enzymes." This sort of construction probably reflects the profound irritation of the intern when the nurses come in the middle of the night to say that Mr. Dickinson has disturbingly low blood pressure. "Oh, he's gonna hurt me bad tonight," the intern might say, inevitably angry at Mr. Dickinson for dropping his pressure and creating a problem.

5   When chemotherapy fails to cure Mrs. Bacon's cancer, what we say is, "Mrs. Bacon failed chemotherapy."

6   "Well, we've already had one hit today, and we're up next, but at least we've got mostly stable players on our team." This means that our team (group of doctors and medical students) has already gotten one new admission today, and it is our turn again, so we'll get whoever is admitted next in emergency, but at least most of the patients we already have are fairly stable, that is, unlikely to drop their pressures or in any other way get suddenly sicker and hurt us bad. Baseball metaphor is pervasive. A no-hitter is a night without any new admissions. A player is always a patient—a nitrate player is a patient on nitrates, a unit player is a patient in the intensive care unit, and so on, until you reach the terminal player.

7   It is interesting to consider what it means to be winning, or doing well, in this perennial baseball game. When the intern hangs up the phone and announces, "I got a hit," that is not cause for congratulations. The team is not scoring points; rather, it is getting hit, being bombarded with new patients. The object of the game from the point of view of the doctors, considering the players for whom they are already responsible, is to get as few new hits as possible.

8   This special language contributes to a sense of closeness and professional spirit among people who are under a great deal of stress. As a medical student, I found it exciting to discover that I'd finally cracked the code, that I could understand what doctors said and wrote, and could use the same formulations myself. Some people seem to become enamored of the jargon for its own sake, perhaps because they are so deeply thrilled with the idea of medicine, with the idea of themselves as doctors.

9   I knew a medical student who was referred to by the interns on the team as Mr. Eponym because he was so infatuated with eponymous terminology, the more obscure the better. He never said "capillary pulsations" if he could say "Quincke's pulses." He would lovingly tell over the multinamed syndromes—Wolff-Parkinson-White, Lown-Ganong-Levine, Schönlein-Henoch—until the temptation to suggest Schleswig-Holstein or Stevenson-Kefauver or Baskin-Robbins became irresistible to his less reverent colleagues.

10   And there is the jargon that you don't ever want to hear yourself using. You know that your training is changing you, but there are certain changes you think would be going a little too far.

11   The resident was describing a man with devastating terminal pancreatic cancer. "Basically he's CTD," the resident concluded. I reminded myself that I had resolved not to be shy about asking when I didn't understand things. "CTD?" I asked timidly.

12   The resident smirked at me. "Circling The Drain."

13   The images are vivid and terrible. "What happened to Mrs. Melville?"

14   "Oh, she boxed last night." To box is to die, of course.

15   Then there are the more pompous locutions that can make the beginning medical student nervous about the effects of medical training. A friend of mine was told by his resident, "A pregnant woman with sickle-cell represents a failure of genetic counseling."

16   Mr. Eponym, who tried hard to talk like the doctors, once explained to me, "An infant is basically a brainstem preparation." The term "brainstem preparation," as used in neurological research, refers to an animal whose higher brain functions have been destroyed so that only the most primitive reflexes remain, like the sucking reflex, the startle reflex, and the rooting reflex.

17   And yet at other times the harshness dissipates into a strangely elusive euphemism. "As you know, this is a not entirely benign procedure," some doctor will say, and that will be understood to imply agony, risk of complications, and maybe even a significant mortality rate.

18   The more extreme forms aside, one most important function of medical jargon is to help doctors maintain some distance from their patients. By reformulating a patient's pain and problems into a language that the patient doesn't even speak, I suppose we are in some sense taking those pains and problems under our jurisdiction and also reducing

their emotional impact. This linguistic separation between doctors and patients allows conversations to go on at the bedside that are unintelligible to the patient. "Naturally, we're worried about adeno-CA," the intern can say to the medical student, and lung cancer need never be mentioned.

19   I learned a new language this past summer. At times it thrills me to hear myself using it. It enables me to understand my colleagues, to communicate effectively in the hospital. Yet I am uncomfortably aware that I will never again notice the peculiarities and even atrocities of medical language as keenly as I did this summer. There may be specific expressions I manage to avoid, but even as I remark them, promising myself I will never use them, I find that this language is becoming my professional speech. It no longer sounds strange in my ears—or coming from my mouth. And I am afraid that as with any new language, to use it properly you must absorb not only the vocabulary but also the structure, the logic, the attitudes. At first you may notice these new and alien assumptions every time you put together a sentence, but with time and increased fluency you stop being aware of them at all. And as you lose that awareness, for better or for worse, you move closer and closer to being a doctor instead of just talking like one.

A.   Comprehension

Choose the answer that best completes each statement. Do not refer to the selection while doing this exercise.

1.   Klass writes that during her first three months working in the hospital as a medical student, she has learned (a) the importance of using correct medical terminology; (b) endless abbreviations and medical jargon; (c) the appropriate ways to communicate to patients; (d) the hierarchy that exists among hospital personnel.

2.   The phrase "LOL in NAD" stands for "Little Old Lady," and "NAD" stands for (a) "New Admissions Directory"; (b) "Not Ambulatory or Diagnosable"; (c) Not Apparently Dead"; (d) "No Apparent Distress."

3.   Klass writes that medical personnel are particular fond of using metaphors from the field of (a) high technology; (b) football; (c) baseball; (d) politics.

4.   For the author the expressions "Circling The Drain" and "to box" are particularly vivid and (a) insulting; (b) useful; (c) terrible; (d) humiliating.

5.   The phrase from which the title of the book comes, "a not entirely benign procedure" is a euphemism meaning that the procedure (a) is guaranteed to succeed; (b) has never been tried before; (c) is probably more harmful than helpful; (d) is highly risky.

6.   Despite her dislike of some of the jargon she has learned, Klass con-
     cludes that her new language (a) is necessary if she is going to commu-
     nicate effectively with patients; (b) gives her a new insight on the diffi-
     culties of practicing medicine; (c) allows her to communicate effectively
     with other medical personnel; (d) is just another irritating requirement
     for all medical students.

B.   Inferences

On the basis of the evidence in the passage, mark these statements as follows: PA for inferences that are probably accurate; PI for inferences that are
probably inaccurate; and IE for insufficient evidence. You may refer to the
selection to answer the questions in this section and in all the remaining
sections.

_____ 1.   Klass and her fellow medical students learned medical jargon
             and abbreviations by taking a required class.
_____ 2.   According to medical jargon derived from baseball, winning
             means admitting several new patients at once on the same
             shift.
_____ 3.   The interns nicknamed a medical student Mr. Eponym because
             they thought he sounded ridiculous.
_____ 4.   It is a good idea for doctors to become emotionally involved in
             their patients' illnesses and to form strong emotional bonds
             with them.
_____ 5.   Sometimes doctors use medical jargon to prevent the patient
             from knowing the risks involved in a medical procedure or the
             harsh truth.

C.   Structure

Choose the best answer.

1.   The mode of discourse in this essay is primarily (a) narration; (b) de-
     scription; (c) exposition; (d) persuasion.
2.   Mark any of the following methods of development that are evident in
     paragraphs 1–17. (a) example; (b) analogy; (c) contrast; (d) steps in a
     process; (e) classification.
3.   Explain in your own words the function of the first sentence in para-
     graph 8 as it relates to the essay as a whole.

_____

4.   The method of development in paragraphs 17 and 18 is
     (a) comparison; (b) example; (c) steps in a process; (d) cause and
     effect; (e) illustration.

5. Klass concludes by stressing the positive side of learning medical jargon, which was, for her, _____

   _____

D. Vocabulary

For each italicized word from the selection, choose the best definition according to the context in which it appears.

1. a state of *primeval* innocence [paragraph 2]: (a) charming; (b) original; (c) misunderstood; (d) crude.
2. baseball metaphor is *pervasive* [6]: (a) uncommon; (b) imaginative; (c) overused; (d) present throughout.
3. this *perennial* baseball game [7]: (a) lasting one year; (b) perpetual; (c) competitive; (d) occurring every year at the same time.
4. some people become *enamored of* the jargon [8]: (a) hardened to; (b) accustomed to; (c) captivated by; (d) proficient at.
5. infatuated with *eponymous* terminology [9]: (a) abbreviated; (b) clichéd; (c) name-derived; (d) foreign word.
6. the multinamed *syndromes* [9]: (a) groups of signs and symptoms characterizing a disease; (b) pharmaceutical remedies; (c) mysterious ailments that do not respond to treatment; (d) examples of medical jargon.
7. his less *reverent* colleagues [9]: (a) concerned; (b) respectful; (c) earnest; (d) ambitious.
8. the resident *smirked* at me [12]: (a) winked mischievously; (b) stared rudely; (c) laughed raucously; (d) gave a knowing, smartalecky smile.
9. the more *pompous locutions* [15]: (a) sympathetic terms; (b) self-important, pretentious phrases; (c) concise, direct examples; (d) wise, commonsensical sayings.
10. the harshness *dissipates* [17]: (a) intensifies; (b) significantly changes; (c) vanishes; (d) becomes firmly established.
11. *atrocities* of medical language [19]: (a) misrepresentations; (b) Latin terms; (c) witticisms; (d) horrors.
12. even as I *remark* them [19]: (a) notice; (b) comment on; (c) avoid; (d) challenge.
13. new and *alien* assumptions [19]: (a) unfamiliar; (b) uncomfortable; (c) illogical; (d) intriguing.
14. with time and increased *fluency* [19]: (a) learning a language; (b) ease in using a language; (c) exposure to a language; (d) facility in using a language.

E. Questions for Discussion and Analysis

1. From what Klass writes, what are some specific techniques doctors use to maintain their objectivity and to handle the stress that accompanies working in a hospital?

2. Klass attempts to be objective in her discussion of medical jargon, yet in the end she comes to accept its usefulness. What are some arguments that might be given in support of the contrary position—that such jargon is actually harmful to both doctors and patients?

3. If you are familiar with the special language and jargon of a particular field, choose some examples and, as Klass does, classify them according to their function.

7

Tone

In this last chapter of Part II we examine how a writer's words—whether denotative or connotative—contribute to the tone of a piece of writing. In addition to tone, you will be introduced to the subtleties of irony, wit, sarcasm, and cynicism. The chapter ends with a brief discussion of special effects, allusion, and symbolism.

An Explanation of Tone

Some of the exercises in the preceding chapters have asked you to identify the tone of a passage, so the term should not be completely unfamiliar. *Tone* refers to the feeling, mood, or emotional quality of a piece of writing. In technical and scientific prose, the author's tone is meant to be objective and impartial as befits the purpose to convey information, not to arouse our emotions. The content is factual and the tone matches it. Newspaper articles as well are usually written in an objective manner, since their purpose is to convey factual information rather than to provide a subjective viewpoint.

But in all other kinds of writing, whether fiction or nonfiction, the writer's tone can reflect any emotional stance one can think of. Here are some examples of adjectives that might characterize tone: sympathetic; bitter; angry; self-serving; resentful; caustic; whining; aggrieved; arrogant; befuddled; earnest; witty; ironic; sarcastic; cynical; hostile; belligerent (like "hostile" but stronger); peevish; concerned; admiring; laudatory (like "admiring" but stronger); charming; humorous; rancorous; annoyed; ingratiating; adamant or inflexible; bored; naive; callous; world-weary. These are only some examples. Like the emotions of

the complex beings we humans are, tone runs the gamut. (If you are not sure of the meanings of some of these descriptive words, check an unabridged dictionary. Sometimes students have difficulty articulating the tone of a passage because they lack the vocabulary to express the emotion it embodies.)

In conversation, a speaker's tone is readily apparent because the listener can also use gestures, tone of voice, vocal pitch (the rise and fall of the voice), and facial expression, in addition to the actual words spoken. We do not even need to see the person's face or gestures, because the tone and pitch of the voice can reveal so much about the speaker's attitude.

For example, read this sentence in two different ways: "How do you know?" The first time, pretend that the speaker has just told you a startling fact, and you want to find out where he or she got the information. What word do you emphasize? If you do this right, you will emphasize the final word, "How do you *know*?"

Now, read the sentence again, this time showing rudeness or disbelief. Indicate that you have reason to question how the person came by the information. Can you hear that you emphasize the third word: "How do *you* know?" Of course, in a reading passage, words the writer intends you to emphasize are seldom italicized; you have to recreate the pitch and tone of voice when you read dialogue in your head.

In contrast, tone in writing is conveyed only by the black print on the white page—by word choice, by choice of details the writer chooses to include, and occasionally by sentence structure, as you will see later. In other words, you must recreate the feelings the printed words are meant to arouse. The best way to do this—as with any other reading skill—is to read widely. Here are several examples of short passages in which a distinctive tone is clearly evident. Study them and the accompanying commentary carefully.

This first example is the first paragraph of Jack London's adventure novel, *White Fang.* As you read it, pay close attention to his word choice.

> Dark spruce forest frowned on either side the frozen waterway. The trees had been stripped by a recent wind of their white covering of frost, and they seemed to lean toward each other, black and ominous, in the fading light. A vast silence reigned over the land. The land itself was a desolation, lifeless, without movement, so lone and cold that the spirit of it was not even that of sadness. There was a hint in it of laughter, but of a laughter more terrible than any sadness—a laughter that was mirthless as the smile of the Sphinx, a laughter cold as the frost and partaking of the grimness of infallibility. It was the masterful and incommunicable wisdom of eternity laughing at the futility of life and the effort of life. It was the Wild, the savage, frozen-hearted Northland Wild.
>
> Jack London, *White Fang*

The highly connotative words indicate a somber, gloomy tone. This passage does not celebrate the freedom of the North or beckon us to savor the adventures of the last frontier. Even the hint of laughter the traveler feels is sinister, almost mocking, as if to challenge humans or animals to survive in such coldness.

Shelby Steele, an associate professor of English at San Jose State University, here discusses the problem of student racism, a phenomenon that has recently increased on American college campuses. (The excerpt is taken from a chapter from his book, *The Content of Our Character.* The entire chapter is reprinted in Part IV.)

In the past few years, we have witnessed what the National Institute Against Prejudice and Violence calls a "proliferation" of racial incidents on college campuses around the country. Incidents of on-campus "intergroup conflict" have occurred at more than 160 colleges in the last two years, according to the institute. The nature of these incidents has ranged from open racial violence—most notoriously, the October 1986 beating of a black student at the University of Massachusetts at Amherst after an argument about the World Series turned into a racial bashing, with a crowd of up to three thousand whites chasing twenty blacks—to the harassment of minority students and acts of racial or ethnic insensitivity, with by far the greatest number of episodes falling in the last two categories. At Yale last year, a swastika and the words "white power" were painted on the university's Afro-American cultural center. Racist jokes were aired not long ago on a campus radio station at the University of Michigan. And at the University of Wisconsin at Madison, members of the Zeta Beta Tau fraternity held a mock slave auction in which pledges painted their faces black and wore Afro wigs. Two weeks after the president of Stanford University informed the incoming freshmen class last fall that "bigotry is out, and I mean it," two freshmen defaced a poster of Beethoven—gave the image thick lips—and hung it on a black student's door.

Shelby Steele, *The Content of Our Character*

Despite the potentially inflammatory subject, the tone of this paragraph is relatively objective. Although the author's use of quotation marks around the words "proliferation" and "intergroup conflict" call those words into question and indicate that he considers them euphemisms, nevertheless they do not overshadow his purpose: to show how widespread such racial incidents have become on college campuses. What does he gain by adopting an objective tone rather than an aggressive or impassioned one?

In the next example, Harvard biologist Edwin O. Wilson discusses the contributions of indigenous people to the world's crops.

From the mostly unwritten archives of native peoples has come a wealth of information about wild and semicultivated crops. It is a remarkable fact that with a single exception, the macadamia nut of Australia, every one of the fruits and nuts used in western countries was grown first by indigenous peoples. The Incas were arguably the all-time champions in creating a reservoir of diverse crops. Without the benefit of wheels, money, iron, or written script, these Andean people evolved a sophisticated agriculture based on almost as many plant species as used by all the farmers of Europe and Asia combined. Their abounding crops, tilled on the cool upland slopes and plateaus, proved especially suited for temperate climates. From the Incas have come lima beans, peppers, potatoes, and tomatoes. But many other species and strains, including a hundred varieties of potatoes, are still confined to the Andes. The Spanish conquerors learned to use a few of the potatoes, but they missed many other representatives of a vast array of cultivated tuberous vegetables, including some that are more productive and savory than the favored crops. The names are likely to be unfamiliar: achira, ahipa, arracacha, maca, mashua, mauka, oca, ulloco, and yacon. One, maca, is on the verge of extinction, limited to 10 hectares in the highest plateau region of Peru and Bolivia. Its swollen roots, resembling brown radishes and rich in sugar and starch, have a sweet, tangy flavor and are considered a delicacy by the handful of people still privileged to consume them.

Edwin O. Wilson, The Diversity of Life

Even though this paragraph is expository, Wilson's tone is admiring, almost laudatory. How does he achieve this? First, many of his words carry positive connotations, for example: "a wealth of information," "a remarkable fact," "the all-time champions," "a sophisticated agriculture," and "their abounding crops." Besides word choice, the content of the paragraph, especially the list of details it provides, reveals admiration. The list is indeed impressive, and we are meant to be impressed with these people's accomplishments, all the more so because, as Wilson observes, these foods were grown "without the benefit of wheels, money, iron, or written script," all inventions that seem like essential prerequisites for agriculture.

In this paragraph, Terry Williams, an African-American writer who has done extensive research on poverty and drugs, describes the appearance of a crackhouse. Again, consider the description and the details he includes to help you determine the tone.

[1]The building is a faded brownstone, five stories tall, faced with green-copper arches. Set between Leona's Discount House and Perfumerie and Victor's Travel Agency, there is not much to distinguish it from hundreds of other buildings in the neighborhood. But there are subtle signs: the

door is jammed open; visitors glance around furtively and step quickly, plunging their hands into their pockets to make sure the glass pipe is out of sight. Multicolored plastic vials crunch underfoot; just inside the door are unshaven lookouts with sunken eyes.

[2]The girls and boys, men and women whose stories are recorded here are the lost souls of the city, visible to outsiders only as menacing apparitions: boys steering customers to a drug location, too-thin girls standing in the stench of the stairwells, pressing passersby for loose change—always trying to get a dollar closer to a "hit."

Terry Williams, *Crackhouse: Notes from the End of the Line*

This passage is somber, too, but in a different way from Jack London's passage earlier. The tone here is more depressing and pathetic. We can infer from the phrase "lost souls of the city" that these users are desperate, their lives ruined by their addiction to crack.

The next passage is by Philip Caputo, a writer and novelist who enlisted in the U.S. Marines immediately after high school and served during the Vietnam War. In this passage from his autobiographical account of his experiences fighting in Vietnam, he describes both the physical environment and the "code of battlefield ethics" that governed the soldiers.

Everything rotted and corroded quickly over there: bodies, boot leather, canvas, metal, morals. Scorched by the sun, wracked by the wind and rain of the monsoon, fighting in alien swamps and jungles, our humanity rubbed off of us as the protective bluing rubbed off the barrels of our rifles. We were fighting in the cruelest kind of conflict, a people's war. It was no orderly campaign, as in Europe, but a war for survival waged in a wilderness without rules or laws; a war in which each soldier fought for his own life and the lives of the men beside him, not caring who he killed in that personal cause or how many or in what manner and feeling only contempt for those who sought to impose on his savage struggle the mincing distinctions of civilized warfare—that code of battlefield ethics that attempted to humanize an essentially inhuman war. According to those "rules of engagement," it was morally right to shoot an unarmed Vietnamese who was running, but wrong to shoot one who was standing or walking; it was wrong to shoot an enemy prisoner at close range, but right for a sniper at long range to kill an enemy soldier who was no more able than a prisoner to defend himself; it was wrong for infantrymen to destroy a village with white-phosphorus grenades, but right for a fighter pilot to drop napalm on it. Ethics seemed to be a matter of distance and technology. You could never go wrong if you killed people at long range with sophisticated weapons. And then there was that inspiring order issued by General

Greene: kill VC.* In the patriotic fervor of the Kennedy years, we had asked, "What can we do for our country?" and our country answered, "Kill VC." That was the strategy, the best our best military minds could come up with: organized butchery. But organized or not, butchery was butchery, so who was to speak of rules and ethics in a war that had none?

Philip Caputo, *A Rumor of War*

*Vietnamese soldiers fighting with or civilians sympathetic to the Vietnamese Liberation Front, the Communist forces against whom the Americans were waging war.

This writer sounds alienated and disillusioned. The physical environment is as corrosive as the moral one. Every man has to look out for his own survival. The tone is harsh, jaded, callous. Caputo sounds like a much older man than someone in his early twenties. The war has emotionally hardened him. He sees through the hypocrisy in the military's code of ethics and knows that it is meaningless.

The next excerpt is from the beginning of an article titled "Uncivil Society" by Todd Gitlin, a professor of sociology at the University of California at Berkeley. Gitlin's thesis is that the Reagan-Bush years were damaging to American society because we were left without a "common ground" or even "common courtesy."

[1]On a recent Saturday night in Berkeley, the audience spills out of the multiplex, having just seen *Grand Canyon,* in which the characters realize with horror just what they have become used to—marauding gangs, helicopters flapping overhead on crime-stopper missions, people pushing their belongings on shopping carts, and for the rich, a lot of stupid work. The audience streams out onto Shattuck Avenue—past two young black women shaking their paper cups for coins. If you are under 18 or so, odds are that this sight is normal. You do not remember a time when the streets of America were not lined with people shaking their cups. Or, if you are older, that time is only a faint memory. And not only in Berkeley, mecca for roustabouts, hobos, what used to be called "street people" before they became "homeless." There is, in America, scarcely a downtown to be found today without its colonies of the desperate and demented, taking their bits of space on the sidewalks, rummaging through garbage cans for bottles, cultivating their panhandling routines or wandering down the streets looking strangely accustomed to their condition. I have seen a young, fit-looking homeless black man wandering hatless through the snow on a January morning in the prosperous college town of Amherst, Mass.

[2]Today, who is not accustomed to such sights? The homeless apply themselves to picking up street smarts while the homeful work out their coping

tactics. The dialogue that takes place, and the internal monologues that animate passersby, are not about why there are hundreds of thousands of these people on the street, and why there aren't enough affordable apartments, but: Should I make eye contact, donate, walk past, give coins? Why don't they go somewhere else? Am I suffering the so-called compassion fatigue I've read about?

[3]The power of a government consists not simply, not even mainly, in its capacity to administer relief or pain. The power of a government also consists in its capacity to accustom people to the way things are. And on this score, the achievement of the last decade or more of American government has been to keep us preoccupied with the minutiae of private decisions. To persuade a majority that the current situation is normal. To persuade those who are fed up to withdraw, either because the wanderers on the street will always be with us, or because they have only themselves to blame. And to demoralize those who aren't persuaded.

Todd Gitlin, "Uncivil Society," Image

Gitlin addresses his remarks to college-age readers—young adults who assume that the homeless problem has always been with us. His discussion suggests deep divisions in our society—those who apply themselves "to picking up street smarts" and those who "work out their coping tactics." His tone can best be described as concerned and troubled by his realization of our easy acceptance of these harsh realities.

This last example is the opening paragraph of a short story, "The Lesson," by Toni Cade Bambara.

Back in the days when everyone was old and stupid or young and foolish and me and Sugar were the only ones just right, this lady moved on our block with nappy hair and proper speech and no makeup. And quite naturally we laughed at her, laughed the way we did at the junk man who went about his business like he was some big-time president and his sorry-ass horse his secretary. And we kinda hated her too, hated the way we did the winos who cluttered up our parks and pissed on our handball walls and stank up our hallways and stairs so you couldn't halfway play hide-and-seek without a goddamn gas mask. Miss Moore was her name. The only woman on the block with no first name. And she was black as hell, cept for her feet, which were fish-white and spooky. And she was always planning these boring-ass things for us to do, us being my cousin, mostly, who lived on the block cause we all moved North the same time and to the same apartment then spread out gradual to breathe. And our parents would yank our heads into some kinda shape and crisp up our clothes so we'd be presentable for travel with Miss Moore, who always looked like she was going to church, though she never did. Which is just one of the things the grown-ups talked about when they talked behind her back like a dog. But

when she came calling with some sachet she'd sewed up or some ginger-bread she'd made or some book, why then they'd all be too embarrassed to turn her down and we'd get handed over all spruced up. She'd been to college and said it was only right that she should take responsibility for the young ones' education, and she not even related by marriage or blood. So they'd go for it. Specially Aunt Gretchen. She was the main gofer in the family. You got some ole dumb shit foolishness you want somebody to go for, you send for Aunt Gretchen. She been screwed into the go-along for so long, it's a blood-deep natural thing with her. Which is how she got saddled with me and Sugar and Junior in the first place while our mothers were in a la-de-da apartment up the block having a good ole time.

Toni Cade Bambara, "The Lesson," Gorilla, My Love

Bambara writes from the vantage point of a child "with attitude." The tone is distinctive because it is sharply irreverent, funny, and smart-alecky. She makes us want to go on reading.

The Ironic Stance

Perceiving irony causes more difficulty for readers than any other stance a writer assumes. The best way to grasp irony is to look at many examples. An *ironic tone* results from a writer's deliberately saying the opposite of what he or she really means. The writer assumes that the reader will see through the pretense and recognize that the words express something different from their literal meaning.

The *American Heritage Dictionary* lists many definitions for irony. These are the three relevant ones:

1. The use of words to convey the opposite of their literal meaning. 2. An expression . . . marked by such a deliberate contrast between apparent and intended meaning. 3. Incongruity between what might be expected and what actually occurs.

Detecting irony is tricky because it is a general term with many shades of meaning, as the first two definitions above suggest—from simple amusement and a keen appreciation of life's absurdities to scathing sarcasm. Richard Altick defines irony like this:

The essence of irony is the implied contrast between what is and what, in a more nearly perfect world, might be; and the effect of irony, similarly, lies in the striking disparity between the writer's apparent attitude—that is, his seeming seriousness, or his pretended lack of seriousness—and what he really means. When an author adopts an ironical manner, he is commenting upon the shortcomings of life, the weaknesses of mankind, or, sometimes, the frailties of individual beings. The ironist often is said to be a disap-

pointed idealist, who laughs only to keep from crying or committing suicide. His disillusionment may be only temporary and may spring from a trivial cause; it may, on the other hand, be almost cosmic in its scope and represent a sweeping rejection of the whole of life and all of mankind. Thus irony has a wide variety of tones and shadings, running the gamut from unmitigated, pathological bitterness to mere gay amusement.

Richard Altick, *Preface to Critical Reading*

Consider these real-life examples of irony. John Wayne was invited to play the role of Matt Dillon in the long-running television western series *Gunsmoke;* however, he turned the offer down because he didn't want to be typecast as a cowboy. Why is this ironic? Because John Wayne was already a famous cowboy movie star.

Another example: In the 1940s and 1950s North America experienced a terrible epidemic of polio. Ironically, according to Geoffrey C. Ward in an article called "War on Polio," this epidemic was a by-product of new standards of middle-class cleanliness. In earlier decades babies and small children had routinely come in contact with the polio virus and developed a lifelong immunity to it. But with new standards of hygiene and increased use of disinfectants in the household, the virus was no longer commonly found in the environment, and when children *were* exposed to it, they had no immunity to it. In other words, while we would *expect* that better hygiene would result in healthier children, the opposite occurred in this case.

Another example of irony is found in a recent newspaper article examining the thinking of many homeless people. Refusing to endure the degrading environment of shelters, they prefer to fend for themselves on the streets. In addition, they refuse to sign up for welfare programs because they don't want to be caught up in a "dependency mentality" or suffer the degradation of standing in long lines or dealing with rude social workers. Do you sense the incongruity in this thinking?

Armed with these definitions and examples of irony, we can now examine the many shades of meaning that encompass this term. The shades of meaning may become clearer if you can imagine a continuum, a horizontal line on which ironic attitudes are plotted. Moving from left to right along the continuum, we move from the most gentle forms of irony to the harshest.

Wit ➡ **Irony** ➡ **Satire** ➡ **Cynicism** ➡ **Sarcasm**

Let us examine each and consider some examples. Keep in mind that these categories are not rigid, but "slippery," in the sense that one kind of irony may slide into the next. The best strategy is to study the examples carefully and discuss them (or others you find) with your instructor.

Wit

Wit implies mental keenness, the ability to discern those elements of a situation or condition that relate to what is comic, and a talent for making a pointed, effective, humorous comment on them.

Here are three well-known examples of wit.

- Oscar Wilde once defined eternity as "two people and a ham."
- Samuel Johnson, commenting on a friend's rather hasty remarriage, once said, "A second marriage is the triumph of hope over experience."
- Ogden Nash once remarked, "Progress was a good thing once but it went on too long."

These next three examples are taken from John Train's book, *Wit*.

- At a lunch party in the country, the company was startled by the sight of two dogs copulating on the lawn.

   "What are they doing?" asked a child.

   Noel Coward [a British actor and composer] spoke soothingly: "You see, my dear, the dog in the front is blind, and the one behind is pushing him where they have to go."
- Dorothy Parker [an American humorist, writer, and critic] once wrote in a book review: "This is not a book to be taken lightly. It is one to be thrown away with great force."
- Princess Anne loves horses. At a dinner party she talked about them through the meal. When the coffee arrived she asked, "Could I have the sugar, please?"

   Her neighbor placed two lumps on his flat palm and held it out.

In this paragraph, Caskie Stinnett, a resident of an island off the coast of Maine, describes the changes (for the worse, according to him) that have occurred there—the result, he complains, of progress, of "Maine's trying to become like everyplace else." Here he cites one example of this misguided progress: the barber shop.

My dog can't go in the barber shop with me anymore, but I don't know why because she curled up by the door and minded her own business until I got out of the chair, when she would gaze at me in astonishment, wondering how I had changed so much in just a few minutes. The sign now says, Sorry, No Dogs. The word *sorry* is pure hypocrisy and I resent it; it gives off a hollow ring like a spurious coin when tapped on the counter. My barber, whom I have called Nick for the past twelve years, has informed me that he is now a stylist, not a barber, and that he would appreciate it if I would call him Mr. Nicholas in the future. I'm looking for a new barber.

Caskie Stinnett, "A Room with a View," *Down East*

How would you describe Stinnett's tone? Even though he has a valid complaint, he seems more amused than angry. He achieves this light-hearted tone by using wit, observing the changes in his world with humor.

Irony

Consider again the three dictionary definitions of *irony* on page 186. We can now examine the ironic stance with a few short examples.

> It finally happened. The waiting is over. It's here now.
>
> The new off-ramp has opened at San Francisco International Airport.
>
> For years we drove into the airport from the Bayshore Freeway on the old off-ramp. The old off-ramp was a concrete cloverleaf that arched over the freeway and deposited the motorist just past the Airport Hilton Hotel.
>
> Ah, but the new off-ramp! The new off-ramp is a concrete cloverleaf that arches over the freeway and deposits the motorist just past the Airport Hilton Hotel.
>
> Steve Rubenstein, *San Francisco Chronicle*

Rubenstein uses irony to good advantage here. His short sentences at the beginning create an atmosphere of expectation and suspense. In using the same words to describe the old and new off-ramps, he is being ironic. We *expect* something as costly as a new freeway off-ramp to be more efficient, more convenient, perhaps wider and safer than the one it replaced. But in this case, the new off-ramp is identical to the old one. He does not have to comment on the wastefulness of spending millions of taxpayer dollars for such a project. The ironic stance allows us to perceive its ridiculousness.

Irony is at the heart of many jokes. In these examples, Page Smith, formerly history professor at the University of California, Santa Cruz, uses irony to illustrate memory failure in older people. In the first, a senior citizen and his wife are sitting on their front porch.

> Wife: "I certainly would appreciate a vanilla ice cream cone."
>
> Husband: "I'll hobble right down to the drugstore and get you one, dear."
>
> Wife: "Now, remember, I want vanilla. You always get chocolate. Write it down. Vanilla."
>
> Husband: "I can certainly remember vanilla. The store is only two blocks away."
>
> Husband comes back with a hamburger and hands it to his wife. She looks at it disgustedly. "I knew you'd forget the mustard," she says.
>
> Page Smith, "Coming of Age: Jokes about Old Age," *San Francisco Chronicle*

Here is another example on the same theme.

An old man sees a friend sitting on a park bench weeping. "How have things been with you, Bob?" he asks his old friend.

"Great. I just married a beautiful young woman."

"Wonderful! But then why are you crying?"

"I can't remember where I live."

Page Smith, "Coming of Age: Jokes about Old Age," San Francisco Chronicle

In this next example, Trevor Fishlock explains what he calls the ambiguity of Alaska, the last frontier. What does Fishlock find ironic about Alaska and the people who move there?

In Alaska there is all the ambiguity of the frontier. The Last Frontier slogan is invested with self-consciousness and sadness. It is meant to sound robustly all-American and celebratory, but it has, too, a note of nostalgic longing, regret for vanishing youth. Otherwise, surely, Alaskans would have called their land, in a more forward-looking way, the New Frontier. Men still journey here to be frontiersmen. They grow their whiskers especially for the purpose. They ransack the trading post catalogues for thick wool shirts, thermal underwear, rifles, Bowie knives and books on how to build log cabins and bear-proof larders. They buy devices to get solar electricity "free from the midnight sun" and consider whether to invest in "the world's most powerful hand gun, 2000 foot-pounds of raw power! Alaska's answer to bear protection." Thus equipped they thrust their eager bushy faces towards the challenging wilderness—and are dismayed to find parking tickets on their windscreens. Anchorage and Fairbanks have traffic jams, parking congestion and severe carbon monoxide pollution. Even in distant Nome, population 2500, there are irksome regulations. *The Nome Nugget,* Alaska's oldest newspaper (the motto on its masthead states: There's no place like Nome), commented regretfully on the installation of the town's first traffic signal in 1984: "It doesn't make us do anything we weren't already supposed to do. So, no cause for alarm yet. It just makes one wonder who will get the first ticket and how long before the first bullet hole shows up. Big city life is creeping up on us."

Trevor Fishlock, The State of America

Satire

A satire is a piece of writing that seeks to expose folly or wickedness, often by means of irony and sarcasm. Jon Carroll, a newspaper columnist who often adopts a satirical stance to poke fun at human folly, here ridicules the owners of various kinds of automobile, classifying them into types. His satire uses a kind of humor called hyperbole (pronounced hī pûr′ bə lē), meaning deliberate exaggeration for effect.

[1]I have been called a bigot. Yes, unthinking, ignorant people have referred to my entirely scientific observations as nothing more than rampant prejudice. But I have facts, friends. Where there are facts, there can be no bigotry.

[2]You too can have facts; you need not take my word for it. I ask that you make this simple experiment. For one week, as you motor about the highways and byways of this great bioregion, note every instance of bad driving that you encounter.

[3]Do not merely curse and scream, although you are free to do that as well. Note carefully the make of vehicle engaged in the bad driving. At the end of the week, tally the results. There is an 82 percent chance that No. 1 on your list of vehicles involved in automotive stupidity and rudeness will be: Volvo.

[4]That is not bigotry! This is not anti-Scandinavian bias! This is the hard, unwaxed truth. Volvos (and, let's face it, Volvo drivers) like to pretend that there are no other cars on the road. Also no other pedestrians, bicycle riders, retail establishments or traffic signs.

[5]They are surrounded by eight tons of metal and an impenetrable aura of smugness. They drive in whatever lane they choose at whatever speed they choose. Maybe they drive in two lanes simultaneously; maybe they drive right next to the curb where the cyclists travel and the children play; c'est la bloody vie, big boy.

[6]The world owes them space: This is the Volvo attitude.

[7]I'd be willing to wager that I could predict the top four places on your list, together with a list of the most common driving errors attributable to each vehicle.

1) Volvo. Oh, look, it's the Queen Mother out for a drive. Her little babies are on board; her dog, Ginger; and her $200 worth of groceries. She's entering the freeway. She's going 13 miles an hour. Oops, was that an accident behind her? There's her off-ramp! But now she's doing 75 in the left lane! No problem! She gives the commoners a gracious wave.

2) Any General Motors car manufactured before 1970. Society sucks. Traffic laws are for fools. He has 385 horses under his hood and power steering that responds at the touch of a finger, if it responds at all. Zow, whooosh, ratatata, hahaha. Brakes pull badly to the left; tail pipe dances like a sailor; Breathalyser a mere formality. Driver still remembers Andrew Dice Clay.

3) Mercedes-Benz. Diesel-powered for maximum choke effect. The driver listens to his tape deck while fiddling with car fax; checks the road only occasionally. Personalized license plate. Drives too fast except when he's on his car phone; then he drives too slow. Coat carefully hung up in back seat. Owns slum property. Changes lanes incessantly in traffic jams, searching for extra edge.

> 4) VW bus. Bumper stickers promote solar power and discredited Central American revolutionary groups. Crystal hangs from rear-view mirror; paisley fabric over rear window. Wildly under-powered; sometimes cannot get across intersection from a standing start before light changes. Karmic route-planning techniques. Will move sideways in wind; needs all five lanes to cross the Bay Bridge.

[8]You already know I'm right; even Volvo drivers know I'm right. They try to improve, but something happens when they get behind the wheel. The movie of those crash tests plays over and over in their brains.

[9]That's the unofficial Volvo slogan: I'm safe no matter what—watch out, America.

Jon Carroll, "By Their Cars Shall Ye Know Them,"
San Francisco Chronicle

Cynicism

Cynicism is as difficult to define as irony. You may find these two definitions for the adjective form *cynical* from the *Random House College Dictionary* helpful.

> 1. Distrusting or disparaging the motives of others. 2. Showing contempt for accepted standards of honesty or morality by one's actions, especially by actions that exploit the scruples of others.

The cynical tone is harsher than the ironic and the satirical. It is characterized, as the definitions above suggest, by scorn for others' motives and virtues. If people have a cynical attitude, they detect falseness in others; they recognize the impurity in others' motives. The cynical tone is mocking and sneering, often bitter. It may or may not involve irony, as the following examples demonstrate.

- When a rich man donates a large sum of money to a charity, the cynic says that his motive was only to get a charitable deduction on his tax return.
- When Elvis Presley died in 1977, one cynic greeted the news of his death with the words, "Good career move!" According to Albert Goldman, one of Presley's biographers, the singer was becoming hard to promote. He was middle-aged, overweight, and addicted to drugs. But, as the cynic observed, if Presley were dead, his image could be promoted free of the nasty realities. (And that is exactly what happened, as evidenced by the popularity of Elvis impersonators, the throngs who gather at Graceland each year on the anniversary of his death, and the frequency of Elvis sightings.)
- Three weeks before President Bush left office, on Christmas Eve in 1992, he pardoned the main Iran-Contra figures: Caspar Weinberger, Elliott Abrams, Duane Clarridge, Robert McFarlane, Alan Fiers, and Clair George. At the same time, it was reported that the State Department, on

orders from someone at the White House, had scrutinized Democratic presidential candidate Bill Clinton's passport file and that of his mother's. In an article written after the pardons were handed down and after the passport incident, Calvin Trillin wrote the following opening paragraph. Can you detect why Trillin's tone is cynical?

> It's a shame that the people who rifled Bill Clinton's passport file during the campaign can't get indicted in time to be pardoned by George Bush. This is just another example, I suppose, of the criminal justice system working too slowly. The Iran-Contra felons have been pardoned, but the people who tried to find evidence that Bill Clinton and his mother were Bolsheviks will probably hit the courts while that same Bill Clinton is in office. The moral of the story may be this: If you think you might want to commit a felony that helps out the president, do it early in his administration.
>
> Calvin Trillin, "Begging His Pardon: The Rifle-Men"

Sarcasm

As defined in the usage notes after the word *wit* in the *American Heritage Dictionary,* sarcasm is "a form of wit intended to taunt, wound, or subject another to ridicule or contempt." It often involves irony, whereby the writer or speaker mockingly points to discrepancies between reality and a more desirable course of action. Sarcasm is often associated with sneering or cutting remarks, as the following two examples demonstrate.

- You bump into a table and nearly upset a lamp while walking through a room, and a not-very-nice acquaintance,—seizing this opportunity to comment on your clumsiness,—remarks "How graceful."
- An English professor is gathering up his lecture notes and books after class. Lying on the podium is his tattered copy of Chaucer's *Canterbury Tales,* the subject of today's lecture. A football player, arriving early for the next class, walks up to the desk, looks at the book, and says to the professor, "Chaucer. I hate Chaucer." The professor looks up and says, "That tells me more about you than it does about Chaucer."

In this excerpt, Beryl Markham, a pioneering bush pilot who lived in Africa for many years, writes about elephants and man's impulse to hunt. After you read it, locate the example of a sarcastic tone. (A *midge,* mentioned in paragraph 1, is a little gnatlike fly.)

> [1]I suppose, if there were a part of the world in which mastodon still lived, somebody would design a new gun, and men, in their eternal impudence, would hunt mastodon as they now hunt elephant. Impudence seems to be the word. At least David and Goliath were of the same species, but, to an elephant, a man can only be a midge with a deathly sting.

[2]It is absurd for a man to kill an elephant. It is not brutal, it is not heroic, and certainly it is not easy; it is just one of those preposterous things that men do like putting a dam across a great river, one tenth of whose volume could engulf the whole of mankind without disturbing the domestic life of a single catfish.

[3]Elephant, beyond the fact that their size and conformation are aesthetically more suited to the treading of this earth than our angular informity, have an average intelligence comparable to our own. Of course they are less agile and physically less adaptable than ourselves—Nature having developed their bodies in one direction and their brains in another, while human beings, on the other hand, drew from Mr. Darwin's lottery of evolution both the winning ticket and the stub to match it. This, I suppose, is why we are so wonderful and can make movies and electric razors and wireless sets—and guns with which to shoot the elephant, the hare, clay pigeons, and each other.

Beryl Markham, *West with the Night*

The next excerpt consists of the opening and closing paragraphs of an article called "The Killing Game" by Joy Williams. Arguing that hunting should be made illegal, she supports this stance by adopting a sarcastic tone in the first paragraph and a strongly critical tone in the last.

[1]Death and suffering are a big part of hunting. A big part. Not that you'd ever know it by hearing hunters talk. They tend to downplay the killing part. To kill is to put to death, extinguish, nullify, cancel, destroy. But from the hunter's point of view, it's just a tiny part of the experience. *The kill is the least important part of the hunt,* they often say, or, *Killing involves only a split second of the innumerable hours we spend surrounded by and observing nature . . .* For the animal, of course, the killing part is of considerably more importance. José Ortega y Gasset, in *Meditations on Hunting,* wrote, *Death is a sign of reality in hunting. One does not hunt in order to kill; on the contrary, one kills in order to have hunted.* This is the sort of intellectual blather that the "thinking" hunter holds dear. The conservation editor of *Field & Stream,* George Reiger, recently paraphrased this sentiment by saying, *We kill to hunt, and not the other way around,* thereby making it truly fatuous. A hunter in West Virginia, one Mr. Bill Neal, blazed through this philosophical fog by explaining why he blows the toes off tree raccoons so that they will fall down and be torn apart by his dogs. *That's the best part of it. It's not any fun just shooting them. . . .*

[2]Hunters' self-serving arguments and lies are becoming more preposterous as nonhunters awake from their long, albeit troubled, sleep. Sport hunting is immoral; it should be made illegal. Hunters are persecutors of nature

who should be prosecuted. They wield a disruptive power out of all proportion to their numbers, and pandering to their interests—the special interests of a group that just wants to kill things—is mad. It's preposterous that every year less than 7 percent of the population turns the skies into shooting galleries and the woods and fields into abattoirs. It's time to stop actively supporting and passively allowing hunting, and time to stigmatize it. It's time to stop being conned and cowed by hunters, time to stop pampering and coddling them, time to get them off the government's duck-and-deer dole, time to stop thinking of wild animals as "resources" and "game," and start thinking of them as sentient beings that deserve our wonder and respect, time to stop allowing hunting to be creditable by calling it "sport" and "recreation." Hunters make wildlife *dead, dead, dead*. It's time to wake up to this indisputable fact. As for the hunters, it's long past check-out time.

Joy Williams, "The Killing Game," *Esquire*

Special Effects

In the foregoing examples, we can see that the writer's choice of descriptive details and connotative language contributes to the sarcastic tone. In the next examples, however, the authors' sarcasm derives not only from the content but from what we might call—for lack of a better phrase—special effects. In the first, television critic John Carman describes the acting debut of Vanna White, better known as the letter-turner on the television game show *Wheel of Fortune,* who appeared in a made-for-television movie, *Goddess of Love.* Carman pokes fun at the movie by writing in overly simple sentences. (For full effect, read this excerpt aloud and exaggerate the simplistic style.)

[1]This is Vanna White. Vanna is the star of her own movie Sunday night on NBC. Vanna's movie is called "Goddess of Love."

[2]Vanna plays Venus in her movie. Venus is a goddess. Venus comes back to life after 3,000 years. General Electric owns NBC. General Electric brings good things to life.

[3]When General Electric brings Venus to life, Venus falls in love with a hair stylist.

[4]Acting is new for Vanna. Vanna says that "it was very hard. It's very hard to sit there for my first major role on television and say, 'Where dost thou slumber?'"

[5]NBC did not let critics see "Goddess of Love." NBC is very smart. The critics are very sad. They wanted very much to see Vanna act and say, "Where dost thou slumber?"

[6]But NBC says it has not seen the movie either. The man who is in charge of NBC movies has not seen "Goddess of Love," even though it will be on TV Sunday (Channel 4, 9 p.m.). Where can it be?

> John Carman, "'G-dd-ss -f L-v' Must Be Vanna,"
> *San Francisco Chronicle*

Another kind of special effect is evident in this excerpt by travel writer Paul Theroux. Using both italicized words to indicate his thoughts and exclamation marks to show his disbelief, Theroux runs through a catalog of things the English do that, to him, seem ridiculous.

Once, from behind a closed door, I heard an Englishwoman exclaim with real pleasure, "They are *funny,* the Yanks!" And I crept away and laughed to think that an English person was saying such a thing. And I thought: *They wallpaper their ceilings! They put little knitted bobble hats on their soft-boiled eggs to keep them warm! They don't give you bags in supermarkets! They say sorry when you step on their toes! Their government makes them get a hundred-dollar license every year for watching television! They issue drivers' licenses that are valid for thirty or forty years—mine expires in the year 2011! They charge you for matches when you buy cigarettes! They smoke on buses! They drive on the left! They spy for the Russians! They say "nigger" and "Jewboy" without flinching! They call their houses Holmleigh and Sparrow View! They sunbathe in their underwear! They don't say "You're welcome"! They still have milk bottles and milkmen, and junk dealers with horse-drawn wagons! They love candy and Lucozade and leftovers called bubble-and-squeak! They live in Barking and Dorking and Shellow Bowells! They have amazing names, like Mr. Eatwell and Lady Inkpen and Major Twaddle and Miss Tosh! And they think* we're *funny?*

> Paul Theroux, "English Traits," *The Kingdom by the Sea*

Exercises: Part 1— Determining Tone

Here are some passages for you to practice with. Read each carefully, paying special attention to word choice (denotation and connotation) and to the quality and "sound" of the prose. Consider the list of possible tones at the beginning of the chapter and the continuum depicting irony. Then decide what the tone is for each excerpt.

Selection 1

[1]DEAR ABBY: This is a message to those men and women who try to prevent women from entering abortion clinics and carry big signs that say, "They Kill Babies Here!"

²Have you signed up to adopt a child? If not, why not? Is it because you don't want one, can't afford one, or don't have the time, patience or desire to raise a child?

³What if a woman who was about to enter a family planning clinic saw your sign, then decided not to have an abortion but chose instead to give her baby to you? Would you accept it? What if the mother belonged to a minority group—or was addicted to drugs, or tested positive for AIDS?

⁴Why are you spending your time carrying a sign? Why aren't you volunteering to baby-sit for a child born to a single mother so she can work? Why haven't you opened your door to a pregnant teenager whose parents have kicked her out when she took your advice and decided not to have an abortion?

⁵As for the taxpayers who resent paying for abortions, who do you think pays for foster care, welfare, social workers and juvenile delinquency? The taxpayers.

⁶Let's talk about something money can't buy: love. Have you ever visited a home for abused and unwanted children? Have you ever been to Juvenile Hall and seen the children who have committed crimes because they were born to mothers who didn't want them?

⁷I'm not thrilled about abortion, but I don't think anyone has the right to tell others not to have one unless he or she has done the things I have mentioned above.

⁸So, to those carrying the signs and trying to prevent women from entering family planning clinics, heed my message: If you must be against abortion, don't be a hypocrite—make your time and energy count.

HATES HYPOCRITES IN SANTA ANA

DEAR HATES: I couldn't have said it better. Or as well.

Signed, "Hates Hypocrites in Santa Ana," Letter to Dear Abby

Selection 2

Lost in the cities of America, the immigrant Jews succumbed to waves of nostalgia for the old world. "I am overcome with longing," wrote an early immigrant, "not only for my Jewish world, which I have lost, but also for Russia." Both the handful of intellectuals and the unlettered masses were now inclined to re-create the life of the old country in their imaginations, so that with time, distance and suffering, the past they had fled took on an attractive glow, coming to seem a way of rightness and order. Not that they forgot the pogroms, not that they forgot the poverty, but that they remembered with growing fondness the inner decorums of *shtetl* life. Desperation induced homesickness, and homesickness coursed through their days like a ribbon of sadness. In Russia "there is more poetry, more music, more feeling, even if our people do suffer appalling persecution. . . . One enjoys life in Russia better than here. . . .

There is too much materialism here, too much hurry and too much prose—and yes, too much machinery." Even in the work of so sophisticated a Yiddish poet as Moshe Leib Halpern, who began to write after the turn of the century, dissatisfaction with the new world becomes so obsessive that he "forgets that his place of birth was very far indeed from being a paradise." "On strange earth I wander as a stranger," wrote Halpern about America, "while strangeness stares at me from every eye."

Irving Howe, *World of Our Fathers*

Selection 3

[1]Arches National Monument has been developed. The Master Plan has been fulfilled. Where once a few adventurous people came on weekends to camp for a night or two and enjoy a taste of the primitive and remote, you will now find serpentine streams of baroque automobiles pouring in and out, all through the spring and summer, in numbers that would have seemed fantastic when I worked there: from 3,000 to 30,000 to 300,000 per year, the "visitation," as they call it, mounts ever upward. The little campgrounds where I used to putter around reading three-day-old newspapers full of lies and watermelon seeds have now been consolidated into one master campground that looks, during the busy season, like a suburban village: elaborate housetrailers of quilted aluminum crowd upon gigantic camper-trucks of Fiberglas and molded plastic; through their windows you will see the blue glow of television and hear the studio laughter of Los Angeles; knobby-kneed oldsters in plaid Bermudas buzz up and down the quaintly curving asphalt road on motorbikes; quarrels break out between campsite neighbors while others gather around their burning charcoal briquettes (ground campfires no longer permitted—not enough wood) to compare electric toothbrushes. The Comfort Stations are there, too, all lit up with electricity, fully equipped inside, though the generator breaks down now and then and the lights go out, or the sewage backs up in the plumbing system (drain fields were laid out in sand over a solid bed of sandstone), and the water supply sometimes fails, since the 3,000-foot well can only produce about 5 gpm—not always enough to meet the demand. Down at the beginning of the new road, at park headquarters, is the new entrance station and visitor center, where admission fees are collected and where the rangers are going quietly nuts answering the same three basic questions five hundred times a day: (1) Where's the john? (2) How long's it take to see this place? (3) Where's the Coke machine?

[2]Progress has come at last to the Arches, after a million years of neglect. Industrial Tourism has arrived.

Edward Abbey, *Desert Solitaire*

Selection 4

[1]In October, 1918, a German corporal had been temporarily blinded by chlorine gas in a British attack near Comines. While he lay in hospital in Pomerania, defeat and revolution swept over Germany. The son of an obscure Austrian

customs official, he had nursed youthful dreams of becoming a great artist. Having failed to gain entry to the Academy of Art in Vienna, he had lived in poverty in that capital and later in Munich. Sometimes as a house-painter, often as a casual labourer, he suffered physical privations and bred a harsh though concealed resentment that the world had denied him success. These misfortunes did not lead him into Communist ranks. By an honourable inversion he cherished all the more an abnormal sense of racial loyalty and a fervent and mystic admiration for Germany and the German people. He sprang eagerly to arms at the outbreak of the war, and served for four years with a Bavarian regiment on the Western Front. Such were the early fortunes of Adolf Hitler.

[2]As he lay sightless and helpless in hospital during the winter of 1918, his own personal failure seemed merged in the disaster of the whole German people. The shock of defeat, the collapse of law and order, the triumph of the French, caused this convalescent regimental orderly an agony which consumed his being, and generated those portentous and measureless forces of the spirit which may spell the rescue or the doom of mankind. The downfall of Germany seemed to him inexplicable by ordinary processes. Somewhere there had been a gigantic and monstrous betrayal. Lonely and pent within himself, the little soldier pondered and speculated upon the possible causes of the catastrophe, guided only by his narrow personal experiences. He had mingled in Vienna with extreme German Nationalist groups, and here he had heard stories of sinister, undermining activities of another race, foes and exploiters of the Nordic world—the Jews. His patriotic anger fused with his envy of the rich and successful into one overpowering hate.

[3]When at length, as an unnoted patient, he was released from hospital still wearing the uniform in which he had an almost schoolboyish pride, what scenes met his newly unscaled eyes? Fearful are the convulsions of defeat. Around him in the atmosphere of despair and frenzy glared the lineaments of Red Revolution. Armoured cars dashed through the streets of Munich scattering leaflets or bullets upon the fugitive wayfarers. His own comrades, with defiant red arm-bands on their uniforms, were shouting slogans of fury against all that he cared for on earth. As in a dream everything suddenly became clear. Germany had been stabbed in the back and clawed down by the Jews, by the profiteers and intriguers behind the front, by the accursed Bolsheviks in their international conspiracy of Jewish intellectuals. Shining before him he saw his duty, to save Germany from these plagues, to avenge her wrongs, and lead the master race to their long-decreed destiny.

Winston Churchill, "Adolf Hitler," *The Gathering Storm*

Selection 5

[1]When people sit down to talk about the world economic situation, one of the points that's almost never brought up is the profusion of stupid license plate mottoes.

[2]Take Pennsylvania's license plate motto: *"You've Got a Friend in Pennsylvania."*

Oh, really? Some friend. Never writes. Never calls. Haven't gotten a Christmas card in years.

[3]Sounds like the kind of friend who never acknowledges your existence until he needs bail money. And you think I'm going to go to Pennsylvania to seek out this guy? No way.

[4]And then there's New Hampshire. The motto on that state's license plates is "Live Free or Die." Interesting sentiment, that one. Especially when you consider that license plates are often made by prison inmates.

[5]And let's not forget Missouri, the "Show-Me State." Show you what? Show you that? You people are a bunch of sickos.

[6]I think it's time for some honesty in license-plate mottoes.

[7]Although I didn't have time to clear my suggestions with the local Chambers of Commerce, I feel sure that they're behind me 100 percent:

Alaska: Petroleum Paradise.

Alabama: The Tractor Pull State.

New Jersey: The Obscene Hand Gesture State.

Wyoming: The Vast Expanses of Basically Nothing State.

California: The Overpriced Real Estate State.

Oklahoma: More Than Just Dust.

Tennessee: The Elvis State.

Arkansas: One of America's 50 States.

Florida: The Mildew State.

Rhode Island: Technically, A State.

Maine: The Freeze-Your-Butt-Off State.

Nevada: Land of Sin.

West Virginia: The Get-Me-Out-Of-Here State.

Kansas: The Dull, Flat State.

Georgia: Land of 10,000,000 Ballcaps.

Texas: The Talk-Funny State.

New York: The Hand-Over-Your-Wallet State.

Michigan: Adventures in Unemployment.

Iowa: Land of Pork State.

North Dakota: The "Other" Dakota.

David Grimes, "Florida—The Mildew State," *Sarasota Herald-Tribune*

Selection 6

In walks these three girls in nothing but bathing suits. I'm in the third checkout slot, with my back to the door, so I don't see them until they're over by the bread. The one that caught my eye first was the one in the plaid green two-piece. She was a chunky kid, with a good tan and a sweet broad soft-looking can with those two crescents of white just under it, where the sun never seems to hit, at the top of the backs of her legs. I stood there with my hand on a box of HiHo crackers trying to remember if I rang it up or not. I ring it up again and the customer starts giving me hell. She's one of these cash-register-watchers, a witch about fifty with rouge on her cheekbones and no eyebrows, and I know it made her day to trip me up. She'd been watching cash registers for fifty years and probably never seen a mistake before.

John Updike, "A & P," *Pigeon Feathers and Other Stories*

Allusions

A writer uses allusions because past associations suggest a new interpretation of things in the present. As Richard D. Altick writes in *Preface to Critical Reading*, "Understanding allusions, as well as making apposite ones in our own writing, is simply one way of bringing the memorable ideas of the past to illuminate what we think and say today." An *allusion* is a pointed and meaningful reference to something outside the text. The reference may be to a biblical, mythological, historical, literary, or musical source. Indeed, it can come from any discipline, though allusions generally come from works or events that educated readers are familiar with.

The reader who misses the associations that an allusion provides misses out not only on the literal content but on the connotative effect as well. The ability to recognize allusions immediately—without turning to reference books—takes years to develop. It is only possible through wide reading and exposure to our cultural tradition. (In the meantime, however, ask your instructor to explain allusions that you do not recognize in your reading or use reference books to help you, since lower-division college students can hardly be expected to have the background in history or literature that adults do.)

Here are three examples of allusions, all of whose meanings can be found in any good unabridged dictionary. Understanding these little references adds immeasurably to your understanding of the whole. The first example is from Helen Keller's autobiography. Deaf and blind since early childhood, Keller describes the way Anne Mansfield Sullivan, her teacher, helped her acquire sign language. Keller describes her feeling at the end of her breakthrough day, when Helen finally understood what words were:

> I learned a great many new words that day. I do not remember what they all were; but I do know that *mother, father, sister, teacher* were among them—words that were to make the world blossom for me, "like Aaron's rod, with flowers." It would have been difficult to find a happier child than I was as I lay in my crib at the close of that eventful day and lived over the joys it had brought me, and for the first time longed for a new day to come.
>
> Helen Keller, *The Story of My Life*

Aaron's rod is defined in *The Random House Dictionary* as "a rod, inscribed with the name of Aaron, that miraculously blossomed and yielded almonds." (The biblical passage from which this allusion comes is Numbers 17:8 in the Old Testament, in case you are interested in reading the whole reference.)

In the next example, Joseph Epstein, a frequent contributor to *The American Scholar* who writes under the pseudonym "Aristides," humor-

ously explains the trepidation he feels when his students evaluate his performance as a teacher. (The entire essay from which this paragraph is taken is reprinted at the end of Part IV.)

> Socrates may have had to take the hemlock, but at least he was spared the indignity of that relatively recent addition to the teaching transaction known as "teacher evaluation." On these evaluations, generally made during the last minutes of the final session of the college term, students, in effect, grade their teachers. Hemlock may on occasion seem preferable, for turnabout here can sometimes be cruel play, especially when students, under the veil of anonymity, take the opportunity of evaluation to comment upon their teacher's dress, or idiosyncrasies, or moral character. For the most part I have not fared too badly on these evaluations, though my clothes have been the subject of faint comedy, my habit of jiggling the change in my pockets and my wretched handwriting have been noted, and in one instance I have been accused of showing favoritism (a charge I choose to interpret as my preference, in the classroom, for calling upon the relatively intelligent over the completely obtuse). None of these student comments, as you can plainly see, affects me in the least; such personal criticisms roll right off me, like buckshot off a duck's heart.
>
> "Aristides" (Joseph Epstein), "Student Evaluations," *The American Scholar*

The allusion in the first sentence is to Socrates, the Athenian teacher and philosopher, who was forced to drink hemlock (a poison) for having corrupted Athenian youth with his teachings. Though Socrates' death was tragic, Aristides's allusion is meant to be playful. It provides a humorous backdrop to his remarks, as does his play on the cliché ("like water rolling off a duck's back") at the end of the paragraph. Can you explain what his last sentence means?

Symbols

You will recall from Chapter 6 that figurative language adds imagination, texture, immediacy to a writer's ideas. In comparing one thing in terms of something else, we are given an intense visual image or a new way of looking at something familiar. A *symbol,* however, is slightly different. It is a representation of an abstract idea.

Fire, for example, can symbolize punishment (eternal burning in Hell for one's wrongdoings on earth) or perhaps ritual purification, as in India. In Western culture the color red can symbolize violence (because of its association with blood) or passion, as we see in Valentine cards. In China, red symbolizes happiness; traditional Chinese brides wear red wedding dresses, and children receive "lucky money" in red envelopes for the New Year.

In our culture green suggests verdant vegetation—the rebirth of life during the spring. But green can also symbolize jealousy, as in Shakespeare's *Othello,* where jealousy is represented symbolically as a "green-eyed monster." In English, we also have the related cliché—"green with envy."

Symbols are often at work in proverbs, as in the old saying "The pen is mightier than the sword," for example. "Pen" symbolizes the persuasive power of writing, and "sword" symbolizes the power of the military. Translated into literal terms, it means that one can exert more influence over others by writing than by using physical coercion. We know that the words "pen" and "sword" in this proverb refer to abstractions and are not to be taken literally.

As with allusions, recognizing symbols takes experience and exposure. You do not need to become a "symbol hunter" when you read literature in particular, fearful that a writer is deliberately throwing in symbols to trick you or to lead you astray. Often the most powerful symbols come from the natural elements, rooted in the yearly cycle of birth, fruition, harvest, and death (represented by the four seasons, spring, summer, autumn, and winter).

Here, Bruce Catton, the eminent Civil War historian, describes a battalion of soldiers—he does not even tell us whether they are Union or Confederate—marching at the end of the war. He weaves in symbols throughout. See if you can locate them and explain the abstract ideas they refer to. How do they reinforce the somber tone?

> The end of the war was like the beginning, with the army marching down the open road under the spring sky, seeing a far light on the horizon. Many lights had died in the windy dark but far down the road there was always a gleam, and it was as if a legend had been created to express some obscure truth that could not otherwise be stated. Everything had changed, the war and the men and the land they fought for, but the road ahead had not changed. It went on through the trees and past the little towns and over the hills, and there was no getting to the end of it. The goal was a going-toward rather than an arriving, and from the top of the next rise there was always a new vista. The march toward it led through wonder and terror and deep shadows, and the sunlight touched the flags at the head of the column.
>
> Bruce Catton, "The Enormous Silence," *A Stillness at Appomattox*

Exercises: Part 2

Selection 1

[1]One of the greatest and most intrepid travelers of all time, Marco Polo, journeyed to the Far East from the Mediterranean in the thirteenth century and spent twenty years in the court of Kublai Khan in China. [2]On his return to

Venice he set down in his book entitled *Description of the World* his impressions of the peoples and places and customs he had seen. [3]There are at least two extraordinary omissions in his account. [4]He says nothing about the art of printing unknown as yet in Europe but in full flower in China. [5]He either did not notice it at all or if he did, failed to see what use Europe could possibly have for it. [6]Whatever reason, Europe had to wait another hundred years for Gutenberg. [7]But even more spectacular was Marco Polo's omission of any reference to the Great Wall of China, nearly 4000 miles long and already more than 1000 years old at the time of his visit. [8]Again, he may not have seen it; but the Great Wall of China is the only structure built by man which is visible from the moon!* [9]Indeed, travelers can be blind.

Chinua Achebe, *Hopes and Impediments*

*About the omission of the Great Wall of China, I am indebted to *The Journey of Marco Polo* as re-created by artist Michael Foreman, published by *Pegasus* magazine, 1974.

A. Vocabulary

For each italicized word from the selection, choose the best definition according to the context in which it appears.

1. *intrepid* [sentence 1]: (a) knowledgeable; (b) famous; (c) untiring; (d) fearless.
2. *omissions* [3 and 7]: (a) things overlooked; (b) things misinterpreted; (c) things not observed; (d) things left out.

B. Content and Structure

1. The main idea of this paragraph is expressed in sentence _____.
2. The method of development is (a) comparison; (b) contrast; (c) analysis; (d) example; (e) analogy.
3. The pattern of organization is (a) deductive; (b) inductive; (c) spatial; (d) chronological; (e) emphatic.
4. If Marco Polo did actually observe that the Chinese knew the art of printing and failed to mention it because he did not see how it could be useful in Europe, such an omission would be an example of (a) a simple oversight; (b) a symbol; (c) cynicism; (d) ignorance; (e) irony.
5. We can infer from sentence 6 that (a) the Chinese gave the idea of the printing press to Gutenberg; (b) Gutenberg traveled to China; (c) Gutenberg invented his printing press independently of the Chinese; (d) Gutenberg's printing process was identical to the Chinese.
6. Why does Achebe mention that the Great Wall of China is the only manmade structure visible from the moon, and how does this fact relate to Marco Polo's stay in China? _____
    _____

7. In relation to the context, the adjectives *extraordinary* (sentence 3) and *spectacular* (sentence 7) are examples of (a) allusions; (b) denotative words; (c) connotative words with positive overtones; (d) connotative words with negative overtones; (e) euphemisms; (f) sneer words.

8. Achebe's tone in this paragraph can best be described as (a) surprised; (b) skeptical; (c) objective; (d) sympathetic; (e) confused.

9. As Achebe points out, it is possible that Marco Polo never observed either the art of printing or the Great Wall; yet what piece of evidence in the paragraph makes this seem unlikely or improbable? _____

_____

10. In a sentence of your own, explain Achebe's observation in the last sentence: "Indeed, travelers can be blind." _____

_____

Selection 2

¹There is something quite deceptive in the sense of acceleration that comes just before a rapid. ²The word "rapid" itself is, in a way, a misnomer. ³It refers only to the speed of the white river relative to the speed of the smooth water that leads into and away from the rapid. ⁴The white water is faster, but it is hardly "rapid." ⁵The Colorado, smooth, flows about seven miles per hour, and, white, it goes perhaps fifteen or, at its whitest and wildest, twenty miles per hour—not very rapid by the standards of the twentieth century. ⁶Force of suggestion creates a false expectation. ⁷The mere appearance of the river going over those boulders—the smoky spray, the scissoring waves—is enough to imply a rush to fatality, and this endorses the word used to describe it. ⁸You feel as if you were about to be sucked into some sort of invisible pneumatic tube and shot like a bullet into the dim beyond. ⁹But the white water, though faster than the rest of the river, is categorically slow. ¹⁰Running the rapids in the Colorado is a series of brief experiences, because the rapids themselves are short. ¹¹In them, with the raft folding and bending—sudden hills of water filling the immediate skyline—things happen in slow motion. ¹²The projector of your own existence slows way down, and you dive as in a dream, and gradually rise, and fall again. ¹³The raft shudders across the ridgelines of water cordilleras to crash softly into the valleys beyond. ¹⁴Space and time in there are something other than they are out here. ¹⁵Tents of water form overhead, to break apart in rags. ¹⁶Elapsed stopwatch time has no meaning at all.

John McPhee, *Encounters with the Archdruid*

A. Vocabulary

For each italicized word from the selection, choose the best definition according to the context in which it appears.

1. *misnomer* [sentence 2]: (a) something misunderstood; (b) something mysterious; (c) something misnamed; (d) something misrepresented.

2. *fatality* [7]: (a) a serious accident; (b) death; (c) a grave mistake; (d) the inevitable, fate.

3. *endorses* [7]: (a) acknowledges; (b) determines; (c) supports; (d) guarantees.

4. *categorically* [9]: (a) typically; (b) ordinarily; (c) theoretically; (d) without exception.

5. *elapsed* [16]: (a) chronological; (b) measured; (c) perceptible; (d) undetected.

B. Content and Structure

Choose the best answer.

1. The main idea of the paragraph is stated in sentence _____.

2. The mode of discourse in this paragraph is primarily (a) narration; (b) description; (c) exposition; (d) persuasion.

3. Specifically, the author's purpose is (a) to explain the meaning and the history of the term *rapid;* (b) to describe the appearance of rapids and the sensation of running them; (c) to persuade the reader to take up white water rafting; (d) to prove that a substitute word should be found for the word *rapid.*

4. Throughout the paragraph, McPhee implies several contrasts. State two specific things that he contrasts. _____

   _____

   _____

5. In sentence 6, McPhee writes, "Force of suggestion creates a false expectation." Paraphrase this sentence. _____

   _____

6. In sentence 8, McPhee uses a figure of speech to describe the feeling when one encounters white water: "you feel as if you were about to be sucked into some sort of invisible pneumatic tube and shot like a bullet into the dim beyond." What sensations do these figures of speech suggest? _____

   _____

7. In sentence 11, McPhee describes the raft as "folding and bending." Is this a literal or metaphorical use of these verbs? _____

   _____

8. In comparing the crests of the water in the rapids to *cordilleras* and the depths to *valleys* (see sentence 13) what is he trying to emphasize about the water? (Use a dictionary, if necessary.) _____

   _____

9. Which of our five senses do these figures of speech appeal to: "the smoky spray," "the scissoring waves," "tents of water," "break apart in rags"? (a) touch; (b) hearing; (c) taste; (d) smell; (e) sight.

10. How would you characterize the tone or emotional quality of this paragraph? _____

Selection 3

¹For some reason, or for no reason, I have never been afraid of elephants. ²This is not courage, which consists of overcoming fear, but stupidity. ³Elephants are large, powerful and wild, and have been so harried and tormented by man almost since mankind began that if every elephant charged every human on sight and trampled him to death the score would not be evened. ⁴It is fear that stops them from doing this, and fear can lead to desperate frenzy as well as to precipitate flight. ⁵Besides, a great many elephants go about with festering wounds, or with memories of man-inflicted pain and terror, and you can never tell whether that creature dozing so peaceably in the shade, and such tempting camera-fodder, bears the scars of bullet-wounds or spearheads. ⁶So it is foolish not to be afraid of elephants. ⁷But, if I had harboured such fears, the elephants of Wamba would have dispelled them.

⁸After the meal, I strolled down to the pool below our camp to enjoy the stillness and the silvery light on leaves and grasses and on the sandy verge of the pool. ⁹A dark-blue sky was bursting with stars. ¹⁰All was quiet, save for now and again a bark from some distant animal, the hoot of an owl, and once an outburst of frog-croak that started up like an orchestra, swelled to a crescendo and suddenly stopped, as if at the touch of a switch. ¹¹Turning to wander back to camp, I looked up to see three elephants standing about fifteen yards away, moonlight illuminating their white tusks, the wrinkles on their foreheads and even a gleam in their eyes. ¹²They were altogether tranquil and relaxed, their big ears slowly moving, trunks hanging slackly down. ¹³Two or three strides and they could have stretched out a trunk and hurled me out of their path, but I sensed their peaceful intention and felt no inclination to turn and fly.

¹⁴"The elephant's a gentleman," Kipling wrote; there is indeed a gentleness about them; they will step aside when a little plover in their path raises her wings to warn them off her nest. ¹⁵There is a legend among both the Kikuyu and the Chagga people of Mount Kilimanjaro that elephants formerly were men and women who, like Adam and Eve, gave offence to God, not in their case by disobedience but by vanity and extravagance. ¹⁶To make themselves look beautiful, they washed in milk. ¹⁷For this, God expelled them from their Eden, inflicting on them milk-white tusks as a perpetual reminder of their folly. ¹⁸Sometimes, it was said, when out of sight, a young elephant would change back into a human. ¹⁹Retreating a few steps, I stood under a tree and watched

them, and they watched me. [20]After about fifteen minutes they half-turned and moved down to the water's edge with the dignity of a high priest bearing votive offerings to a shrine.

Elspeth Huxley, *Out in the Midday Sun*

A. Vocabulary

For each italicized word from the selection, choose the best definition according to the context in which it appears.

1. *harried* [sentence 3]: (a) annoyed by constant attacks; (b) pillaged, raided; (c) exterminated; (d) hunted.
2. *precipitate* [4]: (a) terrified; (b) undignified; (c) rapid; (d) panicky.
3. *festering* [5]: (a) completely healed; (b) infected, supporting; (c) long-remembered; (d) causing death.
4. *harboured* [7] (Note: "harboured" is the British spelling of "harbored"): (a) held, entertained a thought; (b) been kept awake by; (c) repressed, pushed aside; (d) admitted.
5. *dispelled* [7]: (a) made worse; (b) reinforced; (c) encouraged; (d) driven away, rid.
6. *crescendo* [10]: (a) gradual decrease in sound; (b) gradual increase in sound; (c) deafening roar; (d) chorus of whispers.
7. *slackly* [12]: (a) wearily; (b) heavily; (c) loosely; (d) stiffly.
8. *folly* [17]: (a) uselessness; (b) absurdity; (c) excessive pride; (d) foolishness.

B. Content and Structure

Choose the best answer.

1. The best title for this passage would be (a) The Elephants of Wamba; (b) Elephant Behavior; (c) A History of African Elephants; (d) Some Thoughts and Observations about Elephants.
2. Huxley contrasts two quite different images of elephants in this passage. What are they?_____

    _____

3. The predominant mode of discourse in paragraphs 2 and 3 is (a) narration; (b) description; (c) exposition; (d) persuasion.
4. There is an old saying, "An elephant never forgets." What idea from the passage reinforces the truth of this saying? _____

    _____

5. The example in sentence 14 of an elephant's stepping over a little bird so as not to hurt its nest suggests that elephants can be gentle creatures, but it is also ironic. Explain the irony. _____

    _____

6. We can infer from the Kikuyu and Chagga legends regarding the origin of elephants that—at least for some Africans—(a) elephants figure prominently in their culture; (b) they are afraid of elephants; (c) they have long hunted elephants; (d) they consider elephants to be sacred.

7. Explain the meaning of the figure of speech in the last sentence. _____

_____

8. The tone of the second and third paragraphs can best be described as (a) objective, impartial; (b) amused, wry; (c) serious, philosophical; (d) admiring, respectful.

Practice Essay

Venezuela for Visitors
John Updike

One of America's best-known and most prolific writers, John Updike graduated from Harvard College in 1953 and studied at the Ruskin School of Drawing and Fine Arts in England. He has long been associated with The New Yorker, *both as a "Talk of the Town" columnist and as a frequent short story contributor and book reviewer. He is the author of numerous novels, short fiction collections, and nonfiction pieces, among them the* Rabbit *series (*Rabbit, Run, Rabbit Redux, Rabbit Is Rich, *and* Rabbit at Rest*). This essay is from a recent collection of occasional pieces,* Hugging the Shore.

1   All Venezuela, except for the negligible middle class, is divided between the Indians *(los indios)* and the rich *(los ricos)*. The Indians are mostly to be found in the south, amid the muddy tributaries of the Orinoco and the god-haunted *tepuys* (mesas) that rear their fearsome mile-high crowns above the surrounding jungle, whereas the rich tend to congregate in the north, along the sunny littoral, in the burgeoning metropolis of Caracas, and on the semi-circular shores of Lake Maracaibo, from which their sumptuous black wealth is drawn. The negligible middle class occupies a strip of arid savanna in the center of the nation and a few shunned enclaves on the suburban slopes of Monte Avila.

2   The Indians, who range in color from mocha to Dentyne, are generally under five feet tall. Their hair style runs to pageboys and severe bangs, with some tonsures in deference to lice. Neither sex is quite naked: the males wear around their waists a thong to which their foreskins are tied, pulling their penises taut upright; the females, once out of infancy, suffer such adornments as three pale sticks symmetrically thrust into their lower faces. The gazes of both sexes are melting, brown, alert, canny. The visitor, standing among them with his Nikon FE and L. L. Bean fannypack, is shy at first, but warms to their inquisi-

tive touches, which patter and rub across his person with a soft, sandy insistence unlike both the fumblings of children and the caresses one Caucasian adult will give another. There is an infectious, wordless ecstasy in their touches, and a blank eagerness with yet some parameters of tact and irony. *These are human presences,* the visitor comes to realize.

3   The rich, who range in color from porcelain to mocha, are generally under six feet tall. Their hair style runs to chignons and blow-dried trims. Either sex is elegantly clad: the males favor dark suits of medium weight (nights in Caracas can be cool), their close English cut enhanced by a slight Latin flare, and shirts with striped bodies but stark-white collars and French cuffs held by agates and gold; the females appear in a variety of gowns and mock-military pants suits, Dior and de la Renta originals flown in from Paris and New York. The gazes of both sexes are melting, brown, alert, canny. The visitor, standing among them in his funky Brooks Brothers suit and rumpled blue button-down, is shy at first, but warms to their excellent English, acquired at colleges in London or "the States," and to their impeccable manners, which conceal, as their fine clothes conceal their skins, rippling depths of Spanish and those dark thoughts that the mind phrases to itself in its native language. They tell anecdotes culled from their rich international lives; they offer, as the evening deepens, confidences, feelers, troubles. These, too, are human presences.

4   The Indians live in *shabonos*—roughly circular lean-tos woven beautifully of palm thatch in clearings hacked and burned out of the circumambient rain forest. A *shabono* usually rots and is abandoned within three years. The interiors are smoky, from cooking fires, and eye diseases are common among the Indians. They sleep, rest, and die in hammocks *(cinchorros)* hung as close together as pea pods on a vine. Their technology, involving in its pure state neither iron nor the wheel, is yet highly sophisticated: the chemical intricacies of curare have never been completely plumbed, and with their blowpipes of up to sixteen feet in length the Indians can bring down prey at distances of over thirty meters. They fish without hooks, by employing nets and thrashing the water with poisonous lianas. All this sounds cheerier than it is. It is depressing to stand in the gloom of a *shabono,* the palm thatch overhead infested with giant insects, the Indians drooping in their hammocks, their eyes diseased, their bellies protuberant, their faces and limbs besmirched with the same gray-brown dirt that composes the floor, their possessions a few brown baskets and monkey skins. Their lives are not paradise but full of anxiety—their religion a matter of fear, their statecraft a matter of constant, nagging war. To themselves, they are "the people" *(Yanomami);* to others, they are "the killers" *(Waikás).*

5   The rich dwell in *haciendas*—airy long ranch houses whose roofs are of curved tile and, surprisingly, dried sugar-cane stalks. Some *haciendas* surviving in Caracas date from the sixteenth century, when the great valley was all but empty. The interiors are smoky, from candlelit

dinners, and contact lenses are common among the rich. The furniture is solid, black, polished by generations of servants. Large paintings by Diebenkorn, Stella, Baziotes, and Botero adorn the white plaster walls, along with lurid religious pictures in the colonial Spanish style. The appliances are all modern and paid for; even if the oil in Lake Maracaibo were to give out, vast deposits of heavy crude have been discovered in the state of Bolívar. All this sounds cheerier than it is. The rich wish they were in Paris, London, New York. Many have condominiums in Miami. *Haute couture* and abstract painting may not prove bulwark enough. Constitutional democracy in Venezuela, though the last dictator fled in 1958, is not so assured as may appear. Turbulence and tyranny are traditional. Che Guevara is still idealized among students. To themselves, the rich are good, decent, amusing people; to others, they are *"reaccionarios."*

6   Missionaries, many of them United States citizens, move among the Indians. They claim that since Western civilization, with all its diseases and detritus, must come, it had best come through them. Nevertheless, Marxist anthropologists inveigh against them. Foreign experts, many of them United States citizens, move among the rich. They claim they are just helping out, and that anyway the oil industry was nationalized five years ago. Nevertheless, Marxist anthropologists are not mollified. The feet of the Indians are very broad in front, their toes spread wide for climbing avocado trees. The feet of the rich are very narrow in front, their toes compressed by pointed Italian shoes. The Indians seek relief from tension in the use of *ebene,* or *yopo,* a mind-altering drug distilled from the bark of the *ebene* tree and blown into the user's nose through a hollow cane by a colleague. The rich take cocaine through the nose, and frequent mind-altering discotheques, but more customarily imbibe cognac, *vino blanco,* and Scotch, in association with colleagues.

7   These and other contrasts and comparisons between the Indians and the rich can perhaps be made more meaningful by the following anecdote: A visitor, after some weeks in Venezuela, was invited to fly to the top of a *tepuy* in a helicopter, which crashed. As stated, the *tepuys* are supposed by the Indians to be the forbidden haunts of the gods; and, indeed, they present an exotic, attenuated vegetation and a craggy geology to the rare intruder. The crash was a minor one, breaking neither bones nor bottles (a lavish picnic, including *mucho vino blanco,* had been packed). The bottles were consumed, the exotic vegetation was photographed, and a rescue helicopter arrived. In the Cessna back to Caracas, the survivors couldn't get enough of discussing the incident and their survival, and the red-haired woman opposite the visitor said, "I *love* the way you pronounce *'tepuy.'"* She imitated him: *tupooey.* "Real zingy," she said. The visitor slowly realized that he was being flirted with, and that therefore *this woman was middle-class.* In Venezuela, only the negligible middle class flirts. The Indians kidnap or are raped; the

rich commandeer, or languorously give themselves in imperious surrender.

8   The Indians tend to know only three words of Spanish: *"¿Como se llama?"* ("What is your name?"). In Indian belief, to give one's name is to place oneself in the other's power. And the rich, when one is introduced, narrow their eyes and file one's name away in their mysterious depths. Power among them flows along lines of kinship and intimacy. After an imperious surrender, a rich female gazes at her visitor with new interest out of her narrowed, brown, melting, kohl-ringed eyes. He has become someone to be reckoned with, if only as a potential source of financial embarrassment. "Again, what is your name?" she asks.

9   *Los indios* and *los ricos* rarely achieve contact. When they do, *mestizos* result, and the exploitation of natural resources. In such lies the future of Venezuela.

A. Comprehension

Choose the answer that best completes each statement. Do not refer to the selection while doing this exercise.

1.   In Venezuela, the population is essentially divided into (a) the haves and the have-nots; (b) the rich and the Indians; (c) the middle class and the poor; (d) the rich and the poor.

2.   The Indians behaved toward the visitor at first shyly and then (a) cruelly; (b) inquisitively; (c) arrogantly; (d) indifferently.

3.   Updike is particularly concerned, in his description of the Venezuelans, with (a) their appearance and level of education; (b) their family structure and religious beliefs; (c) their appearance and dwellings; (d) their customs and hobbies.

4.   Updike writes that the lives of the Indians are full of (a) happiness and gaiety; (b) sharing and concern for the community; (c) anxiety and fear; (d) deprivation because they lack technology.

5.   The wealth of the rich people in Venezuela comes primarily from (a) cattle ranching; (b) manufacturing; (c) professions like medicine, engineering, and law; (d) oil.

6.   According to Updike, the political situation in Venezuela is traditionally characterized by (a) chaos and corruption; (b) imperialism and imperiousness; (c) turbulence and tyranny; (d) independence and idealism.

B. Inferences

Choose the best answer. You may refer to the selection to answer the questions in this section, and all the remaining sections.

1. When Updike writes at the end of paragraph 1 that the negligible middle class "occupies . . . a few shunned enclaves on the suburban slopes of Mount Avila," who most likely avoids these areas? (a) Updike and other travelers to Venezuela; (b) only the Indians; (c) only the rich; (d) both the rich and the poor.

2. From the beginning sentences of paragraphs 2 and 3, we can accurately infer that (a) the Indians are darker-skinned than the rich; (b) the rich are darker-skinned than the Indians; (c) both the Indians and the rich are dark-skinned; (d) both the Indians and the rich are light-skinned.

3. From paragraph 4 we can infer that curare is (a) a powerful hallucinogenic drug; (b) a staple in the Indians' diet; (c) an animal the Indians hunt; (d) a poison the Indians use in hunting.

4. At the end of paragraph 4, Updike writes that to "others," the Indians are "the killers." Who are the "others"? (a) journalists; (b) other Indian tribes hostile to the Yanomami; (c) the non-Indian population; (d) anthropologists who study the Indians.

5. From all the details we are given in paragraph 5, we can infer that rich Venezuelans (a) are not happy and contented despite their material goods and wealth; (b) are happy and contented with their material goods and wealth; (c) live according to the philosophy of "carpe diem," or "seize the day"; (d) are deeply religious.

6. The visitor mentioned in paragraph 7 and 8 is probably (a) another travel writer; (b) Updike himself; (c) an acquaintance of Updike's; (d) an unidentified visitor that Updike heard about.

C. Structure

1. The main method of development in the essay as a whole is (a) definition; (b) classification; (c) comparison and contrast; (d) analogy; (e) cause-effect.

2. The tone of the essay can best be described as (a) objective, impartial; (b) bewildered, perplexed; (c) hostile, cynical; (d) ironic, sarcastic.

3. According to the information Updike provides about the Indians and the way they live, what is his attitude toward them? (a) sympathetic, feeling pity; (b) indifferent, callous; (c) mocking, insulting; (d) intense dislike.

4. According to the information Updike provides about rich Venezuelans, what does he think of them? (a) He is impressed with their lifestyle; (b) He thinks they are shallow and materialistic; (c) He thinks that they are simple, good people; (d) He thinks that they set a good example for the poorer classes.

5. When Updike writes in paragraphs 4 and 5—in commenting on both groups—that "all this sounds cheerier than it is"—he means something quite different for each group. Explain. _____

_____

6. In paragraph 6, Updike writes, "Foreign experts, many of them United States citizens, move among the rich. They claim that they are just helping out, and that anyway the oil industry was nationalized five years ago." What attitude toward these foreign experts is implied? (a) admiration; (b) skepticism; (c) hostility; (d) envy.

7. An *oxymoron* is a special kind of figure of speech which produces an effect by pairing supposedly contradictory words (for example, "cruel kindness"). Find an oxymoron in paragraph 8. _____

_____

8. Read paragraph 9 again. In relation to Venezuela's future, Updike is (a) decidedly optimistic; (b) decidedly pessimistic; (c) confused, unsure; (d) fearful, anxious.

D. Vocabulary

For each italicized word from the selection, choose the best definition according to the context in which it appears.

1. the *negligible* middle class [paragraph 1]: (a) rapidly increasing; (b) dwindling, decreasing; (c) so trifling as to be insignificant; (d) neglectful, remiss in duty.

2. the *burgeoning* metropolis [1]: (a) growing rapidly; (b) crime-ridden; (c) surrounding; (d) extremely polluted.

3. *parameters* of tact and irony [2]: (a) examples, illustrations; (b) limitations, boundaries; (c) essential characteristics; (d) mathematical variables.

4. anecdotes *culled* from their lives [3]: (a) based on; (b) represented; (c) collected, picked from; (d) experienced in.

5. the *circumambient* rain forest [4] (Note: This word is from the Latin word-parts *circum-*, and *ambient,* meaning literally "to walk around."): (a) overshadowing; (b) surrounding; (c) overlooking; (d) shrinking.

6. their faces and limbs *besmirched* [4]: (a) shriveled; (b) festering; (c) decorated; (d) soiled.

7. *lurid* religious pictures [5]: (a) garish, glowing; (b) tasteful, refined; (c) traditional; (d) delicately ornamented.

8. may not prove *bulwark* enough [5]: (a) amusement; (b) diversion; (c) ammunition; (d) fortification.

9. *turbulence* and tyranny [5]: (a) violent agitation; (b) political uncertainty; (c) revolutionary fervor; (d) oppression.

10. diseases and *detritus* [6]: (a) pollution; (b) debris; (c) remnants; (d) criminal activity.

11. Marxist anthropologists *inveigh* against them [6]: (a) write letters; (b) protest strongly; (c) run in elections; (d) organize militarily.

12. Marxist anthropologists are not *mollified* [6]: (a) bothered; (b) encouraged; (c) pacified; (d) convinced.

13. The rich *commandeer* [7]: (a) seize forcibly; (b) flirt, toy with; (c) give orders to; (d) set an example for.

14. or *languorously* give themselves [7]: (a) sensuously; (b) romantically; (c) indifferently; (d) willingly.

15. in *imperious* surrender [7]: (a) domineering; (b) sweet; (c) insincere; (d) subservient.

E. Questions for Discussion and Analysis

1. Do you find Updike's observations about these two groups of Venezuelans disturbing, exaggerated, humorous, or what? Explain your reactions to this essay.

2. What would you say is the fundamental irony in this essay, particularly in Updike's contrasting descriptions of the rich and the Indians?

III

Reading Critically: Evaluating What You Read

As you have seen in Parts I and II, analytical reading requires thoroughness and careful attention to words and their connotations. In addition to acquiring good comprehension skills, becoming a good reader means developing a critical sense, a means of judging the worth of what you read. This requires keeping an open mind, not *accepting* unquestioningly what you read just because it is in print—and also not *rejecting* ideas simply because they are different from your beliefs. A middle ground is a healthy skepticism.

Once you are sure that you have a firm grasp of a writer's ideas and the vocabulary words used to express them, you can apply the skills you will learn in Part III: locating arguments; detecting unstated assumptions behind an argument; judging the quality of the evidence supporting an argument; distinguishing between deductive and inductive reasoning; telling a valid argument from an invalid one; detecting false appeals and logical fallacies; and recognizing bias and the misuse of authority. In addition, you will learn to recognize false reasoning: generalizations, distortions, even clever manipulation with advertising slogans and statistics. All of these skills will serve you well throughout your life.

Critical Reading Defined

Having a keen critical stance is vital as we wade through or listen to the mass of words that bombards us every day in the form of newspapers, magazines, textbooks, advertising of all stripes, junk mail, political slogans, and speeches. Both to protect our wallets and, more important, to safeguard our ability to think clearly for ourselves, skill in reading critically becomes ever more necessary. The term *critical* reading does not mean "*critical*" in the sense of tearing down or fault-finding; rather it means using careful evaluation, sound judgment, and our reasoning powers.

Some of what is published is very good, some is mediocre, and some is terrible. How do you learn to tell the difference? What criteria should you use to judge prose, to determine whether a piece of writing—particularly persuasive or argumentative writing—is "good" or "bad," to determine whether an argument is sound or unsound? Here are some fundamental standards for judging what you read.

First, the main idea or thesis (or *argument,* in persuasive or argumentative prose) should be clearly stated. The writer should define key words, especially abstract words open to subjective interpretation (like *honor, responsibility, evil*). The language should be clear and unambiguous; words should be used consistently to mean the same thing. The evidence used to support the argument should be logically arranged, and it should be relevant to the main idea. Moreover, the evidence should appeal to our intelligence and to our reason, not solely to our emotions. And finally, there should be sufficient evidence to support the point. In many of the following sections, we will examine some of the ways that writers and their readers—intentionally or unintentionally—go wrong.

The Reader's Responsibility

Perhaps we should begin with our responsibility first. If the writer's task is to muster convincing and fair evidence in support of an argument and to play by the rules of logic, what is the reader's responsibility? Why do we all sometimes misinterpret what we read?

One reason is simple laziness. We may not take the trouble to comprehend accurately. More often, we may not feel like looking up the definitions of key words. Consider this sentence, for example: "The defense attorney used a meretricious argument to get his client's acquittal." Someone might read this and think, "*Meretricious* sounds something like *merit,* and I remember from high school French that *mère* means "mother," so *meretricious* must mean something good." Un-

happily, this is way off the mark. Not only does the word have nothing to do with *merit* or *motherhood,* but it really means "attracting attention in a vulgar manner." (Applied to a person, incidentally, *meretricious* means "resembling or pertaining to a prostitute.") So the student, too lazy to look up the word, reads the sentence and concludes that the lawyer did something noteworthy, when the writer meant something very different.

A second obstacle to good reading is prejudice or bias, letting our narrow personal experience or parochial values get in the way of our reading. Naturally, lower-division college students cannot expect to have the same wealth of experience older people do. Yet sensitivity to connotation and a willingness to see events from another perspective are essential components of critical reading, and they are best developed during the college years, when students have the opportunity to be exposed to a wide assortment of political, social, and philosophical ideas. In the years following college, students can refine their thinking and call upon these skills in every aspect of their lives.

Two incidents that occurred in my critical reading classes will illustrate this problem of misinterpretation due to bias or prejudice. One student, a former Marine in his mid-twenties, worked as a full-time police officer in a large city. When the word *indoctrinate* came up in a passage the class was discussing, he was unable to see that the word could have either a positive or a negative connotation, depending on the context. In the passage, the author was explaining how the Khmer Rouge had rounded up thousands of Cambodians in the 1970s and sent them to "reeducation camps" where they were indoctrinated in Communist theory.

In the student's experience—both in the military and in the police—indoctrination meant being taught certain rules and principles of behavior that needed to be followed for group discipline and survival. To him, therefore, *indoctrinate* suggested something positive. He was unable to see that, in this context, the word carried the suggestion of forcible instruction, something like brainwashing. Lack of flexibility was the culprit here. Critical readers keep an open mind and are sensitive to a word's many possible nuances.

The second example involved another student, also in his mid-twenties, who had recently emigrated from Poland. The class was discussing a newspaper article about Fidel Castro's playing host to Rajiv Gandhi, the prime minister of India. Wanting to give Gandhi a big send-off at the conclusion to his visit, Castro assembled thousands of Cubans, who lined the streets of Havana, cheering and clapping. Here are the pertinent sentences from the article.

> Rounding up a half-million people on short notice is no small task. But it took only a snap of Castro's fingers. By dawn, Havana was abuzz with activity in preparation for Gandhi's midmorning departure. Mass organiza-

tions were alerted and buses normally used to take commuters to their jobs were mobilized. Half a million cheering Cubans saw the Indian leader off that day in 1985.

George Gedda, *San Francisco Examiner*

After reading this passage, the student inferred that Castro had "forced" the population to stop their daily activities and to attend the parade in Gandhi's honor, even though the writer was making only a factual statement and implied no coercion. (One could also infer inaccurately that the people gladly dropped what they were doing simply to get out of work.) Nor does the writer's tone convey anything sinister; the phrase, "Havana was abuzz with activity," for example, is completely neutral.

The student arrived at his incorrect inference by this reasoning. Cuba has been a Communist country for more than thirty years, and traditionally Communist governments have relied on force to quell popular uprisings. (This is, of course, true, though this generalization cannot be applied to every action of those living in a Communist country.) In this case, the student's experience of growing up in a Communist country colored his perception, causing him to read into the writer's words an inference that the writer never implied.

Critical readers try—insofar as it is humanly possible—to maintain objectivity and not allow their expectations, biases, or personal prejudices to interfere with their understanding.

Developing a World View

The etymology of the word *educate* means "a leading out," (from the Latin *ē*, meaning "from" plus *ducāre* meaning "leading"). And although it is impossible for human beings to be completely free of bias and prejudice, we should at least strive to look at ideas from other people's points of view. This requires us to shed our ethnocentric belief that everyone else in the world looks at issues and problems the same way North Americans do. *Ethnocentrism* means a belief in the superiority of one's own ethnic group, or—stated more literally—the belief that one's group is at the center of the universe, and that any other way of perceiving events is somehow wrong or flawed.

A college education will expose you to an enormous range of opinion and thought, and sometimes sorting it all out is difficult. As you grow intellectually and reflect on what you have read, learned, and experienced firsthand, you will develop a "world view": a way of regarding events and issues that reflects your personal point of view.

Where does one's world view come from? Obviously, from the many influences that you have come into contact with during your formative years: your parents, teachers, siblings, friends, acquaintances,

members of the clergy, and coworkers, to name a few. But your world view is also formed by intangibles: the value system you were raised with, your family's economic status, their level of education, race or ethnic group, and religion. All of these intangibles come together to form the person you are—and, for purposes of this discussion—the way you perceive both what goes on around you and what you read.

Our world view is constantly undergoing change, part of the "leading out" process you experience as a student. To characterize your world view, begin by questioning why you think the way you do. You can reflect on your own upbringing and those people who have influenced you most. To what extent does your thinking conform to the way you were brought up? To the way you were educated? Becoming an independent adult—and, along the way, a good thinker and reader—involves developing one's *own* world view, not someone else's views adopted uncritically.

Let us now look at the concept of world view as it connects to reading. The next piece of writing is about the cultural misperceptions of bullfighting. Before you read it, ask yourself these questions to determine your attitude toward the subject. Jot your ideas down on paper so that you are forced to state your thinking in words.

- What do you know/think about bullfighting?
- Do you consider bullfighting to be a sport?
- Where does your opinion come from? What is it based on? For example, have you seen a bullfight on TV? in the movies?
- Have you ever attended a bullfight? If so, what were your reactions? Would you attend another?
- If you answered no to the question above, would you ever attend a bullfight? Why or why not?
- Do you believe bullfighting is a cruel sport?
- Do you believe that bullfighting should be banned?
- Is a bull an intelligent, sensitive animal in the same way, that, say, a dog is?

Now read the article.

[1]A very interesting kind of trouble spot is seen when any element of the form of a complex pattern has different classification or meaning across cultures. The foreign observer gives to the entire pattern the meaning of that different classification of one element.

[2]*Example.* Bullfighting has always been in my observation a source of cross-cultural misinformation. It is a particularly difficult pattern of behavior to explain convincingly to an unsophisticated United States observer. I therefore choose it as a test case.

[3]*Form.* A bullfight has a very precise, complex form. A man, armed with a sword and a red cape, challenges and kills a fighting bull. The form is prescribed in great detail. There are specific vocabulary terms for seemingly minute variations. The bullfighter, the bull, the picadors, the music, the dress, etc., are part of the form.

[4]*Meaning.* The bullfight has a complex of meaning in Spanish culture. It is a sport. It symbolizes the triumph of art over the brute force of a bull. It is entertainment. It is a display of bravery.

[5]*Distribution.* The bullfight shows a complex distribution pattern. There is a season for bullfights on a yearly cycle, there are favored days on a weekly cycle, and there is a favored time on a daily cycle. The bullfight occurs at a specific place, the bull ring, known to the least person in the culture.

[6]*Form, meaning, and distribution to an alien observer.* An American observer seated next to a Spanish or Mexican spectator will see a good deal of the form, though not all of it. He will see a man in a special dress, armed with a sword and cape, challenging and killing the bull. He will see the bull charging at the man and will notice that the man deceives the bull with his cape. He will notice the music, the color, etc.

[7]The meaning of the spectacle is quite different to him, however. It is the slaughter of a "defenseless" animal by an armed man. It is unfair because the bull always gets killed. It is unsportsmanlike—to the bull. It is cruel to animals. The fighter is therefore cruel. The public is cruel.

[8]The distribution constitutes no particular problem to the American observer, since he has the experience of football, baseball, and other spectacles.

[9]*Misinformation.* Is there an element of misinformation here, and if so, wherein is it? I believe there is misinformation. The secondary meaning "cruel" is found in Spanish culture, but it does not attach to the bullfight. The American observer ascribing the meaning cruel to the spectator and fighter is getting information that is not there. Why?

[10]Since the cruelty is interpreted by the American observer as being perpetrated by the man on the bull, we can test to see if those parts of the complex form—the bull and the man—are the same in the two cultures.

[11]*Linguistic evidence.* We find evidence in the language that seems interesting. A number of vocabulary items that are applicable both to animals and to humans in English have separate words for animals and for humans in Spanish. In English both animals and persons have *legs.* In Spanish, animals have *patas,* "animal legs," and humans have *piernas,* "human legs." Similarly, in English, animals and humans have *backs* and *necks,* while in Spanish, animals have *lomo* and *pescuezo,* "animal back" and "animal neck," and humans have *espalda* and *cuello,* "human back" and "human

neck." Furthermore, in English, both animals and humans *get nervous,* have *hospitals,* and have *cemeteries,* named by means of various metaphors. In Spanish, animals do not get nervous, or have hospitals or cemeteries. The linguistic evidence, though only suggestive, points to a difference in the classification of *animal* in the two cultures. In Hispanic culture the distinction between man and animal seems very great, certainly greater than that in American culture.

[12]By further observation of what people say and do one finds additional features of difference. In Spanish culture, man is not physically strong but is skillful and intelligent. A bull is strong but not skillful and not intelligent. In American culture a man is physically strong, and so is a bull. A bull is intelligent. A bull has feelings of pain, sorrow, pity, tenderness—at least in animal stories such as that of *Ferdinand the Bull.* A bull deserves an even chance in a fight; he has that sportsman's right even against a man.

[13]We can, then, hypothesize that the part of the complex form represented by the bull has a different classification, a different meaning, in American culture, and that herein lies the source of the misinformation.

[14]We should test this hypothesis by minimal contrast if possible. We find something akin to a minimal contrast in American culture in tarpon fishing. In tarpon fishing we have a form: a fight to the exhaustion and death of the tarpon at the hands of a man with a line and camouflaged hooks. Much of the form is prescribed in detail. There is no large visible audience, but newspaper stories in a sense represent audience contact. In the complex of meaning, it is a sport, and it represents a triumph of skill over the brute fighting strength of the fish. The distribution seems somewhat different from that of a bullfight, but the difference does not seem relevant as an explanation of the difference we have hypothesized.

[15]We now observe that the very same American who interpreted the bullfight as cruel, and applied that meaning to the spectator and the bullfighter, will sit next to the same spectator on a fishing boat and never think of the fishing game as cruel. I conclude that the part of the complex form represented by the fish is quite distinct from "human being" in both American and Spanish cultures, while the part identified as the bull is much more like "human being" in American culture than in Spanish culture.

[16]Marginal supporting evidence is the fact that in American culture there is a Society for the Prevention of Cruelty to Animals which concerns itself with the feelings of dogs, cats, horses, and other domestic animals. Recently there was a front-page story in the local papers reporting that the Humane Society of New York City had sent a Santa Claus to distribute gifts among the dogs in the New York City pounds. We would not conceive of a society for the prevention of cruelty to fish.

Robert Lado, "How to Compare Two Cultures," Linguistics Across Cultures:
Applied Linguistics for Language Teachers

Has your thinking changed because of this article? Having examined the differences between Spaniards' world view and the North Americans' world views, you may now regard bullfighting differently. You can understand why Spaniards (and other Hispanic cultures) consider bullfighting a sport. The Spaniard's cultural perception and language are different from ours; hence, they consider bullfighting a sport, whereas many North Americans consider it barbaric. Note, however, that having read this article, we are *not* obliged to change our opinion of bullfighting, nor should we feel compelled to attend a bullfight. But we can recognize that there are legitimate cultural differences operating here. Developing cross-cultural awareness means that we have been exposed to different world views from ours.

A final suggestion: Don't be afraid to say that you need more information before you can accept a position on a controversial issue. It is perfectly reasonable to ask what other information you need before you can accept or reject anyone's point of view.

Uncovering Arguments

Before you can evaluate persuasive or argumentative prose, you must first determine what the argument actually is. An *argument,* as the term is used here, is a specific proposition. Whether stated or implied, it is the main idea that the writer wants us to accept. Unlike the subject matter of expository or informative writing, which is usually straightforward, the subject matter of persuasive writing is usually a matter of controversy and a wide variety of opinion surrounds it.

To recognize an argument, first consider the topic and its capacity to incite controversy. Many topics are inherently noncontroversial. No one is going to get worked up about a new program to prevent litter. (After all, who is going to argue seriously that litter is necessary or attractive or that programs to reduce litter are misguided?) But many topics inspire concern, passion, and sometimes even violence: for example, the right of women to seek an abortion without interference; the welfare system; allowing gays who openly admit their sexual orientation to serve in the military; ways to reduce the federal deficit; sexual harassment in the workplace; prayer or "moments of silence" in the public schools; and so forth.

Next, consider the author's stated or underlying purpose. You can tell that the writer wants to convince you to accept a subjective point of view if he or she says that we "should" do such-and-such or that the country "needs" such-and-such. Here are some arguments culled from recent newspaper articles. Notice that each has also been reworded to argue for the exact opposite.

- Elementary school children should be taught in school that other sexual orientations exist besides heterosexuality. (*Contrary argument:* Elementary school children should not be taught in school that sexual orientations exist besides heterosexuality.)
- We as parents must act responsibly and allow high schools to distribute free condoms to any student who requests one. (*Contrary argument:* We as parents must act responsibly and not allow high schools to distribute free condoms to any student who requests one.)
- Women should be prohibited from serving as surrogate mothers for infertile couples and from receiving money to bear them a child. (*Contrary argument:* Women should not be prohibited from serving as surrogate mothers for infertile couples and from receiving money to bear them a child.)
- Retarded or formerly abused people who have been found guilty of murder should not be treated or punished any differently from other murderers, even if it means the death penalty. (*Contrary argument:* Retarded or formerly abused people who have been found guilty of murder should be treated differently from other murderers and should be spared the death penalty.)
- The United States needs to reevaluate its priorities and recognize that we no longer can act as the world's policeman and solve other nations' internal or regional disputes. (*Contrary argument:* The United States needs to recognize that our chief role in the world is to act as the world's moral guide to help solve other nations' internal or regional disputes.)

Arguments may not be so explicitly stated as these. A writer may merely imply what "should" be done or "needs" to be done. Consider these statements:

- English 100 really improved my writing skills. My teacher was helpful and encouraging, and I received an A for all my efforts. It can help you, too. (*Implied argument:* You should take English 100.)
- Buying a computer was the best decision I ever made. My son's attitude toward school has completely turned around, and his grades have improved, too. (*Implied argument:* Buying a computer will improve a child's learning.)
- The continued influx of both legal and illegal immigrants in states like Texas, New York, Florida, and California, has resulted in a serious drain on state budgets and a decline in the quality of life. (*Possible implied arguments:* The United States needs to examine its immigration policy; certain states are bearing an unfair burden resulting from national policy; the United States needs to take more serious steps to halt the flow of illegal immigrants into the country.)

Arguments occur in advertising as well, with the sponsor hoping that the advertising slogan will be clever or convincing enough to make you buy the product. In advertising slogans, the argument ("buy this product") is implied and may rest on dubious, nonspecific, or meaningless claims. For example, study these slogans:

- *"Yuban coffee—the richest coffee in the world."* (TV ad)
- *"Give eggs a break. 22 percent less cholesterol."* (Billboard ad)
- *"It's a great time to be silver."* (TV ad for Centrum Silver vitamins)
- *"Trust the Gorton fisherman."* (TV ad for Gorton's frozen seafood entrees)
- *"Generations will remember this sale at the Waterford Wedgewood store."* (Newspaper ad for a glass and china sale)
- *"More Americans get their news from ABC News."* (TV ad)
- *"What's so different about Turnaround Cream? Its persistence, for one thing. It just won't quit. With nightly use, it operates on a continuous, non-stop basis to rid skin of faults you don't want to see."* (Pamphlet distributed with a Clinique beauty product)

These slogans embody arguments as much as the other examples cited earlier. What is significant about these arguments, however, is the lack of anything meaningful that warrants our accepting the product. The arguments are hidden, couched in vague or pretentious or clever language.

For practice in uncovering arguments, here are two short excerpts from editorials, one stating the argument explicitly, the other implying it. When you finish reading them, state each author's argument in your own words. The first is from an article in which David Segal questions whether states should require welfare mothers to work full-time.

[1]If you've heard politicians podium-pounding about the need to get welfare mothers working, you have a pretty good idea of what direction the welfare reform debate is going. But for a better sense of what's being said—and not being said—in the make-them-work rhetoric, get yourself a copy of *Moving Ahead,* a June 1992 study by three Republican members of the House Human Resources Subcommittee on Ways and Means.

[2]The authors warn that the children of the 3.4 million female-headed families living below the poverty level face greatly increased odds of "having poor school attendance and achievement, dropping out of school, committing crimes," and so on, but they utter not a peep about how these mothers will engage in the "civilizing task" of bringing up their children or how they will keep their kids from the very perils the authors describe. The math of the study's policy prescriptions, for moms with tots of all ages, is predicated on those moms working a 40-hour week. Even Bill Clinton hasn't said anything about welfare mothers actually *parenting*. . . .

[3]The genesis of the recent push for full-time work is traceable to the 1988 Family Support Act, the product of a Democratically controlled Congress and Ronald Reagan, which took the first step to change AFDC from an income-support scheme to a workfare program. Health and Human Services (HHS) mandated that single parents on welfare with children over 4 years old "participate" in job training, school, or, most optimistically, a job for at least 20 hours a week, and required states to provide day care. Teen moms not enrolled full time in classes could be required to go back to school immediately after their children are born.

[4]Since the act was passed, a number of states have applied for waivers that allow them to gnaw away at exemptions and require more moms with younger children to work for more hours. Oregon won a waiver from HHS to mandate full-time participation for any mother with a child over 1 year old. In Michigan, always a trailblazer in welfare reform, mothers with kids age 1 and older can be compelled to work full time or face a cut in benefits.

[5]But is full-time work for mothers one of the rules that mainstream society lives by? Only a third of all married mothers work full time throughout the year. And these women have a partner to assist in rearing the children, plus more money and conveniences—like cars and microwaves—that make juggling the earner and parent roles easier. And of those moms who work, only 23 percent have children under 3.

[6]The children of welfare mothers, like the vast majority of children, need a healthy dose of parental presence in their lives.

David Segal, "Motherload," *The Washington Monthly*

The second excerpt concerns the issue of human control over the natural environment.

[1]China's former leader Mao Zedong once declared war against sparrows, believing they were a pest and a nuisance. In response, millions of Chinese took to the streets, banging on woks and pans to terrify the birds. The idea: force them to stay aloft until they dropped dead of exhaustion. They did just that. The campaign was halted after an infestation of caterpillars, now freed of their feathered predators, devoured the crops, enveloped the trees and rained down upon pedestrians. In that same grand tradition of meddling with nature, Alaska has declared an air war against hundreds of wolves in an effort to boost already abundant populations of caribou and moose. And all to impress hunters and tourists. Never mind that when herds swell, starvation is often close by. Even as Alaska prepares to wage its wolf war, conservationists in the Lower 48 mourn the absence of wolves and seek to reintroduce them.

[2]Chalk another one up to mankind's micromanagement of nature. Recklessly arrogant and myopic, Alaska's decision is rooted in special-interest

economics, not biology. It's all the more distressing for what it tells us about ourselves as a species and our estrangement from nature. Alaska's folly is the product of a theme-park mentality in which nature exists for our amusement, to be enhanced by adding one species and subtracting another. An indiscriminate assault will kill off pack leaders, leaving wolves in hierarchical disarray, and harm eagles, foxes and wolverines, which dine upon the carcasses wolves leave behind. Such contempt for natural order is nothing new, though it comes at a time when many Americans belatedly question both nature's recuperative powers and the human species' claim to a divine right of subjugation.

Ted Gup, "The World Is Not a Theme Park," Time

Throughout the rest of Part III, you will have more opportunities to find the arguments in several reading passages, including editorials.

Unstated Assumptions

All arguments rest on assumptions or premises. Sometimes these assumptions are stated explicitly, but more frequently than not, the writer presumes them to be true and presumes that the reader shares them as well. Unstated assumptions are not necessarily bad or somehow deliberately manipulative. But it is certainly important for us to identify them, especially when they are not included in an argument. Whether or not we accept an argument may depend on whether we can accept the assumptions propping it up. If we cannot accept the underlying assumption, we may surely want to question the proposition it leads to. For example, consider this statement.

- The world's rain forests must be protected at all costs.

    This argument rests on the assumption that rain forests are worth protecting, that their preservation is somehow important for our continued existence.

- Cigarette smoking should be banned in public places.

    The writer's assumption here is that cigarette smoke—so-called secondary or sidestream smoke—harms nonsmokers. Recent studies generally confirm the truth of this unstated assumption: i.e., the rate of ear infections is higher among young children who live with smokers, and the incidence of smoking-related cancer is higher among those who live with smokers. If you accept the premise, then you can accept the argument it leads to.

• John Ventura should be given a full-time position. He is an amazingly good teacher even if he is a part-time instructor teaching at three different community colleges.

This argument rests upon the premise that, for whatever reason, part-time instructors are not as good as full-time faculty. What is the thinking behind such a statement? Propping up the argument is this implied reasoning. Part-time instructors are typically paid an hourly salary, which is considerably less than what full-time faculty receive. (At many community colleges, this is definitely true, with part-time faculty often working for a quarter of what regular faculty earn.) Their low salary, in turn, requires them to work at two or three campuses and to teach more classes than regular faculty do to make ends meet. Therefore, they do not have the financial incentive to teach as well as full-time instructors, nor do they have the time.

Can you accept this assumption? Obviously, some part-time faculty are stretched thin and may not provide as rigorous a course as they might if they had better job security. But the assumption is a generalization. Surely there are many fine, dedicated teachers in the nation's part-time ranks, and every student can point to full-time faculty members who are incompetent. A case *can* be made for the negative effects of having large numbers of part-time teachers on campuses, but generalizing about their ability and commitment is unfair. It may be a good idea to give John Ventura a full-time job because of his teaching abilities, rather than because he does not fit some preconceived stereotype.

• An increasing number of parents who educate their children at home do so, as Richard Viguerie has written, because home-educated children "get along better with adults and many are able to enter college at age fifteen or sixteen." (Quoted in "Thunder on the Right: A Plea for Home Schooling," *San Francisco Chronicle*)

In this example, the writer's argument in favor of home schooling depends on his assumption that primary goals of education are getting along better with adults and entering college early. The first claim seems irrelevant; the second is of questionable value.

Here is one final short example. What is the argument? What unstated assumption underlies it?

• If a student turns in written work with a lot of spelling and grammar errors, the reader will think that he or she is a poor writer.

Kinds of Evidence

The next step is to evaluate the *evidence* the writer uses to support the proposition. This process involves first, determining whether or not the evidence is fair, accurate, sufficient, and relevant to the argument; and second, whether or not the evidence leads to a valid conclusion, that is, whether the conclusion derives logically from the support. In Chapters 2 and 3 of Part I, you studied several methods of paragraph development. Essentially, these methods are derived from the kinds of evidence—examples, analogy, cause and effect, definition, and so on—that a writer may use to develop an idea. These are primarily expository methods.

In this section, we are concerned more with the kinds of evidence used in persuasive and argumentative writing. Without generalizing, it seems fair to say that most good argumentative prose is supported by examples, facts and/or statistics, or good reasons. Naturally, there are exceptions. For example, in Part IV, Richard Wright's essay, "The Ethics of Living Jim Crow," relies on a series of short narratives as the dominant mode of discourse, but he has a secondary purpose: to persuade the reader that a racist environment which uses Jim Crow laws to suppress blacks produces terrible inequities and damages its victims' self-esteem.

Exercises: Part 1— Evaluating Evidence

Here are three articles or excerpts that contain arguments. First, identify the argument and look for any unstated assumptions. (The underlying assumptions may be explicitly stated, as well.) Try to differentiate between the editorials' three parts: argument, evidence in support, conclusion/recommendations. Then decide what kind of evidence the writer relies on; some possibilities are personal experience, facts and statistics, good reasons, narrative examples, definitions of key terms, analogy, or historical analysis. Finally, evaluate the evidence for (a) its relevancy; (b) its reliability; (c) its ability to convince you that the argument is sound.

Selection 1

At the heart of parental loss of control lies the fact that parents today supervise their school-age children less than their counterparts did even ten years and certainly twenty years ago. A new parental casualness is so much the norm these days that only when one compares contemporary children's lives with those of the 1960s and early 1970s does one realize how much earlier the

parental reins are loosened today. There is clear evidence of an overall decrease in parental vigilance about every aspect of children's lives, from the trivial to the life-threatening. Indeed, so universal is children's earlier freedom in today's society that what was once seen as care and nurture is now often regarded as overprotectiveness. Today's children seem to be about two years advanced when compared with children ten years ago. Kids cross the street without holding an adult's hand at four years instead of at six. Seven-year-olds ride the bus alone where once they had to wait until they were nine or ten. Bedtime for seven-year-olds is commonly ten P.M., as it once was for fifth- or sixth-graders, while *those* "young adults"—as they are called in the publishing trade—often don't have any required bedtime at all. (A recent informal survey of fifth- and sixth-graders revealed that the majority no longer consider themselves children. When asked "What are you, then?" they answered "Pre-teenagers" or "Young adults.")

Marie Winn, Children Without Childhood

Selection 2

[1]The so-called "small business" sector can also be a route to wealth and social status. The Census Bureau keeps count of the number of firms owned by black men and women. Its most recent survey found 425,000 such enterprises, numbering about 2.4 percent of the country's corporations, partnerships, and sole proprietorships. By and large, the black businesses are local concerns, with annual receipts averaging around $50,000, and they deal largely in products or services oriented to black clienteles. Indeed, only 70,000 of the 425,000 have any paid employees. In other words, almost 85 percent are one-person enterprises or family-run firms.

[2]Many arguments have been given for the paucity of black-owned enterprises. There is the difficulty of getting start-up loans and capital from banks and investors stemming from biased attitudes about blacks' business abilities. Nor is it easy for blacks to get experience in corporate management as a prelude to branching out on their own. Some blacks have done well providing products and services to their own community. Still, the real challenge is to build a wider clientele. In fact, some firms have been successful in this sphere. Most whites who have bought Park's Sausages and McCall's Patterns do not know that those companies are owned and managed by blacks.

[3]It has occasionally been suggested that black Americans do not have a "culture" that encourages entrepreneurship. But it is best to be wary of such sweeping explanations, since they imply that the roots run very deep. There may be some validity to the view that youngsters who grow up in areas with few locally owned enterprises lack models for business careers. But even this need not be an obstacle, since the decision to start up on your own usually comes later in life. As it happens, in the generation following emancipation, many blacks set up businesses in Southern cities, just as others prospered in farming. Haitian and West Indian immigrants have brought entrepreneurial ambitions with them; and it will be interesting to see what becomes of the West African sidewalk vendors who have become a New York fixture.

PROPORTION OF MEN WHO ARE SELF-EMPLOYED IN 13 ETHNIC GROUPS

Korean	16.5%
Japanese	11.1%
Chinese	9.0%
Cuban	8.3%
White	7.4%
Asian Indian	6.6%
Mexican	4.4%
Hawaiian	3.9%
Eskimo	3.7%
Filipino	3.6%
Black	3.0%
Puerto Rican	2.9%
Vietnamese	2.1%

Source: Andrew Hacker, *Two Nations: Black and White, Separate, Hostile, Unequal*

[4]Considering the advantages and opportunities open to white Americans, it is noteworthy that less than 8 percent of them operate enterprises of their own. The table below provides some census tabulations that suggest that other ethnic groups are well ahead of whites in embarking on entrepreneurship. For this reason, little will be gained by asking whether blacks have a "culture" that inhibits them from establishing their own businesses. Even if that answer is in the affirmative, it also applies to white Americans, 92.6 percent of whom spend their working hours on someone else's payroll.

Selection 3

Compared to the sheer inhumanity of what is happening on an international scale, the justification that is sometimes put forth for limiting the influx of refugees into the U.S. seems almost ludicrous. Many fear that some groups will become long-term welfare burdens, developing a welfare mentality that will result in generation after generation on public support. But in the relatively few years that have passed since the recent refugee movement began, how can accurate predictions be made? Short-term dependency is to be expected; it isn't necessarily indicative of what is to come. Like many of the desperate "economic migrants" we are so unwilling to take, my great-grandmother was illiterate when she arrived in the United States from Russia. She lived here forty years, never spoke a word of English, and had to be supported all her life. There was no welfare in those days, but if there had been, she would have been considered one of those who did not "do well." But her children were neither illiterate nor welfare recipients; like most of their generation, they gave

to American society far more than they took. So it is likely to be with the children of the refugees in this country today. The offspring of the 1975 Vietnamese are thriving; they provide a disproportionate number of high school valedictorians, outdistance their peers in math, and promise to become the brightest in scientific fields. Other groups who came later, from less advantaged backgrounds, may take longer to catch up. But there is evidence that, despite the fears of long-term dependency, they are often doing better than expected. The Hmong from the mountains of Laos, long targeted as a group that "struggles" (that is, takes welfare), are "doing well" in some communities. Even where the statistics aren't promising—as in Fresno, California, where more Hmong live than anywhere else outside Southeastern Asia—innovative local programs have been helping improve a dismal unemployment rate in a still-sluggish economy. Teenage Hmong students are surprising everyone by scoring as well as or better than their American counterparts on certain standardized tests, though so far few are continuing on to college because of cultural traditions. Historically, every incoming group has made ours a more complex and richer culture.

Ellyn Bache, "Vietnamese Refugees: Overcoming Culture Clash," Culture Clash

Balance

Writers of news and feature articles in newspapers and magazines have the journalistic responsibility to present controversial issues fairly. This is called *balance*. Unlike editorial writers, whose works typically appear in magazine editorials or in newspapers' op-ed (opinion-editorial) pages and whose writings are characterized by a subjective point of view, news writers strive to maintain objectivity in presenting both sides of a controversial issue. Such articles do not contain a single argument reflecting the writer's point of view; rather they present all sides of an issue, leaving you free to make up your own mind. Let us examine a recent newspaper article for balance. The subject is the controversy over theme parks' performing whales. After you read the article, take a sheet of paper and draw a vertical line down the middle. Label one column "arguments for" capturing and training whales to perform; label the other "arguments against."

[1]At first glance, Yaka and Vigga—the star cetaceans at Marine World in Vallejo—hardly appear likely candidates for national controversy, as they splash and chatter like carefree children on a beach holiday.

[2]Yet animal welfare advocates argue that the pair of whales and the country's 14 other captive orcas are a disgrace. They charge that the seagoing mammals are ripped from their family groups in the wild and worked to premature death in the arenas of an entertainment industry that insists it is acting to preserve the species and to educate the public.

[3]Now, through demonstrations, lawsuits and pressure on regulatory agencies, animal welfare groups are provoking the industry into a high-stakes standoff.

[4]"We see an animal that has intricate social behaviors, and basically they're forced to spend their lives in something that's just a swimming pool," said John Grandy, vice president of wildlife habitat protection for the Humane Society of the United States. "When a wild orca is taken and put into that, we would view that as a tragedy."

[5]Piegen Barrett, executive director of the Marine Mammal Center at Fort Cronkhite, disputes that view. She says Marine World is an exceptionally humane caretaker and deserves credit for its commitment to rescuing stranded cetaceans, adding that it is wrong to associate the facility with others that have lower standards.

[6]"I do know we're not abusing these animals," Marine World founder and manager Michael Demetrios said in an interview. "The handful we have are ambassadors for their species."

[7]It has taken a generation of experience with captive marine mammals to prompt a debate over the quality of their care and the ethics of displaying them. In the 1960s, families piled into their gas guzzlers and packed the nation's new aquariums, delighted at the spectacle of dolphins leaping through fiery hoops and cavorting in grass skirts and giant sunglasses.

[8]Like Flipper, those days are gone.

[9]"The public is changing its views," Grandy said. ". . . What you're seeing is an evolution of human thought and, perhaps, corporate responsibility."

[10]Since 1989, protesters encouraged by a more skeptical public have claimed credit for restricting a U.S. Navy dolphin program in Puget Sound and blocking the transfer of a dolphin from a private aquarium to the Navy.

[11]Last August, in the first such move since it began monitoring theme parks in 1979, the U.S. Agriculture Department charged a Florida exhibitor with low standards of animal care. And just last month, Great America amusement park in Santa Clara announced that it was dropping its live dolphin show, citing public perceptions and the high costs of the exhibit.

[12]Groups such as In Defense of Animals based in Marin County, are appealing to the emotions of the 15 million Americans who pay money to watch whale shows every year. Hoping to put amusement operators on the defensive and to tweak the consciences of entertainment consumers, they are urging that Yaka and Corky, a killer whale housed at Sea World in San Diego, be returned to their families in Puget Sound.

[13]At the same time, the groups are massing their legal clout for a battle over the Marine Mammal Protection Act, the 1972 law that gives ex-

hibitors the right to capture, import, move and display whales and dolphins in the name of public education. Advocates believe that if enough members of Congress can be swayed to their side by the time the law is up for review in 1993, the industry could wind up saddled with crippling restrictions.

[14]Demetrios, who hopes to expand Marine World and acquire a male killer whale so he can try to breed the animals, said the critics "at some point could become a direct threat." He said Marine World is struggling to break even financially.

[15]Critics not only argue the ethics of capturing marine mammals, they maintain that it is impossible to build adequate facilities for them because so little is known about what they need in order to thrive for many decades.

[16]Pointing to industry disclosures, they say that more than two killer whales have died in captivity for every one now performing in the United States. Stress leaves them vulnerable to disease and injury, Susan Rich of the Earth Island Institute told a National Marine Fisheries Service hearing in Washington, D.C. last month.

[17]Industry executives say the advocates are misleading the public by wrapping self-serving interpretations of mammal longevity in foolish sentimentalism. Further, they say they are the victims of a "protest industry" that deals in warm and fuzzy mammal images for fund-raising. The New England Aquarium was so upset that it fired back at critics with a defamation suit.

[18]"These people protesting are a very small minority of the public," said John Kirtland, spokesman for the International Marine Mammal Trainers Association. "The sad thing is, in an age of oil spills, pollution, and habitat destruction, their focus is on a small group of animals rather than on the critical issues of conservation of species and preservation of habitat."

[19]Jim Mullen, assistant director of marine mammal training for Marine World, and Dr. Laurie Gage, the facility's veterinarian, said protest groups have never bothered to see the whales and dolphins for themselves. If they did, Gage said, they would agree that the creatures are thriving in their performing careers.

[20]Industry supporters acknowledge that plenty of captives died young when parks were in their infancy in the 1960s and 1970s, but they maintain that the average life span of performing whales and dolphins now matches or exceeds that of those in the wild.

[21]In the case of killer whales, the two sides are divided largely because they disagree on how long an animal should be expected to live in the wild. Protest groups argue that orcas can live to 90. But David Bain, a

consultant for the federal fisheries service who has worked with Marine World's two killer whales since 1979, said his research shows that the average life span is about 20 years, although some individuals may last into their 80s.

[22]Yaka is 25 and has been in captivity since 1969. Vigga, 15 years old, was taken in Iceland in 1981.

[23]In any case, industry experts say, it is absurd to suggest that a long-captive animal turned loose again would benefit from the experience. They cite the case of Reno, a harbor seal so named because a Nevada couple picked it up off a San Francisco beach in the early 1970s and fattened it on clams in their bathtub.

[24]Experts at Steinhart Aquarium slimmed down the animal and tried to put it back in the ocean. But Reno just jumped back into the boat.

[25]Still, the concerns over animal welfare are getting through to the public.

[26]Adele Gerz illustrates the new awareness. A contributor to the nonprofit Marine World Foundation since 1985, the 29-year-old Vallejo woman visited the park dozens of times and never questioned its educational mission.

[27]That changed a year ago, when she asked a park guide where Yaka came from and was stunned to learn the five-ton female had been abducted from the sea. Yaka and Vigga are the only killer whales in captivity in Northern California.

[28]"The only conclusion I could draw was that they wanted to open a theme park and have this whale as an attraction," said Gerz, who does not belong to any animal welfare group. "It made me feel kind of sick."

Rick DelVecchio, "Performing Whales Drawing Protests," *San Francisco Chronicle*

Now examine your lists. What is DelVecchio's purpose in writing? How well does DelVecchio maintain his objectivity? Are both sides of the issue presented in roughly the same proportion? Are both sides of the issue presented fairly, in noninflammatory language?

Kinds of Reasoning

In Chapter 4 you learned the difference between deductive and inductive paragraph order. In terms of logic, however, the two kinds of reasoning we will examine here—*deduction* and *induction*—mean something different. They refer to patterns of reasoning—or, more simply, to the way a writer or speaker constructs an argument. In this section you will learn to distinguish between deductive and inductive arguments and to recognize whether they are logically valid or invalid.

Inductive Reasoning

Since the conclusion of an inductive argument can become a major premise in a deductive argument, we will start with induction. An inductive argument is built upon a set of factual statements that serve as evidence. The statements may come from observation or experience, whether personal or scientific. From these statements one may arrive at a generalization or a likely conclusion of what will *probably* occur. It is for this reason that inductive arguments are sometimes called *probability* arguments. For example, pure white cats are supposed to be deaf. (Supposedly a white cat that hears has a grey or black mark somewhere on its body.) Where did this generalization come from? Someone observed a pure white cat; it was deaf. The next pure white cat he or she observed was also deaf; so were pure white cats three and four. The observer concluded: "All pure white cats are deaf." On the basis of *this* observer's experience, the generalization seems reasonable. It remains tentative, however. He or she could not possibly observe all the pure white cats alive today in the world. So the conclusion is based on incomplete information. It might be safer for him or her to say, "All the pure white cats I have observed are deaf."

However, the more examples of pure white cats one can produce with this defect, the stronger the conclusion. And if no one can produce a pure white cat that hears, then the conclusion is valid and true.

Here is another example. Consider this set of factual statements.

Bank tellers at Civic National Bank must know how to use a computer.

The school secretary must know how to use a computer.

Our local gas station owner uses a computer to order auto parts.

Reservation clerks at Midwest Airlines use computers to book flights.

Therefore the person who applies for the new librarian's position at our local branch library will probably have to know how to use a computer.

In this case, the conclusion rests on specific factual statements, from which one could probably conclude that a librarian needs to be computer literate too. Although it is *valid* (that is, it follows logically from the evidence), this conclusion may not actually be *true*. Perhaps the library has no funds for computers and must make do with manual record keeping. As in the pure white cat argument, the more examples of librarians who use computers in their daily work, the stronger the argument becomes and the more valid the generalization derived from these facts will be.

Here is a final example.

No American president has been able to solve the problem of the federal deficit. Since the late 1960s, every president—Nixon, Ford,

Carter, Reagan, and Bush—has tried without success to cut the deficit. It appears likely that Bill Clinton will run into the same difficulty.

Problems with Inductive Reasoning

SWEEPING GENERALIZATION

The most common error in inductive arguments is the sweeping generalization, as you see in this argument.

> You shouldn't buy a fox terrier. All terriers too nervous and high-strung. My neighbor has one that yaps at the least little sound, and he jumps all over people, too.

This argument is different from the pure white cat example at the start of this section. Deafness is verifiable and observable, whereas "nervousness" is relative and calls for a subjective judgment. (What some people might call nervous and high-strung, others might call spirited or lively.) This argument rests on a generalization derived from one example; it is called a sweeping generalization because it sweeps all members of the group into a category. In such an argument, we mentally insert the word *all* before it. However, temperaments among members of any breed of dog vary so widely that this conclusion cannot be safely made, and producing even one serene fox terrier would negate it.

HASTY GENERALIZATION

Like a sweeping generalization, this kind of false reasoning is done in haste, using insufficient evidence.

> The former "boat people" have certainly adjusted well to American life. The store owned by a Cambodian refugee family in my neighborhood is well run and profitable, and it's remarkable how easily the family has assimilated our system of values.

INCORRECT SAMPLING

Inductive arguments often include a *sampling*. For example, "Sixty percent of the Americans we interviewed think that the penalties for drunk driving are too lenient." On the basis of the sample, we could conclude that 60 percent of the population as a whole probably shares this concern. It should be noted, however, that the method of sampling is crucial. The number of people interviewed should be large, and they should be *representative*—i.e., drawn from a cross section of the general population in terms of geographic area, income, ethnicity, religion, and educational level. If you asked the first ten students you see on campus their opinion of drunk-driving penalties, and six of them say that they

are too lenient, you should not infer that 60 percent of the population as a whole shares this opinion. The sample is too small and is not representative.

Here are some real examples of faulty inductive reasoning involving surveys. The first involves a recent newspaper article about the proliferation of sex surveys widely published in national magazines. Critics say that these surveys may make for good reading, but not for good research. The article cites one sex survey in particular, the *Janus Report on Sexual Behavior* (conducted by Samuel Janus, a sex counselor, and his wife, Cynthia), which found, among other questionable conclusions, that Americans over the age of sixty-five have sex more often than do eighteen- to twenty-six-year-olds. Apparently, the Janus researchers interviewed people around the country according to a predetermined quota—so many people of a particular age, so many women, so many blacks, and so forth.

What's wrong with using such a quota system in a national survey? Richard Morin in *The Washington Post*,[1] cites Thomas Smith, director of the General Social Survey at the University of Chicago and a leading expert on sex research. Smith points out many serious defects in the sampling used in the Janus survey, among them this one: In the United States, 2 percent of the adult population is Jewish, 11 percent is "other," and the remainder are Catholic or Protestant. But in the Janus sample 11 percent of the interviews were conducted with Jewish people and 17 percent with people in the "other" category.

As Smith concludes, "They're off by a factor of four or five. If they can't come closer than a factor of four or five on this, why should we believe they're any more accurate on the other questions?" (Notice that this conclusion itself represents an inductive argument. The researchers made errors in their sampling technique. Therefore, their conclusions are probably wrong, too.)

A second example concerns a widely-publicized report done by psychologists Stanley Coren of the University of British Columbia and Diane Halpern of California State University at San Bernadino. Their research showed that left-handed people die an average of nine years earlier than right-handed people. Their study was met with much criticism, skepticism, and more studies, some confirming their findings, others challenging them. Based on their study of mortality rates, Coren and Halpren argued that left-handers are more susceptible to disease and to the risks of using tools and implements designed for right-handed people. As Coren wrote, "Left-handers are being eaten by our environment. They simply don't live as long."[2]

You might wonder how these researchers' findings could be disputed? If the mortality statistics are correct, isn't their conclusion a valid

---

[1]Richard Morin, "A Good Sex Poll Is Hard to Find", *The Washington Post,* April 27, 1993.
[2]Thomas H. Maugh, "Lefties Don't Die Young," *Los Angeles Times,* April 4, 1993.

A Leftward Drift?

Some researchers argue that left-handers are not as prevalent in older popula-tions because parents and teachers early in this century responded to cultural pressures by forcing naturally left-handed children to become right-handed. A new UCLA study offers the first proof of this contention. The researchers found that the percentage of people who said they switched increases in older age groups, largely—but not totally—offsetting the apparent loss of left-han-ders in those groups.

AGE	% LEFT-HANDED	% SWITCHED
21-30	15.5	2.7
31-40	13.0	1.4
41-50	11.8	0.6
51-60	14.0	1.8
61-70	8.0	4.0
71-80	5.0	5.6
81-90	3.8	6.4
91+	0.0	8.0

Source: UCLA

Thomas H. Maugh, "Lefties Don't Die Young," *Los Angeles Times,* April 4, 1993

inductive argument? The most significant rebuttal to the study came from UCLA psychologist Paul Satz and researchers at the University of Bergen in Norway who also studied a group of left-handed adults who were asked which hand they use for a variety of tasks and whether they had been forced to use their right hand when they were children.

The results show that many people over sixty who responded to the survey questions had been forced by parents and schoolteachers to abandon their left-handedness (a very common practice, even as late as the 1950s). So, while it *appeared* that left-handed people do not live as long, the sample was inaccurate. The population of older left-handed people is naturally smaller since so many classify themselves as right-handed. The statistical results of the UCLA/Norway study show a more accurate inductive conclusion.

As you can see, drawing conclusions in inductive arguments can be tricky. One last example. A recent national survey of American college students showed that those students who consumed six or more alco-holic beverages a week consistently had lower grade point averages than those students who drank less or not at all. Even assuming that the sampling was done correctly, is this conclusion valid? Looked at an-other way, which is the cause and which is the effect? Do students' grades suffer because they drink, or do they drink to ease the pain and lowered self-esteem that result from receiving low grades? Later in this section, you will have the opportunity to evaluate some valid and some faulty inductive arguments.

**Deductive
Reasoning**

In Sir Arthur Conan Doyle's first novel, *A Study in Scarlet,* Sherlock Holmes, who has just met Dr. Watson, explains to Watson the usefulness of making deductions in solving mysteries. Watson, apparently, has been skeptical of Holmes's abilities. Holmes says:

> You see I have a lot of special knowledge which I apply to the problem, and which facilitates matters wonderfully. Those rules of deduction laid down in that article which aroused your scorn are invaluable to me in practical work. Observation with me is second nature. You appeared surprised when I told you, on our first meeting, that you had come from Afghanistan.

Watson replies, "You were told, no doubt." And then Holmes demonstrates his deductive powers:

> "Nothing of the sort. I *knew* you came from Afghanistan. From long habit the train of thoughts ran so swiftly through my mind that I arrived at the conclusion without being conscious of intermediate steps. There were such steps, however. The train of reasoning ran: 'Here is a gentleman of a medical type, but with the air of a military man. Clearly an army doctor then. He has just come from the tropics, for his face is dark, and that is not the natural tint of his skin, for his wrists are fair. He has undergone hardship and sickness, as his haggard face says clearly. His left arm has been injured. He holds it in a stiff and unnatural manner. Where in the tropics could an English army doctor have seen much hardship and got his arm wounded? Clearly in Afghanistan.' The whole train of thought did not occupy a second. I then remarked that you came from Afghanistan, and you were astonished."
>
> Sir Arthur Conan Doyle, A Study in Scarlet

As he explains it, Holmes has moved from a set of premises regarding Watson's appearance, dress, and behavior to his conclusion. Since they were consistent with Holmes's observations of other Englishmen who served as doctors in the military in Afghanistan, then he could validly conclude that Watson had performed such service.

A deductive argument moves from reason to conclusion or to specific application with logical necessity. For example, if you know that your textbook is in your backpack and you know that your backpack is in your car, then you can logically deduce that your textbook is in your car. This conclusion must necessarily follow from the two preceding statements, which we call *premises,* if they are true.

Major premise:	My textbook is in my backpack.
Minor premise:	My backpack is in my car.
Conclusion:	Therefore, my textbook is in my car.

Deduction is the opposite of induction because the conclusion can be *logically derived* from the major and minor premises, whereas in an inductive argument, the conclusion is a matter of probability. The reasons *suggest* that the conclusion is true, and as more evidence accumulates, the conclusion becomes stronger. But in an deductive argument, there is no question of probability.

Monroe Beardsley, formerly a professor at Swarthmore College, summarizes these two kinds of arguments like this:

> In a deductive argument, the statements that make up the reason are called *premises,* and the conclusion is said to be "deduced," whether correctly or incorrectly, from the premises. In an inductive argument, the statements that make up the reason are called the *evidence,* and the conclusion is said to be "induced from," or "supported by" the evidence.
>
> Monroe Beardsley, *Thinking Straight*

Here are some examples of deductive arguments, both valid and invalid. They are printed as *syllogisms,* a series of statements expressing a logical deduction.

Major premise:	All men are mortal.
Minor premise:	John is a man.
Conclusion:	John is mortal.

This syllogism is valid because (a) the premises are true and (b) the premises already contain or imply the conclusion. If one accepts the premises, one must also accept the conclusion. Now study this one:

Major premise:	All Italians are good singers.
Minor premise:	Emiliano is Italian.
Conclusion:	Emiliano is a good singer.

This syllogism is logically valid because Emiliano has been placed in a class in which all the members are said to share the same characteristic. Therefore, we can deduce (arrive at the conclusion) that Emiliano also shares that characteristic; therefore, it is *logically valid.* Yet the argument is untrue or unsound because the major premise—that all Italians are good singers—is obviously untrue, since it is a generalization that could be easily invalidated by only one bad singer from Italy. (You should also note that this major premise is the result of an invalid inductive argument that goes something like this. Frederico is Italian and is an excellent singer; Antonio is Italian, and he also sings well; Mario is Italian and is an excellent singer. Therefore, Italians are good singers.)

This distinction between validity and truth leads to the question, what in logic does *true* mean? D. L. McDonald defines truth like this: "It is only when terms are defined and mutually accepted that one can begin marshaling evidence to prove the truth of a statement." McDonald goes on to explain the statement that truth is statistically derived.

A man can insist that fire engines are red because he is expressing a general opinion. Though a "Napoleon" might call them a mass hallucination, he is sure that fire engines exist. Though the color-blind might cavil, he knows they are colored red. And though foreigners or semanticists might do otherwise, he uses the word "red." The reason he speaks the truth and the dissenters do not is that he is in the majority. If the majority did not perceive the engines, or saw them as green, or described them as "rouge," he would be locked up as a babbling, color-blind visionary. "Truth" is what people agree to call true.

D. L. McDonald, *The Language of Argument*

Here is an example of a deductive argument that is invalid for reasons other than that the premise is untrue.

Major premise:	All students who did not write the term paper in English 100 failed the class.
Minor premise:	Dave failed the class.
Conclusion:	Dave must not have written the term paper.

The conclusion does not follow logically from the premises because Dave has not been placed in the group of students who did not write the paper. His failing the class could have been for other reasons—failure to write other papers, poor attendance, or low test grades. Therefore, the conclusion cannot be deduced from the premises, making the argument invalid.

Here is another kind of invalid syllogism.

Major premise:	If Bill doesn't stop smoking, his wife will leave him.
Minor premise:	Bill plans to stop smoking.
Conclusion:	Bill's wife won't leave him.

In this syllogism, the conclusion can be valid only if Bill *doesn't* stop smoking, and the minor premise changes the term (from "smoking" to "stopping smoking"), thereby making the argument invalid. The terms must remain constant within the major and minor premises. Bill's wife may leave him for another reason not contained in the major premise.

Here are two more syllogisms, one valid and the other invalid.

Major premise:	Members of Operation Rescue are opposed to abortion.
Minor premise:	Sue is a member of Operation Rescue.
Conclusion:	Sue is opposed to abortion.

Major premise:	Sue is opposed to abortion.
Minor premise:	Members of Operation Rescue are opposed to abortion.
Conclusion:	Sue must be a member of Operation Rescue.

In the first syllogism, a valid deductive argument, Sue has been put in the class of people who are against abortion. Therefore, the conclusion can be logically deduced from the premises. But in the second example, Sue has not been placed in this group. We can see, in addition, from common sense that one does not have to be a member of Operation Rescue to oppose abortion.

Another kind of invalid deductive argument occurs when one changes the meaning of the terms in the premises.

Major premise:	All lemons are yellow.
Minor premise:	My car is a lemon.
Conclusion:	My car must be yellow.

The syllogism is invalid because the term *lemon* means something different between the two premises. Here is a similar example, leading to an absurd conclusion.

Major premise:	All dogs have tails.
Minor premise:	This airplane has a tail.
Conclusion:	This airplane is a dog.

In this example, the major premise is about dogs, not airplanes, so the premise cannot lead to a conclusion about airplanes.

In the real world, deductive arguments do not present themselves as neat syllogisms with premises and conclusions outlined. Usually the argument is abbreviated with one of the premises, or even the conclusion, omitted. For example, consider this argument:

- This woman shouldn't be allowed to vote because she doesn't speak English.

Recast as a valid, though unsound, syllogism, the argument would be written like this.

Major premise:	Only English speakers should be allowed to vote.
Minor premise:	This woman does not speak English.
Conclusion:	This woman should not be allowed to vote.

In this example, the major premise is assumed.

Here are some examples of everyday deductive arguments, along with their missing or implied parts:

- If you don't vote, then you can hardly criticize the government. (*Missing major premise:* Only voters can criticize the government. This argument is invalid because the major premise is a subjective opinion.)
- To get on that team, you have to be able to do fifty push-ups. Paul couldn't do the push-ups. (*Missing conclusion:* Paul didn't get on the team, a valid conclusion.)

- They say that blondes have more fun, so it's easy to see why Muffie Ferguson is asked out by every man in town. (*Missing minor premise:* Muffie Ferguson has blonde hair. This is a valid argument logically but unsound because of the subjective major premise.)
- Sarah Perkins must be a Deadhead. Did you see that black Grateful Dead T-shirt she's wearing today? (*Missing major premise:* Only Deadheads wear Grateful Dead T-shirts, a false premise leading to a false conclusion, and therefore, an invalid argument.)

Exercises: Part 2— Evaluating Arguments

Based on the explanations and examples of inductive and deductive arguments, evaluate the following arguments according to these steps: (a) Determine whether the argument is deductive or inductive; (b) examine the premises for generalizations; (c) decide whether the argument is valid or invalid; (d) if the argument is deductive, see whether you can determine what part of the argument—major premise, minor premise, or conclusion—is missing.

1. People who go to raves drink "smart" drinks. Kelcey is convinced that these drinks are really beneficial. He must have heard about them at a rave.
2. The whole welfare system is riddled with lazy people who expect to be paid just for living. My neighbor, for example, receives welfare and she hasn't the time to look for work since she spends the whole day watching soap operas.
3. François must be a good lover. He's French, you know.
4. Just look at that Mercedes! The owner must be really rich.
5. It's obvious that the ballot proposition on school vouchers will fail. Why, last week the paper announced the results of a new poll, and nearly 80 percent of the residents of Shady Pines Nursing Home were firmly opposed to the measure.
6. Mayor Winthrop has been in office for a month already, and there are more homeless on the street than before he was elected. He's just like every other politician who makes promises during the campaign and then doesn't keep them once elected. I say we should start a recall petition!
7. It's no wonder Linda Ng scored so high on the math part of the SAT. Everyone knows that Asians are good in math.
8. Ellen has done a lot of writing in all her English courses, so she knows she'll have to write a lot when she takes Mr. Hulbert's critical reading course, English 19.

9. Seven out of ten dentists recommend Trident gum for their patients who chew gum.

10. All roses are red. This rose is red. This flower must be a rose.

11. All A are B. All C are A. Therefore, all C are B.

12. Naturally, Alberto Chavez is a poor driver. What do you expect from someone eighty years old?

13. The Catholic Church should follow the example of the Episcopalians and the Presbyterians and allow women to become priests.

14. If students study this textbook carefully for an hour a day, they will do well in the course. Sarah did well in the course. She must have studied the book faithfully every day.

15. Drinking unpasteurized milk can cause tuberculosis. Katie was just diagnosed as tubercular. I told her not to drink that stuff!

16. "Foreign journalists writing about Africa had often caused problems. . . . The worst case of 'inflammation of information' had occurred when the results of a survey of twenty people from Bissau [a country in Africa], five of whom tested positive for HIV-2, were released to the Portuguese press. The next day there were headlines that twenty-five percent of the people in Guinea-Bissau had AIDS." (Quoted in Alex Shoumatoff, *African Madness*)

17. I don't know what the big deal is about needle exchange programs. Admittedly, the Netherlands has a more liberal drug policy than that of the U.S., but in Amsterdam, police stations offer sterile needles in exchange for used ones, with no names asked. This program has played a major role in stopping the spread of the HIV virus among the city's hard drug users. American cities should follow Amsterdam's example and establish their own exchange programs.

18. If abortions are not granted to women on demand, there will be an increase in the number of unwanted children, and if that happens, we can expect to see an increase in the incidence of child abuse.

19. Charlotte was accepted by four universities with excellent reputations. She must have been a top student in high school.

20. All dogs have four legs. This creature must be a dog.

21. The number of people arrested for drunk driving increased by 100 percent last year in our town. In 1992, in Rockport, population 150, four people were arrested for driving while drunk, but in 1993, eight people were charged. It's obvious that our drunk-driving laws are too lenient.

22. Responsible instructors don't give tests when students aren't prepared for class, so we can safely assume that Mr. Stamps will be nice and not give us a test today.

23. In a *Wall Street Journal* survey of 1,000 students ages eight to seventeen, only 13 percent of girls and only 2 percent of boys said

that they planned to be teachers. It's a shame that occupations still carry sexual stereotypes in this country.

24. I always take my car to Heinrich Muller to be repaired. Germans make the best car mechanics.

25. A recent study compared homicide rates in the U.S., Canada, and South Africa. In the three decades after television was introduced, homicide rates among North American whites rose 90 percent, while dropping 7 percent in South Africa. (Television broadcasting was banned in South Africa until 1975.) But since the introduction of TV in South Africa, the white homicide rate has jumped more than 50 percent. Brandon Centerwall, an epidemiologist at the University of Washington, who conducted the study, concluded that television viewing is the cause of half the homicides committed in the United States each year.

Appeals in Arguments

Now that you can distinguish between induction and deduction and between valid and invalid arguments, we can turn our attention to manipulative devices used in argumentation. The careful persuasive writer uses sound, accurate, appropriate, and convincing evidence, thereby appealing to our intellect. We can accept the argument because the evidence—whether in the form of examples, facts and statistics, or good reasons—persuades us to accept it, or at least to give it some consideration.

You will recall from Chapter 6 in Part II that some writers use slanted language (euphemisms, sneer words, or weasel words) to convince us to accept their point of view or to buy a product. In addition, some writers hope to manipulate our thinking by appealing to various emotions and instincts. Stripping away the emotional appeal allows you to see the argument for itself, unclouded by emotion or sentiment, especially if there is no substantive reasoned discourse for evidence. Let us examine the main types of appeal.

Appeals to the Emotions

Maintaining objectivity in light of controversial issues is difficult, for writer and reader alike. But it is important to recognize when a writer is deliberately firing your emotions and to recognize when you are responding more emotionally than rationally. To paraphrase an old adage, the more emotional the appeal, the weaker the argument. Here are some examples.

- "Lower your taxes. Vote No on Proposition 21!"
- "Stop the land grab! Don't let greedy corporations take your most cherished possession away from you!"

- "Let's get those criminals off the streets and into jail, where they belong."
- "A vote for the school bond issue to build a new gym is a vote for our children."

We respond to emotional appeals on a visceral level because they sound good. After all, who wants higher taxes or criminals roaming the streets? Yet, in the absence of reasoned discourse, arguments resting on emotional appeals are unsound because they rest on oversimplification, and they need not be accepted no matter how good they seem. Here, briefly, are five common emotional appeals.

Transfer

In this kind of appeal, the writer seeks to imply that favorable impressions about one thing will transfer or carry over to something else. This technique is often seen in cigarette or liquor advertisements that show young, attractive, healthy people smoking or drinking. The positive aspects of sociability are meant to be "transferred" to our perceptions of smoking and drinking. The message is that if we smoke or drink, we too can have a good time like these healthy, beautiful people.

In the spring of 1993, President Clinton gave a major address in at the Cooper Union in New York. Behind the podium was a large bust of Abraham Lincoln that Clinton, prior to the address, had requested be placed on the stage. The aim here was to create an association between the two men in viewers' minds, leading them to mentally transfer Lincoln's qualities as president to Clinton.

Just Plain Folks

This appeal lies in the writer's desire to have himself or herself perceived as just an "ordinary citizen" or "just plain folks." It is the opposite of snob appeal. A politician might give a speech to small-town people and use the "plain folks" appeal by stating that he, too, came from a similar little town, went to a school very much like the one there, or came from a family much like theirs. A few years ago, Bartels & Jaymes, the makers of wine coolers, ran some very popular television ads showing two old men dressed in overalls and sitting on a dilapidated front porch of a small house discussing the merits of their beverages. Other examples are restaurants claiming that their food is "just like Mom's" or a brand of pickles named "Aunt Sally's Homemade Pickles." By means of transfer, we are supposed to picture "Mom" or "Aunt Sally" cooking up their old favorites just for us.

Testimonial

Television advertisements abound with appeals that use the testimony of famous people—celebrities, athletes, or other notables who are paid

large sums of money to tout products. One could probably argue that former Chicago Bulls' superstar Michael Jordan is an authoritative representative for Reebok athletic shoes, but we can surely question the opinion of an athlete who endorses a certain brand of automobile or a movie star who is paid to sing the praises of a rental car company. It is hard to see how country singer Willie Nelson could be considered an expert on nutrition when he appears on advertisements for Taco Bell.

Bandwagon Appeal

This appeal asks readers to accept an idea by appealing to their desire to "get on the bandwagon" because it seems that "everybody else thinks so" or out of a desire to be on the winning side. For example, "Don't vote for Proposition P. The polls show it is losing 65 to 35." Or "Everyone knows that pornography is the main cause of rape." Beware of arguments that begin, "Everyone knows" or "Everyone agrees." Look for evidence, not appeals to join the crowd. The crowd can be wrong.

Flattery

A writer who uses flattery tries to put us into a group of people that we might hope to identify with, whether we share their convictions or not. For example, if a writer says, "Every well-educated person knows that James Joyce was one of the most important writers of the twentieth century," we are meant to associate ourselves with "well-educated people." Or this: "All people with good taste shop at Hill's Department Store." We like to think of ourselves as having good taste, so, by means of subtle flattery, we are enticed to become part of the group.

Appeal to Authority

This appeal asks us to accept an argument because some authoritative figure backs it.

- My English teacher says that you should never start a sentence with "and" or "but." He has been teaching for twenty-five years, so he ought to know what's right."
- A recent medical journal article said that there is no correlation between a high-fat diet and certain kinds of cancer. That means I can go ahead and eat all the butter and sour cream I want without worrying about their long-term effects.

Also, do not be deceived by weasly phrases like these that often precede weak arguments: "*Let's face it.* The Constitution is little more than a historical artifact," or "*The fact of the matter is* that gays just don't belong in the military," or "*The truth as I see it is* that we have too many corrupt judges in our courts."

Appeal to Fear   This appeal is obvious. The writer hopes to arouse our fear of what will happen if we adopt a certain course. As with most other appeals, the appeal to fear takes the place of evidence in the form of good reasons or facts.

- It would be a mistake for the United States to intervene in Bosnia's civil war. We might become embroiled in a larger war than anyone imagined, and that could lead to World War III.
- Why would anyone voluntarily move to California? That's earthquake country. After all, the "Big One" is supposed to hit sometime before the end of the century.
- During a strike by the pilots of a national airline in 1985, the newspapers were full of letters to the editor on both sides of the issue. Here is a representative one by a striking pilot: "I am proud to be a member of the striking pilot's association, and I just hope that all those people who have written attacking us for our stand are not caught on some dark and stormy night, strapped in the seat of an aircraft piloted by a scab hired at the last minute who probably hasn't had adequate training."

Appeal to
Patriotism   The appeal to patriotism is a deceptive tactic to make us think that we are being disloyal to our country's system of values if we don't accept an argument. Here are some examples.

- My country, right or wrong!
- Ross Perot against the North American Free Trade Agreement (NAFTA) on a 1993 TV "infomercial" called "Keeping Your Job in the U.S.A.:" "If the United States accepts this agreement, so many U.S. companies will flow south that you will hear a giant sucking sound coming from the U.S.-Mexican border."
- According to Oliver North and John Poindexter, both knew that they were committing illegal acts when they plotted to sell arms to Iran and divert money to the Contras during the Irangate scandal, but they did so out of love for their country.

Appeal to
Prejudice   Like the appeal to fear, this appeal works by inflaming negative feelings, beliefs, or stereotypes about racial, ethnic, or religious groups, gender, or sexual orientation. Once again, emotion replaces reasoned discourse.

- Letting so many immigrants into this country is a mistake. They take jobs away from Americans who are out of work, and they don't share our traditional values.

- It's ridiculous that men want to become nurses. After all, women are traditionally the care-givers in our culture.
- If universities admit large numbers of minorities under affirmative action, soon there won't be any whites in our colleges.

Appeal to Sympathy

By arousing our sympathy, writers and advertisers gain a real advantage over us. We have all seen the advertisements for pet foods using glossy photos of adorable kittens and puppies, for example. Here is another type of example.

- A recent television commercial for StainStick—a prewash product manufactured by DowBrands—showed a mother preparing the wash with her little girl who clearly has Down's syndrome. As the daughter applies StainStick to the spots, the mother says, "We use StainStick because the last place we need a challenge is in the laundry room."

Critics charged that DowBrands was exploiting the child and preying on the viewing public's sympathy to buy the product. In fact, other television ad campaigns are making greater use of the handicapped, showing people in wheelchairs and the like. But the criticism seems justified, since the purpose of the advertisement was to sell StainStick, not to remind us to treat the handicapped fairly.

Here is an additional example.

- Teenage moms really have a tough time. After their boyfriends get them pregnant and abandon them, they have to care for their babies and juggle their schoolwork at the same time. That's why we need on-site day care centers at our high schools.

The situation at issue is clearly tragic, and we have to guard against becoming so jaded and cynical that we harden ourselves to the plight of others. Yet this argument plays *solely* on our sympathy, and the conclusion does not logically derive from the evidence. Whether the local high school is the best place to solve the day-care problems of teenage mothers is open to debate and requires more careful analysis than simply appealing to our sense of outrage or sympathy.

Appeal to Tradition

The appeal to tradition asks us to accept a practice because it has always been done that way, but a variant flatters us with snob appeal, as we see in this first example.

- "Dear Ms. Milan: Our book, *Milans Across America,* represents our informative edition of knowledge about the location of Milan Families in America. If individually researched, it would require you to spend

thousands of dollars or months of work to search through National and State, government and utility records. These records represent the households of over 200 million people. We have found the Milan name to be rare and thus *Milans Across America* is a very special limited edition. There will be less than twenty-five books published and they will only be printed upon your specific request. . . . THIS EDITION WILL NEVER BE PRINTED AGAIN."

- The Roman Catholic Church has forbidden women to become priests for nearly 2,000 years. Why should the Church abandon such a long-standing practice?
- My club shouldn't be required to admit women or minorities. Men should have the right to associate with whomever they want without being hassled or threatened with lawsuits.

Logical Fallacies

In addition to the various deceptive appeals we discussed in the preceding section, some arguments may contain *logical fallacies*, instances of incorrect reasoning that can make them invalid or false. Here, in alphabetical order, are some of the common fallacies and illustrations of arguments employing them. It should be noted that, unlike appeals to emotion and the use of slanted language, not all fallacies are deliberately used to dupe the unwary reader. Many writers lapse into them from ignorance or as a result of sloppy thinking.

Ad Hominem Argument

From the Latin, *ad hominem* means "to the man." This fallacy can take two forms: either attacking the character of the person rather than the principles he or she stands for, or attacking the character and reputation of a position's supporters. In either case, the argument ignores the person's deeds or character. Here are two examples.

- It's a good thing that Gary Hart dropped out of the 1988 presidential race. He's the one who, while still married, was caught with a young woman off the coast in a boat appropriately named "Monkey Business."
- I'm certainly not going to vote for Proposition 16 in the next election. I just looked at the election pamphlet and discovered that the big oil companies are in favor of it. There must be something in it for them.

Begging the Question

In this fallacy, the writer presents a proposition and assumes that it has been proved when it has not. This means that the premise upon which the argument rests and the conclusion are the same, even if they are

worded slightly differently. In other words, the writer assumes to be true that which he or she wants us to accept as the conclusion.

- "Does it make sense to release this murderer so he can commit the same atrocities again and again?" (Prosecuting attorney at a murder trial)

In this example, the prosecutor ignores the real issue, which is to prove whether the defendant actually committed the murder. Therefore, he presumes to be true what it is his duty to prove. Here are more examples:

- If you want miraculously white clothes, use Soapy detergent. It's a washday miracle!
- Because children surely need a mother more than they need a father, women with children should not be allowed to engage in military combat.
- If you can't trust your doctor, whom can you trust?

Either/or Fallacy

Sometimes called *false dilemma,* this fallacy occurs when the writer reduces a complicated issue to only two choices, thereby ignoring other possibilities or alternatives.

- Police officers are either brutal or corrupt.
- A woman should stay home and take care of her house and children. If she wants a career, she should forget about having children.

False Analogy

Although it does not carry the same force as factual evidence or good reasons, arguing by analogy can be effective and persuasive in supporting an argument. An analogy—as you will recall from Chapter 3 in Part I—discusses one subject in terms of another, completely different subject. An analogy is false if there are fewer similarities than differences, if the resemblance is remote or ambiguous, or if there is no resemblance at all.

For example, consider this argument.

- Every red-blooded American serviceman knows that gays should be banned from the military. In the military we're like one big family living in close quarters, and a gay just wouldn't fit in.

This argument rests on the dubious analogy that people living in military quarters are like a family. To see why it's a false analogy, we have to see where it breaks down and to see if there are more dissimilarities than similarities. One chooses to enter the military; one does not

choose which family to be born into. The analogy also implies that military personnel have no privacy whereas family members do. Further, the writer argues that gays should be excluded from the military because other members wouldn't be comfortable being around them, implying—in a contradictory way—that gays can't fit in with a family, either. When you examine the basic differences, the only real connection between the military and a family is that both are social institutions.

Here is another example.

- Student to English department chairperson: "I'm upset that I didn't do well on my English placement essay. I'd like to request another chance because I'm sure I belong in a higher-level class."

   Chairperson: "I'm sorry, that's impossible. You're allowed to write only one placement essay. After all, if your chest x-ray showed that you have tuberculosis, you wouldn't ask for a second x-ray to be taken, would you?"

The chairperson can certainly invoke the one-essay rule, but in doing so, he or she should not base his argument on the assumption that an essay is analogous to a chest x-ray. It is a dubious comparison, because an essay is a subjective examination of one's thinking processes on a given day and on a given subject, whereas an X-ray—assuming that it is properly taken and evaluated—is an objective look at a patient's lungs. Even so, any serious diagnosis should be given a second, or even a third, opinion. For these and other reasons, the chairperson's argument is fallacious.

However, not all analogies used in argumentation are false, and in fact, as noted earlier, this technique can be used effectively and persuasively. To illustrate, in 1987 a group of parents from Minneapolis (a city with one of the highest Native American populations in the country), called the Concerned American Indian Parents, designed a poster that was distributed to local high schools. They were protesting the practice in some high schools of calling their athletic teams the "Indians."

The poster depicted the banner of the real Cleveland Indians football team, along with three other hypothetical banners for the Pittsburgh Negroes, the Kansas City Jews, and the San Diego Caucasians. The slogan at the bottom of the poster read, "Maybe now you know how Native Americans feel." One of the schools that received the poster, Southwest Secondary School in Minneapolis, announced that it had changed the name of one of its teams from the Indians to the Lakers, showing the power of a good analogy.

False Cause

This fallacy presents a false cause-and-effect relationship, either because the cause cited is irrelevant to the effect or because it may be a *remote*

cause, so far back in time that its link with the present effect is only tenuous at best. During the 1992 presidential election, George Bush took credit for playing a decisive role in ending the Cold War, establishing a strong cause-and-effect connection. His opponent, Bill Clinton, responded, "Mr. Bush's taking credit for the ending of the Cold War is like the rooster's taking credit for the dawn." Here are two more examples.

- I knew I should have cancelled my tennis match today. My astrological forecast warned me not to engage in anything competitive, so of course I lost.
- It's no wonder that Sam Anderson was convicted of being an ax murderer. According to an interview I read, he was subjected to a rigid toilet-training regiment when he was a toddler.

Oversimplification

Oversimplification as a fallacy can involve either reducing a complicated issue to overly simple terms or to suppressing information that would strengthen the argument.

- The way to stop drug abuse in this country is to increase dramatically the number of drug enforcement agents and to punish severely anyone caught possessing illegal drugs.

This was the argument used by proponents of the Bush and Reagan administrations' War on Drugs. Some critics of the War on Drugs program, however, charged that this approach was too simplistic and, in fact, hadn't worked despite the billions of dollars poured into the program. They argued that the only effective approach to fighting drug abuse was to attack the *causes* of drug abuse, not simply putting more money into law enforcement.

Moreover, if the people arguing in favor of the War on Drugs failed to disclose damaging data strongly suggesting that police crackdowns and drug busts have not put a dent in the illegal drug market, they would be deliberately suppressing damaging evidence in order to strengthen their case. A good argument presents the facts and does not conveniently omit relevant, though damaging, evidence.

Non Sequitur

A *non sequitur,* taken from the Latin for "it does not follow," is a conclusion that does not follow from the premises or the evidence.

- During the 1950s it was revealed that contestants on quiz shows like *Twenty-One* and the *$64,000 Question* had been fed answers before the programs were aired. The resulting quiz show scandals prompted a national debate about truth and honesty in broadcasting. One quiz

show producer was quoted as saying, in defense of the rigged answers, "If we rig the contest and supply [the contestants] with answers, we'll make intellectualism and learning look glamorous."

Post Hoc, Ergo Propter Hoc	This fallacy is derived from the Latin phrase meaning "after this, therefore because of this." It suggests that, because event B occurred after event A, event A caused event B. The post hoc fallacy is similar to the false cause fallacy, but there is an important difference. With false cause, there is usually a leap from a remote situation to a present one, or a single thing is falsely credited with causing a complicated situation, as for example, in this argument citing a false cause.

- Sweden is a socialist country, and it has one of the highest suicide rates in the world. Socialism must cause suicide.

With the post hoc fallacy, however, the cause-and-effect relationship is based on coincidence, so that one event is seen as causing a second one. For example, a few days after President Clinton was inaugurated in early 1993, he had not yet appointed a White House physician. Dr. Burton Lee, formerly George Bush's personal physician, still serving in this capacity, was asked to give Clinton an allergy shot. He refused and the next day was fired. Lee argued that he was fired (event B) because he refused to give the shot (event A). Clinton claimed that he was acting under his own prerogative to choose his own doctor and that the allergy shot incident had nothing to do with it. (It's hard to know who is right here, because Lee's firing could really have been a matter of coincidence.)

Here is another example.

- According to a company president, "The recent settlement between management and the labor union was a huge mistake. Giving in to the union's demands for a wage increase has resulted in low production figures."

The post hoc fallacy is also the culprit in many silly superstitions, again because of a faulty cause-and-effect relationship. If you walked under a ladder and were hit by a bus ten minutes later, it would be fallacious to argue that the accident occurred because you were foolish enough to defy the superstition of walking under a ladder. A broken mirror does not mean that seven years of bad luck will ensue, nor will stepping on cracks in the sidewalk break your mother's back.

Slippery Slope	The metaphoric name of this fallacy will help you remember it. The slippery slope fallacy suggests that one step in the wrong direction will inevitably lead to more and more dire and undesirable occurrences. The

image invoked is one of a person being unable to halt his or her descent down an icy incline once that first tentative step is taken. Here is an example.

- Legalizing marijuana is a terrible idea. Once marijuana is legalized, users will graduate to progressively more dangerous and addictive drugs, like heroin and crack. Eventually, we'll all be a nation of freaked-out zombies!

Two Wrongs Make a Right

This last fallacy is commonly used to make wrongdoing sound legitimate because others engage in the same practice, as this example shows.

- During the Watergate crisis in 1973 that eventually led to President Nixon's resignation, the President's supporters contended that Nixon had not done anything different from any other president. He just had been caught. In other words, the argument assumes that a precedent exists for bribery, dirty tricks, hush money, and cover-ups of crimes, making other, similar misdeeds acceptable or setting a precedent for one's own activities.

Exercises: Part 3—Identifying Logical Fallacies and False Appeals

For some practice in evaluating arguments, try to determine what particular fallacy or false appeal each of the following examples represents. (Note: Some examples contain more than one fallacy; some contain only a false appeal.)

1. I don't see anything wrong with using the office copy machine to make copies of my personal income tax forms. Just yesterday I saw Mary Thurber making a copy on the office copy machine of that romance novel she's been writing on the side.

2. A dog breeder refused to reimburse a customer who purchased a pedigreed German shepherd that was later found to have a serious defect requiring corrective surgery. The breeder refused to pay even half of the surgery's cost, arguing: "You wouldn't expect your doctor to reimburse you if your child needed surgery, would you?"

3. CONSIDER THE ALTERNATIVES—RECYCLE OR DIE! (Message on a bumpersticker)

4. Yesterday I forgot to take my vitamins, and this morning I woke up with a cold. Now I know that taking vitamins really does prevent colds.

5. Tom remarks to Harry: "I heard that the Asian flu will be worse than usual in the Bay Area this year." Harry replies: "That's because San Francisco has such a large Asian population."

6. Springfield should round up all the homeless sleeping on the streets and make them live in shelters; otherwise, the city will just be a magnet for all destitute people who will end up sleeping in doorways and in our public parks.

7. I'm not going to vote for Senator Snortum in his reelection bid even if his proposal to improve the state's transportation system seems sensible. Last year his wife accused him of having an affair, and now I hear their marriage is rocky.

8. Vanderbilt General Insurance Company, the Big Company with the Big Heart. Fifty thousand satisfied customers can't be wrong!

9. An item from L.M. Boyd's "Grab Bag" in the *San Francisco Examiner* newspaper column submitted by a nurse: "People who don't relate well to other people are the ones with high blood pressure. I'm sure of it. No, I have no documented data. But as a lifelong nurse, I've taken countless blood pressure readings. The loners run high."

10. Try Auntie Em's frozen pies in five delicious flavors. Low-fat, low-cholesterol, and microwaveable, too. Just like Grandma used to make!

11. Escape from the ordinary. Move up to elegance. Test drive a Cheetah X-100 today.

12. Familiar bumpersticker during the Vietnam War era: AMERICA—LOVE IT OR LEAVE IT!

13. During the summer of 1992 at the Earth Summit in Rio de Janeiro, President Bush and the American delegates refused to sign the biodiversity treaty. (This treaty was signed by all the other 172 nations attending the summit.) Bush defended America's refusal to sign by saying that the treaty would cut jobs and profits at the expense of the nation's biotechnical industry.

14. Mother to teenage daughter, whom she has caught smoking: "There isn't anything good about smoking. You know it's bad for you, and you know I don't like the idea of your harming yourself." The daughter replies: "You should be glad I'm just smoking and not doing LSD the way some of my friends are."

15. In the 1992 presidential campaign, George Bush stated, "It's time to make people more important than owls," referring to the controversy in the Pacific Northwest over keeping the spotted owl on the Endangered Species list and thereby preventing logging in old-growth forests.

16. School districts should not provide day-care centers for their unmarried female students with babies. If girls want to go out and get themselves pregnant, they should just drop out of school and take the consequences of their actions.

17. Ad accompanying a Pacific Bell telephone bill:

    "Dear Emma Etiquette: I would like to get Pacific Bell Call Waiting for my phone, but I'm afraid it's rude, What do you think?—Old-Fashioned"

    "Dear Old-Fashioned: It is Emma Etiquette's opinion that today a busy signal is rude. Call Waiting is quite polite, especially when politely handled. Emma Etiquette would simply advise that you observe the normal courtesies. Just as you would not turn your back on one friend to engage in conversation with another, so you should not when using Call Waiting. Simply tell the second caller that you are engaged in another conversation and ask if you can call them back. Most people are decidedly gracious when so treated. In short, Call Waiting is an applaudable convenience, and one on which Emma Etiquette herself relies.—E.E."

18. Excerpt from a chain letter received by the author (the spelling and punctuation errors have been corrected): "This letter has been sent to you for blessings. The original is in New England. It has been around the world nine times. The blessing has been sent to you. You will receive blessings within four days for receiving this letter, provided you send it on. This is no joke. You will receive blessings in the mail. Don't send money, as faith has no price. Do not keep this letter. It must leave your hands within 96 hours. An R.A.R. officer received $70,000. Joe Elliot received $40,000 and lost it because he broke the chain while in the Philippines. Gene Welch lost his wife six days after receiving the letter. He failed to circulate the letter. However, before her death he received $7,755,000. Please send 20 copies and see what happens in four days."

19. Paladin Press is a publisher of how-to books for criminals (for example, how to make explosives and how to commit various kinds of murders). Copies of these books have been found in criminals' libraries. Although no one has sued the company yet, its critics would like to see the government stop it from publishing such material. However, Paladin's right to publish is guaranteed by the Constitution, thus affirming the power of the First Amendment to protect even those who publish advice on how to commit serious crimes. Peter Lund, the president of Paladin Press, defended his company's publications in *The Wall Street Journal,* saying that if someone tried to sue his company, it would be "a travesty of the legal system." He continues, "Do you sue General Motors because a kid runs over his schoolmate in a stolen car?"

20. A recent newspaper article indicated that only 35 percent of National Merit Scholarship winners are girls, although girls get better grades in high school and college than boys do. This discrepancy raises questions about the fairness of the program. According to FairTest, an organization seeking to remove bias from standardized tests, more than 60 percent of the 1993 winners are boys, a pattern consistent with past years.

    Cinthia Schuman, executive director of FairTest, says that the content and form of the test "clearly favor boys." She adds that the multiple-choice test places a premium on speed than on writing, problem solving, and other thinking skills, which are important for success in college courses. However, Elaine Detweiler, a representative of the National Merit Scholarship Corporation, responding to FairTest's criticisms, argues: "To blame the test for the difference between how boys and girls perform is like blaming a yardstick that boys are taller than girls." (Quoted in "Merit Scholarship Test Called Unfair to Girls," *The Los Angeles Times,* May 26, 1993)

21. In early 1993, a nominee for the California State Board of Education was rejected by the California Senate because he supported a bill that would ban the use of state money to educate illegal aliens, a controversial issue in California and other states with large immigrant populations. Senator Nicholas Petris, a Democrat from Oakland, argued against the nominee's candidacy, saying that the wife of the great Greek orator Pericles was considered an illegal immigrant.

22. The right-to-die initiative should be defeated by the voters in the next election. Although the proposition now only includes people with terminal conditions, cooperative doctors will eventually stretch the definition to include people with chronic conditions like Alzheimer's or multiple sclerosis. Pretty soon we won't have any control over who lives or dies. It will be just like ancient Sparta, where babies who did not have the potential to become great warriors were left outside to die.

23. In the debate over high salaries, a recent newspaper article disclosed that the average yearly compensation was $633,000 in 1990 (including benefits and incentives) for chief executives in American corporations. Critics charge that such salaries are immoral, especially when the executives are rewarded for laying off thousands of lower-paid workers by having their own salaries raised still higher.

    In response, Kevin Murphy, a compensation expert and professor at Harvard Business School, replies that this is exactly the kind of situation in which a CEO (chief executive officer) *should* be rewarded: "We have too much capacity [employees] and the right thing for shareholders and society is no longer to grow the firm, but to close plants, to take the painful steps of laying off people and becoming a more efficient operation. Society is just not very well informed if

people are angered by a CEO's pay climbing while he's laying off thousands of people."

Murphy concluded his remarks by saying that limiting executive pay "would be crazy, a disaster" because it would take away an executive's incentive to do an outstanding job. (Quoted in John Eckhouse, "Boards Taking Closer Look at Pay," *San Francisco Chronicle,* May 18, 1992)

24. In many of the nation's prisons, inmates have access to twelve cable channels via cable or satellite dishes. (These channels do not include Playboy or Home Shopping Network, which would be inappropriate for rapists or those imprisoned for credit card fraud.) Florida Attorney General Bob Butterworth is seeking removal of satellite dishes and cable hookups from his state's prisons. In a letter to the *Wall Street Journal* (July 9, 1992), Butterworth wrote: "If satellite dishes are allowed today, what will be allowed in our correctional centers tomorrow? High-definition televisions? Cellular telephones?"

Other Manipulative Techniques

In this last section of Part III, we will look at some other deceptive techniques used in argumentative writing, in politics, and in advertising.

Authority

In the section on appeals, we saw that one kind of emotional appeal is the testimonial—using spokespeople, most often celebrities like movie stars, rock singers, or athletes—in advertising endorsements. We know that we should be skeptical about accepting these endorsers as reliable authorities. First, they are paid—often enormous sums of money—for their kind words. Second, they may not be as knowledgeable about the field as an expert would be. A nutritionist or dietician would be a more reliable authority to speak on the merits or demerits of a product like Jello Pudding-Pops than Bill Cosby.

Besides being knowledgeable about a particular field, an authority should be reliable and relatively unbiased. You cannot expect a butcher, who is an expert on the subject of meat, to speak authoritatively about the dangers of a vegetarian diet. The butcher has an economic stake in your accepting the arguments against vegetarianism.

An authority, finally, should comment on situations in his or her specific field. Stated another way, an authority should not be cited as an authority on an unrelated discipline. For example, Brandon Centerwall, an epidemiologist at the University of Washington, has conducted research showing that there is a strong cause-and-effect relationship be-

tween television programming and homicide rates in North America and South Africa. (See also question 25 of "Evaluating Arguments," page 247.)

Since an epidemiologist is an expert in epidemic diseases, we need to ask whether Centerwall is qualified to speak on this issue. Centerwall is most likely a fine researcher, but his specialty poses a semantic problem. Is homicide an epidemic disease? And if not, then is Centerwall qualified to draw conclusions from research that may be only peripherally related to his field? And finally, if he is not, who *is* an authority on homicide rates and their link with television? Communications experts? Broadcasters? Sociologists? Psychologists? There is no one right answer to any of these questions, but it should point up the necessity of *thinking* about whose words are being cited in support of an argument.

A definite misuse of authority occurs when the high-sounding names of various "research organizations" are used to con the unwary reader or consumer. A particularly blatant instance of this happened in early 1992, when the *New York Times* published an article that informed the reading public that chocolate has cavity-fighting properties. This startling information made headlines. A few days later it was revealed that the information had come from a newsletter published by the Princeton Dental Resource Center and distributed to dentists' offices. (The name of this organization, of course, is meant to sound as if it is affiliated with Princeton University; it is not.) As it turns out, the Princeton Dental Resource Center is actually a front for the M&M/Mars Candy Company.

Bias

The term *bias* refers to the tendency to favor one side over the other, to write or speak from a subjective viewpoint colored by one's own political, economic, social, ethnic or racial, or religious views. Knowing the background of a writer—not merely his or her qualifications for serving as an authority—can alert us to subtle and not-so-subtle attempts to manipulate our thinking.

No one is completely free of prejudice, and it would be impossible for a writer to present *all* the pertinent facts and examples in support of an argument. The fact that a writer must exercise some subjective judgment regarding what material to select and what material to omit is inescapable. Therefore, total objectivity is not humanly possible. But we do have the right to expect that a writer attempt to be fair and objective, especially in presenting news stories. We need to be sure that the writer isn't operating with a "hidden agenda," some secondary motive that might not be readily apparent.

One suggestion is to pay attention to biographical headnotes when you read, for they can contain valuable information about a writer's background and beliefs. A good way to become familiar with the underlying beliefs and agendas of editorial writers is to read several of their

columns over a period of time. After a while you can begin to get a pretty good grasp of their politics. Finally, when you read persuasive prose, you should ask yourself this question: What does the writer stand to gain or lose by accepting (or rejecting) this argument? If you look over the preceding exercises, "Identifying Logical Fallacies and False Appeals," (pages 257–261), you will see that many of these arguments have an ulterior economic incentive. Auntie Em's pies may be very good indeed, but it seems hard to believe that anyone would confuse a frozen pie with a homemade one. And if you fall for the "just-like-Grandma-used-to-make," "just-plain-folks" appeal and buy one of Auntie Em's frozen microwaveable pies, you've enriched the corporate coffers that put out this product, not given Auntie Em herself a little extra spending money.

A good example of bias occurred after the disastrous 1989 oil spill by the tanker *Exxon Valdez* in Alaska, which spilled eleven million gallons of oil, the largest oil spill in U.S. history. A year later, two British scientists were commissioned by Exxon to study the area. Jenifer Baker, a biological consultant from Shrewsbury, England, and Robert B. Clark, a zoology professor emeritus from the University of Newcastle-upon-Tyne, studied the effect of spills on cold-water environments. Their conclusion was that the effect of the spill was likely to be "short-lived."

Alaskan wildlife officials—who knew firsthand the devastation the oil spill had caused—immediately criticized the findings as biased. Because the two scientists had been paid by Exxon to do the study, their findings were tainted by the clear possibility that they had been paid to say the right thing. According to Bruce Batten, a spokesman for Alaska's Fish and Wildlife Service, "It is a mistake to think of the report on environmental recovery by these scientists as being a piece of science. It is not based on any apparent scientific data. It appears to be the result of a two-week sightseeing tour." (Quoted in Carl Nolte, "Two Scientists Paid by Exxon Say Alaska Spill Area Curing Itself," *San Francisco Chronicle,* June 13, 1990.)

Examine the following portion of a news article for bias. What is the author's attitude toward Imelda Marcos? How can you tell? What clue lies in the title (see the source note)? In the author's word choice?

[1]Manila. It was vintage Imelda Marcos.

[2]Sitting in a luxury hotel, where she has taken the $2,000-a-day Imperial Suite and 60 rooms for her entourage, which includes four high-priced American lawyers, 20 American security agents and members of a Washington-based public relations firm, the former first lady told a clamoring crowd of reporters and supporters yesterday that it was time to tell "the truth."

[3]"I come home penniless," she said, appearing to fight back tears.

[4]A similar air of unreality pervaded much of Marcos' first day in the country where she and her late husband Ferdinand are accused of looting billions of dollars during their 21-year dictatorial rule.

[5]There were endless tears and waves of her white lace hanky to the thousands of cheering loyalists who lined streets and rooftops, banged drums, shot fireworks and mobbed her motorcade in near pandemonium for almost three hours under a blazing sun. Many in the crowd then lined up to collect promised payments of $5.56 for their role in the day's carefully scripted drama.

Vow to Philippine People

[6]At a packed rally outside the Philippine Plaza Hotel, she told supporters that she would fight poverty. "As long as there is one Filipino who is poor, Imelda's work will not be over," said the woman best known for her million-dollar shopping sprees and 1,220 pairs of shoes. "I will never turn my back on anyone who suffers in pain."

[7]In an interview with NBC-TV yesterday, Marcos denied having a political agenda, but she later referred at a news conference to the large crowds and told reporters, "I have always said: When the people speak, Imelda follows."

[8]Saying she is neither angry nor bitter, the 62-year-old widow appealed to the heartstrings and tear ducts of the nation that forced her and her husband to flee in disgrace to America in the "people power" revolt of February 1986.

[9]"I will give my heart as the mother of the nation," she said, as supporters wept, chanted and waved placards. "I am appealing on bended knees for us to be united."

Bob Drogin, "'Penniless' Imelda Marcos in $2,000 Suite," *The Los Angeles Times*

The following article is instructive as a model. Although the author takes up a controversial subject—fetal tissue transplants—he presents a balanced mix of scientific explanation and editorial comment. It is obvious that he is in favor of such transplants, but his discussion is measured and reasoned; even if we do not accept his thinking, he has done it well and carefully.

[1]Pioneering medical research frequently provokes ethical controversies. But no research initiative in American medicine has evoked more genuine dishonesty or more hypocrisy than the use of fetal tissue transplants to help treat victims of Parkinson's disease, diabetes and other crippling illnesses. This controversy offers a shameful example of medical innovation mismanagement.

[2]At the center of this controversy are the products of abortion: dead fetuses. Because of its unique biological properties, fetal tissue provides researchers tremendous insights into the workings of the human body. Quite possibly, fetal tissue could prove as vital to healing certain diseases as any blockbuster drug, surgical procedure or transplantable organ.

[3]Transplant research supporters argue that it is sinful to waste the tissue when it could be used to heal the living. Transplant opponents insist that explicitly linking abortion to healing would effectively excuse or encourage the procedure. So although the government funds generic research on fetal tissue, it explicitly refuses to fund transplant research. Arguing that such research is essential, Congress recently voted to lift the funding ban—a move the Bush administration vows to veto.

[4]That debate is political gamesmanship tarted up as public policy. The real issue here isn't fetal tissue transplant research; it's what happens if this research leads to widely practical therapies. Dr. Kenneth Ryan, chairman of obstetrics, gynecology and reproductive biology at Harvard Medical School and a champion of fetal tissue transplant research, believes that work under way in treating Parkinson's disease will generate demand for transplant treatment within three to five years. What happens if fetal tissue proves just as useful in treating diabetes and Alzheimer's? What are the probable consequences of success?

[5]With more than half a million Parkinson's sufferers, nearly three quarters of a million severely affected diabetics and several million potential Alzheimer's victims, the consequences are potentially massive. Theoretically, fetal transplant surgery could become more prevalent than heart surgery.

[6]Shifts in public perception might prove equally dramatic. With transplant technology, an abortion can be transformed from a personal tragedy to a gift of life. Supporters of fetal tissue transplants affirm that there should be a wall between the decision to abort and the decision to donate. But, practically, can there be? Indeed, should there be? Would it be wrong for a doctor to tell a woman who wants an abortion that, if she waits only two weeks, her fetal tissue could help save someone's life? Perhaps that knowledge will ease her trauma. While you're at it, why not offer to pay for the abortion if she is willing to donate? Society does it for blood; why not for fetal tissue?

[7]Let's complicate the question. "What happens when [abortion pill] RU-482 comes to America and there's no tissue?" poses Harvard's Ryan. The economics of fetal tissue availability is quite unlike the economics of kidneys, livers and hearts.

[8]What mother of a crippled Type 1 diabetic girl wouldn't seriously consider the possibility of an induced abortion to save her suffering child? What loving daughter wouldn't explore that possibility to save her father from

the cruel decay of Parkinson's? Indeed, what kind of subtle and overt pressures might women be subjected to if close friends and relatives are similarly stricken? What does "choice" mean under these circumstances?

[9] "If these techniques turn out to be successful, would anyone try to deny that this shifts the process of decision making toward choosing to have an abortion?" asks Dr. James Mason, the assistant secretary for health at the Department of Health and Human Services who champions the Bush Administration's fetal tissue transplant funding ban.

[10] For scientists to divorce fetal tissue transplant research from its therapeutic implications is appallingly dishonest. Simply saying that the difficult ethical choices are up to society is an abdication of responsibility that should disqualify them from public funds. If scientists believe that harvesting aborted fetal tissue or direct family donations are appropriate public policy, then they should defend it and not hide behind the academic veil of "research."

[11] Unfortunately, the Bush administration's stand on fetal tissue transplants isn't only dishonest, it's also breathtakingly hypocritical. While forbidding public funds for fetal transplant research that might lead to induced abortions, the government explicitly allows privately funded fetal tissue transplant research to continue. In other words, it's OK to have a private marketplace in fetal tissue. Mason acknowledges the conflict but says that his department's reach doesn't extend beyond government research funding. At best, that's disingenuous—at worst, it leads to what Harvard's Ryan calls an "anything goes" medical marketplace, much as we have with in vitro fertilization.

[12] That our government and medical establishment duck the life-and-death ethical issues posed by an emerging technique is nothing short of disgraceful. If they treated patients the way they've treated this policy, they would be sued for malpractice.

Michael Schrage, "Behind the Fetal Tissue Transplant Controversy,"
San Francisco Examiner

Lying with the Facts

In politics, where it seems that almost anything goes, a particularly nasty manipulative device turned up in the 1992 election. Called "lying with the facts" (a term invented by Phil Trounstine of the *San Jose Mercury News*), political ads often show a series of assertions, each of which is true, but when taken together, present an untruth. The result is that the viewer sees a biased view of the candidate.

An example: In the bitter 1992 Senate race in California, Gray Davis, the Republican candidate and California Controller, was pitted against the Democratic candidate, Diane Feinstein. Toward the end of the campaign, Davis's organization showed a thirty-second TV ad that made use of "lying with the facts." The ad began by presenting viewers

with "separated-at-birth" photos of Feinstein and Leona Helmsley, the hotel magnate then in prison for tax fraud.

San Francisco Chronicle political reporter Jerry Roberts explains how it's done: "The announcer and the words on the screen then present a series of simple statements (at one point buttressed by a misleading use of *The Chronicle* masthead) that compare Helmsley's criminal conviction to Feinstein's being sued in a civil action for alleged campaign reporting violations: 'Helmsley blames her servants for the felony; Feinstein blames her staff for the lawsuit,' the ad says. 'Helmsley is in jail; Feinstein wants to be a senator.' The individual statements are at least arguably true; the spot's overall, innuendo-filled message is not." (Quoted in Jerry Roberts, "California Primary Finally Heats Up," *San Francisco Chronicle*)

Incidentally, Feinstein won.

Misleading Statistics

The critical reader must also learn to be skeptical of statistics used in the service of an argument. Given the incredible amount of information published on any one subject every day in the information age, it is *very* difficult to ferret out the truth, especially when both sides in a controversy can wave contradictory statistics at each other.

The use of misleading statistics is nicely illustrated in this final example. As the author says, the statistics looked impressive at first glance, but they told only half the story.

[1]I read last week about a 45-year-old skilled machinist who was laid off in March by Moog Inc., a small defense subcontractor in East Aurora, N.Y. Moog was a supplier on an intercontinental ballistic missile program slashed by the Pentagon.

[2]He had been making $40,000 a year, had a wife and three children and was buying a four bedroom house.

[3]The machinist, out of work for five months, has no hope of getting another job as well-paying as the one he lost. He has been offered a few non-machinist jobs paying less than half of what he had been making at Moog.

[4]One of these days he'll have to accept a lower-paying job. It won't quite be flipping burgers at a fast food joint, but the job he'll probably take won't be a morale builder either.

[5]Like the machinist and for millions of other unemployed Americans, the problem is not so much finding a job as finding one that will keep them and their families living above the poverty level.

[6]Until three or four years ago, economist-dreamers and human resources fakirs talked up massive retraining schemes under which laid off autoworkers would, as if by magic, be turned into computer programmers or perhaps astronauts.

[7]Then reality set in. Husky, stubby-fingered assembly-line workers with 20 years experience building cars and trucks were not exactly suited for the programmer business, much less a trip into space. Instead, hundreds of thousands of them swallowed their pride and took janitorial or rent-a-cop jobs at shopping malls for, or only slightly above, the minimum wage.

[8]And by taking those menial jobs the skilled workers contributed to some statistical aberrations as well as keeping the unemployment figures lower than they actually were.

[9]From 1979 through 1989, for example, the Department of Labor reported that the economy grew by 13.6 million jobs.

[10]"Huzza!" cried Ronald Reagan when the numbers were announced on his shift in the White House.

[11]Later George Bush was quoted as saying "Isn't that just peachy news?" when the latest job formation figures were reported.

[12]On the surface it was good news. Numbers don't lie, or do they?

[13]The 13.6 million new jobs figure IS impressive. But another statistic is equally impressive: More than one-third of those new jobs were paying less than $250 a week. That's $13,000 a year, low enough to put a family of four below the poverty level.

[14]That family, which could be headed by a wage earner who once made $40,000 a year, is no longer frolicking in the shopping malls. Nor is it sending much if anything to local, state and federal tax collectors.

Donald K. White, "Breaking the Job Drought," *San Francisco Examiner*

Exercises: Part 4— Analyzing Editorials

The exercises in this final section consist of six examples of persuasive writing to give you practice in implementing your critical reading skills. These eight passages represent editorials on current controversial issues from the op-ed pages of major newspapers. For each selection that your instructor assigns (or that you read on your own), consider these questions:

1. What is the writer's main argument or proposition?
2. What kind of evidence does the writer provide in support of the argument?
3. According to the criteria discussed in this section, is the evidence fair? Does it appear to be reliable? Is it relevant to the argument? Is it sufficient to make the argument convincing or at least worth considering?

4. Is the writer biased or unbiased? Would the writer gain or lose anything by your accepting the argument?
5. Are there any instances of appeals to your emotions, to fear, to sympathy, prejudice, or the like?
6. Are there any logical fallacies?
7. Are there any examples of manipulative language—sneer words, euphemisms, or slanted language?
8. Do you accept the writer's argument? Why or why not? If you need more information, what would you need to know?

Selection 1

The author writes social and political commentary for *The New York Times.*

[1]In September someone pushed a syringe around the edge of a door at the building that houses the Northland Family Planning clinic and sprayed the vestibule with acid. The clinic was one of 14 in Michigan so targeted.

[2]On Christmas Eve, members of a Lutheran church in Omaha received postcards picturing a dismembered fetus. The mass mailing to 250 homes came after a worship service had been disrupted and scriptural graffiti painted in red on a church wall, all because one church member is a doctor who performs abortions.

[3]Next week two events of great moment will take place in Washington, D.C. Bill Clinton will become president. And the 20th anniversary of the Supreme Court decision Roe vs. Wade will be commemorated by foes and proponents of abortion.

[4]But do not be fooled by this timely convergence of the inauguration of a president who supports a woman's right to choose and the anniversary of the decision that recognized that right.

[5]The acid attack, the postal onslaught and many incidents like them tell the real story.

[6]After Clinton's election, some felt the abortion debate was moving toward resolution. The gag rule would be overturned, the abortion pill would be considered on its merits and the man in the Oval Office would sign the Freedom of Choice Act.

[7]All those changes, if they come, will be long overdue. But we have yet to address—or even fully recognize—the problems of everyday procedure. Those will be the battles of the next decade.

[8]Doctors who perform abortions are being besieged by groups like Missionaries to the Pre-Born, which sent the mailing out to the Omaha congregation. Their homes are picketed and their families and patients harassed. It's no wonder that some of them drop out of this particular practice area.

[9]Some are aging out. The 20th anniversary of Roe means that those doctors deeply dedicated to providing abortion services, those who remember the bad old days, are two decades older than when they began. When they retire, there are few young doctors to replace them.

[10]The clinics have aged, too. Their administrators have been through blockades and arsons, and some are weary. Renee Chelian, who oversees three of Michigan's 30 clinics, can still smell the butyric acid someone sprayed inside the building in which her Northland clinic rents space, ruining carpets and paneling and leaving behind noxious fumes.

[11]In one of the other Michigan locations, in a fine bit of irony, an obstetrician had to close his practice for a week because he was afraid inhaling the acid might harm his pregnant patients.

[12]"Protecting the right to abortion and protecting the provision of services are two different things," says Ms. Chelian. One we have fought for relentlessly; the other we have mostly ignored. That has been shortsighted, like lobbying for food for all without noticing the supermarkets closing.

[13]Qualified nurses and physicians' assistants should be permitted to perform uncomplicated early abortions to take up the slack from doctors. Federal officials should use conspiracy statutes to prosecute roving groups who plan acts of vandalism like the acid attacks.

[14]And those who believe that Clinton's election means this issue is somehow settled should realize they are mistaken. The truth is that things may get worse.

[15]For years there have been predictions that the overturn of Roe, if it ever came, would galvanize supporters of legal abortion; we forgot that the election of a pro-choice president could get opponents just as fired up.

[16]For a man like the one who can be heard on the Northeast Indiana Rescue Line, passing on the rumor that the radical Lambs of Christ may be heading for Fort Wayne and adding "Things could get interesting" as though this were a playoff game, a Freedom of Choice Act will only up the ante.

[17]It is good to have a president who believes that a woman must decide this intimate issue for herself. But it does not mark the end of the abortion war, simply the beginning of another kind of battle.

Anna Quindlen, "A New Kind of Battle in the Abortion Wars," *The New York Times*

Selection 2

At the time this editorial was written, the author was a senior at the University of Massachusetts-Amherst and the editor-in-chief of the campus newspaper, *The Daily Collegian*.

[1]Amherst, Mass.

When 200 protesters stormed the offices of the University of Massachusetts' campus newspaper after the Rodney G. King verdict, they destroyed thousands

of dollars worth of office equipment and dampened staff spirits. But the greatest violence was done to the 1st Amendment.

[2]The irony is that the protesters destroyed that freedom in the name of insensitivity to oppression and racism at a newspaper that has tried hard over the years to be inclusive rather than exclusive.

[3]The 102 year-old Collegian is a daily, independent, student paper that receives no financial help from the university. Management positions, including editors, are elected by the staff. Ten percent of the staff are minorities. Seven of the last nine editors-in-chief have been women.

[4]Although only one non-white has held paper's top post, the Collegian has tried to provide a forum for minority voices. The paper's editorials regularly embrace minority views. Still, protesters call the paper racist.

[5]Student sit-ins are a common event at the Collegian. Minorities, unwilling to start their own newspapers even though funds are available, have tried to carve out their own space in the Collegian. They've usually been successful.

[6]Since the creation of a weekly black affairs page in 1975, the flow of "oppressed" groups demanding space for their concerns has been constant. The Collegian has largely complied. Now, the paper's news hole is divvied up for women's issues, multicultural and Third World affairs, and gay, lesbian and bisexual concerns. In response to charges of anti-Semitic articles on the Third World page, a Jewish-affairs editorship was created.

[7]But the protesters wanted more. They called for a new page devoted to women of color. They demanded separate election procedures for editors of the special pages. Only staff members working on those sections would vote. Most important, they called for a new position, a co-editor-in-chief of color.

[8]This person would share power equally with the editor elected by the entire staff. The protesters, in effect, were demanding a paper governed by a separate-but-equal policy. They vowed to reoccupy the Collegian's offices until their demands were met. One protester said "it is not enough for us to have a voice, we need control."

[9]To ensure publication, the staff moved the newspaper's equipment into off-campus apartments. Angered by this, protesters stole all the copies of the May 4 Collegian from distribution points. It was a brazen act of censorship.

[10]What these student protesters forget is that a newspaper's job is to cover and report the news and not be an advocate for every special-interest group that wants to proselytize. The Collegian is the only daily in Amherst and the strongest voice in the liberal Pioneer Valley. Instead of reporting the issues that affect this diverse community, the Collegian has been coerced into printing propaganda.

[11]In essence, a small group of students have taken it upon themselves to decide what is suitable for the community to read. After they decide what that is,

some will resort to threats of force to publish it. One result has been that editors needed police escorts to deliver newspapers on campus. But in the end, this situation is the result of continually caving in to their demands.

[12]The situation illustrates the nearly impossible task of an institution trying to become politically correct. For the Collegian, the process began nearly two decades ago. But like any institution, success will never arrive. It is time for many to realize that there are limits to this PC movement.

[13]The Constitution guarantees equal opportunity, not equal success. Affirmative action can open the door of opportunity. But it fails miserably when imposed, particularly on management positions. The protesters fail to realize that executive positions need to be earned, not given. Journalists feel their hands are tied by a small but vocal minority.

[14]The Collegian's yearly efforts to restructure itself are slowly driving the newspaper into the ground. This spring's demands will likely not be the last. What I have learned about PC protesters is that they are never satisfied.

[15]The system they want provides them with glorified control. But the protesters never want to earn it.

Dan Wetzel, "A Question of Oppression at U. Mass.: Freedom of the Press or Racism?"
The Los Angeles Times

Selection 3

The author, a journalist who lived in Kenya from 1988 to 1992, is also the author of *At the Hand of Man: Peril and Hope for Africa's Wildlife.*

[1]*"It is absurd for a man to kill an elephant. It is not brutal, it is not heroic, and certainly it is not easy: It is just one of those preposterous things that men do like putting a dam across a great river."*

[2]These words of aviator Beryl Markham sum up how I feel about hunting. While I don't share the attitude of animal-rights militants that a hunter is some lower form of the human species (and one that ought to become extinct), I can't fathom why a man picks up a rifle and shoots an elephant, a lion, a leopard or a kudu. But negative feelings about hunters are often knee-jerk. In fact, the establishment conservation ideology that opposes hunting may be counterconservationist.

[3]"I support hunting as a conservation tool," says David Western, an eminent conservationist and director of the Nairobi office of Wildlife Conservation International, the field research arm of the New York Zoological Society. Although Mr. Western is not a hunter, he explains, "To me it's the survival of the wildlife that matters."

[4]Indeed, from a conservation perspective, it can be argued that hunting should be promoted over tourism. While researching a book on conservation in Africa, I discovered that, ecologically, tourists do more damage than hunters, and not

just because there are so many more of the camera clickers. They speed across the plains in their minivans, tearing up the grass, creating dust bowls and cutting ugly ruts. Then they surround a lion pride or rhino, reducing the animals to fright, boredom or what sometimes seems like near tears.

[5]The first offense is a subtle one: Man as tourist is taking the "wild" out of the wildlife in Africa. As recently as the 1970s, the lions in Ngorongoro, a spectacular natural zoo in the bowl of a volcano in northern Tanzania, would "hide from tourist vehicles," one researcher noted. These days, following a steady increase in human visitors, the lions have become so accustomed to man and his car that they yawn and pose.

[6]After so many years of being hounded by tourists, the cheetah, the fastest animal in the kingdom, "no longer lives like a wild animal," says Richard Leakey, director of the Kenya Wildlife Service. Tourists love to stalk the sleek cheetah as it stalks a gazelle or impala. The cheetah reacts by running away or lying down—i.e., giving up its natural activity—until the tourists, bored by the "inactivity," move on.

[7]Tourism may even kill more animals than hunters do. It sometimes prevents mothers from feeding their families. "Harassment of the lions by camera in Serengeti has led to so many kills being missed that lion cubs sometimes starve, Norman Myers, a British conservationist, wrote in 1972 about the northern Tanzania park. (A responsible professional hunter does not shoot a female of a childbearing age, for selfish reasons—the cubs she will bear are the hunter's future prey.)

[8]There is another argument for hunting. Tourists assault the dignity and cultures of indigenous people, snapping pictures as if the person were one of the wild animals, bargaining for jewelry or clothing that the person is wearing and "paying" with a few shillings. The hunter, however, makes only limited contact with local people. Squalid villages with prostitutes and begging children do not spring up near hunters' wilderness camps, as they do near high-rise tourist hotels.

[9]Finally, and perhaps most important for financially exhausted African governments, sport hunting is more profitable than tourism. A lucrative hunting industry can exist with a limited capital investment, without large hotels and minivans, or even roads. Hunters also spend prodigious amounts of money—easily $50,000 for a hunting safari in Tanzania, for example; most of that money stays in Tanzania. By contrast, Europeans can go to Kenya for a week's photo safari for less than $1,000, including air fares. Even a top-of-the-line photographic safari is not likely to cost more than $20,000.

[10]Costa Mlay, the former director of Tanzania's wildlife department, figures that one hunter is worth a hundred nonhunting tourists to his country. Each hunter is required to pay $200 a day to the government—this is in addition to what he pays his professional hunter guide—and there is a 21-day minimum for a hunting safari. The hunter also has to buy a license, and they are expen-

sive—$4,000 for each elephant he plans to shoot, $2,000 for a leopard or lion; $1,300 for a kudu (similar to an antelope). Hunters paid roughly $10,000 each directly to the Tanzanian government during the 1991 hunting season, and the government took in $2.3 million from license fees alone—more than the gate fees tourists paid to enter the country's parks.

[11]Kenya banned hunting in the 1970s—not on moral or ethical grounds, but because of massive corruption. Upon becoming director of the Kenya Wildlife Service in 1989, Mr. Leakey said he would like to reintroduce it. He not only believes in hunting, but in hunting elephants, although he has been careful not to say this publicly. In a 1989 meeting with U.S. officials, which was reported to Washington in a confidential cable, Mr. Leakey urged Washington not to take actions that would prohibit the sport hunting of elephants in Kenya.

[12]Mr. Leakey's reasons for wanting to bring hunters to Kenya are simple—his department desperately needs the money for conservation. It is currently dependent on some $50 million a year from the international community. A 1989 survey concluded that hunters would pay $4 million to the Kenyan wildlife department in license fees alone—four times more than the government had ever earned in a single year from park entrance fee.

[13]Landownership plays a role here. Contrary to what Westerners think, most of Kenya's wildlife is not in parks, but on private lands. Kenya's conservationists realize that the landowners are not going to tolerate wildlife's presence without an incentive—elephants trample crops, lions eat cattle and children. Landowners who earn an average of 70 cents a hectare from tour operators for concessions could earn almost $2 a hectare from selling hunting concessions.

[14]What keeps Kenya, then, from restoring hunting? In part, non-Africans' conventional wisdom about what is good for African wildlife. Mr. Leakey and other Kenyan wildlife officials fear the international community won't approve of a return to hunting. Kenya's tour operators fear that hunting will damage the country's image and could lead to campaigns by the militant animal-rights organizations to boycott Kenya. The result is that Kenya—and many other parts of Africa—cannot follow the most efficient path to conservation.

Raymond Bonner, "A Conservationist Argument for Hunting," *The Wall Street Journal*

Selection 4

The author writes an opinion column for *The Boston Globe*. This editorial was written a few days after the first verdict was handed down in the Rodney King trial, in which four white policemen were acquitted of using excessive force. That verdict resulted in three days of looting and burning in Los Angeles, the worst rioting in U.S. history.

[1]It sure must be marvelous to be white and have a bit of power at the edge of your fingers or the tip of your tongue. Then, if you are employed by a newspaper or—better yet—hold an office like mayor, US senator or president you can

write or say over and over what anybody with an ounce of common sense has grown sick of seeing and hearing these past few days; and the phrase, the clear choice of morons, is: "There can be no excuse for lawlessness."

[2]But the best excuse in the world occurred when a jury from Mars used fear rather than law to acquit bad cops of even worse crimes. And if I had to live in Watts—could not leave, unable even to escape—I think for sure I might have been first man into the appliance store or supermarket in order to steal. After all, the only thing most people there can afford is rage, so why not spend everything at once?

[3]It was amazing, yet some members of that jury had the stupidity to expose themselves on TV to say that if we had seen the video as often as they did, we would realize that, among other things, not all the blows landed on Rodney King. I guess the focus was on aim rather than intent.

[4]Wonderful! This is like me going up to the counter of the J&J Variety Store in Waltham, gun in hand, reaching into the cash drawer and firing off two rounds at poor Danny behind the counter and then getting a "not guilty" because I missed. You are a lousy shot, thus you are a free man.

[5]My God, but this nation is in terrible trouble. And the bulk of it is over the twin demons of race and class. No matter what is said and done, no matter how many programs are proposed or speeches made, we have this continuing inability to simply exist alongside one another. We are so hung up on color and money that we don't even realize we are dying.

[6]Let me tell you a little about Watts. For many months, a long time ago, I would rise early every morning, before the shrouded sun splashed over the rim of the bowl that is the Los Angeles basin, and drive from Torrance into downtown LA.

[7]Every day, I would proceed straight along the ribbon that runs from San Pedro into the city, a road called the Harbor Freeway. All you see as you skim past the exit ramps for Vermont Avenue, Normandie, Crenshaw Boulevard is the tops of huge palm trees swaying in the breeze.

[8]There could be no slum down there, right? These are sights from the tropics. It is warm. People on the sidewalk never freeze. There are all these little bungalows with patches of lawn, no vertical prisons containing the feeble poor.

[9]But, in truth, Watts is merely Orchard Park, part of Mission Hill, half of Harlem or most of Anacostia with a better mean temperature. It is only one more jail for those who have been sentenced to a grim economic and educational death by a system that is absolutely rigged for the rich.

[10]You say, that's an oversimplification. Maybe. I say, the problem is that's precisely what's in too many people's minds if they are black or brown and the rest of us are just unable to walk in their shoes so we don't have a clue as to how deep the bitterness is among those so glibly cast aside.

[11]Certainly, great gains have been made in the past quarter century. An abundance of legislation has been enacted aimed at things like making it easier for black people to vote or attend previously white schools. But you have to have the eye of an eagle in these huge sprawling slums to find a factory.

[12]And all the laws in the world will never come close to providing a human being the dignity that comes with work. The most important word in our language, the most progressive, most meaningful, most liberating is spelled J-O-B.

[13]Jobs bring income. Income means money. Money translates into pride. Pride can conquer drugs. It can hold families and whole blocks together. It can make fathers and mothers seem taller to their children. It sets parents free.

[14]Unfortunately, for 24 years, since Robert F. Kennedy—hurt and wounded himself—traveled the land in the spring of 1968, nearly everyone with a hand on the national lever has lied to both blacks and whites about each other. They lied about learning and lied some more about working and, all the time, they have used the genuine fear of crime and violence to turn those halfway up the ladder against those on the bottom rung.

[15]So this latest municipal carnival of bloodshed in California should not come as any real surprise. This time, the trigger was pulled by 12 morons in Simi Valley. Next time, it could easily be a traffic citation or some poor legitimate white cop making an arrest for drunk and disorderly. But as surely as we sit here this morning—isolated and indifferent—there will be a next time because already all the blind officials are talking about getting things back to normal in Watts, a sewer covered by the shade of palms. And, what we call "normal" is precisely what is slowly choking America to death.

Mike Barnicle, "The Legacy of Lies and Fears," The Boston Globe

---

Selection 5

The author is a former White House speech writer who ran unsuccessfully in the 1992 Republican presidential primary. A nationally syndicated columnist, he is known for his conservative views.

[1]Washington

It was that most innocent of occasions, a recreation center on Benning Road in southeast Washington D.C., a hundred noisy kids jumping in and out of a community pool on a 90-degree day.

[2]Suddenly, a gunman appeared on the hillside. Before he stopped firing with his semi-automatic pistol, six children, 5 to 14, were bleeding from gunshot wounds. In the same 48 hours in which that attempted massacre occurred, 14 people were murdered in the nation's capital.

[3]It was in Jamestown, about 125 miles from San Francisco, that a mother this spring walked into a courtroom and shot to death the smirking pervert charged with molesting her son.

[4]In West Memphis, Ark., three teen-agers are charged in the murder of three 8-year-old boys whose bodies were found in a drainage ditch.

[5]The horror, the anguish of these stories, re-enacted again and again, with trusting children as victims of sex abuse and murder, has induced a terror in the hearts of parents unknown in America.

[6]Parents no longer let children play in the woods or visit parks. When kids are late, apprehension grips many a mother's heart. Many move away from cities where reports of violated children have become common. But there is no place left to hide.

[7]What became of the America we grew up in, where 8-year-olds were given a brown bag with sandwiches in cellophane, and sent off in safety to the play-round for the day?

[8]The day of the pool shooting, a panel of the National Science Foundation reported on the causes of juvenile crime. Among them: "schools that have ability tracking, which works against low-achieving students; a health care system that excludes teenagers . . . the absence of any help for students moving from school to jobs; and a justice system that fails to rehabilitate most adolescent offenders."

[9]Sorry, but the same old sociological explanations just won't do. What we are dealing with here is evil, pure and simple. Our society is sick because the central water supply from which we all must drink—the wellsprings of our thought—is polluted.

[10]Forty years ago, our ideas about right and wrong came out of religious beliefs. Taught in home and school, echoed from pulpits, reflected in film and books, these ideas served as the basis of morality and law.

[11]Today, the conscience-forming, character-forming institutions—family, home, church, school—have broken down. The old ideas of right and wrong are mocked. Popular culture, TV and film, repeat a single theme: Do your own thing.

[12]Into the moral vacuum of weak minds—inhibitions dissolved by TV and film—are slipped the enticements of the forbidden fruits, alluringly presented by pornographic films and magazines, featuring women, even children. From the addiction that follows, from the soul thus corrupted, there ensues the criminal act.

[13]Neither poverty nor unemployment can explain the new barbarism. For, in the 1930s a third of the nation was poor, a fourth without work. Yet, America's cities were decent, safe places.

[14]On finding the 14th victim of our latest murder binge, Lt. Lowell Duckett, president of the D.C. Black Police Caucus, said, "The fear of law enforcement officers is gone. Criminals have to know police will come out against them through any means necessary."

¹⁵America's enemy is not in Mogadishu. He is inside the gates. We will win this war on crime only when the body count of that enemy approaches in number that of the innocent victims of his atrocities.

Pat Buchanan, "It's Evil, Pure and Simple," *San Francisco Examiner*

Selection 6

The author is Albert Schweitzer professor of the humanities at the City University of New York and a winner of Pulitzer Prizes in biography and history. This editorial was written in the late spring of 1993 as the world tried to determine how best to deal with the crisis in Bosnia, a republic in the former Yugoslavia before the fall of the Communist empire.

During 1992 and 1993, Serbia had engaged in a brutal campaign of "ethnic cleansing" to rid its territory of Muslims and Croats. The United States, the European Community, and the United Nations proposed various plans; truces were signed and immediately broken. Part of the national debate concerned America's role in Bosnia—whether to stand by and not intervene in a civil war or to send military forces. It is hoped that by the time this book is published, some peace will have been restored to the Balkans. In any case, Schlesinger's editorial applies to our role in the wider world, not just in Bosnia.

¹The threat of military intervention has persuaded the Bosnian Serbs to say they will go along with the United Nations peace plan. At this point, President Clinton's policy must be accounted a considerable success. But every previous agreement among the warring groups in Yugoslavia has broken down. This one may break down too. What then?

²Secretary of State Christopher is now on a mission to persuade our European friends that, if the agreement does break down, the next step should be limited military intervention—air strikes, arms to the Bosnian Muslims. The administration will also have to persuade a majority of Americans, according to the polls. In short, the Bosnian debate is far from over—the debate that has already produced such strange reversals and odd alliances, turning Anthony Lewis into a hawk on the side of Jeane Kirkpatrick and Abe Rosenthal into a dove on the side of Pat Buchanan.

³On the one hand: It seems unbearable to pass by on the other side while Serbs kill, rape and torture harmless people. Nor is this just a humanitarian concern. Bosnia also places the grand vision of a new world order on test and at risk. If we do not stop aggression there, will not the domino effect spread the infection?—and then no country will be safe. If the agreement collapses, does not the U.S. as the world's only military superpower bear a special and primary responsibility to stop the slaughter of the innocents, punish the ethnic cleansers, murderers, torturers and rapists, and vindicate the essential goal of collective security? What has happened to American idealism? American courage? American decency?

Real Change Unlikely

4On the other hand: What practically can we do if the agreement collapses? President Clinton has wisely ruled out unilateral U.S. intervention. If Washington exerts major pressure, it can probably get Britain and possibly France to join in air strikes and even perhaps in providing arms to the Muslims. Such actions would temporarily ease American consciences by giving the impression that the U.S. is doing *something*. But the object of foreign policy is not to gratify ourselves; it is to bring about real changes in a real world. And suppose limited military intervention fails, what is the next step?

5It is instructive to consider why the European democracies are so reluctant to enter the Yugoslav civil war. It may of course simply be the hope that the U.S. will solve Europe's problems for them. But it may be more than that. It may be that the Europeans have a different assessment as to what is at stake in Bosnia.

6As many Europeans see it, the end of the Cold War encourages the Balkans to be the Balkans again. The Balkan peoples, they say, are fighting among themselves, as they have done throughout their history and, despite the atrocities, there is not much outsiders can do about Yugoslavia until the Yugoslavs get tired of killing each other. Few Europeans subscribe to the apocalyptic interpretation of the Yugoslav civil war.

7The arguments used today for intervention in Bosnia have disquieting echoes of the arguments used 30 years ago for intervention in Vietnam—collective security, domino theory, punishing aggression, defending world order. In 1967, President Johnson sent Clark Clifford on a mission to persuade the Seato allies to increase their token military contributions to Vietnam. Traveling from country to country, Mr. Clifford discovered that the Seato allies, though closer to the scene and more vulnerable to the consequences of a communist victory, did not take the war as tragically as Washington did and were unwilling to put more of their soldiers in the fighting. Mr. Clifford returned from his mission persuaded that there was less at stake in Vietnam than we had supposed.

8In retrospect, the assessment of the Seato allies turned out to be correct. North Vietnam won the war, but there was no domino effect (or rather the dominoes fell not against us but against each other), communist Vietnam attacking communist Cambodia and communist China attacking communist Vietnam, and no encouragement of aggression elsewhere. It may equally be that the assessment of the NATO allies of the stakes in Bosnia is more correct than that of the American interventionists.

9After all, Europeans are more familiar with the territory and will be more endangered by the result. Yet they do not see their vital interests as threatened, nor do they find compelling reasons to send young men to kill and die in Bosnia. Slobodan Milosevic is a wicked scoundrel, but Serbia is not Nazi Germany, nor will it move on from Bosnia to attack Italy and France and Britain. Few Europeans believe that the Yugoslav civil war is going to set off a world war.

[10]And few Europeans believe that, if the agreement breaks down, limited intervention will bring it back to life. Air power is effective in a desert where there is no place to hide. Yugoslavia is not a desert. Bosnia and Serbia are mountainous, forested and filled with places to hide. "Surgical" strikes against Serbian positions are an illusion. As George Ball once remarked, if surgeons used the same criteria that the Air Force does, none of us would ever dare have an operation. We now know that even in the Gulf War the "smart" bombs were not in practice so smart as they were represented as being at the time.

[11]If the agreement breaks down and limited intervention fails to nail that old coonskin to the wall, will the world's only military superpower cravenly retreat? Or, having committed ourselves so far, are we not obligated to go farther and send in ground forces? No doubt in time we could win an all-out war on the ground against Serbia, but it would probably require at least a quarter of a million troops and it would be a messy, murderous affair that no general staff in the West is eager to undertake. And that would not be the end of it. A large military force would have to remain, probably for years, to police a political settlement.

[12]And if we embroil ourselves in the Yugoslav civil war for humanitarian and new world-order reasons, how can we stop with Yugoslavia? What about Armenia/Azerbaijan, Cambodia, Tibet and other countries where the same principles are involved? Do we ignore these suffering peoples because they are not European? Where does our crusade for world redemption end?

[13]One other consideration must weigh heavily on President Clinton's mind. If he leads the U.S. step by step into a Balkan war, he might as well kiss his program of national renovation and reform goodbye. Bosnia will destroy his domestic hopes as surely as Vietnam destroyed Lyndon Johnson's Great Society.

[14]If the agreement breaks down, unless we are prepared to go the distance and send young Americans to kill and die in Bosnia, we may have to settle for longer-run measures of economic and diplomatic ostracism. The barbarous regime in Belgrade cannot hope to escape retribution for the genocidal havoc it has wrought. Should the fighting resume, let us expel Serbia from the U.N., compile the documentation of war crimes and atrocities, and make it clear that, until Serbia has purged itself of its criminal leadership, it cannot return to the fellowship of nations.

Living with Tragedy

[15]Our planet will be filled with barbarism for a long time to come. Violence is epidemic in this post-Cold War world of raging national, religious, ethnic and racial conflict. When vital U.S. interests are directly threatened, of course we must prepare to fight. But in many cases we must accept the sad necessity of living with tragedies that are beyond our power to control and our wisdom to cure.

[16]What President Kennedy said in 1961 applies more than ever today: "We must face the fact that the U.S. is neither omnipotent nor omniscient—that we are only 6% of the world's population—that we cannot impose our will upon the other 94%—that we cannot right every wrong or reverse each adversity—and that therefore there cannot be an American solution to every world problem."

Arthur Schlesinger, Jr., "How to Think about Bosnia," *The Wall Street Journal*

Reading Essays and Articles

Why Read Essays in the First Place?

Why is the essay the staple of reading assignments in composition and reading courses? Before the invention of photocopy machines, anthologies of nonfiction prose were rare; students in freshman English normally were assigned entire texts, which served as the basis for both reading and writing assignments. The photocopy machine, however, made possible the proliferation of anthologies—collections of essays, articles, and short stories.

The result has been that students are presented with a much wider variety of subjects, forms, and styles than was possible before. The essay, after all, can be read in one sitting. Its relatively short length means that a class can discuss a piece thoroughly in one or two meetings. And for the purposes of this book, analytical questions concerning a selection a few pages long are less taxing and overwhelming than they would be if they concerned a book-length work. Although the anthology has been criticized for reprinting "snippets," or taking a cut-and-paste, approach to reading, the anthology does have the advantage of providing suggestions for further reading. If you like one selection, you can easily go to the library and read the entire work of an author you enjoyed.

When a student approaches an assigned essay, he or she should ask: Why should I read this essay? What am I going to get out of it? Aside from the fact that you should read it because your instructor has assigned it(!), you should read it because you will get plenty out of it—both during the reading experience and during class discussion—especially if you give it sufficient time and attention to understand its component parts thoroughly. The truism that practice makes perfect surely applies here. The more experience you have in reading your assignments attentively, the more competent you will become and the more you will enjoy preparing your assignments. There is no advantage in *not* reading. Students who seldom read on their own, who zip through their assignments, or who sit in the back of the classroom or look down, pretending to be engrossed in the text and hoping to avoid being called on, are missing a significant part of the college experience.

When you read an essay, think of yourself as a detective searching for clues to its meaning, looking closely at its parts as though through a magnifying glass, putting the puzzle pieces together until they all fit and you have a thorough appreciation of the whole.

The Characteristics of an Essay

Before we look at the questions to ask yourself as you read, let us examine an essay's characteristics. If the paragraph is an essay in miniature—as it has often been described—then the essay must exemplify the techniques and characteristics that you studied in Chapters 1—4 in Part I. The essay derives from a form of writing established by the seventeenth-century French writer Michel de Montaigne. His short pieces were an attempt to explain human behavior and the customs he had observed. (In French, the verb *essayer* means "to attempt," and an essay—*un essai*—is the work itself.) Today the term *essay* refers to a sustained piece of nonfiction prose in which the author sets down important ideas, describes experience, conveys information, analyzes issues, or sets forth a proposition.

Like the paragraph, a well-written essay has a main idea, called a *thesis;* it has a direction; and it has adequate development, unity, and coherence. Unlike the paragraph, however, which is limited in scope because of its short length, the essay is more flexible and therefore more varied in length, organization, language, and methods of development. Furthermore, except in student writing assignments or in textbooks like this one, paragraphs seldom occur alone, since a single paragraph is usually not sufficient to explore a complex idea. The paragraphs in an essay move the author's ideas forward, and each paragraph logically relates to the others.

The essay has numerous forms. It may be a personal narrative, a description of a thing or an emotion, a presentation of scientific information, a personal confession, an emotional plea to resolve a controversy, a satire on a practice or custom that the writer finds ridiculous, an ex-

planation of a social or political issue, or an examination of a problem and its repercussions. In short, the essay is infinitely adaptable. It may represent any of the four modes of discourse—narration, description, exposition, persuasion—whether singly or in combination, although usually one mode predominates.

Finally, an essay can be any length. Though typically, essays published by professional writers run between 500 and 5,000 words, length is not important in defining the form. If you think back to the practice essays you read in Part II, you can easily see that the form is a remarkably diverse instrument for communicating ideas.

The Parts of an Essay

Like the paragraph, the essay can usually be divided into three parts: the beginning (the introduction); the middle (the body or supporting paragraphs); and the end (the conclusion). The main idea—comparable to a paragraph's topic sentence—is expressed in a *thesis statement,* the writer's central idea or proposition.

Finding the Thesis

The most important skill in reading any piece of prose is finding the main idea. Given its diverse nature and length, the essay poses greater problems for students than single paragraphs. Where should you look? Some writers announce the main idea in the first sentence, although most good writers avoid this overly obvious placement because there is no inducement for the reader to continue on. Other writers save it for the end, so that the supporting paragraphs lead to the thesis. Still other writers do not state the thesis at all, preferring to let the supporting paragraphs reveal it. This method is called the *implied thesis.*

It is impossible to formulate a general rule that will help you locate the thesis in any essay. However, many essays do include a thesis somewhere near the beginning of the essay, often following this classic pattern. The opening paragraphs (perhaps two or three) introduce the general subject and orient us to the topic. These paragraphs may include an anecdote or short narrative; they may provide historical background; or they may introduce us to an issue or problem. Following this prefatory section, the writer states the thesis. Some textbooks call this approach the *funnel pattern.* But don't expect bells and whistles to alert you to the thesis. Few writers announce that a particular sentence is meant to represent the main idea.

Separating the Essay's Parts

Once you have found the thesis, assuming that there is one, you can then separate the essay into its component parts, determining where

286 READING ESSAYS AND ARTICLES

the introduction ends and the body begins and where the body gives way to the conclusion. It cannot be emphasized too strongly how important this skill is. Rather than drowning in the tide of words, your ability to see the logical progression of ideas will help you distinguish the main points from the support. Often, making a brief outline of the tripartite division can help you see the overall structure more clearly, just as an aerial view of a city reveals its layout more clearly than a ground-level view does.

The body portion of the essay develops and supports the thesis by whatever methods of development the writer considers appropriate. A good essay has adequate development. Not only should the writer fully explore the implications of the controlling idea, he or she should also anticipate opposing arguments if the essay's purpose is to convince us or to defend a controversial idea.

Because of its length, it is even more essential that an essay embody the same principles of unity and coherence that you studied in paragraphs. Some methods writers use to ensure clarity are the following: *transitions,* both within as well as between paragraphs; *parallel phrases, clauses, or sentences;* and the *repetition of key words or phrases.* These devices keep us on track. The careful writer also organizes the body paragraphs logically, typically using *emphatic order* (least important to most important).

The essay's conclusion may consist of a summary, a restatement of the main idea, a logical deduction to be drawn from the evidence, a solution or recommendation, a warning for the future, or a challenge. Again, the form the conclusion takes depends on the writer's purpose, subject, and audience.

How to Read an Essay

Armed with this overview of the essay's characteristics and form, you can now turn to the challenge of how to tackle assigned readings. The following suggestions constitute what your English teachers ideally hope their students will do to prepare for class discussion. For each assignment, plan to spend at least an hour preparing—perhaps two hours if the essay is long or difficult. First read the essay through without stopping. Use a pencil to mark any sentences or paragraphs that will require more attention or to underline any words that are not part of your active reading vocabulary.

Then read the piece a second time, slowly and carefully—maybe even a third time to put the pieces together. Of course, during this reading you should also be looking up those troublesome words. While you are reading, keep the questions at the end of this section in mind. When you are done, review the questions to see whether you can answer them in your own words. If something eludes your understanding,

make a note of it so that you can raise the point in class discussion. Taking responsibility for your own learning will serve you well, both in your current English class and in all your other academic courses.

Questions to Consider While Reading

Although your other English texts may provide discussion or "thought" questions after each selection, the following questions are sufficiently extensive and versatile to use with any reading. They constitute the sorts of things your instructors want you to look for when you read. Eventually, the process will become automatic, and you won't have to refer to them each time you have an assignment.

1. Who is the author? In most anthologies, as in this text, the writer is identified by a brief biographical source note or headnote. This information is useful for determining the writer's mastery of the subject (his or her authority), audience, purpose in writing, and point of view (or possible bias).

2. This question follows from the first. Who is the writer writing for? Is the audience the general reading public, or does the vocabulary suggest that the writer is appealing to a narrower group with specialized knowledge? What clues does the author provide that let you know who the audience is?

3. What is the writer's *purpose?* Here, a quick review of the *modes of discourse* in Part I, Chapter 1, might help. Besides the main purpose, does the writer have a secondary purpose in mind as well? If so, what?

4. What is the *thesis?* Where is it located? Is its placement appropriate for the writer's purpose and subject? If its placement is unusual, is there a reason? Once you have located it, can you paraphrase it— i.e., restate it in your own words?

5. What are the main parts of the essay? At what point does the writer stop introducing and offer support? Where does the body end and the conclusion begin? Can you briefly outline the essay's main parts to see how they fit together?

6. Since we read to learn new information, what are we meant to learn? What are the essay's main ideas? Once you locate the thesis, what are the supporting points?

7. What *inferences* are you meant to draw? What conclusions? What has the piece done to educate you about the world? How do the essay's ideas accord with what you already know? What further information do you need?

8.   Aside from unfamiliar words—which you should add to your vocabulary notebook as suggested in Part I—are there any instances of
words used in unusual ways? Any metaphors or similes? Any
strongly connotative words? Is the writer's word choice appropriate
for the purpose, audience, and content?

Before you jump into the fifteen readings in this section, you may
find it useful to examine a classic essay in light of these remarks about
the essay form and the eight questions you have just examined. "The
Spider and the Wasp" by Alexander Petrunkevitch is a widely reprinted
essay that presents a fascinating look at one little part of the insect
world: the deadly confrontation between the tarantula and its arch-
enemy, the digger wasp. After you finish reading it, we will return to
the eight questions posed above and attempt to arrive at some answers.

Sample Essay

The Spider and the Wasp
Alexander Petrunkevitch

*Alexander Petrunkevitch was born in Russia in 1875, and was educated in
Moscow and later at the University of Freiberg, Germany. An authority on
American spiders, he taught at Harvard, Yale, and Indiana universities, in addition to being active as a translator and author on Russian subjects. This
essay was originally published in* Scientific American.

1   In the feeding and safeguarding of their progeny the insects and
spiders exhibit some interesting analogies to reasoning and some crass
examples of blind instinct. The case I propose to describe here is that of
the tarantula spiders and their arch-enemy, the digger wasps of the
genus Pepsis. It is a classic example of what looks like intelligence pitted against instinct—a strange situation in which the victim, though
fully able to defend itself, submits unwittingly to its destruction.

2   Most tarantulas live in the tropics, but several species occur in the
temperate zone and a few are common in the southern U.S. Some varieties are large and have powerful fangs with which they can inflict a
deep wound. These formidable looking spiders do not, however, attack
man; you can hold one in your hand, if you are gentle, without being
bitten. Their bite is dangerous only to insects and small mammals such
as mice; for a man it is no worse than a hornet's sting.

3   Tarantulas customarily live in deep cylindrical burrows, from which
they emerge at dusk and into which they retire at dawn. Mature males
wander about after dark in search of females and occasionally stray into

houses. After mating, the male dies in a few weeks, but a female lives much longer and can mate several years in succession. In a Paris museum is a tropical specimen which is said to have been living in captivity for 25 years.

4   A fertilized female tarantula lays from 200 to 400 eggs at a time; thus it is possible for a single tarantula to produce several thousand young. She takes no care of them beyond weaving a cocoon of silk to enclose the eggs. After they hatch, the young walk away, find convenient places in which to dig their burrows and spend the rest of their lives in solitude. Tarantulas feed mostly on insects and millipedes. Once their appetite is appeased, they digest the food for several days before eating again. Their sight is poor, being limited to sensing a change in the intensity of light and to the perception of moving objects. They apparently have little or no sense of hearing, for a hungry tarantula will pay no attention to a loudly chirping cricket placed in its cage unless the insect happens to touch one of its legs.

5   But all spiders, and especially hairy ones, have an extremely delicate sense of touch. Laboratory experiments prove that tarantulas can distinguish three types of touch: pressure against the body wall, stroking of the body hair and riffling of certain very fine hairs on the legs called trichobothria. Pressure against the body, by a finger or the end of a pencil, causes the tarantula to move off slowly for a short distance. The touch excites no defensive response unless the approach is from above where the spider can see the motion, in which case it rises on its hind legs, lifts its front legs, opens its fangs and holds this threatening posture as long as the object continues to move. When the motion stops, the spider drops back to the ground, remains quiet for a few seconds and then moves slowly away.

6   The entire body of a tarantula, especially its legs, is thickly clothed with hair. Some of it is short and woolly, some long and stiff. Touching this body hair produces one of two distinct reactions. When the spider is hungry, it responds with an immediate and swift attack. At the touch of a cricket's antennae the tarantula seizes the insect so swiftly that a motion picture taken at the rate of 64 frames per second shows only the result and not the process of capture. But when the spider is not hungry, the stimulation of its hairs merely causes it to shake the touched limb. An insect can walk under its hairy belly unharmed.

7   The trichobothria, very fine hairs growing from disklike membranes on the legs, were once thought to be the spider's hearing organs, but we now know that they have nothing to do with sound. They are sensitive only to air movement. A light breeze makes them vibrate slowly without disturbing the common hair. When one blows gently on the trichobothria, the tarantula reacts with a quick jerk of its four front legs. If the front and hind legs are stimulated at the same time, the spider makes a sudden jump. This reaction is quite independent of the state of its appetite.

8 These three tactile responses—to pressure on the body wall, to moving of the common hair and to flexing of the trichobothria—are so different from one another that there is no possibility of confusing them. They serve the tarantula adequately for most of its needs and enable it to avoid most annoyances and dangers. But they fail the spider completely when it meets its deadly enemy, the digger wasp Pepsis.

9 These solitary wasps are beautiful and formidable creatures. Most species are either a deep shiny blue all over, or deep blue with rusty wings. The largest have a wing span of about four inches. They live on nectar. When excited, they give off a pungent odor—a warning that they are ready to attack. The sting is much worse than that of a bee or common wasp, and the pain and swelling last longer. In the adult stage the wasp lives only a few months. The female produces but a few eggs, one at a time at intervals of two or three days. For each egg the mother must provide one adult tarantula, alive but paralyzed. The tarantula must be of the correct species to nourish the larva. The mother wasp attaches the egg to the paralyzed spider's abdomen. Upon hatching from the egg, the larva is many hundreds of times smaller than its living but helpless victim. It eats no other food and drinks no water. By the time it has finished its single gargantuan meal and become ready for wasphood, nothing remains of the tarantula but its indigestible chitinous skeleton.

10 The mother wasp goes tarantula-hunting when the egg in her ovary is almost ready to be laid. Flying low over the ground late on a sunny afternoon, the wasp looks for its victim or for the mouth of a tarantula burrow, a round hole edged by a bit of silk. The sex of the spider makes no difference, but the mother is highly discriminating as to species. Each species of Pepsis requires a certain species of tarantula, and the wasp will not attack the wrong species. In a cage with a tarantula which is not its normal prey the wasp avoids the spider, and is usually killed by it in the night.

11 Yet when a wasp finds the correct species, it is the other way about. To identify the species the wasp apparently must explore the spider with her antennae. The tarantula shows an amazing tolerance to this exploration. The wasp crawls under it and walks over it without evoking any hostile response. The molestation is so great and so persistent that the tarantula often rises on all eight legs, as if it were on stilts. It may stand this way for several minutes. Meanwhile the wasp, having satisfied itself that the victim is of the right species, moves off a few inches to dig the spider's grave. Working vigorously with legs and jaws, it excavates a hole 8 to 10 inches deep with a diameter slightly larger than the spider's girth. Now and again the wasp pops out of the hole to make sure that the spider is still there.

12 When the grave is finished, the wasp returns to the tarantula to complete her ghastly enterprise. First she feels it all over once more with her antennae. Then her behavior becomes more aggressive. She

bends her abdomen, protruding her sting, and searches for the soft membrane at the point where the spider's leg joins its body—the only spot where she can penetrate the horny skeleton. From time to time, as the exasperated spider slowly shifts ground, the wasp turns on her back and slides along with the aid of her wings, trying to get under the tarantula for a shot at the vital spot. During all this maneuvering, which can last for several minutes, the tarantula makes no move to save itself. Finally the wasp corners it against some obstruction and grasps one of its legs in her powerful jaws. Now at last the harassed spider tries a desperate but vain defense. The two contestants roll over and over on the ground. It is a terrifying sight and the outcome is always the same. The wasp finally manages to thrust her sting into the soft spot and holds it there for a few seconds while she pumps in the poison. Almost immediately the tarantula falls paralyzed on its back. Its legs stop twitching; its heart stops beating. Yet it is not dead, as is shown by the fact that if taken from the wasp it can be restored to some sensitivity by being kept in a moist chamber for several months.

13   After paralyzing the tarantula, the wasp cleans herself by dragging her body along the ground and rubbing her feet, sucks the drop of blood oozing from the wound in the spider's abdomen, then grabs a leg of the flabby, helpless animal in her jaws and drags it down to the bottom of the grave. She stays there for many minutes, sometimes for several hours, and what she does all that time in the dark we do not know. Eventually she lays her egg and attaches it to the side of the spider's abdomen with a sticky secretion. Then she emerges, fills the grave with soil carried bit by bit in her jaws, and finally tramples the ground all around to hide any trace of the grave from prowlers. Then she flies away, leaving her descendant safely started in life.

14   In all this the behavior of the wasp evidently is qualitatively different from that of the spider. The wasp acts like an intelligent animal. This is not to say that instinct plays no part or that she reasons as man does. But her actions are to the point; they are not automatic and can be modified to fit the situation. We do not know for certain how she identifies the tarantula—probably it is by some olfactory or chemo-tactile sense—but she does it purposefully and does not blindly tackle a wrong species.

15   On the other hand, the tarantula's behavior shows only confusion. Evidently the wasp's pawing gives it no pleasure, for it tries to move away. That the wasp is not simulating sexual stimulation is certain, because male and female tarantulas react in the same way to its advances. That the spider is not anesthetized by some odorless secretion is easily shown by blowing lightly at the tarantula and making it jump suddenly. What, then, makes the tarantula behave as stupidly as it does?

16   No clear, simple answer is available. Possibly the stimulation by the wasp's antennae is masked by a heavier pressure on the spider's body, so that it reacts as when prodded by a pencil. But the explanation may be

much more complex. Initiative in attack is not in the nature of tarantulas; most species fight only when cornered so that escape is impossible. Their inherited patterns of behavior apparently prompt them to avoid problems rather than attack them. For example, spiders always weave their webs in three dimensions, and when a spider finds that there is insufficient space to attach certain threads in the third dimension, it leaves the place and seeks another, instead of finishing the web in a single plane. This urge to escape seems to arise under all circumstances, in all phases of life and to take the place of reasoning. For a spider to change the pattern of its web is as impossible as for an inexperienced man to build a bridge across a chasm obstructing his way.

17   In a way the instinctive urge to escape is not only easier but often more efficient than reasoning. The tarantula does exactly what is most efficient in all cases except in an encounter with a ruthless and determined attacker dependent for the existence of her own species on killing as many tarantulas as she can lay eggs. Perhaps in this case the spider follows its usual pattern of trying to escape, instead of seizing and killing the wasp, because it is not aware of its danger. In any case, the survival of the tarantula species as a whole is protected by the fact that the spider is much more fertile than the wasp.

Here are some suggested responses to the eight questions on page 287.

1. **Who is the author?** The headnote identifies Petrunkevitch as an expert on spiders (an arachnologist). Although he is a scientist, his style is sufficiently clear that even the technical terms are understandable. We can also assume, at least for the time being, that his report will be a scientific account—objective and impartial in the presentation of ideas.

2. **Who is the audience?** His audience is the general reader, *not* other scientists. The information about the tarantula and digger wasp is described specifically, but the language is not formidable. For example, in paragraph 7 Petrunkevitch uses the technical term, tricobothria, to describe the very fine hairs on the tarantula's legs, yet he also defines the term immediately ("very fine hairs growing from disklike membranes on the legs"). Fellow spider experts would know this term, so including the contextual definition is the clue that Petrunkevitch has a wider audience in mind.

3. **What is the author's purpose?** Petrunkevitch appears to have two purposes. The primary one is to show that the behavior of these two species presents a classic confrontation between reasoning and instinct. The secondary purpose is to explain these species' reproductive habits. The primary mode of discourse is expository, but there are also strong descriptive elements, especially in paragraphs 6 and 7.

4. **What is the thesis?** Paragraph 1 is a good example of the funnel pattern mentioned earlier. Look again at the progression of the first three sentences. Sentence 1 orients us to the general subject: the contrast between intelligence and instinct among insects. Petrunkevitch also includes the specific activities that will demonstrate this conflict: the feeding and safeguarding of their progeny. Sentence 2 introduces the two species he will present as his "case," and sentence 3 states his point of view: that the confrontation is "strange." Sentence 3 also restates the conflict between reasoning and instinct.

    Since the thesis is embodied in bits and pieces in all three sentences, we can suggest this as a paraphrase: *The strange confrontation between the tarantula and its enemy, the digger wasp, is a classic example of the conflict between intelligence and blind instinct.*

5. **What are the main parts of the essay?** Here is a schematic outline of the essay's tripartite division:

    Introduction [paragraph 1]
    Body [paragraphs 2–15]
    Conclusion [paragraphs 16–17]

    The middle portion—the support—can be further subdivided, as follows:

    Explanation and description of tarantulas [paragraphs 2–8]
    Explanation and description of digger wasps [paragraphs 9–10]
    Further explanation of the capturing process [paragraphs 11–13]
    Analysis of the significance of these insects' behavior [paragraphs 14–15]

    During our first reading, we might think that the details about the spider's sense of touch, its body hair, and the three tactile responses are trivial. But the explanation of the process by which the digger wasp nourishes her larva depends on this crucial information. The main point is that the tarantula behaves uncharacteristically ("stupidly," Petrunkevitch says), doing nothing to defend itself against the wasp's molestation. Once we consider the essay's parts as a whole, we can easily see the importance of seemingly insignificant information.

6. **What do we learn from the essay?** This is obviously an individual matter, but the key points in the essay are these: The digger wasp's search for the correct species of tarantula is the case that serves as the essay's focal point. Despite the tarantula's defense mechanisms, it does nothing to defend itself against the wasp's gruesome pawing.

We also learn that the breeding habits and numbers of offspring are vastly different for these two species. The large number of eggs produced by the tarantula contrasts with the wasp's solitary egg, suggesting that the tarantula is a suitable victim and food source. The wasp's predation keeps the tarantula population in check.

Most important, Petrunkevitch's explanation of the tarantula's behavior suggests an implicit definition of intelligence. The wasp acts "intelligently" because her actions are purposeful, and she can modify them. The tarantula behaves "stupidly" because it is not in the nature of spiders to attack and because it operates solely from instinct, as evidenced by its inability to change the pattern of its web. Therefore, it can't adapt its behavior to suit the circumstances. Petrunkevitch's working definition for intelligence or reasoning is the ability to adapt to new situations and to resist attacks.

7. **What inferences and conclusions can we draw?** Nature has provided a mechanism for keeping the tarantula population stable. The essay also challenges the conventional wisdom about the severity of tarantula bites and their supposed aggressiveness.

8. **Is the language unusual?** Most unusual here is the use of *anthropomorphic* words, meaning that Petrunkevitch ascribes human characteristics and motivations to a nonhuman. (Another way to look at this is to say that Petrunkevitch imposes his own interpretation of motives and feelings on the insects' behavior.) Whichever way you characterize the language, its effect is to make the essay more readable but less "scientific," since true scientific writing is meant to be impersonal and objective, with few authorial intrusions or judgments.

Consider these sentences.

- [paragraph 11]: "The tarantula shows an amazing tolerance to this exploration. . . . The molestation is so great and so persistent that the tarantula often rises on all eight legs, as if it were on stilts."
- [paragraph 11]: "Meanwhile the wasp, having satisfied itself that the victim is of the right species, moves off a few inches to dig the spider's grave. . . . Now and again the wasp pops out of the hole to make sure that the spider is still there."
- [paragraph 12]: "When the grave is finished, the wasp returns to the tarantula to complete her ghastly enterprise. First she feels all over once more with her antennae. Then her behavior becomes more aggressive. . . . From time to time, as the exasperated spider slowly shifts ground, the wasp turns on her back and slides along with the aid of her wings, trying to get under the tarantula for a shot at the vital spot. . . ."
- [paragraph 12]: "Now at last the harassed spider tries a desperate but vain defense."

- [paragraph 13]: "Then she emerges, fills the grave with soil carried bit by bit in her jaws, and finally tramples the ground all around to hide any trace of the grave from prowlers. Then she flies away, leaving her descendant safely started in life."

Are such intrusions and anthropomorphic language justified? Yes, if you recall that Petrunkevitch is writing for the layperson, not for spider experts. The language is clear, precise, and evocative. The result is a powerful and evocative description of the spider's struggle against its enemy.

Why Write Summaries?

A summary is a short piece of writing that condenses the essential information of an essay, article, or book. Writing summaries is an excellent intellectual exercise and a good way to measure both your reading and writing skills. Writing a summary requires not only that you understand a piece accurately; it also requires you to weigh the relative worth of ideas, deciding what is essential and what is nonessential, what to retain and what to omit. Further, writing a summary forces you to discern the pattern the writer imposes on the ideas, and it requires you to restate these ideas concisely, accurately, and fairly, without intruding your own opinion or judgment or distorting the thinking. In sum, the true measure of how well you understand something you read is your ability to restate its main points in your own words.

How long should a summary be? If your instructor does not require you to conform to an arbitrary length, then you can use this formula as a guide: a summary of an essay or article should be between 10 and 25 per cent the length of the original.

How to Write a Summary

At the end of this section is a sample essay and a summary of it. But before you read these materials, here are some general suggestions to consider.

- Read through the passage at least twice so that you have a good understanding of the content. Look up any unfamiliar words.
- Underline important words, phrases, and sentences. Another way is to make marginal notations, noting main ideas and key supporting statements. (In the sample essay reprinted later, both techniques are illustrated for you.)
- Copy the underlined or annotated material onto a sheet of paper, using double- or triple-spacing to leave yourself plenty of room to make changes or additions.

- Study this material. You may have to add information from the original or delete what you decide you don't have room for or what you later decide is not important enough to include.
- Then rewrite this material by paraphrasing it, using *your own words* as much as possible.
- Insert transitional words or phrases as necessary to show the relationship between ideas.
- Prepare a final draft by rewriting your sentences. Compare your wording with the author's. Check to see that your summary is accurate and free of your own ideas and opinions. (Note, however, that instructors often assign a summary-response paper, in which they ask the student first to summarize an essay and then to evaluate it by explaining their objections, criticisms, or points of agreement. In this case, your instructor wants you to offer your point of view.)
- Do a rough word count, making sure that your summary is between 10 and 25 per cent of the original's length. For example, the summary of a 2,500-word essay should be between one and two typewritten pages long (250–500 words) to meet the length requirement.

Sample Essay

On the Need for Asylums

Lewis Thomas

The physician Lewis Thomas, who died in 1993, specialized in pathology (the study of the nature of diseases). During his long professional career, he was affiliated with such institutions as the Rockefeller Institute, Tulane University, the University of Minnesota, New York University and Bellevue Hospital, the Yale University School of Medicine, and Memorial Sloan-Kettering Cancer Center in New York. Thomas was also a prolific writer. Among the numerous collections of his writings are The Youngest Science, The Medusa and the Snail, The Lives of a Cell *(which won the National Book Award), and* Late Night Thoughts on Listening to Mahler's Ninth Symphony, *from which this selection comes.*

Structure	*Ideas*	
"Medical miracles" have triumphed over many diseases.	**1**	From time to time, medical science has achieved an indisputable triumph that is pure benefit for all levels of society and deserving of such terms as "breakthrough" and "medical miracle." It is not a long list, but the items are solid bits of encouragement for the future. The conquests of tuberculosis, smallpox, and syphilis of the

Structure   *Ideas*

Paras. 1–3 orient reader
to general subject—
funnel pattern.

central nervous system should be at the top of anyone's list. Rheumatic fever, the most common cause of heart disease forty years ago, has become a rare, almost exotic disorder, thanks to the introduction of antibiotics for treating streptococcal sore throat. Some forms of cancer—notably childhood leukemias, Hodgkin's disease, and certain sarcomas affecting young people—have become curable in a high proportion of patients. Poliomyelitis is no longer with us.

Many serious diseases
still exist.

2 But there is still a formidable agenda of diseases for which there are no cures, needing much more research before their underlying mechanisms can be brought to light. Among these diseases are some for which we have only halfway technologies to offer, measures that turn out to be much more costly than we had guessed and only partly, sometimes marginally, effective. The transplantation of major organs has become successful, but only for a relatively small number of patients with damaged kidneys and hearts, and at a financial cost much too high for applying the technologies on a wide scale. Very large numbers of patients with these fatal illnesses have no access to such treatments. Renal dialysis makes it possible to live for many months, even a few years, with failed kidneys, but it is a hard life.

Focus narrows— a
warning

We may overestimate
medical advances—they
may lead to unforeseen
problems.

3 The overestimation of the value of and advance in medicine can lead to more trouble than anyone can foresee, and a lot of careful thought and analysis ought to be invested before any technology is turned loose on the marketplace. It begins to look as if coronary bypass surgery, for example, is an indispensable operation for a limited number of people, but it was probably not necessary for the large number in whom the expensive procedure has already been employed.

We need to analyze
medical advances care-
fully.

4 There are other examples of this sort of premature, sweeping adoption of new measures in medicine. Probably none has re-

Structure	*Ideas*
Thesis—sentence 2 in para.4.	
	Thorazine, used to treat schizophrenia, is an example of such premature acceptance.
Cause-effect chain: ↓	*Positive results: wild behavior was controlled; mental patients could be released; hospitalization no longer necessary.*
Thorazine ↓	
Control of schizophrenia	
Closing of asylums ↓	*Political side-effects were disastrous.*
Opening of community centers ↓	*New social policies: to open community mental health centers and return patients to community.*

sulted in more untoward social damage than the unpredicted, indirect but calamitous effects of the widespread introduction twenty or so years ago of Thorazine and its chemical relatives for the treatment of schizophrenia. For a while, when it was first used in state hospitals for the insane, the new line of drugs seemed miraculous indeed. Patients whose hallucinations and delusions impelled them to wild, uncontrollable behavior were discovered to be so calmed by the treatment as to make possible the closing down of many of the locked wards in asylums. Patients with milder forms of schizophrenia could return, at least temporarily, to life outside the institutions. It was the first real advance in the treatment of severe mental disease, and the whole world of psychiatry seemed to have been transformed. Psychopharmacology became, overnight, a bright new discipline in medicine.

5 Then came the side effect. Not a medical side effect (although there were some of these) but a political one, and a disaster. On the assumption that the new drugs made hospitalization unnecessary, two social policies were launched with the enthusiastic agreement of both the professional psychiatric community and the governmental agencies responsible for the care of the mentally ill. Brand-new institutions, ambitiously designated "community mental health centers," were deployed across the country. These centers were to be the source of the new technology for treating schizophrenia, along with all other sorts of mental illness: in theory, patients would come to the clinics and be given the needed drugs, and, when necessary, psychotherapy. And at the same time orders came down that most of the patients living in the state hospitals be discharged forthwith to their homes or, lack-

Structure   *Ideas*

ing homes, to other quarters in the community.

6

For a while it looked like the best of worlds, on paper, anyway. Brochures with handsome charts were issued by state and federal agencies displaying the plummeting curves of state hospital occupancy, with the lines coinciding marvelously with the introduction of the new drugs. No one noted that the occupancy of private mental hospitals rose at the same time—though it could not rise very high, with the annual cost of such hospitalization running around $40,000 per bed. The term "breakthrough" was used over and over again, but after a little while it came to be something more like a breakout. The mentally ill were out of the hospital, but in many cases they were simply out on the streets, less agitated but lost, still disabled but now uncared for. The community mental health centers were not designed to take on the task of custodial care. They could serve as shelters only during the hours of appointment, not at night.

Explanation of polit-   *Mentally ill wander*
ical disaster.   *the streets*

Patients dependent on
public facilities were
released—out on the
street now, lost and
abandoned. New centers
provided no custodial
care or shelter.

7

All this is still going on, and it is not working. To be sure, the drugs do work—but only to the extent of allaying some of the most distressing manifestations of schizophrenia. They do not turn the disease off. The evidences of the mind's unhinging are still there, coming and going in cycles of remission and exacerbation just as they have always done since schizophrenia was first described. Some patients recover spontaneously and for good, as some have always done. The chronically and permanently disabled are better off because they are in lesser degrees of mental torment when they have their medication; but they are at the same time much worse off because they can no longer find refuge when they are in need of it. They are, instead, out on the streets, or down in the

Patients have no refuge.

Structure   *Ideas*

Many commit suicide.

subways, or wandering in the parks, or confined in shabby rooms in the shabbiest hotels, alone. Or perhaps they are living at home, but not many of them living happily; nor are many of their families happy to have them at home. One of the high risks of severe mental disease is suicide, and many of these abandoned patients choose this way out, with no one to stop them. It is an appalling situation.

Concession—old hospitals were bad

8   It is claimed that the old state hospitals were even more appalling. They were called warehouses for the insane, incapable of curing anything, more likely to make it worse by the process known in psychiatric circles as "institutionalization," a steady downhill course toward total dependency on the very bleakness of the institution itself. The places were badly managed, always understaffed, repellent to doctors, nurses, and all the other people needed for the care of those with sick minds. Better off without them, it was said. Cheaper too, although this wasn't said so openly.

"Warehouses for the insane"—a downward course of dependency.

Refutation—what could be done.

State hospitals could be decent places.

9   What never seems to have been thought of, or at least never discussed publicly, was changing the state hospitals from bad to good institutions, given the opportunity for vastly improved care that came along with the drugs. It was partly the history of such places that got in the way. For centuries the madhouses, as they were called, served no purpose beyond keeping deranged people out of the public view. Despite efforts at reform in the late nineteenth and early twentieth centuries, they remained essentially lockups.

At least old hospitals provided refuge.

10   But now it is becoming plain that life in the state hospitals, bad as it was, was better than life in the subways or in the doorways of downtown streets, late on cold nights with nothing in the shopping bag to keep a body warm, and no protection at all against molestation by predators or the

Structure	*Ideas*	

sudden urge for self-destruction. What now?

| *Proposal* | *Restore state asylums— spend enough to do it right.* | **11** |

We should restore the state hospital system, improve it, expand it if necessary; and spend enough money to ensure that the patients who must live in these institutions will be able to come in off the streets and live in decency and warmth, under the care of adequately paid, competent professionals and compassionate surrogate friends.

| *Specifics of proposal, continued* | *Mentally ill should live in decency.* | |

12   If there is not enough money, there are ways to save. There was a time when many doctors were glad to volunteer their services on a part-time basis, indeed competed to do so, unpaid by state or federal funds and unreimbursed by insurance companies, in order to look after people unable to care for themselves. We should be looking around again for such doctors, not necessarily specialists in psychiatric medicine, but well-trained physicians possessing affection for people in trouble—a quality on which recruitment to the profession of medicine has always, we hope, been based. We cannot leave the situation of insane human beings where it is today.

| *Conclusion: an ethical and moral challenge* | *Judging by the way we treat our mentally ill, our society has failed. We must change.* | **13** |

A society can be judged by the way it treats its most disadvantaged, its least beloved, its mad. As things now stand, we must be judged a poor lot, and it is time to mend our ways.

(Length: approximately 1,550 words)

Sample Summary

Although medical science has conquered many diseases previously thought incurable, some advances have been enthusiastically embraced and implemented before their potential consequences have been clearly thought out. One example is the use of drugs like Thorazine to treat schizophrenics. Even though they could not cure the

disease, these drugs calmed patients and controlled their bizarre behavior.

Operating under the assumption that hospitalization for mild schizophrenics was no longer necessary, government agencies and the psychiatric community endorsed closing state-owned mental asylums and replacing them with "community mental health centers." The justification was that schizophrenics and other mentally ill patients, on medication, could be released and returned to the community. However good this idea sounded, the political effect was disastrous. These centers offered no custodial care, and many mentally ill people were left to wander the streets uncared for; some become so desperate that they committed suicide. The plight of these released patients is appalling.

Most agree that the old asylums were little better than hellholes, "warehouses for the insane," where patients weren't cured but nonetheless became dependent on the institutions, bleak as they were. But Thomas suggests that state institutions could be good. He proposes reopening and expanding state hospitals and staffing them with a caring, compassionate staff. In answer to the perennial question about adequate funding, Thomas suggests that physicians could volunteer their services on a part-time basis.

If one can judge a culture by the way it treats its mentally ill, then the United States has done a poor job, and it is time for a major change.

(Length: 258 words, or approximately 17 percent)

Comment

Both sets of marginal annotations form the basis of this summary. Those on the far left annotate the essay's structure; those on the right pull out and restate the main points in key paragraphs. Remember that this sample summary is only one person's condensed version of the original ideas; other writers might choose to include other information. For example, one problem I had in preparing this summary was how much weight to give the information in paragraphs 1, 2, and 3, which, at first glance, seemed important. In the original version, I included some of Thomas's examples, like medical breakthroughs to combat tuberculosis, smallpox, various cancers, polio, organ transplants, and coronary bypass surgery. Eventually, however, I realized that paragraphs 1–3 form a classic funnel pattern. Their function is to introduce us to the larger subject of medical advances before the author zeroes in on his real concern—the use of Thorazine to treat schizophrenics and the side effects of this supposed miracle drug. When examined in light of the whole essay, the information in paragraphs 1–3, I realized, could be dispensed with in a single sentence.

The remainder of Part 4 consists of fifteen essays and articles on a variety of subjects. They are divided into three groups, according to their relative levels of difficulty. It is recommended that you read them all, even if your instructor does not assign the entire lot. Any practice you get in addition to your regular assignments will serve you well in improving your comprehension and analytical skills.

Essays: Group 1

Selection 1

A Slave Witness of a Slave Auction
Solomon Northrup

Slave narratives were common before the Civil War, and abolitionists frequently used them in their campaign against slavery. Although many of these narratives were sensational, Northrup's is fairly objective. This narrative was published in 1853 in a book entitled, Twelve Years a Slave: Narrative of Solomon Northrup, a Citizen of New York, Kidnapped in Washington City in 1841, and Rescued in 1853, from a Cotton Plantation near the Red River in Louisiana. *Northrup was finally given his freedom when he was able to get a letter sent to friends in New York. The governor arranged for his release, enabling him to return to his family in Glens Falls, New York.*

1   The very amiable, pious-hearted Mr. Theophilus Freeman, partner or consignee of James H. Burch, and keeper of the slave pen in New-Orleans, was out among his animals early in the morning. With an occasional kick of the older men and women, and many a sharp crack of the whip about the ears of the younger slaves, it was not long before they were all astir, and wide awake. Mr. Theophilus Freeman bustled about in a very industrious manner, getting his property ready for the salesroom, intending, no doubt, to do that day a rousing business.

2   In the first place we were required to wash thoroughly, and those with beards, to shave. We were then furnished with a new suit each, cheap, but clean. The men had hat, coat, shirt, pants and shoes; the women frocks of calico, and handkerchiefs to bind about their heads. We were now conducted into a large room in the front part of the building to which the yard was attached, in order to be properly trained, before the admission of customers. The men were arranged on one side of the room, the women on the other. The tallest was placed at the head of the row, then the next tallest, and so on in the order of their respective heights. Emily was at the foot of the line of women.

Freeman charged us to remember our places; exhorted us to appear smart and lively,—sometimes threatening, and again holding out various inducements. During the day he exercised us in the art of "looking smart," and of moving to our places with exact precision.

3   After being fed, in the afternoon, we were again paraded and made to dance. Bob, a colored boy, who had some time belonged to Freeman, played on the violin. Standing near him, I made bold to inquire if he could play the "Virginia Reel." He answered he could not, and asked me if I could play. Replying in the affirmative, he handed me the violin. I struck up a tune, and finished it. Freeman ordered me to continue playing, and seemed well pleased, telling Bob that I far excelled him—a remark that seemed to grieve my musical companion very much.

4   Next day many customers called to examine Freeman's "new lot." The latter gentleman was very loquacious, dwelling at much length upon our several good points and qualities. He would make us hold up our heads, walk briskly back and forth, while customers would feel of our hands and arms and bodies, turn us about, ask us what we could do, make us open our mouths and show our teeth, precisely as a jockey examines a horse which he is about to barter for or purchase. Sometimes a man or woman was taken back to the small house in the yard, stripped, and inspected more minutely. Scars upon a slave's back were considered evidence of a rebellious or unruly spirit, and hurt his sale.

5   One old gentleman, who said he wanted a coachman, appeared to take a fancy to me. From his conversation with Freeman, I learned he was a resident of the city. I very much desired that he would buy me, because I conceived it would not be difficult to make my escape from New-Orleans on some northern vessel. Freeman asked him fifteen hundred dollars for me. The old gentleman insisted it was too much, as times were very hard. Freeman, however, declared that I was sound and healthy, of a good constitution, and intelligent. He made it a point to enlarge upon my musical attainments. The old gentleman argued quite adroitly that there was nothing extraordinary about the nigger, and finally, to my regret, went out, saying he would call again. During the day, however, a number of sales were made. David and Caroline were purchased together by a Natchez planter. They left us, grinning broadly, and in the most happy state of mind, caused by the fact of their not being separated. Lethe was sold to a planter of Baton Rouge, her eyes flashing with anger as she was led away.

6   The same man also purchased Randall. The little fellow was made to jump, and run across the floor, and perform many other feats, exhibiting his activity and condition. All the time the trade was going on. Eliza was crying aloud, and wringing her hands. She besought the man not to buy him, unless he also bought herself and Emily. She promised, in that case, to be the most faithful slave that ever lived. The man answered that he could not afford it, and then Eliza burst into a paroxysm of grief, weeping plaintively. Freeman turned round to her, savagely,

with his whip in his uplifted hand, ordering her to stop her noise, or he would flog her. He would not have such work—such snivelling; and unless she ceased that minute, he would take her to the yard and give her a hundred lashes. Yes, he would take the nonsense out of her pretty quick—if he didn't, might he be d—d. Eliza shrunk before him, and tried to wipe away her tears, but it was all in vain. She wanted to be with her children, she said, the little time she had to live. All the frowns and threats of Freeman, could not wholly silence the afflicted mother. She kept on begging and beseeching them, most piteously, not to separate the three. Over and over again she told them how she loved her boy. A great many times she repeated her former promises—how very faithful and obedient she would be; how hard she would labor day and night, to the last moment of her life, if he would only buy them all together. But it was of no avail; the man could not afford it. The bargain was agreed upon, and Randall must go alone. Then Eliza ran to him; embraced him passionately; kissed him again and again; told him to remember her—all the while her tears falling in the boy's face like rain.

7   Freeman damned her, calling her a blubbering, bawling wench, and ordered her to go to her place, and behave herself, and be somebody. He swore he wouldn't stand such stuff but a little longer. He would soon give her something to cry about, if she was not mighty careful, and *that* she might depend upon.

8   The planter from Baton Rouge, with his new purchases, was ready to depart.

9   "Don't cry, mama. I will be a good boy. Don't cry," said Randall, looking back, as they passed out of the door.

10   What has become of the lad, God knows. It was a mournful scene indeed. I would have cried myself if I had dared.

A. Comprehension

Choose the answer that best completes each statement. Do not refer to the selection while doing this exercise.

1. Theophilus Freeman was (a) an animal trainer for the city of New Orleans; (b) the keeper of a slave pen in New Orleans; (c) a sympathetic observer at a slave auction; (d) a slave who was going to be sold to a new owner.

2. The slaves were exercised so that (a) they would be in good physical condition for their future labors; (b) they would be kept busy before the auction began; (c) they would be able to compete in athletic contests; (d) they would look sharp for the customers.

3. Scars on a slave's back were evidence of a rebellious or unruly spirit and, consequently, meant that (a) the slave would cost more money;

(b) the slave would cost less to purchase; (c) the sale would be hurt; (d) the slave would be set free.

4. According to what Northrup says, these slaves' primary concern was (a) being separated from their family; (b) being purchased by a kind owner; (c) living in a place from which escape would be easy; (d) living in a congenial environment.

5. The man who purchased Randall claimed that he could not purchase Eliza and Emily too because (a) he needed only one slave; (b) he needed only a male slave; (c) he had room for only one slave; (d) times were hard.

6. The scene when Randall is sold, as Northrup describes it, is (a) embarrassing; (b) unrealistic; (c) pitiful; (d) maudlin.

B. Inferences

On the basis of the evidence in the selection, mark these statements as follows: PA for inferences that are probably accurate; PI for inferences that are probably inaccurate; and IE for insufficient evidence. You may refer to the selection to answer the questions in this section, and all the remaining sections.

_____ 1. Theophilus Freeman was a successful slave broker.

_____ 2. Purchasers preferred docile slaves to those who had been beaten for having a rebellious or unruly nature.

_____ 3. The customers were not allowed to learn much information about the slaves before they purchased them.

_____ 4. Northrup had no intention of trying to escape after his purchase.

_____ 5. Eliza was eventually reunited with her children, Randall and Emily.

C. Structure

1. The mode of discourse in this selection is (a) narration; (b) description; (c) exposition; (d) persuasion.

2. Northrup's specific purpose is (a) to show the reader how slave auctions were conducted; (b) to explain the criteria slaveowners used to purchase slaves; (c) to make us aware of the terrible hardships the auctions imposed on the slaves; (d) to argue for the abolition of slavery as an institution.

3. In paragraph 1, when Northrup describes Theophilus Freeman, keeper of the slave pen, as "amiable" and "pious-hearted," he is being (a) honest; (b) sarcastic; (c) complimentary; (d) overly sympathetic.

4. The method of development used in paragraph 2 is (a) analogy; (b) classification; (c) definition; (d) example; (e) process.

5. In paragraph 3, Northrup describes his violin playing, which calls attention to (a) his desire to ingratiate himself to the slave keeper; (b) his superiority to the other slaves; (c) the disparity between his position as a slave and his culture and education; (d) his love of music and desire to excel.

6. Throughout the essay, Northrup implies that Freeman treated the slaves like (a) family members; (b) objects; (c) luxuries; (d) animals.

7. From Northrup's description of his behavior, Randall acted (a) childishly; (b) stoically; (c) predictably; (d) irrationally.

8. Northrup dwells on the scene with Eliza and her son to emphasize (a) the inhumanity of slavery as an institution; (b) Northrup's own unselfish attempts to intercede on Eliza's behalf; (c) how hard times were, since the planter could not afford to buy the whole family; (d) the long-term emotional effects on slave families.

D. Vocabulary

For each italicized word from the selection, choose the best definition according to the context in which it appears.

1. the very *amiable* Mr. Theophilus Freeman [paragraph 1]: (a) proper; (b) good-natured; (c) honest; (d) religious.

2. the *pious*-hearted Mr. Theophilus Freeman [1]: (a) simple; (b) generous; (c) devoutly religious; (d) superstitious.

3. *exhorted* us to appear [2]: (a) gently encouraged; (b) demanded; (c) urged; (d) threatened.

4. holding out various *inducements* [2]: (a) incentives; (b) threats; (c) bribes; (d) legal pronouncements.

5. the gentleman was very *loquacious* [4]: (a) kindly; (b) talkative; (c) generous; (d) trustworthy.

6. inspected more *minutely* [4]: (a) closely; (b) specifically; (c) with more concern; (d) critically.

7. I was of a good *constitution* [5]: (a) state of health; (b) moral character; (c) physical agility; (d) conscience.

8. the old gentleman argued quite *adroitly* [5]: (a) cleverly; (b) impassionedly; (c) skillfully; (d) convincingly.

9. a *paroxysm* of grief [6]: (a) sudden outburst; (b) emotional crisis; (c) example; (d) loud wailing.

10. weeping *plaintively* [6]: (a) quietly; (b) intensely; (c) mournfully; (d) bitterly.

11. She kept on begging and *beseeching* them [6]: (a) imploring; (b) clutching at; (c) badgering; (d) pursuing.

12.   It was *of no avail* [6]: (a) an impossible matter; (b) a matter of indifference; (c) of no use; (d) of economic gain.

E.   Questions for Analysis and Discussion

1.   Northrup's attitude toward Mr. Freeman shifts during the narrative. What are the purpose and advantage of this seemingly inconsistent point of view?

2.   What is Freeman's attitude toward the slaves? How does Freeman reveal it?

3.   In what way does Northrup's account of Eliza's grief over being separated from her son contrast with his earlier method of reporting?

Selection 2

Mother Tongue

Amy Tan

Amy Tan is a California writer who has written two best-selling books since she began writing fiction in 1985: The Joy Luck Club, *which was a finalist for the National Book Award and the National Book Critics Circle Award, and more recently,* The Kitchen God's Wife, *which is a semi-autobiographical account of her mother's life in China and in the United States. "Mother Tongue" was reprinted in* The Best American Essays 1991, *edited by Joyce Carol Oates. In it, Tan describes the different "Englishes" she uses.*

1   I am not a scholar of English or literature. I cannot give you much more than personal opinions on the English language and its variations in this country or others.

2   I am a writer. And by that definition, I am someone who has always loved language. I am fascinated by language in daily life. I spend a great deal of my time thinking about the power of language—the way it can evoke an emotion, a visual image, a complex idea, or a simple truth. Language is the tool of my trade. And I use them all—all the Englishes I grew up with.

3   Recently, I was made keenly aware of the different Englishes I do use. I was giving a talk to a large group of people, the same talk I had already given to half a dozen other groups. The nature of the talk was about my writing, my life, and my book, *The Joy Luck Club*. The talk was going along well enough, until I remembered one major difference that made the whole talk sound wrong. My mother was in the room. And it was perhaps the first time she had heard me give a lengthy speech, using the kind of English I have never used with her. I was saying

things like, "The intersection of memory upon imagination" and "There is an aspect of my fiction that relates to thus-and-thus"—a speech filled with carefully wrought grammatical phrases, burdened, it suddenly seemed to me, with nominalized forms, past perfect tenses, conditional phrases, all the forms of standard English that I had learned in school and through books, the forms of English I did not use at home with my mother.

4   Just last week, I was walking down the street with my mother, and I again found myself conscious of the English I was using, the English I do use with her. We were talking about the price of new and used furniture and I heard myself saying this: "Not waste money that way." My husband was with us as well, and he didn't notice any switch in my English. And then I realized why. It's because over the twenty years we've been together I've often used that same kind of English with him, and sometimes he even uses it with me. It has become our language of intimacy, a different sort of English that relates to family talk, the language I grew up with.

5   So you'll have some idea of what this family talk I heard sounds like, I'll quote what my mother said during a recent conversation which I videotaped and then transcribed. During this conversation, my mother was talking about a political gangster in Shanghai who had the same last name as her family's, Du, and how the gangster in his early years wanted to be adopted by her family, which was rich by comparison. Later, the gangster became more powerful, far richer than my mother's family, and one day showed up at my mother's wedding to pay his respects. Here's what she said in part:

6   "Du Yusong having business like fruit stand. Like off the street kind. He is Du like Du Zong—but not Tsung-ming Island people. The local people call putong, the river east side, he belong to that side local people. That man want to ask Du Zong father take him in like become own family. Du Zong father wasn't look down on him, but didn't take seriously, until that man big like become a mafia. Now important person, very hard to inviting him. Chinese way, came only to show respect, don't stay for dinner. Respect for making big celebration, he shows up. Mean gives lots of respect. Chinese custom. Chinese social life that way. If too important won't have to stay too long. He come to my wedding. I didn't see, I heard it. I gone to boy's side, they have YMCA dinner. Chinese age I was nineteen."

7   You should know that my mother's expressive command of English belies how much she actually understands. She reads the *Forbes* report, listens to *Wall Street Week,* converses daily with her stockbroker, reads all of Shirley MacLaine's books with ease—all kinds of things I can't begin to understand. Yet some of my friends tell me they understand 50 percent of what my mother says. Some say they understand 80 to 90 percent. Some say they understand none of it, as if she were speaking pure Chinese. But to me, my mother's English is perfectly clear, perfect-

ly natural. It's my mother tongue. Her language, as I hear it, is vivid, direct, full of observation and imagery. That was the language that helped shape the way I saw things, expressed things, made sense of the world.

8   Lately, I've been giving more thought to the kind of English my mother speaks. Like others, I have described it to people as "broken" or "fractured" English. But I wince when I say that. It has always bothered me that I can think of no way to describe it other than "broken," as if it were damaged and needed to be fixed, as if it lacked a certain wholeness and soundness. I've heard other terms used, "limited English," for example. But they seem just as bad, as if everything is limited, including people's perceptions of the limited English speaker.

9   I know this for a fact, because when I was growing up, my mother's "limited" English limited *my* perception of her. I was ashamed of her English. I believed that her English reflected the quality of what she had to say. That is, because she expressed them imperfectly her thoughts were imperfect. And I had plenty of empirical evidence to support me: the fact that people in department stores, at banks, and at restaurants did not take her seriously, did not give her good service, pretended not to understand her, or even acted as if they did not hear her.

10   My mother has long realized the limitations of her English as well. When I was fifteen, she used to have me call people on the phone to pretend I was she. In this guise, I was forced to ask for information or even to complain and yell at people who had been rude to her. One time it was a call to her stockbroker in New York. She had cashed out her small portfolio and it just so happened we were going to go to New York the next week, our very first trip outside California. I had to get on the phone and say in an adolescent voice that was not very convincing, "This is Mrs. Tan."

11   And my mother was standing in the back whispering loudly, "Why he don't send me check, already two weeks late. So mad he lie to me, losing me money."

12   And then I said in perfect English, "Yes, I'm getting rather concerned. You had agreed to send the check two weeks ago, but it hasn't arrived."

13   Then she began to talk more loudly. "What he want, I come to New York tell him front of his boss, you cheating me?" And I was trying to calm her down, make her be quiet, while telling the stockbroker, "I can't tolerate any more excuses. If I don't receive the check immediately, I am going to have to speak to your manager when I'm in New York next week." And sure enough, the following week there we were in front of this astonished stockbroker, and I was sitting there red-faced and quiet, and my mother, the real Mrs. Tan, was shouting at his boss in her impeccable broken English.

14   We used a similar routine just five days ago, for a situation that was far less humorous. My mother had gone to the hospital for an appointment, to find out about a benign brain tumor a CAT scan had re-

vealed a month ago. She said she had spoken very good English, her best English, no mistakes. Still, she said, the hospital did not apologize when they said they had lost the CAT scan and she had come for nothing. She said they did not seem to have any sympathy when she told them she was anxious to know the exact diagnosis, since her husband and son had both died of brain tumors. She said they would not give her any more information until the next time and she would have to make another appointment for that. So she said she would not leave until the doctor called her daughter. She wouldn't budge. And when the doctor finally called her daughter, me, who spoke in perfect English—lo and behold—we had assurances the CAT scan would be found, promises that a conference call on Monday would be held, and apologies for any suffering my mother had gone through for a most regrettable mistake.

15   I think my mother's English almost had an effect on limiting my possibilities in life as well. Sociologists and linguists probably will tell you that a person's developing language skills are more influenced by peers. But I do think that the language spoken in the family, especially in immigrant families which are more insular, plays a large role in shaping the language of the child. And I believe that it affected my results on achievement tests, IQ tests, and the SAT. While my English skills were never judged as poor, compared to math, English could not be considered my strong suit. In grade school I did moderately well, getting perhaps B's, sometimes B-pluses, in English and scoring perhaps in the sixtieth or seventieth percentile on achievement tests. But those scores were not good enough to override the opinion that my true abilities lay in math and science, because in those areas I achieved A's and scored in the ninetieth percentile or higher.

16   This was understandable. Math is precise; there is only one correct answer. Whereas, for me at least, the answers on English tests were always a judgment call, a matter of opinion and personal experience. Those tests were constructed around items like fill-in-the-blank sentence completion, such as, "Even though Tom was _____, Mary thought he was _____." And the correct answer always seemed to be the most bland combinations of thoughts, for example, "Even though Tom was shy, Mary thought he was charming," with the grammatical structure "even though" limiting the correct answer to some sort of semantic opposites, so you wouldn't get answers like, "Even though Tom was foolish, Mary thought he was ridiculous." Well, according to my mother, there were very few limitations as to what Tom could have been and what Mary might have thought of him. So I never did well on tests like that.

17   The same was true with word analogies, pairs of words in which you were supposed to find some sort of logical, semantic relationship—for example, *"Sunset* is to *nightfall* as _____ is to _____." And here you would be presented with a list of four possible pairs, one of which showed the same kind of relationship:

red is to *stoplight, bus* is to *arrival, chills* is to *fever, yawn* is to *boring.* Well, I could never think that way. I knew what the tests were asking, but I could not block out of my mind the images already created by the first pair, "*sunset* is to *nightfall*"—and I would see a burst of colors against a darkening sky, the moon rising, the lowering of a curtain of stars. And all the other pairs of words—red, bus, stoplight, boring—just threw up a mass of confusing images, making it impossible for me to sort out something as logical as saying: "A sunset precedes nightfall" is the same as "a chill precedes a fever." The only way I would have gotten that answer right would have been to imagine an associative situation, for example, my being disobedient and staying out past sunset, catching a chill at night, which turns into feverish pneumonia as punishment, which indeed did happen to me.

18   I have been thinking about all this lately, about my mother's English, about achievement tests. Because lately I've been asked, as a writer, why there are not more Asian Americans represented in American literature. Why are there few Asian Americans enrolled in creative writing programs? Why do so many Chinese students go into engineering? Well, these are broad sociological questions I can't begin to answer. But I have noticed in surveys—in fact, just last week—that Asian students, as a whole, always do significantly better on math achievement tests than in English. And this makes me think that there are other Asian-American students whose English spoken in the home might also be described as "broken" or "limited." And perhaps they also have teachers who are steering them away from writing and into math and science, which is what happened to me.

19   Fortunately, I happen to be rebellious in nature and enjoy the challenge of disproving assumptions made about me. I became an English major my first year in college, after being enrolled as pre-med. I started writing nonfiction as a freelancer the week after I was told by my former boss that writing was my worst skill and I should hone my talents toward account management.

20   But it wasn't until 1985 that I finally began to write fiction. And at first I wrote using what I thought to be wittily crafted sentences, sentences that would finally prove I had mastery over the English language. Here's an example from the first draft of a story that later made its way into *The Joy Luck Club,* but without this line: "That was my mental quandary in its nascent state." A terrible line, which I can barely pronounce.

21   Fortunately, for reasons I won't get into today, I later decided I should envision a reader for the stories I would write. And the reader I decided upon was my mother, because these were stories about mothers. So with this reader in mind—and in fact she did read my early drafts—I began to write stories using all the Englishes I grew up with: the English I spoke to my mother, which for lack of a better term might

be described as "simple"; the English she used with me, which for lack of a better term might be described as "broken"; my translation of her Chinese, which could certainly be described as "watered down"; and what I imagined to be her translation of her Chinese if she could speak in perfect English, her internal language, and for that I sought to preserve the essence, but neither an English nor a Chinese structure. I wanted to capture what language ability tests can never reveal: her intent, her passion, her imagery, the rhythms of her speech and the nature of her thoughts.

22   Apart from what any critic had to say about my writing, I knew I had succeeded where it counted when my mother finished reading my book and gave me her verdict: "So easy to read."

A. **Comprehension**

Choose the answer that best completes each statement. Do not refer to the selection while doing this exercise.

1. For Tan, the English she uses in her writing and the English she grew up with are very different; she characterizes the language she learned in her family as (a) a fractured, ungrammatical language; (b) the language of intimacy; (c) a language that outsiders cannot understand; (d) a mixture of English and Chinese.

2. Apparently, Tan's mother (a) can read English well; (b) refuses to allow English to be spoken in her home; (c) has studied English formally for many years; (d) has little opportunity to practice speaking English.

3. Tan objects to terms like "broken" English or "limited" English because (a) they are not accurate terms; (b) they are insulting terms; (c) they imply something bad about the speaker who uses such English; (d) they imply a kind of linguistic discrimination.

4. One consequence of her mother's inability to communicate well in English is that (a) she leads a sheltered, isolated life; (b) she has to hire an interpreter to deal with outsiders; (c) she is embarrassed about her English and is reluctant to speak to outsiders; (d) people do not take her ideas seriously or give her good service.

5. As a result of the English she learned at home, Tan writes that (a) she was unable to write well in English; (b) she was unable to do well in math or science; (c) her scores on standardized verbal tests like achievement tests or the SAT were not as high as her math scores; (d) she was academically deficient.

6. When Tan began writing, she realized that her mother's English was (a) not suitable for the kinds of stories she wanted to write; (b) marvelously rich in its imagery, rhythms, and thoughts; (c) impossible

to translate onto the printed page; (d) the language she would use only at home with her family members.

B.   Inferences

On the basis of the evidence in the selection, answer these inference questions. You may refer to the selection to answer the questions in this section, and all the remaining sections.

1.   From paragraph 3 we can accurately infer that (a) Tan's mother was impressed with her daughter's formal English; (b) Tan is more comfortable with formal English than with the kind of English she grew up speaking; (c) Tan's mother didn't fit into the group she was speaking to; (d) Tan's manner of address at the talk was more cumbersome, formal, and not as simple as the English she spoke at home.

2.   Look at paragraph 9 again. We can infer that judging people's thoughts by the way they express them is (a) honest; (b) fair; (c) unfair; (d) natural; (e) unrealistic.

3.   From the examples in paragraphs 10–14 we can infer that (a) Tan's pretending to be her mother speaking didn't fool anyone; (b) Tan was effective in getting results for her mother; (c) Tan was embarrassed to play this role; (d) Tan was angry at having to play this role.

4.   From paragraphs 16 and 17 we can infer that Tan had difficulty with analogy questions or fill-in-the-blank completion questions because (a) she was a poor reader; (b) her language abilities were richer and more expressive than the limited answers the questions required; (c) she didn't understand the test directions; (d) the questions required her to use language more expressively and with more imagery than she was accustomed to.

5.   Read again Tan's conclusion in paragraphs 21 and 22. We can conclude that the various "Englishes" Tan uses in her stories are (a) an asset in her writing; (b) a liability in her writing; (c) confusing for the uninitiated or non-Chinese reader; (d) easy to measure on standardized language tests.

C.   Structure

1.   Which of the following best expresses the thesis of the essay? (a) "Recently, I was made keenly aware of the different Englishes I do use"; (b) "It [my English] has become our language of intimacy, a different sort of English that relates to family talk, the language I grew up with"; (c) "Her [my mother's] language, as I hear it, is vivid, direct, full of observation and imagery. That was the language that helped shape the way I saw things, expressed things, made sense of the

world"; (d) "I think my mother's English almost had an effect on limiting my possibilities in life as well."

2. This essay has a clear beginning, middle, and end. Write the numbers of the paragraphs that comprise the introduction, body, and conclusion.

   Introductory paragraphs: _____

   Body paragraphs: _____

   Concluding paragraphs: _____

3. The title of the essay, "Mother Tongue," is a play on words. Explain.

   _____

4. From her recounting of the anecdotes in paragraphs 10–13, Tan appears to be (a) appalled; (b) amused; (c) saddened; (d) bitter; (e) cynical.

5. Look again at paragraph 13 and find a word that is used ironically. (You may have to consult your dictionary.) _____

6. What is the cause-and-effect relationship Tan cites in paragraph 18?

   _____

   _____

7. The method of development in paragraph 21 is (a) analogy; (b) illustration; (c) cause-and-effect; (d) steps in a process; (e) classification.

8. In your own words, explain Tan's attitude(s) toward her mother's English. _____

   _____

D. Vocabulary

For each italicized word from the selection, choose the best definition according to the context in which it appears.

1. the way it can *evoke* an emotion [paragraph 2]: (a) summon, call forth; (b) hide, obscure; (c) express in words; (d) overpower, dominate.

2. filled with carefully *wrought* [past participle of *work*] grammatical phrases [3]: (a) hammered out; (b) appropriate, correct; (c) put together; (d) invented.

3. I *wince* when I say that [8]: (a) become embarrassed; (b) flinch; (c) become anxious; (d) exaggerate.

4. plenty of *empirical* evidence [9]: (a) resting on guesswork, estimates; (b) based on practical experience; (c) derived from accepted theory; (d) originating in an emotional reaction.

5. In this *guise* [10]: (a) brief interlude; (b) awkward moment; (c) preparatory stage; (d) false pretense.
6. her *impeccable* broken English [13]: (a) most comprehensible; (b) flawless; (c) inaudible; (d) raucous, loud.
7. a *benign* brain tumor [14]: (a) inoperable; (b) difficult to detect; (c) malignant, harmful; (d) noncancerous.
8. immigrant families which are more *insular* [15]: (a) isolated, detached; (b) impervious to outside influence; (c) united, standing together; (d) stereotyped.
9. the most *bland* combinations of thoughts [16]: (a) obvious, conspicuous; (b) dull, undistinctive; (c) ridiculous, silly; (d) improbable, illogical.
10. some sort of *semantic* opposites [16]: Describing (a) logical connections between ideas; (b) appearances of objects; (c) symbolic representations of ideas; (d) the meanings of language forms.

E. Questions for Discussion and Analysis

1. In paragraph 9, Tan writes that she was ashamed during her youth of her mother's imperfect English. She says, "I believed that her English reflected the quality of what she had to say. That is, because she expressed them imperfectly her thoughts were imperfect." If possible, discuss this observation with people from other cultures. Specifically, are Americans more likely to equate lower intelligence with imperfect English, or is this a universal phenomenon?
2. In paragraph 18, Tan finds a cause-and-effect relationship between the kind of language Asian Americans grow up with and their ability to do well in math. This observation may indeed be true, but what are some other factors that might account for this phenomenon?

Selection 3

The Ethics of Living Jim Crow
Richard Wright

Born on a plantation near Natchez, Mississippi, in 1908, Richard Wright was one of America's most perceptive black writers of the twentieth century. As a spokesman for the plight of blacks, Wright worked on the Federal Writer's Project as part of the Works Progress Administration (WPA) in 1935. His best-known books are Native Son *(1940) and* Black Boy *(1944). "The Ethics of Living Jim Crow*" comes from his first book, a collection of*

*Jim Crow here refers to the systematic suppression of blacks in the South.

four autobiographical sketches, Uncle Tom's Children, *published in 1938. Like another great African-American writer, James Baldwin, after World War II Wright moved to Paris, where he lived as an expatriate until his death in 1960.*

I

1 My first lesson in how to live as a Negro came when I was quite small. We were living in Arkansas. Our house stood behind the railroad tracks. Its skimpy yard was paved with black cinders. Nothing green ever grew in that yard. The only touch of green we could see was far away, beyond the tracks, over where the white folks lived. But cinders were good enough for me and I never missed the green growing things. And anyhow cinders were fine weapons. You could always have a nice hot war with huge black cinders. All you had to do was crouch behind the brick pillars of a house with your hands full of gritty ammunition. And the first woolly black head you saw pop out from behind another row of pillars was your target. You tried your very best to knock it off. It was great fun.

2 I never fully realized the appalling disadvantages of a cinder environment till one day the gang to which I belonged found itself engaged in a war with the white boys who lived beyond the tracks. As usual we laid down our cinder barrage, thinking that this would wipe the white boys out. But they replied with a steady bombardment of broken bottles. We doubled our cinder barrage, but they hid behind trees, hedges, and the sloping embankments of their lawns. Having no such fortifications, we retreated to the brick pillars of our homes. During the retreat a broken milk bottle caught me behind the ear, opening a deep gash which bled profusely. The sight of blood pouring over my face completely demoralized our ranks. My fellow-combatants left me standing paralyzed in the center of the yard, and scurried for their homes. A kind neighbor saw me and rushed me to a doctor, who took three stitches in my neck.

3 I sat brooding on my front steps, nursing my wound and waiting for my mother to come from work. I felt that a grave injustice had been done me. It was all right to throw cinders. The greatest harm a cinder could do was leave a bruise. But broken bottles were dangerous; they left you cut, bleeding, and helpless.

4 When night fell, my mother came from the white folks' kitchen. I raced down the street to meet her. I could just feel in my bones that she would understand. I knew she would tell me exactly what to do next time. I grabbed her hand and babbled out the whole story. She examined my wound, then slapped me.

5 "How come yuh didn't hide?" she asked me. "How come yuh awways fightin'?"

6 I was outraged, and bawled. Between sobs I told her that I didn't have any trees or hedges to hide behind. There wasn't a thing I could

have used as a trench. And you couldn't throw very far when you were hiding behind the brick pillars of a house. She grabbed a barrel stave, dragged me home, stripped me naked, and beat me till I had a fever of one hundred and two. She would smack my rump with the stave, and, while the skin was still smarting, impart to me gems of Jim Crow wisdom. I was never to throw cinders any more. I was never to fight any more wars. I was never, never, under any conditions, to fight *white* folks again. And they were absolutely right in clouting me with the broken milk bottle. Didn't I know she was working hard every day in the hot kitchens of the white folks to make money to take care of me? When was I ever going to learn to be a good boy? She couldn't be bothered with my fights. She finished by telling me that I ought to be thankful to God as long as I lived that they didn't kill me.

7   All that night I was delirious and could not sleep. Each time I closed my eyes I saw monstrous white faces suspended from the ceiling, leering at me.

8   From that time on, the charm of my cinder yard was gone. The green trees, the trimmed hedges, the cropped lawns grew very meaningful, became a symbol. Even today when I think of white folks, the hard, sharp outlines of white houses surrounded by trees, lawns, and hedges are present somewhere in the background of my mind. Through the years they grew into an overreaching symbol of fear.

9   It was a long time before I came in close contact with white folks again. We moved from Arkansas to Mississippi. Here we had the good fortune not to live behind the railroad tracks, or close to white neighborhoods. We lived in the very heart of the local Black Belt. There were black churches and black preachers; there were black schools and black teachers; black groceries and black clerks. In fact, everything was so solidly black that for a long time I did not even think of white folks, save in remote and vague terms. But this could not last forever. As one grows older one eats more. One's clothing costs more. When I finished grammar school I had to go to work. My mother could no longer feed and clothe me on her cooking job.

10   There is but one place where a black boy who knows no trade can get a job, and that's where the houses and faces are white, where the trees, lawns, and hedges are green. My first job was with an optical company in Jackson, Mississippi. The morning I applied I stood straight and neat before the boss, answering all his questions with sharp yessirs and nosirs. I was very careful to pronounce my *sirs* distinctly, in order that he might know that I was polite, that I knew where I was, and that I knew he was a *white* man. I wanted that job badly.

11   He looked me over as though he were examining a prize poodle. He questioned me closely about my schooling, being particularly insistent about how much mathematics I had had. He seemed very pleased when I told him I had had two years of algebra.

12   "Boy, how would you like to try to learn something around here?" he asked me.

13   "I'd like it fine, sir," I said, happy. I had visions of "working my way up." Even Negroes have those visions.

14   "All right," he said. "Come on."

15   I followed him to the small factory.

16   "Pease," he said to a white man of about thirty-five, "this is Richard. He's going to work for us."

17   Pease looked at me and nodded.

18   I was then taken to a white boy of about seventeen.

19   "Morrie, this is Richard, who's going to work for us."

20   "Whut yuh sayin' there, boy!" Morrie boomed at me.

21   "Fine!" I answered.

22   The boss instructed these two to help me, teach me, give me jobs to do, and let me learn what I could in my spare time.

23   My wages were five dollars a week.

24   I worked hard, trying to please. For the first month I got along O.K. Both Pease and Morrie seemed to like me. But one thing was missing. And I kept thinking about it. I was not learning anything and nobody was volunteering to help me. Thinking they had forgotten that I was to learn something about the mechanics of grinding lenses, I asked Morrie one day to tell me about the work. He grew red.

25   "Whut yuh tryin' t' do, nigger, get smart?" he asked.

26   "Naw; I ain' tryin' t' git smart," I said.

27   "Well, don't, if yuh know whut's good for yuh!"

28   I was puzzled. Maybe he just doesn't want to help me, I thought. I went to Pease.

29   "Say, are yuh crazy, you black bastard?" Pease asked me, his gray eyes growing hard.

30   I spoke out, reminding him that the boss had said I was to be given a chance to learn something.

31   "Nigger, you think you're *white*, don't you?"

32   "Naw, sir!"

33   "Well, you're acting mighty like it!"

34   "But, Mr. Pease, the boss said . . ."

35   Pease shook his fist in my face.

36   "This is a *white* man's work around here, and you better watch yourself!"

37   From then on they changed toward me. They said good-morning no more. When I was just a bit slow in performing some duty, I was called a lazy black son-of-a-bitch.

38   Once I thought of reporting all this to the boss. But the mere idea of what would happen to me if Pease and Morrie should learn that I had "snitched" stopped me. And after all the boss was a white man, too. What was the use?

39   The climax came at noon one summer day. Pease called me to his work-bench. To get to him I had to go between two narrow benches and stand with my back against a wall.

40   "Yes, sir," I said.

41   "Richard, I want to ask you something," Pease began pleasantly, not looking up from his work.

42   "Yes, sir," I said again.

43   Morrie came over, blocking the narrow passage between the benches. He folded his arms, staring at me solemnly.

44   I looked from one to the other, sensing that something was coming.

45   "Yes, sir," I said for the third time.

46   Pease looked up and spoke very slowly.

47   "Richard, *Mr.* Morrie here tells me you called me *Pease.*"

48   I stiffened. A void seemed to open up in me. I knew this was the show-down.

49   He meant that I had failed to call him Mr. Pease. I looked at Morrie. He was gripping a steel bar in his hands. I opened my mouth to speak, to protest, to assure Pease that I had never called him simply *Pease,* and that I had never had any intentions of doing so, when Morrie grabbed me by the collar, ramming my head against the wall.

50   "Now, be careful, nigger!" snarled Morrie, baring his teeth. "*I* heard yuh call 'im *Pease! 'N'* if yuh say yuh didn't, yuh're callin' me a *lie,* see?" He waved the steel bar threateningly.

51   If I had said: No, sir, Mr. Pease, I never called you *Pease,* I would have been automatically calling Morrie a liar. And if I had said: Yes, sir, Mr. Pease, I called you *Pease,* I would have been pleading guilty to having uttered the worst insult that a Negro can utter to a southern white man. I stood hesitating, trying to frame a neutral reply.

52   "Richard, I asked you a question!" said Pease. Anger was creeping into his voice.

53   "I don't remember calling you *Pease,* Mr. Pease," I said cautiously. "And if I did, I sure didn't mean . . ."

54   "You black son-of-a-bitch! You called me *Pease,* then!" he spat, slapping me till I bent sideways over a bench. Morrie was on top of me, demanding:

55   "Didn't yuh call 'im *Pease?* If yuh say yuh didn't, I'll rip yo' gut string loose with this bar, yuh black granny dodger! Yuh can't call a white man a lie 'n' git erway with it, you black son-of-a-bitch!"

56   I wilted. I begged them not to bother me. I knew what they wanted. They wanted me to leave.

57   "I'll leave," I promised. "I'll leave right *now.*"

58   They gave me a minute to get out of the factory. I was warned not to show up again, or tell the boss.

59   I went.

60   When I told the folks at home what had happened, they called me a fool. They told me that I must never again attempt to exceed my boundaries. When you are working for white folks, they said, you got to "stay in your place" if you want to keep working.

II

61 My Jim Crow education continued on my next job, which was portering in a clothing store. One morning, while polishing brass out front, the boss and his twenty-year-old son got out of their car and half dragged and half kicked a Negro woman into the store. A policeman standing at the corner looked on, twirling his night-stick. I watched out of the corner of my eye, never slackening the strokes of my chamois upon the brass. After a few minutes, I heard shrill screams coming from the rear of the store. Later the woman stumbled out, bleeding, crying, and holding her stomach. When she reached the end of the block, the policeman grabbed her and accused her of being drunk. Silently, I watched him throw her into a patrol wagon.

62   When I went to the rear of the store, the boss and his son were washing their hands at the sink. They were chuckling. The floor was bloody and strewn with wisps of hair and clothing. No doubt I must have appeared pretty shocked, for the boss slapped me reassuringly on the back.

63   "Boy, that's what we do to niggers when they don't want to pay their bills," he said, laughing.

64   His son looked at me and grinned.

65   "Here, hava cigarette," he said.

66   Not knowing what to do, I took it. He lit his and held the match for me. This was a gesture of kindness, indicating that even if they had beaten the poor old woman, they would not beat me if I knew enough to keep my mouth shut.

67   "Yes, sir," I said, and asked no questions.

68   After they had gone, I sat on the edge of a packing box and stared at the bloody floor till the cigarette went out.

69   That day at noon, while eating in a hamburger joint, I told my fellow Negro porters what had happened. No one seemed surprised. One fellow, after swallowing a huge bite, turned to me and asked:

70   "Huh! Is tha' all they did t' her?"

71   "Yeah. Wasn't tha' enough?" I asked.

72   "Shucks! Man, she's a lucky bitch!" he said, burying his lips deep into a juicy hamburger. "Hell, it's a wonder they didn't lay her when they got through."

III

73 I was learning fast, but not quite fast enough. One day, while I was delivering packages in the suburbs, my bicycle tire was punctured. I

walked along the hot, dusty road, sweating and leading my bicycle by the handle-bars.

74   A car slowed at my side.

75   "What's the matter, boy?" a white man called.

76   I told him my bicycle was broken and I was walking back to town.

77   "That's too bad," he said. "Hop on the running board."

78   He stopped the car. I clutched hard at my bicycle with one hand and clung to the side of the car with the other.

79   "All set?"

80   "Yes, sir," I answered. The car started.

81   It was full of young white men. They were drinking. I watched the flask pass from mouth to mouth.

82   "Wanna drink, boy?" one asked.

83   I laughed as the wind whipped my face. Instinctively obeying the freshly planted precepts of my mother, I said:

84   "Oh, no!"

85   The words were hardly out of my mouth before I felt something hard and cold smash me between the eyes. It was an empty whisky bottle. I saw stars, and fell backwards from the speeding car into the dust of the road, my feet becoming entangled in the steel spokes of my bicycle. The white men piled out and stood over me.

86   "Nigger, ain' yuh learned no better sense'n tha' yet?" asked the man who hit me. "Ain' yuh learned t' say *sir* t' a white man yet?"

87   Dazed, I pulled to my feet. My elbows and legs were bleeding. Fists doubled, the white man advanced, kicking my bicycle out of the way.

88   "Aw, leave the bastard alone. He's got enough," said one.

89   They stood looking at me. I rubbed my shins, trying to stop the flow of blood. No doubt they felt a sort of contemptuous pity, for one asked:

90   "Yuh wanna ride t' town now, nigger? Yuh reckon yuh know enough t' ride now?"

91   "I wanna walk," I said, simply.

92   Maybe it sounded funny. They laughed.

93   "Well, walk, yuh black son-of-a-bitch!"

94   When they left they comforted me with:

95   "Nigger, yuh sho better be damn glad it wuz us yuh talked t' tha' way. Yuh're a lucky bastard, 'cause if yuh'd said tha' t' somebody else, yuh might've been a dead nigger now."

IV

96   Negroes who have lived South know the dread of being caught alone upon the streets in white neighborhoods after the sun has set. In such a simple situation as this the plight of the Negro in America is graphically symbolized. While white strangers may be in these neighborhoods trying to get home, they can pass unmolested. But the color of a Negro's

skin makes him easily recognizable, makes him suspect, converts him into a defenseless target.

97   Late one Saturday night I made some deliveries in a white neighborhood. I was pedaling my bicycle back to the store as fast as I could, when a police car, swerving toward me, jammed me into the curbing.

98   "Get down and put up your hands!" the policemen ordered.

99   I did. They climbed out of the car, guns drawn, faces set, and advanced slowly.

100   "Keep still!" they ordered.

101   I reached my hands higher. They searched my pockets and packages. They seemed dissatisfied when they could find nothing incriminating. Finally, one of them said:

102   "Boy, tell your boss not to send you out in white neighborhoods after sundown."

103   As usual, I said:

104   "Yes, sir."

V

105   My next job was a hall-boy in a hotel. Here my Jim Crow education broadened and deepened. When the bell-boys were busy, I was often called to assist them. As many of the rooms in the hotel were occupied by prostitutes, I was constantly called to carry them liquor and cigarettes. These women were nude most of the time. They did not bother about clothing, even for bell-boys. When you went into their rooms, you were supposed to take their nakedness for granted, as though it startled you no more than a blue vase or a red rug. Your presence awoke in them no sense of shame, for you were not regarded as human. If they were alone, you could steal sidelong glimpses at them. But if they were receiving men, not a flicker of your eyelids could show. I remember one incident vividly. A new woman, a huge, snowy-skinned blonde, took a room on my floor. I was sent to wait upon her. She was in bed with a thick-set man; both were nude and uncovered. She said she wanted some liquor and slid out of bed and waddled across the floor to get her money from a dresser drawer. I watched her.

106   "Nigger, what in hell you looking at?" the white man asked me, raising himself upon his elbows.

107   "Nothing," I answered, looking miles deep into the blank wall of the room.

108   "Keep your eyes where they belong, if you want to be healthy!" he said.

109   "Yes, sir."

VI

110   One of the bell-boys I knew in this hotel was keeping steady company with one of the Negro maids. Out of a clear sky the police descended

upon his home and arrested him, accusing him of bastardy. The poor boy swore he had had no intimate relations with the girl. Nevertheless, they forced him to marry her. When the child arrived, it was found to be much lighter in complexion than either of the two supposedly legal parents. The white men around the hotel made a great joke of it. They spread the rumor that some white cow must have scared the poor girl while she was carrying the baby. If you were in their presence when this explanation was offered, you were supposed to laugh.

VII

111   One of the bell-boys was caught in bed with a white prostitute. He was castrated and run out of town. Immediately after this all the bell-boys and hall-boys were called together and warned. We were given to understand that the boy who had been castrated was a "mighty, mighty lucky bastard." We were impressed with the fact that next time the management of the hotel would not be responsible for the lives of "trouble-makin' niggers." We were silent.

VIII

112   One night, just as I was about to go home, I met one of the Negro maids. She lived in my direction, and we fell in to walk part of the way home together. As we passed the white night-watchman, he slapped the maid on her buttock. I turned around, amazed. The watchman looked at me with a long, hard, fixed-under stare. Suddenly he pulled his gun and asked:

113   "Nigger, don't yuh like it?"

114   I hesitated.

115   "I asked yuh don't yuh like it?" he asked again, stepping forward.

116   "Yes, sir," I mumbled.

117   "Talk like it, then!"

118   "Oh, yes, sir!" I said with as much heartiness as I could muster.

119   Outside, I walked ahead of the girl, ashamed to face her. She caught up with me and said:

120   "Don't be a fool! Yuh couldn't help it!"

121   This watchman boasted of having killed two Negroes in self-defense.

122   Yet, in spite of all this, the life of the hotel ran with an amazing smoothness. It would have been impossible for a stranger to detect anything. The maids, the hall-boys, and the bell-boys were all smiles. They had to be.

IX

123   I had learned my Jim Crow lessons so thoroughly that I kept the hotel job till I left Jackson for Memphis. It so happened that while in Mem-

phis I applied for a job at a branch of the optical company. I was hired. And for some reason, as long as I worked there, they never brought my past against me.

124   Here my Jim Crow education assumed quite a different form. It was no longer brutally cruel, but subtly cruel. Here I learned to lie, to steal, to dissemble. I learned to play that dual role which every Negro must play if he wants to eat and live.

125   For example, it was almost impossible to get a book to read. It was assumed that after a Negro had imbibed what scanty schooling the state furnished he had no further need for books. I was always borrowing books from men on the job. One day I mustered enough courage to ask one of the men to let me get books from the library in his name. Surprisingly, he consented. I cannot help but think that he consented because he was a Roman Catholic and felt a vague sympathy for Negroes, being himself an object of hatred. Armed with a library card, I obtained books in the following manner: I would write a note to the librarian, saying: "Please let this nigger boy have the following books." I would then sign it with the white man's name.

126   When I went to the library, I would stand at the desk, hat in hand, looking as unbookish as possible. When I received the books desired I would take them home. If the books listed in the note happened to be out, I would sneak into the lobby and forge a new one. I never took any chances guessing with the white librarian about what the fictitious white man would want to read. No doubt if any of the white patrons had suspected that some of the volumes they enjoyed had been in the home of a Negro, they would not have tolerated it for an instant.

127   The factory force of the optical company in Memphis was much larger than that in Jackson, and more urbanized. At least they liked to talk, and would engage the Negro help in conversation whenever possible. By this means I found that many subjects were taboo from the white man's point of view. Among the topics they did not like to discuss with Negroes were the following: American white women; the Ku Klux Klan; France, and how Negro soldiers fared while there; French women; Jack Johnson; the entire northern part of the United States; the Civil War; Abraham Lincoln; U. S. Grant; General Sherman; Catholics; the Pope; Jews; the Republican Party; slavery; social equality; Communism; Socialism; the 13th and 14th Amendments to the Constitution; or any topic calling for positive knowledge or manly self-assertion on the part of the Negro. The most accepted topics were sex and religion.

128   There were many times when I had to exercise a great deal of ingenuity to keep out of trouble. It is a southern custom that all men must take off their hats when they enter an elevator. And especially did this apply to us blacks with rigid force. One day I stepped into an elevator with my arms full of packages. I was forced to ride with my hat on. Two white men stared at me coldly. Then one of them very kindly lifted my hat and placed it upon my armful of packages. Now the most accepted

response for a Negro to make under such circumstances is to look at the white man out of the corner of his eye and grin. To have said: "Thank you!" would have made the white man *think* that you *thought* you were receiving from him a personal service. For such an act I have seen Negroes take a blow in the mouth. Finding the first alternative distasteful, and the second dangerous, I hit upon an acceptable course of action which fell safely between these two poles. I immediately—no sooner than my hat was lifted—pretended that my packages were about to spill, and appeared deeply distressed with keeping them in my arms. In this fashion I evaded having to acknowledge his service, and, in spite of adverse circumstances, salvaged a slender shred of personal pride.

129   How do Negroes feel about the way they have to live? How do they discuss it when alone among themselves? I think this question can be answered in a single sentence. A friend of mine who ran an elevator once told me:

130   "Lawd, man! Ef it wuzn't fer them polices 'n' them ol' lynch-mobs, there wouldn't be nothin' but uproar down here!"

A. Comprehension

Choose the answer that best completes each statement. Do not refer to the selection while doing this exercise.

1. When Wright told his mother that he had been hurt by a broken milk bottle in his fight with neighborhood white boys, (a) she comforted him and spoke to the boys' parents; (b) she was proud that he had stood up for himself; (c) she became angry and punished and lectured him about fighting with white boys; (d) she sent him to bed without any supper.
2. When Wright moved from Arkansas to Mississippi, his family lived (a) near a white neighborhood; (b) next to the railroad tracks; (c) in a racially mixed neighborhood; (d) in an all-black community.
3. When Wright finally got a job working at a local optical company, he came to realize that (a) being an optician would be a good career for him; (b) his boss never intended for him to learn anything about the business; (c) grinding lenses was a boring way to earn a living; (d) the only way he could get ahead was to insist on being trained and not to stay meekly in his place.
4. One particular hazard for blacks in the South that Wright recounts is (a) being in the wrong place at the wrong time; (b) trying to integrate all-white public schools and colleges; (c) refusing to say "sir" to a white man or "ma'am" to a white woman; (d) being caught in a white neighborhood after sundown.
5. In order for Wright to use the local library, (a) he could read any books he was interested in only on the premises; (b) he had to ask a white friend to write a note for him; (c) he had to sneak any books out he

wanted to read; (d) a white friend had to go with Wright and take books out in his name.

6.   According to Wright, the most accepted topics for conversation for blacks and their white coworkers in the optical company he worked at in Mississippi were (a) race relations and women; (b) hunting and fishing; (c) sex and religion; (d) Catholics and Jews.

B.   **Inferences**

On the basis of the evidence in the selection, answer these inference questions in your own words. You may refer to the selection to answer the questions in this and all the remaining sections.

1.   From the selection as a whole, what does Wright mean by the term "Jim Crow education"? _____

_____

2.   According to paragraph 9, what were Wright's feelings about living in an all-black neighborhood when his family moved to Mississippi?

_____

3.   From the sketch about working at the optical company in paragraphs 10–60, what was the real reason Morrie and Pease were so hard on Wright? _____

_____

4.   From Wright's description of the incident in paragraphs 61–72, why did the policeman stand idly by and later arrest the black woman after the store owner had beaten her up? What does this behavior imply about social order and those hired to preserve it in the South? _____

_____

5.   From paragraphs 105–122, what can we infer was the greatest concern among whites about relationships between whites and blacks— especially when the blacks in question were black men? _____

_____

6.   Reread the last paragraph, in which Wright's friend describes how blacks really felt about the way they had to live. Explain what the friend meant in your own words. _____

_____

C.   **Structure**

1.   The mode of discourse in this selection is primarily (a) narration; (b) description; (c) exposition; (d) persuasion.

2.   In paragraphs 12 and 13, when Wright's new boss at the optical company asks him how he would like to learn something about the business, Wright replies, "I'd like it fine, sir." He says that he had visions

of working his way up, adding, "Even Negroes have those visions."
How would you characterize the tone of this last remark? _____
_____

3. In relation to what comes before and after it, what is the purpose of the
   first sentence of paragraph 61? It serves as (a) a conclusion; (b) a
   restatement of the main idea; (c) a transition between parts;
   (d) evidence to support the main idea.

4. Look again at paragraph 66. Explain why the phrase "gesture of
   kindness" is used ironically. _____
   _____

5. Besides using contrast in paragraph 96, another method of
   development embodied in this paragraph is (a) analogy; (b) cause-and-
   effect; (c) classification; (d) steps in a process; (e) definition.

6. With respect to the section comprised of paragraphs 125–128, what is
   the function of paragraph 124? It serves as (a) the main idea; (b) the
   primary evidence; (c) an inductive argument; (d) a conclusion.

D. Vocabulary

For each italicized word from the selection, choose the best definition according to the context in which it appears.

1. our cinder *barrage* [paragraph 2]: (a) pile; (b) defense; (c) outpouring;
   (d) stockade.

2. white faces *leering* at me [7]: (a) scowling maliciously; (b) peering
   curiously; (c) gazing with scornful amusement; (d) glancing lustfully.

3. A *void* seemed to open up in me [48]: (a) emptiness; (b) hostility;
   (c) overabundance of emotion; (d) overpowering hatred.

4. *portering* in a clothing store [61]: (a) stocking shelves; (b) selling
   merchandise; (c) bookkeeping; (d) carrying merchandise.

5. the freshly planted *precepts* of my mother [83]: (a) religious tenets;
   (b) practical suggestions; (c) rules, standards of conduct;
   (d) humorous observations.

6. the *plight* of the Negro [96]: (a) dilemma, choice between two equally
   bad alternatives; (b) difficult situation imposed from the outside;
   (c) political powerlessness; (d) social isolation.

7. *graphically* symbolized [96]: (a) clearly set forth; (b) tragically;
   (c) indisputably; (d) subtly.

8. as I could *muster* [118 and 125]: (a) endure; (b) pretend to have;
   (c) exhibit; (d) summon up.

9. I learned to lie, to steal, to *dissemble* [124]: (a) become violent,
   aggressive; (b) go on the defensive; (c) pretend, conceal the truth;
   (d) utter curses.

10. after a Negro had *imbibed* what scanty schooling the state furnished [125]: (a) taken in; (b) undergone; (c) been subjected to; (d) been corrupted by.
11. a great deal of *ingenuity* [128]: (a) energy; (b) cleverness; (c) intelligence; (d) sophisticated methods.
12. in spite of *adverse* circumstances [128]: (a) unfavorable; (b) fortunate; (c) confusing; (d) contradictory.

E. Questions for Analysis and Discussion

1. List some of the ways that the racists Wright describes denied blacks their humanity. And for their part, examine the ways that blacks learned to cope.
2. Although many of the narrative sketches in this selection are quite strong emotionally, Wright narrates them almost dispassionately. What is the advantage of this point of view?

Selection 4

The View from 80
Malcolm Cowley

Malcolm Cowley (1899–1989) was a man of letters—literary critic, historian, editor, poet, and essayist. His college career at Harvard was interrupted by World War I, in which he drove an ambulance in Europe. After the war he gained fame by serving as the champion of the group of World War I writers called the Lost Generation, which included writers like Ernest Hemingway, William Faulkner, John Dos Passos, e.e. cummings, and F. Scott Fitzgerald. Cowley continued writing and publishing essays and reviews well into his eighties. This excerpt is from his book The View from 80, *an expanded version of an award-winning article originally published in* Life *magazine. Cowley here examines the perils and pleasures of reaching the ninth decade.*

1   They gave me a party on my 80th birthday in August 1978. First there were cards, letters, telegrams, even a cable of congratulation or condolence; then there were gifts, mostly bottles; there was catered food and finally a big cake with, for some reason, two candles (had I gone back to very early childhood?). I blew the candles out a little unsteadily. Amid the applause and clatter I thought about a former custom of the Northern Ojibwas when they lived on the shores of Lake Winnipeg. They were kind to their old people, who remembered and enforced the ancient customs of the tribe, but when an old person became decrepit, it was time for him to go. Sometimes he was simply

abandoned, with a little food, on an island in the lake. If he deserved special honor, they held a tribal feast for him. The old man sang a death song and danced, if he could. While he was still singing, his son came from behind and brained him with a tomahawk.

2   That was quick, it was dignified, and I wonder whether it was any more cruel, essentially, than some of our civilized customs or inadvertences in disposing of the aged. I believe in rites and ceremonies. I believe in big parties for special occasions such as an 80th birthday. It is a sort of belated bar mitzvah, since the 80-year-old, like a Jewish adolescent, is entering a new stage of life; let him (or her) undergo a *rite de passage,* with toasts and a cantor. Seventy-year-olds, or septuas, have the illusion of being middle-aged, even if they have been pushed back on a shelf. The 80-year-old, the octo, looks at the double-dumpling figure and admits that he is old. The last act has begun, and it will be the test of the play.

3   He has joined a select minority that numbers, in this country, 4,842,000 persons (according to Census Bureau estimates for 1977), or about two percent of the American population. Two-thirds of the octos are women, who have retained the good habit of living longer than men. Someday you, the reader, will join that minority, if you escape hypertension and cancer, the two killers, and if you survive the dangerous years from 75 to 79, when half the survivors till then are lost. With advances in medicine, the living space taken over by octos is growing larger year by year.

4   To enter the country of age is a new experience, different from what you supposed it to be. Nobody, man or woman, knows the country until he has lived in it and has taken out his citizenship papers. Here is my own report, submitted as a road map and guide to some of the principal monuments.

5   The new octogenarian feels as strong as ever when he is sitting back in a comfortable chair. He ruminates, he dreams, he remembers. He doesn't want to be disturbed by others. It seems to him that old age is only a costume assumed for those others; the true, the essential self is ageless. In a moment he will rise and go for a ramble in the woods, taking a gun along, or a fishing rod, if it is spring. Then he creaks to his feet, bending forward to keep his balance, and realizes that he will do nothing of the sort. The body and its surroundings have their messages for him, or only one message: "You are old." Here are some of the occasions on which he receives the message:

_____   when it becomes an achievement to do thoughtfully, step by step, what he once did instinctively

_____   when his bones ache

_____ when there are more and more little bottles in the medicine cabinet, with instructions for taking four times a day

_____ when he fumbles and drops his toothbrush (butterfingers)

_____ when his face has bumps and wrinkles, so that he cuts himself while shaving (blood on the towel)

_____ when year by year his feet seem farther from his hands

_____ when he can't stand on one leg and has trouble pulling on his pants

_____ when he hesitates on the landing before walking down a flight of stairs

_____ when he spends more time looking for things misplaced than he spends using them after he (or more often his wife) has found them

_____ when he falls asleep in the afternoon

_____ when it becomes harder to bear in mind two things at once

_____ when a pretty girl passes him in the street and he doesn't turn his head

_____ when he forgets names, even of people he saw last month ("Now I'm beginning to forget nouns," the poet Conrad Aiken said at 80)

_____ when he listens hard to jokes and catches everything but the snapper

_____ when he decides not to drive at night anymore

_____ when everything takes longer to do—bathing, shaving, getting dressed or undressed—but when time passes quickly, as if he were gathering speed while coasting downhill. The year from 79 to 80 is like a week when he was a boy.

6   Those are some of the intimate messages. "Put cotton in your ears and pebbles in your shoes," said a gerontologist, a member of that new profession dedicated to alleviating all maladies of old people except the passage of years. "Pull on rubber gloves. Smear Vaseline over your glasses, and there you have it: instant aging." Not quite. His formula omits the messages from the social world, which are louder, in most cases, than those from within. We start by growing old in other people's eyes, then slowly we come to share their judgment.

7   I remember a morning many years ago when I was backing out of the parking lot near the railroad station in Brewster, New York. There was a near collision. The driver of the other car jumped out and started to abuse me; he had his fists ready. Then he looked hard at me and said, "Why, you're an old man." He got back into his car, slammed the door, and drove away, while I stood there fuming. "I'm only 65," I thought.

"He wasn't driving carefully. I can still take care of myself in a car, or in a fight, for that matter."

8   My hair was whiter—it may have been in 1974—when a young woman rose and offered me her seat in a Madison Avenue bus. That message was kind and also devastating. "Can't I even stand up?" I thought as I thanked her and declined the seat. But the same thing happened twice the following year, and the second time I gratefully accepted the offer, though with a sense of having diminished myself. "People are right about me," I thought while wondering why all those kind gestures were made by women. Do men now regard themselves as the weaker sex, not called upon to show consideration? All the same it was a relief to sit down and relax.

9   A few days later I wrote a poem, "The Red Wagon," that belongs in the record of aging:

> For his birthday they gave him a red express
>   wagon
> with a driver's high seat and a handle that
>   steered.
> His mother pulled him around the yard.
> "Giddyap," he said, but she laughed and went
>   off
> to wash the breakfast dishes.
>
> "I wanta ride too," his sister said,
> and he pulled her to the edge of a hill.
> "Now, sister, go home and wait for me,
> but first give a push to the wagon."
>
> He climbed again to the high seat,
> this time grasping the handle-that-steered.
> The red wagon rolled slowly down the slope,
> then faster as it passed the schoolhouse
> and faster as it passed the store,
> the road still dropping away.
> Oh, it was fun.
>
> But would it ever stop?
> Would the road always go downhill?
> The red wagon rolled faster.
> Now it was in strange country.
> It passed a white house he must have dreamed
>   about,
> deep woods he had never seen,

a graveyard where, something told him, his
    sister was buried.

Far below
the sun was sinking into a broad plain.

The red wagon rolled faster.
Now he was clutching the seat, not even trying
    to steer.
Sweat clouded his heavy spectacles.
His white hair streamed in the wind.

10   Even before he or she is 80, the aging person may undergo another identity crisis like that of adolescence. Perhaps there had also been a middle-aged crisis, the male or the female menopause, but for the rest of adult life he had taken himself for granted, with his capabilities and failings. Now, when he looks in the mirror, he asks himself, "Is this really me?"—or he avoids the mirror out of distress at what it reveals, those bags and wrinkles. In his new makeup he is called upon to play a new role in a play that must be improvised. André Gide, that long-lived man of letters, wrote in his journal, "My heart has remained so young that I have the continual feeling of playing a part, the part of the 70-year-old that I certainly am; and the infirmities and weaknesses that remind me of my age act like a prompter, reminding me of my lines when I tend to stray. Then, like the good actor I want to be, I go back into my role, and I pride myself on playing it well."

11   In his new role the old person will find that he is tempted by new vices, that he receives new compensations (not so widely known), and that he may possibly achieve new virtues. Chief among these is the heroic or merely obstinate refusal to surrender in the face of time. One admires the ships that go down with all flags flying and the captain on the bridge.

12   Among the vices of age are avarice, untidiness, and vanity, which last takes the form of a craving to be loved or simply admired. Avarice is the worst of those three. Why do so many old persons, men and women alike, insist on hoarding money when they have no prospect of using it and even when they have no heirs? They eat the cheapest food, buy no clothes, and live in a single room when they could afford better lodging. It may be that they regard money as a form of power; there is a comfort in watching it accumulate while other powers are dwindling away. How often we read of an old person found dead in a hovel, on a mattress partly stuffed with bankbooks and stock certificates! The bankbook syndrome,[1] we call it in our family, which has never succumbed.

---

[1]A group of signs or symptoms characteristic of a disease or disorder.

13   Untidiness we call the Langley Collyer syndrome. To explain, Langley Collyer was a former concert pianist who lived alone with his 70-year-old brother in a brownstone house on upper Fifth Avenue. The once fashionable neighborhood had become part of Harlem. Homer, the brother, had been an admiralty lawyer, but was now blind and partly paralyzed; Langley played for him and fed him on buns and oranges, which he thought would restore Homer's sight. He never threw away a daily paper because Homer, he said, might want to read them all. He saved other things as well and the house became filled with rubbish from roof to basement. The halls were lined on both sides with bundled newspapers, leaving narrow passageways in which Langley had devised booby traps to catch intruders.

14   On March 21, 1947, some unnamed person telephoned the police to report that there was a dead body in the Collyer house. The police broke down the front door and found the hall impassable; then they hoisted a ladder to a second-story window. Behind it Homer was lying on the floor in a bathrobe; he had starved to death. Langley had disappeared. After some delay, the police broke into the basement, chopped a hole in the roof, and began throwing junk out of the house, top and bottom. It was 18 days before they found Langley's body, gnawed by rats. Caught in one of his own booby traps, he had died in a hallway just outside Homer's door. By that time the police had collected, and the Department of Sanitation had hauled away, 120 tons of rubbish, including, besides the newspapers, 14 grand pianos and the parts of a dismantled Model T Ford.

15   Why do so many old people accumulate junk, not on the scale of Langley Collyer, but still in a dismaying fashion? Their tables are piled high with it, their bureau drawers are stuffed with it, their closet rods bend with the weight of clothes not worn for years. I suppose that the piling up is partly from lethargy and partly from the feeling that everything once useful, including their own bodies, should be preserved. Others, though not so many, have such a fear of becoming Langley Collyers that they strive to be painfully neat. Every tool they own is in its place, though it will never be used again; every scrap of paper is filed away in alphabetical order. At last their immoderate neatness becomes another vice of age, if a milder one.

16   The vanity of older people is an easier weakness to explain, and to condone. With less to look forward to, they yearn for recognition of what they have been: the reigning beauty, the athlete, the soldier, the scholar. It is the beauties who have the hardest time. A portrait of themselves at twenty hangs on the wall, and they try to resemble it by making an extravagant use of creams, powders, and dyes. Being young at heart, they think they are merely revealing their essential persons. The athletes find shelves for their silver trophies, which are polished once a year. Perhaps a letter sweater lies wrapped in a bureau drawer. I remem-

ber one evening when a no-longer-young athlete had guests for dinner and tried to find his sweater. "Oh, that old thing," his wife said. "The moths got into it and I threw it away." The athlete sulked and his guests went home early.

17   Often the yearning to be recognized appears in conversation as an innocent boast. Thus, a distinguished physician, retired at 94, remarks casually that a disease was named after him. A former judge bursts into chuckles as he repeats bright things that he said on the bench. Aging scholars complain in letters (or one of them does), "As I approach 70 I'm becoming avid of honors, and such things—medals, honorary degrees, etc.—are only passed around among academics on a *quid pro quo*[2] basis (one hood capping another)." Or they say querulously, "Bill Underwood has ten honorary doctorates and I have only three. Why didn't they elect me to . . . ?" and they mention the name of some learned society. That search for honors is a harmless passion, though it may lead to jealousies and deformations of character, as with Robert Frost in his later years. Still, honors cost little. Why shouldn't the very old have more than their share of them?

18   To be admired and praised, especially by the young, is an autumnal pleasure enjoyed by the lucky ones (who are not always the most deserving). "What is more charming," Cicero observes in his famous essay *De Senectute,* "than an old age surrounded by the enthusiasm of youth! . . . Attentions which seem trivial and conventional are marks of honor—the morning call, being sought after, precedence, having people rise for you, being escorted to and from the forum. . . . What pleasures of the body can be compared to the prerogatives of influence?" But there are also pleasures of the body, or the mind, that are enjoyed by a greater number of older persons.

19   Those pleasures include some that younger people find hard to appreciate. One of them is simply sitting still, like a snake on a sun-warmed stone, with a delicious feeling of indolence that was seldom attained in earlier years. A leaf flutters down; a cloud moves by inches across the horizon. At such moments the older person, completely relaxed, has become a part of nature—and a living part, with blood coursing through his veins. The future does not exist for him. He thinks, if he thinks at all, that life for younger persons is still a battle royal of each against each, but that now he has nothing more to win or lose. He is not so much above as outside the battle, as if he had assumed the uniform of some small neutral country, perhaps Liechtenstein or Andorra. From a distance he notes that some of the combatants, men or women, are jostling ahead—but why do they fight so hard when the most they can hope for is a longer obituary? He can watch the scroung-

---

[2]Latin for "something for something," in other words, an equal exchange.

ing and gouging, he can hear the shouts of exultation, the moans of the gravely wounded, and meanwhile he feels secure; nobody will attack him from ambush.

20   Age has other physical compensations besides the nirvana of dozing in the sun. A few of the simplest needs become a pleasure to satisfy. When an old woman in a nursing home was asked what she really liked to do, she answered in one word: "Eat." She might have been speaking for many of her fellows. Meals in a nursing home, however badly cooked, serve as climactic moments of the day. The physical essence of the pensioners is being renewed at an appointed hour; now they can go back to meditating or to watching TV while looking forward to the next meal. They can also look forward to sleep, which has become a definite pleasure, not the mere interruption it once had been.

21   Here I am thinking of old persons under nursing care. Others ferociously guard their independence, and some of them suffer less than one might expect from being lonely and impoverished. They can be rejoiced by visits and meetings, but they also have company inside their heads. Some of them are busiest when their hands are still. What passes through the minds of many is a stream of persons, images, phrases, and familiar tunes. For some that stream has continued since childhood, but now it is deeper; it is their present and their past combined. At times they conduct silent dialogues with a vanished friend, and these are less tiring—often more rewarding—than spoken conversations. If inner resources are lacking, old persons living alone may seek comfort and a kind of companionship in the bottle. I should judge from the gossip of various neighborhoods that the outer suburbs from Boston to San Diego are full of secretly alcoholic widows. One of those widows, an old friend, was moved from her apartment into a retirement home. She left behind her a closet in which the floor was covered wall to wall with whiskey bottles. "Oh, those empty bottles!" she explained. "They were left by a former tenant."

22   Not whiskey or cooking sherry but simply giving up is the greatest temptation of age. It is something different from a stoical acceptance of infirmities, which is something to be admired. At 63, when he first recognized that his powers were failing, Emerson wrote one of his best poems, "Terminus":

It is time to be old,
To take in sail:—
The god of bounds,
Who sets to seas a shore,
Came to me in his fatal rounds,
And said: "No more!
No farther shoot
Thy broad ambitious branches, and thy root.

Fancy departs: no more invent;
Contract thy firmament
To compass of a tent."

23   Emerson lived in good health to the age of 79. Within his narrowed firmament, he continued working until his memory failed; then he consented to having younger editors and collaborators. The givers-up see no reason for working. Sometimes they lie in bed all day when moving about would still be possible, if difficult. I had a friend, a distinguished poet, who surrendered in that fashion. The doctors tried to stir him to action, but he refused to leave his room. Another friend, once a successful artist, stopped painting when his eyes began to fail. His doctor made the mistake of telling him that he suffered from a fatal disease. He then lost interest in everything except the splendid Rolls-Royce, acquired in his prosperous days, that stood in the garage. Daily he wiped the dust from its hood. He couldn't drive it on the road any longer, but he used to sit in the driver's seat, start the motor, then back the Rolls out of the garage and drive it in again, back twenty feet and forward twenty feet; that was his only distraction.

24   I haven't the right to blame those who surrender, not being able to put myself inside their minds or bodies. Often they must have compelling reasons, physical or moral. Not only do they suffer from a variety of ailments, but also they are made to feel that they no longer have a function in the community. Their families and neighbors don't ask them for advice, don't really listen when they speak, don't call on them for efforts. One notes that there are not a few recoveries from apparent senility when that situation changes. If it doesn't change, old persons may decide that efforts are useless. I sympathize with their problems, but the men and women I envy are those who accept old age as a series of challenges.

25   For such persons, every new infirmity is an enemy to be outwitted, an obstacle to be overcome by force of will. They enjoy each little victory over themselves, and sometimes they win a major success. Renoir was one of them. He continued painting, and magnificently, for years after he was crippled by arthritis; the brush had to be strapped to his arm. "You don't need your hand to paint," he said. Goya was another of the unvanquished. At 72 he retired as an official painter of the Spanish court and decided to work only for himself. His later years were those of the famous "black paintings" in which he let his imagination run (and also of the lithographs, then a new technique). At 78 he escaped a reign of terror in Spain by fleeing to Bordeaux. He was deaf and his eyes were failing; in order to work he had to wear several pairs of spectacles, one over another, and then use a magnifying glass; but he was producing splendid work in a totally new style. At 80 he drew an ancient man propped on two sticks, with

a mass of white hair and beard hiding his face and with the inscription "I am still learning."

26   Giovanni Papini said when he was nearly blind, "I prefer martyrdom to imbecility." After writing sixty books, including his famous *Life of Christ,* he was at work on two huge projects when he was stricken with a form of muscular atrophy. He lost the use of his left leg, then of his fingers, so that he couldn't hold a pen. The two big books, though never to be finished, moved forward slowly by dictation; that in itself was a triumph. Toward the end, when his voice had become incomprehensible, he spelled out a word, tapping on the table to indicate letters of the alphabet. One hopes never to be faced with the need for such heroic measures.

27   "Eighty years old!" the great Catholic poet Paul Claudel wrote in his journal. "No eyes left, no ears, no teeth, no legs, no wind! And when all is said and done, how astonishingly well one does without them!"

A. Comprehension

Choose the answer that best completes each statement. Do not refer to the selection while doing this exercise.

1. According to Cowley, even before he or she reaches eighty, the aging person may undergo (a) a spiritual crisis; (b) an identity crisis; (c) a feeling of intense loneliness; (d) a period of questioning the worth of his or her life.

2. Cowley states that old people often exhibit three vices: avarice, untidiness, and vanity. Of these three, which does he consider the worst? (a) avarice; (b) untidiness; (c) vanity.

3. Old people hoard money because (a) they are afraid that their remaining assets will dwindle away until there is nothing left; (b) they don't want to leave the money to potentially ungrateful heirs; (c) they see the accumulation of money as a form of power when their other powers are failing; (d) they distrust banks and other financial institutions.

4. The Langley Collyer syndrome illustrates an extreme case of (a) vanity; (b) avarice; (c) untidiness; (d) distrust of outsiders.

5. In discussing the vanity of older people, Cowley writes that old people yearn for recognition of what they used to be and that the people who have the hardest time growing old are (a) athletes; (b) physicians; (c) professors; (d) beauty queens.

6. Cowley quotes Cicero, the Roman orator, as saying, "What is more charming than old age surrounded by" (a) beautiful women; (b) a loving family; (c) the enthusiasm of youth; (d) the pleasures of the body.

7. Old people find pleasures that young people might not appreciate, specifically in (a) the ability to speak their minds on any subject without paying attention to what others think; (b) the possibility of simply sitting still and becoming part of nature; (c) the need to engage in battles as a way of showing that the game is not over; (d) the ability to eat whatever and whenever they want.

8. Cowley believes that the greatest temptation of age is (a) giving up; (b) brooding about death; (c) complaining about your infirmities and physical pain; (d) letting others order you around.

B. Inferences

On the basis of the evidence in the selection, mark these statements as follows: PA for inferences that are probably accurate; PI for inferences that are probably inaccurate; and IE for insufficient evidence. You may refer to the selection to answer the questions in this and all the remaining sections.

_____ 1. Cowley considers barbaric the Northern Ojibwa custom of clobbering an old person to death when his time came.

_____ 2. The majority of the people who die between the ages of seventy-five and seventy-nine die of either cancer or hypertension.

_____ 3. Octogenarians often think they can perform physical activity better than they actually can.

_____ 4. Cowley cannot understand nor is he very sympathetic to old people who hoard money and live like paupers.

_____ 5. Fading beauties who try to recapture their lost youth with creams, powders, and dyes are a bit foolish.

_____ 6. Cowley believes that it is better for an old person to be admired and praised by the young than by one's contemporaries.

_____ 7. Old people gain a perspective about competition and jockeying for status, realizing that ultimately these matters are not very important.

_____ 8. Growing old does not have to be unremittingly gloomy and depressing as long as one refuses to give up or give in.

C. Structure

1. Write the sentence from the selection that best represents the thesis statement of the essay. _____

_____

_____ in paragraph_____.

2. The mode of discourse in the selection as a whole is (a) narration; (b) description; (c) exposition; (d) persuasion.

3. In paragraph 1 Cowley includes the reference to the Northern Ojibwas' method of dealing with their old people to suggest that (a) our so-called civilized methods of dealing with old people may be just as cruel; (b) we have unknowingly adopted some Native American practices; (c) our cultural practices are unquestionably more civilized; (d) we should adopt the Ojibwas' practices.

4. Paragraph 4 uses analogy as the method of development. What is compared metaphorically to what? _____

    _____

5. Which *two* methods of paragraph development are most evident in paragraphs 12–24? (a) steps in a process; (b) cause-and-effect; (c) classification; (d) example; (e) analogy; (f) definition; (g) comparison.

6. Look again at the first sentences of paragraphs 10 and 11 and the last sentence of paragraph 15, all of which serve as (a) main ideas supporting the thesis; (b) transitions from one major section of the essay to another; (c) primary pieces of evidence; (d) statements that appeal to our emotions.

7. Explain in your own words the analogy in the second half of paragraph 19. _____

    _____

8. Read paragraphs 25–27 again. What, apparently, does Cowley admire most about the artists mentioned here? (a) the high quality of their work despite their advanced age; (b) their strong physical constitutions; (c) their refusal to abandon their work and their rebellion against physical infirmities; (d) their exuberant love of life, no matter how feeble they became.

D. Vocabulary

For each italicized word from the selection, choose the best definition according to the context in which it appears.

1. our civilized customs or *inadvertences* [paragraph 2]: (a) oversights, mistakes; (b) religious traditions; (c) deceptions, tricks; (d) concerns, cares.

2. The new octogenarian *ruminates* [5]: (a) expresses regret; (b) complains; (c) meditates at length; (d) repeats the same stories.

3. *alleviating* all maladies [6]: (a) curing; (b) relieving pain; (c) discussing; (d) researching.

4. alleviating all *maladies* [6]: (a) complaints; (b) defects; (c) cancers; (d) diseases.

5. the *infirmities* that remind me of my age [10]: (a) moral weaknesses; (b) subtle changes; (c) lapses of memory; (d) frailties, disabilities.

6. he receives new *compensations* [11]: (a) acquisitions that cost nothing; (b) insights, revelations, perceptions; (c) factors that make up for a loss; (d) goods to foster the competitive spirit.

7. among the vices of age are *avarice* [12]: (a) a desire to amass wealth; (b) a need to compete against others; (c) a compulsion to give away one's possessions and money; (d) an inclination to remain isolated from the outside world.

8. in a *dismaying* fashion [15]: (a) fearful; (b) greatly troubling; (c) encouraging; (d) mildly annoying.

9. the piling up is partly *lethargy* [15]: (a) inborn messiness; (b) a state of unconsciousness; (c) drowsiness; (d) sluggish indifference.

10. The *vanity* of old people [16]: (a) excessive fondness for food and drink; (b) excessive love of spending money; (c) excessive pride in one's appearance or accomplishments; (d) excessive desire to be accepted by others.

11. The vanity of old people is easier to *condone* [16]: (a) argue about; (b) overlook; (c) explain; (d) define.

12. the athlete *sulked* [16]: (a) became sullenly withdrawn; (b) flew into a rage; (c) boasted, bragged; (d) refused to speak.

13. becoming *avid* of honors [17]: (a) interested in; (b) concerned about; (c) indifferent to; (d) eager for.

14. they say *querulously* [17]: (a) bitterly; (b) questioningly; (c) complainingly; (d) obstinately.

15. the *prerogatives* of influence [18]: (a) exclusive rights or privileges; (b) spheres, circles; (c) questions, unsettled issues; (d) pleasures, joys.

16. a delicious feeling of *indolence* [19]: (a) indifference; (b) harmony; (c) independence; (d) laziness.

17. the shouts of *exultation* [19]: (a) triumph; (b) disapproval; (c) outrage; (d) enthusiasm.

18. a *stoical* acceptance of infirmities [22]: (a) pleasurable; (b) inevitable; (c) impassive; (d) complete.

E. Questions for Analysis and Discussion

1. How does what Cowley says accord with your experience with old people?

2. In this selection Cowley writes about his view of life as an eighty-year-old. What is the view from your age? What are the vices, compensations, and virtues of the age you are now?

Anosmia

Diane Ackerman

The author of five books of poetry and recipient of numerous literary prizes, Diane Ackerman is a poet and writer of nonfiction. She has taught at many universities, among them Washington University, New York University, Columbia, and Cornell, where she received an M.F.A. and Ph.D. Ackerman, a resident of upstate New York, is currently a staff writer at The New Yorker. *Described by the* Boston Globe *as a "narrative journey, one that touches upon biology and anthropology, art and human consciousness,"* A Natural History of the Senses, *from which this essay comes, is an engaging look at the wonders to be found in our five senses.*

1   One rainy night in 1976, a thirty-three-year-old mathematician went out for an after-dinner stroll. Everyone considered him not just a gourmet but a wunderkind,[1] because he had the ability to taste a dish and tell you all its ingredients with shocking precision. One writer described it as a kind of "perfect pitch." As he stepped into the street, a slow-moving van ran into him and he hit his head on the pavement when he fell. The day after he got out of the hospital, he discovered to his horror that his sense of smell was gone.

2   Because his taste buds still worked, he could detect foods that were salty, bitter, sour, and sweet, but he had lost all of the heady succulence of life. Seven years later, still unable to smell and deeply depressed, he sued the driver of the van and won. It was understood, first, that his life had become irreparably impoverished and, second, that without a sense of smell his life was endangered. In those seven years, he had failed to detect the smell of smoke when his apartment building was on fire; he had been poisoned by food whose putrefaction he couldn't smell; he could not smell gas leaks. Worst of all, perhaps, he had lost the ability of scents and odors to provide him with heart-stopping memories and associations. "I feel empty, in a sort of limbo," he told a reporter. There was not even a commonly known name for his nightmare. Those without hearing are labeled "deaf," those without sight "blind," but what is the word for someone without smell? What could be more distressing than to be sorely afflicted by an absence without a name? "Anosmia" is what scientists call it, a simple Latin/Greek combination: "without" + "smell." But no casual term—like "smumb," for instance—exists to give one a sense of community or near-normalcy.

---

[1]Pronounced vŏ͝on´ dər kint´, a *wunderkind* is German for "wonder child" or "child prodigy."

3   The "My Turn" column in *Newsweek* of March 21, 1988, by Judith R. Birnberg, contains a deeply moving lament about her sudden loss of smell. All she can distinguish is the texture and temperature of food. "I am handicapped: one of 2 million Americans who suffer from anosmia, an inability to smell or taste (the two senses are physiologically related). . . . We so take for granted the rich aroma of coffee and the sweet flavor of oranges that when we lose these senses, it is almost as if we have forgotten how to breathe." Just before Ms. Birnberg's sense of smell disappeared, she had spent a year sneezing. The cause? Some unknown allergy. "The anosmia began without warning. . . . During the past three years there have been brief periods—minutes, even hours—when I suddenly became aware of odors and knew that this meant that I could also taste. What to eat first? A bite of banana once made me cry. On a few occasions a remission came at dinner time, and my husband and I would dash to our favorite restaurant. On two or three occasions I savored every miraculous mouthful through an entire meal. But most times my taste would be gone by the time we parked the car." Although there are centers for treating smell and taste dysfunction (of which Monell[2] is probably the best known), little can be done about anosmia. "I have had a CAT scan, blood tests, sinus cultures, allergy tests, allergy shots, long-term zinc therapy, weekly sinus irrigations, a biopsy, cortisone injections into my nose and four different types of sinus surgery. My case has been presented to hospital medical committees. . . . I have been through the medical mill. The consensus: anosmia caused by allergy and infection. There can be other causes. Some people are born this way. Or the olfactory nerve is severed as a result of concussion. Anosmia can also be the result of aging, a brain tumor or exposure to toxic chemicals. Whatever the cause, we are all at risk in detecting fires, gas leaks and spoiled food." Finally, she took a risky step and allowed a doctor to give her prednisone, an anti-inflammatory steroid, in an effort to shrink the swelling near olfactory nerves. "By the second day, I had a brief sense of smell when I inhaled deeply. . . . The fourth day I ate a salad at lunch, and I suddenly realized that I could taste everything. It was like the moment in 'The Wizard of Oz' when the world is transformed from black and white to Technicolor. I savored the salad: one garbanzo bean, a shred of cabbage, a sunflower seed. On the fifth day I sobbed—less from the experience of smelling and tasting than from believing the craziness was over."

4   At breakfast the next day, she caught her husband's scent and "fell on him in tears of joy and started sniffing him, unable to stop. His was a comfortable familiar essence that had been lost for so long and was

[2]The Monell Chemical Senses Center in Philadelphia is a research institute where researchers study, as Ackerman says, "the chemistry, psychology, healing properties, and odd characteristics of smell."

now rediscovered. I had always thought I would sacrifice smell to taste if I had to choose between the two, but I suddenly realized how much I had missed. We take it for granted and are unaware that *everything* smells: people, the air, my house, my skin. . . . Now I inhaled all odors, good and bad, as if drunk." Sadly, her pleasures lasted only a few months. When she began reducing the dosage of prednisone, as she had to for safety's sake (prednisone causes bloating and can suppress the immune system, among other unpleasant side effects), her ability to smell waned once more. Two new operations followed. She's decided to go back on prednisone, and yearns for some magical day when her smell returns as mysteriously as it vanished.

5   Not everyone without a sense of smell suffers so acutely. Nor are all smell dysfunctions a matter of loss; the handicap can take strange forms. At Monell, scientists have treated numerous people who suffer from "persistent odors," who keep smelling a foul smell wherever they go. Some walk around with a constant bitter taste in their mouths. Some have a deformed or distorted sense of smell. Hand them a rose, and they smell garbage. Hand them a steak and they smell sulfur. Our sense of smell weakens as we get older, and it's at its peak in middle age. Alzheimer's patients often lose their sense of smell along with their memory (the two are tightly coupled); one day Scratch-and-Sniff tests may help in diagnosis of the disease.

6   Research done by Robert Henkin, from the Center for Sensory Disorders at Georgetown University, suggests that about a quarter of the people with smell disorders find that their sex drive disappears. What part does smell play in lovemaking? For women, especially, a large part. I am certain that, blindfolded, I could recognize by smell any man I've ever known intimately. I once started to date a man who was smart, sophisticated, and attractive, but when I kissed him I was put off by a faint, cornlike smell that came from his cheek. Not cologne or soap: It was just his subtle, natural scent, and I was shocked to discover that it disturbed me viscerally. Although men seldom report such detailed responses to their partner's natural smell, women so often do that it's become a romantic cliché: When her lover is away, or her husband dies, an anguished woman goes to his closet and takes out a bathrobe or shirt, presses it to her face, and is overwhelmed by tenderness for him. Few men report similar habits, but it's not surprising that women should be more keenly attuned to smells. Females score higher than males in sensitivity to odors, regardless of age group. For a time scientists thought estrogen might be involved, since there was anecdotal evidence that pregnant women had a keener sense of smell, but as it turned out prepubescent girls were better sniffers than boys their age, and pregnant women were no more adept at smelling than other women. Women in general just have a stronger sense of smell. Perhaps it's a vestigial bonus from the dawn of our evolution, when we needed it in courtship, mating, or mothering; or it may be that women have

traditionally spent more time around foods and children, ever on the sniff for anything out of order. Because females have often been responsible for initiating mating, smell has been their weapon, lure, and clue.

A. Comprehension

Choose the answer that best completes each statement. Do not refer to the selection while doing this exercise.

1. The mathematician who lost his sense of smell after being hit by a van had a special ability, namely that of identifying by smell (a) human scents; (b) brands of food; (c) wines according to the soil the grapes were grown in; (d) the ingredients in a dish.
2. According to Ackerman, the most serious effect of this man's loss of his sense of smell was his inability (a) to connect smells with memories and associations; (b) to smell spoiled food; (c) to smell smoke or gas leaks; (d) to taste food.
3. The sense of smell is physiologically most closely related to our (a) sense of touch; (b) sense of hearing; (c) sense of sight; (d) sense of taste; (e) memory.
4. For Judith Birnberg, the most precious scent to her when she temporarily regained her sense of smell was that of (a) her own skin; (b) her husband; (c) a green salad; (d) her house.
5. According to Ackerman, our sense of smell is strongest during (a) our youth; (b) young adulthood; (c) middle age; (d) old age.
6. According to scientific research, (a) women and men are equally sensitive to smells; (b) men are more sensitive to smells than women are; (c) women are more sensitive to smells than men are; (d) children are more sensitive to smells than adults are.

B. Inferences

On the basis of the evidence in the selection, mark these statements as follows: PA for inferences that are probably accurate; PI for inferences that are probably inaccurate; and IE for insufficient evidence. You may refer to the selection to answer the questions in this and all the remaining sections.

_____ 1. The ability to identify precisely the ingredients in a dish is a rare talent.

_____ 2. People who lose their sense of smell feel more isolated than blind or deaf people do.

_____ 3. Since no nonscientific word exists in English for someone without smell, this disorder must not be as common as blindness or deafness.

_____ 4. "Smumb" is a word the author made up, combining "smell" and perhaps "numb."

_____ 5. A keen sense of smell is essential for one to lead a normal, relatively happy life.

_____ 6. Judith Birnberg's sense of smell returned as mysteriously as it disappeared.

_____ 7. Estrogen apparently plays an important role in a woman's ability to smell.

_____ 8. Scientists do not know the exact causes of anosmia.

C. Structure

1. The main idea is that (a) anosmia is a physical disorder characterized by loss of the ability to smell; (b) victims of anosmia experience serious emotional trauma as a result of losing their sense of smell; (c) research must be done to find a cure for victims of anosmia; (d) anosmia is only one of many smell dysfunctions.

2. The mode of discourse in this essay is (a) narration; (b) description; (c) exposition; (d) persuasion.

3. The pattern of organization in the first six sentences of paragraph 2 is (a) deductive; (b) inductive; (c) variation of deductive; (d) emphatic.

4. Look again at paragraph 3 and find a phrase that represents a controlling idea for the details in both paragraphs 3 and 4. _____

5. State the cause-and-effect relationship Ackerman makes in the first four sentences of paragraph 6. _____

_____

6. Look again at this remark from paragraph 6: "it's not surprising that women should be more keenly attuned to smells." The method of development in this statement and the remaining sentences in the paragraph is (a) classification; (b) example; (c) cause and effect; (d) analogy; (e) steps in a process; (f) definition.

D. Vocabulary

For each italicized word from the selection, choose the best definition according to the context in which it appears.

1. the heady _succulence_ of life [paragraph 2]: (a) fascination, interest; (b) juiciness, tenderness; (c) spirit, animation; (d) indulgence, enjoyment.

2. his life had become _irreparably_ impoverished [2]: (a) definitely; (b) unable to be explained; (c) unable to be repaired; (d) permanently.

3. food whose _putrefaction_ he couldn't smell [2]: (a) chemical additives; (b) pesticides and herbicides; (c) spicy aroma; (d) rottenness.

4.   a deeply moving *lament* [3]: (a) expression of grief, remorse;
     (b) spasm of envy, jealousy; (c) surge of anger, bitterness; (d) moment
     of sarcasm, cynicism.

5.   a *remission* came at dinner time [3]: (a) a serious worsening of
     symptoms; (b) a lessening of symptoms; (c) an unexplainable and
     temporary cure; (d) a return of one's memory.

6.   smell and taste *dys*function [3 and 5]: The prefix *dys*- means (a) well;
     (b) faulty; (c) typical; (d) two.

7.   the *olfactory* nerve [3]: (a) taste-related (b) smell-related; (c) hearing-
     related; (d) touch-related; (e) sight-related.

8.   her ability to smell *waned* [4]: (a) gradually improved; (b) gradually
     decreased; (c) became tolerable; (d) stayed the same.

9.   it disturbed me *viscerally* [6]: (a) illogically, irrationally; (b) profoundly,
     deeply; (c) intensely, emotionally; (d) slightly, moderately.

10. more keenly *attuned to* smells [6]: (a) accustomed to as with a special
     perception; (b) involved with for research; (c) being in harmony with;
     (d) intrigued or fascinated by.

11. *anecdotal* evidence [6]: (a) factual, historical; (b) brief, cursory;
     (c) rumored, reported; (d) scientific, proven.

12. Perhaps it's a *vestigial* bonus [6]: (a) extra, unnecessary; (b) not clearly
     understood; (c) innate, inborn; (d) a visible trace of something that no
     longer exists.

E.   Questions for Analysis and Discussion

1.   Consider again the last part of paragraph 6 where Ackerman discusses
     some possible theories about women's superior ability to smell. How
     plausible do you find these theories? Can you think of any others that
     might account for this phenomenon, assuming, of course, that it is
     true?

2.   Of your five senses, which do you think would be the most difficult to
     be deprived of?

Essays: Group 2

Selection 6

Harmless Lying
Sissela Bok

*Sissela Bok teaches courses in ethics and decision-making at Harvard Medical
School. The following excerpt is from her book,* Lying: Moral Choice in Pub-

lic and Private Life, *which examines something we probably all admit to doing—telling white lies. Bok first defines white lies and raises some interesting ethical and philosophical concerns about the long-term effects of these supposedly harmless or trivial untruths.*

1   White lies are at the other end of the spectrum of deception from lies in a serious crisis. They are the most common and the most trivial forms that duplicity can take. The fact that they are so common provides their protective coloring. And their very triviality, when compared to more threatening lies, makes it seem unnecessary or even absurd to condemn them. Some consider all well-intentioned lies, however momentous, to be white; in this book, I shall adhere to the narrower usage: a white lie, in this sense, is a falsehood not meant to injure anyone, and of little moral import. I want to ask whether there are such lies; and if there are, whether their cumulative consequences are still without harm; and, finally, whether many lies are not defended as "white" which are in fact harmful in their own right.

2   Many small subterfuges may not even be intended to mislead. They are only "white lies" in the most marginal sense. Take, for example, the many social exchanges: "How nice to see you!" or "Cordially Yours." These and a thousand other polite expressions are so much taken for granted that if someone decided, in the name of total honesty, not to employ them, he might well give the impression of an indifference he did not possess. The justification for continuing to use such accepted formulations is that they deceive no one, except possibly those unfamiliar with the language.

3   A social practice more clearly deceptive is that of giving a false excuse so as not to hurt the feelings of someone making an invitation or request: to say one "can't" do what in reality one may not *want* to do. Once again, the false excuse may prevent unwarranted inferences of greater hostility to the undertaking than one may well feel. Merely to say that one can't do something, moreover, is not deceptive in the sense that an elaborately concocted story can be.

4   Still other white lies are told in an effort to flatter, to throw a cheerful interpretation on depressing circumstances, or to show gratitude for unwanted gifts. In the eyes of many, such white lies do no harm, provide needed support and cheer, and help dispel gloom and boredom. They preserve the equilibrium and often the humaneness of social relationships, and are usually accepted as excusable so long as they do not become excessive. Many argue, moreover, that such deception is so helpful and at times so necessary that it must be tolerated as an exception to a general policy against lying. Thus Bacon observed:

> Doth any man doubt, that if there were taken out of men's minds vain opinions, flattering hopes, false valuations, imaginations as one would,

and the like, but it would leave the minds of a number of men poor shrunken things, full of melancholy and indisposition, and unpleasing to themselves?

5   Another kind of lie may actually be advocated as bringing a more substantial benefit, or avoiding a real harm, while seeming quite innocuous to those who tell the lies. Such are the placebos given for innumerable common ailments, and the pervasive use of inflated grades and recommendations for employment and promotion.

6   A large number of lies without such redeeming features are nevertheless often regarded as so trivial that they should be grouped with white lies. They are the lies told on the spur of the moment, for want of reflection, or to get out of a scrape, or even simply to pass the time. Such are the lies told to boast or exaggerate, or on the contrary to deprecate and understate; the many lies told or repeated in gossip; Rousseau's lies told simply "in order to say something"; the embroidering on facts that seem too tedious in their own right; and the substitution of a quick lie for the lengthy explanations one might otherwise have to provide for something not worth spending time on.

7   Utilitarians often cite white lies as the *kind* of deception where their theory shows the benefits of common sense and clear thinking. A white lie, they hold, is trivial; it is either completely harmless, or so marginally harmful that the cost of detecting and evaluating the harm is much greater than the minute harm itself. In addition, the white lie can often actually be beneficial, thus further tipping the scales of utility. In a world with so many difficult problems, utilitarians might ask: Why take the time to weigh the minute pros and cons in telling someone that his tie is attractive when it is an abomination, or of saying to a guest that a broken vase was worthless? Why bother even to define such insignificant distortions or make mountains out of molehills by seeking to justify them?

8   Triviality surely does set limits to when moral inquiry is reasonable. But when we look more closely at practices such as placebo-giving, it becomes clear that all lies defended as "white" cannot be so easily dismissed. In the first place, the harmlessness of lies is notoriously disputable. What the liar perceives as harmless or even beneficial may not be so in the eyes of the deceived. Second, the failure to look at an entire practice rather than at their own isolated case often blinds liars to cumulative harm and expanding deceptive activities. Those who begin with white lies can come to resort to more frequent and more serious ones. Where some tell a few white lies, others may tell more. Because lines are so hard to draw, the indiscriminate use of such lies can lead to other deceptive practices. The aggregate harm from a large number of marginally harmful instances may, therefore, be highly undesirable in the end—for liars, those deceived, and honesty and trust more generally.

9   Just as the life-threatening cases showed the Kantian analysis to be too rigid, so the cases of white lies show the casual utilitarian calculation to be inadequate. Such a criticism of utilitarianism does not attack its foundations, because it does not disprove the importance of weighing consequences. It merely shows that utilitarians most often do not weigh enough factors in their quick assumption that white lies are harmless. They often fail to look at *practices* of deception and the ways in which these multiply and reinforce one another. They tend to focus, rather, on the individual case, seen from the point of view of the individual liar.

10   In the post-Watergate period, no one need regard a concern with the combined and long-term effects of deception as far-fetched. But even apart from political life, with its peculiar and engrossing temptations, lies tend to spread. Disagreeable facts come to be sugar-coated, and sad news softened or denied altogether. Many lie to children and to those who are ill about matters no longer peripheral but quite central, such as birth, adoption, divorce, and death. Deceptive propaganda and misleading advertising abound. All these lies are often dismissed on the same grounds of harmlessness and triviality used for white lies in general.

A. Comprehension

Choose the answer that best completes each statement. Do not refer to the selection while doing this exercise.

1. Bok defines white lies as (a) serious falsehoods with significant moral consequences; (b) harmless lies used only to flatter others or to cover one's errors; (c) falsehoods not meant to injure anyone and of little moral import; (d) trivial examples of common civility that all of us can see through.

2. Many people believe that white lies preserve social relationships, accepting them as excusable (a) if they deal with a trivial subject; (b) as long as they do not become excessive; (c) if they are easily perceived as lies; (d) if they are easier than telling the truth.

3. The author defines utilitarians as people who believe that white lies (a) are never acceptable, even to avoid hurting others' feelings; (b) destroy mutual trust between two people; (c) are trivial, harmless, and sometimes even beneficial; (d) are a way to alleviate boredom or to make dull facts more interesting.

4. Choose the *two* concerns Bok expresses about white lies: (a) the deceived person may not perceive such lies as harmless; (b) liars often have trouble keeping their lies straight; (c) lying is no longer seen as morally wrong; (d) liars become blind to the cumulative harm of

lying, which may in turn lead to more serious deceptive practices; (e) liars develop a reputation for lying so that nothing they say can be trusted.

5. The problem with dismissing white lies as harmless is that we also consider harmless other lies like (a) misleading advertising; (b) political campaign promises; (c) those told to avoid hurting others' feelings; (d) elaborate excuses to get out of doing something we don't want to do.

6. Fundamentally, Bok's concern with harmless lying in general is that (a) they tend to spread; (b) they lead to political scandals like Watergate; (c) they really fool no one; (d) they undermine our trust in those around us.

B. Inferences

On the basis of the evidence in the selection, answer these inference questions in your own words. You may refer to the selection to answer the questions in this and all the remaining sections.

1. From the essay as a whole, what is Bok's opinion about the commonly accepted definition of white lies as well intentioned and having little moral import? _____

_____

2. According to paragraphs 2 and 3, which lie is more harmful: saying how nice it is to see someone again or saying that we can't do something we don't want to do? _____

_____

3. From what Bok suggests in paragraph 8, why should we look at the whole pattern of lying rather than simply isolated examples of white lies? _____

_____

4. From what Bok implies in paragraph 10, why have we become accustomed to and tolerant of misleading advertising, sugar-coated facts, and deceptive propaganda? _____

_____

C. Structure

1. The author wrote the essay (a) to provide a reasonable definition of white lies; (b) to examine contemporary attitudes about white lies and our reasons for telling them; (c) to question the ethics and to examine some long-term effects of telling white lies; (d) to cite specific instances when telling white lies is preferable to telling the truth.

2. Look again at the last sentence of paragraph 1, which in relation to the essay as a whole, serves as (a) a transition; (b) a statement of the author's purpose; (c) supporting evidence; (d) a rhetorical question asked only for effect.

3. Which method of paragraph development is most evident in the section from paragraphs 2–6? _____
And which *two* methods of development are evident in paragraph 8?
_____

4. The author's tone can be best described as (a) self-righteous, "holier-than-thou"; (b) complaining, aggrieved; (c) objective, impartial; (d) serious, philosophical; (e) angry, hostile.

5. Which of the following seems to be the most reasonable conclusion we can draw from this essay? (a) White lies are often acceptable if they save others from being hurt; (b) The circumstances when we tell white lies should be limited, and we should think very carefully about their many repercussions before resorting to them; (c) Everyone tells white lies; it's simply human nature; (d) White lies are often more convenient and less harmful in the long run than telling the truth.

D. Vocabulary

For each italicized word from the selection, choose the best definition according to the context in which it appears.

1. the most trivial forms that *duplicity* can take [paragraph 1]:
   (a) deliberate deception; (b) conscious imitation; (c) immoral behavior; (d) questionable ethics.

2. of little moral *import* [1]: (a) value; (b) concern; (c) question; (d) significance.

3. Many small *subterfuges* [2]: (a) pertinent illustrations; (b) related concepts; (c) evasive tactics; (d) capital crimes.

4. may prevent *unwarranted* inferences [3]: (a) unjustified; (b) unconnected; (c) unproven; (d) unfounded.

5. They preserve the *equilibrium* [4]: (a) integrity; (b) status quo; (c) balance; (d) character.

6. seeming quite *innocuous* [5]: (a) dangerous; (b) purposeful; (c) relevant; (d) harmless.

7. for *want* of reflection [6]: (a) desire; (b) necessity; (c) lack; (d) goal.

8. to *deprecate* and understate [6]: (a) complain; (b) whine about; (c) exaggerate; (d) belittle.

9. *Utilitarians* often cite white lies [7]: (a) those who place what is beautiful over what is morally right; (b) believers in what is practical over what is ethical; (c) upholders of what is morally right over what is

the easy course; (d) those who put more value on what is a public matter than on what is a private matter.

10. The *aggregate* harm [8]: (a) necessary; (b) numerical; (c) total; (d) incalculable.

11. matters no longer *peripheral* [10]: (a) inessential, outside the center; (b) clear, identifiable; (c) concerning basic survival; (d) crucial, very important.

12. Deceptive propaganda and misleading advertising *abound* [10]: (a) no longer surprise; (b) confuse, bewilder; (c) establish the norm; (d) exist in great amount.

E. Questions for Analysis and Discussion

1. Do you agree with Bok's assertion that telling white lies, first, injures the people who are lied to and, second, has cumulative consequences that far override the liars' claim that such untruths are legitimate, beneficial, or trivial?

2. How has this essay changed your perception about white lies in particular and about lying in general?

Selection 7

A Bad Time

Nancy Mitford

Born in 1904 to a rather eccentric, freewheeling upper-class English family, Nancy Mitford, the oldest of the six Mitford girls, was educated at home. Their unconventional upbringing is described in Daughters and Rebels *an amusing account written by her sister, Jessica Mitford, also a famous writer who now lives in the U.S. Nancy Mitford was admired both for her novels and for her two nonfiction works, among them* The Pursuit of Love, The Sun King, *and* Voltaire in Love. *"A Bad Time," written in 1962 and published posthumously in a collection of essays,* The Water Beetle, *chronicles Captain Scott's ill-fated expedition in 1910 to the South Pole.*

1   Apsley Cherry Garrard has said that 'polar exploration is at once the cleanest and most isolated way of having a bad time that has yet been devised'.[1] Nobody could deny that he and the twenty-four other members of Captain Scott's expedition to the South Pole had a bad time; in fact, all other bad times, embarked on by men of their own free

---

[1]Unless otherwise stated, the quotations in this essay are from *The Worst Journey in the World,* by Cherry Garrard.

will, pale before it. Theirs is the last of the great classic explorations; their equipment, though they lived in our century, curiously little different from that used by Captain Cook. Vitamin pills would probably have saved the lives of the Polar party, so would a wireless transmitter; an electric torch have mitigated the misery of the Winter Journey. How many things which we take completely as a matter of course had not yet been invented, such a little time ago! Scott's *Terra Nova* had the advantage over Cook's *Resolution* of steam as well as sail. Even this was a mixed blessing, as it involved much hateful shovelling, while the coal occupied space which could have been put to better account in the little wooden barque (764 tons). Three motor-sledges lashed to the deck seemed marvellously up-to-date and were the pride and joy of Captain Scott.

2   The *Terra Nova* sailed from London 15th June 1910 and from New Zealand 26th November. She was fearfully overloaded; on deck, as well as the motor-sledges in their huge crates, there were 30 tons of coal in sacks, 2½ tons of petrol in drums, 33 dogs, and 19 ponies. She rode out a bad storm by a miracle. 'Bowers and Campbell were standing upon the bridge and the ship rolled sluggishly over until the lee combings of the main hatch were under the sea . . . as a rule, if a ship goes that far over she goes down.' It took her thirty-eight days to get to McMurdo Sound,[2] by which time the men were in poor shape. They had slept in their clothes, lucky if they got five hours a night, and had had no proper meals. As soon as they dropped anchor they began to unload the ship. This entailed dragging its cargo over ice floes which were in constant danger of being tipped up by killer whales, a very tricky business, specially when it came to moving ponies, motor sledges and a pianola. Then they built the Hut which was henceforward to be their home. Scott, tireless himself, always drove his men hard and these things were accomplished in a fortnight. The *Terra Nova* sailed away; she was to return the following summer, when it was hoped that the Polar party would be back in time to be taken off before the freezing up of the sea forced her to leave again. If not, they would be obliged to spend a second winter on McMurdo Sound. Winter, of course, in those latitudes, happens during our summer months and is perpetual night, as the summer is perpetual day. The stunning beauty of the scenery affected the men deeply. When the sun shone the snow was never white, but brilliant shades of pink, blue and lilac; in winter the aurora australis[3] flamed across the sky and the summit of Mount Erebus glowed.

[2]An inlet along the coast of Antarctica on the Ross Sea directly south of New Zealand. [ed.]
[3]The "southern lights"; these colored lights flash in the sky at night in the southern hemisphere. The "northern lights," seen in the Arctic Circle, are called aurora borealis. [ed.]

3   The Hut, unlike so much of Scott's equipment, was a total success. It was built on the shore, too near the sea, perhaps, for absolute security in the cruel winter storms, under the active volcano Mount Erebus, called after the ship in which Ross discovered these regions in 1839. It was 50 feet by 25, 9 feet high. The walls had double boarding inside and outside the frames, with layers of quilted seaweed between the boards. The roof had six layers of alternate wood, rubber and seaweed. Though 109 degrees of frost was quite usual, the men never suffered from cold indoors; in fact, with twenty-five of them living there, the cooking range at full blast and a stove at the other end, they sometimes complained of stuffiness.

4   Life during the first winter was very pleasant. Before turning in for good they had done several grueling marches, laying stores in depots along the route of the Polar journey; they felt they needed and had earned a rest. Their only complaint was that there were too many lectures; Scott insisted on at least three a week and they seem to have bored the others considerably—except for Ponting's magic lantern slides of Japan. A gramophone and a pianola provided background music and there was a constant flow of witticisms which one assumes to have been unprintable until one learns that Dr Wilson would leave the company if a coarse word were spoken. In the Hut they chiefly lived on flesh of seals, which they killed without difficulty, since these creatures are friendly and trustful by nature. 'A sizzling on the fire and a smell of porridge and seal liver heralded breakfast which was at 8 a.m. in theory and a good deal later in practice.' Supper was at 7. Most were in their bunks by 10 p.m., sometimes with a candle and a book; the acetylene was turned off at 10.30 to economize the fuel. Cherry Garrard tells us that the talk at meals was never dull. Most of these men were from the Royal Navy, and sailors are often droll, entertaining fellows possessing much out-of-the-way information. (Nobody who heard them can have forgotten the performances of Commander Campbell on the B.B.C.—he was one of the greatest stars they ever had, in my view.) Heated arguments would break out on a diversity of subjects, to be settled by recourse to an encyclopedia or an atlas or sometimes a Latin dictionary. They wished they had also brought a *Who's Who*. One of their discussions, which often recurred, concerned 'Why are we here? What is the force that drives us to undergo severe, sometimes ghastly hardships of our own free will?' The reply was The Interests of Science—it is important that man should know the features of the world he lives in, but this was not a complete answer. Once there was a discussion as to whether they would continue to like Polar travel if, by the aid of modern inventions, it became quite easy and comfortable. They said no, with one accord. It seems as if they really wanted to prove to themselves how much they could endure. Their rewards were a deep spiritual satisfaction and relationships between men who had become more than brothers.

5   Their loyalty to each other was fantastic—there was no jealousy, bickering, bullying or unkindness. Reading between the lines of their diaries and records it is impossible to guess whether anybody disliked anybody else. As for The Owner, as they called Scott, they all worshipped and blindly followed him. Cherry Garrard, the only one who could be called an intellectual and who took a fairly objective view of the others, gives an interesting account of Scott's character: subtle, he says, full of light and shade. No sense of humour—peevish by nature, highly strung, irritable, melancholy and moody. However, such was his strength of mind that he overcame these faults, though he could not entirely conceal long periods of sadness. He was humane, so fond of animals that he refused to take dogs on long journeys, hauling the sledge himself rather than see them suffer. His idealism and intense patriotism shone through all he wrote. Of course, he had the extraordinary charm without which no man can be a leader. In his diaries he appears as an affectionate person, but shyness or the necessary isolation of a sea-captain prevented him from showing this side to the others. He was poor; he worried about provision for his family when it became obvious that he would never return to them. Indeed, he was always hampered by lack of money and never had enough to finance his voyages properly. Lady Kennet, his widow, once told me that Scott only took on Cherry Garrard because he subscribed £2,000 to the expedition. He thought him too young (23), too delicate and too short-sighted, besides being quite inexperienced; he was the only amateur in the party. It is strange and disgraceful that Scott, who was already a world-famous explorer, should have had so little support from the Government for this prestigious voyage.

6   These men had an enemy, not with them in the Hut but ever present in their minds. His shadow fell across their path before they left New Zealand, when Captain Scott received a telegram dated from Madeira, with the laconic message *Am going South Amundsen.* Now, Amundsen[4] was known to be preparing Nansen's[5] old ship, the *Fram,* for a journey, having announced that he intended to do some further exploring in the Arctic. Only when he was actually at sea did he tell his crew that he was on his way to try and reach the South Pole. There seemed something underhand and unfair about this. Scott's men were furious; they talked of finding the Amundsen party and having it out with them, but Scott put a good face on it and pretended not to mind at all. The two leaders could hardly have been more different. Amundsen was cleverer than Scott, 'an explorer of a markedly intellectual type rather Jewish than Scandinavian'. There was not much humanity or idealism about him, he was a tough,

---

[4]Roald Amundsen (1872–1928), Norwegian Arctic and Antarctic explorer. [ed.]
[5]Fridtjof Nansen (1861–1930), Norwegian Arctic explorer. [ed.]

brave professional. He had a sense of humour and his description of flying over the North Pole in a dirigible with General Nobile is very funny indeed. Nobile was for ever in tears and Amundsen on the verge of striking him, the climax coming when, over the Pole, Nobile threw out armfuls of huge Italian flags which caught in the propeller and endangered their lives. All the same, Amundsen died going to the rescue of Nobile in 1928.

7   No doubt the knowledge that 'the Norskies' were also on their way to the Pole was a nagging worry to Scott all those long, dark, winter months, though he was very careful to hide his feelings and often remarked that Amundsen had a perfect right to go anywhere at any time. 'The Pole is not a race,' he would say. He (Scott) was going in the interests of science and not in order to 'get there first'. But he knew that everybody else would look on it as a race; he was only human, he longed to win it.

8   The chief of Scott's scientific staff and his greatest friend was Dr Wilson. He was to Scott what Sir Joseph Hooker had been to Ross. (Incredible as it seems, Hooker only died that very year, 1911. Scott knew him well.) Wilson was a doctor of St George's Hospital and a zoologist specializing in vertebrates. He had published a book on whales, penguins and seals and had prepared a report for the Royal Commission on grouse disease. While he was doing this Cherry Garrard met him, at a shooting lodge in Scotland, and became fired with a longing to go south. Wilson was an accomplished water-colourist. Above all, he was an adorable person: 'The finest character I ever met,' said Scott. Now Dr Wilson wanted to bring home the egg of an Emperor Penguin.[6] He had studied these huge creatures when he was with Scott on his first journey to the Antarctic and thought that their embryos would be of paramount biological interest, possibly proving to be the missing link between bird and fish. The Emperors, who weigh 6½ stone,[7] look like sad little men and were often taken by early explorers for human natives of the South Polar regions, are in a low state of evolution (and of spirits). They lay their eggs in the terrible mid-winter, because only thus can their chicks, which develop with a slowness abnormal in birds, be ready to survive the next winter. They never step on shore, even to breed; they live in rookeries on sea-ice. To incubate their eggs, they balance them on their enormous feet and press them against a patch of bare skin on the abdomen protected from the cold by a lappet of skin and feathers. Paternity is the only joy known to these wretched birds and a monstrous instinct for it is implanted in their breasts; male and female hatch out the eggs and nurse the chicks, also on their feet, indiscrimi-

---

[6]See David Attenborough's essay, "Penguins," at the end of Chapter 4 for a similar description. [ed.]
[7]A British unit of weight equalling 14 pounds. Six and a half stone is about 90 pounds. [ed.]

nately. When a penguin has to go in the sea to catch his dinner he leaves egg or chick on the ice; there is then a mad scuffle as twenty childless birds rush to adopt it, quite often breaking or killing it in the process. They will nurse a dead chick until it falls to pieces and sit for months on an addled egg or even a stone. All this happens in darkness and about a hundred degrees of frost. I often think the R.S.P.C.A.[8] ought to do something for the Emperor Penguins.

9   Dr Wilson had reason to suppose that there was a rookery of Emperors at Cape Crozier, about sixty miles along the coast. When the ghastly winter weather had properly set in he asked for two volunteers to go with him and collect some eggs. It was one of the rules in the Hut that everybody volunteered for everything, so Wilson really chose his own companions: 'Birdie' Bowers, considered by Scott to be the hardest traveller in the world, and Cherry Garrard. The three of them left the light and warmth and good cheer of the Hut to embark upon the most appalling nightmare possible to imagine. The darkness was profound and invariable. (They steered by Jupiter.) The temperature was generally in the region of 90 degrees of frost, unless there was a blizzard, when it would rise as high as 40 degrees of frost, producing other forms of discomfort and the impossibility of moving. The human body exudes a quantity of sweat and moisture, even in the lowest temperatures, so the men's clothes were soon frozen as stiff as boards and they were condemned to remain in the bending position in which they pulled their sleigh. It was as though they were dressed in lead. The surface of the snow was so bad that they had to divide their load and bring it along by relays. They could never take off their huge gloves for fear of losing their hands by frostbite; as it was, their fingers were covered with blisters in which the liquid was always frozen, so that their hands were like bunches of marbles. The difficulty of performing the simplest action with them may be imagined; it sometimes took over an hour to light a match and as much as nine hours to pitch their tent and do the work of the camp. Everything was slow, slow. When they had a discussion it lasted a week. If Cherry Garrard had written his book in a more uninhibited age he would no doubt have told us how they managed about what the Americans call going to the bathroom.[9] As it is, this interesting point remains mysterious. Dr Wilson insisted on them spending seven hours out of the twenty-four (day and night in that total blackness were quite arbitrary) in their sleeping-bags. These were always frozen up, so that it took at least an hour to worm their way in and then they suffered the worst of all the tortures. Normally on such journeys the great comfort was sleep. Once in their warm dry sleeping-bags

---

[8]Royal Society for the Prevention of Cruelty to Animals [ed.]
[9]'They [the savages] go to the bathroom in the street.' (Report from a member of the Peace Corps in the Congo).

the men went off as if they were drugged and nothing, neither pain nor worry, could keep them awake. But now the cold was too intense for Wilson and Cherry Garrard to close an eye. They lay shivering until they thought their backs would break, enviously listening to the regular snores of Birdie. They had got a spirit lamp—the only bearable moments they knew were when they had just swallowed a hot drink; for a little while it was like a hot-water bottle on their hearts; but the effect soon wore off. Their teeth froze and split to pieces. Their toe-nails came away. Cherry Garrard began to long for death. It never occurred to any of them to go back. The penguin's egg assumed such importance in their minds, as they groped and plodded their four or five miles a day, that the whole future of the human race might have depended on their finding one.

10   At last, in the bleakest and most dreadful place imaginable, they heard the Emperors calling. To get to the rookery entailed a long, dangerous feat of mountaineering, since it was at the foot of an immense cliff. Dim twilight now glowed for an hour or two at midday, so they were able to see the birds, about a hundred of them, mournfully huddled together, trying to shuffle away from the intruders without losing the eggs from their feet and trumpeting with curious metallic voices. The men took some eggs, got lost on the cliff, were nearly killed several times by falling into crevasses and broke all the eggs but two. That night there was a hurricane and their tent blew away, carried out to sea, no doubt. Now that they faced certain death, life suddenly seemed more attractive. They lay in their sleeping-bags for two days waiting for the wind to abate and pretending to each other that they would manage somehow to get home without a tent, although they knew very well that they must perish. When it was possible to move again Bowers, by a miracle, found the tent. 'We were so thankful we said nothing.' They could hardly remember the journey home—it passed like a dreadful dream, and indeed they often slept while pulling their sleigh. When they arrived, moribund, at the Hut, exactly one month after setting forth, The Owner said: 'Look here, you know, this is the hardest journey that has ever been done.'

11   I once recounted this story to a hypochondriac friend, who said, horrified, 'But it must have been so *bad* for them.' The extraordinary thing is that it did them no harm. They were quite recovered three months later, in time for the Polar journey, from which, of course, Wilson and Bowers did not return, but which they endured longer than any except Scott himself. Cherry Garrard did most of the Polar journey; he went through the 1914 war, in the trenches much of the time, and lived until 1959.

12   As for the penguins' eggs, when Cherry Garrard got back to London the first thing he did was to take them to the Natural History Museum. Alas, nobody was very much interested in them. The Chief Custodian, when he received Cherry Garrard after a good long delay, simply put

them down on an ink stand and went on talking to a friend. Cherry Garrard asked if he could have a receipt for the eggs? 'It's not necessary. It's all right. You needn't wait,' he was told.

13 The Winter Journey was so appalling that the journey to the Pole, which took place in daylight and in much higher temperatures seemed almost banal by comparison; but it was terribly long (over seven hundred miles each way) and often very hard. Scott left the Hut at 11 p.m. on 1st November. He soon went back, for a book; was undecided what to take, but finally chose a volume of Browning. He was accompanied by a party of about twenty men with two motor-sledges (the third had fallen into the sea while being landed), ponies and dogs. Only four men were to go to the Pole, but they were to be accompanied until the dreaded Beardmore glacier had been climbed. The men in charge of the motors turned back first, the motors having proved a failure. They delayed the party with continual breakdowns and only covered fifty miles. The dogs and their drivers went next. The ponies were shot at the foot of the glacier. The men minded this; they had become attached to the beasts, who had done their best, often in dreadful conditions. So far the journey had taken longer than it should have. The weather was bad for travelling, too warm, the snow too soft; there were constant blizzards. Now they were twelve men, without ponies or dogs, man-hauling the sledges. As they laboured up the Beardmore, Scott was choosing the men who would go to the Pole with him. Of course, the disappointment of those who were sent home at this stage was acute; they had done most of the gruelling journey and were not to share in the glory. On 20th December Cherry Garrard wrote: 'This evening has been rather a shock. As I was getting my finesko on to the top of my ski Scott came up to me and said he had rather a blow for me. Of course, I knew what he was going to say, but could hardly grasp that I was going back—tomorrow night. . . . Wilson told me it was a toss-up whether Titus [Oates] or I should go on; that being so I think Titus will help him more than I can. I said all I could think of—he seemed so cut up about it, saying "I think somehow it is specially hard on you." I said I hoped I had not disappointed him and he caught hold of me and said "No, no—no", so if that is the case all is well.'

14 There was still one more party left to be sent back after Cherry Garrard's. Scott said in his diary: 'I dreaded this necessity of choosing, nothing could be more heartrending.' He added: 'We are struggling on, considering all things against odds. The weather is a constant anxiety.' The weather was against them; the winter which succeeded this disappointing summer set in early and was the worst which hardened Arctic travellers had ever experienced.

15 Scott had always intended to take a party of four to the Pole. He now made the fatal decision to take five. Oates was the last-minute choice; it is thought that Scott felt the Army ought to be represented.

So they were: Scott aged 43, Wilson 39, Seaman Evans 37, Bowers 28, and Oates 32. The extra man was *de trop*[10] in every way. There were only four pairs of skis; the tent was too small for five, so that one man was too near the outside and always cold; worst of all, there were now five people to eat rations meant for four. It was an amazing mistake, but it showed that Scott thought he was on a good wicket.[11] The returning parties certainly thought so; it never occurred to them that he would have much difficulty, let alone that his life might be in danger. But they were all more exhausted than they knew and the last two parties only got home by the skin of their teeth, after hair-raising experiences on the Beardmore. Scott still had 150 miles to go.

16   On 16th January, only a few miles from the Pole, Bowers spied something in the snow—an abandoned sledge. Then they came upon dog tracks. Man Friday's footsteps on the sand were less dramatic. They knew that the enemy had won. 'The Norwegians have forestalled us,' wrote Scott, 'and are first at the Pole. . . . All the day dreams must go; it will be a wearisome return'. And he wrote at the Pole itself: 'Great God! This is an awful place!'

17   Amundsen had left his base on 20th October with three other men, all on skis, and sixty underfed dogs to pull his sleighs. He went over the Axel Herberg glacier, an easier climb than the Beardmore, and reached the Pole on 16th December with no more discomfort than on an ordinary Antarctic journey. His return only took thirty-eight days, by which time he had eaten most of the dogs, beginning with his own favourite. When the whole story was known there was a good deal of feeling in England over these animals. At the Royal Geographical Society's dinner to Amundsen the President, Lord Curzon, infuriated his guest by ending his speech with the words, 'I think we ought to give three cheers for the dogs.'

18   And now for the long pull home. Evans was dying, of frostbite and concussion from a fall. He never complained, just staggered along, sometimes wandering in his mind. The relief when he died was tremendous, as Scott had been tormented by feeling that perhaps he ought to abandon him, for the sake of the others. When planning the Winter Journey, Wilson had told Cherry Garrard that he was against taking seamen on the toughest ventures—he said they simply would not look after themselves. Indeed, Evans had concealed a wound on his hand which was the beginning of his troubles. A month later, the party was again delayed, by Oates's illness; he was in terrible pain from frostbitten feet. He bravely committed suicide, but too late to save the others. Scott wrote: 'Oates' last thoughts were of his mother, but immediately before he took pride in thinking that his regiment would be pleased at the

[10]French for "too much." [ed.]
[11]A British expression, derived from the sport of cricket, meaning "in a good situation." [ed.]

bold way in which he met his death. . . . He was a brave soul. He slept through the night, hoping not to wake; but he woke in the morning, yesterday. It was blowing a blizzard. He said "I am just going outside and may be some time.'"

19   All, now, were ill. Their food was short and the petrol for their spirit lamp, left for them in the depots, had mostly evaporated. The horrible pemmican,[12] with its low vitamin content, which was their staple diet was only bearable when made into a hot stew. Now they were eating it cold, keeping the little fuel they had to make hot cocoa. (This business of the petrol was very hard on the survivors. When on their way home, the returning parties had made use of it, carefully taking much less than they were told was their share. They always felt that Scott, who never realized that it had evaporated, must have blamed them in his heart for the shortage.) Now the weather changed. 'They were in evil case but they would have been all right if the cold had not come down upon them; unexpected, unforetold and fatal. The cold in itself was not so tremendous until you realize that they had been out four months, that they had fought their way up the biggest glacier in the world, in feet of soft snow, that they had spent seven weeks under plateau conditions of rarified air, big winds and low temperatures.' They struggled on and might just have succeeded in getting home if they had had ordinary good luck. But, eleven miles from the depot which would have saved them, a blizzard blew up so that they could not move. It blew for a week, at the end of which there was no more hope. On 29th March Scott wrote:

> My dear Mrs Wilson. If this reaches you, Bill and I will have gone out together. We are very near it now and I should like you to know how splendid he was at the end—everlastingly cheerful and ready to sacrifice himself for others, never a word of blame to me for leading him into this mess. He is suffering, luckily, only minor discomforts.
>
> His eyes have a comfortable blue look of hope and his mind is peaceful with the satisfaction of his faith, in regarding himself as part of the great scheme of the Almighty. I can do no more to comfort you than to tell you that he died, as he lived, a brave, true man—the best of comrades and staunchest of friends. My whole heart goes out to you in pity.
>
> Yours R. Scott.

20   And to Sir James Barrie:[13]

21   'We are pegging out[14] in a very comfortless spot . . . I am not at all afraid of the end but sad to miss many a humble pleasure which I had planned for the future on our long marches. . . . We have had four days of storm

---

[12]A food consisting of dried strips of meat pounded into paste, mixed with fat and berries, and formed into little cakes; used for emergency rations. [ed.]
[13]Author of "Peter Pan." [ed.]
[14]A British euphemism for "dying." [ed.]

in our tent and nowhere's food or fuel. We did intend to finish ourselves when things proved like this but we have decided to die naturally in the track.'

22   On 19th March Cherry Garrard and the others in the Hut, none of them fit, began to be worried. The *Terra Nova* had duly come back, with longed-for mails and news of the outer world. They had to let her go again, taking those who were really ill. On 27th March Atkinson, the officer in charge, and a seaman went a little way to try and meet the Polar party, but it was a hopeless quest, and they were 100 miles from where Scott was already dead when they turned back. They now prepared for another winter in the Hut, the sadness of which can be imagined. Long, long after they knew all hope was gone they used to think they heard their friends coming in, or saw shadowy forms that seemed to be theirs. They mourned them and missed their company. Scott, Wilson and Bowers had been the most dynamic of them all, while 'Titus' or 'Farmer Hayseed' (Oates) was a dear, good-natured fellow whom everybody loved to tease. The weather was unimaginably awful. It seemed impossible that the Hut could stand up to the tempests which raged outside for weeks on end and the men quite expected that it might collapse at any time. When at last the sun reappeared they set forth to see if they could discover traces of their friends. They hardly expected any results, as they were firmly convinced that the men must have fallen down a crevasse on the Beardmore, a fate they had all escaped by inches at one time or another. Terribly soon, however, they came upon what looked like a cairn; it was, in fact, Scott's tent covered with snow.

23   'We have found them. To say it has been a ghastly day cannot express it. Bowers and Wilson were sleeping in their bags. Scott had thrown the flaps of his bag open at the end. His left hand was stretched over Wilson, his lifelong friend.' Everything was tidy, their papers and records in perfect order. Atkinson and Cherry Garrard read enough to find out what had happened and packed up the rest of the papers unopened. They built a cairn over the tent, which was left as they found it. Near the place where Oates disappeared they put up a cross with the inscription: 'Hereabouts died a very gallant gentleman, Captain E. G. Oates of the Inniskilling Dragoons. In March 1912, returning from the Pole, he walked willingly to his death in a blizzard to try and save his comrades, beset by hardship.'

24   In due course Cherry Garrard and the others were taken off by the *Terra Nova*. When they arrived in New Zealand Atkinson went ashore to send cables to the dead men's wives. 'The Harbour Master came out in the tug with him. "Come down here a minute," said Atkinson to me and "It's made a tremendous impression. I had no idea it would make so much," he said.' Indeed it had. The present writer well remembers this impression, though only seven at the time.

25   Amundsen had won the race, but Scott had captured his fellow countrymen's imagination. It is one of our endearing qualities, perhaps

unique, that we think no less of a man because he has failed—we even like him better for it. In any case, Amundsen complained that a year later a Norwegian boy at school in England was being taught that Captain Scott discovered the South Pole.

26   I don't quite know why I have felt the need to write down this well-known story, making myself cry twice, at the inscription on Oates's cross and when Atkinson said, 'It has made a tremendous impression.' Perhaps the bold, bald men who get, smiling, into cupboards, as if they were playing sardines, go a little way (about as far as from London to Manchester) into the air and come out of their cupboards again, a few hours later, smiling more than ever, have put me in mind of other adventurers. It is fifty years to the day, as I write this, that Scott died. Most of the wonderful books which tell of his expedition are out of print now, but they can easily be got at second hand. I should like to feel that I may have induced somebody to read them again.

A.   Comprehension

Choose the answer that best completes each statement. Do not refer to the selection while doing this exercise.

1.   Apsley Cherry Garrard is quoted by Mitford as saying that "polar exploration is at once the cleanest and most isolated way of"
(a) "testing one's ability to endure the elements"; (b) "having a bad time that has yet been devised"; (c) "serving God and country"; (d) "reducing life to its simplest, most elemental terms."

2.   For Scott and his fellow explorers, life during the first winter living in the Hut was (a) miserable and discouraging; (b) filled with relentless hard work and deprivations; (c) pleasant, often amusing, and filled with good company; (d) ominous, portending what was to come.

3.   Mitford emphasizes that the chief characteristic among the members of Scott's party was their intense (a) ambition; (b) competitive spirit; (c) dislike for each other; (d) loyalty to one another.

4.   Amundsen, who also led an expedition to the South Pole at the same time as Scott, was (a) German; (b) Swedish; (c) Norwegian; (d) Russian.

5.   During the ill-conceived search for an Emperor Penguin's egg, Wilson and the other men on the month-long expedition suffered most from (a) lack of food and water; (b) the intense cold and wind; (c) loneliness and isolation; (d) frostbite.

6.   According to Mitford, Scott's fatal error in planning the expedition to the South Pole was his decision (a) to go himself and leave the others behind; (b) to take too many horses and dogs; (c) to take an unproven route that was supposedly a shortcut; (d) to take five rather than four men.

7. Amundsen reached the South Pole first because he (a) had fewer men to worry about; (b) chose an easier glacier to climb than Scott had; (c) had better, more sophisticated equipment; (d) encountered better weather than Scott's party.

8. Mitford writes that, in England, Scott (a) was widely reviled as a failure; (b) was considered to have discovered the South Pole; (c) captured his countrymen's imagination; (d) was posthumously knighted for his bravery.

B. Inferences

On the basis of the evidence in the selection, answer these inference questions. You may refer to the selection to answer the questions in this and all the remaining sections.

1. From paragraph 1 we can infer that (a) Scott had not outfitted his expedition party sufficiently; (b) Scott's expedition was equipped with the latest technological devices; (c) devices invented after Scott's journey might have saved their lives; (d) no number of new inventions could have saved Scott's party.

2. Near the end of paragraph 4 Mitford questions the men's reasons for undertaking such hardships "of their own free will" and strongly suggests that (a) their real reason was to help science; (b) they all had something to escape in their past; (c) their motivation was fame and fortune; (d) they wanted to test their endurance in intolerable conditions.

3. From paragraphs 5, 6, and 17 we can infer that Mitford (a) admired Scott more than Amundsen; (b) admired Amundsen more than Scott; (c) admired both explorers equally but for different reasons; (d) considered both explorers flawed and difficult to admire.

4. From paragraph 9, we can infer that Dr. Wilson and the two men who accompanied him in his quest for an Emperor Penguin's egg (a) were not surprised by the harsh conditions they encountered on their journey; (b) realized the ridiculousness of their mission; (c) lost their perspective about the importance of their mission; (d) suffered long-term effects as a result of the hardships they endured.

5. Look again at paragraph 13. Why were the ponies shot instead of being sent back with the drivers and the dogs? (a) Mitford implies that the ponies were weak and exhausted and could not have survived the trip back to the Hut; (b) Mitford implies that the ponies could not have climbed the Beardmore glacier; (c) Mitford implies that the ponies had become a liability, causing the journey to take longer than it should have; (d) Mitford does not supply a plausible reason.

6. From Mitford's description of Scott's reaction to Amundsen's reaching the South Pole first, we can infer that he felt (a) great anger; (b) bitter disappointment; (c) great relief; (d) acute emotional depression.

C. Structure

1. Find the sentence in the essay that represents the thesis.

_____

_____

_____

2. Mitford's primary purpose is to tell the story of Scott's expedition to Antarctica, but she has a secondary purpose as well. Look through the essay and find the section where she states it. _____

_____

3. Throughout the essay Mitford emphasizes that (a) everything, but especially the weather, conspired against Scott's expedition to ensure its failure; (b) Scott's own weaknesses should be blamed for the expedition's failure; (c) Scott failed to plan his expedition carefully enough, thus ensuring its failure; (d) great explorers should be given more credit for the risks and hardships they endure.

4. From Mitford's description in paragraph 8, we see the Emperor Penguins and their breeding process as (a) ridiculously pathetic and wretched; (b) awe-inspiring; (c) heartwarming, acutely moving; (d) amusing, entertaining.

5. Ironies abound in the events that Mitford describes. Look through the essay and find two or three examples of ironic twists and state them in your own words. _____

_____

_____

6. Using your own words, characterize Captain Scott as a picture of him emerges in this narrative. _____

_____

_____

D. Vocabulary

For each italicized word from the selection, choose the best definition according to the context in which it appears.

1. all other bad times *pale* before it [paragraph 1]: (a) assume more importance; (b) decrease in relative importance; (c) develop a historical significance; (d) gradually become forgotten.

2. *mitigated* the misery [1]: (a) stopped; (b) contributed to; (c) rewritten; (d) lessened.

3. several *gruelling* marches [4 and 13]: (a) physically exhausting; (b) long; (c) patriotic; (d) fatal.

4. sailors are often *droll* [4]: (a) dull; (b) eccentric; (c) comical; (d) weird.

5. settled by *recourse to* an encyclopedia [4]: (a) briefly reading about; (b) turning to for help; (c) fighting over; (d) being amused by.
6. *peevish* by nature [5]: (a) excessively generous; (b) passionate; (c) given to tantrums; (d) ill-tempered.
7. the *laconic* message [6]: (a) terse; (b) rude; (c) taunting; (d) upsetting.
8. of *paramount* biological importance [8]: (a) relatively insignificant; (b) moderate; (c) primary; (d) revolutionary.
9. nurse the chicks *indiscriminately* [8]: (a) in a confused, disorganized way; (b) done at random by both male and female; (c) characterized by hovering or near-smothering; (d) showing great prejudice or favoritism.
10. sit for months on an *addled* egg [8]: (a) unbroken; (b) rotten; (c) precious; (d) stolen.
11. waiting for the wind to *abate* [10]: (a) disappear; (b) increase in intensity; (c) lessen in intensity; (d) shift direction.
12. When they arrived, *moribund,* at the Hut [10]: (a) worn out; (b) starving; (c) elated by victory; (d) at the point of death.
13. seemed almost *banal* by comparison [13]: (a) amusing, comical; (b) dull, trite; (c) of mythic proportions; (d) absurd, ridiculous.
14. what looked like a *cairn* [22 and 23]: (a) a gravesite marked by stones; (b) a stone shelter (c) a pile of stones used as a memorial; (d) a religious shrine built on stones.
15. *induced* somebody to read them again [26]: (a) influenced; (b) offered; (c) required; (d) urged.

E. Questions for Analysis and Discussion

1. In paragraph 1, Mitford writes, "How many things which we take completely as a matter of course had not yet been invented, such a little time ago!" Consider some specific inventions that have been invented in your lifetime and examine the impact they have had on our daily lives.
2. What characteristics of Scott and the members of his party does Mitford appear to admire most?

Selection 8

Solitary Confinement
Nien Cheng

"Solitary Confinement" is a chapter from Nien Cheng's autobiographical work, Life and Death in Shanghai, *published in 1986. It represents the*

account of her persecution and imprisonment in the 1960s during Mao Ze-dong's Cultural Revolution. Because she had been an employee of the Anglo-Dutch company, Shell Oil, Cheng was accused of spying for the British government. Refusing to make a false confession, she was imprisoned for six and a half years. This excerpt relates her arrival at the No. 1 Detention House in Shanghai. (Note: Even though the repression of the Cultural Revolution is now history, the political situation in China remains greatly troubled. In June 1989 the Chinese army fired on students protesting in Tienanmen Square in Beijing for increased democracy, killing hundreds.)

1   The streets of Shanghai, normally deserted at nine o'clock in the evening, were a sea of humanity. Under the clear autumn sky in the cool breeze of September, people were out in thousands to watch the intensified activities of the Red Guards. On temporary platforms erected everywhere, the young Revolutionaries were calling upon the people in shrill and fiery rhetoric to join in the Revolution, and conducting small-scale struggle meetings against men and women they seized at random on the street and accused of failing to carry Mao's Little Red Book of quotations or simply wearing the sort of clothes the Red Guards disapproved of. Outside private houses and apartment buildings, smoke rose over the garden walls, permeating the air as the Red Guards continued to burn books indiscriminately.

2   Fully loaded trucks containing household goods confiscated from capitalist families were parked along the sidewalks ready to be driven away. With crowds jamming the streets and moving in all directions, buses and bicycles could only crawl along. The normal life of the city was making way for the Cultural Revolution, which was rapidly spreading in scope and increasing in intensity.

3   Loudspeakers at street corners were broadcasting such newly written revolutionary songs as "Marxism is one sentence: revolution is justified," "To sail the ocean we depend on the Helmsman; to carry out a revolution we depend on the Thought of Mao Zedong," and "The Thought of Mao Zedong glitters with golden light." If one heard only the marching rhythm of the music but not the militant words of the songs, if one saw only the milling crowd but not the victims and the Red Guards, one might easily think the scene was some kind of fair held on an autumn night to provide the people with entertainment, rather than a political campaign full of sinister undertones designed to stir up mutual mistrust and class hatred among the populace.

4   Both my body and my mind were paralyzed with fatigue from continued stress and strain, not only from the last few hours of the struggle meeting but also from the events of the preceding two and a half months. I had no idea where I was being taken, and I did not speculate. But I was indignant and angry about the way I was being treated, because I had never done anything against the People's Government.

The accusation that I had committed crimes against my own country was so ludicrous that I thought it was just an excuse for punishing me because I had dared to live well. Clearly I was a victim of class struggle. As my friend Winnie had said, since Shell had closed its Shanghai office, the Maoists among the Party officials in Shanghai believed they should bring me down to the level of the masses.

5   Whenever the police vehicle in which I was being transported was forced to halt momentarily, a curious crowd pressed forward to peer at the "class enemy" inside; some applauded the victory of the proletariat* in exposing yet another enemy, while others simply gazed at me with curiosity. A few looked worried and anxious, suddenly turning away from the ominous sight of another human being's ill fortune.

6   In Mao Zedong's China, going to prison did not mean the same thing as it did in the democracies. A man was always presumed guilty until he could prove himself innocent. The accused were judged not by their own deeds but by the acreage of land once possessed by their ancestors. A cloud of suspicion always hung over the heads of those with the wrong class origins. Furthermore, Mao had once declared that 3 to 5 percent of the population were enemies of socialism. To prove him correct, during the periodically launched political movements, 3 to 5 percent of the members of every organization, whether it was a government department, a factory, a school, or a university, must be found guilty of political crimes or heresy against socialism or Mao Zedong Thought. Among those found guilty, a number would be sent either to labor camps or to prison. Under such circumstances, the imprisonment of completely innocent persons was a frequent occurrence. Going to prison no longer carried with it the stigma of moral degeneration or law infringement. In fact, the people were often skeptical about government claims of anybody's guilt, and those unhappy with their lot in Communist China looked on political prisoners with a great deal of sympathy.

7   From the moment I became involved in the Cultural Revolution in early July and decided not to make a false confession, I had not ruled out the possibility of going to prison. I knew that many people, including seasoned Party members, made ritual confessions of guilt under pressure, hoping to avoid confrontation with the Party or to lessen their immediate suffering by submission. Many others became mentally confused under pressure and made false confessions because they had lost control. When a political campaign ended, some of them were rehabilitated. Many were not. In the Reform through Labor camps that dotted the landscape of China's remote and inhospitable provinces, such as Gansu and Qinghai, many innocent men and

---

*The group constituting the working class, who because they do not possess capital, must depend on their labor to survive.

women were serving harsh sentences simply because they had made false confessions of guilt. It seemed to me that making a false confession when I was innocent was a foolish thing to do. The more logical and intelligent course was to face persecution no matter what I might have to endure.

8   As I examined my own position, I realized that the preliminary period of my persecution was drawing to a close. Whatever lay ahead, I would have to redouble my efforts to frustrate my persecutor's attempt to incriminate me. As long as they did not kill me, I would not give up. So, while I sat in the jeep, my mood was not one of fear and defeat but one of resolution.

9   When the jeep reached the business section of the city, the crowds became so dense that the car made very slow progress and was forced to stop every few blocks. The man in the tinted glasses told the driver to switch on the siren. It was an eerie wail with a pulsating rhythm changing from high to low and back again, rising above the sound of the revolutionary songs and drowning all other noise as well. Everybody turned to watch as the crowd parted to make way for the jeep. The driver sped up, and we proceeded through the streets with no further hindrance. Soon the jeep stopped outside a double black iron gate guarded by two armed sentries with fixed bayonets that glistened under the street lamps. On one side of the gate was a white wooded board with large black characters: No. 1 Detention House.

10   The gate swung open and the jeep drove in. It was completely dark inside, but in the beams of the jeep's headlights, I saw willow trees on both sides of the drive, which curved to the right. On one side was a basketball court; on the other side were a number of man-sized dummies lying near some poles. They looked like human bodies left carelessly about. It was not until several months later, when I was being taken to a prison hospital, that I had an opportunity to see the dummies in daylight and discovered that they were for target practice by the soldiers guarding the prison compound.

11   I knew that the No. 1 Detention House was the foremost detention house in Shanghai for political prisoners; from time to time it had housed Catholic bishops, senior Kuomintang officials, prominent industrialists, and well-known writers and artists. The irony of the situation was that it was not a new prison built by the Communist regime but an old establishment used by the former Kuomintang government before 1949 to house Communist Party members and their sympathizers.

12   A detention house for political prisoners was an important aspect of any authoritarian regime. Up to now, I had studied Communism in China from the comfort of my home, as an observer. Now I was presented with the opportunity to study it from an entirely different angle, at close range. In a perverse way, the prospect excited me and made me forget momentarily the dangerous situation in which I found myself.

13   The jeep followed the drive and went through another iron gate, passing the guard barracks and stopping in front of the main building in the courtyard. The two men jumped out and disappeared inside. A female guard in a khaki cap with its red national emblem at center front led me into a bare room where another uniformed woman was waiting. She closed the door, unlocked the handcuffs on my wrists, and said, "Undress!"

14   I took my clothes off and laid them on the table, the only piece of furniture in the room. The two women searched every article of my clothing extremely thoroughly. In my trouser pocket they found the envelope containing the 400 yuan I had intended to give my gardener.

15   "Why have you brought so much money?" asked one of the guards.

16   "It's for my gardener. I was waiting for him to come to my house to get it. But he didn't come. Perhaps someone could give it to him for me," I said.

17   She handed me back my clothes except for my brassiere, an article of clothing the Maoists considered a sign of decadent Western influence. When I was dressed, the female guard led me into another room across a dimly lit narrow passage.

18   A man with the appearance and complexion of a peasant from North China was seated there behind a counter, under an electric light bulb dangling from the ceiling. The female guard indicated a chair facing the counter but a few feet away from it and told me to sit down. She placed the envelope with the money on the counter and said something to the man. He lifted his head to look at me. Then, in a surprisingly mild voice, he asked me for my name, age, and address, all of which he entered into a book, writing slowly and laboriously as if not completely at home with a pen and having difficulty remembering the strokes of each character. That he was doubtless barely literate did not surprise me, as I knew the Communist Party assigned men jobs for their political reliability rather than for their level of education.

19   When the man had finally finished writing, he said, "While you are here, you will be known by a number. You'll no longer use your name, not even to the guards. Do you understand?"

20   I nodded.

21   We were interrupted by a young man carrying a camera with a flash. He walked into the room and said to me, "Stand up!" Then he took several photographs of me from different angles and swaggered out of the room. I sat down again, wishing they would hurry up with the proceedings, for I was dead-tired.

22   The man behind the counter resumed in a slow and bored manner, "Eighteen-oh-six is your number. You will be known henceforth as eighteen-oh-six. Try to remember it."

23   I nodded again.

24   The female guard pointed to a sheet of paper pasted on the wall and said, "Read it aloud!"

25   It was a copy of the prison regulations. The first rule was that all prisoners must study the books of Mao Zedong daily to seek reform of their thinking. The second rule was that they must confess their crimes without reservation and denounce others involved in the same crimes. The third rule was that they must report to the guards any infringement of prison rules by inmates in the same cell. The rest of the rules dealt with meals, laundry, and other matters of daily life in the detention house.

26   When I had finished reading, the female guard said, "Try to remember the rules and abide by them."

27   The man told me to dip my right thumb in a shallow inkpot filled with sticky red paste and make a print in the registration book. After I had done so, I asked the man for a piece of paper to wipe my thumb.

28   "Hurry up!" The female guard was getting impatient and shouted from the door. But the man was good-natured. He pulled open a drawer and took out a wrinkled piece of paper, which he handed to me. I hastily wiped my thumb and followed the woman out of the room and the building.

29   My admission into the No. 1 Detention House had been done in a leisurely manner; the attitude of the man and of the female guards was one of casual indifference. To them my arrival was merely routine. For me, crossing the prison threshold was the beginning of a new phase of my life that, through my struggle for survival and for justice, was to make me a spiritually stronger and politically more mature person. The long hours I spent alone reexamining my own life and what had gone on in China since 1949 when the Communist Party took power also enabled me to form a better understanding of myself and the political system under which I was living. Though on the night of September 27, 1966, when I was taken to the detention house I could not look into the future, I was not afraid. I believed in a just and merciful God, and I thought he would lead me out of the abyss.

30   It was pitch-dark outside, and the ground was unevenly paved. As I followed the female guard, I breathed deeply the sweet night air. We walked around the main building, passed through a peeling and faded red gate with a feeble light, and entered a smaller courtyard where I saw a two-story structure. This was where the women prisoners were housed.

31   From a room near the entrance, another female guard emerged yawning. I was handed over to her in silence.

32   "Come along," she said sleepily, leading me through a passage lined with bolted, heavily padlocked doors. My first sight of the prison corridor was something I have never been able to forget. In subsequent years, in my dreams and nightmares, I saw again and again, in the dim light, the long line of doors with sinister-looking bolts and padlocks outside, and felt again and again the helplessness and frustration of being locked inside.

33   When we reached the end of the corridor, the guard unlocked a door on the left to reveal an empty cell.

34   "Get in," she said. "Have you any belongings?"

35   I shook my head.

36   "We'll notify your family in the morning and get them to send you your belongings. Now go to sleep!"

37   I asked her whether I could go to the toilet. She pointed to a cement fixture in the left-hand corner of the room and said, "I'll lend you some toilet paper."

38   She pushed the bolt in place with a loud clang and locked the door. I heard her moving away down the corridor.

39   I looked around the room, and my heart sank. Cobwebs dangled from the ceiling; the once whitewashed walls were yellow with age and streaked with dust. The single naked bulb was coated with grime and extremely dim. Patches of the cement floor were black with dampness. A strong musty smell pervaded the air. I hastened to open the only small window, with its rust-pitted iron bars. To reach it, I had to stand on tiptoe. When I succeeded in pulling the knob and the window swung open, flakes of peeling paint as well as a shower of dust fell to the floor. The only furniture in the room was three narrow beds of rough wooden planks, one against the wall, the other two stacked one on top of the other. Never in my life had I been in or even imagined a place so primitive and filthy.

40   The guard came back with several sheets of toilet paper of the roughest kind, which she handed to me through a small square window in the door of the cell, saying, "There you are! When you get your supply, you must return to the government the same number of sheets. Now go to sleep. Lie with your head towards the door. That's the regulation."

41   I could not bring myself to touch the dust-covered bed. But I needed to lie down, as my legs were badly swollen. I pulled the bed away from the dirty wall and wiped it with the toilet paper. But the dirt was so deeply ingrained that I could only remove the loose dust. Then I lay down anyhow and closed my eyes. The naked bulb hanging from the center of the ceiling was directly above my head. Though dim, it irritated me. I looked around the cell but could not see a light switch anywhere.

42   "Please, excuse me!" I called, knocking on the door with my hand.

43   "Quiet! Quiet!" The guard hurried over and slid open the shutter on the small window.

44   "I can't find the light switch," I told her.

45   "We don't switch off the light at night here. In future, when you want to speak to the guards, just say, 'Report.' Don't knock on the door. Don't say anything else."

46   "Could you lend me a broom to sweep the room? It's so dirty."

47   "What nonsense! It's past two o'clock. You just go to sleep!" She closed the shutter but remained outside and watched me through the peephole to make sure I obeyed her orders.

48   I lay down on the bed again and turned to face the dusty wall to avoid the light. I closed my eyes to shut out the sight of the wall, but I had to inhale the unpleasant smell of dampness and dust that surrounded me. In the distance, I heard faintly the crescendo of noise from the crowds on the streets. While it no longer menaced me, I worried about my daughter. I hoped my removal to the detention house would free her from any further pressure to denounce me. If that were indeed the case and she could be treated as just a member of the masses, I would be prepared to put up with anything.

49   Suddenly a horde of hungry mosquitoes descended on me. I sat up and tried to ward them off with my arms, but they were so stubborn and persistent that I was badly bitten. The itchy welts greatly added to my discomfort and annoyance.

50   Just before daybreak, the electric light in the cell was switched off. In the darkness, the dirt and ugliness of the room disappeared. I could imagine myself elsewhere. It was a moment of privacy and relief; I felt as if a tight band around me had been loosened. But not for long. Soon the narrow strip of sky turned gray and then white. Daylight slowly poured into the cell, bringing its ugly features into focus again. However, during all the years I spent in that prison cell, the short time of darkness after the light was switched off and before daybreak was always a moment when I recovered the dignity of my being and felt a sense of renewal, simply because I had a precious moment of freedom when I was not under the watchful eyes of the guards.

51   Footsteps in the passage approached. "Get up! Get up!" It was the voice of the same guard calling at the door of each cell. I could hear the muted sound of people stirring all over the building, and whispering voices and movements in the cell above mine.

52   The shutter of the small window on the door was pushed open. A young women called, "Water," and pushed the spout of a watering can through the opening.

53   When I told her I had no utensil for the water, she withdrew the can but pressed her pale young face against the opening to look at me. When our eyes met, she smiled. A few days later, I caught a glimpse of a square piece of white cloth pinned on her jacket front stating that she was a prisoner serving a sentence of Labor Reform. After that, whenever there was an opportunity, we would smile at each other to acknowledge the painful fate we shared as prisoners of the state. This silent contact and the flicker of a smile I observed on her pale face came to mean a great deal to me in the years I spent in the detention house. When she disappeared, perhaps having completed her sentence, I experienced a deep sense of loss and felt despondent for days.

54   The shutter opened again. An oblong aluminum container appeared. A woman's voice said impatiently, "Come over, come over!"

55   When I took the container from her, she said, "In future, stand here at mealtimes and wait." She also handed me a pair of bamboo chopsticks that were wet and worn thin with prolonged usage.

56   The battered container was three-quarters full of lukewarm watery rice porridge with a few strips of pickled vegetables floating on top. I wiped the edge of the container with a piece of toilet paper and took a tentative sip. The rice tasted smoky for some reason, and the saltiness of the pickled vegetables made it bitter. The food was worse than I could possibly have imagined, but I made a determined effort to drink half of it. When the woman opened the small window again, I handed her back the container and the chopsticks.

57   In a little while, another female guard came. She said, "Why didn't you eat your rice?"

58   I did eat some of it. May I see a responsible person?" I asked her. Chinese Communist officials did not like to be called "officials" unless they were addressed by their exact titles, such as "Minister Wang" or "Director Chang." Generally speaking, the officials were known as *ganbu,* which the standard Chinese-English dictionary translates as "cadres." Minor officials were usually referred to as "responsible persons," which could mean cadres or just clerks.

59   "What's the hurry? You have only just arrived. When the interrogator is ready, he will call you. What you should do now is to consider the crime you have committed. When he calls you, you must show true repentance by making a full confession in order to obtain lenient treatment. If you denounce others, you'll gain a point of merit for yourself."

60   "I've never committed a crime," I declared emphatically.

61   "Ah, a lot of you say this when you first come here. That's a foolish attitude to assume. Just think, there are ten million people in this city. Why should you have been brought here rather than someone else? You have certainly committed a crime."

62   It seemed pointless to argue with her. But her words convinced me that I was going to be there for some time. The dirt in the cell was intolerable. I simply had to deal with it if I was to live in that cell for another night. Besides, I had always found physical work soothing for frayed nerves. Since I was deeply unhappy to find myself in prison and terribly worried about my daughter, I asked her whether I could borrow a broom to sweep the floor.

63   "You are allowed to borrow a broom on Sundays only. But since you have just come, I'll lend you one today."

64   A few moments later she came back with an old, worn broom, which she squeezed through the small window to me. I pulled the bed around the cell and stood on it to reach the cobwebs. When I brushed the walls, the cell was enveloped in a cloud of dust.

65   The shutter opened again. A sheet of paper was pushed through to me. Looking out, I saw a male guard standing there.

66   "The money you brought here last night has been banked for you. This is your receipt. You are allowed to use the money to buy daily necessities such as toilet paper, soap, and towels," he said.

67   "That's just what I need. Could I buy some now?" I asked him.

68   "You may buy what you need," the man said.

69   "Please get me a washbasin, two enameled mugs for eating and drinking, some sewing thread, needles, soap, towels, a toothbrush and toothpaste, and some toilet paper. Am I allowed to buy some cold cream?"

70   "No, only necessities."

71   Soon he returned with a washbasin decorated with two large roses, six towels with colorful stripes, a stack of toilet paper, six cakes of the cheapest kind of laundry soap, two enameled mugs with lids, a toothbrush, a tube of toothpaste, and two spools of coarse cotton thread. He told me that prisoners were not allowed to have needles in the cell but they could borrow them from the guards on Sundays.

72   The guard had to open the cell door to hand me the washbasin. While it was still open, another male guard brought me the clothes and bedding left me by the Red Guards, as well as *The Collected Works of Mao Zedong* and the Little Red Book of Mao's quotations. After I had signed the receipt for these things, the two guards locked the door and departed.

73   I looked through everything very carefully, hoping to find a hidden note from my daughter. There was nothing. I sat on the edge of the bed, weary with disappointment and sadness. I longed for a moment with my daughter and prayed for her safety. After some time, I felt more peaceful. I decided to tackle the dirty room. What I needed was some water.

74   "Report!" I went to the door and called.

75   It was another female guard who pushed open the shutter and said sternly, "You don't have to shout!" Now what do you want?"

76   I knew from her tone of voice that she would probably refuse whatever I might request. To forestall such a possibility, I quickly recited a quotation of Mao that said, "To be hygienic is glorious; to be unhygienic is a shame." Then I asked, "May I have some water to clean the cell?"

77   She walked away without saying a word. I waited and waited. Eventually the Labor Reform girl came and gave me enough water to fill the new washbasin as well as the one brought from my home with my things. First I washed the bed thoroughly; then I climbed onto my rolled-up bedding to wipe the dust-smeared windowpanes so that more light could come into the room. After I had washed the cement toilet built into the corner of the cell, I still had enough cold water left to bathe myself and rinse out my dirty blouse. When hot water for drinking was issued, I sat on the clean bed and drank it with enjoyment. Plain boiled water had never tasted so good.

78   The midday meal was dry rice and some boiled green cabbage. With a portion of the rice I made a paste that I used to glue sheets of toilet paper onto the dirty wall along the bed so that I and my bedclothes would not touch it while I was sleeping. After that I felt much better. When the guard came to tell me to walk about in the cell for exercise, I said, "May I return the broom, please?"

79   She opened the small window to accept the broom and saw the toilet paper I had pasted onto the wall.

80   "It's against regulations to make changes in the cell," she said. I remained silent, wondering how best to deal with the situation if she should order me to remove the paper. But she only picked up the broom and closed the shutter. A moment later, I heard her upstairs calling from cell to cell, "Exercise! Exercise!"

81   I could hear footsteps of many people walking around and around in the room above mine. When the guard called for everybody to sit down at the end of the exercise period, I heard many prisoners flopping down onto the floor. Evidently in the multiple cell upstairs there were no beds; the inmates were sleeping and sitting on the bare floor. The wall between the next-door cell and mine was too thick for me to hear any sound, but I could hear quite clearly every word spoken aloud in the cell above. The sound of the women prisoners moving overhead and the murmuring of their voices when the guard was not near somewhat mitigated my acute feeling of loneliness and isolation.

82   The contrast of color and shape and the blending of different sounds that please the senses in normal life were completely absent in prison. Everywhere I looked I saw ugly shapes and a uniform shade of depressing, dirty gray. There was nothing other than the guard's cold and indifferent voice of authority to break the ominous silence. Sitting in the cell, I found my gaze straying often to the window. I would stare at the narrow strip of sky through the iron bars for hours at a time. It was not only that light and fresh air came in through the window to sustain my life; the window was also the only channel through which I maintained a tenuous link with the world outside. Often, while my body sat in the cell, my spirit would escape through the window to freedom. One of my most vivid memories of prison life is watching the shifting shadow of the window bars on the cement floor. With its slow movement across the cell, I watched the passage of time while I waited and waited day after day and year after year, sometimes for the next meal, sometimes for the next interrogation, but above all for some political development that would curb the power of the Maoist Revolutionaries.

83   Daylight faded, and the electric light was switched on. I ate another portion of rice and green cabbage. The guard on night duty was another woman. She handed me the newspaper. Putting her face to the small opening on the door, she shouted, "What have you done to the cell?"

84   "I cleaned it according to Chairman Mao's teaching on hygiene," I answered.

85   "If you heed the teaching of our Great Leader Chairman Mao, why are you locked in a prison cell?" she yelled. "Did the Chairman tell you to commit a crime?"

86   "I've never committed a crime. There has been a mistake. It can be cleared up by investigation and examination of the facts," I said.

87   "You have a glib tongue, that I can see. You're trying to bring your capitalist way of life into this place, aren't you? I advise you to think less of your own personal comfort and more of your criminal deeds. Give the matter serious consideration. When you are called, be sure to give a full confession so that you can earn lenient treatment." She closed the small window so that I could not answer back.

88   I was getting very tired of this talk of confession and how it could earn lenient treatment for the prisoner. Perhaps it was true, I thought, that a really guilty person could earn a lighter sentence by confessing voluntarily. But I was not guilty. It was infuriating to be told so often that I had committed a crime when I had not.

89   I picked up the newspaper and stood directly under the feeble light to read it. Like other newspapers in China, the *Shanghai Liberation Daily* was published, financed and completely controlled by the People's Government. The journalists were officials appointed by the Party's propaganda department; their job was to select and often distort news, especially foreign news, for propaganda purposes and to write articles praising government policies. The newspaper is used everywhere in China, including in the prisons, for the education of the people.

90   The Chinese people had long ago learned that the only way to read the newspaper was to read between the lines and pay attention to the omissions as well as to the printed items. In fact, the real source of news for the Chinese people was not the newspaper at all, but political gossip passed from one person to another in low whispers, often in the language of symbols and signs, with no names mentioned. This was called "footpath news," meaning that it did not come openly by the main road, that is, official channels. In the past, before the Communist Party took control of the country, its underground organizations had used "footpath news" effectively to undermine the Chinese people's confidence in the Kuomintang government. Now they themselves were plagued by it. When the people mistrusted the official newspapers and could not obtain news freely, they were naturally more than eager to listen to and believe in whatever they could pick up in the way of political gossip.

91   In the detention house, the *Shanghai Liberation Daily* was my sole source of information about what went on outside the prison walls. I read it very carefully, sometimes going over the same news item or article twice, in order to follow the course of the Cultural Revolution and

evaluate the political development that was taking place. From the way items of news were presénted, the subjects of special articles, the tone of the editorials, and the quotation of Mao Zedong selected for use on a certain day, I could often discern what the Maoists hoped to accomplish or what had not gone according to plan. However, my full understanding of the details of the struggle for power within the Communist Party came only after my release. I succeeded then in gathering together a collection of uncensored Red Guard publications and had the opportunity to question young people who had taken part in the revolutionary activities.

92   When Sunday came around, I asked the guard for the loan of a needle. I joined two of the newly purchased towels to make a seat for the cement toilet, sewed together layers of toilet paper to make a cover for one of the washbasins I used for storing water, and cut up a handkerchief to make an eyeshade to cover my eyes at night. When I asked to use scissors, the guard stood at the small window to watch me, taking them back as soon as I had finished cutting. Doing something practical to improve my daily life made me feel better. I found sewing, in particular, a soothing occupation.

93   Several days passed. I made a request every day to see the interrogator, without result. One sunny morning, the prisoners were told to get ready for outdoor exercise. The guard went to each cell calling, *"Fangfeng!"* ("Out to get air!")

94   Eager for sunshine and fresh air, I jumped up, laid down the book of Mao's I had been reading, and rushed to stand by the door. But I had to wait for quite some time before being let out. The No. 1 Detention House had an elaborate system to prevent inmates of different cells from meeting one another. I had to wait until the prisoner in the cell next to mine turned the corner and was out of sight before being allowed to leave my cell. Guards were posted along the route to watch the prisoners and to lead them to the exercise yards.

95   The exercise yard I was locked into was spacious but in a state of dismal neglect. Broken plaster on the walls exposed the bricks underneath. The ground was covered with dirt and loose gravel. I saw something green in one corner and discovered a cluster of resilient weeds struggling to keep alive. Pleased to see something growing in this inhospitable place, I went over to examine it closely and saw tiny pink flowers at the tip of each stem. Every flower had five perfectly formed petals that were no bigger than a seed. In the midst of dirt and gravel, the plant stood proudly in the sunshine giving a sign of life in this dead place. Gazing at the tiny flowers, which seemed incredibly beautiful to me, I felt an uplifting of my spirit.

96   "Walk about! Walk about with your head bowed! You are not allowed to stop walking!" a guard shouted at me from the raised platform on the walls of the exercise yard. There were two pavilions on the plat-

form, one open and one enclosed with glass windows. As the weather was fine, the guards were watching the prisoners from the open pavilion.

97   I started to walk around in the exercise yard; gradually the heaviness on my chest loosened, and I breathed more easily. The autumn air was cool and dry; the sun was warm on my face. Time passed slowly in prison, with each day endlessly long. But not so during outdoor exercise periods. Even in the depths of winter when my clothes could not keep my starved body warm and I shivered incessantly in the bitter north wind, the outdoor exercise period passed altogether too quickly for me.

98   The male guard who led me back to my cell could not find the right key for the door. While he was trying one key after another, I took the opportunity to make another request to see the interrogator.

99   "I've been here such a long time already. May I see the interrogator?" I asked him.

100   "A long time already?" He straightened up and turned to face me. "You talk nonsense. I know you've been here less than a month. A month is not a long time. There are people who have been here for years, and their cases are not yet resolved. Why are you so impatient? You are always asking to see the interrogator. What are you going to say to him when you do see him? Are you ready to make a full confession?"

101   "I'll ask the interrogator to investigate my case and clarify the misunderstanding."

102   "What misunderstanding?" He appeared genuinely puzzled.

103   "The misunderstanding that brought me here," I said.

104   "You are here because you committed a crime against the People's Government. There is no misunderstanding. You mustn't talk in riddles."

105   "I've never committed a crime in my whole life," I said firmly.

106   "If you have not committed a crime, why are you locked up in prison? Your being here proves you have committed a crime."

107   His logic appalled me. It was based on the assumption that the Party and the government could not be mistaken. I could not argue with him without appearing to offend the Party and the People's Government, so I merely said, "Honestly, I have never committed a crime. There has been a mistake."

108   "Perhaps there was something you did that you don't remember. Prisoners often need help and guidance from the interrogator to confess."

109   "I don't think I could forget if I had committed a crime," I told him. I recalled hearing of cases where the interrogator fed the prisoner with things to say while confessing. All of it was written down and held against the prisoner eventually.

110   "Perhaps you did not realize you were committing a crime at the time. You are probably still quite muddled," the guard said. He seemed quite sincere.

111   Could it be possible that what I considered innocent behavior had really been interpreted by others as criminal deeds against the state? Although I had followed political and economic developments in China carefully and tried to acquire an intelligent understanding of events, I had never studied the Communist government's penal code. I decided to make good this omission without further delay. So I said to the guard, "In that case, I'll study the lawbooks to see if I have indeed committed a crime inadvertently. Will you please lend me your lawbooks?"

112   "What lawbooks? You talk just like the capitalist intellectuals who are being denounced in this Cultural Revolution. You think in terms of lawbooks, rules, and regulations. We are the proletariat, we do not have anything like that." He seemed highly indignant, as if my assumption that they had lawbooks were an insult.

113   "If you do not have lawbooks, what do you go by? How do you decide whether a man has committed a crime or not?"

114   "We go by the teachings of our Great Leader Chairman Mao. His words are our criteria. If he says a certain type of person is guilty and you belong to that type, then you are guilty. It's much simpler than depending on a lawbook," he said. To him, it was perfectly good and logical to have the fate of men decided arbitrarily by the words of Mao Zedong, which varied depending on his priorities during a particular period and were often so vague that local officials could interpret them to suit themselves. The absolute infallibility of Mao's words was a part of his personality cult. But I wondered how the guard would have felt if not I but he had been the victim.

115   After he had locked me into the cell again, I made no further request to see an interrogator. Instead I settled down to study assiduously and seriously *The Collected Works of Mao Zedong*. I wanted to know how his words could be used against me, and I wanted to see if I could not use his words to refute my accusers. I thought I should learn to speak Mao's language and be fluent in using his quotations when the time came for me to face the interrogator.

116   Many weeks passed. One day merged into another. Prolonged isolation heightened my feeling of depression. I longed for some news of my daughter. I missed her terribly and worried about her constantly. Often I would be so choked with emotion that breathing became difficult. At other times, a heavy lump would settle on my stomach, so that I had difficulty swallowing food.

117   Outside the prison walls, the Cultural Revolution seemed to be increasing in intensity. The loudspeaker of the nearby high school was blaring all day long. Instead of revolutionary songs, angry denunciations of local officials and prominent scholars were pouring out. I strained my ears to listen to them, trying to catch a word here and a phrase there when the wind was in the right direction. Within the gloomy cell,

I studied Mao's books many hours a day, reading until my eyesight became blurred.

118   One day, in the early afternoon, when my eyes were too tired to distinguish the printed words, I lifted them from the book to gaze at the window. A small spider crawled into view, climbing up one of the rust-eroded bars. The little creature was no bigger than a good-sized pea; I would not have seen it if the wooden frame nailed to the wall outside to cover the lower half of the window hadn't been painted black. I watched it crawl slowly but steadily to the top of the iron bar, quite a long walk for such a tiny thing, I thought. When it reached the top, suddenly it swung out and descended on a thin silken thread spun from one end of its body. With a leap and swing, it secured the end of the thread to another bar. The spider then crawled back along the silken thread to where it had started and swung out in another direction on a similar thread. I watched the tiny creature at work with increasing fascination. It seemed to know exactly what to do and where to take the next thread. There was no hesitation, no mistake, and no haste. It knew its job and was carrying it out with confidence. When the frame was made, the spider proceeded to weave a web that was intricately beautiful and absolutely perfect, with all the strands of thread evenly spaced. When the web was completed, the spider went to its center and settled there.

119   I had just watched an architectural feat by an extremely skilled artist, and my mind was full of questions. Who had taught the spider how to make a web? Could it really have acquired the skill through evolution, or did God create the spider and endow it with the ability to make a web so that it could catch food and perpetuate its species? How big was the brain of such a tiny creature? Did it act simply by instinct, or had it somehow learned to store the knowledge of web making? Perhaps one day I would ask an entomologist. For the moment, I knew I had just witnessed something that was extraordinarily beautiful and uplifting. Whether God had made the spider or not, I thanked Him for what I had just seen. A miracle of life had been shown me. It helped me to see that God was in control. Mao Zedong and his Revolutionaries seemed much less menacing. I felt a renewal of hope and confidence.

120   My cell faced southwest. For a brief moment, the rays of the setting sun turned the newly made web into a glittering disc of rainbow colors, before it shifted further west and sank below the horizon. I did not dare to go up to the window in case I should frighten the spider away. I remained where I was, watching it. Soon I discovered it was not merely sitting there waiting for its prey but was forever vigilant. Whenever a corner of the web was ruffled or torn by the breeze, the spider was there in an instant to repair the damage. And as days passed, the spider renewed the web from time to time; sometimes a part of it was remade, sometimes the whole web was remade.

121 I became very attached to the little creature after watching its activities and gaining an understanding of its habits. First thing in the morning, throughout the day, and last thing at night, I would look at it and feel reassured when I saw that it was still there. The tiny spider became my companion. My spirits lightened. The depressing feeling of complete isolation was broken by having another living thing near me, even though it was so tiny and incapable of response.

122 Soon it was November. The wind shifted to the northwest. With each rainy day the temperature fell further. I watched the spider anxiously, not wishing to close the window and shut it out. It went on repairing the wind-torn web and patiently making new ones. However, one morning when I woke up, I found the spider gone. Its derelict web was in shreds. I felt sad but hopefully kept the window open in case it should come back. Then I chanced to look up and saw my friend sitting in the center of a newly made web in the corner of the ceiling. I quickly closed the window and felt happy to know that my friend had not deserted me.

123 Towards the end of November one morning, I woke up with a streaming cold and a severe headache. Blowing my nose and feeling miserable, I sat on the edge of the bed wondering whether I should ask for some medicine. When the watery rice was given to me, I made myself drink it up, hoping the warm liquid might give me some relief, but I could not eat the dry rice and boiled cabbage at noon. I returned it to the woman from the kitchen untouched. Throughout the afternoon, the guard on duty came frequently to watch me through the peephole. She made no attempt to speak to me until evening, when she suddenly pushed open the small window and said, "You have been crying!"

124 "Oh, no," I said, "I have a cold."

125 "You are crying. You are crying because you are not used to the living conditions here. You find everything quite intolerable, don't you? We have been watching you trying to improve things. Also you are crying because you miss your daughter. You are wondering what's happening to her," the guard said.

126 "No, really, I just have a cold. May I have an aspirin?"

127 "Aspirin isn't going to help you. What's bothering you is in your mind. Think over your own position. Assume the correct attitude. Be repentant," she said.

128 I sat in the cell for the rest of the evening with my face averted from the door and tried not to blow my nose or wipe my eyes. When rice was given to me in the evening, I ate some and tipped the rest into the toilet, pouring water in to wash it away. Nevertheless, so firmly did the guards believe I was crying because I could not endure the hardship of prison life that they seized on what they thought was a psychological weak moment and called me for interrogation the next day.

A. Comprehension

Choose the answer that best completes each statement. Do not refer to the selection while doing this exercise.

1. Before Cheng was arrested, she observed the Red Guards in Shanghai burning (a) trucks; (b) belongings confiscated from capitalists; (c) Western records and cassette tapes; (d) books.

2. Cheng was accused of (a) writing inflammatory articles against Mao Zedong; (b) socializing with foreigners; (c) committing crimes against her country; (d) hiding people who were likely to be arrested.

3. During the Cultural Revolution, a person was always (a) presumed innocent until he could be proven guilty; (b) presumed guilty until he could prove himself innocent; (c) found guilty no matter what evidence he brought up in his own defense; (d) found guilty only if he or his family owned property.

4. Cheng writes that she firmly refused (a) to go to prison; (b) to criticize the Communist regime; (c) to memorize revolutionary slogans and quotations; (d) to make a false confession of guilt.

5. With respect to her persecutors, Cheng's mood was one of (a) resolution and determination; (b) fear and defeat; (c) terror and anxiety; (d) feigned indifference.

6. The No. 1 Detention House where Cheng was taken was a prison for (a) hard-core felons; (b) potential political exiles—those who were eventually to be banished from China; (c) political prisoners; (d) minor criminals, those who had merely committed misdemeanors.

7. Cheng describes her cell as being (a) tiny and cramped; (b) small but comfortable; (c) austere but clean; (d) primitive and filthy.

8. According to Cheng, the term "footpath news" referred to (a) news that came from official channels; (b) information that was published in the official newspaper, *Shanghai Liberation Daily;* (c) political gossip passed from one person to another; (d) prison rumors.

9. During the Cultural Revolution, a prisoner's guilt was largely determined according to (a) Chairman Mao's words; (b) legal precedents from other revolutionary periods; (c) arbitrary decisions of the guards, prison officials, and judges; (d) laws codified and written down in textbooks.

10. The appearance of the spider in Cheng's cell filled her with (a) dread; (b) hope; (c) homesickness; (d) melancholy.

B. Inferences

On the basis of the evidence in the selection, mark these statements as follows: *PA* for inferences that are probably accurate; *PI* for inferences that are probably inaccurate; and *IE* for insufficient evidence. You may

refer to the selection to answer the questions in this section, and all the remaining sections.

_____ 1. Cheng's husband and daughter were also arrested for political crimes against the regime.

_____ 2. Because Cheng was considered to be a capitalist, her personal possessions and household goods were probably confiscated.

_____ 3. Cheng had not committed crimes against her country; she was persecuted only because she was a victim of a class struggle.

_____ 4. Cheng was considered "well off" by Chinese Communist standards.

_____ 5. If one's ancestors owned land in China, he or she was sure to be persecuted by Mao's Revolutionary Guards.

_____ 6. The only people who were sent to prison during the Cultural Revolution were moral degenerates or people who had deliberately broken the law.

_____ 7. Some people made false confessions of guilt only to receive a more lenient prison sentence.

_____ 8. As would be expected, prison etiquette made informing the authorities about another prisoner's activities unacceptable.

_____ 9. Cheng was squeamish about the living conditions in her cell.

_____ 10. In the No. 1 Detention House, the guards assumed one was guilty merely from the fact that he or she was imprisoned.

_____ 11. Cheng adapted to prison life quickly, by learning to play the game and by spending her time in useful pursuits.

_____ 12. Chinese citizens generally believed every word published in the newspapers and never questioned the veracity of news articles.

_____ 13. The prison officials' refusal to allow Cheng to see an interrogator was probably an attempt to break her spirit.

_____ 14. During the Cultural Revolution, legal precedents for determining one's guilt or innocence were set aside and replaced by a set of arbitrary rules.

_____ 15. The guards were sympathetic about Cheng's cold and realized that she was truly sick.

C. Structure

1. Which of the following sentences *best* expresses the main idea of the selection? (a) The Cultural Revolution was . . . "a political campaign full of sinister undertones designed to stir up mutual mistrust and class hatred among the populace"; (b) "From the moment I became involved in the Cultural Revolution in early July and decided not to make a false confession, I had not ruled out the possibility of going to

prison"; (c) "Often, while my body sat in the cell, my spirit would escape through the window to freedom"; (d) "For me, crossing the prison threshold was the beginning of a new phase of my life that, through my struggle for survival and justice, was to make me a spiritually stronger and politically more mature person."

2. The primary mode of discourse in the selection is (a) narration; (b) description; (c) exposition; (d) persuasion.

3. From Cheng's discussion of the Red Guards' activities before her arrest, we can infer that she felt (a) apprehension and fear; (b) resignation and accommodation; (c) despair and hopelessness; (d) happy excitement and anticipation.

4. Cheng strongly implies throughout the selection that (a) she actually was guilty and was just covering up her past involvement in criminal activities; (b) apart from Mao Zedong, the leaders of the Cultural Revolution were a fairly ignorant lot; (c) she trusted the legal system and believed that she would eventually be vindicated; (d) she believed in the goals of the Cultural Revolution and was merely a victim of its excesses.

5. Look again at paragraph 6. Write the sentence that represents the main idea. _____

   _____

6. The method of development in paragraph 6 is (a) analogy; (b) definition; (c) analysis; (d) comparison; (e) contrast.

7. Look again at paragraph 25. The method of development is (a) example; (b) definition; (c) classification; (d) analysis; (e) cause–effect.

8. In paragraph 29 the method of development is (a) example; (b) illustration; (c) comparison; (d) contrast; (e) analogy.

9. The pattern of organization in paragraph 39 is (a) deductive; (b) variation of deductive; (c) spatial; (d) inductive; (e) chronological.

10. When Cheng quoted Chairman Mao by saying, "To be hygienic is glorious; to be unhygienic is a shame," she was being (a) arrogant; (b) clever; (c) conscientious; (d) virtuous.

11. Cheng's attitude toward her imprisonment and those who imprisoned her can best be described as (a) self-pitying; (b) aggrieved, complaining; (c) straightforward, determined; (d) hostile, belligerent.

12. The spider that took up residence in Cheng's cell helped her to see that (a) persistence always meets with reward; (b) patience is a virtue; (c) God is in control of our lives; (d) God indeed does exist; (e) there is a connection between all living things.

D. Vocabulary

For each italicized word from the selection, choose the best definition according to the context in which it appears.

1. to burn books *indiscriminately* [1]: (a) menacingly; (b) savagely; (c) haphazardly; (d) indifferently.
2. the *ominous* sight [5 and 83]: (a) unusual; (b) welcome; (c) terrifying; (d) threatening.
3. guilty of political crimes or *heresy* [6]: (a) sabotage, deliberate subversion; (b) dissension from established doctrine; (c) looting, pillaging; (d) sabotage.
4. the *stigma* of moral degeneration [6]: (a) mark of disgrace; (b) symptom; (c) presumption; (d) type of behavior.
5. my persecutors' attempt to *incriminate* [8]: (a) falsely imprison; (b) find guilty of a crime; (c) charge with a crime; (d) fabricate criminal charges.
6. a sign of *decadent* Western influences [17]: Characterized by (a) trendiness; (b) deceit; (c) moral decay; (d) inferiority.
7. they must *denounce* others involved [25, 48, and 59]: (a) rehabilitate; (b) openly condemn; (c) give permission to; (d) mildly criticize.
8. I felt *despondent* for days [53]: (a) ill at ease; (b) anxiety; (c) dejected; (d) intimidated.
9. To *forestall* such a possibility [76]: (a) prevent; (b) perdict; (c) give up; (d) get ahead of.
10. their voices somewhat *mitigated* my feeling of loneliness [81]: (a) heightened; (b) intensified; (c) made milder; (d) completely relieved.
11. I maintained a *tenuous* line [82]: (a) tense; (b) stubborn; (c) important; (d) weak.
12. One of my most *vivid* memories [82]: (a) active, lifelike; (b) terrifying, fearsome; (c) unusual, different; (d) pleasant, serene.
13. You have a *glib* tongue [87]: (a) easy, fluent; (b) nasty, vindictive; (c) insincere, superficial; (d) idle, lazy.
14. I could often *discern* [91]: (a) connect; (b) perceive; (c) discriminate; (d) understand.
15. a cluster of *resilient* weeds [95]: (a) having the ability to bounce back; (b) having the ability to reproduce easily; (c) resplendent; (d) unsightly.
16. His words are our *criteria* [114]: (a) words of wisdom; (b) philosophical doctrine; (c) standards for judging; (d) rules to live by.
17. the fate of men decided *arbitrarily* [114]: Describing a decision that is made (a) by a mediator; (b) on one's whim or caprice; (c) under protest; (d) without a rational explanation.
18. The absolute *infallibility* of Mao's words [114]: Incapability of being (a) misunderstood; (b) wrong; (c) acceptable; (d) correct.
19. I settled down to study *assiduously* [115]: (a) with great interest; (b) with little interest; (c) diligently; (d) conscientiously.

20. to *refute* my accusers [115]: (a) turn away; (b) disprove; (c) attack; (d) challenge.

E. Questions for Analysis

1. Compare the political system Cheng describes in this selection with the imperialist system as it is revealed in George Orwell's selection "Shooting an Elephant." What do these systems have in common? What are the differences?

2. What personal qualities or characteristics helped Cheng survive her imprisonment?

3. What do you suppose would be the purpose of the Maoist regime stirring up "mutual mistrust and class hatred among the populace," as Cheng writes at the end of paragraph 3?

Selection 9

Wounded Chevy at Wounded Knee
Diana Hume George

A professor of English and women's studies at Pennsylvania State University, Diana Hume George is a frequent contributor of essays, poetry, and reviews to many journals. Her works have been published in The Missouri Review, The Georgia Review, *and* Spoon River Quarterly. *Her book of literary criticism,* Blake and Freud, *was nominated for the Pulitzer Prize. "Wounded Chevy at Wounded Knee," originally published in* The Missouri Review *and chosen for inclusion in* The Best American Essays 1991 *presents George's personal reflections on Native American culture and what she sees as its imminent demise.*

1   *Pine Ridge Sioux Reservation, July 1989*
"If you break down on that reservation, your car belongs to the Indians. They don't like white people out there." This was our amiable motel proprietor in Custer, South Dakota, who asked where we were headed and then propped a conspiratorial white elbow on the counter and said we'd better make sure our vehicle was in good shape. To get to Wounded Knee, site of the last cavalry massacre of the Lakota in 1890 and of more recent confrontations between the FBI and the American Indian Movement, you take a road out of Pine Ridge on the Lakota reservation and go about eight miles. If you weren't watching for it you could miss it, because nothing is there but a hill, a painted board explaining what happened, a tiny church, and a cemetery.

2   The motel man told us stories about his trucking times, when by day his gas stops were friendly, but by night groups of Indian men who'd been drinking used to circle his truck looking for something to steal—or so he assumed. He began carrying a .357 Magnum with him "just in case." Once he took his wife out to Pine Ridge. "She broke out in hives before we even got there." And when they were stopped on the roadside and a reservation policeman asked if they needed help, she was sure he was going to order her out of the car, steal it, and, I suppose, rape and scalp her while he was at it. As the motel man told us these contradictory stories, he seemed to be unaware of the irony of warning us that the Indians would steal our car if they got a chance and following with a story about an Indian who tried to help them just in case they might be having trouble.

3   He did make a distinction between the reservation toughs and the police. He wasn't a racist creep, but rather a basically decent fellow whose view of the world was narrowly white. I briefly entertained the notion of staying awhile, pouring another cup of coffee, and asking him a few questions that would make him address the assumptions behind his little sermon, but I really wanted to get on my way, and I knew he wasn't going to change his mind about Indians here in the middle of his life in the middle of the Black Hills.

4   Mac and I exchanged a few rueful remarks about it while we drove. But we both knew that the real resistance to dealing with Indian culture on these trips that have taken us through both Pueblo and Plains Indian territories hasn't come from outside of our car or our minds, but rather from within them. More specifically, from within me. For years Mac has read about the Plains Indians with real attentiveness and with an openness to learning what he can about the indigenous peoples of North America. He reads histories, biographies, novels, and essays, thinks carefully about the issues involved, remembers what he has read, informs himself with curiosity and respect about tribes that have occupied the areas we visit. For a couple of years he urged me toward these materials, many of which have been visible around our home for years: *Black Elk Speaks, In a Sacred Manner We Live, Bury My Heart at Wounded Knee,* studies of Indian spiritual and cultural life. While we were in Lakota country this time, he was reading Mari Sandoz's biography of Crazy Horse. But he has long since given up on getting me to pay sustained attention to these rich materials, because my resistance has been firm and long-standing. I am probably better informed about Indian life than most Americans ever thought of being, but not informed enough for a thoughtful reader and writer. My resistance has taken the form of a mixture of pride and contempt: pride that I already know more than these books can tell me, and contempt for the white liberal intellectual's romance with all things Indian. But my position has been very strange perhaps, given that I was married to an American Indian for five years, lived on a reservation, and am the mother of a half-Indian son.

5   I've been mostly wrong in my attitudes, but it's taken me years to understand that. Wounded Knee is where I came to terms with my confusion, rejection, and ambivalence, and it happened in a direct confrontation with past events that are now twenty years old. My resistance broke down because of an encounter with a young Lakota named Mark, who is just about my own son's age.

6   I grew up in the 1950s and 1960s in a small white community on the edge of the Cattaraugus Seneca Indian Reservation in western New York State. Relations between Indians and whites in my world were bitter, and in many respects replicated the dynamics between whites and blacks in the South, with many exceptions due to the very different functions and circumstances of these two groups of people of color in white America. The school system had recently been integrated after the closing of the Thomas Indian School on the reservation. The middle-class whites wanted nothing to do with the Indians, whom they saw as drunkards and degenerates, in many cases subhuman. When I rebelled against the restraints of my white upbringing, the medium for asserting myself against my parents and my world was ready-made, and I grabbed it.

7   I began hanging out on the reserve with young Indians and shifted my social and sexual arena entirely to the Indian world. I fell in love with an idea of noble darkness in the form of an Indian carnival worker, got pregnant by him, married him, left the white world completely, and moved into his. Despite the fact that this was the sixties, my actions weren't politically motivated; or, rather, my politics were entirely personal at that point. While my more aware counterparts might have done some of the same things as conscious political and spiritual statements, I was fifteen when I started my romance with Indians, and I only knew that I was in love with life outside the constricting white mainstream, and with all the energy that vibrates on the outer reaches of cultural stability. My heart and what would later become my politics were definitely in the right place, and I have never regretted where I went or what I came to know. But for twenty years that knowledge spoiled me for another kind of knowing.

8   Whatever my romantic notions were about the ideal forms of American Indian wisdom—closeness to the land, respect for other living creatures, a sense of harmony with natural cycles, a way of walking lightly in the world, a manner of living that could make the ordinary and profane into the sacred—I learned that on the reservation I was inhabiting a world that was contrary to all these values. American Indian culture at the end of the road has virtually none of these qualities. White America has destroyed them. Any culture in its death throes is a grim spectacle, and there can be no grimmer reality than that endured by people on their way to annihilation.

9   I did not live among the scattered wise people or political activists of the Seneca Nation. I did not marry a nominal American Indian from

a middle-class family. I married an illiterate man who dropped out of school in the seventh grade and was in school only intermittently before that. He traveled around the East with carnivals, running a Ferris wheel during the summer months, and logged wood on the reservation during the winter—when he could get work. Home base was an old trailer without plumbing in the woods, where his mother lived. He drank sporadically but heavily, and his weekends, often his weekdays, were full of pool tables, bar brawls, the endlessness of hanging out with little to do. He didn't talk much. How I built this dismal life into a romanticized myth about still waters running deep gives me an enduring respect for the mythopoeic, self-deluding power of desire, wish, will.

10   When I was married to him my world was a blur of old cars driven by drunk men in the middle of the night, of honky-tonk bars, country music, late night fights with furniture flying, food stamps and welfare lines, stories of injury and death. The smell of beer still sickens me slightly. I was sober as a saint through all of this, so I didn't have the insulation of liquor, only of love. I lived the contrary of every white myth about Indian life, both the myths of the small-town white racists and those of the smitten hippies. When I finally left that life behind, extricating myself and my child in the certain knowledge that to stay would mean something very like death for both of us, I removed myself in every respect. I knew how stupid white prejudice was, understood the real story about why Indians drank and wasted their lives, felt the complexities so keenly that I couldn't even try to explain them to anyone white. But similarly, I knew how birdbrained the lovechild generation's romance with Indian culture was.

11   My husband went on to a career of raping white women that had begun during—or maybe before—our marriage. When he was finally caught, convicted, and sent to Attica, I was long since done with that part of my life. My son pulled me back toward it with his own love for his father, and I still keep in touch with my husband's mother on the reservation, sometimes helping her to handle white bureaucracy, but that's all. I heard at a remove of miles, of eons, it seemed, about the early deaths of young men I'd known well—deaths due to diabetes, to lost limbs, or to car wrecks at high speed—and I felt something, but I didn't have to deal with it. When I tried to think about that past life in order to put it into some kind of perspective, no whole picture emerged. When I tried to write about it, no words would come. And when I tried to be open to learning something new about Indians in America on my trips, my heart closed up tight, and with it my mind. When I went to Wounded Knee, the wounds of these other Indians half a continent and half a lifetime away were a part of the landscape.

12   We pull off to the side of the road to read the billboard that tells what happened here. "Massacre of Wounded Knee" is the header, but upon close inspection you see that "Massacre" is a new addition, painted over

something else. "Battle," perhaps? What did it used to say, I wonder, and hope I'll run into a local who can tell me. While I'm puzzling over this, an old Chevy sputters into the pull-off and shakes to a stop. It's loaded with dark faces, a young man and an older woman with many small children. The man gets out and walks slowly to the front of the car, rolling up his T-shirt over his stomach to get air on his skin. As he raises the hood, a Comanche truck pulls in beside him with one woman inside. It's very hot, and I weave a little in the glare of sun. Suddenly I see the past, superimposed on this hot moment. I've seen it before, again and again, cars full of little Indian kids in the heat of summer on the sides of roads. I glance again, see the woman in the front seat, know that she's their mother or their aunt. She looks weary and resigned, not really sad. She expects this.

13   And then in another blink it's not only that I have seen this woman; I have *been* this woman, my old car or someone else's packed with little kids who are almost preternaturally quiet, wide-eyed and dark-skinned and already knowing that this is a big part of what life is about, sitting in boiling back seats, their arms jammed against the arms of their brother, their sister, their cousin. There is no use asking when they'll get there, wherever "there" is. It will happen when it happens, when the adults as helpless as they figure out what to do. In the meantime they sweat and stare. But I am not this woman anymore, not responsible for these children, some of whose intelligent faces will blank into a permanent sheen of resignation before they're five. I am a tourist in a new Plymouth Voyager, my luggage rack packed with fine camping equipment, my Minolta in my hand to snap pictures of the places I can afford to go.

14   When Mac suggests that we offer to help them, I am not surprised at my flat negative feeling. He doesn't know what that means, I surmise, and I don't have any way to tell him. Help them? Do you want to get anywhere today, do you have the whole afternoon? The young man's shoulders bend over the motor. He is fit and beautiful, his good torso moves knowingly but powerlessly over the heat rising from beneath the hood. I recognize him, as well as the woman. He has no job. He talks about getting off the reservation, finding work, living the dreams he still has. He'll talk this way for a few more years, then give up entirely. He drinks too much. He has nothing to do. Drinking is the only thing that makes him really laugh, and his only way to release rage. I also know that whatever else is wrong with it the car is out of gas, and that these people have no money. Okay, sure, I say to Mac, standing to one side while he asks how we can help. Close to the car now, I see that the woman is the young man's mother. These kids are his brothers and sisters.

15   The car is out of gas and it needs a jump. The battery is bad. The woman in the other car is the young man's aunt, who can give him a jump but has no money to give him for gas—or so she says. I know her,

too. She is more prosperous than her relatives, and has learned the hard way never to give them any money because she needs it herself, and if she gives it to them she'll never see it again. She made her policy years ago, and makes it stick no matter what. She has to.

16   Well, then, we'll take them to the nearest gas station. Do they have a gas can? No, just a plastic washer-fluid jug with no top. Okay, that will have to do. How far is the nearest gas? Just up the road a couple of miles. But they don't have any money because they were on their way to cash his mother's unemployment check when they ran out of gas, and the town where they can do that is many miles away. So can we loaned them some money for gas? We can. He gets in the front seat. I get in the back, and as we pull away from the windy parking area, I look at the woman and the kids who will be sitting in the car waiting until we return. She knows she can't figure out how soon that will be. She stares straight ahead. I don't want to catch her eye, nor will she catch mine.

17   Right here up this road. Mark is in his early twenties. Mac asks him questions. He is careful and restrained in his answers at first, then begins to open up. No there's no work around here. Sometimes he does a little horse breaking or fence mending for the ranchers. All the ranches here are run by whites who had the money to make the grim land yield a living. They lease it from the Lakota. Mark went away to a Job Corps camp last year, but he had to come back because his twenty-one-year-old brother died last winter, leaving his mother alone with the little ones. He froze to death. He was drinking at a party and went outside to take a leak. Mark said they figured he must have just stopped for a minute to rest, and then he fell asleep. They found him frozen in the morning. Mark had to come back home to bury his brother and help his mother with the kids.

18   As we bounce over the dirt road, I stare at the back of Mark's head and at his good Indian profile when he turns toward Mac to speak. He is so familiar to me that I could almost reach out to touch his black straight hair, his brown shoulder. He is my husband, he is my son. I want to give him hope. He speaks about getting out of here, going to "Rapid"—Lakota shorthand for Rapid City—and making a life. He is sick of having nothing to do, he wants work, wants an apartment. But he can't leave yet; he has to stay to help his mother. But things are going to be okay, because he has just won a hundred thousand dollars and is waiting for them to send the check.

19   What?

20   "You know the Baja Sweepstakes?" He pronounces it "Bay-jah." "Well, I won it, I think I won it, I got a letter. My little brother sent in the entry form we got with my CD club and he put my name on it, and it came back saying that I'm one of a select few chosen people who've won a hundred thousand dollars. That's what it said, it said that, and I had to scratch out the letters and if three of them matched it means I

win, and they matched, and so I sent it back in and now I'm just waiting for my money. It should come pretty soon and then everything will
be okay." He repeats it over and over again in the next few minutes:
he's one of a select few chosen people.

21   As he speaks of this, his flat voice becomes animated. Slowly I
begin to believe that he believes this. Whatever part of him knows better is firmly shelved for now. This hope, this belief that hundreds of
thousands of dollars are on the way, is what keeps him going, what
keeps him from walking out into the sky—or to the outhouse in the
winter to take a leak and a nap in the snow. What will you do with the
money, I ask. Well, first he is going to buy his mother and the kids a
house.

22   The first gas stop is a little shack that's closed when we finally get
there. Sandy wind and no sign of life. Miles on down the road is a small
Lakota grocery store with only a few items on the shelves and a sign
that reads "Stealing is not the Lakota way." Mac hands Mark a five dollar bill. You can kiss that five bucks goodbye, I say to Mac. I know, he
nods. When Mark comes back out he has the gas, and also a big cup of
7-Up and a bag of nachos. You want some, he asks me? He hands Mac a
buck fifty in change. On the way back I hold the gas can in the back
seat, placing my hand over the opening. Despite the open windows, the
van fills with fumes. My head begins to ache. I am riding in a dream of
flatness, ranch fences, Mark's dark head in front of me wishing away his
life, waiting for the break that takes him to Rapid. Later I learn that we
are in Manderson, and this is the road where Black Elk lived.

23   Mark is talking about white people now. Yes, they get along okay.
For "yes" he has an expression of affirmation that sounds sort of like
"huh." Mari Sandoz spells it "hou" in her books on the Lakota. The
Lakota are infiltrated in every way by whites, according to Mark. Lots
of people in charge are white, the ranchers are white. And there's a
place in Rapid called Lakota Hills, fancy houses meant for Lakotas,
but whites live in them. Later it occurs to us that this is probably a
development named Lakota Hills that has nothing at all to do with
the Indians, but it has their name and so Mark thinks it belongs to
them. I am angry for him that we borrow their name this way and
paste it on our air-conditioned prosperity. I don't have anything to
say to him. I lean back and close my eyes. It would be easy to be one
of them again. I remember now how it's done. You just let everything flatten inside.

24   And when we return to Wounded Knee, the pull-off is empty.
Mother, children, car, aunt, all are gone. There's nothing but wind and
dust. This doesn't surprise me. Mark's mother knows better than to wait
for her son's return if other help comes along. Mark means well, but
maybe she has learned that sometimes it's hours before he gets back
with gas—hours and a couple of six-packs if he has the chance. Now we
face the prospect of driving Mark around the reservation until we can

find them. I have just resigned myself to this when his aunt pulls back in and says they're broken down again a couple of miles up. We can leave now. Mark thanks us, smiles, and shyly allows us the liberty of having his aunt take a picture of all three of us. I am feeling a strange kind of shame, as though I had seen him naked, because he told us his secret and I knew it was a lie.

25   Unemployment, high rates of suicide and infant mortality, fetal alcohol syndrome, death by accident, and drinking-related diseases such as diabetes: these are now the ways that American Indians are approaching their collective demise. Over a century ago, American whites began this destruction by displacing and killing the *pte,* the Indian name for the buffalo the Plains Indians depended upon. We herded them together in far crueler ways than they had herded the bison, whose sacredness the Indians respected even as they killed them for food and shelter. The history of our genocide is available in many historical and imaginative sources. What is still elusive, still amazingly misunderstood, is how and why the Indians seem to have participated in their own destruction by their failure to adapt to changed circumstances.

26   Whites can point to the phenomenal adjustments of other non-Caucasian groups in America, most recently the Asians, who were badly mistreated and who have nevertheless not only adapted but excelled. Indians even come off badly in comparison to the group in some respects most parallel to them, American blacks, whose slowness in adapting seems at first glance to have more justification. Blacks were, after all, our slaves, brought here against their will, without close cultural ties to keep them bound together in a tradition of strength; and on the whole blacks are doing better than Indians. However slowly, a black middle class is emerging in America. What's the matter with Indians? Why haven't they adjusted better as a group?

27   The American Indian Movement is of course strong in some areas, and Indians have articulate, tough leaders and savvy representatives of their cause who are fighting hard against the tide of despair gripping the heart of their race. But they're still losing, and they know it. Estimates of unemployment on the Pine Ridge and Rosebud reservations run as high as 85 percent. Health officials at Pine Ridge estimate that as many as 25 percent of babies born on the reservation now have fetal alcohol syndrome. This culturally lethal condition cannot be overemphasized, since it means that the next generation of Lakota are genetically as well as socioeconomically crippled; one of the consequences of fetal alcohol syndrome is not only physical disability but mental retardation. The prospects are extremely depressing for Lakota leaders whose traditional values are associated with mental acuity and imaginative wisdom. Mark is vastly ignorant and gullible, but he is intelligent enough. Many of his younger brothers and sisters are not only underprivileged and without educational advantages, but also—let the word be spo-

ken—stupid. When the light of inquiry, curiosity, mental energy, dies out in the eyes of young Indians early in their stunted lives because they have nowhere to go and nothing to do, it is one kind of tragedy. When it is never present to die out in the first place, the magnitude of the waste and devastation is exponentially increased. Indian leaders who are now concentrating on anti-alcohol campaigns among their people are doing so for good reasons.

28   Indian leaders disagree about culpability at this point. Essentially the arguments become theories of genocide or suicide. On one end of the spectrum of blame is the theory that it is all the fault of white America. The evidence that can be marshaled for this point of view is massive: broken treaties, complete destruction of the Indian ways of life, welfare dependency established as the cheapest and easiest form of guilt payment, continued undermining of Indian autonomy and rights. The problem with this perspective, say others, is that it perpetuates Indian desperation and permits the easy way out—spend your life complaining that white America put you here, and drink yourself into the oblivion of martyrdom instead of taking responsibility for your own life. Some Indians say they've heard enough about white America's culpability, and prefer to transfer responsibility—not blame, but responsibility—to the shoulders of their own people. "White people aren't doing this to us—we're doing it to ourselves," said one Pine Ridge health official on National Public Radio's *Morning Edition* recently. She sees the victim stance as the lethal enemy now.

29   The situation is as nearly hopeless as it is possible to be. Assimilation failed the first time and would fail if tried concertedly again, because Indian culture is rural and tribal and tied to open land, not urban airlessness. The Indian model is the encampment or village—the latter more recently and under duress—and not the city. Even the more stationary pueblo model is by definition not urban. The only real hope for Indian prosperity would be connected to vast tracts of land—not wasteland, but rich land. Nor are most Indians farmers in the sense that white America defines the farm. Though they might be, and have been, successful farmers under pressure, this is not their traditional milieu. Supposing that many tribes could adapt to the farming model over hunting and gathering, they would need large tracts of fine land to farm, and there are none left to grant them.

30   When the American government gave the Lakota 160 acres apiece and said "Farm this," they misunderstood the Indians completely; and even if Indians had been able to adapt readily—a change approximately as difficult as asking a yuppie to become a nomad moving from encampment to encampment—the land they were given was inadequate to the purpose. Grubbing a living out of the land we have given them, in what John Wesley Powell called "the arid region" west of the one hundredth meridian—takes a kind of know-how developed and perfected by white Americans, and it also takes capital. It is no coincidence

that the large ranches on Pine Ridge are almost entirely leased by whites who had the initial wherewithal to make the land yield.

31   The Sioux were a people whose lives were shaped by a sense of seeking and vision that white America could barely understand even if we were to try, and we do not try. The life of a Sioux of a century and a half ago was framed by the Vision Quest, a search for goals, identity, purpose. One primary means of fulfillment was self-sacrifice. Now, as Royal Hassrick has written, "No longer is there anything which they can deny themselves, and so they have sacrificed themselves in pity." Whereas they were once people whose idea of being human was bound to creative self-expression, their faces now reflect what Hassrick calls "apathy and psychic emaciation." Collectively and individually they have become a people without a vision.

32   Why do they drink themselves into obliteration and erasure? Why not? When white America approaches the problem from within our own ethnocentric biases, we can't see why people would allow themselves to be wasted in this way, why they would not take the initiative to better themselves, to save themselves through the capitalist individuality that says, "*I* will make it out of this." But in fact part of their problem is that they have tried to do this, as have most Indian peoples. They've bought the American dream in part, and become greedy for money and material goods. Life on an Indian reservation—almost any reservation—is a despairing imitation of white middle-class values. In this respect Indians are like all other minority groups in ghettos in America, and this explains why Mark has a CD player instead of the more modest possessions we would not have begrudged him. If he is anything like the Indians I lived with, he also has a color TV, though he may well live in a shack or trailer without plumbing and without siding.

33   Their own dreams have evaded them, and so have ours. Mark and his brothers and sisters have been nourished on memories of a culture that vanished long before they were born and on the promises of a different one, from whose advantages they are forever excluded. Does Mark really believe he has won the sweepstakes? What he got was obviously one of those computer letters that invite the recipient to believe he has won something. Without the education that could teach him to read its language critically, or to read it adequately at all, he has been deceived into believing that a *deus ex machina** in the form of the Baja Sweepstakes will take him out of his despair.

34   In 1890, the year of the final defeat of the Sioux at Wounded Knee, the Ghost Dance was sweeping the plains. Begun by a few leaders, especially the Paiute seer Wovoka, the Ghost Dance promised its practition-

---

*From the Latin, literally "god from a machine"; any unexpected character or event suddenly introduced, traditionally in a play, to untangle the plot or resolve a situation.

ers among the warriors that the buffalo would return and the white man would be defeated. Ghost Dancers believed that their ceremonial dancing and the shirts they wore would make them proof against the white man's bullets. Among the Sioux warriors at Wounded Knee, the willing suspension of disbelief was complete. It made the warriors reckless and abandoned, throwing normal caution and survival strategy to the wind.

35   A tragically inverted form of the self-delusion embodied in the Ghost Dance is practiced today on the Pine Ridge and other Sioux reservations. The original Ghost Dance has beauty and vitality, as well as desperation, as its sources. Now many Sioux men who would have been warriors in another time behave as though liquor and passivity will not kill them. Mark chooses to suspend his disbelief in white promises and to wait for a hundred thousand dollars to arrive in the mail.

36   Hank Doctor was my husband's best friend on the Seneca reservation. He was raunchy, hard drinking, outrageous in behavior and looks. His hair was long and scraggly, his nearly black eyes were genuinely wild, and his blue jeans were always caked with dust and falling down his hips. His wit was wicked, his laugh raucous, dangerous, infectious. Hank was merciless toward me, always making white-girl jokes, telling me maybe I better go home to my mama, where I'd be safe from all these dark men. He wanted me to feel a little afraid in his world, told me horrible stories about ghost-dogs that would get me on the reservation if I ventured out at night—and then he'd laugh in a way that said hey, white girl, just joking, but not entirely. He alternated his affection toward me with edgy threats, made fun of the too-white way I talked or walked, took every opportunity to make me feel foolish and out of place. He was suspicious that I was just slumming it as a temporary rebellion—maybe taking notes in my head—and that I'd probably run for home when the going got too tough. Of course he was right, even though I didn't know it at the time. I liked him a lot.

37   A few years ago, my son Bernie went through a period when he chose to remove himself from my world and go live in his father's, from which I'd taken him when he was three. I didn't try to stop him, even though I knew he was hanging out with people who lived dangerously. I used to lie in bed unable to go to sleep because I was wondering what tree he'd end up wrapped around with his dad. He was a minor, but I was essentially helpless to prevent this. If I'd forced the issue, it would only have made his desire to know a forbidden world more intense. He lived there for months, and I slowly learned to get to sleep at night. Mothers can't save their children. And he had a right.

38   The day I knew he'd ultimately be okay was when he came home and told me about Hank. He wondered if I'd known Hank. He'd never met him before because Hank had been out west for years. Now he was back home, living in a shack way out in the country, terribly crippled

with diabetes and other ailments from drinking, barely able to walk. Hank would have been in his mid-forties at this time. Bernie and his dad took rabbits to Hank when they went hunting so that Hank would have something to eat. During these visits, Hank talked nonstop about the old days, reminding big Bernard of all their bar brawls, crowing to young Bernie that the two of them could beat anyone then they fought as a team, recounting the times they'd dismantled the insides of buildings at four in the morning. He told his stories in vivid, loving detail. His gift for metaphor was precise and fine, his memory perfect even if hyperbolic. He recalled the conversations leading up to fights, the way a person had leaned over the bar, and who had said what to whom just before the furniture flew.

39   Bernie was impressed with him, but mostly he thought it was pathetic, this not-yet-old man who looked like he was in his seventies, with nothing to remember but brawls. I told Bernie to value Hank for the way he remembered, the way he could make a night from twenty years ago intensely present again, his gift for swagger and characterization, his poetry, his laughter. In another time Hank would have been a tribal narrator, a story catcher with better exploits to recount. He would have occupied a special place in Seneca life because of his gifts.

40   My son left the reservation valuing and understanding important things about his father's world, but not interested in living in its grip. He lives in Florida where he's a chef in a resort, and he's going to college. A month ago his daughter, my granddaughter, was born. She is named Sequoia, after the Cherokee chief who gave his people an alphabet and a written language. Bernie took her to the reservation on his recent visit north and introduced the infant Sequoia to her great-grandmother. My husband's mother says that big Bernard is drinking again, using up her money, and she doesn't know how much more she can take. I know she'll take as much as she has to. I hope I'll see Bernard someday soon to say hello, and maybe we can bend together over our granddaughter, for whom I know we both have many hopes.

41   Just before we leave Wounded Knee, I walk over to Aunt Lena's Comanche and point to the tribal sign that tells the story. "It says 'Massacre' there, but it used to say something else." I ask her if she knows what it said before. She looks over my shoulder and laughs. "That's funny," she says, "I've lived here all my life, but you know, I never did read that sign." We're miles down the road before I realize that I never finished reading it myself.

A. Comprehension

Choose the answer that best completes each statement. Do not refer to the selection while doing this exercise.

1. The author decided that the motel proprietor they encountered in Custer, South Dakota, was not a "racist creep," but rather a basically decent fellow with (a) little or no education; (b) a narrowly white view of the world; (c) typically Indian antiwhite sentiments; (d) irrational fears and prejudices.

2. The author confesses that she feels at once pride in her knowledge of Indian life and contempt for those who profess to have a romance with all things Indian, an attitude most often held by (a) the authors of books and articles about Indian life; (b) government bureaucrats like those who work for the Bureau of Indian Affairs; (c) white liberals and hippies; (d) back-to-nature types.

3. When the author became rebellious during her teen years, she (a) did a lot of drugs and read books on Indian religious customs; (b) became a spokesperson for the Indian liberation movement; (c) rejected the white world by running away and marrying an Indian carnival worker; (d) began doing volunteer work on the local Indian reservation.

4. According to George, reservation life is destroying American Indian culture because fundamentally (a) that life is contrary to traditional Indian values; (b) the Indians do not have enough government support to improve their lives; (c) the natural resources in these locations have been depleted; (d) no one in power cares about the Indians' fate.

5. The author confronted her memories and feelings about both her experiences and the situation facing Indians today when she (a) read *Black Elk Speaks;* (b) returned to the Seneca reservation in New York State; (c) took a trip to Wounded Knee in South Dakota and encountered Mark; (d) returned to live with her former husband's family on a Lakota reservation.

6. The history of white genocide of the Indians is well understood, but what is not so well understood is why Indians (a) do not adapt well to urban life; (b) statistically have higher rates of alcoholism than other ethnic groups; (c) have apparently participated in their own destruction by not changing with the times; (d) refuse to be integrated into the larger society.

7. Among all the problems facing Indian tribes like the Lakota, the one that George finds potentially most destructive for the next generation is (a) the high unemployment rates; (b) fetal alcohol syndrome and the resulting retardation and disabilities; (c) a lack of good educational facilities; (d) Indian resistance to change.

8. Essentially, the arguments about who is responsible for the plight of Indians today boil down to a conflict between two factors: (a) unemployment vs. alcohol; (b) the individual vs. the community; (c) white neglect vs. white interference; (d) genocide by the whites vs. Indian suicide.

B. Inferences

On the basis of the evidence in the selection, answer these inference questions. You may refer to the selection to answer the questions in this and all the remaining sections.

1. From paragraph 3, we can infer that the author decided not to argue with the motel proprietor because (a) she knew deep down that he was right; (b) she didn't want to attract others' attention; (c) she knew arguing against him wouldn't change his opinions; (d) she realized that Mac would take his side.

2. Read paragraph 4 again, from which learn that George and Mac's thinking about Indian life comes from different sources. George implies that (a) book knowledge is superior to practical experience; (b) practical experience is superior to book knowledge; (c) book knowledge and practical experience are equally good (d) practical experience has hardened her against anything books might say.

3. From the details George provides in paragraphs 9 and 10, we can infer that her husband was (a) fairly typical of young men who grew up on the Seneca reservation; (b) proud of his Indian heritage; (c) soundly criticized by his family for marrying a white girl; (d) incapable of holding onto a full-time job.

4. George implies in paragraphs 14 and 16 that she agreed to help Mark, the driver of the Chevy, most likely because (a) she wanted to interview Mark and learn about his life; (b) she knew that no one else would stop to help; (c) she felt sorry for Mark's mother and the little kids; (d) she would feel guilty and embarrassed if she told Mac the truth, that she really didn't want to help; (e) she was suffering from "white guilt" and wanted to atone for past atrocities committed against Indians.

5. We can infer from the first part of paragraph 27 that (a) no matter how strong, Indian leaders cannot counteract the terrible influences that are destroying their culture; (b) most Indians find jobs off the reservations; (c) Indian leaders need to work more closely with the government to fund jobs on reservations; (d) the plight of the Indians is reversible.

6. In paragraphs 28–33, George analyzes some reasons to explain the Indians' plight, specifically their willingness to destroy themselves by alcohol. Read this section carefully and decide who, according to George, should bear the *major* part of the responsibility for this situation. (a) She believes that both whites and Indians are equally responsible; (b) She blames the Indians' plight on the failure of the American dream—promising wealth that never materialized; (c) She blames the Indians for adopting a victim's stance; (d) Her own opinion in this controversy is not evident.

7. Mark any of the following reasons that you can reasonably infer from paragraphs 29 and 30 that answer this statement: The Indian

reservations have failed chiefly because (a) the government did not pressure Indians enough to become successful farmers; (b) Indians are traditionally hunters and gatherers who are tied to open land; (c) the government gave the Plains Indians poor land and no money to farm it; (d) Indians simply refuse to make the reservation system work; (e) Indians are incapable of adapting to new circumstances.

8. From what George writes in paragraphs 5, 8, and 11, we can infer that George's thoughts about Indians and their life and culture are (a) straightforward but rigid; (b) ambivalent and confused; (c) hostile, overwhelmingly negative; (d) vague and unformed.

C. Structure

1. Which of these modes of discourse are evident in the essay? (a) narration; (b) description; (c) exposition; (d) persuasion. Defend your choice(s). _____

_____

_____

_____

2. The main idea of the essay is that (a) for various reasons—some historical, some contemporary—American Indian culture is being annihilated; (b) American Indian culture is fighting against harmful white practices; (c) today's American Indians have become people without a vision; (d) many Americans have romantic, misguided, and deceptive ideas about the realities of Indian life.

3. Consider again these words in paragraph 8: ". . . the ideal forms of American Indian wisdom—closeness to the land, respect for other living creatures, a sense of harmony with natural cycles, a way of walking lightly in the world, a manner of living that could make the ordinary and profane into the sacred. . . ." What is the logical relationship between the two groups of words on either side of the dash? (a) cause and effect; (b) general statement and specific examples; (c) steps in a process; (d) comparison; (e) contrast.

4. From George's discussion in paragraphs 20 and 21, we are meant to see that (a) Mark is definitely going to win the lottery; (b) winning the lottery would ultimately not make much difference in Mark's life; (c) Mark's belief that he is going to win the lottery is understandable but pathetically naive; (d) the lottery is just a way for the club to get Mark and members like him to buy more CDs.

5. The logical relationship between the two parts of the first sentence in paragraph 25 (separated by the colon) is (a) steps in a process; (b) general term and a definition of it; (c) contrast; (d) cause and effect; (e) general term and supporting examples.

6. In paragraph 25, consider this sentence, "We herded them together in

far crueler ways than they had herded the bison." What specifically
does the pronoun "them" refer to? _____
And in this sentence from the end of paragraph 27, "When it is never
present to die out in the first place . . . ," what does the pronoun "it"
refer to? _____

D. Vocabulary

For each italicized word from the selection, choose the best definition according to the context in which it appears.

1. exchanged a few *rueful* remarks [paragraph 4]: (a) casual; (b) pointed;
    (c) humorous; (d) faintly sardonic.
2. the *indigenous* peoples of North America [4]: (a) oppressed; (b) native;
    (c) nomadic; (d) alien.
3. my confusion, rejection, and *ambivalence* [5]: (a) mutually conflicting
    feelings; (b) apprehension, dread; (c) compassion, sorrow; (d) shared
    feelings with the community.
4. *replicated* the dynamics between blacks and whites [6]: (a) recalled;
    (b) intensified; (c) segregated; (d) repeated.
5. make the *profane* into the sacred [8]: (a) ancient traditions and
    customs; (b) worldly things; (c) the rule of law; (d) one's elders.
6. a *nominal* American Indian [9]: (a) typical, ordinary; (b) downtrodden;
    (c) brave, fearless; (d) not real, in name only.
7. those of the *smitten* [past participle of *smite*] hippies [10]:
    (a) charmed, affected deeply by; (b) destroyed, damaged; (c) filled
    with pretense; (d) drugged, intoxicated.
8. *extricating* myself and my child [10]: (a) rescuing from harm;
    (b) interrupting, interfering; (c) complicating, straining; (d) releasing
    from an entanglement.
9. kids almost *preternaturally* quiet [13]: (a) excessively; (b) minimally;
    (c) abnormally; (d) impressively.
10. The Lakota are *infiltrated* by whites [23]: (a) openly deceived;
    (b) influenced surreptitiously; (c) well-respected; (d) permanently
    abandoned.
11. approaching their collective *demise* [25]: (a) corruption; (b) transfer;
    (c) degradation; (d) death.
12. still *elusive,* still amazingly misunderstood [25]: (a) unsolved;
    (b) escaping understanding; (c) clear; (d) awe-inspiring.
13. *savvy* representatives of their cause [27]: (a) smart, knowledgeable;
    (b) politically powerful; (c) economically powerful; (d) deeply
    committed.
14. mental *acuity* and imaginative wisdom [27]: (a) adaptability;
    (b) anguish; (c) keenness; (d) cleverness.

15. the *magnitude* of the waste is increased [27]: (a) greatness in size; (b) area of discussion; (c) degree of seriousness; (d) justification.

16. white America's *culpability* [28]: (a) solutions for the problem; (b) responsibility for wrong; (c) political and economic tactics; (d) deliberate suppression.

17. it *perpetuates* Indian desperation [28]: (a) aggravates, makes worse; (b) speeds up; (c) prolongs the existence of; (d) relieves, makes less painful.

18. this is not their traditional *milieu* [pronounced mĭl-yōō´ [29]: (a) behavior; (b) custom; (c) rite of passage; (d) environment.

19. the initial *wherewithal* [30]: (a) necessary financial means; (b) opportunity for advancement; (c) foresight; (d) determination to succeed.

20. his memory perfect even if *hyperbolic* [38]: (a) bizarre; (b) filled with gaps; (c) demented; (d) deliberately exaggerated.

E. Questions for Analysis and Discussion

1. What are the origins of most Americans' attitudes toward American Indians? How does George dispel these attitudes in her essay?

2. It is evident that George harbors many conflicting emotions and attitudes in this essay. Trace these feelings as they emerge stage-by-stage in her chronicle.

3. How effective is George's analysis of the American Indians' plight and the underlying reasons for it? Do you agree with her rather grim assessment or not? What extra information might you need before you could accept or reject her thinking?

Selection 10

The Recoloring of Campus Life
Shelby Steele

Shelby Steele is a professor of English at San Jose State University in California. A frequent contributor to publications like the New York Times Magazine, Commentary, The Washington Post, *and* American Scholar, *Steele writes eloquently and candidly about race relations in the United States. The book from which this selection comes,* The Content of Our Character, *won the National Book Critics Circle Award. The book, subtitled "Student Racism, Academic Pluralism, and the End of a Dream," examines subtle and not-so-subtle recent changes in race relations on American college campuses and analyzes the reasons for them.*

1 In the past few years, we have witnessed what the National Institute Against Prejudice and Violence calls a "proliferation" of racial inci-

dents on college campuses around the country. Incidents of on-campus "intergroup conflict" have occurred at more than 160 colleges in the last two years, according to the institute. The nature of these incidents has ranged from open racial violence—most notoriously, the October 1986 beating of a black student at the University of Massachusetts at Amherst after an argument about the World Series turned into a racial bashing, with a crowd of up to three thousand whites chasing twenty blacks—to the harassment of minority students and acts of racial or ethnic insensitivity, with by far the greatest number of episodes falling in the last two categories. At Yale last year, a swastika and the words "white power" were painted on the university's Afro-American cultural center. Racist jokes were aired not long ago on a campus radio station at the University of Michigan. And at the University of Wisconsin at Madison, members of the Zeta Beta Tau fraternity held a mock slave auction in which pledges painted their faces black and wore Afro wigs. Two weeks after the president of Stanford University informed the incoming freshmen class last fall that "bigotry is out, and I mean it," two freshmen defaced a poster of Beethoven—gave the image thick lips— and hung it on a black student's door.

2   In response, black students around the country have rediscovered the militant protest strategies of the sixties. At the University of Massachusetts at Amherst, Williams College, Penn State University, University of California–Berkeley, UCLA, Stanford University, and countless other campuses, black students have sat in, marched, and rallied. But much of what they were marching and rallying about seemed less a response to specific racial incidents than a call for broader action on the part of the colleges and universities they were attending. Black students have demanded everything from more black faculty members and new courses on racism to the addition of "ethnic" foods in the cafeteria. There is the sense in these demands that racism runs deep. Is the campus becoming the battleground for a renewed war between the races? I don't think so, not really. But if it is not a war, the problem of campus racism does represent a new and surprising hardening of racial lines within the most traditionally liberal and tolerant of America's institutions—its universities.

3   As a black who has spent his entire adult life on predominantly white campuses, I found it hard to believe that the problem of campus racism was as dramatic as some of the incidents seemed to make it. The incidents I read or heard about often seemed prankish and adolescent, though not necessarily harmless. There is a meanness in them but not much menace; no one is proposing to reinstitute Jim Crow on campus. On the California campus where I now teach, there have been few signs of racial tension.

4   And, of course, universities are not where racial problems tend to arise. When I went to college in the mid-sixties, colleges were oases of calm and understanding in a racially tense society; campus life—with its traditions of tolerance and fairness, its very distance from the "real"

world—imposed a degree of broad-mindedness on even the most provincial students. If I met whites who were not anxious to be friends with blacks, most were at least vaguely friendly to the cause of our freedom. In any case, there was no guerrilla activity against our presence, no "mine field of racism" (as one black student at Berkeley recently put it to me) to negotiate. I wouldn't say that the phrase "campus racism" is a contradiction in terms, but until recently it certainly seemed an incongruence.

5   But a greater incongruence is the generational timing of this new problem on the campuses. Today's undergraduates were born after the passage of the 1964 Civil Rights Act. They grew up in an age when racial equality was for the first time enforceable by law. This too was a time when blacks suddenly appeared on television, as mayors of big cities, as icons of popular culture, as teachers, and in some cases even as neighbors. Today's black and white college students, veterans of "Sesame Street" and often of integrated grammar and high schools, have had more opportunities to know each other than any previous generation in American history. Not enough opportunities, perhaps, but enough to make the notion of racial tension on campus something of a mystery, at least to me.

6   To look at this mystery, I left my own campus with its burden of familiarity and talked with black and white students at California schools where racial incidents had occurred: Stanford, UCLA, and Berkeley. I spoke with black and white students—not with Asians and Hispanics—because, as always, blacks and whites represent the deepest lines of division, and because I hesitate to wander onto the complex territory of other minority groups. A phrase by William H. Gass—"the hidden internality of things"—describes, with maybe a little too much grandeur, what I hoped to find. But it is what I wanted to find, for this is the kind of problem that makes a black person nervous, which is not to say that it doesn't unnerve whites as well. Once every six months or so someone yells "nigger" at me from a passing car. I don't like to think that these solo artists might soon make up a chorus, or worse, that this chorus might one day soon sing to me from the paths of my own campus.

7   I have long believed that the trouble between the races is seldom what it appears to be. It was not hard to see after my first talks with students that racial tension on campus is a problem that misrepresents itself. It has the same look, the archetypal pattern, of America's timeless racial conflict—white racism and black protest. And I think part of our concern over it comes from the fact that it has the feel of a relapse, illness gone and come again. But if we are seeing the same symptoms, I don't believe we are dealing with the same illness. For one thing, I think racial tension on campus is more the result of racial equality than inequality.

8   How to live with racial difference has been America's profound so-

cial problem. For the first hundred years or so following emancipation it was controlled by a legally sanctioned inequality that kept the races from each other. No longer is this the case. On campuses today, as throughout society, blacks enjoy equality under the law—a profound social advancement. No student may be kept out of a class or a dormitory or an extracurricular activity because of his or her race. But there is a paradox here: on a campus where members of all races are gathered, mixed together in the classroom as well as socially, differences are more exposed than ever. And this is where the trouble starts. For members of each race—young adults coming into their own, often away from home for the first time—bring to this site of freedom, exploration, and (now, today) equality, very deep fears, anxieties, inchoate feelings of racial shame, anger, and guilt. These feelings could lie dormant in the home, in familiar neighborhoods, in simpler days of childhood. But the college campus, with its structures of interaction and adult-level competition—the big exam, the dorm, the mixer—is another matter. I think campus racism is born of the rub between racial difference and a setting, the campus itself, devoted to interaction and equality. On our campuses, such concentrated micro-societies, all that remains unresolved between blacks and whites, all the old wounds and shames that have never been addressed, present themselves for attention—and present our youth with pressures they cannot always handle.

9   I have mentioned one paradox: racial fears and anxieties among blacks and whites, bubbling up in an era of racial equality under the law, in settings that are among the freest and fairest in society. But there is another, related paradox, stemming from the notion of—and practice of—affirmative action. Under the provisions of the Equal Employment Opportunity Act of 1972, all state governments and institutions (including universities) were forced to initiate plans to increase the proportion of minority and women employees and, in the case of universities, of students too. Affirmative action plans that establish racial quotas were ruled unconstitutional more than ten years ago in *University of California v. Bakke*, but such plans are still thought by some to secretly exist, and lawsuits having to do with alleged quotas are still very much with us. But quotas are only the most controversial aspect of affirmative action; the principal of affirmative action is reflected in various university programs aimed at redressing and overcoming past patterns of discrimination. Of course, to be conscious of past patterns of discriminations—the fact, say, that public schools in the black inner cities are more crowded and employ fewer top-notch teachers than a white suburban public school, and that this is a factor in student performance—is only reasonable. But in doing this we also call attention quite obviously to difference: in the case of blacks and whites, racial difference. What has emerged on campus in recent years—as a result of the new equality and of affirmative action and, in a sense, as a result of progress—is a *politics of difference*, a troubling, volatile politics in which

each group justifies itself, its sense of worth and its pursuit of power, through difference alone.

10   In this context, racial, ethnic, and gender differences become forms of sovereignty, campuses become balkanized,* and each group fights with whatever means are available. No doubt there are many factors that have contributed to the rise of racial tension on campus: What has been the role of fraternities, which have returned to campus with their inclusions and exclusions? What role has the heightened notion of college as some first step to personal, financial success played in increasing competition, and thus tension? But mostly, what I sense is that in interactive settings, fighting the fights of "difference," old ghosts are stirred and haunt again. Black and white Americans simply have the power to make each other feel shame and guilt. In most situations, we may be able to deny these feelings, keep them at bay. But these feelings are likely to surface on college campuses, where young people are groping for identity and power, and where difference is made to matter so greatly. In a way, racial tension on campus in the eighties might have been inevitable.

11   I would like, first, to discuss black students, their anxieties and vulnerabilities. The accusation black Americans have always lived with is that they are inferior—inferior simply because they are black. And this accusation has been too uniform, too ingrained in cultural imagery, too enforced by law, custom, and every form of power not to have left a mark. Black inferiority was a precept accepted by the founders of this nation; it was a principle of social organization that relegated blacks to the sidelines of American life. So when young black students find themselves on white campuses surrounded by those who have historically claimed superiority, they are also surrounded by the myth of their inferiority.

12   Of course, it is true that many young people come to college with some anxiety about not being good enough. But only blacks come wearing a color that is still, in the minds of some, a sign of inferiority. Poles, Jews, Hispanics, and other groups also endure degrading stereotypes. But two things make the myth of black inferiority a far heavier burden—the broadness of its scope and its incarnation in color. There are not only more stereotypes of blacks than of other groups, but these stereotypes are also more dehumanizing, more focused on the most despised human traits: stupidity, laziness, sexual immorality, dirtiness, and so on. In America's racial and ethnic hierarchy, blacks have clearly been relegated to the lowest level—have been burdened with an ambiguous, animalistic humanity. Moreover, this is made unavoidable for blacks by sheer visibility of black skin, a skin that evokes the myth of

---

*The process by which an entity is progressively divided into smaller units that are hostile to one another, as occurred in this century in the countries of the Balkan Peninsula.

inferiority on sight. Today this myth is sadly reinforced for many black students by affirmative action programs, under which blacks may often enter college with lower test scores and high school grade point averages than whites. "They see me as an affirmative action case," one black student told me at UCLA. This reinforces the myth of inferiority by implying that blacks are not good enough to make it into college on their own.

13   So when a black student enters college, the myth of inferiority compounds the normal anxiousness over whether he or she will be good enough. This anxiety is not only personal but also racial. The families of these students will have pounded into them the fact that blacks are not inferior. And probably more than anything it is this pounding that finally leaves the mark. If I am not inferior, why the need to say so?

14   This myth of inferiority constitutes a very sharp and ongoing anxiety for young blacks, the nature of which is very precise: it is the terror that somehow, through one's actions or by virtue of some "proof" (a poor grade, a flubbed response in class), one's fear of inferiority—inculcated in ways large and small by society—will be confirmed as real. On a university campus where intelligence itself is the ultimate measure, this anxiety is bound to be triggered.

15   A black student I met at UCLA was disturbed a little when I asked him if he ever felt vulnerable—anxious about "black inferiority"—as a black student. But after a long pause, he finally said, "I think I do." The example he gave was of a large lecture class he'd taken with over three hundred students. Fifty or so black students sat in the back of the lecture hall and "acted out every stereotype in the book." They were loud, ate food, came in late—and generally got lower grades than whites in the class. "I knew I would be seen like them, and I didn't like it. I never sat by them." Seen like what, I asked, though we both knew the answer. "As lazy, ignorant, and stupid," he said sadly.

16   Had the group at the back been white fraternity brothers, they would not have been seen as dumb whites, of course. And a frat brother who worried about his grades would not worry that he be seen "like them." The terror in this situation for the black student I spoke with was that his own deeply buried anxiety would be given credence, that the myth would be verified, and that he would feel shame and humiliation not because of who he was but simply because he was black. In this lecture hall his race, quite apart from his performance, might subject him to four unendurable feelings—diminishment, accountability to the preconceptions of whites, a powerlessness to change those preconceptions, and finally, shame. These are the feelings that make up his racial anxiety, and that of all blacks on any campus. On a white campus a black is never far from these feelings, and even his unconscious knowledge that he is subject to them can undermine his self-esteem. There are blacks on any campus who are not up to doing good college-

level work. Certain black students may not be happy or motivated or in the appropriate field of study—*just like whites.* (Let us not forget that many white students get poor grades, fail, drop out.) Moreover, many more blacks than whites are not quite prepared for college, may have to catch up, owing to factors beyond their control: poor previous schooling, for example. But the white who has to catch up will not be anxious that his being behind is a matter of his whiteness, of his being racially inferior. The black student may well have such a fear.

17   This, I believe, is one reason why black colleges in America turn out 37 percent of all black college graduates though they enroll only 16 percent of black college students. Without whites around on campus, the myth of inferiority is in abeyance and, along with it, a great reservoir of culturally imposed self-doubt. On black campuses, feelings of inferiority are personal; on campuses with a white majority, a black's problems have a way of becoming a "black" problem.

18   But this feeling of vulnerability a black may feel, in itself, is not as serious a problem as what he or she does with it. To admit that one is made anxious in integrated situations about the myth of racial inferiority is difficult for young blacks. It seems like admitting that one is racially inferior. And so, most often, the student will deny harboring the feelings. This is where some of the pangs of racial tension begin, because denial always involves distortion.

19   In order to deny a problem we must tell ourselves that the problem is something different from what it really is. A black student at Berkeley told me that he felt defensive every time he walked into a classroom of white faces. When I asked why, he said, "Because I know they're all racists. They think blacks are stupid." Of course it may be true that some whites feel this way, but the singular focus on white racism allows this student to obscure his own underlying racial anxiety. He can now say that his problem—facing a classroom of white faces, *fearing* that they think he is dumb—is entirely the result of certifiable white racism and has nothing to do with his own anxieties, or even that this particular academic subject may not be his best. Now all the terror of his anxiety, its powerful energy, is devoted to simply *seeing* racism. Whatever evidence of racism he finds—and looking this hard, he will no doubt find some—can be brought in to buttress his distorted view of the problem while his actual deep-seated anxiety goes unseen.

20   Denial, and the distortion that results, places the problem *outside* the self and in the world. It is not that I have any inferiority anxiety because of my race; it is that I am going to school with people who don't like blacks. This is the shift in thinking that allows black students to reenact the protest pattern of the sixties. *Denied racial anxiety—distortion—reenactment* is the process by which feelings of inferiority are transformed into an exaggerated white menace—which is then protested against with the techniques of the past. Under the sway of this process, black students believe that history is repeating itself, that it's

just like the sixties, or fifties. In fact, it is not-yet-healed wounds from the past, rather than the inequality that created the wounds, that is the real problem.

21   This process generates an unconscious need to exaggerate the level of racism on campus—to make it a matter of the system, not just a handful of students. Racism is the avenue away from the true inner anxiety. How many students demonstrating for black theme dorms—demonstrating in the style of the sixties, when the battle was to win for blacks a place on campus—might be better off spending their time reading and studying? Black students have the highest dropout rate and the lowest grade point average of any group in American universities. This need not be so. And it is not the result of not having black theme dorms.

22   It was my very good fortune to go to college in 1964, when the question of black "inferiority" was openly talked about among blacks. The summer before I left for college, I heard Martin Luther King speak in Chicago, and he laid it on the line for black students everywhere: "When you are behind in a footrace, the only way to get ahead is to run faster than the man in front of you. So when your white roommate says he's tired and goes to sleep, you stay up and burn the midnight oil." His statement that we were "behind in a footrace" acknowledged that, because of history, of few opportunities, of racism, we were, in a sense, "inferior." But this had to do with what had been done to our parents and their parents, not with inherent inferiority. And because it was acknowledged, it was presented to us as a challenge rather than a mark of shame.

23   Of the eighteen black students (in a student body of one thousand) who were on campus in my freshman year, all graduated, though a number of us were not from the middle class. At the university where I currently teach, the dropout rate for black students is 72 percent, despite the presence of several academic support programs, a counseling center with black counselors, an Afro-American studies department, black faculty, administrators, and staff, a general education curriculum that emphasizes "cultural pluralism," an Educational Opportunities Program, a mentor program, a black faculty and staff association, and an administration and faculty that often announce the need to do more for black students.

24   It may be unfair to compare my generation with the current one. Parents do this compulsively and to little end but self-congratulation. But I don't congratulate my generation. I think we were advantaged. We came along at a time when racial integration was held in high esteem. And integration was a very challenging social concept for both blacks and whites. We were remaking ourselves—that's what one did at college—and making history. We had something to prove. This was a profound advantage; it gave us clarity and a challenge. Achievement in

the American mainstream was the goal of integration, and the best thing about this challenge was its secondary message—that we *could* achieve.

25   There is much irony in the fact that black power would come along in the late sixties and change all this. Black power was a movement of uplift and pride, and yet it also delivered the weight of pride—a weight that would burden black students from then on. Black power "national-ized" the black identity, made blackness itself an object of celebration, an allegiance. But if it transformed a mark of shame into a mark of pride, it also, in the name of pride, required the denial of racial anxiety. Without a frank account of one's anxieties, there is no clear direction, no concrete challenge. Black students today do not get as clear a message from their racial identity as my generation got. They are not filled with the same urgency to prove themselves because black pride has said, *You're already proven, already equal, as good as anybody.*

26   The "black identity" shaped by black power most forcefully contributes to racial tensions on campuses by basing entitlement more on race than on constitutional rights and standards of merit. With integration, black entitlement derived from constitutional principles of fairness. Black power changed this by skewing the formula from rights to color—if you were black, you were entitled. Thus the United Coalition Against Racism (UCAR) at the University of Michigan could "demand" two years ago that all black professors be given immediate tenure, that there is a special pay incentive for black professors, and that money be provided for an all-black student union. In this formula, black becomes the very color of entitlement, an extra right in itself, and a very danger-ous grandiosity is promoted in which blackness amounts to specialness.

27   Race is, by any standard, an unprincipled source of power. And on campuses the use of racial power by one group makes racial, ethnic, or gender difference a currency of power for all groups. When I make my *difference* into power, other groups must seize upon their difference to contain my power and maintain their position relative to me. Very quickly a kind of politics of difference emerges in which racial, ethnic, and gender groups are forced to assert their entitlement and vie for power based on the single quality that makes them different from one another.

28   On many campuses today academic departments and programs are established on the basis of difference—black studies, women's studies, Asian studies, and so on—despite the fact that there is nothing in these "difference" departments that cannot be studied within traditional aca-demic disciplines. If their rationale is truly past exclusion from the mainstream curriculum, shouldn't the goal now be complete inclusion rather than separateness? I think this logic is overlooked because those groups are too interested in the power their difference can bring, and they insist on separate departments and programs as tribute to that power.

29   This politics of difference makes everyone on campus a member of a minority group. It also makes racial tension inevitable. To highlight one's difference as a source of advantage is also, indirectly, to inspire the enemies of that difference. When blackness (and femaleness) become power, then white maleness is also sanctioned as power. A white male student I spoke with at Stanford said, "One of my friends said the other day that we should get together and start up a white student union and come up with a list of demands."

30   It is certainly true that white maleness has long been an unfair source of power. But the sin of white male power is precisely its use of race and gender as a source of entitlement. When minorities and women use their race, ethnicity, and gender in the same way, they not only commit the same sin but also, indirectly, sanction the very form of power that oppressed them in the first place. The politics of difference is based on a tit-for-tat sort of logic in which every victory only calls one's enemies to arms.

31   This elevation of difference undermines the communal impulse by making each group foreign and inaccessible to others. When difference is celebrated rather than remarked, people must think in terms of difference, they must find meaning in difference, and this meaning comes from an endless process of contrasting one's group with other groups. Blacks use whites to define themselves as different, women use men, Hispanics use whites and blacks, and on it goes. And in the process each group mythologizes and mystifies its difference, puts it beyond the full comprehension of outsiders. Difference becomes inaccessible preciousness toward which outsiders are expected to be simply and uncomprehendingly reverential. But beware: in this world, even the insulated world of the college campus, preciousness is a balloon asking for a needle. At Smith College graffiti appears: "Niggers, spics, and chinks. Quit complaining or get out."

32   I think that those who run our colleges and universities are every bit as responsible for the politics of difference as are minority students. To correct the exclusions once caused by race and gender, universities—under the banner of affirmative action—have relied too heavily on race and gender as criteria. So rather than break the link between difference and power, they have reinforced it. On most campuses today, a well-to-do black student with two professional parents is qualified by his race for scholarship monies that are not available to a lower-middle-class white student. A white female with a private school education and every form of cultural advantage comes under the affirmative action umbrella. This kind of inequity is an invitation to backlash.

33   What universities are quite rightly trying to do is compensate people for past discrimination and the deprivations that followed from it. But race and gender alone offer only the grossest measure of this. And the failure of universities has been their backing away from the challenge of identifying principles of fairness and merit that make finer and

more equitable distinctions. The real challenge is not simply to include a certain number of blacks, but to end discrimination against all blacks and to offer special help to those with talent who have also been economically deprived.

34   With regard to black students, affirmative action has led universities to correlate color with poverty and disadvantage in so absolute a way as to encourage the politics of difference. But why have they gone along with this? My belief is that it is due to the specific form of racial anxiety to which whites are most subject.

35   Most of the white students I talked with spoke as if from under a faint cloud of accusation. There was always a ring of defensiveness in their complaints about blacks. A white student I spoke to at UCLA told me: "Most white students on this campus think the black student leadership here is made up of oversensitive crybabies who spend all their time looking for things to kick up a ruckus about." A white student at Stanford said, "Blacks do nothing but complain and ask for sympathy when everyone really knows that they don't do well because they don't try. If they worked harder, they could do as well as everyone else."

36   That these students felt accused was most obvious in their compulsion to assure me that they were not racist. Oblique versions of some-of-my-best-friends-are stories came ritualistically before or after critiques of black students. Some said flatly, "I am not a racist, but . . ." Of course, we all deny being racist, but we only do this compulsively, I think, when we are working against an accusation of bias. I think it was the color of my skin itself that accused them.

37   This was the meta-message that surrounded these conversations like an aura, and it is, I believe, the core of white American racial anxiety. My skin not only accused them; it judged them. And this judgment was a sad gift of history that brought them to account whether they deserved such accountability or not. It said that wherever and whenever blacks were concerned, they had reason to feel guilt. And whether it was earned or unearned, I think it was guilt that set off the compulsion in these students to disclaim. I believe it is true that, in America, black people make white people feel guilty.

38   Guilt is the essence of white anxiety just as inferiority is the essence of black anxiety. And the terror that it carries for whites is the terror of discovering that one has reason to feel guilt where blacks are concerned—not so much because of what blacks might think but because of what guilt can say about oneself. If the darkest fear of blacks is inferiority, the darkest fear of whites is that their better lot in life is at least partially the result of their capacity for evil—their capacity to dehumanize an entire people for their own benefit and then to be indifferent to the devastation their dehumanization has wrought on successive generations of their victims. This is the terror that whites are vulnerable

to regarding blacks. And the mere fact of being white is sufficient to feel it, since even whites with hearts clean of racism benefit from being white—benefit at the expense of blacks. This is a conditional guilt having nothing to do with individual intentions or actions. And it makes for a very powerful anxiety because it threatens whites with a view of themselves as inhuman, just as inferiority threatens blacks with a similar view of themselves. At the dark core of both anxieties is a suspicion of incomplete humanity.

39   So, the white students I met were not just meeting me; they were also meeting the possibility of their own inhumanity. And this, I think, is what explains how some young white college students in the late eighties could so frankly take part in racially insensitive and outright racist acts. They were expected to be cleaner of racism than any previous generation—they were born into the Great Society. But this expectation overlooks the fact that, for them, color is still an accusation and judgment. In black faces there is a discomforting reflection of white collective shame. Blacks remind them that their racial innocence is questionable, that they are the beneficiaries of past and present racism, and the sins of the father may well have been visited on the children.

40   And yet young whites tell themselves that they had nothing to do with the oppression of black people. They have a stronger belief in their racial innocence than any previous generation of whites and a natural hostility toward anyone who would challenge that innocence. So (with a great deal of individual variation) they can end up in the paradoxical position of being hostile to blacks as a way of defending their own racial innocence.

41   I think this is what the young white editors of the *Dartmouth Review* were doing when they harassed black music professor William Cole. Weren't they saying, in effect, I am so free of racial guilt that I can afford to attack blacks ruthlessly and still be racially innocent? The ruthlessness of these attacks was a form of denial, a badge of innocence. The more they were charged with racism, the more ugly and confrontational their harassment became (an escalation unexplained even by the serious charges against Professor Cole). Racism became a means of rejecting racial guilt, a way of showing that they were not, ultimately, racists.

42   The politics of difference sets up a struggle for innocence among all groups. When difference is the currency of power, each group must fight for the innocence that entitles it to power. To gain this innocence, blacks sting whites with guilt, remind them of their racial past, accuse them of new and more subtle forms of racism. One way whites retrieve their innocence is to discredit blacks and deny their difficulties, for in this denial is the denial of their own guilt. To blacks this denial looks like racism, a racism that feeds black innocence and encourages them

to throw more guilt at whites. And so the cycle continues. The politics of difference leads each group to pick at the vulnerabilities of the other.

43   Men and women who run universities—whites, mostly—participate in the politics of difference because they handle their guilt differently than do many of their students. They don't deny it, but still they don't want to *feel* it. And to avoid this feeling of guilt they have tended to go along with whatever blacks put on the table rather than work with them to assess their real needs. University administrators have too often been afraid of guilt and have relied on negotiation and capitulation more to appease their own guilt than to help blacks and other minorities. Administrators would never give white students a racial theme dorm where they could be "more comfortable with people of their own kind," yet more and more universities are doing this for black students, thus fostering a kind of voluntary segregation. To avoid the anxieties of integrated situations blacks ask for theme dorms; to avoid guilt, white administrators give theme dorms.

44   When everyone is on the run from their anxieties about race, race relations on campus can be reduced to the negotiation of avoidances. A pattern of demand and concession develops in which both sides use the other to escape themselves. Black studies departments, black deans of student affairs, black counseling programs, Afro houses, black theme dorms, black homecoming dances and graduation ceremonies—black students and white administrators have slowly engineered a machinery of separatism that, in the name of sacred difference, redraws the ugly lines of segregation.

45   Black students have not sufficiently helped themselves, and universities, despite all their concessions, have not really done much for blacks. If both faced their anxieties, I think they would see the same thing: academic parity with all other groups should be the overriding mission of black students, and it should also be the first goal that universities have for their black students. Blacks can only *know* they are as good as others when they are, in fact, as good—when their grades are higher and their dropout rate lower. Nothing under the sun will substitute for this, and no amount of concessions will bring it about.

46   Universities can never be free of guilt until they truly help black students, which means leading and challenging them rather than negotiating and capitulating. It means inspiring them to achieve academic parity, nothing less, and helping them to see their own weaknesses as their greatest challenge. It also means dismantling the machinery of separatism, breaking the link between difference and power, and skewing the formula for entitlement away from race and gender and back to constitutional rights.

47   As for the young white students who have rediscovered swastikas and the word "nigger," I think that they suffer from an exaggerated

sense of their own innocence, as if they were incapable of evil and beyond the reach of guilt. But it is also true that the politics of difference creates an environment that threatens their innocence and makes them defensive. White students are not invited to the negotiating table from which they see blacks and others walk away with concessions. The presumption is that they do not deserve to be there because they are white. So they can only be defensive, and the less mature among them will be aggressive. Guerrilla activity will ensue. Of course this is wrong, but it is also a reflection of an environment where difference carries power and where whites have the wrong "difference."

48   I think universities should emphasize commonality as a higher value than "diversity" and "pluralism"—buzzwords for the politics of difference. Difference that does not rest on a clearly delineated foundation of commonality is not only inaccessible to those who are not part of the ethnic or racial group, but also antagonistic to them. Difference can enrich only the common ground.

49   Integration has become an abstract term today, having to do with little more than numbers and racial balances. But it once stood for a high and admirable set of values. It made difference second to commonality, and it asked members of all races to face whatever fears they inspired in each other. I doubt the word will have a new vogue, but the values, under whatever name, are worth working for.

A. Comprehension

Choose the answer that best completes each statement. Do not refer to the selection while doing this exercise.

1. Steele writes that when he was a college student in the mid-sixties, colleges were (a) wholly segregated, reflecting sharp racial divisions in American society; (b) just beginning to adopt affirmative action guidelines to solve the problem of past racial discrimination; (c) held hostage by various racial and ethnic groups, each demanding separate facilities and academic curricula; (d) oases of calm and understanding, quite removed from the racial tensions in American society.

2. The author finds an "incongruence" in the fact that racism exists on college campuses today, because today's students were born (a) during the Vietnam War; (b) after the passage of the 1964 Civil Rights Act; (c) after the assassination of Martin Luther King, Jr.; (d) after the 1972 Equal Employment Opportunity Act.

3. When Steele spoke with students on California campuses where racial incidents had occurred, he deliberately spoke only to blacks and whites, and not to Asians or Hispanics, for these *two* reasons: (a) he did not

want to intrude on the territory of other minority groups; (b) these two groups have not been the targets of any racial incidents; (c) more Asians and Hispanics attend college than blacks; (d) blacks and whites represent the deepest lines of racial division; (e) Asian and Hispanic students have been less vocal in their protests and demands.

4. Steele believes that today's racial tension on college campuses is less the result of racial inequality than it is the result of (a) a lack of communication; (b) a lack of equal educational opportunities; (c) a new racial equality, specifically affirmative action programs; (d) a lack of experience and contact with racial minorities.

5. Steele calls the new political situation that has emerged on college campuses the politics of (a) meaning; (b) indifference; (c) difference; (d) racial identities.

6. College campuses traditionally promote tolerance, fairness, freedom, and equality, but tension is nonetheless present in this environment from students who bring with them (a) racist ideas taught at home; (b) unresolved feelings of guilt, anger, and shame about race; (c) an unwillingness to deal with minority groups' conflicts and fears; (d) vague, unformed opinions about their own racial identity and that of others.

7. Steele observes that affirmative action programs, by implying that blacks aren't good enough to get into college on their own merits, (a) reinforce the myth of their inferiority; (b) are merely quota systems with a fancy, euphemistic name; (c) discriminate against students with better academic records; (d) guarantee that unprepared students will do poorly.

8. Steele partly blames minority students for contributing to renewed racial tensions, but he also blames (usually white) university administrators for (a) being insensitive to black students' demands for separate facilities or programs; (b) being too soft on those who engage in racist behavior; (c) being indifferent to the new segregation that now exists on college campuses; (d) giving into black demands for concessions to assuage their white guilt.

B. Inferences

On the basis of the evidence in the paragraphs indicated, mark these statements as follows: PA for inferences that are probably accurate; PI for inferences that are probably inaccurate; and IE for insufficient evidence. You may refer to the selection to answer the questions in this and all the remaining sections.

_____   1.   Racial incidents have been more common on the campuses

of private universities than at public colleges. [paragraphs 1 and 2]

_____ 2. Black students think that adoption of new courses on racism and increased numbers of minority faculty will help stop the number of racial incidents directed against them. [paragraph 2]

_____ 3. Increased contact between whites and blacks—both in real life and in the media—and a new push for racial equality have not resulted in an improvement in race relations. [paragraph 5]

_____ 4. It makes little sense for blacks to feel inferior and vulnerable today simply because of their race. [paragraph 11]

_____ 5. Lower graduation rates for blacks attending predominantly white colleges than for those who attend black colleges may be the result of their inability to do well academically in an environment where they stand out as different or feel inferior. [paragraph 17]

_____ 6. Ironically, despite the gains of the civil rights movement and the push for racial equality, black students today have a harder time in college than the author did in the 1960s. [paragraphs 22–25]

_____ 7. The trend toward the politics of difference, wherein each group asserts its entitlement and vies for power based on the quality that makes it different, is inevitable but not a cause for serious concern. [paragraphs 27–29]

_____ 8. University administrators should stop giving in to black students' demands for separate departments, deans, counseling programs, dorms, and the like. [paragraph 44]

C. Structure

1. Steele's thesis is that (a) black students have rediscovered the political effectiveness of militant protests to achieve their demands; (b) on American college campuses, white students feel anxiety because of their perceived guilt and black students feel anxiety over their perceived inferiority; (c) establishing separate facilities for students of different races is the solution for long-simmering racial tensions on college campuses; (d) the new incidents of racism on college campuses reflect a hardening of racial lines as differences between racial groups are emphasized.

2. In what way do paragraphs 1 and 2 represent the classic "funnel" pattern of essay introductions? _____

3. The predominant mode of discourse in the essay is (a) narration; (b) description; (c) exposition; (d) persuasion.

4. The *two* methods of paragraph development most evident throughout the essay as a whole are (a) example; (b) analogy; (c) definition; (d) analysis; (e) steps in a process; (f) cause-and-effect.

5. Explain the irony implied in paragraph 30. _____

6. In your own words, summarize the solutions Steele suggests in paragraphs 33 and 45–49? _____

7. The author's tone can best be described as (a) admonishing, reproving; (b) critical yet reasonable and sympathetic; (c) objective, impartial; (d) sarcastic, cynical; (e) conciliatory, forgiving.

8. One can reasonably conclude from his analysis that the author thinks affirmative action programs (a) have successfully compensated minority groups for past discrimination against them; (b) are more appropriate for correcting inequities in employment than in college admissions; (c) should be reexamined and perhaps even eliminated because they work against the desired goals of commonality and integration; (d) should continue for a few more years because the problems they have caused may work themselves out in time.

D. Vocabulary

For each italicized word from the selection, choose the best definition according to the context in which it appears.

1. it certainly seemed an *incongruence* [paragraphs 4 and 5]: (a) incomprehensible term; (b) incompatible pairing; (c) insensitive formulation; (d) inaccurate summary.

2. the same look, the *archetypal* pattern [7]: (a) historical; (b) older; (c) original; (d) architectural.

3. controlled by legally *sanctioned* inequality [8]: (a) prohibited; (b) authorized; (c) determined; (d) defended.

4. there is a *paradox* here [8 and 9]: (a) an important question; (b) a lesson to be learned; (c) a dangerous situation; (d) an apparent contradiction.

5. *inchoate* feelings of racial shame, anger, and guilt [8]: (a) just beginning; (b) deeply embedded; (c) lying on the surface; (d) confused, ambivalent.

6. a troubling, *volatile* politics [9]: (a) corrupt; (b) explosive; (c) intolerant; (d) underhanded.

7. Black inferiority was a *precept* [11]: (a) rule, principle; (b) requirement, necessity; (c) myth, illusion; (d) tradition, custom.

8. its *incarnation* in color [12]: (a) reception; (b) realization; (c) vague image; (d) manifestation in bodily form.

9. *inculcated* in ways large and small [14]: (a) reaffirmed; (b) instilled; (c) passed down from generation to generation; (d) codified.

10. his anxiety would be given *credence* [16]: (a) consideration; (b) supporting evidence; (c) acceptance as true; (d) special treatment.

11. the myth of inferiority is *in abeyance* [17]: (a) being questioned, examined; (b) being temporarily set aside; (c) under discussion; (d) being destroyed permanently.

12. to *obscure* his own underlying racial anxiety [19]: (a) conceal from view; (b) share; (c) reconcile; (d) focus on.

13. *skewing* the formula from rights to color [26]: (a) redirecting; (b) calculating precisely; (c) substituting; (d) distorting.

14. a very dangerous *grandiosity* is promoted [26]: (a) feigned grandeur; (b) historical precedent; (c) revolutionary fervor; (d) unwarranted indulgence.

15. *vie* for power based on the single quality [27]: (a) aim; (b) compete; (c) grab; (d) relinquish.

16. This kind of *inequity* [32]: (a) indecision; (b) exclusiveness; (c) special treatment; (d) injustice.

17. led universities to *correlate* color with poverty [34]: (a) establish a relationship; (b) substitute; (c) distinguish; (d) redefine.

18. *Oblique* versions of some-of-my-best-friends-are stories [36]: (a) trite, overused; (b) transparent, easily seen through; (c) updated, revised; (d) evasive, not straightforward.

19. The *ruthlessness* of these attacks [41]: (a) mercilessness; (b) unfairness; (c) randomness; (d) violence.

20. relied on negotiation and *capitulation* [43] (See also *capitulating* in 46): (a) diplomacy; (b) force; (c) surrender; (d) good will.

E. Questions for Analysis and Discussion

1. Steele observes that everyone involved—blacks, whites, and university administrators—can be blamed for the current spate of racial incidents on college campuses. Does he treat each group fairly? Can you find any instances of favoritism for one group over another?

2. What was your attitude toward affirmative action programs before you read this essay? What was the basis of this opinion? What have been your experiences? your observations? Now, which of Steele's points do you agree with? disagree with?

Essays: Group 3

Selection 11

The Brown Wasps

Loren Eiseley

A native of Lincoln, Nebraska, Loren Eiseley (1907–1977) had a long and distinguished career as an anthropologist and scientific historian. After finishing his degree at the University of Nebraska, he completed graduate work in anthropology at the University of Pennsylvania. During his career, he taught at many colleges, among them Oberlin College in Ohio, Harvard and Columbia universities, and the universities of California and Pennsylvania. For many years he was active in the search for early postglacial man in the western United States. His best known works are The Immense Journey *(1957) and* The Night Country *(1971), in which "The Brown Wasps" was first published.*

1   There is a corner in the waiting room of one of the great Eastern stations where women never sit. It is always in the shadow and overhung by rows of lockers. It is, however, always frequented—not so much by genuine travelers as by the dying. It is here that a certain element of the abandoned poor seeks a refuge out of the weather, clinging for a few hours longer to the city that has fathered them. In a precisely similar manner I have seen, on a sunny day in midwinter, a few old brown wasps creep slowly over an abandoned wasp nest in a thicket. Numbed and forgetful and frost-blackened, the hum of the spring hive still resounded faintly in their sodden tissues. Then the temperature would fall and they would drop away into the white oblivion of the snow. Here in the station it is in no way different save that the city is busy in its snows. But the old ones cling to their seats as though these were symbolic and could not be given up. Now and then they sleep, their gray old heads resting with painful awkwardness on the backs of the benches.

2   Also they are not at rest. For an hour they may sleep in the gasping exhaustion of the ill-nourished and aged who have to walk in the night. Then a policeman comes by on his round and nudges them upright.

3   "You can't sleep here," he growls.

4   A strange ritual then begins. An old man is difficult to waken. After a muttered conversation the policeman presses a coin into his hand and passes fiercely along the benches prodding and gesturing toward the door. In his wake, like birds rising and settling behind the passage of a farmer through a cornfield, the men totter up, move a few paces, and subside once more upon the benches.

5   One man, after a slight, apologetic lurch, does not move at all. Tubercularly thin, he sleeps on steadily. The policeman does not look back. To him, too, this has become a ritual. He will not have to notice it again officially for another hour.

6   Once in a while one of the sleepers will not awake. Like the brown wasps, he will have had his wish to die in the great droning center of the hive rather than in some lonely room. It is not so bad here with the shuffle of footsteps and the knowledge that there are others who share the bad luck of the world. There are also the whistles and the sounds of everyone, everyone in the world, starting on journeys. Amidst so many journeys somebody is bound to come out all right. Somebody.

7   Maybe it was on a like thought that the brown wasps fell away from the old paper nest in the thicket. You hold till the last, even if it is only to a public seat in a railroad station. You want your place in the hive more than you want a room or a place where the aged can be eased gently out of the way. It is the place that matters, the place at the heart of things. It is life that you want, that bruises your gray old head with the hard chairs; a man has a right to his place.

8   But sometimes the place is lost in the years behind us. Or sometimes it is a thing of air, a kind of vaporous distortion above a heap of rubble. We cling to a time and a place because without them man is lost, not only man but life. This is why the voices, real or unreal, which speak from the floating trumpets at spiritualist seances are so unnerving. They are voices out of nowhere whose only reality lies in their ability to stir the memory of a living person with some fragment of the past. Before the medium's cabinet both the dead and the living revolve endlessly about an episode, a place, an event that has already been engulfed by time.

9   This feeling runs deep in life; it brings stray cats running over endless miles, and birds homing from the ends of the earth. It is as though all living creatures, and particularly the more intelligent, can survive only by fixing or transforming a bit of time into space or by securing a bit of space with its objects immortalized and made permanent in time. For example, I once saw, on a flower pot in my own living room, the efforts of a field mouse to build a remembered field. I have lived to see this episode repeated in a thousand guises, and since I have spent a large portion of my life in the shade of a nonexistent tree I think I am entitled to speak for the field mouse.

10   One day as I cut across the field which at that time extended on one side of our suburban shopping center, I found a giant slug feeding from a runnel of pink ice cream in an abandoned Dixie cup. I could see his eyes telescope and protrude in a kind of dim uncertain ecstasy as his dark body bunched and elongated in the curve of the cup. Then, as I stood there at the edge of the concrete, contemplating the slug, I began to realize it was like standing on a shore where a different type of life creeps up and fumbles tentatively among the rocks and sea wrack. It knows its place and will only creep so far until something changes. Little by little as I stood there I began to see more of this shore that surrounds the place of man. I looked with sudden care and attention at things I had been running over thoughtlessly for years. I even waded out a short way into the grass and the wild-rose thickets to see more. A huge black-belted bee went droning by and there were some indistinct scurryings in the underbrush.

11   Then I came to a sign which informed me that this field was to be the site of a new Wanamaker suburban store. Thousands of obscure lives were about to perish, the spores of puffballs would go smoking off to new fields, and the bodies of little white-footed mice would be crunched under the inexorable wheels of the bulldozers. Life disappears or modifies its appearances so fast that everything takes on an aspect of illusion—a momentary fizzing and boiling with smoke rings, like pouring dissident chemicals into a retort. Here man was advancing, but in a few years his plaster and bricks would be disappearing once more into the insatiable maw* of the clover. Being of an archaeological cast of mind, I thought of this fact with an obscure sense of satisfaction and waded back through the rose thickets to the concrete parking lot. As I did so, a mouse scurried ahead of me, frightened of my steps if not of that ominous Wanamaker sign. I saw him vanish in the general direction of my apartment house, his little body quivering with fear in the great open sun on the blazing concrete. Blinded and confused, he was running straight away from his field. In another week scores would follow him.

12   I forgot the episode then and went home to the quiet of my living room. It was not until a week later, letting myself into the apartment, that I realized I had a visitor. I am fond of plants and had several ferns standing on the floor in pots to avoid the noon glare by the south window.

13   As I snapped on the light and glanced carelessly around the room, I saw a little heap of earth on the carpet and a scrabble of pebbles that had been kicked merrily over the edge of one of the flower pots. To my astonishment I discovered a full-fledged burrow delving downward among the fern roots. I waited silently. The creature who had made the

---

*An opening that appears to have a voracious appetite.

burrow did not appear. I remembered the wild field then, and the flight of the mice. No house mouse, no *Mus domesticus,* had kicked up this little heap of earth or sought refuge under a fern root in a flower pot. I thought of the desperate little creature I had seen fleeing from the wild-rose thicket. Through intricacies of pipes and attics, he, or one of his fellows, had climbed to this high green solitary room. I could visualize what had occurred. He had an image in his head, a world of seed pods and quiet, of green sheltering leaves in the dim light among the weed stems. It was the only world he knew and it was gone.

14   Somehow in his flight he had found his way to this room with drawn shades where no one would come till nightfall. And here he had smelled green leaves and run quickly up the flower pot to dabble his paws in common earth. He had even struggled half the afternoon to carry his burrow deeper and had failed. I examined the hole, but no whiskered twitching face appeared. He was gone. I gathered up the earth and refilled the burrow. I did not expect to find traces of him again.

15   Yet for three nights thereafter I came home to the darkened room and my ferns to find the dirt kicked gaily about the rug and the burrow reopened, though I was never able to catch the field mouse within it. I dropped a little food about the mouth of the burrow, but it was never touched. I looked under beds or sat reading with one ear cocked for rustlings in the ferns. It was all in vain. I never saw him. Probably he ended in a trap in some other tenant's room.

16   But before he disappeared I had come to look hopefully for his evening burrow. About my ferns there had begun to linger the insubstantial vapor of an autumn field, the distilled essence, as it were, of a mouse brain in exile from its home. It was a small dream, like our dreams, carried a long and weary journey along pipes and through spider webs, past holes over which loomed the shadows of waiting cats, and finally, desperately, into this room where he had played in the shuttered daylight for an hour among the green ferns on the floor. Every day these invisible dreams pass us on the street, or rise from beneath our feet, or look out upon us from beneath a bush.

17   Some years ago the old elevated railway in Philadelphia was torn down and replaced by a subway system. This ancient El with its barn-like stations containing nut-vending machines and scattered food scraps had, for generations, been the favorite feeding ground of flocks of pigeons, generally one flock to a station along the route of the El. Hundreds of pigeons were dependent upon the system. They flapped in and out of its stanchions and steel work or gathered in watchful little audiences about the feet of anyone who rattled the peanut-vending machines. They even watched people who jingled change in their hands, and prospected for food under the feet of the crowds who gathered between trains. Probably very few among the waiting people who tossed a crumb to an eager pigeon realized that this El was like a food-bearing

river, and that the life which haunted its banks was dependent upon the running of the trains with their human freight.

18   I saw the river stop.

19   The time came when the underground tubes were ready; the traffic was transferred to a realm unreachable by pigeons. It was like a great river subsiding suddenly into desert sands. For a day, for two days, pigeons continued to circle over the El or stand close to the red vending machines. They were patient birds, and surely this great river which had flowed through the lives of unnumbered generations was merely suffering from some momentary drought.

20   They listened for the familiar vibrations that had always heralded an approaching train; they flapped hopefully about the head of an occasional workman walking along the steel runways. They passed from one empty station to another, all the while growing hungrier. Finally they flew away.

21   I thought I had seen the last of them about the El, but there was a revival and it provided a curious instance of the memory of living things for a way of life or a locality that has long been cherished. Some weeks after the El was abandoned workmen began to tear it down. I went to work every morning by one particular station, and the time came when the demolition crews reached this spot. Acetylene torches showered passers-by with sparks, pneumatic drills hammered at the base of the structure, and a blind man who, like the pigeons, had clung with his cup to a stairway leading to the change booth, was forced to give up his place.

22   It was then, strangely, momentarily, one morning that I witnessed the return of a little band of the familiar pigeons. I even recognized one or two members of the flock that had lived around this particular station before they were dispersed into the streets. They flew bravely in and out among the sparks and the hammers and the shouting workmen. They had returned—and they had returned because the hubbub of the wreckers had convinced them that the river was about to flow once more. For several hours they flapped in and out through the empty windows, nodding their heads and watching the fall of girders with attentive little eyes. By the following morning the station was reduced to some burned-off stanchions in the street. My bird friends had gone. It was plain, however, that they retained a memory for an insubstantial structure now compounded of air and time. Even the blind man clung to it. Someone had provided him with a chair, and he sat at the same corner staring sightlessly at an invisible stairway where, so far as he was concerned, the crowds were still ascending to the trains.

23   I have said my life has been passed in the shade of a nonexistent tree, so that such sights do not offend me. Prematurely I am one of the brown wasps and I often sit with them in the great droning hive of the station, dreaming sometimes of a certain tree. It was planted sixty years ago by a boy with a bucket and a toy spade in a little Nebraska town.

That boy was myself. It was a cottonwood sapling and the boy remembered it because of some words spoken by his father and because everyone died or moved away who was supposed to wait and grow old under its shade. The boy was passed from hand to hand, but the tree for some intangible reason had taken root in his mind. It was under its branches that he sheltered; it was from this tree that his memories, which are my memories, led away into the world.

24   After sixty years the mood of the brown wasps grows heavier upon one. During a long inward struggle I thought it would do me good to go and look upon that actual tree. I found a rational excuse in which to clothe this madness. I purchased a ticket and at the end of two thousand miles I walked another mile to an address that was still the same. The house had not been altered.

25   I came close to the white picket fence and reluctantly, with great effort, looked down the long vista of the yard. There was nothing there to see. For sixty years that cottonwood had been growing in my mind. Season by season its seeds had been floating farther on the hot prairie winds. We had planted it lovingly there, my father and I, because he had a great hunger for soil and live things growing, and because none of these things had long been ours to protect. We had planted the little sapling and watered it faithfully, and I remembered that I had run out with my small bucket to drench its roots the day we moved away. And all the years since it had been growing in my mind, a huge tree that somehow stood for my father and the love I bore him. I took a grasp on the picket fence and forced myself to look again.

26   A boy with the hard bird eye of youth pedaled a tricycle slowly up beside me.

27   "What'cha lookin' at?" he asked curiously.

28   "A tree," I said.

29   "What for?" he said.

30   "It isn't there," I said, to myself mostly, and began to walk away at a pace just slow enough not to seem to be running.

31   "What isn't there?" the boy asked. I didn't answer. It was obvious I was attached by a thread to a thing that had never been there, or certainly not for long. Something that had to be held in the air, or sustained in the mind, because it was part of my orientation in the universe and I could not survive without it. There was more than an animal's attachment to a place. There was something else, the attachment of the spirit to a grouping of events in time; it was part of our mortality.

32   So I had come home at last, driven by a memory in the brain as surely as the field mouse who had delved long ago into my flower pot or the pigeons flying forever amidst the rattle of nut-vending machines. These, the burrow under the greenery in my living room and the red-bellied bowls of peanuts now hovering in midair in the minds of pigeons, were all part of an elusive world that existed nowhere and yet

everywhere. I looked once at the real world about me while the persistent boy pedaled at my heels.

33   It was without meaning, though my feet took a remembered path. In sixty years the house and street had rotted out of my mind. But the tree, the tree that no longer was, that had perished in its first season, bloomed on in my individual mind, unblemished as my father's words. "We'll plant a tree here, son, and we're not going to move any more. And when you're an old, old man you can sit under it and think how we planted it here, you and me, together."

34   I began to outpace the boy on the tricycle.

35   "Do you live here, Mister?" he shouted after me suspiciously. I took a firm grasp on airy nothing—to be precise, on the bole of a great tree. "I do," I said. I spoke for myself, one field mouse, and several pigeons. We were all out of touch but somehow permanent. It was the world that had changed.

A. Comprehension

Choose the answer that best completes each statement. Do not refer to the selection while doing this exercise.

1. For the brown wasps who return to it, the abandoned hive represents (a) a refuge from harsh winter weather; (b) the spring hive of earlier days; (c) a place of shelter; (d) a sad memory.

2. According to Eiseley, the people who frequent the waiting room of the great Eastern station are (a) arriving and departing travelers; (b) the dying and the abandoned poor; (c) homeless derelicts and panhandlers; (d) former mental patients.

3. From Eiseley's observations throughout the essay, we learn that a central feeling shared by all organisms—humans and animals alike—is that of (a) exile and alienation; (b) autonomy and independence; (c) self-consciousness and self-awareness; (d) nostalgia and melancholy.

4. Eiseley writes that the field mouse burrowing in the plant in his living room was looking for (a) a place to build a new nest; (b) a suburban shopping center; (c) a world of seed pods and sheltering leaves; (d) a cozy and familiar burrow.

5. For the pigeons who gathered there, the Philadelphia El served as (a) shelter; (b) a nesting site; (c) a place to prospect for food; (d) a place of refuge from the city's noise and grime.

6. When the author returned to his childhood home in Nebraska to see the cottonwood tree that he and his father had planted sixty years ago and that had been growing in his mind all that time, he found (a) that the house no longer existed; (b) the tree was large and healthy, just as he had imagined it; (c) the tree had been cut down for a later owner; (d) the tree had apparently died soon after it was planted.

B. Inferences

On the basis of the evidence in the selection, answer these inference questions in your own words. You may refer to the selection to answer the questions in this and all the remaining sections.

1. Look again at paragraphs 4–5. What can we infer about the way the policeman's order for the men to move is heeded? _____

_____

_____

2. In paragraph 6, why exactly do these old people congregate in the waiting room? _____

_____

3. Read paragraph 11 again. What is Eiseley's opinion of the new Wanamaker suburban store? _____

4. What are the two reasons implied by Eiseley in paragraph 22 to explain the return of the pigeons to the old elevated railway site? _____

_____

_____

5. From what he writes in paragraphs 30–35, what can you infer about Eiseley's feelings when he realized that the cottonwood tree no longer existed? _____

_____

C. Structure

1. The main idea of the selection is that (a) life is not only impermanent but also incomprehensible; (b) there is a nearly universal tendency among all living things to cling to a time and a place; (c) as we grow older, we become more observant of both human and animal behavior; (d) part of our mortality is the way the spirit is attached to events in time.

2. Paragraph 1 metaphorically compares the corner of the waiting room and the old men who frequent it to an abandoned wasp nest and the brown wasps who return to it. Explain the meaning of this dual metaphor in your own words. _____

_____

_____

3. Paraphrase this expression from paragraph 1: "save that the city is busy in its snows." _____

_____

4. In paragraph 6, Eiseley writes: "There are also the whistles and sounds of everyone, everyone in the world, starting on journeys. Amidst so

many journeys somebody is bound to come out all right. Somebody."
These sentences emphasize that the corner's occupants are (a) about to
take a train trip; (b) optimistic about their health and future welfare;
(c) desperate, possibly even suicidal; (d) alienated from society, but still
determined to be part of it.

5. Consider again the description of the field and the little field mouse in
    paragraph 11. What emotion does Eiseley intend us to feel for the
    mouse? _____

6. In paragraphs 17–19, Eiseley writes that for the pigeons, the elevated
    railway metaphorically represented _____

    _____

7. Look again at the first sentence of paragraph 32. This sentence, coming
    close to Eiseley's conclusion, provides (a) paragraph coherence;
    (b) more supporting evidence for the thesis; (c) thematic unity; (d) the
    author's subjective opinion; (e) an appropriate analogy.

8. Eiseley's tone can best be described as (a) sorrowful, mournful;
    (b) nostalgic, lamenting; (c) uncertain, bewildered; (d) philosophical,
    ruminative; (e) childish, adolescent.

D. Vocabulary

For each italicized word from the selection, choose the best definition according to the context in which it appears.

1. It is always *frequented* [paragraph 1]: (a) constantly inhabited;
    (b) bustling, busy; (c) frequently visited; (d) associated with.

2. The hum still *resounded* faintly [1]: (a) resembled; (b) reverberated;
    (c) returned; (d) proclaimed widely.

3. in their *sodden* tissues [1]: (a) worn-out; (b) diseased; (c) saturated;
    (d) healthy.

4. the white *oblivion* of the snow [1]: (a) obsolescence; (b) confusion;
    (c) purity, freshness; (d) forgetfulness.

5. the men totter up and *subside* [4 and 19]: (a) settle back down; (b) fall
    down; (c) lurch, stagger; (d) become less active.

6. a kind of *vaporous* distortion [8]: (a) fanciful, imaginary; (b) vague,
    ephemeral; (c) crazy, bizarre; (d) imperceptible.

7. repeated in a thousand *guises* [9]: (a) scenes; (b) ways; (c) images;
    (d) appearances.

8. Thousands of *obscure* lives . . . an *obscure* sense of satisfaction [11].
    This word, which is used twice in this paragraph, means two different
    things. Be sure to choose *two* definitions, one for each usage: (a) dark,
    gloomy; (b) dingy, dull; (c) inconspicuous, unnoticed; (d) vague, not
    clearly understood; (e) undistinguished, of humble station.

9. the *inexorable* wheels of the bulldozers [11]: (a) unyielding;
    (b) notorious; (c) detestable; (d) infernal.

10. into the *insatiable* maw of clover [11]: (a) inedible; (b) invisible; (c) incapable of being satisfied; (d) undetectable by smell.
11. that *ominous* Wanamaker sign [11]: (a) offensive; (b) menacing; (c) distorted; (d) fearful.
12. a mouse brain in *exile* from its home [16]: (a) forced removal; (b) expectation; (c) a new location; (d) flight.
13. a *realm* unreachable by pigeons [19]: (a) position; (b) place; (c) kingdom; (d) possibility.
14. for some *intangible* reason [23]: (a) irrational; (b) not precisely defined; (c) unclear, vague; (d) inescapable.
15. part of an *elusive* world [32]: (a) carefree; (b) difficult to appreciate; (c) subtle, not immediately apparent; (d) evading grasp or perception.

E. Questions for Analysis and Discussion

1. In what ways does Eiseley consider himself similar to a field mouse and a flock of pigeons?
2. Why does Eiseley return to his childhood home? What image of the tree has he held in his mind for sixty years, and why is it so important to him?

Selection 12

America's Decadent Puritans
The Economist

How do other countries perceive the United States? The author of this unsigned article looks at America from an outsider's perspective and observes some troubling developments, specifically concerning the direction in which American culture is heading. The Economist, *in which the article was published on July 28, 1990, is a British weekly political and economic magazine founded in 1843. It is influential in business and industrial circles and tends to support the conservative point of view, although, as the author states, it is also "unashamedly Americanophile," meaning that it is generally friendly toward American interests.*

1   Considering the alternatives, it has been easy to admire the American way these past few decades. It was and is demonstrably better at making its average citizens rich and free than rival systems. Culturally, too, the world has voted for America by seeking everything from jeans to Michael Jackson. Yet if, today, you stop the average European, or Japanese, or Latin American, or, for full effect, Canadian in the street and ask him what he thinks about America, you are as likely to hear contempt as praise.

2   The Japanese will probably mention idleness and self-indulgence, the European philistinism and naivety, the Latin American insensitivity and boorishness. Someone will use the word materialist. Drugs, guns and crime will feature; so will a television culture catering to the lowest common denominator of public taste, a political system corruptible by money, shocking contrasts of wealth and poverty, and a moralistic and litigious approach to free expression.

3   America attracts such bile partly because it is more self-critical than other nations. Hypocrisy is often in the eye of the beholder: how dare a European look down his nose at a country to whose universities his brightest fellow-citizens choose to flock? Foreign criticism often attacks American habits that the critics themselves happily adopt a few years later: from refrigerators and Elvis Presley to negative campaigning and aerobics. To criticise America is to criticise what the future holds in store.

4   This newspaper is unashamedly Americanophile, knowing that the British pot is at least as black as the American kettle. But it has misgivings about the direction in which some of America's "culture" is heading—precisely because the American way today tends to be the way of the world tomorrow. By culture we mean not painting and music, but way of living. The worry is about what might be called a "decadent puritanism" within America: an odd combination of ducking responsibility and telling everyone else what to do.

5   The decadence lies in too readily blaming others for problems, rather than accepting responsibility oneself. America's litigiousness is virtually banishing the concept of bad luck. The most notorious (and overexposed) examples come from tort law. A hotel refuses to allow an able-bodied guest to swim in its shallow rooftop pool because there is no lifeguard on duty. A drunken driver can sue his host for allowing him to get drunk. But there are other examples. If a prominent citizen becomes an alcoholic or is caught indulging some illegal appetite, he all too often claims he is a victim, not a fool. The habit of pleading insanity as an excuse for a crime is spreading. Increasingly, too, people are blaming their genes and finding sympathetic (and often foolish) scientific support. The exaggerated claims by a few scientists that they have found "genes for" alcoholism, or aggression, are well couched to prevent people taking the rap for their own actions.

6   To allow legal redress for negligence, or to seek to rehabilitate rather than punish victims—these are worthy aims. But fair redress is not always appropriate; sometimes the buck must simply stop. Just as an over-padded welfare state breeds a habit of blaming and expecting help from government, so America's legalism breeds a habit of shifting burdens on to somebody else. It saps initiative out of an economy quite as effectively as the state-sponsored variety.

7   Another facet of this phenomenon is the warped idea that the problem with America's underclass is a lack of self-esteem, and that the answer to poor educational performance is to teach more self-esteem.

Bunk. The characteristic that in the past drove generations of immigrants from the underclass to prosperity was not self-esteem, it was self-discipline. The reason that Japanese schoolchildren—and the children of Asian immigrants in America—learn so much more than their American counterparts is discipline, not self-esteem.

Don't Fire Someone. Let Him Go.

8   To see how far such evasiveness has caught on, look at the new abundance of euphemism. Prisons have become "rehabilitative correctional facilities," housewives are "homemakers," deaf people are "hearing-impaired," the Cerebral Palsy society tells journalists never to use the word "suffer" about those with that "disease" (forbidden), "affliction" (forbidden), condition (allowed). Jargon cannot alter reality. How refreshing to hear a politician who favours both abortion and the death penalty described bluntly as "pro-death."

9   Take race. There are few countries on earth in which people are generally less prejudiced about colour than America, stereotypes of the old South and Bensonhurst notwithstanding. Yet there are few countries where the issue looms so large; where pressure groups are so quick to take offence at a careless remark, or where words are made to carry such a weight of meaning. "Black" is fast following negro into the lexicon of the forbidden, to be replaced by "African-American" in the never-ending search for a label without overtones. Some universities, egged on by their students, have recently imposed disgraceful restrictions on free speech rather than let bigots speak out on campus and be judged for what they are.

10   As for puritanism, America's search for fairness has begun to conflict with its famous tolerance for new peoples, new ideas and new technologies. A conformist tyranny of the majority, an intolerance of any eccentricity, is creeping into America, the west coast in particular. An increasingly puritanical approach to art, married to a paranoid suspicion of child-abuse, has made a photographer who takes pictures of parents with their children naked on the beach into a target for the FBI. Add to that sort of thing the ruthless prudishness of the television networks about anything except gratuitous violence, and the gradual assertion of "correct" ways of thinking about such things as smoking and affirmative action. It all adds up to a culture of conformity that would rather bore than shock.

11   A television script-writer recently admitted that he puts cigarettes into the hands only of baddies. A whole industry of pressure groups has arisen to try to persuade television producers to push "correct" ideas on their (fictional) programmes: smoking is bad for you, concern for the homeless is right, plastic bags are bad for the environment. All true, all admirable. But fiction is fiction, not a set of cautionary tales. (Perhaps the success of the surreal serial "Twin Peaks" will reverse this trend.)

12   As Americans get ever richer, they seem to grow more risk-averse, so that they become paranoid about hazardous waste in their district, obsessed with their cholesterol levels, and ready to spend large premiums for organic vegetables. It being a free world, they are welcome to do so, even if the risks from hazardous waste are exaggerated, or the risks from natural carcinogens in organic vegetables greater than from pesticides. But must they become killjoys in the process? Being bossed by faddish doctors is something people have come to expect. But neighbours and friends (and advertisers) have no need to be ruthlessly disapproving of the fellow who prefers cream and an early coronary to self-absorption in a costly gym building muscles he will never need.

13   None of these things is confined to America, but—like everything else—they breed faster and more lushly in America. And now the infection has spread to politicians, who have discovered that a quick way to television prominence is to take outraged offence at every imagined slight. Careers can collapse because of a single "gaffe" that does not pass some ideological litmus test. Television seems to have done its best to drive humour out of politics. Can you imagine Lyndon Johnson getting away with half of his witticisms today? If we are all to enjoy the twenty-first century, America must lighten up a bit.

A.   Comprehension

Complete the following statements in your own words. Do not refer to the selection while doing this exercise.

1. The author begins by stating that there is much to admire about American culture, but continues by listing several troubling characteristics that outsiders find troubling. List three that are mentioned. _____

_____

_____

2. What is the author's main concern about the way American culture is going? _____

_____

3. How does the author define "culture"? _____

_____

4. Explain what the author means by the phrase "decadent puritanism."

_____

_____

5. According to the article, what do alcoholics, addicts, aggressive people increasingly name as the reason for their problems? _____

6. The author rejects the notion that America's underclass needs more self-esteem, stating that good educational performance can be achieved only through _____

7. To support the idea that Americans have become overly evasive about the truth, the author cites several examples. List two. _____
_____

8. What is the author's chief complaint about what he calls the "culture of conformity"? _____

B. Inferences

On the basis of the evidence in the selection, mark these statements as follows: PA for inferences that are probably accurate; PI for inferences that are probably inaccurate; and IE for insufficient evidence. You may refer to the selection to answer the questions in this section, and all in the remaining sections.

_____   1. American culture influences other nations only in entertainment and fashion trends.

_____   2. It is hypocritical of nations to criticize America when those nations eventually adopt elements of our culture.

_____   3. Tort law refers to civil liability—the result of negligence, damage, or wrongdoing—rather than to criminal liability.

_____   4. It is foolish for drug addicts or alcoholics to blame their affliction on their genetic inheritance.

_____   5. America should admit more immigrants from diverse nations so that we do not become too insular or culturally uniform.

_____   6. A culture that promotes only "correct" ways of thinking will eventually stifle both creativity and free expression.

_____   7. Television is an appropriate forum for inducing people to accept certain ideas, like the hazards associated with cigarette smoking.

_____   8. The conclusion that America "must lighten up a bit" means that we must reclaim our traditional tolerance for the eccentric and not be so quick to take offense.

C. Structure

1. The mode of discourse in the article is (a) narration; (b) description; (c) exposition; (d) persuasion.

2. Write the sentence that best represents the thesis of the article. _____
_____

_____

3. The method of development in paragraph 2 is (a) definition; (b) contrast; (c) steps in a process; (d) example; (e) cause-and-effect.

4. Look again at paragraph 4. Explain what the author means by this expression, "the British pot is at least as black as the American kettle,"

which represents a play on an old proverb. _____

_____

_____

5. An *oxymoron* is a figure of speech in which two words are joined
    together to produce an apparent contradiction, for example, "cruel
    kindness." Find an example of an oxymoron in paragraph 4.

    _____

6. The author finds a strong connection between America's increasing
    litigiousness (i.e., Americans' propensity for filing lawsuits) and

    _____

7. Read paragraph 12 again, specifically studying the examples used as
    support. What seems to be the author's main point here? _____

    _____

8. In your own words, characterize the author's tone or attitude toward
    the current state of American culture. _____

    _____

D. Vocabulary

For each italicized word from the selection, choose the best definition according to the context in which it appears.

1. idleness and *self-indulgence* [paragraph 2]: (a) excessively giving in to
    one's own desires; (b) overly concerned with one's own status; (c)
    overly concerned with one's own importance; (d) being too hard on
    oneself for mistakes or misfortunes.

2. *philistinism* and naivety [2]: (a) being innocent of the ways of the
    world; (b) lack of culture; (c) excessive preoccupation with sex; (d)
    concern for the plight of others.

3. insensitivity and *boorishness* [2]: (a) indifference; (b) ruthlessness;
    (c) the condition of being boring; (d) the condition of being ill-
    mannered.

4. a *litigious* approach to free expression [2]. (See also *litigiousness* in 5):
    (a) engaging in frequent lawsuits; (b) quarrelsome; (c) repressive;
    (d) acting like a censor.

5. a "*decadent* puritanism" [4]. (See also *decadence* in 5): (a) unhealthy;
    (b) neurotic; (c) declining, deteriorating; (d) militant.

6. exaggerated claims are well *couched* [5]: (a) accepted; (b) received;
    (c) ambushed; (d) phrased.

7. To allow legal *redress* for negligence [6]: (a) amends for wrongs done
    to someone; (b) judgment in a court of law; (c) retribution, revenge;
    (d) full financial responsibility.

8. the *warped* idea [7]: (a) reasonable, rational; (b) ludicrous, absurd;
    (c) twisted, distorted; (d) debatable, moot.

9. To see how far such *evasiveness* has caught on [8]: (a) vagueness, avoiding reality; (b) avoidance to escape detection; (c) verbal corruption; (d) lack of responsibility.

10. stereotypes of the old South and Bensonhurst *notwithstanding* [9]: (a) in concert with; (b) in spite of; (c) to name a couple; (d) to go along with.

11. the *lexicon* of the forbidden [9]: (a) hidden areas; (b) way, route; (c) premises, territory; (d) vocabulary, list of terms.

12. A conformist *tyranny* of the majority [10]: (a) conspiracy; (b) absolute power; (c) formula; (d) complete overthrow.

13. the ruthless *prudishness* of the television networks [10]: (a) regard for tradition; (b) concern with the profit motive; (c) extreme modesty or propriety; (d) exercise of good judgment.

14. *gratuitous* violence [10]: (a) unnecessary, unjustified; (b) free of charge; (c) senseless, random; (d) uninhibited, unrestrained.

15. a single "*gaffe*" [13]: (a) criminal act; (b) change of heart; (c) mistake in pronunciation; (d) clumsy blunder.

E. Questions for Analysis and Discussion

1. The author of this article enumerates many criticisms of American culture. Is the author fair? Is there sufficient evidence to back up these claims?

2. What specifically are the author's criticisms of American television? Are they justified?

3. Look through the article and find example of slanted language—loaded adjectives, pejoratively used words, and the like. Does this use of slanted language enhance or detract from the author's point?

Selection 13

Ode to Thanksgiving

Michael J. Arlen

Michael J. Arlen was born in 1930 in London, England, and graduated from Harvard College in 1952. He has been a staff writer and television critic for The New Yorker *since 1957, and he has won numerous awards for broadcast journalism. Three of his published books are collections of essays about television and American culture:* Living-Room War, The View from Highway One, *and* The Camera Age, *from which this satirical essay is taken.*

1   It is time, at last, to speak the truth about Thanksgiving, and the truth is this. Thanksgiving is really not such a terrific holiday. Consider the traditional symbols of the event: Dried cornhusks hanging

on the door! Terrible wine! Cranberry jelly in little bowls of extremely doubtful provenance which everyone is required to handle with the greatest of care! Consider the participants, the merrymakers: men and women (also children) who have survived passably well throughout the years, mainly as a result of living at considerable distances from their dear parents and beloved siblings, who on this feast of feasts must apparently forgather (as if beckoned by an aberrant Fairy God-mother), usually by circuitous routes, through heavy traffic, at a common meeting place, where the very moods, distempers, and obtrusive personal habits that have kept them all happily apart since adulthood are then and there encouraged to slowly ferment beneath the corn-husks, and gradually rise with the aid of the terrible wine, and finally burst forth out of control under the stimulus of the cranberry jelly! No, it is a mockery of a holiday. For instance: *Thank you, O Lord, for what we are about to receive.* This is surely not a gala concept. There are no presents, unless one counts Aunt Bertha's sweet rolls a present, which no one does. There is precious little in the way of costumery: miniature plastic turkeys and those witless Pilgrim hats. There is no sex. Indeed, Thanksgiving is the one day of the year (a fact known to everybody) when all thoughts of sex completely vanish, evaporating from apartments, houses, condominiums, and mobile homes like steam from a bathroom mirror.

2   Consider also the nowhereness of the time of year: the last week or so in November. It is obviously not yet winter: winter, with its death-dealing blizzards and its girls in tiny skirts pirouetting on the ice. On the other hand, it is certainly not much use to anyone as fall: no golden leaves or Oktoberfests, and so forth. Instead, it is a no-man's-land between the seasons. In the cold and sobersides northern half of the country, it is a vaguely unsettling interregnum of long, mournful walks beneath leafless trees: the long, mournful walks following the midday repast with the dread inevitability of pie following turkey, and the leaf-less trees looming or standing about like eyesores, and the ground either as hard as iron or slightly mushy, and the light snow always beginning to fall when one is halfway to the old green gate—flecks of cold, watery stuff plopping between neck and collar, for the reason that, it being not yet winter, one has forgotten or not chosen to bring along a muffler. It is a corollary to the long, mournful Thanksgiving walk that the absence of this muffler is quickly noticed and that four weeks or so later, at Christmastime, instead of the Sony Betamax one had secretly hoped the children might have chipped in to purchase, one receives another muffler: by then the thirty-third. Thirty-three mufflers! Some walk! Of course, things are more fun in the warm and loony southern part of the country. No snow there of any kind. No need of mufflers. Also, no long, mournful walks, because in the warm and loony southern part of the country everybody drives. So everybody drives over to Uncle Jasper's house to watch the Cougars play the Gators, a not entirely

unimportant conflict which will determine whether the Gators get a
Bowl bid or must take another post-season exhibition tour of North
Korea. But no sooner do the Cougars kick off (an astonishing end-over-
end squiggly thing that floats lazily above the arena before plummeting
down toward K.C. McCoy and catching him on the helmet) than Auntie Em starts hustling turkey. Soon Cousin May is slamming around the
bowls and platters, and Cousin Bernice is oohing and ahing about "all
the fixin's," and Uncle Bob is making low, insincere sounds of appreciation: "Yummy, yummy, Auntie Em, I'll have me some more of these delicious yams!" Delicious yams? Uncle Bob's eyes roll wildly in his head.
Billy Joe Quaglino throws his long bomb in the middle of Grandpa
Morris saying grace, Grandpa Morris speaking so low nobody can hear
him, which is just as well, since he is reciting what he can remember of
his last union contract. And then, just as J.B. (Speedy) Snood begins his
ninety-two-yard punt return, Auntie Em starts dealing everyone second
helpings of her famous stuffing, as if she were pushing a controlled substance, which it well might be, since there are no easily recognizable ingredients visible to the naked eye.

3   Consider for a moment the Thanksgiving meal itself. It has become
a sort of refuge for endangered species of starch: cauliflower, turnips,
pumpkin, mince (whatever "mince" is), those blessed yams. Bowls of
luridly colored yams, with no taste at all, lying torpid under a lava flow
of marshmallow! And then the sacred turkey. One might as well try to
construct a holiday repast around a fish—say, a nice piece of boiled haddock. After all, turkey tastes very similar to haddock: same consistency,
same quite remarkable absence of flavor. But then, if the Thanksgiving
pièce de résistance were a nice piece of boiled haddock instead of turkey,
there wouldn't be all that fun for Dad when Mom hands him the ster-
ling-silver, bone-handled carving set (a wedding present from her parents and not sharpened since) and then everyone sits around pretending
not to watch while he saws and tears away at the bird as if he were trying
to burrow his way into or out of some grotesque, fowl-like prison.

4   What of the good side to Thanksgiving, you ask. There is always a
good side to everything. Not to Thanksgiving. There is only a bad side
and then a worse side. For instance, Grandmother's best linen tablecloth is a bad side: the fact that it is produced each year, in the manner
of a red flag being produced before a bull, and then is always spilled
upon by whichever child is doing poorest at school that term and so is
in need of greatest reassurance. Thus: "Oh, my God, *Veronica,* you just
spilled grape juice [or plum wine or tar] on Grandmother's best linen
tablecloth!" But now comes worse. For at this point Cousin Bill, the one
who lost all Cousin Edwina's money on the car dealership three years
ago and has apparently been drinking steadily since Halloween,
bizarrely chooses to say: "Seems to me those old glasses are always
falling over." To which Auntie Meg is heard to add: "Somehow I don't
remember receivin' any of those old glasses." To which Uncle Fred

replies: "That's because you and George decided to go on vacation to Hawaii the summer Grandpa Sam was dying." Now Grandmother is sobbing, though not so uncontrollably that she can refrain from murmuring: "I think that volcano painting I threw away by mistake got sent me from Hawaii, heaven knows why." But the gods are merciful, even the Pilgrim-hatted god of cornhusks and soggy stuffing, and there is an end to everything, even to Thanksgiving. Indeed, there is a grandeur to the feelings of finality and doom which usually settle on a house after the Thanksgiving celebration is over, for with the completion of Thanksgiving Day the year itself has been properly terminated: shot through the cranium with a high-velocity candied yam. At this calendrical nadir, all energy on the planet has gone, all fun has fled, all the terrible wine has been drunk.

5   But then, overnight, life once again begins to stir, emerging, even by the next morning, in the form of Japanese window displays and Taiwanese Christmas lighting, from the primeval ooze of the nation's department stores. Thus, a new year dawns, bringing with it immediate and cheering possibilities of extended consumer debt, office-party flirtations, good—or, at least, mediocre—wine, and visions of Supersaver excursion fares to Montego Bay. It is worth noting, perhaps, that this true new year always starts with the same mute, powerful mythic ceremony: the surreptitious tossing out, in the early morning, of all those horrid aluminum-foil packages of yams and cauliflower and stuffing and red, gummy cranberry substance which have been squeezed into the refrigerator as if a reenactment of the siege of Paris were shortly expected. Soon afterward, the phoenix of Christmas can be observed as it slowly rises, beating its drumsticks, once again goggle-eyed with hope and unrealistic expectations.

A. Comprehension

1. According to Arlen, the truth about Thanksgiving is that it is (a) the most boring day of the year; (b) a pretentious, self-congratulatory celebration; (c) a mockery of a holiday; (d) an outmoded way to remember the Pilgrims and Indians.

2. Arlen complains that Thanksgiving is missing some features common to other holidays. Which is *not* mentioned? (a) costumes; (b) gifts; (c) sex; (d) good food; (e) a series of festive parties.

3. The season when Thanksgiving occurs is described as (a) depressing; (b) uninspiring; (c) nowhere—neither here or there; (d) mournful.

4. An activity that competes with the Thanksgiving dinner for the diners' attention is (a) watching football games on television; (b) taking long walks in the snow; (c) playing games like Monopoly or Trivial Pursuit; (d) arguing over money.

5. The chief component of the Thanksgiving meal is, according to Arlen, (a) sugar; (b) starch; (c) protein; (d) alcohol; (e) overcooked vegetables.

6. For Arlen, Thanksgiving has (a) an equal number of bad and good sides; (b) more good sides than bad sides; (c) more bad sides than good sides; (d) a bad side and a worse side.

B. Inferences

On the basis of the evidence in the selection, mark these statements as follows: PA for inferences that are probably accurate; PI for inferences that are probably inaccurate; and IE for insufficient evidence. You may refer to the selection to answer the questions in this and all the remaining sections.

_____ 1. Arlen refuses to celebrate Thanksgiving with his family.
_____ 2. Family reunions at Thanksgiving tend to make the participants irritable and quarrelsome.
_____ 3. Arlen lives in the Eastern part of the country.
_____ 4. Arlen thinks football is a silly game.
_____ 5. The only part of the Thanksgiving dinner that Arlen likes is the turkey.
_____ 6. Arlen prefers Christmas to Thanksgiving.

C. Structure

1. The mode of discourse in the essay is (a) narration; (b) description; (c) exposition; (d) persuasion.
2. Write the sentence from the essay that represents the thesis.

_____

_____

3. Arlen's purpose is (a) to satirize the way Americans celebrate Thanksgiving; (b) to complain about his family reunions at Thanksgiving; (c) to explain why our expectations of most holidays are unrealistic; (d) to poke fun at the way television dominates our lives.
4. The tone of the selection can best be described as (a) hostile, scornful; (b) silly, frivolous; (c) irreverent, derisively witty; (d) earnest, solemn.
5. In describing the football plays in paragraph 2 and the traditional Thanksgiving meal in paragraph 3, Arlen relies extensively on (a) hyperbole, deliberate exaggeration for effect; (b) restatement of the main ideas; (c) euphemisms as a substitute for offensive words and phrases; (d) logical fallacies in the form of sweeping generalizations.
6. Find a metaphor in paragraph 3. What is being compared to what?
    _____ is compared to _____ Explain the metaphor. _____

    _____

7. What are the details and the dialogue in paragraph 4 meant to suggest about Thanksgiving? (a) that fighting and squabbling among family

members are part of the traditional ritual; (b) that the celebrants drink too much and say things they don't really mean; (c) that the participants act insincere just to keep up the tradition; (d) that they are not really having any fun.

8. Look at the last sentence of paragraph 5 again. Look up "phoenix" in the dictionary if you are unsure of its meaning. What is compared to the phoenix? _____

    _____

    Finally, why is this an appropriate metaphor with which to end the essay? _____

    _____

D. Vocabulary

1. in little bowls of doubtful *provenance* [paragraph 1]: (a) value; (b) origin; (c) quality; (d) ownership.

2. men and women who have survived *passably* well [1]: (a) outstandingly; (b) not very; (c) satisfactorily; (d) superficially.

3. beckoned by an *aberrant* Fairy Godmother [1]: (a) deviating from the proper or expected; (b) physically and morally defective; (c) cruel, evil; (d) obstinate, willful.

4. by *circuitous* routes [1]: (a) well-traveled; (b) circular; (c) indirect; (d) impassable.

5. this is surely not a *gala* concept [1]: (a) festive; (b) acceptable; (c) popular; (d) satisfactory.

6. it is a vaguely unsettling *interregnum* [2]: (a) difficult period; (b) natural phenomenon; (c) interval of time; (d) interrelationship.

7. long, mournful walks following the midday *repast* [2]: (a) nap; (b) reminiscences about the past; (c) cooking; (d) meal.

8. it is a *corollary* [2]: (a) natural consequence, effect; (b) tradition, ritual; (c) amusing observation; (d) unwelcome event.

9. bowls of *luridly* colored yams [3]: (a) bizarrely; (b) beautifully; (c) repulsively; (d) glowingly.

10. lying *torpid* under a lava flow of marshmallow [3]: (a) scorching, burning; (b) stiffly, inactively; (c) colorfully, vibrantly; (d) invitingly, temptingly.

11. the Thanksgiving *pièce de résistance* [French expression, pronounced pyĕs də rā zē stäns´] [3]: (a) principal dish at a meal; (b) culinary disaster; (c) traditional holiday fare; (d) inedible substance.

12. a *grandeur* to the feelings of finality and doom [4]: (a) feeling of hopelessness; (b) greatness, splendor; (c) sense of inevitability; (d) feeling of elation.

13. at this calendrical *nadir* [4]: (a) highest point; (b) lowest point; (c) difficult time; (d) festive time.

14. from the *primeval* ooze [5]: (a) the medieval; (b) present; (c) earliest; (d) evil, corrupt.

15. the *surreptitious* tossing out [5]: (a) secret, stealthy; (b) hurried, hasty; (c) suspicious, questionable; (d) final, conclusive.

E. Questions for Analysis and Discussion

1. The *American Heritage Dictionary* defines a *satire* as "a literary work in which irony, derision, or wit in any form is used to expose folly or wickedness." In what way does "Ode to Thanksgiving" represent a satire? What specifically is the target of Arlen's humor?

2. As the headnote indicates, this essay was published in a collection of pieces about television called *The Camera Age.* Although it is really secondary to his purpose, what does Arlen suggest about the influence of TV on American culture in the piece?

3. Do you find Arlen's piece funny. Why or why not? How would you characterize his humor?

Selection 14

Carrie Buck's Daughter

Stephen Jay Gould

Stephen Jay Gould teaches geology, biology, and the history of science at Harvard University. He writes widely on scientific subjects like genetics, biology, and paleontology for the general reader. His best-known books include The Panda's Thumb, Hen's Teeth *and* Horse's Toes, *and the collection of essays from which this selection comes,* The Flamingo's Smile: Reflections in Natural History. *"Carrie Buck's Daughter" presents the case of a young Virginia woman who was a unwitting victim of eugenics (the branch of science concerned with improving humans' genetic stock) and the compulsory sterilization laws popular during the 1920s.*

1   The Lord really put it on the line in his preface to that prototype of all prescription, the Ten Commandments:

> . . . for I, the Lord thy God, am a jealous God, visiting the iniquity of the fathers upon the children unto the third and fourth generation of them that hate me (Exod. 20:5).

2   The terror of this statement lies in its patent unfairness—its promise to punish guiltless offspring for the misdeeds of their distant forebears.

3   A different form of guilt by genealogical association attempts to remove this stigma of injustice by denying a cherished premise of West-

ern thought—human free will. If offspring are tainted not simply by the deeds of their parents but by a material form of evil transferred directly by biological inheritance, then "the iniquity of the fathers" becomes a signal or warning for probable misbehavior of their sons. Thus Plato, while denying that children should suffer directly for the crimes of their parents, nonetheless defended the banishment of a personally guiltless man whose father, grandfather, and great-grandfather had all been condemned to death.

4   It is, perhaps, merely coincidental that both Jehovah and Plato chose three generations as their criterion for establishing different forms of guilt by association. Yet we maintain a strong folk, or vernacular, tradition for viewing triple occurrences as minimal evidence of regularity. Bad things, we are told, come in threes. Two may represent an accidental association; three is a pattern. Perhaps, then, we should not wonder that our own century's most famous pronouncement of blood guilt employed the same criterion—Oliver Wendell Holmes's defense of compulsory sterilization in Virginia (Supreme Court decision of 1927 in *Buck* v. *Bell*): "three generations of imbeciles are enough."

5   Restrictions upon immigration, with national quotas set to discriminate against those deemed mentally unfit by early versions of IQ testing, marked the greatest triumph of the American eugenics movement—the flawed hereditarian doctrine, so popular earlier in our century and by no means extinct today, that attempted to "improve" our human stock by preventing the propagation of those deemed biologically unfit and encouraging procreation among the supposedly worthy. But the movement to enact and enforce laws for compulsory "eugenic" sterilization had an impact and success scarcely less pronounced. If we could debar the shiftless and the stupid from our shores, we might also prevent the propagation of those similarly afflicted but already here.

6   The movement for compulsory sterilization began in earnest during the 1890s, abetted by two major factors—the rise of eugenics as an influential political movement and the perfection of safe and simple operations (vasectomy for men and salpingectomy, the cutting and tying of Fallopian tubes, for women) to replace castration and other socially unacceptable forms of mutilation. Indiana passed the first sterilization act based on eugenic principles in 1907 (a few states had previously mandated castration as a punitive measure for certain sexual crimes, although such laws were rarely enforced and usually overturned by judicial review). Like so many others to follow, it provided for sterilization of afflicted people residing in the state's "care," either as inmates of mental hospitals and homes for the feebleminded or as inhabitants of prisons. Sterilization could be imposed upon those judged insane, idiotic, imbecilic, or moronic, and upon convicted rapists or criminals when recommended by a board of experts.

7   By the 1930s, more than thirty states had passed similar laws, often with an expanded list of so-called hereditary defects, including alcoholism and drug addiction in some states, and even blindness and deafness in others. These laws were continually challenged and rarely enforced in most states; only California and Virginia applied them zealously. By January 1935, some 20,000 forced "eugenic" sterilizations had been performed in the United States, nearly half in California.

8   No organization crusaded more vociferously and successfully for these laws than the Eugenics Record Office, the semiofficial arm and repository of data for the eugenics movement in America. Harry Laughlin, superintendent of the Eugenics Record Office, dedicated most of his career to a tireless campaign of writing and lobbying for eugenic sterilization. He hoped, thereby, to eliminate in two generations the genes of what he called the "submerged tenth"—"the most worthless one-tenth of our present population." He proposed a "model sterilization law" in 1922, designed

> to prevent the procreation of persons socially inadequate from defective inheritance, by authorizing and providing for eugenical sterilization of certain potential parents carrying degenerate hereditary qualities.

9   This model bill became the prototype for most laws passed in America, although few states cast their net as widely as Laughlin advised. (Laughlin's categories encompassed "blind, including those with seriously impaired vision; deaf, including those with seriously impaired hearing; and dependent, including orphans, ne'er-do-wells, the homeless, tramps, and paupers.") Laughlin's suggestions were better heeded in Nazi Germany, where his model act inspired the infamous and stringently enforced *Erbgesundheitsrecht*,* leading by the eve of World War II to the sterilization of some 375,000 people, most for "congenital feeblemindedness," but including nearly 4,000 for blindness and deafness.

10   The campaign for forced eugenic sterilization in America reached its climax and height of respectability in 1927, when the Supreme Court, by an 8–1 vote, upheld the Virginia sterilization bill in *Buck* v. *Bell*. Oliver Wendell Holmes, then in his mid-eighties and the most celebrated jurist in America, wrote the majority opinion with his customary verve and power of style. It included the notorious paragraph, with its chilling tag line, cited ever since as the quintessential statement of eugenic principles. Remembering with pride his own distant experiences as an infantryman in the Civil War, Holmes wrote:

> We have seen more than once that the public welfare may call upon the best citizens for their lives. It would be strange if it could not call upon

*German term meaning a program promoting inherited good health.

those who already sap the strength of the state for these lesser sacrifices.
. . . It is better for all the world, if instead of waiting to execute degener-
ate offspring for crime, or to let them starve for their imbecility, society
can prevent those who are manifestly unfit from continuing their kind.
The principle that sustains compulsory vaccination is broad enough to
cover cutting the Fallopian tubes. Three generations of imbeciles are
enough.

11   Who, then, were the famous "three generations of imbeciles," and
why should they still compel our interest?

12   When the state of Virginia passed its compulsory sterilization law
in 1924, Carrie Buck, an eighteen-year-old white woman, lived as an
involuntary resident at the State Colony for Epileptics and Feeble-
Minded. As the first person selected for sterilization under the new act,
Carrie Buck became the focus for a constitutional challenge launched,
in part, by conservative Virginia Christians who held, according to eu-
genical "modernists," antiquated views about individual preferences
and "benevolent" state power. (Simplistic political labels do not apply
in this case, and rarely in general for that matter. We usually regard eugenics as a conservative movement and its most vocal critics as members of the left. This alignment has generally held in our own decade.
But eugenics, touted in its day as the latest in scientific modernism, attracted many liberals and numbered among its most vociferous critics
groups often labeled as reactionary and antiscientific. If any political
lesson emerges from these shifting allegiances, we might consider the
true inalienability of certain human rights.)

13   But why was Carrie Buck in the State Colony and why was she selected? Oliver Wendell Holmes upheld her choice as judicious in the
opening lines of his 1927 opinion:

> Carrie Buck is a feeble-minded white woman who was committed to the
> State Colony. . . . She is the daughter of a feeble-minded mother in the
> same institution, and the mother of an illegitimate feeble-minded child.

14   In short, inheritance stood as the crucial issue (indeed as the driving force behind all eugenics). For if measured mental deficiency arose
from malnourishment, either of body or mind, and not from tainted
genes, then how could sterilization be justified? If decent food, upbringing, medical care, and education might make a worthy citizen of Carrie
Buck's daughter, how could the State of Virginia justify the severing of
Carrie's Fallopian tubes against her will? (Some forms of mental deficiency are passed by inheritance in family lines, but most are not—a
scarcely surprising conclusion when we consider the thousand shocks
that beset us all during our lives, from abnormalities in embryonic
growth to traumas of birth, malnourishment, rejection, and poverty. In
any case, no fair-minded person today would credit Laughlin's social
criteria for the identification of hereditary deficiency—ne'er-do-wells,

the homeless, tramps, and paupers—although we shall soon see that Carrie Buck was committed on these grounds.)

15   When Carrie Buck's case emerged as the crucial test of Virginia's law, the chief honchos of eugenics understood that the time had come to put up or shut up on the crucial issue of inheritance. Thus, the Eugenics Record Office sent Arthur H. Estabrook, their crack fieldworker, to Virginia for a "scientific" study of the case. Harry Laughlin himself provided a deposition, and his brief for inheritance was presented at the local trial that affirmed Virginia's law and later worked its way to the Supreme Court as *Buck* v. *Bell.*

16   Laughlin made two major points to the court. First, that Carrie Buck and her mother, Emma Buck, were feebleminded by the Stanford-Binet test of IQ, then in its own infancy. Carrie scored a mental age of nine years, Emma of seven years and eleven months. (These figures ranked them technically as "imbeciles" by definitions of the day, hence Holmes's later choice of words—though his infamous line is often misquoted as "three generations of idiots." Imbeciles displayed a mental age of six to nine years; idiots performed worse, morons better, to round out the old nomenclature of mental deficiency.) Second, that most feeblemindedness resides ineluctably in the genes, and that Carrie Buck surely belonged with this majority. Laughlin reported:

> Generally feeble-mindedness is caused by the inheritance of degenerate qualities; but sometimes it might be caused by environmental factors which are not hereditary. In the case given, the evidence points strongly toward the feeble-mindedness and moral delinquency of Carrie Buck being due, primarily, to inheritance and not to environment.

17   Carrie Buck's daughter was then, and has always been, the pivotal figure of this painful case. I noted in beginning this essay that we tend (often at our peril) to regard two as potential accident and three as an established pattern. The supposed imbecility of Emma and Carrie might have been an unfortunate coincidence, but the diagnosis of similar deficiency for Vivian Buck (made by a social worker, as we shall see, when Vivian was but six months old) tipped the balance in Laughlin's favor and led Holmes to declare the Buck lineage inherently corrupt by deficient heredity. Vivian sealed the pattern—*three* generations of imbeciles are enough. Besides, had Carrie not given illegitimate birth to Vivian, the issue (in both senses) would never have emerged.

18   Oliver Wendell Holmes viewed his work with pride. The man so renowned for his principle of judicial restraint, who had proclaimed that freedom must not be curtailed without "clear and present danger"—without the equivalent of falsely yelling "fire" in a crowded theater—wrote of his judgment in *Buck* v. *Bell:* "I felt that I was getting near the first principle of real reform."

19   And so *Buck* v. *Bell* remained for fifty years, a footnote to a moment of American history perhaps best forgotten. Then, in 1980, it reemerged to prick our collective conscience, when Dr. K. Ray Nelson, then director of the Lynchburg Hospital where Carrie Buck had been sterilized, researched the records of his institution and discovered that more than 4,000 sterilizations had been performed, the last as late as 1972. He also found Carrie Buck, alive and well near Charlottesville, and her sister Doris, covertly sterilized under the same law (she was told that her operation was for appendicitis), and now, with fierce dignity, dejected and bitter because she had wanted a child more than anything else in her life and had finally, in her old age, learned why she had never conceived.

20   As scholars and reporters visited Carrie Buck and her sister, what a few experts had known all along became abundantly clear to everyone. Carrie Buck was a woman of obviously normal intelligence. For example, Paul A. Lombardo of the School of Law at the University of Virginia, and a leading scholar of *Buck* v. *Bell,* wrote in a letter to me:

> As for Carrie, when I met her she was reading newspapers daily and joining a more literate friend to assist at regular bouts with the crossword puzzles. She was not a sophisticated woman, and lacked social graces, but mental health professionals who examined her in later life confirmed my impressions that she was neither mentally ill nor retarded.

21   On what evidence, then, was Carrie Buck consigned to the State Colony for Epileptics and Feeble-Minded on January 23, 1924? I have seen the text of her commitment hearing; it is, to say the least, cursory and contradictory. Beyond the bald and undocumented say-so of her foster parents, and her own brief appearance before a commission of two doctors and a justice of the peace, no evidence was presented. Even the crude and early Stanford-Binet test, so fatally flawed as a measure of innate worth (see my book *The Mismeasure of Man,* although the evidence of Carrie's own case suffices) but at least clothed with the aura of quantitative respectability, had not yet been applied.

22   When we understand why Carrie Buck was committed in January 1924, we can finally comprehend the hidden meaning of her case and its message for us today. The silent key, again as from the first, is her daughter Vivian, born on March 28, 1924, and then but an evident bump on her belly. Carrie Buck was one of several illegitimate children borne by her mother, Emma. She grew up with foster parents, J.T. and Alice Dobbs, and continued to live with them as an adult, helping out with chores around the house. She was raped by a relative of her foster parents, then blamed for the resulting pregnancy. Almost surely, she was (as they used to say) committed to hide her shame (and her rapist's identity), not because enlightened science had just discovered her true

mental status. In short, she was sent away to have her baby. Her case never was about mental deficiency; Carrie Buck was persecuted for supposed sexual immorality and social deviance. The annals of her trial and hearing reek with the contempt of the well-off and well-bred for poor people of "loose morals." Who really cared whether Vivian was a baby of normal intelligence; she was the illegitimate child of an illegitimate woman. Two generations of bastards are enough. Harry Laughlin began his "family history" of the Bucks by writing: "These people belong to the shiftless, ignorant and worthless class of anti-social whites of the South."

23   We know little of Emma Buck and her life, but we have no more reason to suspect her than her daughter Carrie of true mental deficiency. Their supposed deviance was social and sexual; the charge of imbecility was a cover-up, Mr. Justice Holmes notwithstanding.

24   We come then to the crux of the case, Carrie's daughter, Vivian. What evidence was ever adduced for her mental deficiency? This and only this: At the original trial in late 1924, when Vivian Buck was seven months old, a Miss Wilhelm, social worker for the Red Cross, appeared before the court. She began by stating honestly the true reason for Carrie Buck's commitment:

> Mr. Dobbs, who had charge of the girl, had taken her when a small child, had reported to Miss Duke [the temporary secretary of Public Welfare for Albemarle County] that the girl was pregnant and that he wanted to have her committed somewhere—to have her sent to some institution.

25   Miss Wilhelm then rendered her judgment of Vivian Buck by comparing her with the normal granddaughter of Mrs. Dobbs, born just three days earlier:

> It is difficult to judge probabilities of a child as young as that, but it seems to me not quite a normal baby. In its appearance—I should say that perhaps my knowledge of the mother may prejudice me in that regard, but I saw the child at the same time as Mrs. Dobbs' daughter's baby, which is only three days older than this one, and there is a very decided difference in the development of the babies. That was about two weeks ago. There is a look about it that is not quite normal, but just what it is, I can't tell.

26   This short testimony, and nothing else, formed all the evidence for the crucial third generation of imbeciles. Cross-examination revealed that neither Vivian nor the Dobbs grandchild could walk or talk, and that "Mrs. Dobbs' daughter's baby is a very responsive baby. When you play with it or try to attract its attention—it is a baby that you can play with. The other baby is not. It seems very apathetic and not responsive." Miss Wilhelm then urged Carrie Buck's sterilization: "I think,"

she said, "it would at least prevent the propagation of her kind." Several years later, Miss Wilhelm denied that she had ever examined Vivian or deemed the child feebleminded.

27   Unfortunately, Vivian died at age eight of "enteric colitis" (as recorded on her death certificate), an ambiguous diagnosis that could mean many things but may well indicate that she fell victim to one of the preventable childhood diseases of poverty (a grim reminder of the real subject in *Buck* v. *Bell*). She is therefore mute as a witness in our reassessment of her famous case.

28   When *Buck* v. *Bell* resurfaced in 1980, it immediately struck me that Vivian's case was crucial and that evidence for the mental status of a child who died at age eight might best be found in report cards. I have therefore been trying to track down Vivian Buck's school records for the past four years and have finally succeeded. (They were supplied to me by Dr. Paul A. Lombardo, who also sent other documents, including Miss Wilhelm's testimony, and spent several hours answering my questions by mail and Lord knows how much time playing successful detective in re Vivian's school records. I have never met Dr. Lombardo; he did all this work for kindness, collegiality, and love of the game of knowledge, not for expected reward or even requested acknowledgment. In a profession—academics—so often marred by pettiness and silly squabbling over meaningless priorities, this generosity must be recorded and celebrated as a sign of how things can and should be.)

29   Vivian Buck was adopted by the Dobbs family, who had raised (but later sent away) her mother, Carrie. As Vivian Alice Elaine Dobbs, she attended the Venable Public Elementary School of Charlottesville for four terms, from September 1930 until May 1932, a month before her death. She was a perfectly normal, quite average student, neither particularly outstanding nor much troubled. In those days before grade inflation, when C meant "good, 81-87" (as defined on her report card) rather than barely scraping by, Vivian Dobbs received A's and B's for deportment and C's for all academic subjects but mathematics (which was always difficult for her, and where she scored D) during her first term in Grade 1A, from September 1930 to January 1931. She improved during her second term in 1B, meriting an A in deportment, C in mathematics, and B in all other academic subjects; she was placed on the honor roll in April 1931. Promoted to 2A, she had trouble during the fall term of 1931, failing mathematics and spelling but receiving A in deportment, B in reading, and C in writing and English. She was "retained in 2A" for the next term—or "left back" as we used to say, and scarcely a sign of imbecility as I remember all my buddies who suffered a similar fate. In any case, she again did well in her final term, with B in deportment, reading, and spelling, and C in writing, English, and mathematics during her last month in school. This daughter of "lewd and immoral" women excelled in deportment and performed adequately, although not brilliantly, in her academic subjects.

30   In short, we can only agree with the conclusion that Dr. Lombardo has reached in his research on *Buck* v. *Bell*—there were no imbeciles, not a one, among the three generations of Bucks. I don't know that such correction of cruel but forgotten errors of history counts for much, but I find it both symbolic and satisfying to learn that forced eugenic sterilization, a procedure of such dubious morality, earned its official justification (and won its most quoted line of rhetoric) on a patent falsehood.

31   Carrie Buck died last year. By a quirk of fate, and not by memory or design, she was buried just a few steps from her only daughter's grave. In the umpteenth and ultimate verse of a favorite old ballad, a rose and a brier—the sweet and the bitter—emerge from the tombs of Barbara Allen and her lover, twining about each other in the union of death. May Carrie and Vivian, victims in different ways and in the flower of youth, rest together in peace.

A. Comprehension

Choose the answer that best completes each statement. Do not refer to the selection while doing this exercise.

1. The basic assumption proponents of eugenics and compulsory sterilization hold is that (a) parents should be held legally responsible for their children's crimes; (b) human free will should take precedence over all other considerations; (c) the propensity for evil or for mental deficiency is inherited and can be passed down from generation to generation; (d) the Ten Commandments established historical precedents for sterilization.

2. Guilt by association partly depends on the observation that two similar occurrences could simply be a coincidence, but that three similar occurrences represent (a) a magical number; (b) the Holy Trinity; (c) a mathematical formula; (d) a pattern.

3. Gould writes that the eugenics movement, which he characterizes as flawed, specifically advocated preventing biologically unfit people from reproducing and encouraged (a) scientific research in the new field of genetics; (b) people who were biologically fit to reproduce; (c) increased immigration to the U.S. to diversify the gene pool; (d) people with mental deficiencies to submit to voluntary sterilization.

4. The campaign for forced eugenic sterilization reached its height of respectability in the Supreme Court case, *Buck* v. *Bell,* which resulted in the famous phrase, "Three generations of imbeciles are enough," written by the well-respected jurist (a) John Jay; (b) Louis Brandeis; (c) Oliver Wendell Holmes; (d) Earl Warren.

5. The ostensible or *stated* reason that Carrie Buck was selected for involuntary sterilization was that (a) she had inherited criminal tendencies from her mother; (b) she, her mother, and her daughter

were all feebleminded; (c) she suffered from a sexually-transmitted disease; (d) she had a mental age of nine years according to the Stanford-Binet IQ test.

6. According to Gould, the *real* reason Carrie Buck was confined to a mental institution and sterilized is that (a) her foster parents wanted to get rid of her; (b) she was homeless and had nowhere else to go; (c) she was widely regarded in Charlottesville as a person of "loose morals"; (d) she was illegitimate herself, and after she was raped, produced an illegitimate offspring.

7. Vivian Buck, Carrie Buck's daughter, was judged mentally defective at the age of six months by a social worker, Miss Wilhelm, who (a) studied the baby intensively for several days; (b) looked at the baby briefly and concluded that she didn't look quite right in comparison with another baby of the same age; (c) compared her with her own granddaughter who was also mentally defective; (d) administered the Stanford-Binet IQ test to her.

8. The school records for Vivian Buck, Carrie Buck's daughter, reveal that she was (a) a gifted child who had a promising academic career ahead of her; (b) as mentally deficient as her mother; (c) an average student who made acceptable progress; (d) a troublemaker, but not mentally deficient.

B. Inferences

On the basis of the evidence in the selection, answer these inference questions. You may refer to the selection to answer the questions in this and all the remaining sections.

1. Gould implies in paragraph 5 that (a) mentally defective people should not be allowed to immigrate to the U.S.; (b) eugenics is a crackpot theory; (c) it would be difficult to prevent supposedly inferior people from procreating; (d) the IQ tests should have been used to measure intelligence, not biological fitness.

2. From paragraph 5 and the essay as a whole, we can infer that (a) it is morally wrong for science or government to tamper with people's reproductive rights; (b) no one takes eugenics seriously any longer; (c) feeblemindedness is a genetic trait that can be handed down to the next generation; (d) eugenics has some positive tenets, among them weeding out undesirables from the population.

3. From paragraph 6 we know that the law requiring castration for people convicted of sex crimes was not always enforced, and we can infer that (a) the law requiring sterilization of the mentally deficient was similarly not enforced; (b) the mentally ill were routinely sterilized; (c) sterilizing the mentally ill was illegal; (d) sterilizing the mentally ill kept the numbers of mentally deficient children low.

4. Gould implies in paragraphs 8 and 9 that Harry Laughlin (a) believed that blindness, deafness, and poverty were hereditary conditions; (b) was not very effective in his campaign to promote eugenic sterilization; (c) ignored those who criticized his eugenics campaign; (d) had solid scientific evidence behind his campaign to stop the "submerged one-tenth of the population" from procreating.

5. From the end of paragraph 12 we can infer that the phrase "the true inalienability of certain human rights" probably refers to the right to (a) life, liberty, and the pursuit of happiness; (b) bear arms; (c) defend one's own property; (d) bear children.

6. We can infer from paragraphs 16 and 20 that (a) Harry Laughlin knew Carrie Buck well; (b) the Stanford-Binet test administered to Carrie Buck was a reliable measure of her intelligence; (c) the Stanford-Binet test administered to Carrie Buck was an unreliable measure of her intelligence; (d) Harry Laughlin lied in court about Carrie Buck's intelligence.

7. Gould implies in paragraph 18 that, in his handling of *Buck* v. *Bell,* Oliver Wendell Holmes (a) indeed showed judicial restraint; (b) did not show judicial restraint; (c) was uncertain about Laughlin's eugenic theories; (d) established a significant legal precedent that still exists today.

8. From the essay as a whole and from paragraph 22, we can infer that Carrie Buck (a) was a victim of repressive sexual mores characteristic of earlier times; (b) spoke out vehemently in her own defense but was unsuccessful; (c) lost her civil rights because she had been committed in to a state hospital; (d) was committed and later sterilized because she refused to name her rapist.

C. Structure

1. The primary mode of discourse in the essay is (a) narration; (b) description; (c) exposition; (d) persuasion. Defend your answer.

    _____

    _____

    _____

2. Gould's purpose in writing this essay is, specifically, (a) to trace the history of an important Supreme Court decision; (b) to tell the story of Carrie Buck's sad life; (c) to analyze the defects in eugenic theories; (d) to set the record straight about forced eugenic sterilization, using the case of Carrie Buck as the focus.

3. In a sentence or two, summarize the ideas in paragraphs 2 and 3.

    _____

    _____

    _____

    _____

4. Which of the following statements is crucial to understanding the wrong that was done to Carrie Buck? (a) California and Virginia applied forced sterilization more zealously than other states; (b) Three generations of imbeciles are enough; (c) [Her] supposed deviance was social and sexual; the charge of imbecility was a cover-up; (d) Inheritance stood as the crucial issue (indeed as the driving force behind all eugenics).

5. With regard to the essay as a whole, paragraphs 5–10 serve as (a) important explanatory background about the eugenics movement; (b) legal evidence in the case against Carrie Buck; (c) the author's own scientific theories; (d) a discussion of constitutional law.

6. Find examples of slang in paragraph 15. _____

    _____

    What is their effect? _____

    (Why does Gould put quotation marks around the word "scientific"?

    _____

7. The opinion of Dr. Paul A. Lombardo, whom Gould praises for his generous assistance in researching this case, is included because (a) he is an authority on *Buck* v. *Bell*; (b) he interviewed Carrie Buck and found her of normal intelligence; (c) he is a personal friend of Gould's; (d) he also does not accept the theories of eugenics supporters.

8. Why is this essay titled "Carrie Buck's Daughter" and not, say, "The Case of Carrie Buck"? _____

    _____

D. Vocabulary

For each italicized word from the selection, choose the best definition according to the context in which it appears.

1. that *prototype* of all prescription [paragraphs 1 and 9]: (a) relevant example; (b) original model; (c) written document; (d) set of legal precepts.

2. visiting the *iniquity* of the fathers upon the children [1 and 3]: (a) hereditary influence; (b) personality traits; (c) physical characteristics; (d) sin, wickedness.

3. lies in its *patent* unfairness [2 and 30]: (a) exclusive; (b) unsealed; (c) obvious; (d) protected.

4. the misdeeds of their distant *forebears* [2]: (a) descendants; (b) ancestors; (c) relatives; (d) siblings.

5. to remove this *stigma* of injustice [3]: (a) mark of disgrace; (b) principle; (c) representation; (d) damage.

6. their *criterion* for establishing forms of guilt [4]. (See also *criteria,* the plural form, in 14): (a) evaluation; (b) rationale; (c) motivation; (d) standard for judging.

7. those *deemed* biologically unfit [5]: (a) defended as; (b) declared free of; (c) considered, judged; (d) stereotyped as.

8. *abetted* by two major factors [6]: (a) encouraged; (b) supported; (c) proved; (d) justified.

9. a *punitive* measure for certain sexual crimes [6]: (a) corrupting; (b) penalty; (c) definitive; (d) revolutionary.

10. only California and Virginia applied them *zealously* [7]: (a) sparingly; (b) randomly; (c) uniformly; (d) enthusiastically.

11. No organization crusaded more *vociferously* [8]. (See also *vociferous* in 12): (a) loudly, vehemently; (b) effectively, productively; (c) openly, above board; (d) obsessively, compulsively.

12. his customary *verve* and power of style [10]: (a) flair; (b) eloquence; (c) liveliness; (d) forcefulness.

13. the *quintessential* statement of eugenic principles [10]: (a) definitive, authoritative; (b) pure, concentrated; (c) lucid, clear; (d) rational, reasonable.

14. held *antiquated* views [12]: (a) outmoded, obsolete; (b) absurd, ridiculous; (c) traditional, customary; (d) right-wing, reactionary.

15. *touted* as the latest in scientific modernism [12]: (a) revealed; (b) published; (c) praised; (d) identified.

16. the old *nomenclature* of mental deficiency [16]: (a) system of naming; (b) description; (c) hierarchy; (d) analytical model.

17. most feeblemindedness resides *ineluctably* in the genes [16]: (a) invisibly; (b) unavoidably; (c) unobtrusively; (d) indestructibly.

18. *covertly* sterilized [19]: (a) quickly; (b) effectively; (c) openly; (d) secretly.

19. the *crux* of the case [24]: (a) basic point; (b) highlight; (c) supporting evidence; (d) main argument.

20. a procedure of such *dubious* morality [30]: (a) wise; (b) high-minded; (c) doubtful; (d) clear-cut.

E. Questions for Analysis and Discussion

1. How effective is Gould at presenting information exonerating Carrie Buck and uncovering the real story behind her forced sterilization?

2. As Gould states in paragraph 5, the science of eugenics is not extinct today. With the increased availability of genetic counseling, prospective parents can learn the genetic makeup of their unborn children. Those who study ethics fear that soon parents will be able to choose an

offspring that meets a certain genetic model (height, eye color, intelligence level, and the like). Comment on this phenomenon. Does it pose ethical concerns for you?

Selection 15

Student Evaluations
Aristides

"Aristides" is the pen name of Joseph Epstein, professor of English at Northwestern University as well as an editor of and regular contributor to The American Scholar, *a publication of the Phi Beta Kappa Society. (Aristides "the Just" was a fifth-century political leader in Athens.) Epstein has published many books, among them* Plausible Prejudices *(1985) and* Ambition: The Secret Passion *(1980). This essay, which appeared in* The American Scholar, *is partly a confessional piece, in which Epstein discusses his own failings as a student, and partly an examination of teachers' expectations of students, written with Epstein's characteristic wit and self-deprecating humor.*

1   Socrates may have had to take the hemlock, but at least he was spared the indignity of that relatively recent addition to the teaching transaction known as "teacher evaluation." On these evaluations, generally made during the last minutes of the final session of the college term, students, in effect, grade their teachers. Hemlock may on occasion seem preferable, for turn-about here can sometimes be cruel play, especially when students, under the veil of anonymity, take the opportunity of evaluation to comment upon their teacher's dress, or idiosyncrasies, or moral character. For the most part I have not fared too badly on these evaluations, though my clothes have been the subject of faint comedy, my habit of jiggling the change in my pockets and my wretched handwriting have been noted, and in one instance I have been accused of showing favoritism (a charge I choose to interpret as my preference, in the classroom, for calling upon the relatively intelligent over the completely obtuse). None of these student comments, as you can plainly see, affects me in the least; such personal criticisms roll right off me, like buckshot off a duck's heart.

2   Unless they have long since been rendered catatonic by boredom, or are people on whom everything is lost, teachers of course make similar observations about their students—certainly this teacher does—and the one subject on which all teachers ought to be connoisseurs is that of the studentry. The difference is that teachers, unlike contemporary students, must keep these observations to themselves. Yet observe one will, nothing for it, and sometimes, as I am standing before a class, the subject of observation, I am myself observing my observers observing

me. In this particular zoo, it is not always clear who is the tourist and who is the ape. I do know that I carry the mental equivalent of a camera with me whenever I step into a classroom, and it is always clicking away, the monster of observation in me perpetually at work. To alter Christopher Isherwood slightly, "I am a chimera."*

3   "Ah, Miss Fogelson, you nod exuberantly, smiling in broad agreement, as if to say, 'I take your point exactly.' All quarter long you imply that you have taken my points. Your smiling nods are meant to convey that we are in some sort of intellectual complicity and are obviously on the same wave length. But beneath that nodding, invariably agreeable smile, why do I sense that in the high noon of your soul you are tuned to a hard rock AM station?"

4   "Mr. Gold, you scowl, sometimes fully glower, at what I say, which implies passion for and penetration into the subject under discussion, which your contemptuous countenance suggests I am making a terrible hash of. I would more readily believe in your perturbation had I not had the displeasure of having read your midterm examination, which reveals you to have greater control over your facial muscles than over your punctuation."

5   "Mr. Kantor, sitting in the back of the room, what are you whispering to and then laughing with Miss Reilly about? Have I stumbled verbally—committed a lip-o, the aural equivalent of a typo—resulting in my having mistakenly said something lewd? Is there a shred of broccoli from lunch stuck between my front teeth? Can my fly be open? Damn it, kiddo, what is so blasted amusing?"

6   "Miss Simpson, need you look so young and fresh and uncomplicatedly beautiful? Your earnest, not very clever presence in this hall of learning is a distraction to a dry man in a cold month, being without much joy, waiting for brains."

7   Thus does my mental camera click away, ever on the lookout for one or another kind of student performance. Of course, I much prefer the genuine article, bright students truly interested in learning, of whom I have had more than my fair share. But my mind is naturally attracted to falsity in student behavior, for I have in my own time been a nodder and smiler, a scowler and glowerer, a whisperer and laugher. For the better part of my sixteen years of formal schooling, I was a fake, a boy and then a young man who in the classroom aspired no higher than to mediocrity and frequently fell well short of the mark. I was precisely the kind of student whom today, as a teacher, I should view as obviously hopeless. Lest this seem false humility of a retrospective kind, an attempt to display a phony set of before and after photographs, let me hasten to add that, were I forced to return to school as a student

---

*A pun on Christopher Isherwood's book *I Am a Camera,* later made into a Broadway musical and movie, *Cabaret.* A *chimera* was a mythical fire-breathing she-monster who had the head of a lion, the body of a goat, and a tail like a serpent's.

now, I am reasonably confident that I would still be a bad student; and this for reasons I am not altogether clear about but shall nonetheless attempt to discover.

8   The question of what it is that makes for a good or a bad student never occurred to me quite so vividly as it did five or six years ago, when I served on a committee for student awards at the university where I teach. As a member of this committee, I read the classroom essays of an English major—an English major?, Lionel Trilling joked in his story "Of This Time, Of That Place." In what regiment?—who was a shoo-in candidate for the best junior-year student in the department. These essays were, each one of them, impeccable. Cold *A*'s, every one—not a semicolon out of place, flawlessly typed, perfectly shaped paragraphs led off by tidy topic sentences. Here was a boy who knew his job, who could deliver the goods.

9   It was only taken together that I found his classroom papers despicable. For a Marxist professor, this boy produced a correctly down-the-line analysis of *Sister Carrie;* for a survey course, he wrote a tribute to Benjamin Franklin as a hero of the American way of pragmatism and capitalist good sense; for a Freudian-minded teacher of nineteenth-century fiction, he discovered unresolved complexes and sexual tensions in *David Copperfield.* (Had he taken one of my courses, doubtless he would have played for me whatever intellectual music it is I wish to hear.) To each of his teachers he gave what he or she asked for—no less and a little bit more. As I read these essays en bloc, I grew first to feel uncomfortable about, then to dislike, finally actively to despise this young man, whom I thought of as an academic stock boy happily filling orders. He went on the following year to graduate with all possible honors. I hope I may be forgiven when I say that I do not wish him any too well. Like others who have chosen early in life to go with the flow, may he one day before too long be made to taste a little lava.

10   I was not a bad student in the way in which I think of this young man, who combined real intellectual gifts with real sycophancy, as a bad student. I did not give my teachers what they wanted; and I was distinctly not a sycophant, for the sound reason that I hadn't the basic skills to mount anything like a decent campaign to please my teachers. I was a bad student in the fundamental sense of being an inept student. Although I believe I was mildly precocious as a very young child—I could print my name before I went to school and my father gave me columns of numbers that I added up with alacrity and joy—once I hit the classroom my brain all but ceased functioning. I was not a discipline problem, I had no learning disabilities, but I was absolutely, even profoundly mediocre. Almost all the things one was called upon to do in the early grades, I could not do. I could not draw, and my coloring with crayons always strayed outside the lines; I sang badly off key; and my printing and early handwriting looked like the work of an incipient psychopath. I did not use scissors well, I could not draw a straight line,

I made my inkwells look as if they were Oklahoma gushers that had just come in, and with paste I was simply out of control. In later grades I brought something like the same impressive ineptitude to making outlines, diagramming sentences, assembling one or another kind of notebook. I remember especially those notebooks in which a student pasted down and catalogued the various kinds of leaves—you're nondeciduous now, so whaddaya gonna do?—easily marking the nadir of my grade-school productions; it was at least four or five full cuts down from disgraceful.

11   I used to say that I had too happy a childhood ever to bother learning grammar. But it would be more accurate to say that I did not learn anything that I found uninteresting. This might put me in the same category as George Santayana, who, reflecting on his years at the Boston Latin School, remarked that "I have always been recalcitrant about studying what doesn't interest me." One of the many differences between Santayana and me, however, is that almost nothing interested me, with the possible exception of spelling. I was all right at spelling, chiefly, I believe, because it was competitive, or at any rate competitively taught through the exercises known as spelldowns, from which I, for some reason, didn't wish to be too soon eliminated. I hope no one reading this will think that, had my teachers taken more "creative" approaches to learning, I would have been a better student, for I am convinced that I would have been even worse. Thinking back on my own early days of schooling, I realize that I reacted to only two stimuli, fear and competition, and when both were absent, so, mentally, was I.

12   As for competition, in my case it was highly selective. I rarely competed when I didn't have a decent chance of, if not winning, at least finishing respectably. I very early knew that I could not compete with the bright kids in my class who had a special aptitude for science, so by the time I was, say, ten or eleven, all science became uninteresting to me. So it went with other subjects. A few of my classmates had only to show strong aptitudes for me to show a countervailingly strong apathy. This, combined with my ability to take my pleasure in life from being a fair playground athlete and a more than fair general screw-off, left me a perfectly mediocre student—one of those children who merely gets by. If I was in any way in doubt about my own mediocrity as a student, I had it confirmed for me when, before going off to high school, I learned that I was not recommended to take Latin, as even the minimally bright students were.

13   Having myself been such a poor student, I naturally adore stories about geniuses who were judged to have been either poor or indifferent students in their day—in the way, I suppose, that failed writers take special delight in learning about classic works that were sorely neglected in their day. The most famous such story is about Albert Einstein's difficulties with mathematics in secondary school, though there is reason to believe that this may be a myth. But it is not mythical that St. Thomas

Aquinas when a student was known as "the dumb ox." In the class-room, Henry James was no great shakes. Theodore Dreiser made a rather poor showing in his single year at Indiana University. The physi-cist and philosopher Ernst Mach was deemed by his teachers to be ut-terly without talent, and they suggested that he be apprenticed to a cabinetmaker. (I blithely pass by all those geniuses who were splendid students right out of the starting gate.) Yet my guess is that all these men I have named probably failed to do well in school because they were dreamy, or unorthodox, or ran their trains of thought along differ-ent, wider-gauged, more farreaching tracks than conventional teaching could accommodate.

14   Along with distinctly not being a genius, I was not dreamy, or un-orthodox, or anything other than prodigiously uninterested. I went to a high school with lots of bright kids, but with no intellectual traditions. Anti-intellectual traditions ran much stronger. What are now called "street smarts" were greatly valued, but if there was wisdom in the world, surely no one in his right mind at my high school expected to find it in the words of teachers or in books. "In my school crowd, inso-far as I had one," Mary McCarthy has recently recounted of her high-school days, "nobody read." If anyone in my school crowd read, he kept it a secret. I had read the sports stories of John R. Tunis in grade school. I must have been assigned the dreary little project known as "book reports" in high-school English, but I evidently gave mine from Classic Comics, the comic book versions of great works of literature. Many years later, in New York, I met a free-lance writer down on his luck who had actually written some of the scripts for Classic Comics. Acknowledging his important contribution to my education, I thanked him warmly.

15   Over the course of four years in high school, I have no recollection of doing any homework, with the exception of preparation for geome-try. Here, I must report, fear operated. I quickly realized that I could not fake or finagle my way through this subject as I could—in fact, did—through every other. Besides, I happened to like geometry, the intellec-tual order and clarity of it; I also rather enjoyed manipulating theorems and axioms, and being able to close an argument with one of Euclid's rhythmic punch lines: "The angle of the dangle equals the flip of the zip," or "If the square of the hypotenuse equals the longest side, then the giraffe emits a laugh." The point I would underscore, however, is that, liking geometry and working at it, I nonetheless received for my efforts a *C*.

16   One of the fine shiny sociological clichés of our day is contained in the phrase "peer pressure." It might be mildly comforting to me to think that I did so poorly in school owing to peer pressure. Yet I cannot re-member feeling any such pressure; it is far more likely that I was one of those peers who put the pressure on other kids. I recall the rather light-hearted contempt with which my friends and I viewed the category of

students we referred to as "science bores." These were students who took an earnest interest in such subjects as math, physics, and chemistry (as opposed to my own circle's interest in gin rummy, blackjack, and poker), and who were usually identified by a uniform that consisted of thickish spectacles, rumpled cotton-flannel shirts, unmanageable curly hair, and a light coat of acne. I used to believe that there were no good teachers at my high school, but then it occurred to me that if a teacher was thought to be good—which meant serious and demanding—I steered clear of him. I remember a teacher of chemistry named Dr. Davidson, one of those gallant pedagogues with a Ph.D. who preferred to teach in the trenches of a city public high school. He was dark, with a receding hairline, a perpetually furrowed brow, and rimless glasses. He taught and walked the corridors in a white lab coat and, with every gesture, radiated an air of high intellectual purpose. I would just as soon have taken Dr. Davidson's chemistry course then as I would enter myself in a backwards naked marathon now.

17   I was able to get through what was then called "the general course" in high school without learning a thing—apart from the instruction available in the air provided by Dr. O.S. Mosis—and yet without ever actually failing a single subject. Lest anyone misread this as a chronicle of misgiving, let me hasten to add that during this time I enjoyed myself hugely, while devoting my days to the extracurricular and my nights to the paracurricular. I was able to achieve this through the application of mother wit and the careful selection of the weakest courses taught by the poorest teachers.

18   My parents had a respect for education but, not having gone to college themselves, they had very little interest in schooling. When I would bring home my invariably dismal report cards—a couple of *C*'s, a *D*, a rare *B*, a more frequent *A* in gym—my father would read it, recite a little homily to me about trying harder to do my best, sign it, and let it go at that. I gather that my parents must have concluded that their eldest son's talents, if he had any at all, lay outside the classroom. I am grateful to them for this, especially today when, as a teacher, I regularly encounter students who work under the extreme pressure of parents who have grandiose educational plans for them and who have not been able to conceal their disappointment that their child did not get admitted to Harvard or Yale, Princeton or Brown. (What, I have long wondered, was Brown's first name? Somehow I have the feeling that it wasn't Irving.) If you are looking for a big tax write-off under medical expenses (therapy chiefly), my advice is that you get behind your children and push them really hard to get into the very best universities.

19   Far from being pushed, I decided quite on my own to go to college. (After about the age of ten, it occurs to me, I made all the educational decisions in my life.) If I had chosen not to go to college but instead directly to work, no one would have been in the least surprised and no one certainly would have been aggrieved. To give my mediocrity a nu-

meric character, I graduated 152 in a class of 211. Today it would be difficult to find a respectable college for a student who had done so poorly —finishing just above the lowest quarter of his class. But in the middle fifties, if you were a resident of the state, the University of Illinois had to accept you as a student, with the single proviso that students who finished in the bottom quarter of their high-school graduating classes were accepted on probation. This can be a bit tricky to explain to the young, but college then was at once more casual and more serious than it is now. Getting in was not so difficult—I never, for example, had to take the College Board Examinations, as I believe the SAT's were then called—but flunking out was much easier. Nowadays the reverse seems to be the case. A friend who has taught at Harvard in recent years remarked to me that, by and large, students at Harvard did not seem to him all that interested in what goes on in classrooms there. "After all," he said, "what is likely to be the greatest achievement in most of their lives has already taken place—this is that they have been admitted to Harvard."

20   In England, in France, in Germany, a boy who had done as poorly as I in secondary school would have been scrubbed, washed up, finished. In education, however, America is the land of the second chance, a condition of which I, for reasons not entirely impersonal, vastly approve. My own experience has left me a half-hearted elitist—someone who feels that everything possible should be done to single out, encourage, and promote true talent, yet who also knows that talent has a way of sometimes not showing up on schedule. In *Out of Step*, his soon-to-be-published autobiography, the philosopher Sidney Hook reveals himself to have been a rebellious high-school student of the wise-guy type; I recently read, in a collection of his letters, that the widely talented poet and painter Weldon Kees never received other than mediocre grades in school. Doubtless hundreds of other names of talented men and women could be adduced who performed poorly in school, and out of this list a National Dishonor Society could be formed, though where exactly the dishonor ought to fall—on the students for not working very hard, or on their teachers for not contriving to get the best of them—is by no means clear. My own rather jaded view is that no matter how efficient and finely meshed an educational system one devises, many children will slip through it and some among them will be the (secretly) talented. A few may scarcely need any schooling at all. "The only school Beethoven attended, and then only for a short time," reports J.W.N. Sullivan in his study of the composer's spiritual development, "was a lower grade public school in Bonn called the Tirocinium."

21   I blush to speak of the talented, even the secretly talented, for if I had any talent at eighteen, when I went off to the state university that by law was compelled to accept me, it was certainly a secret to me. I had, however, a very keen sense of the talents that I did *not* possess. Most of the friends with whom I went off to the University of Illinois

were majoring in business, a subject that I, too, should no doubt have majored in, if only because, in the context of the rather philistine middle-class culture in which I grew up, business sounded so splendidly purposeful. But to major in business meant one had to take several courses in accounting, and I knew, in the nuclei of the cells of the marrow of my smallest bones, that with my handwriting, my penchant for disorder, my unearned disdain for clerical detail, I could turn enrollment in an introductory accounting course into a Venetian tragedy. Out of fear of accounting, then, I chose to study something called "liberal arts," a phrase I heard for the first time only after I had arrived on the campus of the University of Illinois in Champaign–Urbana.

22   If fear of accounting sent me into the liberal arts, fear of flunking out of college kept me studying them, I will not say with intelligence but with ferocious energy. I was less than handsomely equipped for the task of staying in school: I had an unsure grasp of English grammar, knowledge of no foreign language beyond the level of *el burro es un animal importante,* a mind unclogged with even the rudiments of general science, a storehouse of historical fact learned exclusively at the movies, and no study habits whatsoever. My approach to college study was quite simple—I merely memorized everything set before me. Biological taxonomy, French verbs, seventeenth-century English sonnets—hey, as they say nowadays, no problem, I memorized them all. In a composition course then somewhat grandly entitled Rhetoric, I learned that I had a very small knack for writing, a knack I didn't overstrain by doing anything fancy; and anything fancy included using a semicolon, which looked to me like a combination of a Hebrew vowel and a Chinese ideograph and which I wouldn't have touched with a ten-foot dash. Fear of humiliation goading me on all the way, I was able to achieve something like a *B* average at the close of my first semester.

23   Out of the Crockpot into the Cuisinart, I transferred a year later to the University of Chicago, which must have been rather hard up for undergraduates if it accepted me, though I am very grateful that it did. Graduate students greatly outnumbered undergraduates at the University of Chicago, and the school's graduate students set the tone for the place, which was bohemian, slightly neurotic, and very serious. What made the University of Chicago seem especially impressive, at least to my untrained eyes, were the Europeans on its faculty, refugees from Hitler's depredations in Europe. The undergraduates I encountered were kilometers ahead of me intellectually; the representative undergraduate struck me then as being someone from New York who had been reading the *New Republic* from the age of eleven and decided against going to an Ivy League school because they were all deemed too lightweight. Some among them possessed what seemed to me startlingly arcane information about history, early music, philosophy, politics. Once, in a poetry class taught by Elder Olson, Olson began chanting, quite beautifully and in French, a poem by Baudelaire. He was presently joined in his

chant by the student sitting next to me, whose name was Martha Silverman, who also had the poem by heart and in French. Sensing more vividly than ever before how much over my head I was, I felt a strong wave of utter hopelessness wash over me. Oh, Martha, what has become of you since that brilliant performance on that dark morning in Elder Olson's classroom? Did you, I wonder, peak at that very moment, to fall thenceforth gently into decline?

24   I had become more earnest as a student, but I was clearly in the camp of the drones. Even among drones I was a drone. In three years at the University of Chicago I do not believe I ever said anything in a classroom that advanced the discussion in any useful way. On the rare occasions when I spoke at all, usually after being called upon to do so, no teacher ever capped my comments by saying, "A point well taken," or "That is nicely formulated," or "Good, but can you say a little more?" or even "Interesting." The only time I ever knew an answer that no one else in the room knew was when, in a course on the novel, Morton Dauwen Zabel asked if anyone knew what other famous book besides *Madame Bovary* was then—it was 1957—in its centenary year. I happened to have read somewhere, perhaps in the News Notes of *Poetry,* that 1957 was the centenary of *Les Fleurs du Mal.* I raised my hand, decided not to risk the French, and when called upon said, "Charles Baudelaire's *The Flowers of Evil.*" "Correct," said Zabel. "Thank you." I felt flush, as if I had just won the lottery.

25   On the few occasions when I attempted to slip free of dronedom, it proved a mistake. In a course on satire, a very nice professor put forth his theory of satire, which I thought half-baked, and I criticized it in a term paper in which I put forth a completely raw theory of my own. The result was a charitable *C.* In a course in Greek history, I was asked to do an essay on why Philip of Macedon chose Aristotle for his son Alexander's tutor. Cutting through a good deal of historico-political claptrap, I said it was really quite simple: Philip, being no dope, wanted the best possible teacher for his son, and there was none better than Aristotle in the whole of the Peloponnesus. Another icy *C,* this time accompanied by the gentle remonstrance that I should try to control a tendency toward glibness. The evidence was beginning to weigh in: as a drone, I was a *B* student; as an original thinker, I was a *C.*

26   I should have been delighted if, when I was young, some teacher had taken me aside and said, or in his behavior implied, "There is something special in you, and I want to help you develop it." None ever did. But, then, it occurs to me to add, there wasn't anything special in me. I was a rough without a diamond in it. It would be convenient for me now to say of myself that I was obviously a late developer; that, at any rate, is the conventional category in which my intellectual autobiography would seem to fit. But I do not truly think I am a late developer. (I began publishing in magazines, somewhat precociously, in my early twenties.) I think instead that I am someone who has never

been able to profit much from the kind of education that is available in classrooms and lecture halls. I may be, in the strict schoolroom sense of the term, ineducable.

27   Not that I was entirely impervious to my teachers, but such influence as they exerted upon me was, in the main, stylistic. Watching a lecture delivered in the grand European manner, or a social scientist unsentimentally dissecting a serious subject, or an art historian passionately conveying his love for Guido Reni—all this was very exciting to me, yet the problem may have been that I *watched* it so intently that I never quite *heard* what they were saying. Observing my professors seemed so much more interesting than actually listening to them.

28   Had I gone on to graduate school, which I never for a moment contemplated doing, I might have fallen under the sway of some powerful teacher and become, say, a Straussian, or Wintersian, or Leavisite. Yet I rather doubt it. I was plenty ignorant, but I wasn't gullible. I had a strong father at home and wasn't looking for one away from home. I also had a street-learned skepticism, and I believed with Santayana (whom I hadn't yet read) that "skepticism is the chastity of the intellect, and it is shameful to surrender it too soon or to the first comer. . . ." In any case, I think I should have bridled under too firm an intellectual influence. One of the things that college taught me was that I cannot be taught in the conventional manner. Autodidactically, I have to go about things in my own pokey way, obliquely acquiring on my own such intellectual skills as I have, assembling such learning as I possess from my odd, unsystematic reading. Are there many such people as I? The inefficacy of teaching in his own life, if I may say so, is an unusual thing to have to admit on the part of a man who himself spends a good part of his own time teaching others. But there it is— or, rather, there I am.

29   As a former poor student who is now a teacher, I study good students rather as Malinowski did the Trobriand Islanders—as an outsider, someone, that is, who is distinctly not one of them. I am tempted to steal a formulation from Tolstoy and say that all good students are alike while every bad student is bad in his own way, except that I don't quite believe it is so. My quotation in the previous paragraph from Santayana reminds me that one of Santayana's best students was Walter Lippmann, whom he asked to stay on to be his assistant at Harvard, though that young man had other ideas about his career. Traditionally, good students at Harvard have been thought to have a certain intellectual sophistication and suavity without being very deep, whereas good students at the University of Chicago have been thought to be deep but without much in the way of intellectual sophistication or suavity. Owing perhaps to such go-getter alumni as Henry Luce, William Benton, and Chester Bowles, one tends to think of good students at Yale as training themselves for success in the world, while at Princeton the social question—that is to say, snobbery—still seems uppermost, though

this may be a hangover from F. Scott Fitzgerald days (Fitzgerald was himself a very poor student, and so was another famous Princetonian named Adlai Stevenson). Good students at St. John's in Annapolis seem almost too earnest—the good life is all very well, but leading it surely cannot entail talking about it so much, as all "great books" education seems to require of its students. But good students have a way of popping up in odd places; and, besides, it is probably more sensible today to refer not to good schools—viewed close up, no contemporary school seems very good—but instead to schools that are difficult to get into.

30   Still, I remain astonished at the sheer proficiency of certain students. When I was myself a student, I was much impressed with the type of good student known as "the quick study." The girl-friend of a friend of mine at the University of Chicago, who did not appear to be more than mildly interested in intellectual things, seemed unable to score poorly on an examination or to write an unsuccessful paper. One felt about Dottie that she could write a *B+* paper on John Stuart Mill while sitting under a tree during a monsoon, or score an *A–* on a mathematics exam administered to her during a car crash. At the school where I teach, I have come across a number of students with the happy knack of knocking out term papers that quite simply cannot be given less than an *A*. These students are like beautifully trained retrievers: "T.S. Eliot and Catholicism"—OK, girl, fetch! "Dostoyevsky's Politics"— C'mon, boy, go get it! And they do: efficiently, tidily, sometimes quite brilliantly. Often behind what I have called "the happy knack"—my old tendency toward glibness is still intact, I see—is a great deal of effort; and careful writing is, after all, the best evidence going for having an orderly and lucid mind. And yet the superior writers among my students are often merely those students who best sense what is wanted of them and, through skills they have developed over the years, are able to deliver it. I am generally delighted, in the locution of the car dealers, "to take delivery." Still, in my intellectual greed, I hope that my best students will be more than merely good at school.

31   Everyone who teaches must at some point ask himself what he wants from his students. If one is teaching a science, or a foreign language, or the skills required for such vocations as law or journalism, the answer ought to be clear—one wants one's students to master the material in the course. But in the teaching of literature, which is what I teach, I don't believe the materials are quite masterable; I have no notion how one masters Henry James or Joseph Conrad. Far from having mastered the materials I teach, I frequently find that, from semester to semester, I cannot even remember them myself, and so have to reread five- and six-hundred-page novels. It would be foolish to expect one's students to be better at this than one is oneself.

32   In my case the matter is complicated by the fact that, so far as I know, I teach no strict doctrine, no clear method; I have no architectonic ideas, or even any very tonic ones. I try to make sense of literary

works, convey my appreciation for their subtlety and power and beauty, and make plain their significance. If my teaching has a central message, it is probably the intellectual equivalent of "Don't accept any wooden nickels." (Usually these intellectual wooden nickels have "isms" attached to them.) All this being so, my ideal student is one who has that intolerance for nonsense otherwise known as skepticism. But his must be skepticism of a certain kind—skepticism reinforced by seriousness. By seriousness I mean the understanding that art and ideas have real consequences—consequences over the long haul as great and sometimes greater than those of politics and technology—that life is at once a gift and a puzzle, and that the attempt to make the most of this life through coming to an understanding of the puzzle is not the only game in town but surely the most important one. Of course, in the young such seriousness is almost always inchoate, but it does from time to time turn up, and when it does it is immensely impressive and makes merely being good at school—you will pardon the expression—academic.

33   As a teacher who was not himself good at school, I have a special sympathy for students who do not perform well in class. I rather prize C students—were my younger self to walk into one of my current courses, he would doubtless get a C, perhaps a C+—for in the current day of grade inflation, to be able to give a student a C helps convince a teacher that he still has high standards. When I sense a student's nervousness, my own nervousness as a student comes back to me. In a sense, I still am a poor student, or at least have the psychology of a poor student. When an undergraduate, I would occasionally have what I think of as student nightmares: these usually involved my having to take an exam in some branch of higher mathematics or some language, such as Persian, for which I was wholly unprepared. Now, generally near the beginning of a new term, I can count on a teaching nightmare: these usually involve my having lost my notes before a lecture, or being unable to find the room in which I am to teach, or knowing nothing whatever about the subject in which I am to instruct others. Today, even awake, when giving an examination, I feel a slight shudder of terror pass over me—terror and relief at not having to take another college examination myself.

34   A few years after I began teaching, it occurred to me that being a teacher—not being a student—provides the best education. "To teach is to learn twice," wrote Joubert, in a simple-sounding maxim that could have several different meanings. It could mean that one first learns when getting up the material one is about to teach and then tests and relearns it in the actual teaching. It could mean that being a teacher offers one a fine chance for a second draft on one's inevitably inadequate initial education. It could mean that learning, like certain kinds of love, is better the second time around. It could mean that we are not ready for education, at any rate of the kind that leads on to wisdom, until we

are sixty, or seventy, or beyond. I favor this last interpretation, for it accounts for the strange feeling that I have had every year of my adult life, which is that only twelve months ago I was really quite stupid.

A. Comprehension

Choose the answer that best completes each statement. Do not refer to the selection while doing this exercise.

1. Aristides writes that he observes his students carefully, identifying the obviously bright ones but also looking out for (a) the glowerers and scowlers; (b) budding but undiscovered geniuses; (c) bad students who need extra encouragement; (d) students who are fakes, the way he was as a student.

2. One kind of bad student that Aristides encountered when he served on a student awards committee was a young man who (a) refused to take responsibility for his own learning; (b) produced flawless papers reflecting exactly what each professor wanted; (c) submitted plagiarized essays; (d) exhibited no real intellectual curiosity.

3. As a student, Aristides reacted to only two stimuli: (a) threats from his parents and warnings from the principal; (b) threats from his teachers and competition; (c) fear of humiliation and competition; (d) the desire to get into a good college and to achieve status among his peers.

4. The only subject Aristides studied for, simply because he couldn't fake his way through it, was (a) physics; (b) English; (c) geometry; (d) poetry.

5. Aristides characterizes himself as a student as (a) concerned only with his social life; (b) lazy and unmotivated; (c) skeptical of teachers' attempts to find what he was good at; (d) profoundly mediocre.

6. When the author was assigned book reports to write in high school, he (a) diligently read the assigned books but pretended he hadn't to his friends; (b) watched the movies made from the books; (c) read the Classic Comic versions instead; (d) didn't bother to do the assignment.

7. When Aristides wrote papers in college in which he tried to say something original, (a) he received lower grades than when he gave the professors what they wanted; (b) he received higher grades; (c) he was accused of plagiarism; (d) he received approving, highly complimentary comments.

8. Aristides defines the ideal student as one who (a) takes responsibility for his or her own learning; (b) organizes his or her time efficiently and hands assignments in on time; (c) develops a philosophy based on reading, observation, and thinking; (d) develops a healthy skepticism tempered by a serious appreciation of the importance of ideas.

B. Inferences

On the basis of the evidence in the paragraphs indicated, mark these statements as follows: PA for inferences that are probably accurate; PI for inferences that are probably inaccurate; and IE for insufficient evidence. You may refer to the selection to answer the questions in this section, and all in the remaining sections.

_____   1. Aristides believes that college students should not have the right to evaluate their teachers. [paragraph 1]

_____   2. The other members of the student awards committee shared Aristides' contempt for the English major's essays. [8]

_____   3. The fear that Aristides says was one of his primary motivations for doing well in spelling bees probably refers to his fear of being embarrassed in front of his peers. [11]

_____   4. Aristides' teachers recognized his innate talents but were unsuccessful in their attempts to motivate him. [11]

_____   5. Aristides deliberately sought out the weakest, least demanding teachers so that he could get mediocre grades for doing little work. [16–17]

_____   6. The author decided to go to the University of Illinois probably because he realized that he had wasted his high school years. [19]

_____   7. Teachers are as much to blame for their students turning in unoriginal work as the students are themselves. [8, 9, and 25]

_____   8. Far from being truly mediocre, as his academic performance suggested, the author simply was not equipped to learn in the conventional classroom and with conventional methods. [26]

_____   9. Aristides is very impressed with the quality of education at universities like Harvard, Princeton, and Yale. [29]

_____   10. Because of his own experience during his student days, Aristides is probably more sympathetic to mediocre, unmotivated students than most teachers are. [33]

C. Structure

1. Explain in your own words what you consider Aristides' primary purpose in writing this essay. _____
_____
_____

2. The main idea of the essay is that (a) American teachers do not provide enough academic challenges for their students; (b) the American educational system fosters mediocrity; (c) the author's mediocre academic performance was no indication of his real talents and intellectual skills; (d) students today do not know what being a good student requires.

3. Look again at the last sentence in paragraph 1. Explain the simile and explain why it is funny. _____

    _____

    _____

4. In paragraph 2, Aristides writes, "Yet observe one will, nothing for it. . . ." Paraphrase this expression. _____

    _____

5. In paragraphs 3–6, Aristides gives us imaginary comments on hypothetical students as his mental camera clicks away. Briefly explain what Aristides says about each student:
    Miss Fogelson [3] _____

    _____

    Mr. Gold [4]   _____

    _____

    Mr. Kantor [5] _____

    _____

    Miss Simpson [6] _____

    _____

6. In the metaphor at the end of paragraph 9, _____ is compared to _____. What does the metaphor mean?

    _____

    _____

7. In paragraph 13, Aristides mentions the names of geniuses who were supposedly terrible students because (a) he doesn't believe these stories; (b) he includes himself in this group; (c) he would like to think that he was part of the group, even though he knows he isn't; (d) he wants to prove that geniuses are self-made, not taught.

8. How would you characterize the tone in the second half of paragraph 18? (a) sincere, earnest; (b) ironic, mocking; (c) objective, impartial; (d) complaining, aggrieved.

9. In your own words, explain the point Aristides is trying to make in paragraphs 24–25. _____

    _____

    _____

10. The tone of the essay as a whole can best be described as (a) confessional, humorous, yet serious; (b) straightforward and objective; (c) philosophical and reflective; (d) confessional, humorous, and arrogant.

D. Vocabulary

For each italicized word from the selection, choose the best definition according to the context in which it appears.

1. comment on their *idiosyncracies* [paragraph 1]: (a) peculiar characteristics; (b) personal weaknesses; (c) inherited traits; (d) virtues, strengths.
2. the relatively *obtuse* [1]: (a) intellectually gifted; (b) slow to understand; (c) comatose, unresponsive; (d) shy, reticent.
3. some sort of intellectual *complicity* [3]: (a) model for correct behavior; (b) majority opinion; (c) conspiracy or partnership; (d) competition.
4. your contemptuous *countenance* [4]: (a) mannerism; (b) appearance; (c) discourse; (d) tone of voice.
5. believe in your *perturbation* [4]: (a) determination; (b) competitive spirit; (c) anger; (d) agitation.
6. These essays were *impeccable* [8]: (a) brilliant; (b) boring; (c) flawless; (d) difficult to criticize.
7. As I read these essays *en bloc* (A French expression, pronounced än blŏk´ [9]: (a) one by one; (b) as a single group; (c) quickly, cursorily; (d) in anticipation.
8. I was distinctly not a *sycophant.* [10] (See also *sychophancy,* 10): (a) a person with a creative mind; (b) a docile, easily led person; (c) a troublemaker; (d) a servile flatterer.
9. the work of an *incipient* psychopath [10]: (a) dangerous; (b) violent; (c) long-established; (d) beginning.
10. an *inept* student [10]. (See also *ineptitude,* 10): (a) indifferent; (b) self-indulgent; (c) passive; (d) incompetent.
11. the *nadir* of my grade-school productions [10]: (a) lowest point; (b) highest point; (c) main point; (d) ridiculous joke.
12. I have always been *recalcitrant* about studying [11]: (a) eager, enthusiastic; (b) stubbornly resistant; (c) uncompromising, inflexible; (d) difficult to motivate.
13. because they were *unorthodox* [13 and 14]: (a) eccentric; (b) habitually lying; (c) unconventional; (d) disorganized.
14. *prodigiously* uninterested [14]: (a) enormously; (b) seriously; (c) slightly; (d) obsessively.
15. one of those gallant *pedagogues* [16]: (a) politicians; (b) diplomats; (c) taskmasters; (d) schoolteachers.
16. recite a little *homily* to me [18]: (a) short poem; (b) list of rules; (c) moralizing sermon; (d) humorous anecdote.
17. no one certainly would have been *aggrieved* [19]: (a) surprised; (b) interested; (c) distressed; (d) stirred up.

18. My own rather *jaded* view [20]: (a) deviant; (b) world-weary; (c) unique; (d) irrational.

19. Fear of humiliation *goading* me on [22]: (a) urging; (b) yanking; (c) gently nudging; (d) nagging.

20. startlingly *arcane* information [23]: (a) earthshaking; (b) deeply philosophical; (c) understood by only a select few; (d) available to everyone.

21. control a tendency toward *glibness* [25 and 30]: (a) shallowness, superficiality; (b) pretentiousness, arrogance; (c) awkwardness, clumsiness; (d) stupidity, dullness.

22. Not that I was entirely *impervious* to my teachers [27]: (a) irresistible; (b) rude; (c) incapable of being appreciative; (d) incapable of being affected.

23. I should have *bridled* under too firm an influence [28]: (a) become resentful; (b) become more disciplined; (c) improved; (d) conformed.

24. *Autodidactically,* I have to go about things [28]: (a) slow to learn; (b) self-taught; (c) eager to absorb new knowledge; (d) self-restrained.

25. such seriousness is almost always *inchoate* [32]: (a) fully formed; (b) primitive, undeveloped; (c) in its initial stage; (d) impossible to detect.

E. Questions for Analysis and Discussion

1. Comment on Aristides' humor. How would you characterize it?

2. Aristides confesses that he was a bad, or at least a mediocre, student. Do you agree with this assessment? In the long run, does it matter? Is there any particular advantage to his academic mediocrity in high school and college?

Reading Short Stories

Literature, Aristotle wrote, serves to delight and to instruct. Modern critics do not consider it fashionable to speak of the *didactic* (instructional) aspects of literature; the term has gotten a bad name from moralistic poetry and fiction that has been popular at various times throughout literary history. Aristotle's phrase does not mean that literature "instructs" us in the moralistic sense. Rather, it means that we read literature for enjoyment and for its revelation of human experience and behavior. We learn, through the actions of a story's characters, about our own humanity. We learn about all of human experience, far beyond what we as individuals could possibly experience in a lifetime.

Short stories are included in this book, not only to provide you with a different opportunity for sharpening and round out your reading skills, but also to round out your reading experiences and to give you enjoyment. This is the reason that you should read the four stories in Part V, even if they are not all assigned to you.

Analyzing the Short Story

Students commonly complain when they study literature—particularly in high school and introductory college courses—that analysis ruins the pleasure of reading, as if examining the structure of a story (or of a

poem or a play) somehow destroys their appreciation of it. Surely, literary analysis is unrewarding and meaningless if you are asked to consider irrelevant topics like the one a college classmate of mine was asked to write on in her American literature survey: "Brand Names in William Faulkner's Fiction." This is trivia, not analysis.

Analysis, as you may recall from Part II, means breaking down a subject to see how each part functions in relation to the whole. Rather than killing your enthusiasm or spontaneous enjoyment, analysis of literature has—or at least should have—the opposite effect: to increase your understanding. And the more you understand how a story or a poem works, the more likely you will "delight" (as Aristotle wrote) in the experience of reading it.

The Short Story Defined

A story can be broadly defined as a fairly brief piece of narrative prose. It is fiction (that is, the people and events in it are made up), as opposed to nonfiction (or prose writing on real topics), such as the essays you have been reading in Part IV. The length is not particularly important. Roughly speaking, a short story can be anywhere from two or three pages to as many as thirty or forty pages long. Stories longer than that are usually classified as *novellas,* ("little novels").

More important than length is what the story accomplishes. Typically, a *short story* presents a series of actions or events that reveal a single aspect of a character. In contrast, a *novel* reveals many aspects of the life and experience of a character or of several characters. Whereas a novel may describe a character's entire life, or even the lives of several generations of characters, the action of a short story is tightly compressed, so that we see a character at a particular time in his or her life. "Miss Brill" by Katherine Mansfield illustrates this compression well. We see Miss Brill at one stage of her life, and we infer only a few bare facts about her life. She is old and supports herself by giving English lessons and reading aloud to an invalid. She lives alone somewhere on the French coast; she spends her Sunday afternoons at the public garden listening to the music and observing people. The exposition (or background) is subtly woven into the story's brief content, and the bulk of the action, such as it is, takes place on a single Sunday afternoon.

The Parts of a Short Story

A story's action is divided into two parts: rising action and falling action. During the *rising action,* the author provides the background or ex-

position, introduces the character(s), establishes the setting (location, environment, and often weather or season), and sets the action in motion. The main character, called the *protagonist,* encounters a conflict, a tension between himself or herself and something else—perhaps another character (termed the *antagonist*), a custom or belief at odds with his own nature, an element in the physical or social environment, or perhaps even an element in his own nature.

For example, "The Lady with the Pet Dog" by Chekhov, the first story in Part V, conveys two conflicts, one external and the other internal. Gurov, the main character, is at odds with himself. At the beginning of the story, he despises women, calling them "the lower race," but as his affair with Anna Sergeyevna progresses, he falls in love with her, and has difficulty reconciling his feelings of tenderness and compassion with his former hostility. The external conflict is between the characters and the larger society they inhabit and the strict mores of late-nineteenth-century Russia. Trapped in unhappy marriages with divorce apparently unthinkable, Anna and Gurov appear doomed.

In "Miss Brill," the outward conflict is generational, as shown in the scene in which the two young people rudely mock the older woman. But within herself, Miss Brill embodies another conflict, the classic one between illusion—her self-deceptive but harmless means of coping with her loneliness—and reality—the harsher view of herself and her life the young people force her to confront.

In most stories, the tension or conflict increases as the events proceed until a *crisis,* or turning point, is reached. After the crisis, the action changes to a *falling action,* in which the character resolves the conflict or, increasingly in modern fiction, is defeated by it, or is changed in some way. In Raymond Carver's story, "Cathedral," the main character exhibits an attitude of barely disguised sarcasm toward his wife's blind friend. During the falling action of the story, however, he experiences an *epiphany*—a sudden flash of revelation or recognition—when the blind man asks him to draw a picture of a cathedral.

Not all stories have "happy endings," in which tensions and problems are ironed out and we are led to believe that everyone will live happy lives. In this collection, only "Cathedral" ends on a positive note. But despite the unhappy or unsatisfactory endings in the other three stories, we have learned something about human experience and human relationships. In Bobbie Ann Mason's story, "Shiloh," we learn how married people can drift apart when communication falters and when people change. In "Miss Brill," we see the terrible loneliness of the old. And in "The Lady with the Pet Dog" we learn about the dangers of idle flirtation and the unhappiness that results from marrying the wrong person. The essential principle in each case is that the story's action, the conflict or tension, and the crisis reveal something new to us about the character—an aspect or truth that we did not know at the story's beginning.

Diagramming the Plot

The *plot*—or sequence of events—of a typical story can be diagrammed as follows. (Keep in mind that not every story you read will conform exactly to this model.)

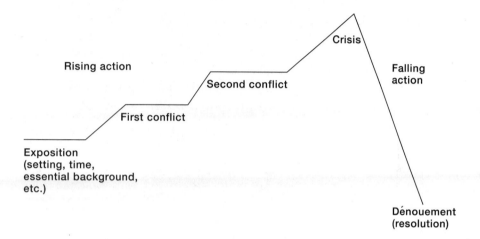

Besides plot, the second primary element in fiction is *character*—the people in the story as they are described and revealed to us, their actions, their responses to events around them, their motivations, their behavior. Out of plot and character comes the third basic element in fiction—*theme*. The theme is the underlying idea that the author wishes to get across, the idea that gives rise to plot and character. In other words, the theme is embodied in the story's events and in the way the characters respond to them.

Other considerations are important, too. For example, from whose point of view do we observe the story's events? (Who is the narrator?) What tone do the author's words reveal? Does the weather or the season of the year have a symbolic meaning? In "The Lady with the Pet Dog," for example, the passion of Anna and Gurov's love affair is symbolically reflected in the steamy but oppressive heat of Yalta, the seaside resort where they meet. Later, when Gurov returns to his family in Moscow, winter has arrived unseasonably early, suggesting both the death of their love affair and his frozen emotions.

In fiction, everything works together, and in a good short story, everything counts. The reader's task is complex, requiring attention not just to structure and event but to little things as well. Little, seemingly insignificant details *are* important. The careful writer embellishes a story with detail to provide texture and reality and to suggest some strength or foible in the characters.

For example, in Bobbie Ann Mason's short story, "Shiloh," the main character, Leroy, Norma Jean's husband, is disabled, the result of an accident, and is living on disability, no longer able to work as a long-distance trucker. When we are introduced to Leroy, we learn that Leroy spends his day making things from craft kits. For example, he has made a miniature log cabin from notched Popsicle sticks (which later inspires him to dream of building a log cabin for him and Norma Jean from notched logs and plunking it down in one of the numerous subdivisions ringing their Kentucky town). He has made pictures out of string and black velvet, a snap-together B-17 plane, a macramé owl, and a lamp out of a model truck.

We also know about Leroy that he gets his information from *Donahue;* that he drives aimlessly around the town, pondering the changes in his life; that he buys marijuana from a doctor's teenage son; and that he does nothing around the house. What do the details about his craft kits suggest, then? When we add them to other things we know about Leroy, we see that he is drifting. His choice of crafts—all a little tacky, definitely artificial and unnecessary—suggests that he has no idea what to do with himself or what Norma Jean would like or need. And as the story unfolds and we learn more about Leroy and Norma Jean's marriage, we see that their relationship is as fragile as these useless knick-knacks.

In other words, the details add a dimension and a subtlety to their growing conflict, heightening it and making us more aware of it. They are not included as useless decoration.

Questions about Short Stories

Each of the four stories in Part V is followed by questions for discussion, analysis, and writing. However, they are by no means meant to exhaust the possibilities for analysis and discussion. Here are some general questions on plot, character, and theme that you can ask yourself after you read each story.

Questions about Plot

1. How are the incidents that make up the plot related to each other? Is there a cause-and-effect relationship between them?
2. Does the plot suggest conflict? If so, who or what is responsible for it?
3. Where in the story does the crisis occur? What provokes it?
4. Is the conflict resolved, and if it is, is it resolved satisfactorily?

5. Is there any evidence of irony in the plot? (In literature, *irony* refers to knowledge or information that the reader has that the characters are unaware of.)

6. Does the plot suggest an additional interpretation, one which perhaps the reader can see but which the characters cannot?

Questions about Character

1. Define each character in terms of his or her "essence," behavior, and motivation.

2. How are the characters revealed to us (through direct comment, through contact with others, through behavior)?

3. Why do the characters behave as they do? Are their actions consistent with what has been revealed about them?

4. Do any characters change during the course of the story?

5. What is your response to each character? What is the basis for your attitude?

6. Do any of the characters stand for something greater than themselves—that is, can their actions be interpreted as symbolic?

Questions about Theme

1. What is the theme and how is it embodied in the story?

2. In what ways do plot and character work to convey the theme?

3. Are there minor themes?

4. What do we learn about human existence and human nature from the story?

Short Story 1

The Lady with the Pet Dog
Anton Chekhov

Born in Russia, Anton Chekhov was the grandson of a serf (peasant servant) whose father abandoned his family when Chekhov was sixteen to escape going to debtors' prison. Chekhov learned early on to shift for himself. He studied medicine on scholarship at the University of Moscow. However, literature became more important to him than his medical practice, and today, he is universally regarded as one of the world's great writers of the nineteenth century. He wrote short stories, masterful little gems with carefully sketched

characters, as "The Lady with the Pet Dog" well illustrates. He is also known for his plays, some of the most famous being The Sea Gull, Three Sisters, *and* The Cherry Orchard. *In 1904, Chekhov died of tuberculosis at the age of forty-four.*

I

They were saying a new face had been seen on the esplanade: a lady with a pet dog. Dmitry Dmitrich Gurov, who had already spent two weeks in Yalta* and regarded himself as an old hand, was beginning to show an interest in new faces. He was sitting in Vernet's coffeehouse when he saw a young lady, blonde and fairly tall, wearing a beret and walking along the esplanade. A white Pomeranian was trotting behind her.

Later he encountered her several times a day in the public gardens or in the square. She walked alone, always wearing the same beret, and always accompanied by the Pomeranian. No one knew who she was, and people called her simply "the lady with the pet dog."

"If she is here alone without a husband or any friends," thought Gurov, "then it wouldn't be a bad idea to make her acquaintance."

He was under forty, but he already had a twelve-year-old daughter and two boys at school. He had married young, when still a second-year student at college, and by now his wife looked nearly twice as old as he did. She was a tall, erect woman with dark eyebrows, dignified and imposing, who called herself a thinking person. She read a good deal, used simplified spelling in her letters, and called her husband Dimitry instead of Dmitry. Though he secretly regarded her as a woman of limited intelligence, narrow-minded and rather dowdy, he stood in awe of her and disliked being at home. Long ago he had begun being unfaithful to her, and he was now constantly unfaithful, and perhaps that was why he nearly always spoke ill of women, and whenever they were discussed in his presence he would call them "the lower race."

It seemed to him that he had been so schooled by bitter experience that he was entitled to call them anything he liked, but he was unable to live for even two days without "the lower race." In the company of men he was bored, cold, ill at ease, and uncommunicative, but felt at home among women, and knew what to say to them and how to behave; and even when he was silent in their presence he felt at ease. In his appearance, in his character, in his whole nature, there was something charming and elusive, which made him attractive to women and cast a spell over them. He knew this, and was himself attracted to them by some mysterious power.

*A resort city on the southern Crimean Peninsula, now part of Ukraine. After World War II, when it was part of the former USSR, Yalta was the site of a postwar conference in 1945 attended by Churchill, Roosevelt, and Stalin [ed.]

Repeated and bitter experience had taught him that every fresh intimacy, which at first seems to give the spice of variety to life and a sense of delightful and easy conquest, inevitably ends by introducing excessively complicated problems, and creating intolerable situations— this is particularly true of the well-intentioned Moscow people, who are irresolute and slow to embark on adventures. But with every new encounter with an interesting woman he forgot all about his former experiences, and the desire to live surged in him, and everything suddenly seemed simple and amusing.

One evening when he was dining in the public gardens, the lady in the beret came strolling up and sat down at the next table. Her expression, her clothes, her way of walking, the way she did her hair, suggested that she belonged to the upper classes, that she was married, that she was paying her first visit to Yalta, and that she was alone and bored. . . . Stories told about immorality in Yalta are largely untrue, and for his part Gurov despised them, knowing they were mostly invented by people who were only too ready to sin, if they had the chance. . . . But when the lady sat down at the next table a few yards away from him, he remembered all those stories of easy conquests and trips to the mountains, and he was suddenly possessed with the tempting thought of a quick and temporary liaison, a romance with an unknown woman of whose very name he was ignorant.

He beckoned invitingly at the Pomeranian, and when the little dog came up to him, he shook his finger at it. The Pomeranian began to bark. Then Gurov wagged his finger again.

The lady glanced up at him and immediately lowered her eyes.

"He doesn't bite!" she said, and blushed.

"May I give him a bone?" Gurov said, and when she nodded, he asked politely: "Have you been long in Yalta?"

"Five days."

"And I am dragging through my second week."

There was silence for a while.

"Time passes so quickly, and it is so dull here," she said without looking at him.

"It's quite the fashion to say it is boring here," he replied. "People who live out their lives in places like Belevo or Zhizdro are not bored, but when they come here they say: 'How dull! All this dust!' One would think they live in Granada!"

She laughed. Then they both went on eating in silence, like complete strangers, but after dinner they walked off together and began to converse lightly and playfully like people who are completely at their ease and contented with themselves, and it is all the same to them where they go or what they talk about. They walked and talked about the strange light of the sea, the soft warm lilac color of the water, and the golden pathway made by the moonlight. They talked of how sultry it was after a hot day. Gurov told her he came from Moscow, that he

had been trained as a philologist, though he now worked in a bank, that at one time he had trained to be an opera singer, but had given it up, and he told her about the two houses he owned in Moscow. From her he learned that she grew up in St. Petersburg and had been married in the town of S——, where she had been living for the past two years, that she would stay another month in Yalta, and perhaps her husband, who also needed a rest, would come to join her. She was not sure whether her husband was a member of a government board or on the zemstvo council, and this amused her. Gurov learned that her name was Anna Sergeyevna.

Afterwards in his room at the hotel he thought about her, and how they would surely meet on the following day. It was inevitable. Getting into bed, he recalled that only a little while ago she was a schoolgirl, doing lessons like his own daughter, and he remembered how awkward and timid she was in her laughter and in her manner of talking with a stranger—it was probably the first time in her life that she had found herself alone, in a situation where men followed her, gazed at her, and talked with her, always with a secret purpose she could not fail to guess. He thought of her slender and delicate throat and her lovely gray eyes.

"There's something pathetic about her," he thought, as he fell asleep.

II

A week had passed since they met. It was a holiday. Indoors it was oppressively hot, but the dust rose in clouds out of doors, and the people's hats whirled away. All day long Gurov was plagued with thirst, and kept going to the soft-drink stand to offer Anna Sergeyevna a soft drink or an ice cream. There was no refuge from the heat.

In the evening when the wind dropped they walked to the pier to watch the steamer come in. There were a great many people strolling along the pier: they had come to welcome friends, and they carried bunches of flowers. Two peculiarities of a festive Yalta crowd stood out distinctly: the elderly ladies were dressed like young women, and there were innumerable generals.

Because there was a heavy sea, the steamer was late, and already the sun was going down. The steamer had to maneuver for a long time before it could take its place beside the jetty. Anna Sergeyevna scanned the steamer and the passengers through her lorgnette, as though searching for someone she knew, and when she turned to Gurov her eyes were shining. She talked a good deal, with sudden abrupt questions, and quickly forgot what she had been saying; and then she lost her lorgnette in the crush.

The smartly dressed people went away, and it was now too dark to recognize faces. The wind had dropped, but Gurov and Anna Sergeyev-

na still stood there as though waiting for someone to come off the steamer. Anna Sergeyevna had fallen silent, and every now and then she would smell her flowers. She did not look at Gurov.

"The weather is better this evening," he said. "Where shall we go now? We might go for a drive."

He gazed at her intently and suddenly embraced her and kissed her on the lips, overwhelmed by the perfume and moisture of the flowers. And then, frightened, he looked around—had anyone observed them?

"Let us go to your . . ." he said softly.

They walked away quickly.

Her room was oppressively hot, and there was the scent of the perfume she had bought at a Japanese shop. Gurov gazed at her, and all the while he was thinking: "How strange are our meetings!" Out of the past there came to him the memory of other careless, good-natured women, happy in their love-making, grateful for the joy he gave them, however short, and then he remembered other women, like his wife, whose caresses were insincere and who talked endlessly in an affected and hysterical manner, with an expression which said this was not love or passion but something far more meaningful; and then he thought of the few very beautiful cold women on whose faces there would suddenly appear the glow of a fierce flame, a stubborn desire to take, to wring from life more than it can give: women who were no longer in their first youth, capricious, imprudent, unreflecting, and domineering, and when Gurov grew cold to them, their beauty aroused his hatred, and the lace trimming of their lingerie reminded him of fish scales.

But here there was all the shyness and awkwardness of inexperienced youth: a feeling of embarrassment, as though someone had suddenly knocked on the door. Anna Sergeyevna, "the lady with the pet dog," accepted what had happened in her own special way, gravely and seriously, as though she had accomplished her own downfall, an attitude which he found odd and disconcerting. Her features faded and drooped away, and on both sides of her face the long hair hung mournfully down, while she sat musing disconsolately like an adulteress in an antique painting.

"It's not right," she said. "You're the first person not to respect me."

There was a watermelon on the table. Gurov cut off a slice and began eating it slowly. For at least half an hour they were silent.

There was something touching about Anna Sergeyevna, revealing the purity of a simple and naïve woman who knew very little about life. The single candle burning on the table barely illumined her face, but it was clear that she was deeply unhappy.

"Why should I not respect you?" Gurov said. "You don't know what you are saying."

"God forgive me!" she said, and her eyes filled with tears. "It's terrible!"

"You don't have to justify yourself."

"How can I justify myself? No, I am a wicked, fallen woman! I despise myself, and have no desire to justify myself! It isn't my husband I have deceived, but myself! And not only now, I have been deceiving myself for a long time. My husband may be a good, honest man, but he is also a flunky! I don't know what work he does, but I know he is a flunky! When I married him I was twenty. I was devoured with curiosity. I longed for something better! Surely, I told myself, there is another kind of life! I wanted to live! To live, only to live! I was burning with curiosity. You won't understand, but I swear by God I was no longer in control of myself! Something strange was going on in me. I could not hold back. I told my husband I was ill, and I came here. . . . And now I have been walking about as though in a daze, like someone who has gone out of his senses. . . . And now I am nothing else but a low, common woman, and anyone may despise me!"

Gurov listened to her, bored to death. He was irritated with her naïve tone, and with her remorse, so unexpected and so out of place. But for the tears in her eyes, he would have thought she was joking or playing a part.

"I don't understand," he said gently. "What do you want?"

She laid her face against his chest and pressed close to him.

"Believe me, believe me, I beg you," she said. "I love all that is honest and pure in life, and sin is hateful to me. I don't know what I am doing. There are simple people who say: 'The Evil One led her astray,' and now I can say of myself that the Evil One has led me astray."

"Don't say such things," he murmured.

Then he gazed into her frightened, staring eyes, kissed her, spoke softly and affectionately, and gradually he was able to quieten her, and she was happy again; and then they both began to laugh.

Afterwards when they went out, there was not a soul on the esplanade. The town with its cypresses looked like a city of the dead, but the sea still roared and hurled itself against the shore. A single boat was rocking on the waves, and the lantern on it shone with a sleepy light.

They found a cab and drove to Oreanda.

"I discovered your name in the foyer just now," he said. "It was written up on the board—von Diederichs. Is your husband German?"

"No, I believe his grandfather was German, but he himself is an Orthodox Russian."

At Oreanda they sat on a bench not far from the church and gazed below at the sea and were lost in silence. Yalta was scarcely visible through the morning mist. Motionless white clouds covered the mountaintops. No leaves rustled, but the cicadas sang, and the monotonous muffled thunder of the sea, coming up from below, spoke of the peace, the eternal sleep awaiting us. This muffled thunder rose from the sea when neither Yalta nor Oreanda existed, and so it roars and will roar, dully, indifferently, after we have passed away. In this constancy of the

sea, in her perfect indifference to our living and dying, there lies perhaps the promise of our eternal salvation, the unbroken stream of life on earth, and its unceasing movement toward perfection. Sitting beside the young woman, who looked so beautiful in the dawn, Gurov was soothed and enchanted by the fairylike scene—the sea and the mountains, the clouds and the broad sky. He pondered how everything in the universe, if properly understood, would be entirely beautiful, but for our own thoughts and actions when we lose sight of the higher purposes of life and our human dignity.

Someone came up to them—probably a coast guard—looked at them and then walked away. His coming seemed full of mystery and beauty. Then in the glow of the early dawn they saw the steamer coming from Feodossia, its lights already doused.

"There is dew on the grass," said Anna Sergeyevna after a silence.

"Yes, it's time to go home."

They went back to the town.

Thereafter they met every day at noon on the esplanade, lunched and dined together, went out on excursions, and admired the sea. She complained of sleeping badly and of the violent beating of her heart, and she kept asking the same questions over and over again, alternately surrendering to jealousy and the fear that he did not really respect her. And often in the square or in the public gardens, when there was no one near, he would suddenly draw her to him and kiss her passionately. Their perfect idleness, those kisses in the full light of day, exchanged circumspectly and furtively for fear that anyone should see them, the heat, the smell of the sea, the continual glittering procession of idle, fashionable, well-fed people—all this seemed to give him a new lease of life. He kept telling Anna Sergeyevna how beautiful and seductive she was; he was impatient and passionate for her; and he never left her side, while she brooded continually, always trying to make him confess that he had no respect for her, did not love her at all, and saw in her nothing but a loose woman. Almost every evening at a late hour they would leave the town and drive out to Oreanda or to the waterfall, and these excursions were invariably a success, while the sensations they enjoyed were invariably beautiful and sublime.

All this time they were waiting for her husband to come, but he sent a letter saying he was having trouble with his eyes and imploring her to come home as soon as possible. Anna Sergeyevna made haste to obey.

"It's a good thing I am going away," she told Gurov. "It is fate."

She took a carriage to the railroad station, and he went with her. The drive took nearly a whole day. When she had taken her seat in the express train, and when the second bell had rung, she said: "Let me have one more look at you! Just one more! Like that!"

She did not cry, but looked sad and ill, and her face trembled.

"I shall always think of you and remember you," she said. "God be

with you! Think kindly of me! We shall never meet again—that's all for the good, for we should never have met. God bless you!"

The train moved off rapidly, and soon its lights vanished, and in a few moments the sound of the engine grew silent, as though everything were conspiring to put an end to this sweet oblivion, this madness. Alone on the platform, gazing into the dark distance, Gurov listened to the crying of the cicadas and the humming of the telegraph wires with the feeling that he had only just this moment woken up. And he told himself that this was just one more of the many adventures in his life, and it was now over, and there remained only a memory. . . . He was confused, sad, and filled with a faint sensation of remorse. After all, this young woman whom he would never meet again, had not been happy with him. He had been affectionate and sincere, but in his manner, his tone, his caresses, there had always been a suggestion of irony, the insulting arrogance of a successful male who was almost twice her age. And always she had called him kind, exceptional, noble: obviously he had seemed to her different from what he really was, and unintentionally he had deceived her. . . .

Here at the railroad station there was the scent of autumn in the air; and the evening was cold.

"It's time for me to go north, too," Gurov thought as he left the platform. "High time!"

III

At home in Moscow winter was already at hand. The stoves were heated, and it was still dark when the children got up to go to school, and the nurse would light the lamp for a short while. Already there was frost. When the first snow falls, and people go out for the first time on sleighs, it is good to see the white ground, the white roofs: one breathes easily and lightly, and one remembers the days of one's youth. The old lime trees and birches have a kindly look about them: they lie closer to one's heart than cypresses and palms; and below their branches one has no desire to dream of mountains and the sea.

Gurov, a native of Moscow, arrived there on a fine, frosty day, and when he put on his fur coat and warm gloves and went for a stroll along the Petrovka, and when on Saturday evening he heard the church bells ringing, then his recent travels and all the places he had visited lost their charm for him. Little by little he became immersed in Moscow life, eagerly read three newspapers a day, and declared that on principle he never read Moscow newspapers. Once more he was caught up in a whirl of restaurants, clubs, banquets, and celebrations, and it was flattering to have famous lawyers and actors visiting his house, and flattering to play cards with a professor at the doctors' club. He could eat a whole portion of *selyanka,* a cabbage stew, straight off the frying pan. . . .

So a month would pass, and the image of Anna Sergeyevna, he thought, would vanish into the mists of memory, and only rarely would she visit his dreams with her touching smile, like the other women who appeared in his dreams. But more than a month went by, soon it was the dead of winter, and the memory of Anna Sergeyevna remained as vivid as if he had parted from her only the day before. And these memories kept glowing with an even stronger flame. Whether it was in the silence of the evening when he was in his study and heard the voices of his children preparing their lessons, or listening to a song or the music in a restaurant or a storm howling in the chimney, suddenly all his memories would spring to life again: what happened on the pier, the misty mountains in the early morning, the steamer coming in from Feodossia, their kisses. He would pace up and down the room for a long while, remembering it all and smiling to himself, and later these memories would fill his dreams, and in his imagination the past would mingle with the future. When he closed his eyes, he saw her as though she were standing before him in the flesh, younger, lovelier, tenderer than she had really been; and he imagined himself a finer person than he had been in Yalta. In the evenings she peered at him from the bookshelves, the fireplace, a corner of the room; he heard her breathing and the soft rustle of her skirts. In the street he followed the women with his eyes, looking for someone who resembled her.

He began to feel an overwhelming desire to share his memories with someone. But in his home it was impossible for him to talk of his love, and away from home—there was no one. The tenants who lived in his house and his colleagues at the bank were equally useless. And what could he tell them? Had he really been in love? Was there anything beautiful, poetic, edifying, or even interesting, in his relations with Anna Sergeyevna? He found himself talking about women and love in vague generalities, and nobody guessed what he meant, and only his wife twitched her dark eyebrows and said: "Really, Dimitry, the role of a coxcomb does not suit you at all!"

One evening he was coming out of the doctors' club with one of his card partners, a government official, and he could not prevent himself from saying: "If you only knew what a fascinating woman I met in Yalta!"

The official sat down in the sleigh, and was driving away when he suddenly turned round and shouted: "Dmitry Dmitrich!"

"What?"

"You were quite right just now! The sturgeon wasn't fresh!"

These words, in themselves so commonplace, for some reason aroused Gurov's indignation: they seemed somehow dirty and degrading. What savage manners, what awful faces! What wasted nights, what dull days devoid of interest! Frenzied card playing, gluttony, drunkenness, endless conversations about the same thing. Futile pursuits and

conversations about the same topics taking up the greater part of the day and the greater part of a man's strength, so that he was left to live out a curtailed, bobtailed life with his wings clipped—an idiotic mess—impossible to run away or escape—one might as well be in a madhouse or a convict settlement.

Gurov, boiling with indignation, did not sleep a wink that night, and all the next day he suffered from a headache. On the following nights, too, he slept badly, sitting up in bed, thinking, or pacing the floor of his room. He was fed up with his children, fed up with the bank, and had not the slightest desire to go anywhere or talk about anything.

During the December holidays he decided to go on a journey and told his wife he had to go to St. Petersburg on some business connected with a certain young friend of his. Instead he went to the town of S——. Why? He hardly knew himself. He wanted to see Anna Sergeyevna and talk with her and if possible arrange a rendezvous.

He arrived at S—— during the morning and took the best room in the hotel, where the floor was covered with gray army cloth and on the table there was an inkstand, gray with dust, topped by a headless rider holding a hat in his raised hand. The porter gave him the necessary information: von Diederichs lived on Old Goncharnaya Street in a house of his own not far from the hotel; lived on a grand scale, luxuriously, and kept his own horses; the whole town knew him. The porter pronounced the name "Driderits."

He was in no hurry. He walked along Old Goncharnaya Street and found the house. In front of the house stretched a long gray fence studded with nails.

"You'd run away from a fence like that," Gurov thought, glancing now at the windows of the house, now at the fence.

He thought: "Today is a holiday, and her husband is probably at home. In any case it would be tactless to go up to the house and upset her. And if I sent her a note it might fall into her husband's hands and bring about a catastrophe! The best thing is to trust to chance." So he kept walking up and down the street by the fence, waiting for the chance. He saw a beggar entering the gates, only to be attacked by dogs, and about an hour later he heard someone playing on a piano, but the sounds were very faint and indistinct. Probably Anna Sergeyevna was playing. Suddenly the front door opened, and an old woman came out, followed by the familiar white Pomeranian. Gurov thought of calling out to the dog, but his heart suddenly began to beat violently and he was so excited he could not remember the dog's name.

As he walked on, he came to hate the gray fence more and more, and it occurred to him with a sense of irritation that Anna Sergeyevna had forgotten him and was perhaps amusing herself with another man, and that was very natural in a young woman who had nothing to look

at from morning to night but that damned fence. He went back to his hotel room and for a long while sat on the sofa, not knowing what to do. Then he ordered dinner and took a long nap.

"How absurd and tiresome it is!" he thought when he woke and looked at the dark windows, for evening had fallen. "Well, I've had some sleep, and what is there to do tonight?"

He sat up in the bed, which was covered with a cheap gray blanket of the kind seen in hospitals, and he taunted himself with anger and vexation.

"You and your lady with the pet dog. . . . There's a fine adventure for you! You're in a nice fix now!"

However, at the railroad station that morning his eye had been caught by a playbill advertising in enormous letters the first performance of *The Geisha*. He remembered this, and drove to the theater.

"It's very likely that she goes to first nights," he told himself.

The theater was full. There, as so often in provincial theaters, a thick haze hung above the chandeliers, and the crowds in the gallery were fidgeting noisily. In the first row of the orchestra the local dandies were standing with their hands behind their backs, waiting for the curtain to rise, while in the governor's box the governor's daughter, wearing a boa, sat in front, the governor himself sitting modestly behind the drapes, with only his hands visible. The curtain was swaying; the orchestra spent a long time tuning up. While the audience was coming in and taking their seats, Gurov was looking impatiently around him.

And then Anna Sergeyevna came in. She sat in the third row, and when Gurov looked at her his heart seemed to stop, and he understood clearly that the whole world contained no one nearer, dearer, and more important than Anna. This slight woman, lost amid a provincial rabble, in no way remarkable, with her silly lorgnette in her hands, filled his whole life: she was his sorrow and his joy, the only happiness he desired for himself; and to the sounds of the wretched orchestra, with its feeble provincial violins, he thought how beautiful she was. He thought and dreamed.

There came with Anna Sergeyevna a young man with small side whiskers, very tall and stooped, who inclined his head at every step and seemed to be continually bowing. Probably this was the husband she once described as a flunky one day in Yalta when she was in a bitter mood. And indeed in his lanky figure, his side whiskers, his small bald patch, there was something of a flunky's servility. He smiled sweetly, and in his buttonhole there was an academic badge like the number worn by a waiter.

During the first intermission the husband went away to smoke, and she remained in her seat. Gurov, who was also sitting in the orchestra, went up to her and said in a trembling voice, with a forced smile: "How are you?"

She looked up at him and turned pale, then glanced at him again

in horror, unable to believe her eyes, tightly gripping the fan and the lorgnette, evidently fighting to overcome a feeling of faintness. Both were silent. She sat, he stood, and he was frightened by her distress, and did not dare sit beside her. The violins and flutes sang out as they were tuned. Suddenly he was afraid, as it occurred to him that all the people in the boxes were staring down at them. She stood up and walked quickly to the exit; he followed her, and both of them walked aimlessly up and down the corridors, while crowds of lawyers, teachers, and civil servants, all wearing the appropriate uniforms and badges, flashed past; and the ladies, and the fur coats hanging from pegs, also flashed past; and the draft blew through the place, bringing with it the odor of cigar stubs. Gurov, whose heart was beating wildly, thought: "Oh Lord, why are these people here and this orchestra?"

At that moment he recalled how, when he saw Anna Sergeyevna off at the station in the evening, he had told himself it was all over and they would never meet again. But how far away the end seemed to be now!

Anna paused on a narrow dark stairway which bore the inscription: "This way to the upper balcony."

"How you frightened me!" she said, breathing heavily, pale and stunned. "How you frightened me! I am half dead! Why did you come? Why?"

"Do try to understand, Anna—please understand . . ." he said in a hurried whisper. "I implore you, please understand . . ."

She looked at him with dread, with entreaty, with love, intently, to retain his features all the more firmly in her memory.

"I've been so unhappy," she went on, not listening to him. "All this time I've thought only of you, I've lived on thoughts of you. I tried to forget, to forget—why, why have you come?"

A pair of schoolboys were standing on the landing above them, smoking and peering down, but Gurov did not care, and drawing Anna to him, he began kissing her face, her cheeks, her hands.

"What are you doing? What are you doing?" she said in terror, pushing him away from her. "We have both lost our senses! Go away now—tonight! . . . I implore you by everything you hold sacred. . . . Someone is coming!"

Someone was climbing up the stairs.

"You must go away . . ." Anna Sergeyevna went on in a whisper. "Do you hear, Dmitry Dmitrich? I'll come and visit you in Moscow. I have never been happy. I am miserable now, and I shall never be happy again, never! Don't make me suffer any more! I swear I'll come to Moscow! We must separate now. My dear precious darling, we have to separate!"

She pressed his hand and went quickly down the stairs, all the while gazing back at him, and it was clear from the expression in her eyes that she was miserable. For a while Gurov stood there, listening to

her footsteps, and then all sounds faded away, and he went to look for his coat and left the theater.

IV

And Anna Sergeyevna began coming to see him in Moscow. Every two or three months she would leave the town of S——, telling her husband she was going to consult a specialist in women's disorders, and her husband neither believed her nor disbelieved her. In Moscow she always stayed at the Slavyansky Bazaar Hotel, and the moment she arrived she would send a redcapped hotel messenger to Gurov. He would visit her, and no one in Moscow ever knew about their meetings.

One winter morning he was going to visit her as usual. (The messenger from the hotel had come the evening before, but he was out.) His daughter accompanied him. He was taking her to school, and the school lay on the way to the hotel. Great wet flakes of snow were falling.

"Three degrees above freezing, and it's still snowing," he told his daughter. "That's only the surface temperature of the earth—the other layers of the atmosphere have other temperatures."

"Yes, Papa. But why are there no thunderstorms in winter?"

He explained that, too. He talked, and all the while he was thinking about his meeting with the beloved, and not a living soul knew of it, and probably no one would ever know. He was living a double life: an open and public life visible to all who had any need to know, full of conventional truth and conventional lies, exactly like the lives of his friends and acquaintances, and another which followed a secret course. And by one of those strange and perhaps accidental circumstances everything that was to him meaningful, urgent, and important, everything about which he felt sincerely and did not deceive himself, everything that went to shape the very core of his existence, was concealed from others, while everything that was false and the shell where he hid in order to hide the truth about himself—his work at the bank, discussions at the club, conversations about women as "an inferior race," and attending anniversary celebrations with his wife—all this was on the surface. Judging others by himself, he refused to believe the evidence of his eyes, and therefore he imagined that all men led their real and meaningful lives under a veil of mystery and under cover of darkness. Every man's intimate existence revolved around mysterious secrets, and it was perhaps partly for this reason that all civilized men were so nervously anxious to protect their privacy.

Leaving his daughter at the school, Gurov went on to the Slavyansky Bazaar Hotel. He removed his fur coat in the lobby, and then went upstairs and knocked softly on the door. Anna Sergeyevna had been exhausted by the journey and the suspense of waiting for his arrival—she had in fact expected him the previous evening. She was wearing her fa-

vorite gray dress. She was pale, and she looked at him without smiling, and he had scarcely entered the room when she threw herself in his arms. Their kisses were lingering and prolonged, as though two years had passed since they had seen each other.

"How were things down there?" he said. "Anything new?"

"Please wait. . . . I'll tell you in a moment. . . . I can't speak yet!"

She could not speak because she was crying. She turned away from him, pressing a handkerchief to her eyes.

"Let her have her cry," he thought. "I'll sit down and wait." And he sat down in an armchair.

Then he rang and ordered tea, and while he drank the tea she remained standing with her face turned to the window. . . . She was crying from the depth of her emotions, in the bitter knowledge that their life together was so weighed down with sadness, because they could only meet in secret and were always hiding from people like thieves. And that meant surely that their lives were shattered!

"Oh, do stop crying!" he said.

It was evident to him that their love affair would not soon be over, and there was no end in sight. Anna Sergeyevna was growing more and more passionately fond of him, and it was beyond belief that he would ever tell her it must one day end; and if he had told her, she would not have believed him.

He went up to her and put his hands on her shoulders, intending to console her with some meaningless words and to fondle her; and then he saw himself in the mirror.

His hair was turning gray. It struck him as strange that he should have aged so much in these last years, and lost his good looks. Her shoulders were warm and trembling at his touch. He felt pity for her, who was so warm and beautiful, though probably it would not be long before she would begin to fade and wither, as he had done. Why did she love him so much? Women had always believed him to be other than what he was, and they loved in him not himself but the creature who came to life in their imagination, the man they had been seeking eagerly all their lives, and when they had discovered their mistake, they went on loving him. And not one of them was ever happy with him. Time passed, he met other women, became intimate with them, parted from them, never having loved them. It was anything you please, but it was not love.

And now at last, when his hair was turning gray, he had fallen in love—real love—for the first time in his life.

Anna Sergeyevna and he loved one another as people who are very close and dear love one another: they were like deeply devoted friends, like husband and wife. It seemed to them that Fate had intended them for one another, and it was beyond understanding that one had a wife, the other a husband. It was as though they were two birds of passage, one male, one female, who had been trapped and were now compelled

to live in different cages. They had forgiven one another for all they were ashamed of in the past, they forgave everything in the present, and felt that this love of theirs changed them both.

Formerly in moments of depression he had consoled himself with the first argument that came into his head, but now all such arguments were foreign to him. He felt a deep compassion for her, and desired to be tender and sincere. . . .

"Don't cry, my darling," he said. "You've cried enough. Now let us talk, and we'll think of something. . . ."

Then they talked it over for a long time, trying to discover some way of avoiding secrecy and deception, and living in different towns, and being separated for long periods. How could they free themselves from their intolerable chains?

"How? How?" he asked, holding his head in his hands. "How?"

And it seemed as though in a little while the solution would be found and a lovely new life would begin for them; and to both of them it was clear that the end was still very far away, and the hardest and most difficult part was only beginning.

Questions for Discussion and Analysis

1. How would you describe Gurov's character at the beginning of the story?
2. What qualities of Anna Sergeyevna's attract him when they meet in Yalta?
3. How does Gurov change at different points during the course of the story? When he returns to Moscow? When he visits Anna for the first time? At what point in the story does he experience an epiphany?
4. Are Gurov and Anna doomed? Is this story a tragedy?
5. What glimpse of late-nineteenth-century Russian life does this story provide? What Russian attitudes toward love and marriage do the story's events subtly convey?
6. How does setting (specifically the weather and the climate) contribute to our understanding of the story and its significance?

Short Story 2

Shiloh
Bobbie Ann Mason

One of the new young writers to have emerged from the American South, Bobbie Ann Mason won the PEN/Hemingway Award for best fiction. She has written a novel, In Country, *and her stories have been published in two collections:* Shiloh and Other Stories, *from which this story comes, and* Love Life. *Many of Mason's stories are set in Kentucky, where she grew up. She*

now lives in rural Pennsylvania. The title "Shiloh" refers to the area in south-western Tennessee that was the site of the decisive Civil War battle in which the Union soldiers soundly defeated the Confederate Army.

Leroy Moffitt's wife, Norma Jean, is working on her pectorals. She lifts three-pound dumbbells to warm up, then progresses to a twenty-pound barbell. Standing with her legs apart, she reminds Leroy of Wonder Woman.

"I'd give anything if I could just get these muscles to where they're real hard," says Norma Jean. "Feel this arm. It's not as hard as the other one."

"That's 'cause you're right-handed," says Leroy, dodging as she swings the barbell in an arc.

"Do you think so?"

"Sure."

Leroy is a truckdriver. He injured his leg in a highway accident four months ago, and his physical therapy, which involves weights and a pulley, prompted Norma Jean to try building herself up. Now she is attending a body-building class. Leroy has been collecting temporary disability since his tractor-trailer jackknifed in Missouri, badly twisting his left leg in its socket. He has a steel pin in his hip. He will probably not be able to drive his rig again. It sits in the backyard, like a gigantic bird that has flown home to roost. Leroy has been home in Kentucky for three months, and his leg is almost healed, but the accident frightened him and he does not want to drive any more long hauls. He is not sure what to do next. In the meantime, he makes things from craft kits. He started by building a miniature log cabin from notched Popsicle sticks. He varnished it and placed it on the TV set, where it remains. It reminds him of a rustic Nativity scene. Then he tried string art (sailing ships on black velvet), a macramé owl kit, a snap-together B-17 Flying Fortress, and a lamp made out of a model truck, with a light fixture screwed in the top of the cab. At first the kits were diversions, something to kill time, but now he is thinking about building a full-scale log house from a kit. It would be considerably cheaper than building a regular house, and besides, Leroy has grown to appreciate how things are put together. He has begun to realize that in all the years he was on the road he never took time to examine anything. He was always flying past scenery.

"They won't let you build a log cabin in any of the new subdivisions," Norma Jean tells him.

"They will if I tell them it's for you," he says, teasing her. Ever since they were married, he has promised Norma Jean he would build her a new home one day. They have always rented, and the house they live in is small and nondescript. It does not even feel like a home, Leroy realizes now.

Norma Jean works at the Rexall drugstore, and she has acquired an amazing amount of information about cosmetics. When she explains to

Leroy the three stages of complexion care, involving creams, toners, and moisturizers, he thinks happily of other petroleum products—axle grease, diesel fuel. This is a connection between him and Norma Jean. Since he has been home, he has felt unusually tender about his wife and guilty over his long absences. But he can't tell what she feels about him. Norma Jean has never complained about his traveling; she has never made hurt remarks, like calling his truck a "widow-maker." He is reasonably certain she has been faithful to him, but he wishes she would celebrate his permanent homecoming more happily. Norma Jean is often startled to find Leroy at home, and he thinks she seems a little disappointed about it. Perhaps he reminds her too much of the early days of their marriage, before he went on the road. They had a child who died as an infant, years ago. They never speak about their memories of Randy, which have almost faded, but now that Leroy is home all the time, they sometimes feel awkward around each other, and Leroy wonders if one of them should mention the child. He has the feeling that they are waking up out of a dream together—that they must create a new marriage, start afresh. They are lucky they are still married. Leroy has read that for most people losing a child destroys the marriage—or else he heard this on *Donahue*. He can't always remember where he learns things anymore.

At Christmas, Leroy bought an electric organ for Norma Jean. She used to play the piano when she was in high school. "It don't leave you," she told him once. "It's like riding a bicycle."

The new instrument had so many keys and buttons that she was bewildered by it at first. She touched the keys tentatively, pushed some buttons, then pecked out "Chopsticks." It came out in an amplified fox-trot rhythm, with marimba sounds.

"It's an orchestra!" she cried.

The organ had a pecan-look finish and eighteen preset chords, with optional flute, violin, trumpet, clarinet, and banjo accompaniments. Norma Jean mastered the organ almost immediately. At first she played Christmas songs. Then she bought *The Sixties Songbook* and learned every tune in it, adding variations to each with the rows of brightly colored buttons.

"I didn't like these old songs back then," she said. "But I have this crazy feeling I missed something."

"You didn't miss a thing," said Leroy.

Leroy likes to lie on the couch and smoke a joint and listen to Norma Jean play "Can't Take My Eyes Off You" and "I'll Be Back." He is back again. After fifteen years on the road, he is finally settling down with the woman he loves. She is still pretty. Her skin is flawless. Her frosted curls resemble pencil trimmings.

Now that Leroy has come home to stay, he notices how much the town has changed. Subdivisions are spreading across western Kentucky like

an oil slick. The sign at the edge of town says "Pop: 11,500"—only seven hundred more than it said twenty years before. Leroy can't figure out who is living in all the new houses. The farmers who used to gather around the courthouse square on Saturday afternoons to play checkers and spit tobacco juice have gone. It has been years since Leroy has thought about the farmers, and they have disappeared without his noticing.

Leroy meets a kid named Stevie Hamilton in the parking lot at the new shopping center. While they pretend to be strangers meeting over a stalled car, Stevie tosses an ounce of marijuana under the front seat of Leroy's car. Stevie is wearing orange jogging shoes and a T-shirt that says CHATTAHOO-CHEE SUPER-RAT. His father is a prominent doctor who lives in one of the expensive subdivisions in a new white-columned brick house that looks like a funeral parlor. In the phone book under his name there is a separate number, with the listing "Teenagers."

"Where do you get this stuff?" asks Leroy. "From your pappy?"

"That's for me to know and you to find out," Stevie says. He is slit-eyed and skinny.

"What else you got?"

"What you interested in?"

"Nothing special. Just wondered."

Leroy used to take speed on the road. Now he has to go slowly. He needs to be mellow. He leans back against the car and says, "I'm aiming to build me a log house, soon as I get time. My wife, though, I don't think she likes the idea."

"Well, let me know when you want me again," Stevie says. He has a cigarette in his cupped palm, as though sheltering it from the wind. He takes a long drag, then stomps it on the asphalt and slouches away.

Stevie's father was two years ahead of Leroy in high school. Leroy is thirty-four. He married Norma Jean when they were both eighteen, and their child Randy was born a few months later, but he died at the age of four months and three days. He would be about Stevie's age now. Norma Jean and Leroy were at the drive-in, watching a double feature (*Dr. Strangelove* and *Lover Come Back*), and the baby was sleeping in the back seat. When the first movie ended, the baby was dead. It was the sudden infant death syndrome. Leroy remembers handing Randy to a nurse at the emergency room, as though he were offering her a large doll as a present. A dead baby feels like a sack of flour. "It just happens sometimes," said the doctor, in what Leroy always recalls as a nonchalant tone. Leroy can hardly remember the child anymore, but he still sees vividly a scene from *Dr. Strangelove* in which the President of the United States was talking in a folksy voice on the hot line to the Soviet premier about the bomber accidentally headed toward Russia. He was in the War Room, and the world map was lit up. Leroy remembers Norma Jean standing catatonically beside him in the hospital and himself thinking: Who is this strange girl? He had forgotten who she was.

Now scientists are saying that crib death is caused by a virus. Nobody knows anything, Leroy thinks. The answers are always changing.

When Leroy gets home from the shopping center, Norma Jean's mother, Mabel Beasley, is there. Until this year, Leroy has not realized how much time she spends with Norma Jean. When she visits, she inspects the closets and then the plants, informing Norma Jean when a plant is droopy or yellow. Mabel calls the plants "flowers," although there are never any blooms. She always notices if Norma Jean's laundry is piling up. Mabel is a short, overweight woman whose tight, brown-dyed curls look more like a wig than the actual wig she sometimes wears. Today she has brought Norma Jean an off-white dust ruffle she made for the bed; Mabel works in a custom-upholstery shop.

"This is the tenth one I made this year," Mabel says. "I got started and couldn't stop."

"It's real pretty," says Norma Jean.

"Now we can hide things under the bed," says Leroy, who gets along with his mother-in-law primarily by joking with her. Mabel has never really forgiven him for disgracing her by getting Norma Jean pregnant. When the baby died, she said that fate was mocking her.

"What's that thing?" Mabel says to Leroy in a loud voice, pointing to a tangle of yarn on a piece of canvas.

Leroy holds it up for Mabel to see. "It's my needlepoint," he explains. "This is a *Star Trek* pillow cover."

"That's what a woman would do," says Mabel. "Great day in the morning!"

"All the big football players on TV do it," he says.

"Why, Leroy, you're always trying to fool me. I don't believe you for one minute. You don't know what to do with yourself—that's the whole trouble. Sewing!"

"I'm aiming to build us a log house," says Leroy. "Soon as my plans come."

"Like *heck* you are," says Norma Jean. She takes Leroy's needlepoint and shoves it into a drawer. "You have to find a job first. Nobody can afford to build now anyway."

Mabel straightens her girdle and says, "I still think before you get tied down y'all ought to take a little run to Shiloh."*

"One of these days, Mama," Norma Jean says impatiently.

Mabel is talking about Shiloh, Tennessee. For the past few years,

---

*Of the battle of Shiloh, the Civil War historian Bruce Catton writes, "Nor have many battles been more decisive, in their effect on the course of the war. Shiloh represented a supreme effort on the part of the Confederacy to turn the tables, to recoup what had been lost along the Tennessee-Kentucky line, to win a new chance to wage war west of the Appalachians on an equal footing. It failed. After this, the Southern Nation could do no more than fight an uphill fight to save part of the Mississippi Valley—the great Valley of American empire without which the war could not be won." *Terrible Swift Sword,* Doubleday & Company, Inc., Garden City, New York, 1963, p. 238.

she has been urging Leroy and Norma Jean to visit the Civil War battleground there. Mabel went there on her honeymoon—the only real trip she ever took. Her husband died of a perforated ulcer when Norma Jean was ten, but Mabel, who was accepted into the United Daughters of the Confederacy in 1975, is still preoccupied with going back to Shiloh.

"I've been to kingdom come and back in that truck out yonder," Leroy says to Mabel, "but we never yet set foot in that battleground. Ain't that something? How did I miss it?"

"It's not even that far," Mabel says.

After Mabel leaves, Norma Jean reads to Leroy from a list she has made. "Things you could do," she announces. "You could get a job as a guard at Union Carbide, where they'd let you set on a stool. You could get on at the lumberyard. You could do a little carpenter work, if you want to build so bad. You could—"

"I can't do something where I'd have to stand up all day."

"You ought to try standing up all day behind a cosmetics counter. It's amazing that I have strong feet, coming from two parents that never had strong feet at all." At the moment Norma Jean is holding on to the kitchen counter, raising her knees one at a time as she talks. She is wearing two-pound ankle weights.

"Don't worry," says Leroy. "I'll do something."

"You could truck calves to slaughter for somebody. You wouldn't have to drive any big old truck for that."

"I'm going to build you this house," says Leroy. "I want to make you a real home."

"I don't want to live in any log cabin."

"It's not a cabin. It's a house."

"I don't care. It looks like a cabin."

"You and me together could lift those logs. It's just like lifting weights."

Norma Jean doesn't answer. Under her breath, she is counting. Now she is marching through the kitchen. She is doing goose steps.

Before his accident, when Leroy came home he used to stay in the house with Norma Jean, watching TV in bed and playing cards. She would cook fried chicken, picnic ham, chocolate pie—all his favorites. Now he is home alone much of the time. In the mornings, Norma Jean disappears, leaving a cooling place in the bed. She eats a cereal called Body Buddies, and she leaves the bowl on the table, with the soggy tan balls floating in a milk puddle. He sees things about Norma Jean that he never realized before. When she chops onions, she stares off into a corner, as if she can't bear to look. She puts on her house slippers almost precisely at nine o'clock every evening and nudges her jogging shoes under the couch. She saves bread heels for the birds. Leroy watches the birds at the feeder. He notices the peculiar way goldfinches fly past the window. They close their wings, then fall, then spread their wings to catch and lift themselves. He wonders if they close their eyes when they

fall. Norma Jean closes her eyes when they are in bed. She wants the lights turned out. Even then, he is sure she closes her eyes.

He goes for long drives around town. He tends to drive a car rather carelessly. Power steering and an automatic shift make a car feel so small and inconsequential that his body is hardly involved in the driving process. His injured leg stretches out comfortably. Once or twice he has almost hit something, but even the prospect of an accident seems minor in a car. He cruises the new subdivisions, feeling like a criminal rehearsing for a robbery. Norma Jean is probably right about a log house being inappropriate here in the new subdivisions. All the houses look grand and complicated. They depress him.

One day when Leroy comes home from a drive he finds Norma Jean in tears. She is in the kitchen making a potato and mushroom-soup casserole, with grated-cheese topping. She is crying because her mother caught her smoking.

"I didn't hear her coming. I was standing here puffing away pretty as you please," Norma Jean says, wiping her eyes.

"I knew it would happen sooner or later," says Leroy, putting his arm around her.

"She don't know the meaning of the word 'knock,'" says Norma Jean. "It's a wonder she hadn't caught me years ago."

"Think of it this way," Leroy says. "What if she caught me with a joint?"

"You better not let her!" Norma Jean shrieks. "I'm warning you, Leroy Moffitt!"

"I'm just kidding. Here, play me a tune. That'll help you relax."

Norma Jean puts the casserole in the oven and sets the timer. Then she plays a ragtime tune, with horns and banjo, as Leroy lights up a joint and lies on the couch, laughing to himself about Mabel's catching him at it. He thinks of Stevie Hamilton—a doctor's son pushing grass. Everything is funny. The whole town seems crazy and small. He is reminded of Virgil Mathis, a boastful policeman Leroy used to shoot pool with. Virgil recently led a drug bust in a back room at a bowling alley, where he seized ten thousand dollars' worth of marijuana. The newspaper had a picture of him holding up the bags of grass and grinning widely. Right now, Leroy can imagine Virgil breaking down the door and arresting him with a lungful of smoke. Virgil would probably have been alerted to the scene because of all the racket Norma Jean is making. Now she sounds like a hard-rock band. Norma Jean is terrific. When she switches to a Latin-rhythm version of "Sunshine Superman," Leroy hums along. Norma Jean's foot goes up and down, up and down.

"Well, what do you think?" Leroy says, when Norma Jean pauses to search through her music.

"What do I think about what?"

His mind has gone blank. Then he says, "I'll sell my rig and build us a house." That wasn't what he wanted to say. He wanted to know what she thought—what she *really* thought—about them.

"Don't start in on that again," says Norma Jean. She begins playing "Who'll Be the Next in Line?"

Leroy used to tell hitchhikers his whole life story—about his travels, his hometown, the baby. He would end with a question: "Well, what do you think?" It was just a rhetorical question. In time, he had the feeling that he'd been telling the same story over and over to the same hitchhikers. He quit talking to hitchhikers when he realized how his voice sounded—whining and self-pitying, like some teenage-tragedy song. Now Leroy has the sudden impulse to tell Norma Jean about himself, as if he had just met her. They have known each other so long they have forgotten a lot about each other. They could become reacquainted. But when the oven timer goes off and she runs to the kitchen, he forgets why he wants to do this.

The next day, Mabel drops by. It is Saturday and Norma Jean is cleaning. Leroy is studying the plans of his log house, which have finally come in the mail. He has them spread out on the table—big sheets of stiff blue paper, with diagrams and numbers printed in white. While Norma Jean runs the vacuum, Mabel drinks coffee. She sets her coffee cup on a blueprint.

"I'm just waiting for time to pass," she says to Leroy, drumming her fingers on the table.

As soon as Norma Jean switches off the vacuum, Mabel says in a loud voice, "Did you hear about the datsun dog that killed the baby?"

Norma Jean says, "The word is 'dachshund.'"

"They put the dog on trial. It chewed the baby's legs off. The mother was in the next room all the time." She raises her voice. "They thought it was neglect."

Norma Jean is holding her ears. Leroy manages to open the refrigerator and get some Diet Pepsi to offer Mabel. Mabel still has some coffee and she waves away the Pepsi.

"Datsuns are like that," Mabel says. "They're jealous dogs. They'll tear a place to pieces if you don't keep an eye on them."

"You better watch out what you're saying, Mabel," says Leroy.

"Well, facts is facts."

Leroy looks out the window at his rig. It is like a huge piece of furniture gathering dust in the backyard. Pretty soon it will be an antique. He hears the vacuum cleaner. Norma Jean seems to be cleaning the living room rug again.

Later, she says to Leroy, "She just said that about the baby because she caught me smoking. She's trying to pay me back."

"What are you talking about?" Leroy says, nervously shuffling blueprints.

"You know good and well," Norma Jean says. She is sitting in a kitchen chair with her feet up and her arms wrapped around her knees. She looks small and helpless. She says, "The very idea, her bringing up a subject like that! Saying it was neglect."

"She didn't mean that," Leroy says.

"She might not have *thought* she meant it. She always says things like that. You don't know how she goes on."

"But she didn't really mean it. She was just talking."

Leroy opens a king-sized bottle of beer and pours it into two glasses, dividing it carefully. He hands a glass to Norma Jean and she takes it from him mechanically. For a long time, they sit by the kitchen window watching the birds at the feeder.

Something is happening. Norma Jean is going to night school. She has graduated from her six-week body-building course and now she is taking an adult-education course in composition at Paducah Community College. She spends her evenings outlining paragraphs.

"First you have a topic sentence," she explains to Leroy. "Then you divide it up. Your secondary topic has to be connected to your primary topic."

To Leroy, this sounds intimidating. "I never was any good in English," he says.

"It makes a lot of sense."

"What are you doing this for, anyhow?"

She shrugs. "It's something to do." She stands up and lifts her dumbbells a few times.

"Driving a rig, nobody cared about my English."

"I'm not criticizing your English."

Norma Jean used to say, "If I lose ten minutes' sleep, I just drag all day." Now she stays up late, writing compositions. She got a B on her first paper—a how-to theme on soup-based casseroles. Recently Norma Jean has been cooking unusual foods—tacos, lasagna, Bombay chicken. She doesn't play the organ anymore, though her second paper was called "Why Music Is Important to Me." She sits at the kitchen table, concentrating on her outlines, while Leroy plays with his log house plans, practicing with a set of Lincoln Logs. The thought of getting a truckload of notched, numbered logs scares him, and he wants to be prepared. As he and Norma Jean work together at the kitchen table, Leroy has the hopeful thought that they are sharing something, but he knows he is a fool to think this. Norma Jean is miles away. He knows he is going to lose her. Like Mabel, he is just waiting for time to pass.

One day, Mabel is there before Norma Jean gets home from work, and Leroy finds himself confiding in her. Mabel, he realizes, must know Norma Jean better than he does.

"I don't know what's got into that girl," Mabel says. "She used to go to bed with the chickens. Now you say she's up all hours. Plus her a-smoking. I like to died."

"I want to make her this beautiful home," Leroy says, indicating the Lincoln Logs. "I don't think she even wants it. Maybe she was happier with me gone."

"She don't know what to make of you, coming home like this."

"Is that it?"

Mabel takes the roof off his Lincoln Log cabin. "You couldn't get *me* in a log cabin," she says. "I was raised in one. It's no picnic, let me tell you."

"They're different now," says Leroy.

"I tell you what," Mabel says, smiling oddly at Leroy.

"What?"

"Take her on down to Shiloh. Y'all need to get out together, stir a little. Her brain's all balled up over them books."

Leroy can see traces of Norma Jean's features in her mother's face. Mabel's worn face has the texture of crinkled cotton, but suddenly she looks pretty. It occurs to Leroy that Mabel has been hinting all along that she wants them to take her with them to Shiloh.

"Let's all go to Shiloh," he says. "You and me and her. Come Sunday."

Mabel throws up her hands in protest. "Oh, no, not me. Young folks want to be by theirselves."

When Norma Jean comes in with groceries, Leroy says excitedly, "Your mama here's been dying to go to Shiloh for thirty-five years. It's about time we went, don't you think?"

"I'm not going to butt in on anybody's second honeymoon," Mabel says.

"Who's going on a honeymoon, for Christ's sake?" Norma Jean says loudly.

"I never raised no daughter of mine to talk that-a-way," Mabel says.

"You ain't seen nothing yet," says Norma Jean. She starts putting away boxes and cans, slamming cabinet doors.

"There's a log cabin at Shiloh," Mabel says. "It was there during the battle. There's bullet holes in it."

"When are you going to *shut up* about Shiloh, Mama?" asks Norma Jean.

"I always thought Shiloh was the prettiest place, so full of history," Mabel goes on. "I just hoped y'all could see it once before I die, so you could tell me about it." Later, she whispers to Leroy, "You do what I said. A little change is what she needs."

"Your name means 'the king,'" Norma Jean says to Leroy that evening. He is trying to get her to go to Shiloh, and she is reading a book about another century.

"Well, I reckon I ought to be right proud."

"I guess so."

"Am I still king around here?"

Norma Jean flexes her biceps and feels them for hardness. "I'm not fooling around with anybody, if that's what you mean," she says.

"Would you tell me if you were?"

"I don't know."

"What does *your* name mean?"

It was Marilyn Monroe's real name."

"No kidding!"

"Norma comes from the Normans. They were invaders," she says. She closes her book and looks hard at Leroy. "I'll go to Shiloh with you if you'll stop staring at me."

On Sunday, Norma Jean packs a picnic and they go to Shiloh. To Leroy's relief, Mabel says she does not want to come with them. Norma Jean drives, and Leroy, sitting beside her, feels like some boring hitch-hiker she has picked up. He tries some conversation, but she answers him in monosyllables. At Shiloh, she drives aimlessly through the park, past bluffs and trails and steep ravines. Shiloh is an immense place, and Leroy cannot see it as a battleground. It is not what he expected. He thought it would look like a golf course. Monuments are everywhere, showing through the thick clusters of trees. Norma Jean passes the log cabin Mabel mentioned. It is surrounded by tourists looking for bullet holes.

"That's not the kind of log house I've got in mind," says Leroy apologetically.

"I know *that.*"

"This is a pretty place. Your mama was right."

"It's O.K.," says Norma Jean. "Well, we've seen it. I hope she's satisfied."

They burst out laughing together.

At the park museum, a movie on Shiloh is shown every half hour, but they decide that they don't want to see it. They buy a souvenir Confederate flag for Mabel, and then they find a picnic spot near the cemetery. Norma Jean has brought a picnic cooler, with pimiento sandwiches, soft drinks, and Yodels. Leroy eats a sandwich and then smokes a joint, hiding it behind the picnic cooler. Norma Jean has quit smoking altogether. She is picking cake crumbs from the cellophane wrapper, like a fussy bird.

Leroy says, "So the boys in gray ended up in Corinth. The Union soldiers zapped 'em finally. April 7, 1862."

They both know that he doesn't know any history. He is just talking about some of the historical plaques they have read. He feels awkward, like a boy on a date with an older girl. They are still just making conversation.

"Corinth is where Mama eloped to," says Norma Jean.

They sit in silence and stare at the cemetery for the Union dead and, beyond, at a tall cluster of trees. Campers are parked nearby, bumper to bumper, and small children in bright clothing are cavorting and squealing. Norma Jean wads up the cake wrapper and squeezes it tightly in her hand. Without looking at Leroy, she says, "I want to leave you."

Leroy takes a bottle of Coke out of the cooler and flips off the cap.

He holds the bottle poised near his mouth but cannot remember to take a drink. Finally he says, "No, you don't."

"Yes, I do."

"I won't let you."

"You can't stop me."

"Don't do me that way."

Leroy knows Norma Jean will have her own way. "Didn't I promise to be home from now on?" he says.

"In some ways, a woman prefers a man who wanders," says Norma Jean. "That sounds crazy, I know."

"You're not crazy."

Leroy remembers to drink from his Coke. Then he says, "Yes, you *are* crazy. You and me could start all over again. Right back at the beginning."

"We *have* started all over again," says Norma Jean. "And this is how it turned out."

"What did I do wrong?"

"Nothing."

"Is this one of those women's lib things?" Leroy asks.

"Don't be funny."

The cemetery, a green slope dotted with white markers, looks like a subdivision site. Leroy is trying to comprehend that his marriage is breaking up, but for some reason he is wondering about white slabs in a graveyard.

"Everything was fine till Mama caught me smoking," says Norma Jean, standing up. "That set something off."

"What are you talking about?"

"She won't leave me alone—*you* won't leave me alone." Norma Jean seems to be crying, but she is looking away from him. "I feel eighteen again. I can't face that all over again." She starts walking away. "No, it *wasn't* fine. I don't know what I'm saying. Forget it."

Leroy takes a lungful of smoke and closes his eyes as Norma Jean's words sink in. He tries to focus on the fact that thirty-five hundred soldiers died on the grounds around him. He can only think of that war as a board game with plastic soldiers. Leroy almost smiles, as he compares the Confederates' daring attack on the Union camps and Virgil Mathis's raid on the bowling alley. General Grant, drunk and furious, shoved the Southerners back to Corinth, where Mabel and Jet Beasley were married years later, when Mabel was still thin and good-looking. The next day, Mabel and Jet visited the battleground, and then Norma Jean was born, and then she married Leroy and they had a baby, which they lost, and now Leroy and Norma Jean are here at the same battleground. Leroy knows he is leaving out a lot. He is leaving out the insides of history. History was always just names and dates to him. It occurs to him that building a house out of logs is similarly empty—too simple. And the real inner workings of a marriage, like most of history, have escaped him. Now he sees that building a log house is the dumbest idea he

could have had. It was clumsy of him to think Norma Jean would want a log house. It was a crazy idea. He'll have to think of something else, quickly. He will wad the blueprints into tight balls and fling them into the lake. Then he'll get moving again. He opens his eyes. Norma Jean has moved away and is walking through the cemetery, following a serpentine brick path.

Leroy gets up to follow his wife, but his good leg is asleep and his bad leg still hurts him. Norma Jean is far away, walking rapidly toward the bluff by the river, and he tries to hobble toward her. Some children run past him, screaming noisily. Norma Jean has reached the bluff, and she is looking out over the Tennessee River. Now she turns toward Leroy and waves her arms. Is she beckoning to him? She seems to be doing an exercise for her chest muscles. The sky is unusually pale—the color of the dust ruffle Mabel made for their bed.

Questions for Discussion and Analysis

1. At the beginning of the story, how would you describe Leroy and Norma Jean? What are their interests and motivations? What are they doing with their lives?
2. From the details the narrator provides, what do we know about their marriage? What accommodations has each made?
3. Do you see any significance in Leroy's hobbies? What does the narrator suggest about their quality?
4. In terms of the story as a whole, what is significant about Mabel's catching Norma Jean smoking?
5. What is ironic about Leroy's and Norma Jean's names and their origins?
6. Why does Norma Jean decide to leave Leroy? Is the breakup of their marriage a tragedy?

Short Story 3

Miss Brill
Katherine Mansfield

Born in 1888 Wellington, New Zealand, Katherine Mansfield published her first book of stories, In a German Pension, *in 1911. Two more collections followed:* Bliss and Other Stories *(1920) and* The Garden Party *(1922). Like Chekhov, she died of tuberculosis at the peak of her success. She was thirty-four years old.*

Although it was so brilliantly fine—the blue sky powdered with gold and great spots of light like white wine splashed over the Jardins Publiques—Miss Brill was glad that she had decided on her fur. The air

was motionless, but when you opened your mouth there was just a faint chill, like a chill from a glass of iced water before you sip, and now and again a leaf came drifting—from nowhere, from the sky. Miss Brill put up her hand and touched her fur. Dear little thing! It was nice to feel it again. She had taken it out of its box that afternoon, shaken out the moth-powder, given it a good brush, and rubbed the life back into the dim little eyes. "What has been happening to me?" said the sad little eyes. Oh, how sweet it was to see them snap at her again from the red eiderdown! . . . But the nose, which was of some black composition, wasn't at all firm. It must have had a knock, somehow. Never mind—a little dab of black sealing-wax when the time came—when it was absolutely necessary. . . . Little rogue! Yes, she really felt like that about it. Little rogue biting its tail just by her left ear. She could have taken it off and laid it on her lap and stroked it. She felt a tingling in her hands and arms, but that came from walking, she supposed. And when she breathed, something light and sad—no, not sad, exactly—something gentle seemed to move in her bosom.

There were a number of people out this afternoon, far more than last Sunday. And the band sounded louder and gayer. That was because the Season had begun. For although the band played all the year round on Sundays, out of season it was never the same. It was like someone playing with only the family to listen; it didn't care how it played with only the family to listen; it didn't care how it played if there weren't any strangers present. Wasn't the conductor wearing a new coat, too? She was sure it was new. He scraped with his foot and flapped his arms like a rooster about to crow, and the bandsmen sitting in the green rotunda blew out their cheeks and glared at the music. Now there came a little "flutey" bit—very pretty!—a little chain of bright drops. She was sure it would be repeated. It was; she lifted her head and smiled.

Only two people shared her "special" seat: a fine old man in a velvet coat, his hands clasped over a huge carved walking-stick, and a big old woman, sitting upright, with a roll of knitting on her embroidered apron. They did not speak. This was disappointing, for Miss Brill always looked forward to the conversation. She had become really quite expert, she thought, at listening as though she didn't listen, at sitting in other people's lives just for a minute while they talked round her.

She glanced, sideways, at the old couple. Perhaps they would go soon. Last Sunday, too, hadn't been as interesting as usual. An Englishman and his wife, he wearing a dreadful Panama hat and she button boots. And she'd gone on the whole time about how she ought to wear spectacles; she knew she needed them; but that it was no good getting any; they'd be sure to break and they'd never keep on. And he'd been so patient. He'd suggested everything—gold rims, the kind that curved round your ears, little pads inside the bridge. No, nothing would please her. "They'll always be sliding down my nose!" Miss Brill had wanted to shake her.

The old people sat on the bench, still as statues. Never mind, there

was always the crowd to watch. To and fro, in front of the flower-beds and the band rotunda, the couples and groups paraded, stopped to talk, to greet, to buy a handful of flowers from the old beggar who had his tray fixed to the railings. Little children ran among them, swooping and laughing; little boys with big white silk bows under their chins, little girls, little French dolls, dressed up in velvet and lace. And sometimes a tiny staggerer came suddenly rocking into the open from under the trees, stopped, stared, and suddenly sat down "flop," until its small high-stepping mother, like a young hen, rushed scolding to its rescue. Other people sat on the benches and green chairs, but they were nearly always the same, Sunday after Sunday, and—Miss Brill had often noticed—there was something funny about nearly all of them. They were odd, silent, nearly all old, and from the way they stared they looked as though they'd just come from dark little rooms or even—even cupboards!

Behind the rotunda the slender trees with yellow leaves down drooping, and through them just a line of sea, and beyond the blue sky with gold-veined clouds.

Tum-tum-tum tiddle-um! tum tiddley-um tum ta! blew the band.

Two young girls in red came by and two young soldiers in blue met them, and they laughed and paired and went off arm-in-arm. Two peasant women with funny straw hats passed, gravely, leading beautiful smoke-coloured donkeys. A cold, pale nun hurried by. A beautiful woman came along and dropped her bunch of violets, and a little boy ran after to hand them to her, and she took them and threw them away as if they'd been poisoned. Dear me! Miss Brill didn't know whether to admire that or not! And now an ermine toque and a gentleman in grey met just in front of her. He was tall, stiff, dignified, and she was wearing the ermine toque she'd bought when her hair was yellow. Now everything, her hair, her face, even her eyes, was the same colour as the shabby ermine, and her hand, in its cleaned glove, lifted to dab her lips, was a tiny yellowish paw. Oh, she was so pleased to see him—delighted! She rather thought they were going to meet that afternoon. She described where she'd been—everywhere, here, there, along by the sea. The day was so charming—didn't he agree? And wouldn't he, perhaps? . . . But he shook his head, lighted a cigarette, slowly breathed a great deep puff into her face, and, even while she was still talking and laughing, flicked the match away and walked on. The ermine toque was alone; she smiled more brightly than ever. But even the band seemed to know what she was feeling and played more softly, played tenderly, and the drum beat, "The Brute! The Brute!" over and over. What would she do? What was going to happen now? But as Miss Brill wondered, the ermine toque turned, raised her hand as though she'd seen someone else, much nicer, just over there, and pattered away. And the band changed again and played more quickly, more gaily than ever, and the old couple on Miss Brill's seat got up and marched away, and such a funny old

man with long whiskers hobbled along in time to the music and was nearly knocked over by four girls walking abreast.

Oh, how fascinating it was! How she enjoyed it! How she loved sitting here, watching it all! It was like a play. It was exactly like a play. Who could believe the sky at the back wasn't painted? But it wasn't till a little brown dog trotted on solemn and then slowly trotted off, like a little "theater" dog, a little dog that had been drugged, that Miss Brill discovered what it was that made it so exciting. They were all on the stage. They weren't only the audience, not only looking on; they were acting. Even she had a part and came every Sunday. No doubt somebody would have noticed if she hadn't been there; she was part of the performance after all. How strange she'd never thought of it like that before! And yet it explained why she made such a point of starting from home at just the same time each week—so as not to be late for the performance—and it also explained why she had quite a queer, shy feeling at telling her English pupils how she spent her Sunday afternoons. No wonder! Miss Brill nearly laughed out loud. She was on the stage. She thought of the old invalid gentleman to whom she read the newspaper four afternoons a week while he slept in the garden. She had got quite used to the frail head on the cotton pillow, the hollowed eyes, the open mouth and the high pinched nose. If he'd been dead she mightn't have noticed for weeks; she wouldn't have minded. But suddenly he knew he was having the paper read to him by an actress! "An actress!" The old head lifted; two points of light quivered in the old eyes. "An actress—are ye?" And Miss Brill smoothed the newspaper as though it were the manuscript of her part and said gently: "Yes, I have been an actress for a long time."

The band had been having a rest. Now they started again. And what they played was warm, sunny, yet there was just a faint chill—a something, what was it?—not sadness—no, not sadness—something that made you want to sing. The tune lifted, lifted, the light shone; and it seemed to Miss Brill that in another moment all of them, all the whole company, would begin singing. The young ones, the laughing ones who were moving together, they would begin, and the men's voices, very resolute and brave, would join them. And then she too, she too, and the others on the benches—they would come in with a kind of accompaniment—something low, that scarcely rose or fell, something so beautiful—moving. . . . And Miss Brill's eyes filled with tears and she looked smiling at all the other members of the company. Yes, we understand, we understand, she thought—though what they understood she didn't know.

Just at that moment a boy and a girl came and sat down where the old couple had been. They were beautifully dressed; they were in love. The hero and heroine, of course, just arrived from his father's yacht. And still soundlessly singing, still with that trembling smile, Miss Brill prepared to listen.

"No, not now," said the girl. "Not here, I can't."

"But why? Because of that stupid old thing at the end there?" asked the boy. "Why does she come here at all—who wants her? Why doesn't she keep her silly old mug at home?"

"It's her fu-fur which is so funny," giggled the girl. "It's exactly like a fried whiting."

"Ah, be off with you!" said the boy in an angry whisper. Then: "Tell me, ma petite chérie—"

"No, not here," said the girl. "Not *yet.*"

On her way home she usually bought a slice of honey-cake at the baker's. It was her Sunday treat. Sometimes there was an almond in her slice, sometimes not. It made a great difference. If there was an almond it was like carrying home a tiny present—a surprise—something that might very well not have been there. She hurried on the almond Sundays and struck the match for the kettle in quite a dashing way.

But to-day she passed the baker's by, climbed the stairs, went into the little dark room—her room like a cupboard—and sat down on the red eiderdown. She sat there for a long time. The box that the fur came out of was on the bed. She unclasped the necklet quickly; quickly, without looking, laid it inside. But when she put the lid on she thought she heard something crying.

Questions for Discussion and Analysis

1. Who is Miss Brill? From the details Mansfield provides, what sort of life does she lead?

2. How does Miss Brill perceive herself? How does she perceive those around her? How does she perceive herself as different from the usual occupants of the Jardins Publiques (the public gardens)?

3. Look again at the exchange between the "ermine toque" and the "gentleman in grey"? Who are these people? Whose eyes do we see them through? What has taken place between these two?

4. What is ironic about the description of Miss Brill's reading to the old invalid gentleman?

5. In what way does Miss Brill change during the course of the story? What is the impetus for that change? What is crying when she puts her fur back into its box?

6. Is Miss Brill tragic or merely silly? How are we to see her?

Short Story 4

Cathedral

Raymond Carver

By the time of his untimely death in 1988 of lung cancer at the age of forty-nine, Raymond Carver had established himself as one of America's most influential short story writers. Twice awarded grants from the National Endowment for the Arts, Carver also was a Guggenheim Fellow in 1979. His stories are about ordinary people who somehow survive whatever befalls them. "Cathedral," reprinted from the short story collection of the same name, is one of Carver's best-known works, and it is a masterpiece of subtle sardonic humor that ultimately has a serious edge. Two other collections of his stories are Will You Please Be Quiet, Please? *and* What We Talk About When We Talk About Love.

This blind man, an old friend of my wife's, he was on his way to spend the night. His wife had died. So he was visiting the dead wife's relatives in Connecticut. He called my wife from his in-laws'. Arrangements were made. He would come by train, a five-hour trip, and my wife would meet him at the station. She hadn't seen him since she worked for him one summer in Seattle ten years ago. But she and the blind man had kept in touch. They made tapes and mailed them back and forth. I wasn't enthusiastic about his visit. He was no one I knew. And his being blind bothered me. My idea of blindness came from the movies. In the movies, the blind moved slowly and never laughed. Sometimes they were led by seeing-eye dogs. A blind man in my house was not something I looked forward to.

That summer in Seattle she had needed a job. She didn't have any money. The man she was going to marry at the end of the summer was in officers' training school. He didn't have any money, either. But she was in love with the guy, and he was in love with her, etc. She'd seen something in the paper: "HELP WANTED—*Reading to Blind Man,* and a telephone number. She phoned and went over, was hired on the spot. She'd worked with this blind man all summer. She read stuff to him, case studies, reports, that sort of thing. She helped him organize his little office in the county social-service department. They'd become good friends, my wife and the blind man. How do I know these things? She told me. And she told me something else. On her last day in the office, the blind man asked if he could touch her face. She agreed to this. She told me he touched his fingers to every part of her face, her nose—even her neck! She never forgot it. She even tried to write a poem about it. She was always trying to write a poem. She wrote a poem or two every year, usually after something really important had happened to her.

When we first started going out together, she showed me the poem.

In the poem, she recalled his fingers and the way they had moved around over her face. In the poem, she talked about what she had felt at the time, about what went through her mind when the blind man touched her nose and lips. I can remember I didn't think much of the poem. Of course, I didn't tell her that. Maybe I just don't understand poetry. I admit it's not the first thing I reach for when I pick up something to read.

Anyway, this man who'd first enjoyed her favors, the officer-to-be, he'd been her childhood sweetheart. So okay. I'm saying that at the end of the summer she let the blind man run his hands over her face, said goodbye to him, married her childhood etc., who was now a commissioned officer, and she moved away from Seattle. But they'd kept in touch, she and the blind man. She made the first contact after a year or so. She called him up one night from an Air Force base in Alabama. She wanted to talk. They talked. He asked her to send him a tape and tell him about her life. She did this. She sent the tape. On the tape, she told the blind man about her husband and about their life together in the military. She told the blind man she loved her husband but she didn't like it where they lived and she didn't like it that he was a part of the military-industrial thing. She told the blind man she'd written a poem and he was in it. She told him that she was writing a poem about what it was like to be an Air Force officer's wife. The poem wasn't finished yet. She was still writing it. The blind man made a tape. He sent her the tape. She made a tape. This went on for years. My wife's officer was posted to one base and then another. She sent tapes from Moody AFB, McGuire, McConnell, and finally Travis, near Sacramento, where one night she got to feeling lonely and cut off from people she kept losing in that moving-around life. She got to feeling she couldn't go it another step. She went in and swallowed all the pills and capsules in the medicine chest and washed them down with a bottle of gin. Then she got into a hot bath and passed out.

But instead of dying, she got sick. She threw up. Her officer—why should he have a name? he was the childhood sweetheart, and what more does he want?—came home from somewhere, found her, and called the ambulance. In time, she put it all on a tape and sent the tape to the blind man. Over the years, she put all kinds of stuff on tapes and sent the tapes off lickety-split. Next to writing a poem every year, I think it was her chief means of recreation. On one tape, she told the blind man she'd decided to live away from her officer for a time. On another tape, she told him about her divorce. She and I began going out, and of course she told her blind man about it. She told him everything, or so it seemed to me. Once she asked me if I'd like to hear the latest tape from the blind man. This was a year ago. I was on the tape, she said. So I said okay, I'd listen to it. I got us drinks and we settled down in the living room. We made ready to listen. First she inserted the tape into the player and adjusted a couple of dials. Then she pushed a lever.

The tape squeaked and someone began to talk in this loud voice. She lowered the volume. After a few minutes of harmless chitchat, I heard my own name in the mouth of this stranger, this blind man I didn't even know! And then this: "From all you've said about him, I can only conclude—" But we were interrupted, a knock at the door, something, and we didn't ever get back to the tape. Maybe it was just as well. I'd heard all I wanted to.

Now this same blind man was coming to sleep in my house.

"Maybe I could take him bowling," I said to my wife. She was at the draining board doing scalloped potatoes. She put down the knife she was using and turned around.

"If you love me," she said, "you can do this for me. If you don't love me, okay. But if you had a friend, any friend, and the friend came to visit, I'd make him feel comfortable." She wiped her hands with the dish towel.

"I don't have any blind friends," I said.

"You don't have *any* friends," she said. "Period. Besides," she said, "goddamn it, his wife's just died! Don't you understand that? The man's lost his wife!"

I didn't answer. She'd told me a little about the blind man's wife. Her name was Beulah. Beulah! That's a name for a colored woman.

"Was his wife a Negro?" I asked.

"Are you crazy?" my wife said. "Have you just flipped or something?" She picked up a potato. I saw it hit the floor, then roll under the stove. "What's wrong with you?" she said. "Are you drunk?"

"I'm just asking," I said.

Right then my wife filled me in with more detail than I cared to know. I made a drink and sat at the kitchen table to listen. Pieces of the story began to fall into place.

Beulah had gone to work for the blind man the summer after my wife had stopped working for him. Pretty soon Beulah and the blind man had themselves a church wedding. It was a little wedding—who'd want to go to such a wedding in the first place?—just the two of them, plus the minister and the minister's wife. But it was a church wedding just the same. It was what Beulah had wanted, he'd said. But even then Beulah must have been carrying the cancer in her glands. After they had been inseparable for eight years—my wife's word, *inseparable*—Beulah's health went into a rapid decline. She died in a Seattle hospital room, the blind man sitting beside the bed and holding on to her hand. They'd married, lived and worked together, slept together—had sex, sure—and then the blind man had to bury her. All this without his having ever seen what the goddamned woman looked like. It was beyond my understanding. Hearing this, I felt sorry for the blind man for a little bit. And then I found myself thinking what a pitiful life this woman must have led. Imagine a woman who could never see herself as she was seen in the eyes of her loved one. A woman who could go on

day after day and never receive the smallest compliment from her beloved. A woman whose husband could never read the expression on her face, be it misery or something better. Someone who could wear makeup or not—what difference to him? She could, if she wanted, wear green eye-shadow around one eye, a straight pin in her nostril, yellow slacks and purple shoes, no matter. And then to slip off into death, the blind man's hand on her hand, his blind eyes streaming tears—I'm imagining now—her last thought may be this: that he never even knew what she looked like, and she on an express to the grave. Robert was left with a small insurance policy and half of a twenty-peso Mexican coin. The other half of the coin went into the box with her. Pathetic.

So when the time rolled around, my wife went to the depot to pick him up. With nothing to do but wait—sure, I blamed him for that—I was having a drink and watching the TV when I heard the car pull into the drive. I got up from the sofa with my drink and went to the window to have a look.

I saw my wife laughing as she parked the car. I saw her get out of the car and shut the door. She was still wearing a smile. Just amazing. She went around to the other side of the car to where the blind man was already starting to get out. This blind man, feature this, he was wearing a full beard! A beard on a blind man! Too much, I say. The blind man reached into the back seat and dragged out a suitcase. My wife took his arm, shut the car door, and, talking all the way, moved him down the drive and then up the steps to the front porch. I turned off the TV. I finished my drink, rinsed the glass, dried my hands. Then I went to the door.

My wife said, "I want you to meet Robert. Robert, this is my husband. I've told you all about him." She was beaming. She had this blind man by his coat sleeve.

The blind man let go of his suitcase and up came his hand.

I took it. He squeezed hard, held my hand, and then he let it go.

"I feel like we've already met," he boomed.

"Likewise," I said. I didn't know what else to say. Then I said, "Welcome. I've heard a lot about you." We began to move then, a little group, from the porch into the living room, my wife guiding him by the arm. The blind man was carrying his suitcase in his other hand. My wife said things like, "To your left here, Robert. That's right. Now watch it, there's a chair. That's it. Sit down right here. This is the sofa. We just bought this sofa two weeks ago."

I started to say something about the old sofa. I'd liked that old sofa. But I didn't say anything. Then I wanted to say something else, small-talk, about the scenic ride along the Hudson. How going *to* New York, you should sit on the right-hand side of the train, and coming *from* New York, the left-hand side.

"Did you have a good train ride?" I said. "Which side of the train did you sit on, by the way?"

"What a question, which side!" my wife said. "What's it matter which side?" she said.

"I just asked," I said.

"Right side," the blind man said. "I hadn't been on a train in nearly forty years. Not since I was a kid. With my folks. That's been a long time. I'd nearly forgotten the sensation. I have winter in my beard now," he said. "So I've been told, anyway. Do I look distinguished, my dear?" the blind man said to my wife.

"You look distinguished, Robert," she said. "Robert," she said. "Robert, it's just so good to see you."

My wife finally took her eyes off the blind man and looked at me. I had the feeling she didn't like what she saw. I shrugged.

I've never met, or personally known, anyone who was blind. This blind man was late forties, a heavy-set, balding man with stooped shoulders, as if he carried a great weight there. He wore brown slacks, brown shoes, a light-brown shirt, a tie, a sports coat. Spiffy. He also had this full beard. But he didn't use a cane and he didn't wear dark glasses. I'd always thought dark glasses were a must for the blind. Fact was, I wished he had a pair. At first glance, his eyes looked like anyone else's eyes. But if you looked close, there was something different about them. Too much white in the iris, for one thing, and the pupils seemed to move around in the sockets without his knowing it or being able to stop it. Creepy. As I stared at his face, I saw the left pupil turn in toward his nose while the other made an effort to keep in one place. But it was only an effort, for that eye was on the roam without his knowing it or wanting it to be.

I said, "Let me get you a drink. What's your pleasure? We have a little of everything. It's one of our pastimes."

"Bub, I'm a Scotch man myself," he said fast enough in this big voice.

"Right," I said. Bub! "Sure you are. I knew it."

He let his fingers touch his suitcase, which was sitting alongside the sofa. He was taking his bearings. I didn't blame him for that.

"I'll move that up to your room," my wife said.

"No, that's fine," the blind man said loudly. "It can go up when I go up."

"A little water with the Scotch?" I said.

"Very little," he said.

"I knew it," I said.

He said, "Just a tad. The Irish actor, Barry Fitzgerald? I'm like that fellow. When I drink water, Fitzgerald said, I drink water. When I drink whiskey, I drink whiskey." My wife laughed. The blind man brought his hand up under his beard. He lifted his beard slowly and let it drop.

I did the drinks, three big glasses of Scotch with a splash of water in each. Then we made ourselves comfortable and talked about Robert's travels. First the long flight from the West Coast to Connecticut, we

covered that. Then from Connecticut up here by train. We had another drink concerning that leg of the trip.

I remembered having read somewhere that the blind didn't smoke because, as speculation had it, they couldn't see the smoke they exhaled. I thought I knew that much and that much only about blind people. But this blind man smoked his cigarette down to the nubbin and then lit another one. This blind man filled his ashtray and my wife emptied it.

When we sat down at the table for dinner, we had another drink. My wife heaped Robert's plate with cube steak, scalloped potatoes, green beans. I buttered him up two slices of bread. I said, "Here's bread and butter for you." I swallowed some of my drink. "Now let us pray," I said, and the blind man lowered his head. My wife looked at me, her mouth agape. "Pray the phone won't ring and the food doesn't get cold," I said.

We dug in. We ate everything there was to eat on the table. We ate like there was no tomorrow. We didn't talk. We ate. We scarfed. We grazed that table. We were into serious eating. The blind man had right away located his foods, he knew just where everything was on his plate. I watched with admiration as he used his knife and fork on the meat. He'd cut two pieces of meat, fork the meat into his mouth, and then go all out for the scalloped potatoes, the beans next, and then he'd tear off a hunk of buttered bread and eat that. He'd follow this up with a big drink of milk. It didn't seem to bother him to use his fingers once in a while, either.

We finished everything, including half a strawberry pie. For a few moments, we sat as if stunned. Sweat beaded on our faces. Finally, we got up from the table and left the dirty plates. We didn't look back. We took ourselves into the living room and sank into our places again. Robert and my wife sat on the sofa. I took the big chair. We had us two or three more drinks while they talked about the major things that had come to pass for them in the past ten years. For the most part, I just listened. Now and then I joined in. I didn't want him to think I'd left the room, and I didn't want her to think I was feeling left out. They talked of things that had happened to them—to them!—these past ten years. I waited in vain to hear my name on my wife's sweet lips: "And then my dear husband came into my life"—something like that. But I heard nothing of the sort. More talk of Robert. Robert had done a little of everything, it seemed, a regular blind jack-of-all-trades. But most recently he and his wife had had an Amway distributorship, from which, I gathered, they'd earned their living, such as it was. The blind man was also a ham radio operator. He talked in his loud voice about conversations he'd had with fellow operators in Guam, in the Philippines, in Alaska, and even in Tahiti. He said he'd have a lot of friends there if he ever wanted to go visit those places. From time to time, he'd turn his blind face toward me, put his hand under his beard, ask me something.

How long had I been in my present position? (Three years.) Did I like my work? (I didn't.) Was I going to stay with it? (What were the options?) Finally, when I thought he was beginning to run down, I got up and turned on the TV.

My wife looked at me with irritation. She was heading toward a boil. Then she looked at the blind man and said, "Robert, do you have a TV?"

The blind man said, "My dear, I have two TVs. I have a color set and a black-and-white thing, an old relic. It's funny, but if I turn the TV on, and I'm always turning it on, I turn on the color set. It's funny, don't you think?"

I didn't know what to say to that. I had absolutely nothing to say to that. No opinion. So I watched the news program and tried to listen to what the announcer was saying.

"This is a color TV," the blind man said. "Don't ask me how, but I can tell."

"We traded up a while ago," I said.

The blind man had another taste of his drink. He lifted his beard, sniffed it, and let it fall. He leaned forward on the sofa. He positioned his ashtray on the coffee table, then put the lighter to his cigarette. He leaned back on the sofa and crossed his legs at the ankles.

My wife covered her mouth, and then she yawned. She stretched. She said, "I think I'll go upstairs and put on my robe. I think I'll change into something else. Robert, you make yourself comfortable," she said.

"I'm comfortable," the blind man said.

"I want you to feel comfortable in this house," she said.

"I am comfortable," the blind man said.

After she'd left the room, he and I listened to the weather report and then to the sports roundup. By that time, she'd been gone so long I didn't know if she was going to come back. I thought she might have gone to bed. I wished she'd come back downstairs. I didn't want to be left alone with a blind man. I asked him if he wanted another drink, and he said sure. Then I asked if he wanted to smoke some dope with me. I said I'd just rolled a number. I hadn't, but I planned to do so in about two shakes.

"I'll try some with you," he said.

"Damn right," I said. "That's the stuff."

I got our drinks and sat down on the sofa with him. Then I rolled us two fat numbers. I lit one and passed it. I brought it to his fingers. He took it and inhaled.

"Hold it as long as you can," I said. I could tell he didn't know the first thing.

My wife came back downstairs wearing her pink robe and her pink slippers.

"What do I smell?" she said.

'We thought we'd have us some cannabis," I said.

My wife gave me a savage look. Then she looked at the blind man and said, "Robert, I didn't know you smoked."

He said, "I do now, my dear. There's a first time for everything. But I don't feel anything yet."

"This stuff is pretty mellow," I said. "This stuff is mild. It's dope you can reason with," I said. "It doesn't mess you up."

"Not much it doesn't, bub," he said, and laughed.

My wife sat on the sofa between the blind man and me. I passed her the number. She took it and toked and then passed it back to me. "Which way is this going?" she said. Then she said, "I shouldn't be smoking this. I can hardly keep my eyes open as it is. That dinner did me in. I shouldn't have eaten so much."

"It was the strawberry pie," the blind man said. "That's what did it," he said, and he laughed his big laugh. Then he shook his head.

"There's more strawberry pie," I said.

"Do you want some more, Robert?" my wife said.

"Maybe in a little while," he said.

We gave our attention to the TV. My wife yawned again. She said, "Your bed is made up when you feel like going to bed, Robert. I know you must have had a long day. When you're ready to go to bed, say so." She pulled his arm. "Robert?"

He came to and said, "I've had a real nice time. This beats tapes, doesn't it?"

I said, "Coming at you," and I put the number between his fingers. He inhaled, held the smoke, and then let it go. It was like he'd been doing it since he was nine years old.

"Thanks, bub," he said. "But I think this is all for me. I think I'm beginning to feel it," he said. He held the burning roach out for my wife.

"Same here," she said. "Ditto. Me, too." She took the roach and passed it to me. "I may just sit here for a while between you two guys with my eyes closed. But don't let me bother you, okay? Either one of you. If it bothers you, say so. Otherwise, I may just sit here with my eyes closed until you're ready to go to bed," she said. "Your bed's made up, Robert, when you're ready. It's right next to our room at the top of the stairs. We'll show you up when you're ready. You wake me up now, you guys, if I fall asleep." She said that and then she closed her eyes and went to sleep.

The news program ended. I got up and changed the channel. I sat back down on the sofa. I wished my wife hadn't pooped out. Her head lay across the back of the sofa, her mouth open. She'd turned so that her robe had slipped away from her legs, exposing a juicy thigh. I reached to draw her robe back over her, and it was then that I glanced at the blind man. What the hell! I flipped the robe open again.

"You say when you want some strawberry pie," I said.

"I will," he said.

I said, "Are you tired? Do you want me to take you up to your bed? Are you ready to hit the hay?"

"Not yet," he said. "No, I'll stay up with you, bub. If that's all right. I'll stay up until you're ready to turn in. We haven't had a chance to talk. Know what I mean? I feel like me and her monopolized the evening." He lifted his beard and he let it fall. He picked up his cigarettes and his lighter.

"That's all right," I said. Then I said, "I'm glad for the company."

And I guess I was. Every night I smoked dope and stayed up as long as I could before I fell asleep. My wife and I hardly ever went to bed at the same time. When I did go to sleep, I had these dreams. Sometimes I'd wake up from one of them, my heart going crazy.

Something about the church and the Middle Ages was on the TV. Not your run-of-the-mill TV fare. I wanted to watch something else. I turned to the other channels. But there was nothing on them, either. So I turned back to the first channel and apologized.

"Bub, it's all right," the blind man said. "It's fine with me. Whatever you want to watch is okay. I'm always learning something. Learning never ends. It won't hurt me to learn something tonight. I got ears," he said.

We didn't say anything for a time. He was leaning forward with his head turned at me, his right ear aimed in the direction of the set. Very disconcerting. Now and then his eyelids drooped and then they snapped open again. Now and then he put his fingers into his beard and tugged, like he was thinking about something he was hearing on the television.

On the screen, a group of men wearing cowls was being set upon and tormented by men dressed in skeleton costumes and men dressed as devils. The men dressed as devils wore devil masks, horns, and long tails. This pageant was part of a procession. The Englishman who was narrating the thing said it took place in Spain once a year. I tried to explain to the blind man what was happening.

"Skeletons," he said. "I know about skeletons," he said, and he nodded.

The TV showed this one cathedral. Then there was a long, slow look at another one. Finally, the picture switched to the famous one in Paris, with its flying buttresses and its spires reaching up to the clouds. The camera pulled away to show the whole of the cathedral rising above the skyline.

There were times when the Englishman who was telling the thing would shut up, would simply let the camera move around over the cathedrals. Or else the camera would tour the countryside, men in fields walking behind oxen. I waited as long as I could. Then I felt I had to say something. I said, "They're showing the outside of this cathedral

now. Gargoyles. Little statues carved to look like monsters. Now I guess they're in Italy. Yeah, they're in Italy. There's paintings on the walls of this one church."

"Are those fresco paintings, bub?" he asked, and he sipped from his drink.

I reached for my glass. But it was empty. I tried to remember what I could remember. "You're asking me are those frescoes?" I said. "That's a good question. I don't know."

The camera moved to a cathedral outside Lisbon. The differences in the Portuguese cathedral compared with the French and Italian were not that great. But they were there. Mostly the interior stuff. Then something occurred to me, and I said, "Something has occurred to me. Do you have any idea what a cathedral is? What they look like, that is? Do you follow me? If somebody says cathedral to you, do you have any notion what they're talking about? Do you know the difference between that and a Baptist church, say?"

He let the smoke dribble from his mouth. "I know they took hundreds of workers fifty or a hundred years to build," he said. "I just heard the man say that, of course. I know generations of the same families worked on a cathedral. I heard him say that, too. The men who began their life's work on them, they never lived to see the completion of their work. In that wise, bub, they're no different from the rest of us, right?" He laughed. Then his eyelids drooped again. His head nodded. He seemed to be snoozing. Maybe he was imagining himself in Portugal. The TV was showing another cathedral now. This one was in Germany. The Englishman's voice droned on. "Cathedrals," the blind man said. He sat up and rolled his head back and forth. "If you want the truth, bub, that's about all I know. What I just said. What I heard him say. But maybe you could describe one to me? I wish you'd do it. I'd like that. If you want to know, I really don't have a good idea."

I stared hard at the shot of the cathedral on the TV. How could I even begin to describe it? But say my life depended on it. Say my life was being threatened by an insane guy who said I had to do it or else.

I stared some more at the cathedral before the picture flipped off into the countryside. There was no use. I turned to the blind man and said, "To begin with, they're very tall." I was looking around the room for clues. "They reach way up. Up and up. Toward the sky. They're so big, some of them, they have to have these supports. To help hold them up, so to speak. These supports are called buttresses. They remind me of viaducts, for some reason. But maybe you don't know viaducts, either? Sometimes the cathedrals have devils and such carved into the front. Sometimes lords and ladies. Don't ask me why this is," I said.

He was nodding. The whole upper part of his body seemed to be moving back and forth.

"I'm not doing so good, am I?" I said.

He stopped nodding and leaned forward on the edge of the sofa. As he listened to me, he was running his fingers through his beard. I wasn't getting through to him, I could see that. But he waited for me to go on just the same. He nodded, like he was trying to encourage me. I tried to think what else to say. "They're really big," I said. "They're massive. They're built of stone. Marble, too, sometimes. In those olden days, when they built cathedrals, men wanted to be close to God. In those olden days, God was an important part of everyone's life. You could tell this from their cathedral-building. I'm sorry," I said, "but it looks like that's the best I can do for you. I'm just no good at it."

"That's all right, bub," the blind man said. "Hey, listen. I hope you don't mind my asking you. Can I ask you something? Let me ask you a simple question, yes or no. I'm just curious and there's no offense. You're my host. But let me ask if you are in any way religious? You don't mind my asking?"

I shook my head. He couldn't see that, though. A wink is the same as a nod to a blind man. "I guess I don't believe in it. In anything. Sometimes it's hard. You know what I'm saying?"

"Sure, I do," he said.

"Right," I said.

The Englishman was still holding forth. My wife sighed in her sleep. She drew a long breath and went on with her sleeping.

"You'll have to forgive me," I said. "But I can't tell you what a cathedral looks like. It just isn't in me to do it. I can't do any more than I've done."

The blind man sat very still, his head down, as he listened to me.

I said, "The truth is, cathedrals don't mean anything special to me. Nothing. Cathedrals. They're something to look at on late-night TV. That's all they are."

It was then that the blind man cleared his throat. He brought something up. He took a handkerchief from his back pocket. Then he said, "I get it, bub. It's okay. It happens. Don't worry about it," he said. "Hey, listen to me. Will you do me a favor? I got an idea. Why don't you find us some heavy paper? And a pen. We'll do something. We'll draw one together. Get us a pen and some heavy paper. Go on, bub, get the stuff," he said.

So I went upstairs. My legs felt like they didn't have any strength in them. They felt like they did after I'd done some running. In my wife's room, I looked around. I found some ballpoints in a little basket on her table. And then I tried to think where to look for the kind of paper he was talking about.

Downstairs, in the kitchen, I found a shopping bag with onion skins in the bottom of the bag. I emptied the bag and shook it. I brought it into the living room and sat down with it near his legs. I moved some things, smoothed the wrinkles from the bag, spread it out on the coffee table.

The blind man got down from the sofa and sat next to me on the carpet.

He ran his fingers over the paper. He went up and down the sides of the paper. The edges, even the edges. He fingered the corners.

"All right," he said. "All right, let's do her."

He found my hand, the hand with the pen. He closed his hand over my hand. "Go ahead, bub, draw," he said. "Draw. You'll see. I'll follow along with you. It'll be okay. Just begin now like I'm telling you. You'll see. Draw," the blind man said.

So I began. First I drew a box that looked like a house. It could have been the house I lived in. Then I put a roof on it. At either end of the roof, I drew spires. Crazy.

"Swell," he said. "Terrific. You're doing fine," he said. "Never thought anything like this could happen in your lifetime, did you, bub? Well, it's a strange life, we all know that. Go on now. Keep it up."

I put in windows with arches. I drew flying buttresses. I hung great doors. I couldn't stop. The TV station went off the air. I put down the pen and closed and opened my fingers. The blind man felt around over the paper. He moved the tips of his fingers over the paper, all over what I had drawn, and he nodded.

"Doing fine," the blind man said.

I took up the pen again, and he found my hand. I kept at it. I'm no artist. But I kept drawing just the same.

My wife opened up her eyes and gazed at us. She sat up on the sofa, her robe hanging open. She said, "What are you doing? Tell me, I want to know."

I didn't answer her.

The blind man said, "We're drawing a cathedral. Me and him are working on it. Press hard," he said to me. "That's right. That's good," he said. "Sure. You got it, bub. I can tell. You didn't think you could. But you can, can't you? You're cooking with gas now. You know what I'm saying? We're going to really have us something here in a minute. How's the old arm?" he said. "Put some people in there now. What's a cathedral without people?"

My wife said, "What's going on? Robert, what are you doing? What's going on?"

"It's all right," he said to her. "Close your eyes now," the blind man said to me.

I did it. I closed them just like he said.

"Are they closed?" he said. "Don't fudge."

"They're closed," I said.

"Keep them that way," he said. He said, "Don't stop now. Draw."

So we kept on with it. His fingers rode my fingers as my hand went over the paper. It was like nothing else in my life up to now.

Then he said, "I think that's it. I think you got it," he said. "Take a look. What do you think?"

But I had my eyes closed. I thought I'd keep them that way for a little longer. I thought it was something I ought to do.

"Well?" he said. "Are you looking?"

My eyes were still closed. I was in my house. I knew that. But I didn't feel like I was inside anything.

"It's really something," I said.

Questions for Discussion and Analysis

1. What is the advantage of having the main character serve as first-person narrator?

2. Read the first paragraph again, preferably aloud. What tone is embodied in the narrator's voice?

3. The scene in which the narrator describes the blind man's request to feel his wife's face is an example of *foreshadowing,* a technique whereby the author uses one action to suggest a more important action to come. What incident in the story does this point toward?

4. How would you characterize the narrator's attitude toward the blind man? The blind man's attitude toward the husband?

5. In what ways does Robert break the stereotype usually associated with blind people?

6. The narrator experiences an epiphany, a dramatic revelation at the end of the story. What causes it? What happens? What does he learn?

Reading and Studying Textbook Material

The Structure of Modern Textbooks

Reading textbooks requires a different approach to reading from what you have been doing in the other parts of this book. When you read a textbook, your purpose is to extract information. As a result, intensive analysis of rhetorical patterns, recognizing subtleties in tone, and determining the connotations of words are not as relevant.

This is not to say, however, that you should ignore the structure of textbook chapters. Writers of texts use methods of paragraph development and patterns of organization for the same reason that other nonfiction writers do—to make the material easy to follow. Since you have undoubtedly gained some skill in recognizing these techniques, both your comprehension and your ability to remember what you read should be stronger now than when you began this course.

In fact, textbook material should present less of a problem for you than other kinds of nonfiction prose, simply because textbook authors set down their ideas in the most straightforward and organized manner

possible. Also, textbook writers typically avoid the subtleties, figurative language, and rhetorical flourishes with which other writers strive to endow their prose.

The organization of the material in textbook chapters is deliberately mechanistic. A typical chapter begins with a brief outline or overview and ends with a quiz, questions for discussion, or a summary—sometimes all three—to ensure that you have isolated the main points and to help you review. In between, in the body of the chapter, the relative importance of the topics discussed is shown graphically with an assortment of typefaces and type sizes. Large letters and boldface type indicate major heads; smaller letters and italicized or regular type denote subheads, and so forth. Look at the layout of the chapter in your standard textbooks to see how this graphic system works. Finally, modern textbooks are filled with charts, graphs, tables, illustrations, photographs, and sometimes even cartoons to provide visual relief and to explain and interpret the main points. All these techniques make reading and studying the modern textbook easier than in the old days when each chapter contained straight text.

Making Efficient Use of Study Time

Given the high cost of a college education today and the fact that so many students need to work part time to survive, it becomes ever more important to make the most efficient use possible of your time. This section offers some suggestions to help you make the most of your study time.

From my twenty-five years of teaching experience, I have observed that many students get into academic trouble in three ways. First, students often overestimate the number of classes they can take and still manage a part-time job. A few weeks into the semester, things often start to slide. Finding it difficult to keep up with their academic load and their job requirements (not to mention such other time-takers as commuting, laundry, and household chores), they slack off, get behind with their studying (and their rest), and end up dropping courses. If you keep in mind that most colleges suggest that students devote two to three hours a week studying *for each hour spent in class,* you will be able to plan both your academic and work schedule more effectively and still lead a balanced life. At the beginning of the semester or quarter, make a realistic appraisal of what your classes will require and set up a workable study and work schedule.

The next impediment to good study habits is something we are all guilty of in one or more areas of our lives—procrastination. It is virtu-

ally impossible to do a month's or two months' worth of studying the night before an exam. Good students use every spare minute to read or to review. You can take advantage of slack times by studying while you are waiting for the bus, by going to the library if you have an hour or more break between classes, and by seriously limiting the amount of television you watch. The SQ3R method introduced in the next section of Part VI will give you specific suggestions for, in effect, learning as you go.

The SQ3R Study Skills Method

Various study skills techniques are taught today in high school and college courses, for example, PQ3R, PQ4R, SQ4R, SQ3R. All derive from a system developed by Francis P. Robinson; all involve the basic principle that students often omit from their study time: preview and review. The method I teach my students is SQ3R, which stands for:

S	Survey
Q	Question
R	Read
R	Recite
R	Review

(The SQ4R and PQ4R methods add an extra "R" step—"Rite" or "Write," meaning that one can take notes after the read step. If you prefer, you can substitute notetaking for the recite step. See the next section for note-taking suggestions.)

Here is how the system works. Before you start to read an assigned textbook chapter, *survey* its contents by quickly reading and thinking about as many of these parts of the chapter as the author provides:

- Chapter title
- Chapter outline
- Chapter introduction
- Main heads and subheads (become familiar with the typefaces)
- Chapter summary
- Review questions or questions for discussion

The survey step gives you a framework, an overview of what the chapter will discuss before you read it. In this way, you provide a focus for your reading, and you can fit the various parts into a coherent whole. This survey step should take no more than ten minutes.

Next, for the *question* step, go back to the beginning of the chapter and turn the main and subheads into questions that will be answered in each section. For example, consider this subhead from an economics textbook: "The Structure of the Federal Reserve System." Such a subhead can lead to many questions beyond the obvious one: How is the federal reserve system structured? Some possibilities are: Who runs the federal reserve system? How is policy determined? How are responsibilities divided up? Where is the power concentrated? How are decisions made? How do its parts fit and work together?

During this question stage, be sure to consider each section as a whole, meaning that you should treat the main head and the text that follows it and the subheads and the text following each of them as a unit. For example, consider this section from a chapter entitled "Prejudice" reprinted from a social psychology textbook:

SOCIAL INEQUALITIES (main head)
Prejudice Rationalizes Inequalities (first subhead)
Religion and Prejudice (second subhead)
Discrimination's Impact: The Self-Fulfilling Prophecy Lurks Again (third subhead)

Taken together, these topics form a discrete section, one that should be previewed, questioned, and read as a unit. Remembering that the chapter is concerned with prejudice, you might ask these questions: What is the relationship between prejudice and social inequalities? Which comes first, social inequalities or prejudice? How does prejudice rationalize inequalities? What is the connection between religion and prejudice? Do religions inadvertently foster prejudicial attitudes? What is the long-term impact of discrimination? Notice that none of these questions can be answered merely with yes or no. Asking yourself if there are in fact inequalities in our society is not particularly helpful.

During these two steps, you should ask yourself what you already know about the material. There is no point in spending time studying what you already know. (Students are often surprised to see that much of what they read in their textbooks, especially social and behavioral science texts, is already familiar to them or a matter of common sense.) The survey and question steps, then, give you a framework for your reading-study time, show what parts of the chapter you should concentrate on, and make what would otherwise be completely unfamiliar material during the read step familiar.

Reading, the third step, is relatively easy if you have laid the groundwork well. As you read each section and subsection, keep in mind the questions you asked and read to find the answers. After you read each section, *recite* the important points. Then go on to the next section, reading and reciting in the same way. As noted earlier, you might want to take brief notes during the recite step.

Once you have finished reading the entire chapter, *review*—immediately! If you do this right away, you can reduce your study time considerably before major exams. To review, look over the chapter once more, restudying the main points in each section, reading the summary, and seeing if you can answer the discussion or review questions.

Applying the SQ3R Method

Two sample sections from standard college textbooks follow. Unless your instructor has other assignments for you, practice the SQ3R method with them. The first is a portion of a chapter from a college social psychology textbook.

Textbook Selection 1

Gender Roles

David G. Myers

The following extract is a part of "Cultural Influences," Chapter 6 of Social Psychology, *Third Edition, McGraw-Hill, 1990.*

Gender Roles

How Do Males and Females Differ?
  Aggression / Empathy and sensitivity / Sexual attitudes and behavior / Social power

Why Do Males and Females Differ?
  Biology / Culture / Biology and culture

Changing Gender Roles

Should There Be Gender Roles?

Gender Roles

The power of socially prescribed roles to shape our attitudes, our behavior, and even our sense of self is nowhere more evident than in society's implanting ideas about masculinity and femininity and how men and women should behave. But before considering gender-role indoctrination, let's first briefly consider what there is to explain: How different are men and women?

How Do Males and Females Differ?

In the last twenty years, *Psychological Abstracts* has indexed more than 20,000 articles on "human sex differences." So what have we learned from these studies comparing hundreds of thousands of males and females?

First, their similarities are considerable. In age of teething and walking, in overall generosity, helpfulness, and intelligence, and in many other ways, males and females are not noticeably different (E. Maccoby, 1980). Even in physical abilities, where the gender gap is greatest, the overlap between the sexes is considerable. In the annual Boston Marathon, the average man finishes about a half hour ahead of the average woman, but some women finish ahead of most of the superbly conditioned men. Don Schollander's world-record-setting 4 minutes 12.2 seconds in the 400-meter swim at the 1964 Olympic Games would have placed him last against the eight women racing in the 1988 Olympics and a full 8.35 seconds behind winner, Janet Evans.

With psychological traits, the gender similarities are even greater. The English scholar Samuel Johnson recognized the much greater variation *within* than between the sexes when asked whether man or woman was more intelligent. His reply: "Which man? Which woman?"

Gender similarities, however, rouse much less interest and publicity than gender-related differences. The difference in, say, males' and females' average scores on the SAT math test elicit much more attention than their similar average scores on the SAT verbal test. Differences excite scientific curiosity and draw media attention and for that reason may exaggerate our perceptions of the differences between women and men, who are assuredly not of *"opposite"* sex, notes Lauren Harris (1979): "Neither in any physiological nor in any psychological sense are males and females contrary or antithetical in nature or tendency. . . ." Moreover, as we will see, *believing* that certain differences exist may lead men and women both to perceive and to enact expected differences, thereby fulfilling the prophecy.

What, then, are these small gender differences in social behavior? Among them are differences in aggressiveness, empathy and nonverbal sensitivity, sexual initiative, and social power.

Aggression

By *aggression,* psychologists refer not to assertiveness but to behavior that intends to hurt. Throughout the world, hunting, fighting, and warring are primarily men's activities. In surveys, men admit to more aggression than do women. In laboratory experiments, men indeed exhibit more physical aggression, for example by administering what they believe are hurtful electric shocks (Eagly & Steffen, 1986; Hyde, 1986). In the United States, men are arrested for violent crimes eight times more often than women—a trend found in every society that has kept crime records (Kenrick, 1987).

Criminal violence is extreme and unusual behavior; this year 99+ percent of people will *not* be arrested for murder or assault. It is a curious feature of statistical distributions that even a small difference between the averages of two groups—say between the overlapping distributions of male and female aggressiveness—can create noticeable differences at the extremes. Only 5 percent of the variation in individuals' activity levels is attributable to gender (Eaton & Enns, 1986), but that's all it takes to make extreme activity—diagnosed as hyperactivity—three times more common in boys than girls. In other words, observing the extremes—say, the preponderance of males among the criminally violent, the hyperactive, and the junior high math whiz kids—can mislead us into exaggerated perceptions of differences between groups.

Empathy and Sensitivity

There is no doubt that the average female *reports* being more empathic, more able to feel what another feels—"to rejoice with those who rejoice, and weep with those who weep." This is especially true when in surveys women and men describe their emotional responses. To some extent it is also true in laboratory studies, in which women have been more likely to cry and to report feeling distressed at another's distress (Eisenberg & Lennon, 1983).

Moreover, many investigators report that women are less competitive and more cooperative than men and more concerned with social relationships (Gilligan, 1982; Knight & Dubro, 1984). Compared to their friendships with men, both men and women report their friendships with women to be higher in intimacy, enjoyment, and nurturance (Sapadin, 1988). Judith Hall (1984) found that in 94 percent of published studies of adult smiling, females smiled more than males. More recent studies outside the laboratory confirm that women's generally greater warmth is frequently expressed as smiling. When Marianne LaFrance (1985) analyzed 9000 college yearbook photos, and when Amy Halberstadt and Martha Saitta (1987) studied 1100 magazine and newspaper photos and 1300 people in shopping malls, parks, and streets, they consistently found that females were more likely to smile. In groups, men contribute more task-oriented behaviors, such as giving information, and women contribute more positive social-emotional behaviors, such as giving help or showing support (Eagly, 1987).

One explanation for this male/female difference in expressed empathy is that women tend to be better at reading others' emotions. In her analysis of 125 studies of men's and women's sensitivity to nonverbal cues, Hall (1984) has discerned that women are generally superior at decoding others' emotional messages. For example, when shown a two-second silent film clip of the face of an upset woman, women tend to guess more accurately whether she is angry or discussing a divorce. Women also are more skilled at expressing emotions nonverbally, reports Hall.

Sexual Attitudes and Behavior

Susan Hendrick and her colleagues (1985) report that many studies, including their own, reveal a gender gap in sexual attitudes: Women are "moderately conservative" about casual sex, and men are "moderately permissive." The American Council on Education's recent survey of a quarter million first-year college students is illustrative. "If two people really like each other, it's all right for them to have sex even if they've known each other for only a very short time," agreed 66 percent of men but only 39 percent of women (Astin et al., 1987).

The gender difference in sexual attitudes carries over to behavior. Across the world, males are more likely to initiate sexual relations and to be less selective about their partners, a pattern that characterizes most animal species (Hinde, 1984; Kenrick & Trost, 1987). Not only in sexual relations, but also in courtship, self-disclosure, and touching, males tend to take more initiative (Hendrick, 1988; Kenrick, 1987).

Social Power

In both modern and traditional societies around the globe, people perceive men to be more dominant, driven, and aggressive, women to be more submissive, nurturant, and affiliative (Williams & Best, 1986). And in every known society, men *are* socially dominant. Iftikhar Hassan (1980) of Pakistan's National Institute of Psychology explains the status of the average Pakistani woman:

> She knows that parents are not happy at the birth of a girl and she should not complain about parents not sending her to school as she is not expected to take up a job. She is taught to be patient, sacrificing, obedient. . . . If something goes wrong with her marriage she is the one who is to be blamed. If any one of her children do not succeed in life, she is the main cause of their failure. And in the rare circumstance that she seeks a divorce or receives a divorce her chances of second marriage are very slim because Pakistani culture is very harsh on divorced women.

In the United States, which prides itself on being more egalitarian than most cultures, women comprise 51 percent of the population, but 5 percent of the 1989 Congress and 3.4 percent of corporate boards of directors (Boyd, 1988). In Canada's 1989 National Parliament, 13 percent are women; in Britain, 6 percent are women. When salaries are paid, those in traditionally male occupations receive more. When asked what pay they deserve, women often expect less than do similarly qualified or competent men (Major, 1987). When juries are formed, 90 percent of foremen—though only half of all jurors—are men (Kerr et al., 1982).

Studies of the links between gender and communication style reveal that men tend to talk more assertively, interrupt more, and look people more directly in the eyes (Hall, 1987; Henley, 1977). Such are

also the behaviors of the more dominant or expert person, as when a professor talks with a student (Dovidio et al., 1988a,b; Ellyson & Dovidio, 1985). Stating the same result from a female perspective, we could say that women's speech tends to be perceived like that of less powerful and warmer people—as less interruptive, more sensitive, less cocky.

Aware of such findings, Nancy Henley (1977) has argued that women should stop feigning smiles, averting their eyes, and tolerating interruptions, and should instead look people in the eye and speak assertively. Judith Hall (1984), however, values women's less autocratic communication style, and therefore objects to the idea

> that women should change their nonverbal style so as to appear more affectively distant and insensitive. . . . What would be sacrificed is the deeper value to self and society of a behavioral style that is adaptive, socially wise, and likely to facilitate positive interaction, understanding, and trust. . . . Whenever it is assumed that women's nonverbal behavior is undesirable, yet another myth is perpetuated: that male behavior is "normal" and that it is women's behavior that is deviant and in need of explanation. (pp. 152–153)

Why Do Males and Females Differ?

These male-female differences in social behavior may be modest, but they provoke interest. Just as detectives are interested in crimes, not in law-abiding behavior, so psychological detectives are intrigued by differences, not similarities. In the case of the male-female differences in aggression, empathy, sexual initiative, and power, the causes for the "crimes" are still under investigation. Preliminary inquiry has identified two suspected culprits: biology and culture.

Biology

Men have penises, women have vaginas. Men produce sperm, women eggs. Men have the muscle mass to throw a spear far, women can breastfeed. Are biological sex differences limited to these obvious distinctions in reproduction and physique? Or do men's and women's genes, hormones, and brains differ in ways that also contribute to their behavioral differences? Social scientists have recently been giving increased attention to biological influences on social behavior. Consider the "biosocial" view of gender differences.

The Evolution of the Sexes

Since Darwin, most biologists have assumed that for millions of years organisms have competed to survive and leave descendants. Genes that increase the odds of an organism's leaving descendants will naturally become more abundant. If those lacking such genes leave few descen-

dants, their genes will fade from the species. In the snowy Arctic environment, for example, polar bear genes programming a thick coat of camouflaging fur have won the genetic competition and now predominate.

Simplified, Darwin assumed that the way organisms evolve is adaptive, otherwise they wouldn't be here. Organisms that are well adapted to their environment are more likely to contribute their genes to posterity. The controversial new field of *sociobiology* studies how this evolutionary process may predispose not just physical traits, such as polar bear coats, but also social behaviors.

The theory offers a ready explanation for why the males of most mammalian species exert more sexual initiative. Sociobiologist Edward O. Wilson explains:

> During the full period of time it takes to bring a fetus to term, from the fertilization of the egg to the birth of the infant, one male can fertilize many females but a female can be fertilized by only one male. Thus if males are able to court one female after another, some will be big winners and others will be absolute losers, while virtually all healthy females will succeed in being fertilized. It pays males to be aggressive, hasty, fickle, and undiscriminating. In theory it is more profitable for females to be coy, to hold back until they can identify males with the best genes. (p. 125)

In other words, past reproductive successes should, over time, spread the genes of sexually assertive males, thereby predisposing more sexual initiative in males than in females.

Wilson and other sociobiologists (Barash, 1979) have also argued that today's men and women bear the imprint of the ancestral division of labor. Men were hunters and warriors; women were food gatherers and bore and nursed the children. Thus natural selection favored the emergence of differing physical traits in males and females, and also of differing psychological traits—aggressiveness in males, and empathy, sensitivity, and nurturance in females.

As you can well imagine, these ideas have provoked controversy. Some assume that sociobiologists are suggesting that women are biologically suited to domestic tasks and men to work outside the home. Actually, even Wilson believes that males and females are but modestly bent by genetic predispositions. Culture, he thinks, more greatly bends the genders.

Without disputing the principle of natural selection—that nature tends to select physical and behavioral traits that contribute to the survival of one's genes—the critics see two problems with sociobiological explanations. First, they are troubled that sociobiological explanation so often starts with an effect (such as the male-female difference in aggression or sexual initiative) and then works backward to conjecture an explanation for it. This approach is reminiscent of "functionalism,"

psychology's dominant theory during the 1920s. "Why does that behavior occur? Because it serves such and such a function." The theorist can hardly lose at this game. Attributing behavior to social norms—after you know what behavior has occurred—is similarly sure to succeed. When one begins by knowing what there is to predict, hindsight almost guarantees a successful "explanation."

Recall that the way to prevent the hindsight bias is to imagine things turning out otherwise. Let's try it. If *women* were the stronger and more aggressive sex, could we conjecture why natural selection might have made it so? I have a hunch we could. After all, since they are the primary caretakers of the young, strong and aggressive women would more successfully protect their young. Thus natural selection maximized strength and aggressiveness in women. Except, of course, it did not.

Or if human males were never known to have extramarital affairs, might we not see the sociobiological wisdom behind their fidelity? After all, males who are loyal to their mates and offspring will more successfully ensure that their young survive to perpetuate their genes. (This is, in fact, a sociobiological explanation for why humans, and certain other species whose young require a heavy parental investment, tend to pair off.)

A hunch is a hunch and mine may well be wrong. Perhaps the male-female differences that exist can be more plausibly explained than their imagined opposites. Even so, as the sociobiologist would remind us, evolutionary wisdom is *past* wisdom. It tells us what behaviors were adaptive in times past. Whether such tendencies are still adaptive and commendable is quite a different question.

Critics also note that while sociobiology might explain some of our commonalities and even some of our differences (a certain amount of diversity can aid survival), our common evolutionary heritage does not predict, say, the enormous cultural variation in human marriage patterns (from one spouse to a succession of spouses to multiple wives to multiple husbands to spouse-swapping). Nor does it explain cultural changes in behavior patterns over mere decades of time. The most significant trait that nature has endowed us with, it seems, is our human capacity to adapt—to learn and to change.

In response to such criticisms, the defenders of sociobiology respond that their ideas are not merely speculations based on hindsight. Rather, they evaluate their hypotheses with data from the behavior of animals, from people in various cultures, and from hormonal and genetic studies. Moreover, as sociobiology's influence in psychology grows, predictions are being introduced that enable its hypotheses to be confirmed or refuted. As the debate continues, the one thing everyone can agree upon is that sociobiology is one of the most provocative theories in social psychology today.

Hormones

The results of architectural blueprints can be seen in physical structures. The effects of genetic blueprints can be seen in bodily structures, such as the sex hormones that differentiate males and females. To what extent do hormonal differences contribute to psychological differences?

Infants have built-in abilities to suck, grasp, and cry. Do mothers have a corresponding built-in predisposition to respond? Advocates of the biosocial perspective, such as sociologist Alice Rossi (1978), argue that they do. Behaviors critical to survival, such as the attachment of nursing mothers to their dependent infants, tend to be innate and culturally universal. For example, an infant's crying and nursing stimulates in the mother the secretion of oxytocin, the same sex hormone that causes the nipples to erect during lovemaking. For most of human history, the physical pleasure of breast feeding probably helped forge the mother-infant bond. Thus Rossi finds it not surprising that, while many cultures expect men to be loving fathers, *all* cultures expect women to be closely attached to their young children. Likely, she would also not be surprised that in one study of more than 7000 passers-by in a Seattle shopping mall, teenage and young adult women were more than twice as likely as similar-age men to pause to look at a baby (Robinson et al., 1979).

A universal behavior pattern—one found in every known society—likely has some biological predisposition. In a book that helped rekindle interest in *The Psychology of Sex Differences,* Eleanor Maccoby and Carol Jacklin (1974) enumerated reasons for supposing that the culturally universal male-female aggression difference is partly biological: It appears in subhuman primates (from an early age, male monkeys are more aggressive than females); it appears early in life (before cultural pressures would have much effect); and it can be influenced by sex hormones. In monkey experiments, females given male hormones become as aggressive and dominant as males. Moreover, human females who receive excess male hormones during fetal development (due to a glandular malfunction or to injections their mothers received) tend as prepubertal children to be aggressive and "tomboyish" (Money, 1987). None of these lines of evidence is by itself conclusive (perhaps the tomboyish girls were treated differently). But taken together, they do convince most scholars that sex hormones make a difference.

Culture

No one disputes culture's enormous impact on **gender roles.** Our whole sense of what it means to be male or female is socially constructed. From birth onward culture teaches us the importance of sex as a social category. People's first question—"Is it a boy or a girl?"—helps them know how to categorize and relate to the newborn. Infants are dressed as girls or boys, preschoolers are given either girls' or boys' toys, school-

children are often seated, lined up, and engaged in play as girls or boys. But do such cultural practices create gender differences or merely reflect them? Cultural variations in gender roles, supplemented by experiments on gender roles, leave no doubt that culture helps construct our gender categories.

Cultural Differences in Gender Roles

We've already noted a few cultural universals: Virtually all societies are patriarchal—ruled by men. Men fight the wars and hunt large game; women gather food and tend the children (a division of labor that makes evolutionary sense to a sociobiologist). In their book, *The Longest War,* Carol Tavris and Carole Wade (1984) illustrate another universal. See if you can detect and state it:

> Among the Toda of India, men do the domestic chores; such work is too sacred for a mere female. If the women of a tribe grow sweet potatoes and men grow yams, yams will be the tribe's prestige food, the food distributed at feasts. . . . And if women take over a formerly all-male occupation, it loses status, as happened to the professions of typing and teaching in the United States, medicine in the Soviet Union, and cultivating cassavas in Nigeria. (p. 21)

The rule is this, say Tavris and Offir: Men's work, no matter what it is, is most prestigious.

So there are cross-cultural similarities. But cultural differences are more numerous. In nonwesternized regions, agricultural food-accumulating societies tend to restrict women to child-related activities and men tend to regard such activities with contempt. In more nomadic hunting-gathering societies, women have greater freedom and gender-role distinctions are not so sharp (Van Leeuwen, 1978). Moreover, although every culture distinguishes masculinity from femininity, the traits and jobs assigned men in one culture are, in another, sometimes those assigned women. In some tribes, men do the weaving; in other tribes, weaving is a woman's work.

In the United States, most physicians and dentists are men. In Denmark, dentistry is predominantly a woman's occupation, as is medicine in the Soviet Union. A biological explanation of the U.S. male predominance in these occupations would require human biology to be different in Denmark and the Soviet Union. Plainly, such is not the case. Even in the United States, secretaries, nurses, and teachers used to be mostly men. Has the biological suitability of men for these occupations somehow lessened?

Cultures vary not only in the tasks and occupations deemed suitable for women and men but in the sexes' social behavior. In the United States, males have less intimate same-sex friendships than do females,

especially after marrying (Tschann, 1988). In India, men need not be rugged individualists. Thus men and women are equally free to share intimate feelings and worries with their best friends (Berman et al., 1988).

Experiments on Gender Roles

The discussion of cultural variation has asked a simple question: If we hold biology constant but vary cultural expectations, what do we get? Answer: A big effect of culture. Social psychologists ask the same question when they experimentally explore the social origins of gender differences. In the laboratory, too, social factors significantly affect how males and females behave.

Recall from Chapters 4 and 5 that our social ideas are often self-confirming. People expected to be hostile, extraverted, or gifted may actually exhibit hostility, extraversion, or high achievement. Mark Zanna and his colleagues wondered whether being stereotyped in a gender role would, similarly, lead one to fulfill the stereotype. In one experiment, Zanna and Susan Pack (1975) had Princeton University undergraduate women answer a questionnaire on which they described themselves to a tall, unattached, senior man they expected to meet. Women led to believe that the man's ideal woman was "traditional" (deferent to her husband, emotional, home-oriented) presented themselves as more conventionally feminine than did women expecting to meet a man who supposedly liked independent, competitive, ambitious women. Moreover, when given a problem-solving test, those expecting to meet the nonsexist man behaved more intelligently: They solved 18 percent more problems than those expecting to meet the man with the traditional views. This adapting of themselves to fit the man's image was much less pronounced if the man was less desirable—a short, already attached freshman.

Aware that three-fourths of television's roles are played by men (Gerbner et al., 1986), and that women have played stereotyped roles on programs and in ads, social psychologists have questioned such portrayals. For example, Florence Geis and her colleagues (1984) had their University of Delaware students view either re-creations of four typical sex-stereotyped commercials or the same commercials with the gender roles reversed (for example, a little man proudly serves a delicious package dinner to his hungry wife, who is just home from work). When the women viewers then wrote essays about what they envisioned their lives to be "ten years from now," those who viewed the nontraditional commercials were more likely to express career aspirations. A follow-up experiment revealed that women who viewed the nontraditional commercials were also less conforming in a laboratory test and more self-confident when delivering a speech (Jennings et al., 1980).

If viewing but four vivid commercials has even a temporary effect on women's aspirations and behavior, one must wonder about the cu-

mulative effect of the 350,000 commercials commonly viewed during the growing-up years and of the many more instances of gender stereo-typing in television's programs. Recent experiments by Christine Hansen (1988; Hansen & Hansen, 1988) show that viewing rock music videos can color people's impressions of other social interactions. After viewing images of a macho man and sexually acquiescent woman, sub-jects tended to view a woman whom they observed as more submissive and sexual.

Biology and Culture

The cultural variations in gender roles and the experiments on gender roles illustrate this chapter's central message: Cultural norms subtly but powerfully affect our attitudes and behavior. But they needn't do so in-dependent of biology. What biology initiates, culture may accentuate. If males' genes and hormones predispose them to be more physically ag-gressive than females, culture may amplify this difference by socializing males to be tough and females to be the kinder, gentler sex.

Biology and culture may also ***interact.*** In humans, biological traits influence how the environment reacts. People respond differently to a Sylvester Stallone than to a Woody Allen. Men, being 8 percent taller and averaging almost double the proportion of muscle mass, may like-wise have different experiences than women (Kenrick, 1987). Or con-sider this: There is a very strong cultural norm dictating that males should be taller than their female mates. In one recent study, only 1 in 720 married couples violated this norm (Gillis & Avis, 1980). With hindsight, we can speculate a psychological explanation: Perhaps being taller (and older) helps men perpetuate their social power over women. But we can also speculate biological wisdom that might underlie the cultural norm: If people preferred partners of the same height, tall men and short women would often be without partners. As it is, biology dic-tates that men tend to be taller than women, and culture dictates such within couples. So the height norm might well be biology *and* culture, hand in hand.

In her book on *Sex Differences in Social Behavior,* Alice Eagly (1987) theorizes a process by which biology and culture interact. She believes that a variety of factors, including biological influences and childhood socialization experiences, have traditionally predisposed a sexual divi-sion of labor. In adult life the immediate causes of gender differences in social behavior are the *roles* that reflect this sexual division of labor. Given that men tend to be found in roles demanding social and physi-cal power, and women in more nurturant roles, each sex tends to exhib-it the behaviors expected of those who fill such roles. As they do so their skills and beliefs are shaped accordingly. Thus the effects of biol-ogy and socialization may be important insofar as they influence the social roles that people are playing in the here and now.

Changing Gender Roles

From the perspective of evolution, Act I of the human drama may be drawing to a close. Gender roles that were biologically adaptive in ages when women were pregnant both often and unpredictably may be less adaptive now that most women spend far more time working outside the home than mothering. Let us see how gender roles have changed in recent years and then ponder how they might change in the future.

Gender roles are converging. In 1962, only a third of women in the metropolitan Detroit area disagreed with the statement, "Most of the important decisions in the life of the family should be made by the man of the house." Fifteen years later, more than two-thirds disagreed. And three-fourths disagreed that some work is meant for men and other work for women (Thornton & Freedman, 1979).

But as noted in the Chapter 2 discussion of attitudes and actions, people don't always act out the attitudes they express. It's one thing for a man to say he approves "the changes in women's roles" (which, according to a Louis Harris poll, most men say they do); it's another for him to cook dinner. As one well-known actress remarked, "I've been married to a fascist and married to a Marxist, and neither one of them took out the garbage" (Tavris & Wade, 1984, p. 366).

In some ways, however, behavior *is* changing. Between 1965 and 1985, American women were spending progressively less time in household tasks, men progressively more time—thus raising the total proportion of housework done by men from 15 to 33 percent (Robinson, 1988). From 1947 to 1989 the proportion of U.S. women in the labor force rose from 32 to 57 percent. When the class of 1991 began college in 1987, one-third of the women—five times the percentage of twenty years earlier—were intending to pursue careers in business, law, medicine, or engineering (Astin et al., 1987a,b). During these same two decades, the percentage of first-year students agreeing that "The activities of married women are best confined to the home and family" plunged from 57 to 26 percent. As Figure 6-3 shows, for increasing numbers of women the dream of a doctoral degree has become a reality.

Assuming the continuation of these trends, imagine eventually reaching a point where nearly all men and women have full-time jobs. If such occurs, will gender roles—for better or for worse—disappear? Carol Tavris and Carole Wade (1984) have analyzed societies where, already, nearly all women are employed. For example, based on the Marxist ideology of the equality of the sexes, the communist governments in the Soviet Union and China revolutionized the roles of women. Similarly, Israel's communal kibbutz communities have consciously liberated women from housework. Yet each of these social experiments in equality has failed to achieve its egalitarian goals. In all three societies, women have less political and social power than men. In the Soviet Union, for example, women have made up nearly half the work force but only 5 percent of the Communist Party's Central Committee. As

Nikita Khrushchev once admitted, "It turns out that it is men who do the administering and women who do the work" (1980, p. 65). And when you ask, "Who works in the communal child-care nurseries?" and "Who cooks dinner?" the answers are usually as predictable as those given in the United States. Women may share increasingly in the bread-winning, but they still do most of the bread baking. Thus Tavris and Wade conclude that while

> increasing numbers of women are taking their place alongside men in the working world, men are not taking their place alongside women in the nursery and the kitchen. No country has given the question top priority. Until they do the hand that rocks the cradle will be too tired to rule the world. (p. 366)

Why is it easier to prescribe than to practice the elimination of sex roles? The answer again lies with the controversy of biology versus culture. "Aha!" some say, "this feminist attempt to abolish gender roles goes against our natural state. Sure, with enough effort, some people can overcome biological dispositions for awhile, but once they slack off, they go right back to their biologically prescribed maleness or female-ness." Others point to the existence of enormous cultural variation, and suggest, "In just one or two generations you can't possibly expect to overturn a long history of male supremacy."

However, in at least one sense, men may now actually be the *less* liberated sex: Male gender roles, some researchers believe, are the more rigidly defined. Consider some instances: Both parents and children are more tolerant of girls playing "like a boy" than boys playing "like a girl" (Carter & McCloskey, 1983-84; O'Leary & Donoghue, 1978). Better a tomboy than a sissy. Moreover, women feel freer to become doctors than men to become nurses. And social norms now allow married women increased freedom to choose whether or not to have a paying vocation; men who shun a job and assume the domestic role are "shift-less" and "lazy." In these areas, at least, it is men who are more pre-dictable, more locked into their role.

Should There Be Gender Roles?

Describing traditional gender roles does not make them wrong and an-other set of norms right. A description of what *is* needn't provide a pre-scription of what *ought* to be. Nevertheless, many of the social scientists who study human norms have strong personal convictions about what ought to be. Most favor eliminating or modifying gender roles so all persons can develop their own potentialities, unhindered by considera-tion of their sex.

There are at least three ways in which we might minimize gender roles: by (1) socializing females to behave more like males (such as through assertiveness training); (2) socializing males to exhibit tradi-

tional feminine qualities (sensitivity, nurturance, cooperativeness); or (3) socializing everyone to become **androgynous**—to develop both "masculine" and "feminine" traits, so they may draw upon whichever are appropriate in given situations.

In research studies, androgynous subjects are those who describe themselves as having both "masculine" assertiveness, independence, and so forth, *and* "feminine" warmth, compassion, and so forth. Some initial reports suggested that androgynous people feel better about themselves than do gender-typed masculine men and feminine women. But dozens of follow-up studies, from North American to India, revealed that, for both men and women, masculine qualities were associated with high self-regard (Orlofsky & O'Heron, 1987; Sethi & Bala, 1983; Whitley, 1985).

For personal relationships, however, traditional feminine qualities make for greater satisfaction (Ickes, 1985; Kurdek & Schmitt, 1986). William Ickes and Richard Barnes (1978) discovered this when they arranged brief blind dates in the laboratory for forty couples. Ten of the couples were composed of a masculine male and feminine female, the rest included at least one androgynous person. Did "opposites attract" in the ten couples with complementary masculine/feminine qualities? Hardly. During their 5 minutes, the macho-man-meets-sweet-woman couples did less talking, mutual gazing, smiling, and laughing than did the other couples. Afterward they expressed much less attraction for each other.

Strong masculine qualities seem to interfere with intimacy. In a study of 108 married couples in Sydney, Australia, John Antill (1983) found that when either the wife or husband had traditionally feminine qualities such as gentleness, sensitivity, and affectionateness—or better yet, when *both* did—marital satisfaction was higher. Having the personal attributes of Rambo may be good for self-esteem, but both husbands and wives report that it's much more satisfying to be married to someone who is nurturant, sensitive, and emotionally supportive.

Such a relationship contributes not only to a happy marriage but to a satisfying life. Grace Baruch and Rosaline Barnett (1986) of the Wellesley College Center for Research on Women report that for women what influences overall happiness is not so much which roles a woman occupies—as paid worker, wife, and/or mother—but the quality of her experience in those roles. Happiness is having work that fits your interests and provides a sense of competence and accomplishment; having a partner who is a close, supportive companion; having loving children of whom you feel proud.

So, should gender roles be eliminated? Some say that biological gender differences make social differences inevitable. Sociologist Alice Rossi (1978) has warned that "We cannot just toss out the physiological equipment that centuries of adaptation have created. [Our vision of

equality should be] respectful of natural body processes and of the differences between individuals. . . ." Concern also exists that making androgyny the ideal—one person having to be all things—takes Western individualism to the extreme (Sampson, 1977; Wallston, 1981). Might it therefore be better to accept and value our differences? Two people, like two sides of a coin, can be different yet equal.

Others, like Sandra Bem (1987), grant there may be some "biologically based sex differences in behavior," but believe that culture's version of gender greatly exaggerates the small sex differences that exist naturally. If, given social conditions that do not restrain people because of their sex,

> it turns out that more men than women become engineers or that more women than men decide to stay at home with their children, I'll live happily with those sex differences as well as with any others that emerge. But I am willing to bet that the sex differences that emerge under those conditions will not be nearly as large or as diverse as the ones that currently exist in our society.

The second excerpt is Chapter 2 of a widely-used speech textbook, The Art of Public Speaking. *Not only is this chapter useful for practicing study skills, but the content—learning to become a better listener—is something every one of us, and especially college students who must listen to daily lectures—can benefit from.*

Textbook Selection 2

Listening

Stephen E. Lucas

The following extract is Chapter 2 of The Art of Public Speaking, *Fourth Edition, McGraw-Hill, 1992.*

Listening Is Important

Listening and Critical Thinking

Four Causes of Poor Listening

   Not Concentrating

   Listening Too Hard

   Jumping to Conclusions

   Focusing on Delivery and Personal Appearance

How to Become a Better Listener
  Take Listening Seriously
  Resist Distractions
  Don't Be Diverted by Appearance or Delivery
  Suspend Judgment
  Focus Your Listening
  Develop Note-Taking Skills
Summary

It had been a long day at the office, and the going-home traffic was bumper to bumper. By the time Rick Peterson pulled his late-model car into the driveway at home, he was exhausted. As he trudged into the house, he routinely asked his wife, "How did things go with you at work today?"

"Oh, pretty well," she replied, "except for the terrorist attack in the morning and the outbreak of bubonic plague in the afternoon."

Rick nodded his head as he made his way toward the sofa. "That's nice," he said. "At least someone had a good day. Mine was awful."

This story illustrates what one research study after another has revealed—most people are shockingly poor listeners. We fake paying attention. We can look right at someone, appear interested in what that person says, even nod our head or smile at the appropriate moments—all without really listening.

Not listening doesn't mean we don't hear. *Hearing* is a physiological process, involving the vibration of sound waves on our eardrums and the firing of electrochemical impulses from the inner ear to the central auditory system of the brain. But *listening* involves paying close attention to, and making sense of, what we hear. Even when we think we are listening carefully, we usually grasp only 50 percent of what we hear. After two days we can remember only half of that—or 25 percent of the original message. It's little wonder that listening has been called a neglected art.

Listening Is Important

Although most people listen poorly, there are exceptions. Top-flight business executives, successful politicians, brilliant teachers—nearly all are excellent listeners. So much of what they do depends on absorbing information that is given verbally—and absorbing it quickly and accurately. If you had an interview with the president of a major corporation, you might be shocked (and flattered) to see how closely that per-

son listened to your words. One business executive admitted, "Frankly, I had never thought of listening as an important subject by itself. But now that I am aware of it, I think that perhaps 80 percent of my work depends upon my listening to someone, or upon someone listening to me." A recent survey by Brigham Young University asked business managers to rank-order the skills most crucial to their jobs. They ranked listening number one.

Skilled listeners weren't born that way. They have *worked* at learning how to listen effectively. Even if you don't plan to be president of a corporation, the art of listening can be helpful in almost every part of your life. This is not surprising when you realize that people spend more time listening than doing any other communicative activity—more than reading, more than writing, more even than speaking. Parents and children, husbands and wives, doctors and patients, teachers and students—all depend on the apparently simple skill of listening. Regardless of your profession or walk of life, you never escape the need for a well-trained ear.

Listening is also important to you as a speaker. It is probably the way you get most of your ideas and information—from television, radio, conversation, and lectures. If you do not listen well, you will not understand what you hear and may pass along your misunderstanding to others.

Besides, in class—as in life—you will listen to many more speeches than you give. It is only fair to pay close attention to your classmates' speeches; after all, you want them to listen carefully to *your* speeches. An excellent way to improve your own speeches is to listen attentively to the speeches of other people. One student, reflecting on her speech class, said, "As I listened to the speeches, I discovered things that seemed to work—things I could try. I also learned what didn't work—what to avoid. That helped a lot in my own speeches." Over and over, teachers find that the best speakers are usually the best listeners.

A side benefit of your speech class is that it offers an ideal opportunity to work on the art of listening. During the 95 percent of the time when you are not speaking, you have nothing else to do but listen and learn. You can sit there like a stone—or you can use the time profitably to master a skill that will serve you in a thousand ways.

Listening and Critical Thinking

One of the ways listening can serve you is by enhancing your skills as a critical thinker. Experts identify four kinds of listening:

Appreciative listening—listening for pleasure or enjoyment, as when we listen to music, to a comedy routine, or to an entertaining speech.

Empathic listening—listening to provide emotional support for the speaker, as when a psychiatrist listens to a patient or when we lend a sympathetic ear to a friend in distress.

Comprehensive listening—listening to understand the message of a speaker, as when we attend a classroom lecture or listen to directions for finding a friend's house.

Critical listening—listening to evaluate a message for purposes of accepting or rejecting it, as when we listen to the sales pitch of a used-car dealer, the campaign speech of a political candidate, or the closing argument of an attorney in a jury trial.

Although all four kinds of listening are important, this chapter deals primarily with the last two—comprehensive listening and critical listening. They are the kinds of listening you will use most often when listening to speeches in class, when taking lecture notes in other courses, when communicating at work, and when responding to the barrage of commercials and other persuasive appeals you face every day in our fast-paced society. They are also the kinds of listening that are most closely tied to critical thinking.

As we saw in Chapter 1, critical thinking involves a number of skills. Some of those skills—summarizing information, recalling facts, distinguishing main points from minor points—are central to comprehensive listening. Other skills of critical thinking—separating fact from opinion, spotting weaknesses in reasoning, judging the soundness of evidence—are especially important in critical listening. When you engage in comprehensive listening or critical listening, you must use your mind as well as your ears. When your mind is not actively involved, you may be hearing, but you are not *listening*. In fact, listening and critical thinking are so closely allied that one researcher has concluded that training in listening is really training in how to think.

At the end of this chapter, we'll discuss steps you can take to improve your skills in comprehensive listening and critical listening. If you follow these steps, you may also find yourself becoming a better critical thinker at the same time.

Four Causes of Poor Listening

Not Concentrating

The brain is incredibly efficient. Although we talk at a rate of 125 to 150 words a minute, the brain can process from 400 to 800 words a minute. This would seem to make listening very easy, but actually it has the opposite effect. Because we can take in a speaker's words with ease and still have plenty of spare "brain time," we are tempted to interrupt our listening by thinking about other things. And thinking about other things is just what we do. Here's what happens:

Joel Nevins is the youngest member of the public relations team for a giant oil company. He is pleased to be included in the biweekly staff meetings. After two dozen or so meetings, however, he is beginning to find them tedious.

This time the vice president is droning on about executive speech writing—an area in which Joel is not directly concerned. The vice president says, "When the draft of a speech hits the president's desk . . ."

"Desk," thinks Joel. "That's my big problem. It's humiliating to have a metal desk when everyone else has wood. There must be some way to convince my boss that I need a new wooden desk." In his imagination, Joel sees himself behind a handsome walnut desk. He is conducting an interview, and his visitor is so impressed . . .

Sternly, Joel pulls his attention back to the meeting. The vice president has moved on to a public relations problem in Latin America. Joel listens carefully for a while, until he hears the words "especially in the Caribbean."

"Oh, if only I could get away for a winter vacation this year," he thinks. He is lost in a reverie featuring white beaches, tropical drinks, exotic dances, scuba-diving, sailboats, himself tanned and windblown . . .

". . . will definitely affect salary increases this year" brings him back to the meeting with a jolt. What did the vice president say about salary increases? Oh, well, he can ask someone else after the meeting. But now the vice president is talking about budgets. All those dreary figures and percentages . . . And Joel is off again.

His date last night, Margie, really seems to like him and yet . . . Was it something he did that made her say goodnight at the door and go inside alone? Could she have been *that* tired? The last time she invited him in for coffee. Of course, she really did have a rough day. Anybody can understand that. But still . . .

". . . an area that Joel has taken a special interest in. Maybe we should hear from him." Uh, oh! *What* area does the vice president mean? Everyone is looking at Joel, as he tries frantically to recall the last words said at the meeting.

It's not that Joel *meant* to lose track of the discussion. But there comes a point at which it's so easy to give in to physical and mental distractions—to let your thoughts wander rather than to concentrate on what is being said. After all, concentrating is hard work. Louis Nizer, the famous trial lawyer, says, "So complete is this concentration that at the end of a court day in which I have only listened, I find myself wringing wet despite a calm and casual manner."

Later in this chapter, we will look at some things you can do to concentrate better on what you hear.

Listening Too Hard

Until now we have been talking about not paying close attention to what we hear. But sometimes we listen *too* hard. We turn into human sponges, soaking up a speaker's every word as if every word were equal-

ly important. We try to remember all the names, all the dates, all the places. In the process we often miss the speaker's point by submerging it in a morass of details. What is worse, we may end up confusing the facts as well.

> The car with out-of-state plates and ski racks on the roof pulled up outside a Vermont farmhouse. The driver called out to the farmer, "Can you tell us how to get to Green Mountain Lodge?"
>
> "Well," replied the farmer, "I guess you know it's not there anymore. Terrible thing. But if you want to know where it *used* to be, you go down the road two miles, take a left at the blinking light, make the next right at the cheese shop, and follow the mountain road for about eight miles until you get to the top. Really a sad thing it's all gone."
>
> "Let me make sure I heard you right," said the driver. "Two miles down the road, and then a left at the light, a right at the cheese shop, and then up the mountain road for eight miles to the top?"
>
> "That's it," answered the farmer. "But you won't find much when you get there."
>
> "Thanks a lot," called the driver, as the car drove away.
>
> When the car had pulled out of sight, the farmer turned to his son. "Do you suppose," he said, "they don't know the lodge burned down last summer?"

This is a typical example of losing the main message by concentrating on details. The driver of the car had set his mind to remember directions—period. In so doing, he blocked out everything else—including the information that his destination no longer existed.

The same thing can happen when you listen to a speech: you pick up the details but miss the point. It just isn't possible to remember everything a speaker says. Efficient listeners usually concentrate on main ideas and evidence. We'll discuss these things more thoroughly later in the chapter.

Jumping to Conclusions

Janice and David are married. One day they both come home from work exhausted. While Janice struggles to get dinner on the table, David pours a glass of wine for each of them and then falls down in front of the television set to watch the evening news. Over dinner, this conversation takes place:

JANICE: There's going to be a big change around here.

DAVID: I know, I know. I haven't been pulling my share of the cooking and cleaning, but I'm really going to try to be better about it.

JANICE: Well, that's certainly true, but it's not the only thing . . .

DAVID: Look, I *know* I didn't take out the garbage last night and you had to do it. I promise I won't forget the next time.

JANICE: No, you're not listening. I'm talking about a much more basic change, and . . .

DAVID: I hope you don't want to write up a formal schedule saying who does what on which days. Because I think that's ridiculous. We can work this out sensibly.

JANICE: No, I don't mean that at all. You're not paying attention. I mean something a *lot* more basic, and . . .

DAVID: Janice, we're both reasonable, intelligent people. We can work this out if we just approach it rationally.

JANICE: Of course we can. If you would only *listen* for a minute. I'm trying to tell you I had a call from my sister today. She's lost her job and she doesn't have any money. I told her she could stay with us for a few months until she finds another one.

Why is there so much confusion here? Clearly, Janice is unhappy about the amount of household work David does and has mentioned it several times. Equally clearly, David feels guilty about it. So when Janice starts to talk about a "change," David jumps to a conclusion and assumes Janice is going to bring up household work again. This results in a breakdown of communication. The whole problem could have been avoided if, when Janice said "There's going to be a big change . . . ," David had asked "What change?"—and then *listened*.

This is one form of jumping to conclusions—putting words into a speaker's mouth. It is one reason why we sometimes communicate so poorly with people we are closest to. Because we are so sure we know what they mean, we don't listen to what they actually say. Sometimes we don't even hear them out.

Another way of jumping to conclusions is prematurely rejecting a speaker's ideas as boring or misguided. We may decide early on that a speaker has nothing valuable to say. Suppose you are passionately committed to animal rights and a speaker's announced topic is "The Importance of Animals to Scientific Research." You may decide in advance not to listen to anything the speaker has to say. This would be a mistake. You might pick up useful information that could either strengthen or modify your thinking. In another situation, you might jump to the conclusion that a speech will be boring. Let's say the announced topic is "Looking Toward Jupiter: Science and the Cosmos." It sounds dull. So you tune out—and miss a fascinating discussion of possible extraterrestrial life forms.

Nearly every speech has something to offer you—whether it be information, point of view, or technique. You are cheating yourself if you prejudge and choose not to listen.

Focusing on Delivery and Personal Appearance

George Matthews had just received his engineering degree from a major university—magna cum laude and Phi Beta Kappa. Several good firms were

interested in hiring him. At his first interview the company's personnel manager took him to meet the hiring executive, with whom George spent nearly an hour. At the end of the interview George felt he had made an excellent impression.

Later, the personnel manager called the executive and asked, "What did you think of Matthews?" The executive replied, "He won't do. He's a lightweight. Everything he said made me think he's not serious about a career in engineering."

"Funny," said the personnel manager, "he didn't seem like a lightweight to me. What exactly did he say?"

The executive hemmed and hawed. He couldn't remember the *precise* words, but the guy was definitely a lightweight. He would not be able to handle the work load or make a contribution to the firm. Still the personnel manager persisted. What was the problem? Finally, the executive was pinned down.

"The man wouldn't fit in," he said. "He had on a double-knit suit, and we're a Brooks Brothers type of company. To tell you the truth, I didn't hear a word he said, because the minute he walked in I knew he wouldn't do. For crying out loud, he was wearing yellow socks!"

This story illustrates a very common problem. We tend to judge people by the way they look or speak and therefore don't listen to what they *say.* Some people are so put off by personal appearance, regional accents, speech defects, or unusual vocal mannerisms that they can't be bothered to listen. This kind of emotional censorship is less severe in the United States now than it was a decade or two ago, but we need always to guard against it. Nothing is more deadly to communication.

How to Become a Better Listener

Take Listening Seriously

The first step to improvement is always self-awareness. Analyze your shortcomings as a listener and commit yourself to overcoming them. Good listeners are not born that way. They have *worked* at learning how to listen effectively. Good listening does not go hand in hand with intelligence, education, or social standing. Like any other skill, it comes from practice and self-discipline.

You should begin to think of listening as an active process. So many aspects of modern life encourage us to listen passively. We "listen" to the radio while studying or "listen" to the television while moving about from room to room. This type of passive listening is a habit— but so is active listening. We can learn to identify those situations in which active listening is important. If you work seriously at becoming a more efficient listener, you will reap the rewards in your schoolwork, in your personal and family relations, and in your career.

Resist Distractions

In an ideal world, we could eliminate all physical and mental distractions. In the real world, however, this is not possible. Because we think so much faster than a speaker can talk, it's easy to let our attention wander while we listen. Sometimes it's very easy—when the room is too hot, when construction machinery is operating right outside the window, when the speaker is tedious. But our attention can stray even in the best of circumstances—if for no other reason than a failure to stay alert and make ourselves concentrate.

Whenever you find this happening, make a conscious effort to pull your mind back to what the speaker is saying. Then force it to stay there. One way to do this is to think a little ahead of the speaker—try to anticipate what will come next. This is not the same as jumping to conclusions. When you jump to conclusions, you put words into the speaker's mouth and don't actually listen to what is said. In this case you *will* listen—and measure what the speaker says against what you had anticipated.

Another way to keep your mind on a speech is to review mentally what the speaker has already said and make sure you understand it. Yet another is to listen between the lines and assess what a speaker implies verbally or says nonverbally with body language. Suppose a politician is running for reelection. During a campaign speech to her constituents she makes this statement: "Just last week I had lunch with the President, and he assured me that he has a special concern for the people of our state." The careful listener would hear this implied message: "If you vote for me, there's a good chance more tax money will flow into the state."

To take another example, suppose a speaker is introducing someone to an audience. The speaker says, "It gives me great pleasure to present to you my very dear friend, Mrs. Smith." But the speaker doesn't shake hands with Mrs. Smith. He doesn't even look at her—just turns his back and leaves the podium. Is Mrs. Smith really his "very dear friend"? Certainly not.

Attentive listeners can pick up all kinds of clues to a speaker's real message. At first you may find it difficult to listen so intently. If you work at it, however, your concentration is bound to improve.

Don't Be Diverted by Appearance or Delivery

If you had attended Abraham Lincoln's momentous Cooper Union speech of 1860, this is what you would have seen:

> The long, ungainly figure upon which hung clothes that, while new for this trip, were evidently the work of an unskilled tailor; the large feet and clumsy hands, of which, at the outset, at least, the orator seemed to be un-

duly conscious; the long, gaunt head, capped by a shock of hair that seemed not to have been thoroughly brushed out, made a picture which did not fit in with New York's conception of a finished statesman.

But although he seemed awkward and uncultivated, Lincoln had a powerful message about the moral evils of slavery. Fortunately, the audience at Cooper Union did not let his appearance stand in the way of his words.

Similarly, you must be willing to set aside preconceived judgments based on a person's looks or manner of speech. Einstein had frizzy, uncombed hair and wore sloppy clothes. Gandhi was a very unimpressive-looking man who often spoke dressed in a loincloth or wrapped in a blanket. Helen Keller, deaf and blind from earliest childhood, always had trouble articulating words distinctly. Yet imagine if no one had listened to them. Even though it may tax your tolerance, patience, and concentration, don't let negative feelings about a speaker's appearance or delivery keep you from listening to the message.

On the other hand, try not to be misled if the speaker has an unusually attractive appearance. It's all too easy to assume that because someone is good-looking and has a polished delivery he or she is speaking eloquently. Some of the most unscrupulous speakers in history have been handsome people with hypnotic delivery skills. Again, be sure you respond to the message, not to the package it comes in.

Suspend Judgment

Unless we listen only to people who think exactly as we do, we are going to hear things with which we disagree. When this happens, our natural inclination is to argue mentally with the speaker or to dismiss everything he or she says. But neither response is fair—to the speaker or to ourselves. In both cases we blot out any chance of learning or being persuaded.

Does this mean you must agree with everything you hear? Not at all. It means you should hear people out *before* reaching a final judgment. Try to understand their point of view. Listen to their ideas, examine their evidence, assess their reasoning. *Then* make up your mind. If you're sure of your beliefs, you need not fear listening to opposing views. If you're not sure, you have every reason to listen carefully. It has been said more than once that a closed mind is an empty mind.

Focus Your Listening

As we have seen, skilled listeners do not try to absorb a speaker's every word. Rather, they focus on specific things in a speech. Here are three suggestions to help you focus your listening.

Listen for Main Points

Most speeches contain from two to four main points. Here, for example, are the main points of a recent speech by Robert J. Aaronson, President of the Air Transport Association:

1.   Outmoded facilities and an overburdened air traffic control system have seriously eroded the quality of air travel in the United States.
2.   Solving the problem will require decisive government action to expand and modernize the entire U.S. aviation system.

These main points are the heart of Aaronson's message. As with any speech, they are the most important things to listen for.

Unless a speaker is terribly scatterbrained, you should be able to detect his or her main points with little difficulty. Often at the outset of a speech, a speaker will give some idea of the main points to be developed. For example, in his introduction Aaronson said: "Flying isn't as much fun as it used to be. . . . After I tell you why, I want to tell you what can be done about it." Noticing this, a sharp listener would have been prepared for a speech with two main points—the first detailing a problem (why "flying isn't as much fun as it used to be"), the second presenting a solution to that problem ("what can be done about it").

Listen for Evidence

Identifying a speaker's main points, however, is not enough. You must also listen for supporting evidence. By themselves, Aaronson's main points are only assertions. You may be inclined to believe them just because they come from the president of a respected public organization such as the Air Transport Association. Yet a careful listener will be concerned about evidence no matter who is speaking. Had you been listening to Aaronson's speech, you would have heard him support his claim about the problems facing America's air-travel system with a mass of verifiable evidence. Here is an excerpt:

We are operating essentially the same-sized airport and airways system here in the United States that we were in 1970. That should tell you something, because the number of people flying in that system will have grown from 170 million in 1970 to about 470 million by the end of this year. . . .

In the last 10 years, daily airline traffic has increased 43 percent, to about 1.2 million passenger boardings each day. The number of flights has increased 22 percent to more than 18,000 daily.

But if you fly today, the chances are about one in five that your flight will be late. Why? Because we have roughly the same number of air traffic controllers that we did 10 years ago, and those that we have are, on average, less experienced than the 1980 controllers.

Also, the Federal Aviation Authority is operating the air traffic control system with a lot of the same equipment used 10, 20, even 30 years ago. And we haven't built a big, new airport in this country for 15 years.

There are four basic questions to ask about a speaker's evidence:

Is it *accurate?*
Is it taken from *objective* sources?
Is it *relevant* to the speaker's claim?
Is it *sufficient* to support the speaker's point?

In Aaronson's case, the answer to each question is yes. His figures about the increase in daily airline traffic, the chances of having a flight delayed, the number of air traffic controllers, and the age of equipment used by the FAA are well established in the public record and can be verified independently. They are clearly relevant to Aaronson's claim about the declining quality of America's air-travel system, and they are sufficient to support that claim. If Aaronson's evidence were inaccurate, biased, irrelevant, or insufficient, you should be wary of accepting his claim.

We will discuss these—and other—tests of evidence in detail in Chapters 6 and 14. For now, it is enough to know that you should be on guard against unfounded assertions and sweeping generalizations. Keep an ear out for the speaker's evidence and for its accuracy, objectivity, relevance, and sufficiency.

Listen for Technique

We said earlier that you should not let a speaker's delivery distract you from the message, and this is true. However, if you want to become an effective speaker, you should study the methods other people use to speak effectively. When you listen to speeches—in class and out—focus above all on the content of a speaker's message; but also pay attention to the techniques the speaker uses to get the message across.

Analyze the introduction: What methods does the speaker use to gain attention, to relate to the audience, to establish credibility and good will? Assess the organization of the speech: Is it clear and easy to follow? Can you pick out the speaker's main points? Can you follow when the speaker moves from one point to another?

Study the speaker's language: Is it accurate, clear, vivid, appropriate? Does the speaker adapt well to the audience and occasion? Finally, diagnose the speaker's delivery: Is it fluent, dynamic, convincing? Does it strengthen or weaken the impact of the speaker's ideas? How well does the speaker use eye contact, gestures, and visual aids?

As you listen, focus on both the speaker's strengths and weaknesses. If the speaker is not effective, try to determine why. If he or she is effective, try to pick out techniques you can use in your own speeches. If you listen in this way, you will be surprised how much you can learn about successful speaking.

This is why many teachers require students to complete evaluation

forms on their classmates' speeches. To fill in such forms conscientiously, you must listen carefully. But the effort is well worth the rewards. Not only will you provide valuable feedback to your classmates about their speeches, you will also find yourself becoming a much more efficient listener.

Develop Note-Taking Skills

Speech students are often amazed at how easily their teacher can pick out a speaker's main points, evidence, and techniques. Of course, the teacher knows what to listen for and has had plenty of practice. But the next time you get an opportunity, watch your teacher during a speech. Chances are he or she will be listening with pen and paper. When note taking is done properly, it is a sure-fire way to improve your concentration and keep track of a speaker's ideas.

The key words here are *when done properly.* Unfortunately, many people don't take notes effectively. Some try to write down everything a speaker says. They view note taking as a race, pitting their penmanship agility against the speaker's rate of speech. As the speaker starts to talk, the note taker starts to write. But soon the speaker is winning the race. In a desperate effort to keep up, the note taker slips into a scribbled writing style with incomplete sentences and abbreviated words. Even this is not enough. The speaker pulls so far ahead that the note taker can never catch up. Finally, the note taker concedes defeat and spends the rest of the speech grumbling in frustration.

Some people go to the opposite extreme. They arrive armed with pen, notebook, and the best of intentions. They know they can't write down everything, so they settle comfortably in their seats and wait for the speaker to say something that grabs their attention. Every once in a while the speaker rewards them with a joke, a dramatic story, or a startling fact. Then the note taker seizes pen, jots down a few words, and leans back dreamily to await the next fascinating tidbit. By the end of the lecture the note taker has a set of tidbits—and little or no record of the speaker's important ideas.

As these examples illustrate, most inefficient note takers suffer from one or both of two problems: they don't know *what* to listen for, and they don't know *how* to record what they do listen for. The solution to the first problem is to focus on a speaker's main points and evidence. But once you know what to listen for, you still need a sound method of note taking.

Although there are a number of systems, most students find the *key-word outline* best for listening to classroom lectures and formal speeches. As its name suggests, this method briefly notes a speaker's main points and supporting evidence in rough outline form. Suppose a speaker says:

Elephants have long been hunted for their ivory tusks. In the 1920s thousands of elephants were killed to meet demand in the United States for 60,000 ivory billiard balls every year and hundreds of thousands of piano keys. Today the ivory trade is centered in the Far East, where ivory ornaments are highly prized. Hong Kong is the world's ivory marketplace. According to *Time* magazine, more than 3,900 tons of ivory were imported into Hong Kong during the 1980s. That represents the death of more than 400,000 elephants.

How serious is this problem? The Associated Press notes that just ten years ago, 1.3 million elephants roamed Africa. Now that number has been cut in half. In Kenya, the elephant population has been reduced by 70 percent over the past ten years. *U.S. News & World Report* states that if the carnage continues, elephants could be threatened with extinction.

A key-word note taker would record something like this:

Elephants long hunted
   1920s—U.S.
   Today—Far East
     Hong Kong ivory marketplace
     400,000 elephants in 1980s
How serious a problem?
   African elephants down 50 percent
   Kenya reduced 70 percent
   U.S. News: could threaten extinction

Notice how brief the notes are. They contain only 34 words (compared to the speaker's 148), yet they accurately summarize the speaker's ideas. Also notice how clear the notes are. By separating main points from subpoints and evidence, the outline format shows the relationships among the speaker's ideas.

Perfecting this—or any other—system of note taking requires practice. But with a little effort you should see results soon. As you become a better note taker, you will become a better listener. There is also a good chance you will become a better student. Common sense and experience suggest that students who take effective notes usually get higher grades than those who do not.

Summary

Most people are poor listeners. Even when we think we are listening carefully, we usually grasp only half of what we hear, and we retain even less. Improving your listening skills can be helpful in every part of your life—including speechmaking. The best speakers are often the best listeners. Your speech class gives you a perfect chance to work on your listening skills as well as your speaking skills.

The most important cause of poor listening is giving in to physical and mental distractions. Many times we let our thoughts wander rather than concentrating on what is being said. Sometimes, however, we listen *too* hard. We try to remember every word a speaker says, and we lose the main message by concentrating on details. In other situations, we may jump to conclusions and prejudge a speaker without hearing out the message. Finally, we often judge people by their appearance or speaking manner instead of listening to what they say.

You can overcome these poor listening habits by taking several steps. First, take listening seriously. Think of listening as an active process and commit yourself to becoming a better listener. Second, resist distractions. Make a conscious effort to keep your mind on what the speaker is saying. Third, try not to be diverted by appearance or delivery. Set aside preconceived judgments based on a person's looks or manner of speech. Fourth, suspend judgment until you have heard the speaker's entire message—even if you think you are going to disagree. Fifth, focus your listening by paying attention to main points, to evidence, and to the speaker's techniques. Finally, develop your note-taking skills. When done properly, note taking is an excellent way to improve your concentration and to keep track of a speaker's ideas. It almost forces you to become a more attentive and creative listener.

Review Questions

After reading this chapter, you should be able to answer the following questions:

1. What is the difference between hearing and listening?
2. Why is listening important to you as a public speaker?
3. What are the four main causes of poor listening?
4. What are six ways to become a better listener?

Permissions Acknowledgments

"Manatees" from *The Wildlife Stories of Faith McNulty* (Doubleday). © 1979 Faith McNulty. Originally in *The New Yorker*.

Nancy Mitford, "A Bad Time," *The Water Beetle*. Reprinted by permission of Peters Fraser & Dunlop Group Ltd., London.

Genelle G. Morain, "Kinesis and Cross-Cultural Understanding," *Language in Education: Theory and Practice*. No. 7, 1978. Washington, DC. Center for Applied Linguistics. ERIC Clearinghouse on Languages and Linguistics. Reprinted by permission.

David G. Myers, "Gender Roles," from Chapter 6, *Social Psychology*, 3/e, McGraw-Hill, Inc., 1990, pp. 180–195. Reproduced with permission of McGraw-Hill.

"Chickens of the Sea." Originally published in *Florida*, the Sunday magazine of the *Orlando Sentinel*, November 24, 1991. Reprinted by permission.

Susan Orlean, "All Mixed Up." Reprinted by permission; © 1992 Susan Orlean. Originally in *The New Yorker*.

From "The Spider and the Wasp," by Alexander Petrunkevitch, *Scientific American*, August 1952, pp. 21–23. Copyright 1952 by Scientific American, Inc. All rights reserved.

Richard Preston, "Profiles: David and Gregory Chudnovsky" from "The Mountains of Pi." Reprinted by permission; © 1992 Richard Preston. Originally in *The New Yorker*.

Anna Quindlen, "A New Kind of Battle in the Abortion Wars," originally titled "Public and Private/The Third Decade," *The New York Times*, January 13, 1993. Copyright © 1993 by The New York Times Company. Reprinted by permission.

Tom Regan, *Matters of Life and Death*, 3/e, 1993, McGraw-Hill, Inc. Reproduced with permission of McGraw-Hill.

From *Going to Miami* by David Rieff. Copyright © 1987 by David Rieff. By permission of Little, Brown and Company. First published by *The New Yorker*.

Arthur Schlesinger, Jr., "How to Think About Bosnia," *The Wall Street Journal*, May 3, 1993. Reprinted by permission.

Michael Schrage, "Behind the Fetal Tissue Transplant Controversy." Copyright © 1991 by Los Angeles Times Syndicate. Reprinted with permission.

David Segal, "Motherload." Reprinted with permission from *The Washington Monthly*. Copyright by The Washington Monthly Company, 1611 Connecticut Avenue, NW, Washington D.C. 20009. (202) 462-0128.

From Neil and Susan Sheehan *After the War Was Over*, Random House, 1992. Originally published in *The New Yorker*.

Page Smith, "To Sleep (II): Perchance to Dream," *San Francisco Chronicle*, November 25, 1990. Reprinted by permission of the author.

From *Killing the Spirit* by Page Smith. Copyright © 1990 by Page Smith. Used by permission of Viking Penguin, a division of Penguin Books USA Inc.

The Content of Our Character, Shelby Steele. Copyright © 1990 by Shelby Steele. St. Martin's Press, Inc., New York, NY. Reprinted by permission.

James Stevenson, "People Start Running." Reprinted by permission; © 1980 James Stevenson. Originally in *The New Yorker*.

Amy Tan, "Mother Tongue." Copyright © 1989 by Amy Tan. As first appeared in *Three-Penny Review*. Reprinted by permission of the author.

"Clever Animals," copyright © 1982 by Lewis Thomas, "On the Need for Asylums," copyright © 1981 by Lewis Thomas, from *Late Night Thoughts on Listening to Mahler's Ninth* by Lewis Thomas. Used by permission of Viking Penguin, a division of Penguin Books USA Inc.

Lewis Thomas, "Man's Role on Earth," *The New York Times*, April 1984. Copyright © 1984 by The New York Times Company. Reprinted by permission.

Solomon Northrup, "A Slave Witness of a Slave Auction," *A Southern Reader*, edited by Willard Thorp. Alfred A. Knopf, 1955. Reprinted by permission of the Willard Thorp Estate.

Index

Abbey, Edward, *Desert Solitaire*, 198
Achebe, Chinua, *Hopes and Impediments*, 203–204
Ackerman, Diane, 342
  "Anosmia," 342–345
  A Natural History of the Senses, 106, 133–134, 139
Ad hominem (logical fallacy), 252
Adler, Mortimer, "How to Mark a Book," *Saturday Review*, 31
Aesop's fables:
  "It Is Easy to Despise What You Cannot Get," *Folk-Lore and Fable: Aesop, Grimm, Andersen*, 33
  "The Wind and the Sun," 129–130
Analogies:
  compared to metaphors, 162
  false, 253–254
  in paragraph development, 77–80
Antonyms as context clues, 11
Appeals in arguments, 247–252
  authority, 249
  bandwagon, 249
  emotions, 247–248
  fear, 250
  flattery, 249
  just plain folks, 248
  patriotism, 250
  prejudice, 250–251
  sympathy, 251
  testimonial, 248–249
  tradition, 251–252
  transfer, 248
  unstated assumptions in, 228–229

Arguments:
  uncovering, 224–228
  validity in, 242
  (*See also* Appeals in arguments)
Allusions, 201–202
Altick, Richard, *Preface to Critical Reading*, 186–187
"America's Decadent Puritans," *The Economist*, 431–434
Analysis in paragraph development, 71–74
Antonym as context clues, 11
Aristides (Joseph Epstein), 456
  "Student Evaluations," 456–458
Arlen, Michael J., 437
  "Ode to Thanksgiving," 437–440
Armalagos, George, *Consuming Passions: The Anthropology of Eating*, 41–42, 52–53
Attenborough, David, 115
  "Penguins," 115–118
  The Living Planet, 27
Atwood, Margaret, "The View from the Backyard," *The Nation*, 169–170
Author, purpose of, and modes of discourse, 32–40
Authority, appeal to:
  in arguments, 249
  as manipulative technique, 261–262

Bache, Ellyn, "Vietnamese Refugees: Overcoming Culture Clash," *Culture Clash*, 232–233

Balance in presentation of information, 233–236

Baldwin, James, "Fifth Avenue, Uptown: A Letter from Harlem," *Nobody Knows My Name: More Notes of a Native Son,* 6–7

Bambara, Toni Cade, "The Lesson," *Gorilla, My Love,* 185–186

Bandwagon appeal in arguments, 249

Barich, Bill, "Still Truckin'," *The New Yorker,* 81

Barnicle, Mike, "The Legacy of Lies and Fears," *The Boston Globe,* 274–276

Beard, Henry, *The Official Politically Correct Dictionary and Handbook,* 158

Begging the question (logical fallacy), 252–253

Bellah, Robert N., *Habits of the Heart,* 73

Bias, role of, in manipulative techniques, 262–263

Billington, Ray Allen, "The Frontier Disappears," *The American Story,* 148–149

Bok, Sissela, 347–348
  "Harmless Lying," 348–350
  Lying: Moral Choice in Public and Private Life, 76

Bonner, Raymond, "A Conservationist Argument for Hunting," *The Wall Street Journal,* 272–274

Boulding, Kenneth, *The Image,* 102

Buchanan, Pat, "It's Evil, Pure and Simple," *San Francisco Examiner,* 276–278

Cadwallader, Mervyn, "Marriage as a Wretched Institution," *The Atlantic Monthly,* 2

Caputo, Philip, *A Rumor of War,* 183–184

Carman, John, "'G-dd-ss -f L-v' Must Be Vanna," *San Francisco Chronicle,* 195–196

Carroll, Jon, "By Their Cars Shall Ye Know Them," *San Francisco Chronicle,* 191–192

Carver, Raymond, 509
  "Cathedral," 509–521

Catton, Bruce, "The Enormous Silence," *The Stillness at Appomattox,* 203

Cause and effect:
  false, 254–255
  in paragraph development, 74–77

Cerf, Christopher, *The Official Politically Correct Dictionary and Handbook,* 158

Chandler, Raymond, *The High Window,* 34

Chekhov, Anton, 478–479
  "The Lady with the Pet Dog," 478–492

Cheng, Nien, 367–368
  Life and Death in Shanghai, 127, 367–383

"Chickens of the Sea," *Harper's,* 155

Chronological order in paragraphs, 100–101

Churchill, Winston, "Adolf Hitler," *The Gathering Storm,* 198–199

Classification in paragraph development, 71–74

Clichés, 160

Coherence in paragraphs, 94–96

Cohn, Lowell, "It's Time for Stanford to Shift Gears," *San Francisco Chronicle,* 163–164

Colons, meaning of, 108–109

Combination of methods in paragraph development, 80–81

Commas, meaning of, 107–108

Comparison in paragraph development, 56–57

Connotation, 146–150

Context clues, 20
  antonyms, 11
  examples, 11–12
  illustrations, 11–12
  opinion, 12
  synonyms, 10
  tone, 12
  using, 10

Contrast in paragraph development, 56–57

Controlling idea, 19–22

Cost, Bruce, "Mom Might Faint, But It's OK to Slurp in Chinese Eateries," *San Francisco Chronicle,* 54

Cowley, Malcolm, 329
  "The View from 80," 329–338

Critical reading, definition of, 218

Cynicism, 192–193

Dashes, meaning of, 109–110

Dear Abby, letter to, 196–197

Deductive order in paragraphs, 103–104
  variation of, 104–105

Deductive reasoning, 241–245
  syllogisms in, 242–245

Definition:
 in paragraph development, 57–60
 in traditional rhetoric, 59
Del Castillo, Rose Guilbault, 65
 "Book of Dreams: The Sears Roebuck
  Catalog," 65–68
Denotation, 146–150
Description in discourse, 34–37
Dickens, Charles, *David Copperfield,* 150
Didion, Joan, *Miami,* 57
Dillard, Annie, "Living Like Weasels,"
 *Teaching a Stone to Talk: Expeditions
 and Encounters,* 35–37
Discourse, modes of:
 combination of methods, 35–37, 40
 description, 34–37
 exposition, 37–38
 narration, 33–34
 persuasion, 38–40
Doublespeak, 156–157
Doyle, Arthur Conan, *A Study in Scarlet,*
 241
Drogin, Bob, "'Penniless' Imelda Marcos
 in $2,000 Suite," *Los Angeles Times,*
 263–264
D'Sousa, Dinesh, *Illiberal Education,* 38
Durrell, Gerald, *The Overloaded Ark,*
 166–167

Early, Gerald, "Life with Daughters:
 Watching the Miss America
 Pageant," *The Kenyon Review,* 39–40
Ehrlich, Greta, *The Solace of Open Spaces,*
 29
Eiseley, Loren, 422
 "The Brown Wasps," 422–428
Either/or (logical fallacy), 253
Elkind, David, *All Grown Up and No Place
 to Go,* 75–76
Emotions, appeal to, in arguments,
 247–248
Emphatic order, in paragraphs, 106
Epstein, Joseph (*see* Aristides)
Epstein, Joseph, 456
 "Student Evaluations," 456–468
Essays:
 characteristics of, 284–285
 how to read, 286–287
 parts of, 285–286
 questions to consider, 287–288
Euphemisms, 154–155
Evidence, kinds of, 230
Examples:
 as context clues, 11–12

 in paragraph development, 51–53
Exposition in discourse, 37–38

Fallacies, logical (*see* Logical fallacies)
Fallows, James, "No Hard Feelings," *The
 Atlantic Monthly,* 40
False analogy (logical fallacy), 253–254
False cause (logical fallacy), 254–255
Faludi, Susan, *Backlash: The Undeclared
 War Against Women,* 58–59
Farb, Peter, 87
 *Consuming Passions: The Anthropology of
 Eating,* 41–42, 52–53
 "How to Talk about the World," 87–90
Fear, appeal to, in arguments, 250
Figurative language, 161–164
Finnegan, William, "Surfing," *The New
 Yorker,* 55–56, 76–77
Fishlock, Trevor, *The State of America,* 190
Flattery, appeal, in arguments, 249
Fraiberg, Selma, *The Magic Years,* 22
Frazier, Ian, "Bear News," *The New Yorker,*
 134–135
Funk, Charles Earle, *Thereby Hangs a Tale:
 Stories of Curious Word Origins,* 58

George, Diana Hume, 388
 "Wounded Chevy at Wounded Knee,"
  388–399
Good readers (*see* Readers)
Gooderham, Mary, "Khat—The Drug
 That Saps Somalia," *San Francisco
 Chronicle,* 5
Gould, Stephen Jay, 443
 "Carrie Buck's Daughter," 443–451
Grimes, David, "Florida—the Mildew
 State," *Sarasota Herald-Tribune,*
 199–200
Gup, Ted, "The World Is Not a Theme
 Park," *Time,* 227–228

Hacker, Andrew, *Two Nations: Black and
 White, Separate, Hostile, Unequal,*
 99–100
Hall, Donald, "A Fear of Metaphors," *New
 York Times Magazine,* 159
Hall, Edward T., *The Hidden Dimension,* 60
Harris, Eddy L., *Native Stranger,* 79–80
Harris, Marvin, *Cows, Pigs, Wars, and
 Witches,* 26
Hasty generalization in inductive
 reasoning, 238

Haugh, Thomas M., "Lefties Don't Die Young," *Los Angeles Times,* 240
Herriot, James, *All Creatures Great and Small,* 104–105
Hirsch, E. D., Jr., *Cultural Literacy: What Every American Needs to Know,* 38–39
Howe, Irving, *World of Our Fathers,* 197–198
Huxley, Elspeth, *Out in the Midday Sun,* 207–208

Illustrations:
  as context clues, 51–53
  in paragraph development, 51–53
Incorrect sampling in inductive reasoning, 238–240
Inductive order in paragraphs, 105–106
Inductive reasoning, 237–240
  hasty generalization, 238
  incorrect sampling, 238–240
  sweeping generalization, 238
Inferences:
  defined, 125–126
  open-ended, 133–134
  practice in making, 126–133
Irony, 189–190

Jargon, 158–160
Just plain folks appeal in arguments, 248

Kahn, E. J., *The Big Drink,* 131–132
Keller, Hellen, *The Story of My Life,* 201
Kinkead, Eugene, "Tennessee Small Fry," *The New Yorker,* 100–101
Klass, Perri, 172
  "Learning the Language," 172–175
Kluger, Richard, 45
  "Topeka, 1951," 45–48
Knopf, Olga, *Successful Aging,* 96

Lado, Robert, "How to Compare Two Cultures," *Linguistics across Cultures: Applied Linguistics for Language Teachers,* 221–223
Langewiesche, William, "The World in Its Extreme," *The Atlantic Monthly,* 54–55
Language, 146–164
  antonyms, 11
  clichés, 160

  connotation, 146–150
  denotation, 146–150
  doublespeak, 156–157
  euphemisms, 154–155
  figurative, 161–164
  jargon, 158–160
  politically correct, 157–158
  similes, 161–162
  sneer words, 155–156
  weasel words, 151–154
  synonyms, 10
  (*See also* Analogies; Metaphors)
Leakey, Richard E. and Roger Lewin, *Origins,* 103–104
Leffland, Ella, *Rumors of Peace,* 168
Leonard, Jonathan Norton, *Ancient America,* 110–111
Logical fallacies, 252–257
  ad hominem, 252
  begging the question, 252–253
  either/or, 253
  false analogy, 253–254
  false cause, 254–255
  non sequitur, 255–256
  oversimplification, 255
  post hoc, ergo propter hoc, 256
  slippery slope, 256–257
  two wrongs make a right, 257
London, Jack, *White Fang,* 180
Lucas, Stephen E., "Listening," 541–555
Lutz, William D., *Quarterly Review of Doublespeak,* 156
Lying with facts, as manipulative technique, 266–267

Main idea, 19–32
  and paragraph structure, 19–22
  placement of, 26–30
  delayed, 27–28
  support for, levels of, 30–32
Manipulative techniques, use of, 261–268
  authority, appeal to, 261–262
  bias, 262–266
  lying with facts, 266–267
  statistics, misleading, 267–268
Mansfield, Katherine, 504
  "Miss Brill," 504–508
Marin, Peter, "Helping and Hating the Homeless," *The New York Times,* 128
Marius, Richard, *A Writer's Companion,* 23–25
Markham, Beryl, *West with the Night,* 193–194

Mason, Bobbie Ann, 492–493
  "Shiloh," 504
Maugham, W. Somerset, "Death Speaks,"
  Sheppey, 130
McKibben, Bill, "Reflections: Television,"
  The New Yorker, 56–57, 136–137
McNulty, Faith, "Manatees," *The New
  Yorker,* 80–81
McPhee, John, *Encounters with the
  Archdruid,* 205
Metaphors, 161–162
  compared to analogies, 162
Miller, Mark Crispin, "Black and White,"
  Boxed In: The Culture of TV, 63
Misleading statistics, use of, 267–268
Mitford, Nancy, 353
  "A Bad Time," 353–364
Moraine, Genelle G., "Kinesis and Cross-
  Cultural Understanding," *Language
  in Education: Theory and Practice,*
  37, 105–106
Morris, Desmond, *Manwatching: A Field
  Guide to Human Behaviour,* 32, 82
Myers, David G., "Gender Roles," 527–541

Narration in discourse, 33–34
Non sequitur (logical fallacy), 255–256
Northrup, Solomon, 303
  "A Slave Witness of a Slave Auction,"
  303–305

O'Flaherty, Liam, "The Sniper," *Spring
  Sowing,* 41
Opinion as context clue, 12
Orleans, Susan, "All Mixed Up," *The New
  Yorker,* 30
Orwell, George, "Some Thoughts on the
  Common Toad," *The Orwell Reader,*
  97–98
Oversimplification (logical fallacy), 255

Paragraph development methods, 51–93
  analogy, 77–80
  analysis, 71–74
  cause and effect, 74–77
  classification, 71–74
  comparison, 56–57
  contrast, 56–57
  definition, 57–60
  examples, 51–53
  illustrations 51–53
  process, 53–56

Paragraph organization, patterns of,
  94–106
  chronological, 100–101
  deductive, 103–104
    variation of, 104–105
  emphatic, 106
  inductive, 105–106
  spatial, 101–102
  transitions and their functions,
  96–100
Paragraphs:
  coherence in, 94–96
  direction of, 22–25
  structure of, 19–22
  support in, 30–32
  unity in, 94–96
  (*See also* Paragraph development
    methods; Paragraph organization,
    patterns of)
Parentheses, meaning of, 109
Patriotism, appeal to, in arguments, 250
Persuasion in discourse, 38–40
Petrunkevitch, Alexander, 288
  "The Spider and the Wasp," 25, 31,
  288–292
Politically correct language, 157–158
Post hoc, ergo propter hoc (logical
  fallacy), 256
Prejudice, appeal to, in arguments, 250–251
Preston, Richard, "Profiles: David and
  Gregory Chudnovsky," *The New
  Yorker,* 74
Process in paragraph development, 53–56
Punctuation, meaning of, 106–110

Quindlen, Anna, "A New Kind of Battle
  in the Abortion Wars," *The New
  York Times,* 269–270

Readers:
  good, characteristics of, 1–2
  development of world view by, 220–224
  responsibility of, in critical reading,
  218–224
Reasoning, kinds of, 236–245
  deductive, 241–245
  inductive, 237–240
Regan, Tom, *Matters of Life and Death,*
  28–29
Reid, T. R., "New Yellowstone to Rise
  from Ashes," *Washington Post,*
  79
Rhetoric, traditional, definition in, 59

Rick DelVecchio, "Performing Whales Drawing Protests," *San Francisco Chronicle*, 233–236
Rieff, David, "The Second Havana," *The New Yorker*, 28
Rosten, Leo, *Rome Wasn't Built in a Day*, 53
Rubenstein, Steve, *San Francisco Chronicle*, 189

Sarcasm, 193–195
Satire, 190–192
Schrage, Michael, "Behind the Fetal Tissue Transplant Controversy," *San Francisco Chronicle*, 264–266
Schlesinger, Arthur, Jr., "How to Think about Bosnia," *The Wall Street Journal*, 278–281
Segal, David, "Motherload," *The Washington Monthly*, 226–227
Semicolons, meaning of, 108
Sheehan, Neil and Susan Sheehan, "Vietnam," *The New Yorker*, 26–27
Short stories, 473–478
   analyzing, 473–474
   defined, 474
   character, 478
   plot, 476–477
   theme, 478
   parts of, 474–475
Shoumatoff, Alex, "The Emperor Who Ate His People" *African Madness*, 72–73
Similes, 161–162
Slippery slope (logical fallacy), 257
Smith, Page:
   Killing the Spirit: Higher Education in America, 95–96
   "To Sleep (II): Perchance to Dream," *San Francisco Chronicle*, 72, 189–190
Sneer words, 155–156
Spatial order, in paragraphs, 101–102
Special effects (in tone of writing), 195–196
SQ3R study skills method, 525–527
Statistics, misleading, use of, 267–268
Steele, Shelby, 404
   "The Recoloring of Campus Life," *The Content of Our Character*, 181, 404–417
Steinbeck, John, *America and Americans*, 148

Stevenson, James, "People Start Running," *The New Yorker*, 43–44
Stinnett, Caskie, "Room with a View," *Down East*, 188
Study time, efficient use of, 524–525
   SQ3R method for, 525–527
Summaries, writing, 295–296
   sample, 301–302
Support, levels of, in paragraphs, 30–32
Sweeping generalization in inductive reasoning, 238
Syllogisms, in deductive reasoning, 242–245
Symbols in representation of abstract ideas, 202–203
Sympathy, appeal to, in arguments, 251
Synonyms, as context clues, 10

Tan, Amy, 308
   "Mother Tongue," 308–313
Testimonial, appeal, via, in arguments, 248–249
Textbooks, structure of, 523–524
Theroux, Paul:
   "English Traits," *The Kingdom by the Sea*, 196
   Riding the Red Rooster, 35
Thesis of essay, 285
Thomas, Lewis, 296
   "Clever Animals," *Late Night Thoughts on Listening to Mahler's Ninth Symphony*, 61–62
   "The Long Habit," *Lives of a Cell*, 33–34, 103
   "Man's Role on Earth," *The New York Times*, 149–150
   "On the Need for Asylums," *Late Night Thoughts on Listening to Mahler's Ninth Symphony*, 296–301
Tisdale, Sallie:
   "The Only Harmless Great Thing," 83–84
   "The Pacific Northwest," 101–102
Todd Gitlin, "Uncivil Society," *Image*, 184–185
Tone, 179–196
   allusions, 201–202
   as context clue, 12
   cynicism, 192–193
   explanation of, 179–180
   irony, 189–190
   sarcasm, 193–195
   satire, 190–192

Tone *(Cont.)*
  special effects, 195–196
  wit, 188–189
Topic sentence *(see* Main idea)
Tradition, appeal to, in arguments,
    251–252
Transfer, appeal via, in arguments, 248
Transitions and their junctions in
    paragraphs, 96–100
Trillin, Calvin, "Begging His Pardon: The
    Rifle-Men," 193
Trimble, Jeff, and Dianne Rinehart, *U.S.
    News & World Report,* 78
Twain, Mark, *Life on the Mississippi,* 85–86
Two wrongs make a right (logical fallacy),
    257

Uncovering arguments, 224–228
Unity in paragraphs, 94–96
Unstated assumptions in arguments,
    228–229
Updike, John, 209
  "A & P," *Pigeon Feathers and Other
    Stories,* 200
  "Venezuela for Visitors," 209–212

Validity in arguments, 242
Vocabulary, improving, 4–10
  dictionaries, use of, 8–9
  importance of, 4–8
  system for, 9–10

Weasel words, 151–154
Weschler, Lawrence, "A Reporter at Large:
    Poland," *The New Yorker,* 78
Wetzel, Dan, "A Question of Oppression
    at U. Mass.: Freedom of the Press
    or Racism?" *Los Angeles Times,*
    270–272
Williams, Joy, "The Killing Game,"
    Esquire, 194–195
Williams, Terry, *Crackhouse: Notes from the
    End of the Line,* 182–183
Wilson, Edwin O., *The Diversity of Life,*
    59–60, 113–114, 182
Wit, 188–189
"Wind and the Sun," *Aesop's Fables,*
    129–130
Winn, Marie:
  Children without Childhood, 230–231
  The Plug-In Drug, 56
Woiwode, Larry, 141
  "Guns," 141–142
Words *(see* Language, Vocabulary,
    improving)
World view, development of, 220–224
Wright, Richard, 316–317
  "The Ethics of Living Jim Crow,"
    317–326
Wrighter, Carl, *I Can Sell You Anything,*
    151–154

Yoors, Jan, *The Gypsies,* 112